Europe Today

A Twenty-first Century Introduction

Third Edition

Edited by Ronald Tiersky and Erik Jones

ROWMAN & LITTLEFIELD PUBLISHERS, INC.
Lanham • Boulder • New York • Toronto • Plymouth, UK

ROWMAN & LITTLEFIELD PUBLISHERS, INC.

Published in the United States of America
by Rowman & Littlefield Publishers, Inc.
A wholly owned subsidary of The Rowman & Littlefield Publishing Group, Inc.
4501 Forbes Boulevard, Suite 200, Lanham, Maryland 20706
www.rowmanlittlefield.com
Estover Road, Plymouth PL6 7PY, United Kingdom

Statistical information for individual countries is from the *IMF World Economic Outlook Database*, September 2006; *World Population Data Sheet*, 2005; and Psephos: Adam Carr's Election Archive (http://psephos.adam-carr.net/).

British Library Cataloguing in Publication Information Available

Library of Congress Cataloging-in-Publication Data

Europe today : a twenty-first century introduction / [edited by] Ronald Tiersky and Erik Jones.—3rd ed.
      p. cm.
   Includes bibliographical references and index.
   ISBN-13: 978-0-7425-5501-3 (pbk. : alk. paper)
   ISBN-10: 0-7425-5501-1 (pbk. : alk. paper)
   1. European Union countries—Politics and government—21st century.   2. Europe—Politics and government—21st century.   3. Europe—Forecasting. I. Tiersky, Ronald, 1944–   II. Jones, Erik.
   JN30.E82475 2007
   320.94—dc22   2006101838

Printed in the United States of America

Europe Today
Series Editor: Ronald Tiersky

Contents

Preface

A Note to Students

Introductory textbooks are notoriously difficult for professors to write. Success demands from authors not only a mastery of subject matter but an ability to explain things to beginning students without talking down to them. The job isn't easy.

For your part, you, the student, must be willing to read seriously and to engage the book in good faith. You must be willing to try to imagine what many or most of you have not yet seen, that is, Europe and its vividly different countries and societies. You must begin with nothing more than a willingness to get interested—an intellectual curiosity about the world outside the United States. We can assure you that cosmopolitan knowledge will repay you in ways that you will understand only later. You will discover the empowerment of traveling with your mind. You will, we hope, go to Europe and feel after a day or two that you are not completely a stranger in London, Paris, Berlin, Rome, Stockholm, or Warsaw, or even Brussels, home of the often-confusing European Union (EU).

Understanding international politics first requires familiarity with particular countries, so as to possess a sort of foundational stone of knowledge upon which to build a progressively larger view of the world. One must be a specialist before becoming a generalist. You will find several country chapters in this book, but you will find the separate countries again in every European-gauge chapter. Be aware that your job is to hold the two ends of a rope—to know separate countries and to understand the European Union.

As students just arriving on the scene, you have the advantage of naïveté, meaning a relative lack of prejudices and stereotypes. How fortunate you are, we think, not to begin with the heavy baggage of the past! Yet how much you don't know of what you need to know—that is, the past!

A Note to Teachers

In our note to students, we've put teachers on the spot. We've asked students for imagination in addition to information; we're asking the same of teachers. We hope that at the end of your courses you will feel that this book has done its part by giving you what you need to do an important job.

Some teachers have raised the issue of whether the country chapters or the European-integration chapters should come first. There is no obvious or completely satisfactory answer. At those moments when integration stalls, as after the demise of the European Union's Constitutional Treaty in 2004, putting the country chapters first seems best. When integration advances, as when the euro and monetary union were achieved with unexpected ease in 1999–2002 and the Constitutional Treaty was being discussed in 2002–2004, placing the European Union chapters first seemed right. After some consideration, we're presenting the country chapters first, as in the first edition. Teachers, obviously, can use the book from either direction according to their own inclinations.

Nor should teachers feel obliged to teach entirely "with the book" in order to get the most out of it. Each chapter in some way is a debate rather than a monologue. Teaching partly against rather than with the author of a chapter can be a powerful pedagogical strategy.

Above all, *Europe Today,* Third Edition, strives to be teacher- as well as student-friendly. We welcome comments about how the book can be improved.

—∙∙∙—

In closing, we should give credit where credit is due. Three groups of people from the Johns Hopkins Bologna Center provided vital production assistance. Barbara Wiza formatted the different drafts to a common template and put together the final manuscript. Timo Behr and Frederick Hood helped with the country data, the timeline, and the glossary. Suzanne Platt, Maria Sadowska, and Saskia van Genugten redesigned the supporting website (http://www.jhubc.it/europe-today).

Finally, it's a pleasure once again to thank Susan McEachern, our editor at Rowman & Littlefield Publishers, who has been so important in the success of the Europe Today series. She makes a great deal happen and she saves us from many mistakes.

The European Union

Member States |||| Candidate Countries

Country Abbreviations: ⊛ Capitals (selected)

Belg. = Belgium	Mont. = Montenegro
Cr. = Croatia	Neth. = Netherlands
L. = Liechtenstein	Sl. = Slovenia
Lux. = Luxembourg	Slov. = Slovak Republic
Mac. = Macedonia	S.M. = San Marino
Mon. = Monoco	Switz. = Switzerland

City Abbreviations:

Br. = Bratislava	Sa. = Sarajevo
L. = Ljubljana	T. = Tirana
P.= Podgorica	Z. = Zagreb
S. = Skojpe	

European Union
Statistical Information

Population (million):	463.5
Area in Square Miles:	1,425,000
GDP (in billion dollars, 2005):	$13,502.8
GDP per capita (PPP, 2005):	$26,900

Performance of Key Political Parties in Parliamentary Elections of June 10–13, 2004

European People's Party/European Democrats (EPP-ED)	32.3%
Party of European Socialists (PES)	25.0%
Alliance of Liberals and Democrats for Europe (ALDE)	10.9%
Greens/European Free Alliance	6.6%
Confederal Group of the European United Left/Nordic Green Left (G/EFA)	6.0%
Independence and Democracy (ID)	5.2%
Union for a Europe of Nations (UEN)	3.8%
Far-Right Parties	3.4%
Non-Affiliated Parties	6.8%

Main Office Holders: President of the European Parliament: Josep Borrell Fontelles (Spain)—PES (2004–2007); expected to be succeeded by Hans-Gert Pöttering (German)—EPP (2007–2009); President of the European Commission: José Manuel Durão Barroso (Portugal)—in office since 2004; High Representative for CFSP: Francisco Javier Solana Madariaga (Spain)—in office since 1999.

Membership in Key International Organizations in Europe

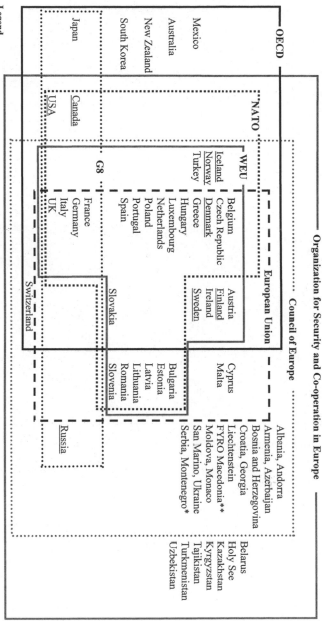

Timeline of Events Leading to the Current State of the European Union

May 1945	End of World War II in Europe.
June 1945	The United Nations is founded.
June 1947	The Marshall Plan (European Recovery Program) is launched.
April 1948	Organization for European Economic Cooperation (OEEC) is established.
May 1949	Council of Europe is founded.
April 1951	Treaty of Paris signed, which establishes the European Coal and Steel Community (ECSC).
March 1957	Treaties of Rome are signed, which establish the European Atomic Energy Community (Euratom) and the European Economic Community (EEC). Members of EEC are France, Netherlands, Belgium, Luxembourg, Germany, and Italy.
February 1958	Benelux Economic Union is founded.
July 1958	Common Agricultural Policy (CAP) is proposed.
December 1960	OEEC is reorganized into the Organization for Economic Cooperation and Development (OECD).
August 1961	Denmark, Ireland, and the UK apply for EEC membership. (President de Gaulle of France vetoes British application twice; in January 1963 and November 1967.)
April 1962	Norway applies for EEC membership.
April 1965	Merger Treaty signed, which consolidates the institutions created by the Treaty of Paris and the Treaties of Rome.
July 1968	EEC customs union is finalized and the CAP is enacted.
January 1972	EEC negotiations concluded with UK, Denmark, Ireland, and Norway.
September 1972	National referendum in Norway goes against its membership in EEC.
January 1973	UK, Denmark, and Ireland join EEC.
January 1974	Creation of European Social Fund.

January 1975	Creation of European Regional Development Fund.
June 1975	Greece applies for EEC membership.
March 1977	Portugal applies for EEC membership.
July 1977	Spain applies for EEC membership.
March 1979	European Monetary System (EMS) established.
June 1979	First direct elections of the European Parliament (EP).
January 1981	Greece joins EEC.
January 1986	Spain and Portugal join the EEC.
February 1986	Single European Act signed in Luxembourg removing most of the remaining physical, fiscal, and technical barriers to the formation of a European common market. EEC now referred to simply as EC.
June 1987	Turkey applies for EC membership.
July 1989	Austria applies for EC membership.
December 1989	Turkey's membership application is rejected.
July 1990	Malta and Cyprus apply for EC membership.
October 1990	German Reunification brings the former East Germany into the EC.
July 1991	Sweden applies for EC membership.
February 1992	Treaty on European Union (Maastricht Treaty) signed, which expands process of European integration and creates a timetable for European Monetary Union (EMU). The European Community (EC) is now referred to as the European Union (EU).
March 1992	Finland applies for EU membership.
June 1992	Danish voters reject Maastricht Treaty.
May 1993	Danish voters approve Maastricht Treaty after certain compromises are inserted into treaty.
January 1995	Austria, Sweden, and Finland join the EU after respective national referendums favor membership. National referendum in Norway rejects EU membership.
October 1997	Treaty of Amsterdam signed, which aims, among other things, to equalize tax structures among members of the EU in preparation for upcoming monetary union.
January 1999	EMU goes into effect. The eleven EU member states participating are Austria, Belgium, Finland, France, Germany, Ireland, Italy, Luxembourg, the Netherlands, Portugal, and Spain.
May 1999	Treaty of Amsterdam enters into force.
September 1999	EP approves new European Commission (EC) led by Romano Prodi.
December 1999	European Council meeting in Helsinki decides to open accession negotiations with Bulgaria, Latvia, Lithuania,

	Malta, Romania, and the Slovak Republic and to recognize Turkey as a candidate country.
June 2000	A new partnership agreement (2000–2020) between the EU and the African-Caribbean-Pacific (ACP) countries is signed in Cotonou, Benin.
December 2000	European Council agrees on Treaty of Nice (to be ratified by all member states). EU leaders formally proclaim the charter of Fundamental Rights of the European Union.
January 2001	Greece joins the "euro area."
February 2001	Regulation adopted establishing the Rapid Reaction Force.
Jan.–Feb. 2002	The euro becomes legal tender and permanently replaces national currencies in EMU countries.
December 2002	Copenhagen European Council declares that Cyprus, Czech Republic, Estonia, Hungary, Latvia, Lithuania, Malta, Poland, Slovak Republic, and Slovenia will become EU members by May 1, 2004.
February 2003	The Treaty of Nice enters into force.
April 2003	Treaty of Accession (2003) is signed in Athens.
May 2004	Cyprus, Czech Republic, Estonia, Hungary, Latvia, Lithuania, Malta, Poland, Slovak Republic, and Slovenia become EU member states.
October 2004	President-designate of the European Commission, José-Manuel Barroso is forced to withdraw his proposal for the new European Commission. EU leaders sign the treaty establishing a constitution for Europe.
November 2004	The EP approves the new Commission proposed by Barroso.
February 2005	Spain holds the first referendum on the European Constitution; the Spanish people accept it.
April 2005	The EP gives its approval to the accession of Bulgaria and Romania to the EU by 2007.
May 2005	The French electorate reject the European Constitution in a national referendum.
June 2005	The Dutch electorate reject the European Constitution in a national referendum.
October 2005	European accession negotiations open with Croatia and Turkey.
January 2007	Bulgaria and Romania become EU member states; Slovenia joins the "euro area."

Introduction
The European Scene

Ronald Tiersky

Europe, for all its historical importance, is a deceptively small place. There were fifteen member countries of the European Union (EU) in 2004, when eight former Soviet-bloc countries (and two islands, Malta and the Greek half of Cyprus) joined up, making twenty-five. In 2007, two more former Soviet-bloc countries (Romania and Bulgaria) were awarded membership. In all, by plausibly counting European countries still further to the east, the whole of Europe comprises forty-six countries and a myriad of languages, cultures, and subcultures. Such numbers would appear to require a huge continent, but it only makes for a small, crowded place compared to the others. Moreover, strictly speaking, Europe is not even a continent, just the modest northwestern peninsula of the huge landmass known as Eurasia.

If we do consider it as a continent, Europe is the smallest one by far. It is about half the size of the United States or China, and about two-thirds the size of Brazil. (And Brazil, astonishingly, is sixteen times larger than France.)

If there is one generalization to make about European development since the last edition of this textbook, it is that recent events have reemphasized that nation-states remain the fundamental building blocks of the European integration process. Creating the European Monetary System with the European Central Bank (ECB) and the euro currency in 1999–2002 marked the high point of recent European Union pooling of sovereignty.

The May 2004 enlargement to the east was certainly an achievement of historical importance: the European continent was unified at last after the half-century-long "kidnapping" of Eastern Europe by the Soviet Union. In political life there is always more than one effect out of a given cause, very often an unintended consequence. The second effect of the 2004 enlargement on EU life was to bring in a large number of new member states with their own problems and national interests. The number of seats at the EU's negotiating tables increased from fifteen to twenty-five, making compromises more difficult to reach while simultaneously making them more necessary.

In 2005 the return of the nation-state in European integration was taken to a new level by the defeat of a proposed constitution for the European Union. The debates in the different member states (including the new countries) demonstrated a bewildering variety of national circumstances and attitudes toward supranational integration. "Euro-skepticism," a variety of attitudes throwing into question the desirability of more integration, became stronger than it had been, more or less throughout the EU.

This zigzag of opinion about the value of integration is where the EU and the entire process of European integration find themselves today, and explaining the interplay of nation-states and integration is a persistent theme of this book.

Yet the fact remains that, after a horrendously bloody and tyrannical twentieth century, Europe today is by and large a continent of peace and prosperity. The structure and functioning of the European Union have become models for other regions of the world. And as a promise of political development to come, the EU, along with the United Nations, is doubtless the most original institutional innovation of the last century.

European integration in the EU is constructed on the dissection of national sovereignty into parts that are then "pooled" at the European level to create European structures that overarch and complement all the remaining structures of sovereign decisionmaking, national policies, and distinctive political cultures and traditions. (The clearest example is the single European currency, the euro, which has replaced the old national currencies—the German mark, the French franc, the Italian lira, etc.)

The EU is nevertheless by no means a "United States of Europe" and will not become one, as far as can be reasonably forecast. Yet the rethinking, breaking apart, and refashioning of national sovereignty into combined sovereignty in certain policy areas is the European Union's historical originality. It represents a kind of unexpected discovery by the Europeans that getting beyond the nation-state is not entirely impossible, and in many ways it is necessary or simply unavoidable. The Europeans, who three centuries ago invented the modern nation-state, have in the last fifty years invented the first example of what a postnational world order might look like. One writer has said that, "The world's economy is global; its politics are national. This, in a nutshell, is the dilemma of global governance."[1] This is too abrupt. The EU (and the WTO, the IMF and the World Bank, etc.) demonstrates that in some respects political governance, that is, political globalization, may follow economic globalization.

In sum, Europe today, while still comprised of nation-states with conflicting national interests and residual sovereign powers, is the most supranational of the continents, the world region farthest "beyond the nation-state." Whatever its defects and shortcomings, European integration is a revolution in world political development.

The Political and Moral Significance of European Integration

Political stability and reliability, domestic and international peace, the rule of law, liberal democracy, protection of minority rights, and growth-oriented market economies constitute the substance and justification of European integration. The European Union acts as a security umbrella and a solidarity guarantee for all, especially the new and poor member states. In return, each country, according to its capacities, is a guarantee of European integrity.

EU membership has been decisive in transforming once numerous dictatorships—in the 1970s the former post-Fascist regimes in Spain, Greece, Portugal; in the 1990s the former Soviet-bloc countries that had become independent when the USSR collapsed in December 1991. The prospect of membership continues to promote positive developments in new candidate countries, such as Romania and Bulgaria before their membership in 2007, and yet other countries such as Turkey and beyond.

Skeptics today question whether European integration's momentum has been lost, and even whether integration will unravel.

There is some evidence for this possibility beyond the failure of the constitutional draft in 2005 and the subsequent resurgence of national interests as opposed to willingness to compromise.

The EU is structured in such a way that countries have the freedom to opt out of joining certain of its institutions. Sometimes called "cafeteria Europe," "Europe a la carte," or "variable geometry Europe," this freedom has resulted in few countries being members of every EU internal institution. The so-called euro zone is again the clearest example. Twelve of fifteen eligible countries (the fifteen members before the 2004 enlargement) have adopted the single currency, while Britain, Sweden, and Denmark have opted out.

If resistance to the draft constitution is any guide for the coming years, picking and choosing may become an increasingly common EU member-state strategy. This might not be a bad thing in certain respects. In foreign and security policy matters, for example, the biggest military powers, Britain and France, along with Germany and Italy, could plausibly lead a group of member states committed to a stronger European influence in the international order, leaving the less powerful and less interested states to go their own way. In the economic realm, the number of euro-zone countries (those that have adopted the euro currency) may increase, but debate about resigning from it has already occurred in some countries (e.g., Italy). The single interest rate set by the federal European Central Bank is always beneficial to certain countries and harmful to others. Generally less competitive countries or those at a specific downturn in the business cycle will suffer from a high interest rate and a high euro-to-dollar exchange rate. Stronger economies, to the contrary, will want a higher interest rate to tamp down inflation.

These examples demonstrate that because member states' national interests remain inevitably in conflict, supranational sovereignty can legitimately be opposed, brutally if necessary. The choice for war or peace is the fundamental situation, as was shown in the wrenching European disagreements regarding the Iraq invasion. No country wants to be dragooned into war. We have long known that nationalism can be destructive. Now it is clear that supranationalism poses its own dilemmas. A moral guide to the proper balance between national and European-level interest would be a difficult book to write.

Europe in the World Order: If Americans Are Still from Mars, Are Europeans Still from Venus?

In 2002, the American intellectual Robert Kagan ignited a great transatlantic controversy with a metaphor. Americans, he said, are "from Mars," while Europeans are "from Venus." The U.S. does the heavy lifting in international crises while the Europeans generally shy from their proper share of strategic-level international responsibilities, especially where military force might be needed. Were Europeans, now liberated from the Cold War by the Soviet Union's exit from history, now willing to play a heavy-duty role in world-order problems? The answer, he said, seemed to be quite negative.

In a paradoxical sense, the issue was that the Cold War policy of "containment" of Soviet communism had succeeded all too well. Europe had solved its own security problems (or rather, the U.S. had done the solving for them). A peaceful, prosperous Europe, Kagan wrote, left the Europeans content to shift the burden of guaranteeing the world order to the United States, even concerning certain European vital interests such as guaranteeing oil supplies and keeping the sea lanes open for trade.

The intensity of European response to Kagan's arguments showed that the polemic had struck home.

During the Cold War, the Europeans were necessarily more onlookers than providers of their own security. True enough, the détente and "eastern" policies of the French leader Charles de Gaulle and the German chancellor Willy Brandt attempted to dilute Cold War dangers and tensions. But the Soviet threat to West European political independence meant that Western Europeans became accustomed to dependence, to being a U.S. protectorate, while the Eastern Europeans had to accept Soviet power and local communist regimes, like it or not.

Western Europe, largely freed from the heaviest investments in their own defense, became internally focused. While this created a psychology of depend-

Box I.1   Mars and Venus: Truth or Myth?

It is time to stop pretending that Europeans and Americans share a common view of the world, or even that they occupy the same world. On the all-important question of power—the efficacy of power, the morality of power, the desirability of power—American and European perspectives are diverging. Europe is turning away from power, or to put it a little differently, it is moving beyond power into a self-contained world of laws and rules and transnational negotiation and cooperation. It is entering a post-historical paradise of peace and relative prosperity, the realization of Immanuel Kant's "perpetual peace." Meanwhile, the United States remains mired in history, exercising power in an anarchic Hobbesian world where international laws and rules are unreliable, and where true security and the defense and promotion of a liberal order still depend on the possession and use of military might. That is why on major strategic and international questions today, Americans are from Mars and Europeans are from Venus.

(*Source:* Robert Kagan, *Of Paradise and Power: America and Europe in the New World Order*, New York: Alfred A. Knopf, 2003, p. 3.)

ence, it also facilitated European integration. The various steps toward the current European Union were thus a paradoxical result of the Cold War. In this sense, Kagan was certainly correct. The U.S. military security guarantee against the threat from the East fostered reconciliation (above all, between Germany and France) and prosperity within Western Europe. The problem was, as de Gaulle had warned in the 1960s, that even an unavoidable dependence on others can create a permanent psychology.

When the Cold War ended, Europeans had suddenly to face the consequences of freedom and independence in international relations. Foreign policy strength ultimately depends on two factors: a strong domestic economy and, as much or more so, on a nation's willingness to pay the price for "influence." The question was whether Europeans actually wanted more responsibilities in the world order and, if so, whether they were willing to make the effort necessary for success.

One U.S. political commentator said caustically that the Europeans "had come to see their global mission as embodying civilization, not defending it."[2] This may or may not be true. What is clear in any case is that whether Europe will count for more in terms of maintaining international stability is one of the most important issues of the coming years.[3]

One salient example is the war in Afghanistan. The Europeans have played a significant role in Afghanistan, where, at this writing, the struggle continues to stabilize the country in the wake of the October 2001 U.S.-led overthrow of the Taliban regime that had provided safe haven and training areas for the global terrorist organization Al-Qaeda. The British government of Tony Blair was the most important ally of the Bush administration in overthrowing the Taliban regime, as it was again in the March 2003 invasion to oust Saddam Hussein from power in Iraq. But French, German, and other European military contingents have also been important. In 2006, NATO forces, mainly European, took over the peace-building mission in Afghanistan, but not the counterinsurgency combat operations still run by the United States and Britain.

Beyond Afghanistan and Iraq, the Europeans face a serious problem of military overstretch, although it is different from the dilemma of fielding sufficient combat troops around the world while fighting two wars.

Peacekeeping has become a European specialty. Britain and France are the most active suppliers, but other countries are raising their commitments. According to International Institute for Strategic Studies data, in 2005 twenty-one EU governments had sent troops to Kosovo, nineteen had soldiers in Afghanistan, eighteen in Bosnia, and nine in Iraq. Eighteen other countries also had EU peacekeeping soldiers on the ground.[4] As the demand for European peacekeepers grows, so does pressure to expand military spending and armed forces.

EUROPE AND THE MIDDLE EAST

A growing European responsibility has become evident in the Israeli-Palestinian conflict as a consequence of the July–August 2006 war in Lebanon.

It goes without saying that Europe has vital interests in the greater Middle East. In terms of oil, the "addiction" of Western economies, Europe, and Japan makes them far more dependent on Middle Eastern supplies than the United States. In spite of this, it is the United States that has long guaranteed access to reliable Middle Eastern oil supplies. The United States always suffers the disadvantages, as well as reaps the benefits, of being the only great power with a global reach. The Europeans have been allowed choices by U.S. willingness to act in the Middle East. Whether they have done as much as they should or whether they have been in no power position to do more is a matter of importance in gauging what Europeans might do, and be asked to do, in the coming years.

The George W. Bush administration, beginning in 2000, unilaterally raised the strategic stakes in the region by declaring its intention to force democratization in the greater Middle East. Overthrowing Saddam Hussein's regime in Iraq was a first step that has left a devastatingly violent postwar situation.

European governments, during the diplomatic run-up to the invasion, were irreconcilably divided about whether to become part of the Bush administration's "coalition of the willing." Britain, as has been said, was the most important Bush administration ally, and friendly governments such as those of Spain, Poland, and Italy also joined up in spite of fierce antiwar feeling among their own populations. France and Germany (joined by Belgium) led an antiwar coalition that had external endorsement from Russia and China.

As the Iraq crisis continued, Iran's nuclear ambitions created another dilemma for the United States and Europe. Tehran was suspected, entirely plausibly, of hiding the intent to produce nuclear weapons behind a declared intention of producing only nuclear energy for domestic purposes. Whereas no weapons of mass destruction had been found in Iraq (the main Bush administration justification for invading the country in the first place), Iran's nuclear program was quite real, and its design seemed unsuited to strictly civilian nuclear energy production. Furthermore, Tehran had dissembled for years to the outside world, including the United Nations' watchdog International Atomic Energy Agency, first about the very existence of its program and then about the nature of it and the extent of its construction facilities.

The Europeans in 2004–2006 played a new and potentially significant role in dealing with Tehran, leading diplomatic negotiations in which they represented the United States, the European Union, Russia, and the UN. The foreign ministers of Britain, France, and Germany, the so-called E-3, shuttled to Tehran in the hope of negotiating Iran's renunciation of nuclear enrichment in exchange for a package of economic incentives and international security guarantees. The Bush administration stayed out of these negotiations, appearing as a "bad cop" in the background with an implied threat of military action in the case of Iranian noncompliance. Although a façade was maintained, the Europeans alone were never taken seriously by the Iranians. In 2006 the Bush administration finally agreed to join the negotiations.

It was of some significance for European integration—in this case, the intention to develop a single or common European foreign policy—that the EU's chief foreign policy official, the Spaniard Javier Solana, was then authorized to negotiate on behalf of all the "P5" countries (i.e., the permanent members of the UN Security Council) plus Germany. But the result was no better. Negotiations about the Iranian nuclear program between Solana and the Iranian representative, Ali Larijani, collapsed in fall 2006. North Korea's unexpected nuclear test in October 2006 further complicated the Iranian conundrum.

Iran's influence was a grave concern in other ways. Iran sponsors global terrorist operations that threaten Europe, the United States, and perhaps other outside powers such as Russia. Its revolution, overthrowing the shah in 1979, put in place a theocratic Islamist regime that has become an example, or at least an inspiration, for Islamist movements around the world.[5] Through its financial and military sponsorship of organizations such as Hezbollah in Lebanon and other Shi'a organizations in Iraq and elsewhere, Iran seems intent on a hegemonic role in the greater Middle East.

These concerns about Afghanistan, Iraq, and Iran—and terrorism—have been sobering for the Europeans. If they are to be taken seriously in dealing with world-order security issues, a more effective united diplomacy, backed by a more determined political will and, surely, greater military capacity, is necessary. European policy can't be successful if all it has to offer are words and carrots.

Following the war in Lebanon, the Europeans have taken on new responsibilities in the Israeli-Palestinian conflict. Europeans are leading a renovated United Nations interposition force (UNIFIL) placed on the Lebanese border. The UN Security Council created UNIFIL originally in 1978 to monitor Israel's withdrawal from Lebanon at the time of an earlier conflict. After the 2006 war, the Council expanded UNIFIL significantly and gave it a more robust mandate—to monitor the truce and help the Lebanese army to deploy in its southern territory up to the Israeli border, which meant dealing with Hezbollah's control of the area.

Potentially more important, UNIFIL military forces (led by Italy and France) were given rules of engagement that included the right to defend themselves militarily if attacked. This signified that European governments had taken the political decision to reenter the highly inflamed Israel-Palestine conflict, taking casualties if necessary that it would have to explain to public opinion at home.[6]

In other words, Americans are surely still from Mars, but Europeans may be returning from Venus. The transatlantic partners live in a single, still very dangerous solar system in which responsibilities must be shared and partners must deal realistically with each other in a common enterprise.

The European Economy

A strong and growing economy is necessary for at least three aspects of a country's national life. A good economy is the basis of prosperity. It provides the tax receipts necessary to fund social policies. And, as already mentioned, the economy, along with the will of the political class, is the basis of a country's influence in the world order.

Strong economies generate the money to fund social guarantees. Stagnant economies generate unemployment and insufficient tax revenues to fund redistributive programs. Whether social programs are a matter of the limited safety net provided by U.S.-style market economy countries or the full "European Social Model" welfare state benefits of more highly regulated continental European countries such as France, Germany, and Italy, a sufficient tax base is necessary to both.

Collapse of the communist myth of postcapitalist plenty, along with the much-less-remarked failure of radical but gradualist European "democratic socialist" parties to create postcapitalist societies, has left widespread agreement that free-market economies are the best bet for strong economic growth, good jobs, and high standards of living. The private sector rather than government is understood to be the primary engine of job creation and tolerable unemployment levels. The problem of even a highly redistributive social market economy is thus an issue of where, how, and how much to regulate, rather than abolishing the market.

In today's Europe, various balances are struck, as exemplified by differences between more liberal economies and the more social democratic economies. The general model can be called a historic compromise between socialism and capitalism—"capitalism with a human face," or capitalism with social democratic characteristics.[7] Each European country has its own distinctive national structures and policies. And even the European Union's common structures and policies turn out to have different effects in different countries according to the structures into which they are inserted.[8]

Finally, actual national results, for example GDP growth, inflation, trade balances, or national debt, can differ significantly, although it must be remembered that assessments of economic "success" or "failure" are always matters for debate.

THE EUROPEAN ECONOMY TODAY

The transatlantic economy linking Europe and the United States remains Europe's single most important economic relationship. It is also the most intense and lucrative economic relationship in the world. This is reflected in trade statistics, but even more in foreign direct investment (FDI), meaning business investments abroad, either by setting up new companies in other countries, or through mergers and acquisitions in those countries. European FDI in the United States, and U.S. FDI in Europe, are much more significant than European-U.S. trade as such.[9]

Globalization also affects European economic competitiveness and results. In recent years, the northern European Union countries, especially the Nordic countries (Sweden, Denmark, Norway and Finland), have performed better internationally than the continental countries of Germany, France, Italy, and smaller countries such as Greece and Portugal. Compared to the "social-model" countries, Britain, Northern Ireland (Europe's new "economic miracle"), the Scandinavian countries, and the new EU eastern member states have marked stronger growth and lower unemployment. Success of the European Monetary Union has tamed inflation in both areas, with most national economies hovering around the European Central Bank's target range of 2 percent.

The northern European countries face many economic challenges, but economic stagnation in the big continental countries has been most worrisome. Although in 2006 anemic growth began to increase and sky-high unemployment began to decline, the social-model economies have performed badly over the past decade, some for two decades.

Economic growth during this period has been flat. It might rise to 1–2 percent in good years in countries such as France and Germany, but it has hovered around zero or recession levels in bad years, in a country such as Italy. Unemployment was locked in at 10 percent or higher for twenty years in France and for over a decade in Germany, since German reunification in 1989 brought in the much poorer regions of the former East Germany. Unemployed millions in the social-market countries cannot take much comfort from low inflation.

Government deficits have been necessarily high in order to finance the welfare state on an insufficient fiscal base. Deficits, high labor costs (salary plus fringe benefits), and low birth rates are a threat not only to domestic prosperity but to Europe's global economic competitiveness.

Traditionally generous levels of universal medical care, unemployment insurance, pensions, and family and child welfare support are consequently being cut across the board. Demographic trends increase the strain because Europe's baby boom generation is beginning to retire from the work force, and the steady increase of those on pension will place an increasing tax burden, already at high levels, on new generations. While there were three or four workers for every retiree in the economic golden years of the 1960s, there will soon be only one or two. A common problem across the social-model countries is thus popular resistance to budget cuts in social programs. Europeans generally understand that cuts are necessary, but they are unwilling to volunteer for them. Whereas street demonstrations in the hundreds of thousands used to demand the abolition of capitalism, today their demands are to keep things the way they are. As the title of the French actress Simone Signoret's memoirs put it years ago, "Nostalgia isn't what it used to be." However, she was referring (in 1976) to the disillusion of leftish intellectuals like herself with the Soviet Union.

The "social solidarity" principle of the European Social Model, as opposed to U.S.-style goals of personal success, is under siege. Young Europeans worry about becoming a "Kleenex generation," used and discarded, that is, obliged to pay for their parents' retirements while they themselves will never reach their parents' standard of living.

THE ISSUE OF LABOR MARKET "FLEXIBILITY"

Any return to strong economic growth will depend on a combination of factors involving business entrepreneurship, appropriate government policies, and, most painfully, adjustments in the mind-set and living conditions of salaried workers long accustomed to generous social-model guarantees and benefits.

Lowering traditionally high social-model corporate tax rates and loosening excessive regulation of business are necessary.

But the main obstacle is the difficult issue of what liberal economic thinking calls "labor market reform," or "labor market flexibility." In simpler terms this means thinning the labor market's dense networks of worker-favorable laws, won by strong trade unions in the postwar decades of leftwing militancy, combined with high economic growth.

It is obvious why "flexibility" worries employees so much. Deregulation of job-protection laws leaves workers in a more precarious working situation. It would be an acceptable reform in their eyes only if future opportunities look promising. No one wants to accept unemployment on a promise of a new job that never materializes. Abolishing job-market protection laws amounts, for a worker, to risking his job today—even if it is already threatened—for the promised medium- and long-term gain of more good jobs for everyone. And even workers with apparently secure jobs are worried about loosened corporate restrictions, for example regarding mergers and acquisitions, that might result in being "downsized" into long-term unemployment.[10] Globalization and outsourcing add to the worry, creating political conflicts in every European country (as well as in the United States).

Yet deregulation and increased labor market flexibility are not entirely unreasonable, in that they reduce high labor costs and lifetime business commitments to employees. Higher profits enable business to invest more and to hire new workers without the worry that every new worker hired is a lifetime investment for a company. "Flexibility," in other words, is plausibly overall a good bet for salaried workers in general, even if not for any worker in particular.

The best balance to strike between job market deregulation, reduced social-model benefits, and lower corporate taxes is obviously a question that has no single correct answer. In each country the situation is particular. Yet the general pattern of conflicts of interest is pervasive across the European Union area.[11]

The so-called Lisbon Agenda, which was adopted by the European Union in March 2000, was an ambitious charter for a new era of European economic renewal and increased international competitiveness that would create "the most competitive and dynamic knowledge-driven economy in the world by the year 2010." It called for an average growth rate of 3 percent in the EU area and the creation of 20 million jobs, mainly by encouraging innovation through government investments in education and technology to reduce structural unemployment levels.

The "big three" countries—Germany, France, and Italy—have not even come close. Their failure stems from a mutually reinforcing combination of uncertain executive leadership, timid parliamentary majorities, and large numbers of people at the grass-roots level ready to take to the streets when changes are presented to them. Luxembourg prime minister Jean-Claude Juncker once summed up the politician's plight: "Everybody knows what reforms we need to implement but nobody knows how to implement them and win an election afterwards."[12]

A strong, renewed European economy is, in sum, crucial to all other aspects of European challenges, successes, and failures. It is the underpinning of a strong foreign policy and international influence, it is vital for sustaining acceptable levels of the European Social Model or even liberal market-style welfare policies that Europeans expect from their governments, and it will be a critical source of social solidarity in attempting to deal with the challenges posed by national minorities and the large numbers of new immigrants that Europe will need for their own good.

Problems of Minorities and Immigration

Every European society, like the United States, faces intense challenges concerning national minorities, immigration laws, and illegal immigrants. This is a worrisome situation portrayed every night on Europe's television screens. But it is also an absolutely normal situation faced by prosperous countries that can offer better lives to those with the determination to seek it. Nation-states certainly have the right, and necessity, to regulate immigration. But they also have a moral obligation to help people who are seeking a better life, as many of them once did themselves. The issue again is what balance to strike, in this case between obligations and capacities—as well as emotionally charged issues concerning how many immigrants an economy and social model can reasonably absorb and how much new "diversity" a given home population is willing to accept.

Similar challenges pervade the continent but important variations exist at the level of the various nation-states.

The Muslim Minorities

The most serious problems of social integration, treatment of minorities and of immigration today concern populations of Muslim origin.

Contrary to the usual impression, most Muslims in Europe are citizens or else legal immigrants in their home countries. Many families have been in their home country for two, three, or even four generations, and it is a cultural issue that even well-established Muslim families may still be viewed as foreigners. The largest Muslim populations in Europe have their origins in North African countries (in particular, those of Algerian extraction in France) and the Turkish-originated minority in Germany. Other significant Muslim populations are Pakistanis, Bangladeshis, and Indians, most of whom live in Britain.

Given the political climate of the past decade in which Islamist terrorism has become such a significant problem in the western countries, it is not surprising that Europe's Muslim communities have become controversial. They are often discriminated against, either because of fears that they are somehow connected to terrorist groups, or because they are simply visible racial and religious minorities facing discriminatory attitudes not unlike those faced by other minorities. Another aspect of the problem is sheer numbers. The 5–7 million Muslims in France and Germany constitute between 6 and 8 percent of the total population. This can be contrasted with the 600,000 or so Jews in France, the largest European Jewish population (not to mention a few hundred thousand Protestants who may still feel some residual discrimination). It is true—and also potentially demagogic—to point out that Islam has become the second-largest religion in France, Germany, and other countries. It is also true, and also potentially demagogic, to remark that, because Muslim dress, practices, and beliefs are often very much outside the mainstream, serious issues arise about the extent to which Islam can (or should be asked to) accommodate itself to traditional European values.

On the other hand, there is much evidence that most Muslims want or are willing to accommodate, and want to become members of society like any others. In any case, at the racist end of "native" European worries about Muslims and Islam is demagogy to the effect that Europe is becoming "Eurabia," with the corollary that Muslims should be sent home, new immigration stopped, and illegal immigrants sent immediately back to their country of origin.

Critics of European attitudes toward Muslim minorities should nevertheless remember that their own countries are usually far from free of problems of discrimination against racial or religious minorities.

CHANGING ATTITUDES TOWARD MINORITIES AND IMMIGRANTS

Indeed, the social climate of Europe as a whole has experienced rapid and dramatic changes in recent years. Even once-tolerant European countries such as Britain, the Netherlands, and the Nordic countries have hardened their attitudes.

In Britain, worries about Muslims have become more highly charged because of the terrorist bombings of the 2005 London public transport system by young Muslim men born and raised in local neighborhoods. In the Netherlands, if present demographic trends continue, by 2020 ethnic minorities will have become majorities in the four biggest cities—Amsterdam, The Hague, Rotterdam, and Utrecht. Animosity is further exacerbated by sensational incidents of violence committed by immigrants or minorities against public figures, including the murders of well-known, sometimes far-right, "native" political or cultural leaders (for example, the film maker Theo Van Gogh in the Netherlands in November 2004).[13]

In addition, rising numbers of illegal immigrants—those who succeed in reaching a European country or those who die trying—are the focus of persistent, often inflammatory media attention, whether it is a matter of "squatters" in Paris apartment buildings or desperate people washed up on Spanish, Italian, or French shores, having risked their lives in exorbitantly expensive and dangerous crossings.

The German Example

Historically speaking, European societies have exhibited a variety of attitudes and policies regarding immigration. Some countries have been de facto widely open to immigration, especially immigration from other European countries. Some have even declared themselves in official policy to be countries of immigration. Still others have explicitly rejected either of these two ways.

In the 1970s, new immigration was halted in several European countries (as well as in the United States). The immediate reason was the economic recession provoked by OPEC's decision to drastically increase oil prices after the 1973 Arab-Israeli war. Since that time, the major avenue for legal immigration has been family reunifications, in which wives, children, and other relatives join legally resident or naturalized family members in their respective host countries.

As new immigration became a permanent crisis in recent years, interior ministers and other officials have met under EU auspices to develop common immigration policies. Usually amounting to new restrictions, the goal of writing common policies stems from the idea that the EU should have a single external border. (Several, although not all, EU countries are members of the "Schengen Agreement" that eliminates all border checks as part of EU's stipulation allowing free movement of people.)[14]

Germany provides a good example of the challenges of integration alongside the more familiar cases of the Mediterranean countries.

In Germany, a long-standing Turkish (as opposed to Arab, African, or Asian) Muslim minority was originally invited as "guest workers" in the 1950s and 1960s when postwar economic growth was exploding and labor shortages were acute. It was naïvely assumed that the guest workers would return home once they were no longer needed. Not surprisingly, most stayed, either because they had become habituated or because they wanted to enjoy the prosperity of Germany as compared to their home country. Wives and children arrived and families and communities were established. Today, 6.7 million strong, the Turkish minority makes up 9 percent of the total German population.[15] Much-criticized German law made it difficult for Turks to acquire citizenship, and only recently was the law widened for even second-generation immigrants, all this in contrast to the automatic "right of return" for immigrants of German origin, a practice that recalled for many people earlier, very damaging German ideas of a right to citizenship based on blood and culture.

In addition to EU-level policies on borders, other kinds of restrictive changes in national immigration requirements are being drafted, for example, in France, Germany, Britain, and Scandinavia. A May 2006 agreement among the interior ministers of Germany's sixteen *Länder* (states) publicly recognized Germany's need for immigrant workers, given Germany's low birth rates, looming labor shortages, and insufficient tax base. Yet the qualifications for immigrants have been made more difficult to meet.[16] Germany and other governments are regularly adopting immigration requirements only recently thought excessive or even constituting the illegitimate cultural targeting of immigrants. The goal is to increase the percentage of selected immigrants in order to limit overall immigration and to raise the education and skill levels of immigrants, as well as to favor candidates who indicate that they intend to integrate socially and culturally.

Candidates for German, British, or Dutch citizenship, for example, will have to take citizenship classes that teach the basic values and principles of a liberal, secular state, so as to facilitate acceptance of the principles of the rule of law and of liberal democratic secular government, including equality between men and women. Tests will assess rudimentary knowledge of national history, literature, culture, personalities, and social issues, and a language test may be required. Applicants must have lived legally in the country of application for a lengthened specified period (in Germany, at least eight years). More-intrusive requirements that were obviously directed at Muslims, such as questioning applicants about their attitudes toward sexuality, gender issues, Islamic fundamentalism, education, and terrorism, were rejected as confusing private matters with state concerns.

Looking Ahead

What is Europe's future? To a significant extent, the answer has to do with Europe's past. True enough, "The past is prologue," as Shakespeare wrote, yet forecasting the future by simple extrapolation of present trends is a fallacy that can have serious consequences.

The British-American historian Tony Judt's magisterial *Postwar: A History of Europe Since 1945* is eloquent on this point.[17] "That history should have weighed so heavily upon European affairs at the start of the twenty-first century was ironic," Judt writes, "considering how lightly it lay upon the shoulders of contemporary Europeans."[18] History, he emphasizes, is not the same thing as memory. Serious reconstruction of the past by historians, that is, professionals, is quite different from the memories of individuals, always idiosyncratic, very often biased or self-serving. Communist rewriting of history is a thing of the past. Yet Europeans as individuals, even groups, tend to ignore their own history, preferring instead what Judt calls "nostalgia" — "The present [is] depicted not as history but as its orphan: cut off from the way things were and the world we have lost."

"History-as-nostalgia" confuses contemporary European attitudes toward European integration and the European Union, if not for the smaller countries, then for nations with a living memory of past grandeur and glory. For France and Britain (not to mention Germany), the "idea of Europe" or the project of building a European identity and international personality is in its very nature an uncomfortable transition. It will be a compromise of "memories," not a conscious choice based on a conscientious understanding of the past and its mistakes.

Nevertheless, even if chastened, and even as Europe's foundation is made from the admixture of nation-states, national consciousness, and national interest, there is more to it than that. Compromise is surely a way forward, especially in a continent as crowded as Europe.

Notes

1. Martin Wolf, "The Dilemma of Global Governance," *Financial Times*, January 24, 2007, p. 4.

2. Michael Mandelbaum, *The Case for Goliath*, New York: Public Affairs Books, 2006. Mandelbaum notes that a 2003 opinion poll asked whether people thought war is sometimes necessary in the cause of justice. Only 12 percent of Europeans said "yes" as opposed to 55 percent of the Americans. More than a few Europeans say they want Europe to play a larger role in world affairs, but not very many say they would pay for the necessary means (p. 213). For example, of 2 million European soldiers under arms, only about 55,000 are deployable at any one time.

3. Two instances in point are Timothy Garten Ash, *Free World: Why a Crisis of the West Reveals the Opportunity of Our Time*, New York: The Penguin Group, 2004; and Pierre Hassner, "The Empire of Force or the Force of Empire?" *EU-ISS Chaillot Papers*, no. 54, September 2000.

4. "Mind the Gap Between Strategy and Capability," *The Financial Times*, September 28, 2006, p. 18.

5. In August 2006 an exhibition of 200 often macabre cartoons satirizing the Holocaust was organized in Tehran after several satirical cartoons of the Prophet Mohammed published in a Danish newspaper, *Jyllands-Posten*, had provoked international Muslim outrage.

6. As of October 2006, the new UNIFIL comprised 6,000 troops. One journalist observed that "heavily armed French marines in battle tanks, Italians in armored personnel carriers, and Spaniards in Humvees have crowded into southern Lebanon, patrolling a space so small that troop convoys create constant traffic jams." Thanassis Cambanis, "UN Force Mobilizes Cautiously in Lebanon," *The Boston Globe*, October 17, 2006, p. 4.

7. Excellent analyses are Peter A. Hall and D. V. Soskice (eds.), *Varieties of Capitalism: The Institutions of Comparative Advantage*, New York: Oxford University Press, 2001; and Vivien A. Schmidt, *The Futures of European Capitalism*, New York: Oxford University Press, 2006.

8. On the differing effects of European law in various countries, see Chapter 9 in this book, by Imelda Maher.

9. See Joseph Quinlin and Daniel Hamilton, *Partners in Prosperity: The Changing Geography of the Transatlantic Economy*, Center for Transatlantic Relations, Washington, DC: The Johns Hopkins School of Advanced International Studies, 2004; and Special Report, *The Transatlantic Economy in 2000: A Partnership for the Future?* Washington, DC: The Atlantic Council, 2005. A new development is the fact that China surpassed the United States as a source of European imports in 2006, while the United States remained Europe's main export market.

10. See for example Chapter 1 on France in this book, discussing the controversy over the 35-hour work week.

11. An outstanding book on these issues is Jonas Pontusson, *Inequality and Prosperity: Social Europe vs. Liberal America*, Ithaca, NY: Cornell University Press, 2005.

12. Richard Bernstein, "Europe Stalls on Road to Economic Change," *New York Times*, April 14, 2006, p. 2.

13. France's Muslim population is estimated at anywhere from 4 to 6 million. (Government policy disallows asking for any information about religious and racial identities in the census.)

14. Migrant workers arriving from Eastern Europe are another case. After the 2004 EU expansion to the east, Britain was the only large country (along with Ireland and Sweden) to waive restrictions that could have been imposed for up to seven years. A study at the time suggested that about 13,000 per year would arrive. In fact, 427,000 Eastern European migrants entered Britain in 2004–2006, not counting the self-employed who made the total about 600,000. This amounts to 1 percent of the total population, the largest single immigration wave in British history. See *The Economist*, August 26, 2006, p. 45. In the fall of 2006 London decided to end this policy.

15. In the years 1970–2005 only 3.2 million foreigners obtained German citizenship, aside from foreigners of German extraction for whom there is an automatic right of return.

16. See Judy Dempsey, *International Herald Tribune*, May 6–7, 2006, p. 1, for this and succeeding points.

17. Tony Judt, *Postwar: A History of Europe Since 1945*, New York: The Penguin Press, 2005.

18. See Judt, *Postwar*, pp. 768–769, for the following quotations.

Suggested Readings

Balanyá, Belén, et al., *Europe Inc.: Regional and Global Restructuring and the Rise of Corporate Power*, 2nd ed., London: Pluto Press, 2003.

Daalder, Ivo H., Nicole Gnesotto, and Philip H. Gordon, *Crescent of Crisis: U.S.-European Strategy for the Greater Middle East*, Washington, DC: Brookings Institution Press, 2006.

Hall, Peter A., and Daniel Soskice (eds.), *Varieties of Capitalism: The Institutions of Comparative Advantage*, New York: Oxford University Press, 2001.

Jabko, Nicholas, and Craig Parsons (eds.), *The State of the European Union*, vol. 7, *With Us or Against US? European Trends in American Perspective*, New York: Oxford University Press, 2005. There are six earlier volumes, comprehensive surveys all, sponsored by the European Union Studies Association.

Judt, Tony, *Postwar: A History of Europe Since 1945*, New York: Penguin Press, 2005.

Kagan, Robert, *Of Paradise and Power: America and Europe in the New World Order*, New York: Alfred A. Knopf, 2003.

Moravscik, Andrew, *The European Union and World Order*, London: Routledge, 2006.

Norman, Peter, *The Accidental Constitution: The Making of Europe's Constitutional Treaty*, 2nd ed., Brussels: EuroComment, 2005.

Schmidt, Vivien A., *The Futures of European Capitalism*, New York: Oxford University Press, 2006.

Schnabel, Rockwell A., *The Next Superpower: The Rise of Europe and Its Challenge to the United States*, Lanham, MD: Rowman & Littlefield, 2005.

Zielonka, Jan, *Europe as Empire: The Nature of the Enlarged European Union*, New York: Oxford University Press, 2006.

PART ONE

COUNTRY STUDIES

CHAPTER 1

France: Hopes and Fears of a New Generation

Ronald Tiersky and Nicolas de Boisgrollier

France

Population (million):	60.7
Area in Square Miles:	212,934
Population Density per Square Mile:	285
GDP (in billion dollars, 2005):	$1,887.5
GDP per capita (PPP, 2005):	$30,104
Joined EC/EU:	January 1, 1958

Performance of Key Political Parties in Parliamentary Elections of June 2002

Greens	4.5%
French Communist Party (PCF)	4.8%
National Front (FN)	11.3%
Socialist Party (PS)	24.1%
Union for French Democracy (UDF)	4.8%
Union for a Presidential Majority [now Union for a Popular Movement] (UMP)	33.3%

Main Office Holders: President: Jacques Chirac—UMP (1995); Prime Minister—Dominique de Villepin—UMP (2005)

France's national soccer team is more than just a world-class competitor; it's a symbol of national hopes, but also of the country's problems.

When "Les Bleus" (for their blue jerseys) won the World Cup in 1998, the French were deliriously happy and patriotic. To be world champions flattered the French desire to be seen as a leading country, to play a model world role that would make France a country that other countries would look to. French political leaders lost no time in claiming that the French national team was like France itself—in the front rank of nations, a special country.

The French team was also said to have a special meaning for French society. Because of its ethnic composition—brown, black, and white—it was called a "rainbow team," an emblem of the country's progress in assimilating its large Muslim North African and mixed Black African minority groups into the "native" French white society.

But the French national team was eliminated in the first round of the 2002 World Cup games, a terrible blow to national pride. At the same time the dilemmas of minority integration, and immigration, seemed to worsen. Social discrimination and economic difficulties were, as they had been, the reality of life for much of France's North African and Black African minority groups. The fig leaf was removed from France's claim to be a "color-blind" society, one in which, according to France's particular ideology of equality before the law, France's "republican model," the state views every citizen apart from any group distinctions. In France, as a matter of constitutional principle, it is illegal even to ask about racial and religious identities in the census.

But the fact was that almost the entire French national team, in 1998 as in 2002—and 2006, when France reached the finals again, losing against Italy—was brown and black (in fact more black than brown), some born in France, others from France's Caribbean possessions, others naturalized. Zinedine Zidane, the French-born football genius who retired in 2006, is the son of Algerian (Berber, not Arab) immigrants.

In November 2005, roving bands of teenage minority youths from the *cités*, the tough housing-project suburbs that surround Paris and other large French cities, went on a rampage of vandalism that lasted weeks. It was touched off by the accidental deaths of two neighborhood boys fleeing a random police check, which is often seen as a form of harassment.

Confounding police and government attempts to stop them, the youths nightly torched hundreds of automobiles across the country, thousands in all. Businesses and schools were trashed, in an old pattern of damage done mainly in the *cités* themselves.[1]

Only a few months later, in February–April 2006, massive nationwide street demonstrations, sit-ins, and occupations of universities erupted. Not a minority teenage rampage, it was a classic "French" protest that recalled the society-wide rebellion against the government of France's historic leader Charles de Gaulle in May–June 1968. Marching for weeks in cities across the country, hundreds of thousands of suddenly mobilized middle-class students, flanked by France's left-wing opposition political parties and trade union movements, were rejecting a minor reform of the French labor code, a new law whose aim was to encourage employment opportunities for young people, especially minorities. Prime Minister Dominique de Villepin and President Jacques Chirac withdrew the law in a humiliating retreat.

The differences between the two episodes outweighed the similarities. Contrary to their self-perception as progressive, the students' demand was conservative, to maintain labor law as it was, which meant accepting longstanding sky-high youth unemployment rates. By contrast, the marauding teenagers in the slum suburbs represented something new in French political culture. It wasn't a traditional rebellion against capitalism and the state. It was vandalism committed with a sense of exhilaration and impunity, violent acting-out as a protest of disrespect, neglect, discrimination, and exclusion, combined with a rudderless moral compass concerning the damage being done to their neighbors and neighborhoods.

Box 1.1

"When France hosted the 1998 World Cup, few French people cared about [soccer]. . . . Football had rarely featured in the national conversation . . . When they won it there was hysteria, not merely on the streets. The president and even serious commentators said the multiracial team would help integrate France. This was exposed as nonsense long before the *banlieues* erupted in riots. Racists revered the Muslim star Zinedine Zidane, while voting for [the far-rightist] Jean-Marie Le Pen. . . . The World Cup transformed not the *banlieues* but French [soccer] . . . When Le Pen complains that France fields too many ethnics, he is speaking for many voters."

(*Source: Financial Times*, July 5, 2006, p. 9.)

"Tahar Illikoud is a Spanish Algerian who has lived in the suburbs of Paris for 30 years. He shares an insightful observation of Zinedine Zidane, France's most popular soccer star. . . . 'Zidane's parents, his mother, his father come from Algeria but he is treated as French. When he plays, he plays for France and when he wins, France wins. But us, we don't know what we are. I live for France, I work for France and everything I do is for France, not for my home country. The only difference is that I have an Arab face. And at the end we don't know if we are French or if we are strangers.'"

(*Source: http://youthoutlook.org/news/view article.html?article id=6ce0f28eafc0819d*, June 12, 2006, accessed July 4, 2006.)

French Troubles, French Successes

France today is a rich country with a quality of life that is still widely envied. But resistance to change and tolerance of social injustices stand out. The future of France is in the hands of a new generation of political and corporate leaders, and none too soon.

THE PASSING OF A POLITICAL GENERATION

In the previous edition of *Europe Today*, author Robert Graham subtitled his chapter on France "Ending the Gaullist Era?"[2] The French presidential election of 2007 indeed marks the passing of this enduring political generation.

President Jacques Chirac, at seventy-four years old, had occupied the office for twelve years, 1995–2007. Remarkably, he had already been prime minister in 1974, was prime minister once again in the 1980s and was elected president in 1995. He has been part of every Fifth Republic government since its founding by Charles de Gaulle in 1958, except between 1981 and 1986.

His predecessor, the Socialist François Mitterrand, had been president of France for fourteen years, 1981–1995. (The seven-year presidential term was changed—because it came to be considered excessive—to five years by constitutional amendment in 2002.) Mitterrand's presidency, to give a comparison, was longer than that of President Franklin D. Roosevelt's.[3]

Compared with other countries, the longevity of the political leadership governing France at the end of the twentieth century was part testimony to talent and part ossification of the political class as a whole.

Jacques Chirac, who began as a rising young Gaullist star in the 1960s, is the last of the generation that produced presidents Georges Pompidou (1969–1974), Valéry Giscard d'Estaing (1974–1981) and Mitterrand, a generation that dominated national political life since de Gaulle, who had already led the anti-Nazi World War II Resistance and presided over the first postwar government in 1944–1946. He resigned in January 1946 when he lost control of the drafting of a new constitution different from the executive-dominated government that he felt was necessary in France's bitterly divided political culture, which already included a huge communist movement loyal to the Soviet Union.

De Gaulle, out of power from 1946 to 1958, was president during 1958–1969, when he resigned again a year after the traumatic anti-Gaullist "events of May–June 1968" that he felt had destroyed his personal legitimacy as France's savior.

Two of the leading candidates for the 2007 election were the conservative Nicolas Sarkozy and the socialist Ségolène Royal, both of them new-style pragmatists rather than old-style ideologists, outspoken critics rather than business-as-usual politicians, innovators rather than time-servers. They, and others who surely will emerge in the next few years, represent the new political generation. They seem to understand that a policy of stalling for time is no longer credible. Facing up to France's problems will require more than the combination of rhetorical elegance and policy timidity so many observers have attributed to Jacques Chirac.[4]

President Chirac's last prime minister, his protégé Dominique de Villepin, is, even though of the younger generation, typical of this elite. Exuding the sophistication that foreigners perceive as typically "French," Villepin's finest moment was his impassioned speech at the UN in February 2003 opposing the Bush's administration's war policy. In France, his approval ratings have been very low.

The Hybrid French Presidential/Parliamentary Constitution

France's governments are formed out of an unusual hybrid of presidential and parliamentary institutions, differing from both a full U.S.-style presidential government and the classical parliamentary regime of countries such as Britain and Germany. The language of the constitution is ambiguous with the result that sometimes the president runs the government and at other times it is the prime minister.

When the president has a majority in the National Assembly, he dominates the government completely. The president is not responsible to parliament, meaning that he cannot be overthrown by a parliamentary vote of "no confidence." But there is also a prime minister who is the president's man. He is responsible to parliament and can be ousted. The prime minister is in effect a lightning rod for criticism and his institutional vulnerability protects the president even though the latter has the real power.

But when a parliamentary election results in a victory of the opposition, the new prime minister suddenly replaces the president as the real leader of the government. The president has some influence, mainly in foreign and security policy. Otherwise the former opposition and its new prime minister are in charge of government policy.

"Cohabitation" is the coquettish name given to this rivalry between a president of one tendency and a parliamentary majority of the other. Cohabitation thus differs from a U.S. legislative deadlock in which a president of one party faces a Congress in which at least one house is controlled by the other party. During periods of cohabitation, the French prime minister and the president are always battling for influence at the margins, made more dramatic by the ideological flamboyancy of French political culture.

Because of the possibility of opposing presidential and parliamentary majorities, that is, a fluctuating center of authority, the Fifth Republic's institutions are denounced by some politicians as intolerably ambiguous and prone to stalemate.

Table 1.1   Fifth Republic Presidents and the Two Cohabitation Periods

1958–1969	Charles de Gaulle (Conservative)
1969–1974	Georges Pompidou (Conservative)
1974–1981	Valéry Giscard d'Estaing (Conservative)
1981–1995	François Mitterrand (Socialist)
1986–1988	Prime Minister Jacques Chirac (Conservative)
1995–2007	Jacques Chirac (Conservative)
1997–2002	Prime Minister Lionel Jospin (Socialist)

Which office, in addition to which party, will control the government is always up for grabs at election time. Government vacillates between a president-dominated "republican monarchy" and a "two-headed" cohabitation arrangement.

But constitutional ambiguity has its advantages, at least in a country such as France where the left-right conflict remains rigid and bipartisan cooperation is unusual. The sharpest critics argue that France should have a new constitution, a Sixth Republic. (Most want a full presidential system.) But in France a pure institutional form could be a ticket to deadlock and escalation.

THE FRENCH ECONOMY: A REBOUND ON THE WAY?

The economies of Japan, Germany, and Italy, in the two decades after World War II, and, in the past ten years, Ireland—among others—share the honor of having been characterized as "miracles" because of their remarkably rapid, successful economic rebirths. And Ireland, so recently economically depressed, is today, along with the perennially successful Netherlands and the Scandinavian countries, often cited as a model for other economically hidebound and stagnant European Union (EU) countries.

France is a different case. Although it did experience a very high growth period from the late 1940s to the late 1970s, called the Trente Glorieuses (the "Thirty Glorious Years" of prosperity), it has never been considered a miracle country, at least economically.

Nevertheless, France is, all things considered, a wealthy, successful, and very modern country. Let us consider some facts and figures. A medium-sized country of 63 million people, France is the sixth-largest economy in the world, the fourth-biggest exporter of services, and the third-largest investor abroad. The French are famous for luxury goods, but France is also a leader when it comes to nuclear energy and space technologies.

The French economy is a multilayered combination of modernity and tradition, of innovation and encrusted special situations. For example, the average French person in the post–World War II decades resisted the arrival of retail banks and checking accounts, as opposed to their traditional post office savings accounts. Then, France launched the chip card revolution, in effect skipping over the checking-account era, much as developing countries today are leaping over the landline telephone era to cellular phones.

France today is one of the leading countries for high-speed Internet usage and fast rail travel, the latter being not only a success at home but one of the country's prestige, big-ticket technological exports. On the Paris-Marseille route, the modestly priced high-speed train completes a distance of 800 kilometers (500 miles) in three hours through wonderful scenery. France's public healthcare system is rated by the World Health Organization as the best in the world. Factors such as these enable the French to live longer than most and enjoy life for the most part, in spite of much complaining that may also be an endemic French characteristic.

In Europe, France's rebounding fertility rate is second only to that of Ireland—although to say this hides the European-wide "demographic deficit." European populations are not replacing themselves and a few countries (Germany and Italy in particular) already are in an absolute population decline. The French fertility rate a few years ago, at 1.65, was considerably lower than the 2.1 children per woman per lifetime replacement rate. Whether this jump in the birthrate to approximately the replacement level represents a signal of renewed French optimism about the future is an important issue, not least in paying for the retirements of current workers.[5]

DO THE FRENCH WORK HARD ENOUGH?
THE 35-HOUR WORK WEEK

A French best-seller of a few years ago was titled *Bonjour paresse*, or "Hello Laziness." Written by an employee of the national electric company (Electricité de France), it is a humorous but devastating critique of the widespread French disdain for business and devotion to jobs, the preference for quality of life, the desire to "work to live," rather than "live to work."[6] Too many French people, critics argue, are committed above all to short work hours and leisure. They are overvigilant about their holidays and coffee breaks but ambivalent about the work ethic and the goal of personal economic and financial success.

Current debate focuses on the 35-hour work week in large and medium-sized companies introduced by the Socialist government of Lionel Jospin (1997–2002). The issue is whether to abolish the 35-hour week (the conservative, market economy view) or to extend it further to small companies, those with twenty employees or less (the Socialist Party proposal).

Continuous reduction of the work week was not a new idea. It was a goal of all the varieties of socialism (Marxist, social democratic, and others) found in French leftist ideology. The worker in a capitalist society is by definition oppressed and alienated. A shorter work week, especially in factories where the "proletariat" is found, creates more family time, leisure and cultural activities, and in short a more humanized life. It is an ideal of social justice and solidarity.

Prime Minister Jospin and his labor minister, Martine Aubry, added a more economic justification—a shorter work week would permit "sharing out" available jobs and various flexible working-hour schemes. Ipso facto, unemployment, the French economic curse of the past few decades, would decline. The Socialists said that 350,000 new jobs would result in the private sector because employers would hire more people to work the aggregate missing hours in order to keep production up.

Jospin later asserted that 200,000–250,000 jobs had been created during his tenure in office, and this was true. But almost all amounted to hiring more people in civil service or government-sponsored or subsidized jobs; there were very few in business. It was the traditional French reliance on government to solve problems by expanding its ranks and increasing its budget deficit.

The 35-hour work week (plus five or six weeks of paid vacation) was much derided abroad, especially in the United States, as a typically "French" self-indulgence. In France itself, it was intensely criticized by French business but quickly became a totem in French left-wing parties and labor unions.

However, in the presidential campaign that began in mid-2006, the taboo was broken by Ségolène Royal, the upstart Socialist politician. She shocked the left-wing establishment (and contradicted her party's electoral platform) not only by emphasizing that few new, solid private-sector jobs had been created, but that even the 35-hour week's social justice effects had not turned out as planned. The shorter work week, she said, really meant that "at the Michelin tire company, managers now have extra vacation days while salaried workers come in on Saturdays. . . . The proportion of people working part time or flexible-hour jobs has increased from 10 to 40 percent, which is more than for American salaried workers." Whereas many corporate executives don't know how to use all their vacation time, working women especially have found that their family lives have become more difficult.[7]

The "European Social Model" and Its Discontents

Debate over the 35-hour work week will continue in the next few years, and it is only one aspect of a larger controversy over the "European Social Model" that characterizes France, Germany, and Italy, sometimes lumped together derisively as "old Europe."

The European Social Model is essentially a very large welfare state based in a society-wide consensus that "social solidarity," organized by government—for

---

Box 1.2   Attitude Toward Business

"The corporate world, alas, has no use for noble passions such as courage, generosity, or devotion to the public good. It doesn't make us dream. And yet . . . if it's not the primary arena where people energetically accomplish real things, why do people with degrees from higher institutions traditionally and overwhelmingly choose to exercise their talents in business—preferably big business.

"When I first started working, big business had wind in its sails, and everything was happening as though business grew out of the same movement toward social mobility and spirit of freedom of the 1960s. However, I quickly became disenchanted. And I've been disenchanted for a long time now and have had the time to notice that they lied to us."

(*Source:* Corinne Maier, *Bonjour Laziness: Jumping Off the Corporate Ladder*, New York, Pantheon Books, 2005, pp. 5–6.)

---

example universal health insurance, generous unemployment insurance, various child subsidies, maternity and paternity leave, and so on—is of more importance than the individualist and competitiveness—the obsession with personal "success"—embodied in the "Anglo-Saxon" (read the U.S. and British) capitalist market economy. French left-wing ideologists call the United States the prime instance of "jungle capitalism."[8]

But, as in Germany and Italy, French social model policies, however praiseworthy, will be impossible to finance at present levels. Over the coming years cuts are unavoidable, not least because the number of retirees of France's baby boomer generation, with all the pensions and services they will require, will increasingly outnumber those in the labor force. France's younger generation is waking up to the fact that it faces the prospect of paying for their parents' (and often their grandparents') senior years while they themselves will have difficulty even reaching their progenitors' standard of living. Young people say they are worried about becoming "the Kleenex generation," i.e., used and discarded.

National unemployment for more than two decades has been an increasing financial, economic, and social burden. Since the 1970s, that is to say, three decades, unemployment has consistently been above 8 percent, and, as of 2006, had been over 10 percent for most of the past twenty years. (By comparison, the U.S. unemployment rate has in general hovered around 4–5 percent.) Youth unemployment, which French statisticians define as people twenty-six or younger who are actively seeking a job, was a quite discouraging 22 percent (which is already 3.5 percent above the EU average). And unemployment among minority youth is estimated at 40 percent or more in some districts, which goes beyond discouragement to despair. The lack of jobs, let alone with a decent salary and some respect, is one cause of France's social troubles, and an underlying fear of the future in parts of French society.

In 2005–2007, during the de Villepin administration, unemployment finally fell below 10 percent, heading (as this is written) toward 8 percent. But private-sector jobs were only a small part of the total, about one-third of the 190,000 increase in 2006. Government-subsidized jobs, through tax advantages, predominated once again. And of these most were modest jobs such as personal services (household help and home nursing for example) and government-subsidized short-term work and temporary job contracts in the private sector. Nothing had changed. Left or right, the Socialist Jospin or the conservative Villepin, the first response to French unemployment has been government jobs and subsidies.

France's appalling unemployment record has many causes. Economic growth, although improving as of 2006–2007, stagnated for thirty years. Even the dot-com boom years of the late 1990s did not break a remarkably high structural unemployment level. As elsewhere in the "social model" countries of continental Europe, the labor market in France is unresponsive to changing circumstances, i.e., business cycle and individual company difficulties, largely because of a dense network of half-century-old labor laws (agreements won by the powerful left-wing Communist and Socialist trade unions of the time) that protect current jobs rather than stimulate economic growth to create new jobs. Companies are naturally reluctant to hire new employees if job guarantees mean the work force can't be reduced in difficult circumstances. But if working people are to accept a "flexible" labor market, they must have confidence that they will benefit.

Government-mandated fringe benefits in France add about 50 percent to an employee's salary (as opposed to about 20 percent in the United States). This "tax wedge" (the difference between the net wage received by employees and the gross labor cost, including benefits, to employers) rigidifies the labor market, often to the detriment rather than benefit of employees. The national minimum wage is too high relative to the productivity level of minimum-wage employees, which means that fewer are hired. (In the United States, of course, the minimum wage is hardly a living wage even though there are more jobs at this level than in France.) The generous and lengthy unemployment benefits often mean that some among the unemployed prefer to live on unemployment insurance rather than seek a job, especially one that may pay little more than the unemployment benefits themselves.

Also, many good job openings remain vacant despite the high number of job seekers. This is partially the result of a traditional French resistance to move to a new city or region, or to change professions in mid-career. But it is also due to the mismatch between the new technical skills sought by companies (science, technology, finance) and the huge numbers of humanities, philosophy, and language majors within the general university system. Thus a surprising number of good private-sector jobs go begging (unbeknown to most young people), and many students, misguided or complacent, end up with disappointing or temporary jobs that have low pay, few job guarantees, and discouraging prospects. Even later on in a career, many people, fearful of not being able to find another position, stay in a job they don't like, increasing the overall level of frustration and reducing the labor market's ability to adjust to changes in economic opportunities. Books about overstressed, unhappy business executives are now commonplace on the best-seller lists.

Remarkably, however, according to the Organization of Economic Cooperation and Development (OECD), "productivity levels in terms of output per hour are high in France—they are probably higher than in the United States—but this has a lot to do with the fact that the labor market excludes many low-skilled people."[9] The low labor participation rate, 2 percent below the OECD average and much lower than that in the United States, is another factor that threatens financing of benefits and entitlements. People join the work force later and retire earlier than is the case in most of France's competitors. The pension problem is European-wide, and extending the retirement age is, in fact, an EU policy recommendation to all member states.

An unfair two-tiered job structure is thus quite evident—in effect, there are two Frances, two categories of jobholders. Most in the public sector or in large companies benefit from significant entitlements and perks, accrued during the high-growth decades, and hold jobs that are highly protected (it is all but impossible to lay off someone from this group). But such advantages are increasingly difficult to sustain across the board, given a consistently mediocre 1–2 percent economic growth rate. Rather than good new jobs, a second-tier job market has thus developed with, as the Socialist Ségolène Royale points out, a surge in often unwanted part-time work and short-term contracts. This split between the insiders and the outsiders reverberates through French society, generating social resentment that could easily turn political, all the more so as it is increasingly difficult for the outsiders to find upward mobility.

This was the issue in the spring 2006 student demonstrations against the new labor law. Despite the fact that French young people on average are on the labor market for several years—sometimes up to six–eight years—before settling into a "real" job, the students rejected the prospect of increased job insecurity during a two-year trial period. Having little faith that French employers would act in good faith or that the number of private-sector jobs would actually grow, they in effect preferred to keep the current system, which is hardly to their advantage. This followed a well-established French pattern. What former Prime Minister Edouard Balladur said about his would-be youth labor law in 1994 could have been said by Prime Minister Dominique de Villepin in April 2006 about his own attempt: "I would like to see an end to the sort of hypocrisy that consists in lamenting youth unemployment while criticizing every single measure we are trying to take." Had the government consulted more widely and allowed lobbying before bringing the law to parliamentary vote—Prime Minister Dominique de Villepin, like all his predecessors, had promised more "social dialogue"—the result would doubtless have been less divisive.

GLOBALIZATION AND "ECONOMIC PATRIOTISM"

French attitudes toward globalization display a broadly similar mentality. Many French companies, small and large, internalized the rules of international competition long ago and make the most of globalization. But there is another France that consists of a substantial civil service, a large public enterprise sector—remarkably, the third-largest in the OECD, behind Poland and Turkey—which includes partially privatized utility companies (for example, electricity and natural gas), and numerous service-sector professions (from pharmacists to taxi drivers) that are largely shielded from genuine forms of competition. The fact that the average wage in the public sector is slightly higher than that in the private sector is a sign of this imbalance. Though not all French people are equally exposed to the risks of globalization, the fear of globalization is widespread in the country.

A stereotypical reaction ensued. In 2005, the concept of "economic patriotism" appeared in France, triggered by rumors of a possible hostile takeover of the French food giant Danone by PepsiCo. Many politicians rallied behind the prime minister to oppose the very idea of the move (some going as far as saying that milk was a commodity of strategic importance!) when at the same time large French corporations such as Alcatel or Bank Crédit Agricole were engaged in takeover operations of their own, which partly explains why France is one of the leading countries when it comes to investing abroad. In fact, the largest French companies, such as Bouygues (construction) or Thales (armaments), undertake an important part (if not most) of their activities in foreign markets and are owned largely by foreigners (about half of the stock of the forty largest French companies is held by foreign individuals and funds). French popular attitudes toward globalization are easy enough to understand, even though they are overblown.

A PERENNIAL ISSUE: CAN THE FRENCH STATE BE MODERNIZED?

The role of the state, of government as such, whether the regime was a monarchy, an empire, or a republic, has been central throughout the history of modern France. In fact, centralization, protectionism, and state-sponsored industries were already key characteristics of the last phase of the French monarchy before the Revolution of 1789. The succession of French republican regimes has essentially put on an old coat in this respect.

Historically, France has been the Etat-Nation (nation-state) par excellence, meaning that French society developed around an all-pervasive state whose political class took on the responsibility to shape the society according to laws and regulations made in Paris. This was quite different from the English case, where civil society constructed a limited constitutional parliamentary monarchy in its image.

The country's top political and economic elites have been, much more than in other countries, a narrow, socially homogenous group educated in highly selective national elite schools (the *grandes écoles*), such as the famous Ecole polytechnique and the Ecole nationale d'administration.[10] As opposed to the United States, where "what's good for business is good for the country," in France, what is good for the state historically was good for the country. This state-centered or statist relationship between government and society was a very French constitutional-ideological mentality, as compared with England (or the United States) for example. Government oversight or "tutelage" of society, as opposed to a society-centered limitation of state powers (British "Whig" government or the Founding Fathers' idea of "limited government"), was reinforced during the Third Republic (1875–1940) by the emergence of socialist ideas in France, including the rise of the French Communist Party and the Communist-dominated trade union, following the Bolshevik Revolution of 1917. Statism and socialism went together, another part of what makes France unique (and hard for foreigners to understand) among the liberal democracies. In France, nationalized and state-created industries (electricity, gas, water, trains, Air France, defense, and others) were normal rather than steps on the road to a Soviet-style government.

Because government jobs and policies have always been crucial to life chances, how the state and its business enterprises are structured—where the good jobs are, who is favored, who is not—has always been a matter of direct self-interest for great numbers of French people. Understandably, then, one of the reasons why globalization is so unpopular in the country today is that the state, and the jobs and benefits it provides, is seen as one of its likely victims. The more power international forces of all kinds gather, the less potent the French state becomes. When former Prime Minister Lionel Jospin said, in the face of massive layoffs by Michelin, that "the state's powers are not limitless [*l'Etat ne peut pas tout*]," many people were shocked—some because the statement was that of a Socialist leader, others depressed by the content of the message itself. More recently, then Prime Minister de Villepin made a politically motivated visit to a factory of the Sogerma corporation (aircraft maintenance) earmarked for closure, creating a false impression that his government was in a position to do something just because the state owned 15 percent of European Aeronautic Defense and Space (EADS), Sogerma's holding company. Once again, the right and the left in France, behind political rhetoric, respond in essentially the same way, creating expectations of government intervention that are increasingly less possible in a modern economy.

According to Nicolas Baverez and other intellectuals, France is a country in historic decline.[11] His book, *La France qui tombe* ("The Fall of France"), published in 2003, became a best-seller, along with others bearing titles such as *The Agony of the Elites* or the *Society of Fear*.

What is clear is that the French state must decrease its size and the number of sectors of society in which it has a key role. (The state-run education system, for example, is France's single largest employer, as all teachers from primary school to universities—except for a small private-school sector—are *fonctionnaires*, i.e., civil servants. Policies to reduce overstaffing are fought by the strong public-education unions, who consider attrition, not replacing retirees, as "an accountant's mentality" concerning education.) Astonishingly, in 2005, about one-quarter of the entire French work force was made up of civil servants and there were 25 percent more civil servants than a quarter of a century before, whereas it should have been the opposite.

The logic driving the French government's mentality is too often means-based rather than organization-driven, meaning that more money and personnel are remedies classically preferred to doing more with less. For instance, it is a typically French illusion, as seen above, that more teachers will inevitably drive educational standards upward. The French state must do fewer things and it must do them better, as per the "smaller is beautiful" concept.

There is also an important issue of fairness. Public servants work fewer years than their counterparts in the private sector and their pensions are based on the salary of their last year on the job rather than some average salary, as in the private sector. And certain categories of public-sector workers in "dangerous" jobs, such as train drivers or electric utility employees, enjoy still further advantages won long ago when such jobs were indeed dangerous. (It is true that public servants live on average several years longer than their private-sector counterparts.)

French Identity: Globalization and *la France profonde*

To understand French culture, it is necessary to understand *la France profonde*. In France, the countryside is not only to grow food. Rural France, agricultural France, France of the provinces, has long been conceived of as a kind of national "garden," an embodiment of the beauty and history of the country as a whole. Rural towns and villages are not merely places where people live and work. With their history-drenched churches, chateaux, and monuments, they are a mosaic of distinctive cultures themselves, each with its own historical memory.

France's different regions—Provence, Brittany, Normandy, Burgundy, Alsace-Lorraine—are much more diverse than the near-homogenous farming areas dotted with fast-food restaurants that the U.S. countryside has become. France is the most visited country in the world, and each part of the country and each village remains culturally to some extent its own world, ensconced in its own history.

Nevertheless, rural France has not escaped the effects of modernization and globalization that it fears, and for which the farmer-intellectual José Bové is the national poster-boy. As the *Wall Street Journal* reported, M. Bové, the son of two prominent crop research scientists, was a university dropout who moved in the mid-1970s to an abandoned farm on the arid Larzac plateau in southern France. "From that remote base, he has developed a career as a professional agitator, honing a skill for headline-grabbing acts of civil disobedience that often sway public opinion. In recent years, he has become one of the few human faces of the diffuse anti-globalization movement."[12]

José Bové became a folk hero in France (and with international antiglobalization coalitions) when he led a group that vandalized a partially built McDonald's restaurant in the town of Millau to protest punitive U.S. import taxes on Roquefort cheese and other European agricultural products. He also lashed out at the global proliferation of what he called *la malbouffe*, i.e., junk food. He was the right man in the right place at the right time. *The World Is Not for Sale: Farmers Against Junk Food*, a crusading book coauthored with a fellow unionist, has been translated into eight languages, including Japanese and Turkish. Characteristically, M. Bové led the French battle to ban sales of hormone-treated U.S. beef, which became a World Trade Organization issue.

LA FRANCE PROFONDE IN PERIL

The traditional French countryside has in many places simply emptied out. Numerous areas (*départments*) of rural France are now statistically depopulated, and too many ancient villages have become ghost towns. Children don't want to take over the family farm, threatened as it is by national and international competition, social isolation, and cultural boredom.

Four-fifths of the French people now live in cities, urbanized towns, or suburbs—more even than in the United States. Today, less than 4 percent of the French earn their living in agriculture and the great bulk of French farming has become "agro-business."

Despite the thinning out of the countryside, French people remain attached to an ill-defined notion of *ruralité* (anything that has to do with the rural world). The French like the idea that they come "from somewhere" and that this somewhere is not a city but a "real" place of roots and family history. Even people who have lived in Paris for generations still like to invoke rural roots, which are often a form of snobbishness but nevertheless a characteristic part of the national psyche. François Mitterrand's official poster during his first successful presidential campaign in 1981 consisted in a picture of his face with, in the back-drop, the "skyline" of a small village with a church, with the byline "*La Force tranquille*" (Quiet Strength). A presidential hopeful could well use a similar poster today.

French Agro-Business: Big Business Indeed

France is Europe's major agricultural exporter and therefore its interests count heavily in European Union agricultural politics and budgets.

The European Union's very costly Common Agriculture Policy (CAP), which subsidizes agricultural production and export, has probably benefited France more than any other EU country. For decades CAP subsidies were liter-ally two-thirds of the European Union's total budget, a triumph for French interests. Today they remain about a third, a contentious use of the hard-won money for European integration. France, after much haggling at EU summits about whether the deal for France is exorbitant, is still the primary beneficiary of the current agricultural budget (2003–2013).

Whatever the advantages granted to France, agriculture can be counted as one of the European Union's successes. Following the devastation of World War II, the European Union became self-sufficient in the 1960s and since then has been a world-class exporter of food products, with France in the lead. Twenty percent of the French population was involved in agriculture when the EU was established, but even with only a few percent today, the protection of farming is still one of France's domestic and European rallying cries, and only partly because a few percent in an election can be critical. When farmers consider that they are being oppressed, they are prompt to use their tractors to block roads and dump some very organic substances into the local prefecture's courtyard. In a country that has France's history of street protests, farmers can indeed be very determined. And they, like other protesting groups, usually can count on sup-port in public opinion against the government.

Interestingly, there is a small but in some ways influential political party called the CNPT, which stands for "Hunting, Nature, Fishing, and Tradition." This party is represented only at the local level. The French senate, the upper house of parliament, is not powerful overall, but it is crucial in its representation of rural areas. Because senators are elected not directly by the people but indi-rectly by local officials such as regional representatives and mayors (France has about 36,000 town and village governments), rural France is overrepresented and senators are highly sensitive to the mood in the countryside.

More generally, the French farming community is well considered in the country. One reason, of course, is that it is entrusted to produce genuine and distinctive products, the raw material of French gastronomy. After all, good milk is helpful to make tasty cheeses and someone has to feed those geese (with good stuff) if their livers are to become foie gras. There are few countries that have appellations of origin, in addition to wine, for mundane produce such as butter, lentils, and chicken. The notion of *terroir*—a reference to the soil and the local traditions attached to it—is essential to understanding the importance of the countryside-kin French culture.

There are in France forty-four country houses per 1,000 inhabitants (not including the many owned by foreigners). Hence the French as a whole sympathize with local communities that fight against the closure of the post office or elementary school for lack of customers or pupils. Increasingly, town halls subsidize convenience stores in small villages. In 1995, a movie titled *Le bonheur est dans le pré* ("Happiness Is the Countryside"), which takes place in a foie gras–making farm in Périgord, was a blockbuster.

Along with the French president and most politicians, a million people visit the annual Paris Agricultural Show—in effect a giant national farm temporarily installed in the capital. Foreigners visit France not only to experience Paris, let alone Euro-Disney, but to discover the richness of a country that spreads out from the Côte d'Azur to the coast of Normandy. A German proverb says a happy man is "as happy as God in France."

Nevertheless, the fact remains that about thirty thousand farms are disappearing every year. French products are increasingly a matter of agro-business replacing the local producer. The French worry, here as elsewhere, that modernization and globalization are destroying what has been so much of what they have considered distinctively French.

CAN THE FRENCH REFORM FRANCE?

The main obstacles to necessary reform of French society are of a psychological and sociological nature. The problem is much less *what* to do—very few of the challenges facing France are new or particular to that country. The problem is *how* to do it, or rather, how to get it done.

Why this strong French inclination to oppose necessary reforms? One reason is that it is a French habit to prefer confrontation to negotiation. France historically has not been a society that tends naturally toward compromise and consensus. Furthermore, French governments are rarely noted for their negotiation skills. Setting unrealistic preconditions for negotiation and quitting the negotiating table in the middle of the process are classic French trade union habits.

For historical reasons, trade unions' assertiveness is inversely proportional to their size. Only 8 percent of French workers belong to a union (5 percent in the private sector, 15 percent in the public sector). This figure is less than in most other industrialized countries, including the United States. This situation, which is also characterized by a large number of organizations, leads to an exacerbation of tensions and to phenomena such as strikes by proxy and free-riding attitudes by other workers (who know that any advantage gained by the unions will benefit them individually because that is how the system is built). Also, unions tend to be strong in public utilities where, as the ultimate insiders, they have, as we mentioned, larger-than-average entitlements to protect and the available tools to bring the country to a standstill (by stopping the trains or interrupting electrical power). Preemptive strikes are sometimes used by French trade unions, just in case. The so-called *droits acquis* (acquired social rights, a key concept in French politics) have become totems to some of these trade unions. Many French people complain that the categories of workers that demonstrate and strike the most (though the occurrence of such events has sharply decreased in the past two decades) are precisely the ones that enjoy the most benefits and whose jobs are the best protected. Here too, duality rather than fairness prevails.

There are other factors as well. The Malthusian mind-set is quite pervasive in France. Rather than seek to enlarge the pie, it is common for people to take its size as a given and spend a huge amount of energy in seeking an equitable way to divide it, as was the case with the 35-hour work week. In addition, many people distrust the motives of the private sector, as demonstrated during the 2006 youth labor law crisis. Overall, an anxiety of downward mobility seems to have gripped the nation: children of immigrants feel they cannot join mainstream France, the youth worry about not being able to reach their parents' standard of living, and the middle-class resent the possibility of getting stuck there. The confidence level of households has seldom been so low. Gloom, leading to a crisis of self-confidence, has engulfed the country.

The concept of reform has become a French political nightmare. "A feeling of distrust toward any reform," as the political commentator Jacques Julliard notes, has developed "within lower social groups."[13] And that feeling is not limited to them.

France's Political Troubles

French political parties have been in a weak position to deal with the reform conundrum. The high level of activism at the extremes of the political spectrum is one of its worrying characteristics. For example, in the first round of the 2002 presidential elections, in which no less than sixteen candidates competed, nearly a third of the electorate voted for an extremist party (not even counting the Communist Party). Astonishingly, the veteran Jean-Marie Le Pen, leader of the far-right xenophobic National Front (FN), came in second, beating out the Socialist prime minister, Lionel Jospin. Le Pen, to the nation's international shame, thus made the runoff ballot against President Chirac. On the far left, the veteran Arlette Laguiller, leader of the splinter far-left "Workers' Struggle"

Party, came in fifth, getting almost 6 percent of the vote. Such a volatile protest electorate indicates why French politics remains almost without any bipartisan consensus, and why the French parliament, unlike England's, has little sense of a "loyal opposition."

The FN, the naughty child of French politics, is the most scrutinized French political party both domestically and internationally. It has never had representation at parliament, except between 1986 and 1988 when a controversial Socialist-sponsored change of the voting system to minimize left-wing losses opened the doors of the National Assembly to thirty-five National Front deputies.

But despite its successes, the extreme right influences the mainstream mainly by tilting the conservative parties further to the right on issues such as national minorities and immigration problems. Mainstream French conservative forces have thus far not been able to reduce their extreme wing, and the National Front's electorate and ideas are an unfortunate characteristic of French domestic politics.

The French left has its own problems. It is important to understand the heritage of the French Communist Party (PCF) in this respect.

When the Socialist president François Mitterrand took four communist ministers into his "Union of the Left" government in 1981, his aim was not to turn France toward communism. He wanted to give the kiss of death to the declining French Communist Party by manipulating it into government so that its rank and file would defect once the PCF inevitably disappointed them. In 1978, the PCF had nearly as many representatives in the National Assembly as did the Socialist Party. Three years later, there was one Communist for six Socialists.

In any case, Mitterrand's strategy was only one of the factors explaining the long-term decline of French communism. The communists had already been on a downward slope, weakened by Charles de Gaulle's return to power in 1958 and its undiminished Stalinism in the 1970s, a period when the Soviet myth was disintegrating and the Italian Communist Party was de-Stalinizing. In France, publication of Alexander Solzhenitsyn's *The Gulag Archipelago* in 1976 was a bombshell after which nostalgic left-leaning French intellectuals had to admit that Soviet communism was a positive regime whose crimes had been only "mistakes."[14]

The PCF—one of the few communist parties in Western Europe that, out of intransigence, has not changed its name—has collapsed as a major political influence. Recently it has been outflanked by smaller extreme-left parties, such as the LCR (Ligue Communiste Révolutionnaire), led by a media-savvy postman in his thirties, Olivier Besancenot. A Chinese communist of today would blush listening to Arlette Laguiller: "It is only at the international level that the proletariat will be able to defeat the bourgeoisie once and for all." Though these parties have no national representation and barely any local roots, they have a capacity to crystallize frustrations that compares well with that of the extreme right. Jospin's defeat on the left in 2002 occurred because voters scattered their first-round ballots on the minor left candidates in order to "send a message of discontent." Extreme-left ideas remain anachronistically powerful in French politics, capable of determining elections.

Given the volatility of the electorate sympathetic to extremist ideologies, use of the referendum, a favorite practice of Charles de Gaulle, has become a dangerous risk in France. Unlike Switzerland or California where voters are invited to vote in numerous referendums, in which the stakes are not always of prime significance, referendums in France are now rare, organized at the national level and usually on fundamental issues. The potential for dramatization and polarization is thus great.

Other factors reinforce these characteristics. Following the tradition of former plebiscites—through which the unelected leader seeks direct support from the people, in the Napoleonic tradition—the referendum remains highly personalized in France: "who" asks the question is as important—if not more—as "what" is being asked, with the voters reformulating the question as they see fit. There is the striking precedent of 1969, when the historic leader de Gaulle resigned following the rejection by voters, in a referendum following the May-June 1968 rebellion against him, of a constitutional reform of secondary importance. Since then each referendum implicitly questions the political legitimacy of the president. This was the case most recently in the failed European Union constitutional referendum of May 2005. Once again, the volatility of the French electorate and the large number of small, protest-thriving parties, means that the timing and context of a referendum are likely to trigger links in the minds of voters that can confuse the issue at stake. As Bruno Frappat, editor of the Catholic daily *La Croix*, once pointed out, "The culture of refusal is a national sport that seeks every opportunity to manifest itself."

In fact, representation in parliament would not suffice to satisfy the demands of the splinter extremist parties. As noted above, the Fifth Republic is a hybrid between a parliamentary system (the prime minister needs the support of a majority in parliament) and a presidential one (the French president is directly elected by the people). In practice, however, parliament has little autonomous power. It is controlled by party discipline, either in favor of the president or a "cohabitation" prime minister. In any case, governments find themselves confronting nonrepresentative trade unions, extremist parties, and all sorts of civil-society groups without a parliament that can act as an intermediary or a source of new ideas. French government has no established system of lobbies, and lobbying remains a suspect, hardly legitimate way to enter parliamentary lawmaking. The result is that even when the government enjoys a significant majority in parliament, it does not hold all the reins of power.

LOOKING AHEAD: THE NEED
FOR A FRENCH NEW DEAL

The French political system clearly needs renewal of its political establishment and institutions. As an ersatz for genuine political breathing space, French voters have systematically voted out the majority in power at each election since 1981.

France also needs a reformed social model, a redefined set of expectations about what government should provide in the way of benefits and guarantees to a rapidly changing society. Most French people realize, even if they don't like it, that the current one is neither sustainable nor adapted to the requirements of a globalized world. A turn toward the Scandinavian "flex-security" model, in which workers can be laid off without crisis but then benefit from a strong support system during their transition back into the job market, would be an arduous if desirable direction. The fundamentals that underpin the social system of these (much smaller) economies—high unionization levels, consensus-seeking societies, absence of extreme social and political actors—do not exist in France.

Although imported ideas can be useful, French political and economic actors must ultimately design their own way forward. Incremental reforms, such as those trimming healthcare and pension entitlements adopted in 2002–2005, are necessary but not sufficient.

In some countries, for example, voting in political elections is compulsory: France could introduce the obligation for all workers to vote for a trade union, turning them into more legitimate and constructive partners for the government and probably rationalizing the trade union landscape. France would also benefit from embracing the principles of simplicity and fairness: one job contract instead of many, a simple fiscal system rather than high taxes with too many complicated exemptions, and the disappearance of anachronistic entitlements for specific groups—all changes that would take France in the right direction. In other words, merge the two Frances into one. This can only be achieved by putting everything on the table and by broadening the issues rather than keeping them separate in small parts that are difficult to deal with. France needs coherence, a sense of destination, and a fully involved parliament, as well as new leaders. And all the more as France has another important challenge to tackle.

MINORITIES AND THE CHALLENGES OF INTEGRATION

France is an old country of immigration. In the late nineteenth century and first part of the twentieth century, there were several waves of immigration from other European countries, such as Portugal, Italy, and Poland. These populations were gradually integrated into French society. To rebuild the country after World War II, workers from these countries but also from North Africa, especially the former colony Algeria, came to France. Today, France is the country in Europe with the largest population of Muslim background, estimated at about 5 million people, that is, 8 percent of a population of 63 million in which about 30 percent are eligible to vote. Notes Justin Vaisse, "Among 'potential Muslims', that is French citizens of African or Turkish origin with at least one parent or grandparent born in Africa or Turkey, 66% identify themselves as Muslims and 20% as having no religion at all."[15]

France, as it widely known, finds it difficult to incorporate its minorities and many factors are at issue.

Whereas previous immigrants originated mainly from Catholic countries (as is the case for France), recent immigration has come from Muslim countries, which are culturally quite different. Also, as growth rates started to decline and unemployment rose in the 1970s, a sense of competition developed between groups of different origins. In the 1980s, immigration became a major political theme and helped the National Front enter the frame, fueling an antagonism between the various communities. The immigration question has since persisted as an electoral issue, at varying levels of intensity. The fact that most immigrants came from former French colonies, with the unease that it occasionally creates on both sides, has been another complicating factor. The emergence of radical Islamic terrorism, which struck France much earlier than it did the United States (albeit never to the same scale) and was essentially a spillover of the Algerian civil war of the 1990s, gave a new resonance to the presence of a large Muslim population, though it is not a key dimension of France's integration challenge.

France has historically championed its own integration model based on the goal of complete assimilation into French society and on strict equality before the law. Immigrants could join French society but as individuals rather than as communities, what is called assimilation rather than *communautarisme*, i.e., the multiculturalist approach of, until recently, Britain. Populations of recent immigrant origins are asked to merge with "French" values rather than living as subcultures.

This "republican ideal of equality" is self-evidently not easily compatible with the development of communities rooted in the country or culture of origin with little interest in blending into society as a whole. In this sense, the French integration model is very different from the U.S. one, which is much more comfortable with the notion of subcultural community and identification of an individual by reference to a given group. Consequently, the concept of positive discriminations, called affirmative action in the United States, is alien to the French "republican tradition." It makes many people uncomfortable and resentful.[16] The exact number of French of Arab or Muslim origin is not even known because it is illegal to seek this information in official census or surveys. A third-generation Algerian immigrant would not refer to him or herself as an "Algerian-French" in the way someone in the United States would say Arab-American or Italian-American.

In fact, despite evident problems, the large minority of Arab and Muslim origin does not translate into France becoming hostage to or a battle ground for radical Islamism. Mosque attendance is low and extremists are rare (and tightly monitored by the authorities). Indeed, to the same extent as the French population has become essentially secular—the reference to France as a Catholic country has become cultural rather than religious, given the low level of regular religious practice in the country today—the population of Arab and Muslim origin could well be taking a similar path. In an April-May 2006 Europe-wide survey, to the question "Do you think of yourself first as a citizen of your country or first as a Muslim?" 42 percent of French Muslims chose "national citizen" and 46 percent said "Muslim." (In Great Britain, the answers to the same question were respectively 7 and 81 percent.[17]) Rates of intermarriage are high, ranging from 20 percent to 50 percent depending on the generation, the country of origin, and the gender of the persons with a Muslim background.[18] (Interestingly, this is also the case of the members of the French 2006 soccer team.) France's integration challenges are real but they are similar to those faced by many other European countries and should not be exaggerated.

The November 2005 riots were not religion-based. The young people involved wanted, as has been said already, the same respect and advantages as everyone else. (The protest group, "AC le feu," whose name is a play on words for "enough fire," was formed to press minority-group grievances on the government.) The violence involved, no doubt exaggerated by sensationalist media coverage, was in fact condemned by all Muslim organizations in France.

In other words, it is inaccurate to simply transpose to the French domestic situation a post–September 11 view of the world, as is sometimes the case in the U.S. media. Islamist terrorism is without question a threat to France, and an influence on French foreign policy. At the same time, French counterterrorism efforts are among the most successful in the world. Historical relationships, for better and worse, between France and many African and Arab countries have left enduring bonds. The French see themselves as particularly knowledgeable about these areas of the world.

President Chirac, who strongly disagreed with the "clash of civilizations" premise, fought tenaciously against both anti-Semitism (he was the first French president to acknowledge the collusion of the French state with the Nazis during their occupation of France in World War II) and anti-Muslim discrimination. Thus, he put in place, then reinforced, the HALDE (Haute Autorité de Lutte contre les Discriminations et pour l'Egalité), an agency dedicated to fighting discrimination, and acknowledged the important role played by African fighters on France's side during both world wars.

Nevertheless, immigration policy is now a permanent issue in French politics as elsewhere in Europe, mainly in the sense of tightening it. A law voted in summer 2006, inspired by Interior Minister Nicolas Sarkozy, restricts the possibilities for family reunification as a justification for immigration and will grant residence visas only to people willing to work in areas where a labor shortage exists, such as construction. One aim is to have greater selectiveness of immigrants to increase those with higher-education qualifications.[19]

France's Role in the World Order

French influence and sense of responsibility on the world stage are perennially controversial, both inside France and among France's friends and partners, probably above all in the United States.

THE FADING LEGACY OF CHARLES DE GAULLE

"Gaullism" was the doctrine of French renewal that sought to revive French national self-confidence after the disasters of World Wars I and II. Charles de Gaulle, France's great Resistance leader, insisted on creating a new regime, a Fifth French Republic in 1958, when he was called back to power by parliament in the midst of a new disaster—the Algerian war in which France sought to keep control of that country by repressing the anticolonialist struggle of the Algerian National Liberation Front.

De Gaulle's longstanding prestige and moral authority pushed through a constitution that set presidential domination of foreign policy and general oversight of domestic government. His World War II intransigence had not diminished at all. He won the argument that French national independence required her own nuclear deterrent as opposed to relying on U.S. protection; he twice vetoed British membership in the European Union on the argument that British strategy was not really European but transatlantic; struggling against Cold War Soviet-U.S. primacy in European political life, he accorded diplomatic recognition to Communist China before any other Western government.

Box 1.3   De Gaulle and Gaullism

All my life I have thought of France in a [special] way. This is inspired by sentiment as much as by reason. The emotional side of me tends to imagine France, like the princess in the fairy stories or the Madonna in the frescoes, as dedicated to an exalted and exceptional destiny. Instinctively I have the feeling that Providence has created her either for complete successes or for exemplary misfortunes. If, in spite of this, mediocrity shows in her acts and deeds, it strikes me as an absurd anomaly, to be imputed to the faults of Frenchmen, not to the genius of the [country]. But the [rational] side of my mind also assures me that France is not really herself unless in the front rank; that only vast enterprises are capable of counterbalancing the ferments of dispersal which are inherent in her people; that our country, as it is, surrounded by the others, as they are, must aim high and hold itself straight, on pain of mortal danger. In short, to my mind, France cannot be France without [grandeur].

(*Source:* Charles de Gaulle, *War Memoirs*, vol. 1, "The Slope," p. 3, New York: Simon & Schuster, 1959; slight alterations in translation by the present authors.)

De Gaulle's dramatic tone and high rhetoric was a backdrop for French domestic politics and foreign policy, something like the place in British history held by Winston Churchill and in U.S. history by Franklin Roosevelt. Not surprisingly, this Gaullist foreign policy outlook, when it resurfaces in today's international relations, is a source of irritation in France's relationship with its European partners and the United States.

FRANCE'S INTERNATIONAL ROLE TODAY

Is France, then, an average middle-sized power with sometimes outsized pretensions, or is there more to it?

Clearly France neither is what it used to be in de Gaulle's time—*a fortiori* in previous centuries—nor is it a superpower. But it does occupy a somewhat special place in international relations for several reasons. First, it holds levers that are associated with power: it is one of the five permanent members of the UN Security Council (and is as such a veto holder) and has been a member of the nuclear club since 1960. Second, it is one of the founding countries of the European Union within which it traditionally played, in tandem with Germany, the central leadership role. Third, France's former glory grants it various channels through which it can leverage its voice, such as close relationships with some former colonies such as Morocco or Senegal. Fourth, as we have mentioned, it remains the sixth economic power and is an important player in world trade and investments. Fifth, French foreign policy uses its influence in the European Union as a megaphone for French national positions and national interests. France and Britain are the two significant military powers in Europe and their conventional military and nuclear cooperation oversee the extent to which Europe might have a successful Common Foreign and Security Policy beyond participation in "coalitions of the willing" such as in the war against the Taliban regime in Afghanistan and the 2006 takeover of the U.S. military role there by the North Atlantic Treaty Organization (NATO). Finally, within the general "soft power" attractiveness of Europe seen as a civilization with its own "European model of society," France possesses a special place through language, culture, and quality of life.

Two facets of France's foreign policy are particularly worth focusing on. One is the country's evolving role in Europe and the other its relationship with the United States.

FRANCE'S EUROPEAN PARADOXES: REJECTING THE DRAFT CONSTITUTION

The May 2005 French rejection of the European draft constitution was not the first French "no." In the 1960s, De Gaulle rejected Great Britain's bid to join the then European Community. But, because the Constitution was brought to a referendum in France, it was the first "no" from the voters themselves, with a resounding 55 percent against. (François Mitterrand's referendum on the Maastricht Treaty in 1992, which was the first time the French electorate was given the chance to vote on European integration, was a close call with only 51 percent in its favor.)

Despite France's leading role in European integration from the very beginning in the 1950s, the French today tend to have ambivalent feelings about its dangers for France as compared with its benefits. Everyone applauds the EU journey away from Europe's war-torn and tormented past, marked above all by the historic Franco-German reconciliation after "three wars in one man's lifetime," as de Gaulle wrote. And most French people recognize that, given a middle power's limitations, France needs to be part of a larger entity if it is to maintain a serious international role.

But at the same time, there is a widespread French anxiety that "Brussels," the location of the main European Union institutions, is growing too powerful, operating without adequate transparency and accountability. This, they feel, compounds the negative effects of globalization. From European and international business competition, to outsourcing of jobs to the new formerly communist member countries in the east, to longstanding pressures on France to agree to reduce EU agricultural subsidies, the average French person probably worries more about European integration than he appreciates it. And Brussels's involvement sometimes gets down to seemingly absurd detail, nitpicking against national and regional traditions by, for example, pushing for systematic cheese pasteurization.

Thus, paradoxically, although key aspects of the European Union are largely France's brainchild and the Constitution might have been written solely by the French, it failed because of French voters. It was replete with the type of social rights the French have learned to love, such as the priority of jobs over market rigors, and the essential role of "social partners." It gave France more voting power in European institutions than it has under the currently-in-effect Nice Treaty of 2001. It attacked the so-called democratic deficit by putting national parliaments in the loop (European Commission documents would have been forwarded to them; they would have been able to object to measures violating the subsidiarity principle, according to which the EU should only take action if a policy can be better achieved at the EU level), as well as augmenting the European Parliament's role. It would have made Turkey's entry in the European Union—a prospect currently rejected by a large majority of the French electorate—more difficult, as the draft document included a Charter of Fundamental Rights that would have turned into a law a political declaration dating from the 2001 Nice summit.

Finally, the Constitution exhorted Europe to become once again a true international power, a *Europe-puissance,* an objective favored by a majority in the country according to opinion polls (although the same polls demonstrate that the French, like Europeans in general, would not be willing to raise taxes in order to pay for a more effective military force to back up diplomacy).

Left-wing politicians criticized the draft Constitution as a product of what they understand as right-wing ideological "economic liberalism," meaning capitalist market economics and deregulation of labor markets as opposed to a strong network of laws to protect jobs and the European Social Model safety net. "Liberalism" has become an inflammatory word in French politics, evoking the specter of precarious jobs and lives. It has resonance far outside left-wing ideology because French people believe it justifies their anxieties about the future.

The structure and functioning of the EU are difficult for outsiders to understand. Its institutional amorphousness and uncertainty of decisionmaking operation make it easy for everyone to present the EU according to their political purposes: for some it is a quasi-federal entity while for others the EU is no more than a political association between nation-states; some argue it is essentially a free market with a political twist, while others see it as a bold political vision in the making. This ambiguity is present, if only implicitly, in most EU-related debates. Hence a third paradox: it may be this ambiguity that has allowed a majority to emerge in favor of the European unification process in the preceding decades. By being different things to different people, the European project won the support of a majority. Europe was in the eyes of the beholder. The withdrawal of the draft Constitution has forced the lifting of this ambiguity, with consequences that are difficult to anticipate.

Finally, the question of Turkey's application for EU membership has occupied an even more central place in French politics than elsewhere in the Union, linked to other issues of French and European choices as well.

Early in October 2004, only days before the European Commission recommended the opening of official entry negotiations with Turkey, the necessity of a referendum on all new proposed memberships (thus Turkey) was inserted as an amendment to the French Constitution. Thus, four words—Europe, Turkey, referendum, and constitution—became confusingly mixed in the minds of many French voters.

French opponents of Turkey's membership in the EU put forward many arguments. According to them, Turkey and "Europe" share neither similar values nor a common culture. The EU should essentially be a Christian club that cannot—and should not have to—deal with the integration of such an important Muslim population. (The fact that Turkey has been governed by an Islamic party, albeit moderate, only reinforces their view.) One of the "no" camp's arguments is the matter-of-fact assertion that Turkey is not situated in Europe, and if Turkey were accepted it would prove difficult to later deny admission to other Mediterranean countries. And in any case, say opponents, extending the frontiers of the EU to those of Iran, Syria, and Iraq (among others) is a very dangerous move to make. In addition, the combination of Turkey's size and its lower level of development is said to be too unaffordable, as well as opening the way to an unmanageable flow of Turkish immigrants. Turkey would dilute the nature and cohesion of the European Union, reducing it to a free-market area (which result, critics say, would explain Washington's support for the Turkish bid).

Two main reasons are given to accept Turkey. The first is that Turkey clearly chose Europe with Mustapha Kemal in the 1920s, when Turkey was a young republic emerging from the ruins of the Ottoman Empire. Among other things, Turkey latinized its alphabet, gave the right of vote to women (at a time when it was not the case in some parts of Western Europe, including France), and opted for secularism, a crucial aspect of modernity. The second reason is geopolitical. Geopolitically, Turkey is more in Asia than it is in Europe. But as a country that occupies a highly strategic position at the edge of a very volatile region and is already part of Europe's security sphere through its membership in NATO, both Turkey and the European Union have as a genuine interest that Turkey be anchored to the European project. Anything less than full membership, e.g., a "privileged partnership," would be better than nothing but less than desirable.

FRANCO-U.S. RELATIONS: A ROCKY RELATIONSHIP SMOOTHED OUT

Since the de Gaulle years in the 1960s, Franco-U.S. relations reached their lowest historical point in 2003 during the Iraq crisis. Where the Bush administration was adamant that Saddam Hussein was a direct threat to world peace and had to be removed by force, President Chirac insisted that the inspection process aimed at determining if Iraq still possessed weapons of mass destruction (WMD) should be carried out until it was conclusive. In fact, until mid-January 2003, Chirac had French military forces preparing to join the coalition before deciding finally that France would veto a clear Security Council resolution to go to war. The French president's decision, in other words, came late, and seemed influenced by the fierce antiwar policy of German chancellor Gerhard Schröder.

Though the following events vindicated France's position—there turned out to be no WMD in Iraq—its adamant opposition to the Bush administration shocked many Americans, as well as some in France. (The Congress was outraged, and some suggested the symbolic reply of changing "French fries" to "Freedom fries.") The resulting Franco-U.S. clash was extremely brutal, and very personal between Bush and Chirac.

Behind the scenes, however, France and the United States had never stopped cooperating. A striking example is intelligence and counterterrorism, which is a French specialty. After September 11—when *Le Monde*, the most important, and not usually pro-U.S. newspaper, headlined "We Are All Americans Today"—the French were, and still are, among the closest and most effective partners of the United States and the international network of counterterrorism against Islamist jihad organizations.[20] Islamist terrorist attacks on French territory go back to the mid-1970s (i.e., when Jacques Chirac was prime minister for the first time), and there were also terrorist attacks on the French during the Algerian war (1954–1962) by the Algerian National Liberation Front. With long experience, French intelligence and counterterrorism services are among the most effective in the world.[21]

Franco-U.S. Rapprochement

French-U.S. relations continue to be delicate at the level of international and strategic policy. But since the invasion of Iraq the fact that overall interests remained essentially identical has brought about a new rapprochement, as it has between the George Bush administration and the antiwar Europeans in general. (The election of the conservative Angela Merkel as German chancellor was a turning point.)

The second Bush administration began with explicit overtures from Washington toward the Europeans, and a more multilateralist attitude, at least rhetorically, toward decisionmaking among the allies. Underneath the smoothed feathers, however, U.S. predominance, Bush's unilateralist instincts, and a reliance on British prime minister Tony Blair had hardly changed.

As for Iraq, the French now said that, whatever the original conflict over whether to invade or not, everyone had a vital interest in working together for a positive outcome, with regard both to oil supplies and resolving the various Middle East conflicts, which could have a ripple effect across world-order problems, including Islamist terrorism, all the more important given the war in the Middle East that broke out suddenly in July 2006.

Differences of global perspective have not abated. The Bush administration's tough rhetoric worries the French, concerned to avoid "clash of civilizations" talk that inflames tensions. French policy also advises a longer-term, less-alarmist view of terrorism than Washington's view that the world has entered an entirely new era of catastrophic dangers.

This combination of rapprochement and continued worries about U.S. geostrategic instincts was apparent elsewhere on the international checkerboard of crises.

In post-Taliban Afghanistan, for example, cooperation has been good. French and U.S. military forces have worked closely on the ground, despite the fact that the Bush administration left NATO as such outside the invasion. France is a leading contributor, both financially and in terms of troops, to NATO endeavors, and was playing a central role in NATO's takeover of key security responsibilities in 2005.[22]

With regard to the Iranian nuclear program, a British-French-German foreign ministers' negotiating team shuttled to Teheran to convince the regime of the ayatollahs that international determination against them warranted giving guarantees that Iran would not produce nuclear weapons and allowing the International Atomic Energy Agency inspections. The Iranian leadership appeared to toy with the "good cop" Europeans, leaving an impression that more serious attention might be paid to "bad cop" Washington, which refused to take any option off the table, a veiled threat of possible military action.

From the point of view of European Union development, the joint foreign ministers' mission did suggest the possibility of a common EU foreign policy, at least in diplomacy if not in military action. But the practical results were meager. Against a determined regime such as Iran's, European policy might be taken seriously only when Washington's military might stands behind it. Thus, not even a European Union megaphone can put France back in the front rank of world powers.

FRANCE, THE ISRAELI-PALESTINIAN CONFLICT, AND THE LEBANON WAR

France has a long history in the Middle East. Napoleon debarked to conquer Egypt in 1798. His reason, according to his memoirs, was "glory," to raise the French flag over the pyramids. The French army did bring back the column that has since adorned the Place de la Concorde in Paris before being defeated in 1801. At the end of World War I, the new League of Nations carved up four territories of the collapsed Ottoman Empire, giving France a mandate to govern Syria and Lebanon and assigning Iraq and Palestine to Britain. In September 1920 France created the State of Greater Lebanon, which achieved its national independence in 1943, with France formally departing in 1945. To some extent Lebanon was created as a protected Christian enclave in the Middle East and France acted as the special guarantor of the Lebanese Maronite Christians.

During the Fourth Republic (1946–1958) France was a friendly ally to Israel, and, along with Britain and Israel, France launched the disastrous Suez invasion of 1956. Charles de Gaulle redirected Fifth Republic foreign policy more toward the Arab states, a tendency that became a full turn as a result of Israel's victory in the 1967 Six Day War. In a famous press conference on November 27, 1967, de Gaulle criticized "the emergence of a warrior State of Israel determined to increase its land area and boundaries." De Gaulle, in a notorious phrase, said that "some people even [fear] that the Jews . . . were still what they had always been, an elite people, sure of themselves and domineering."[23]

Thereafter, all French governments (except François Mitterrand's) took special concern for Arab interests, partly to be evenhanded (in contrast to their perception of a U.S. foreign policy consistently favorable to Israel), and partly because of access to oil and big-ticket exports.[24]

In the past few decades, France along with the other European powers was marginalized in dealing with the Arab-Israeli conflict, until the problem of

Syrian influence in Lebanon (inflamed by the supposed Syrian-sponsored assassination of former Lebanese prime minister Rafik Hariri in 2004) was taken up in the UN Security Council.

In 2004, France (because of its special history with Lebanon) and the U.S. cosponsored UN Security Council resolution 1559, which called for Syria's withdrawal from Lebanon, disarmament of all militias (without saying so, specifically aimed at Hezbollah), and the deployment—never carried out—of the Lebanese army in the Hezbollah-controlled southern territory up to the border with Israel.

France participated in the cutoff of European aid to the Palestinian Hamas government in 2006, demanding that Hamas meet the international community's three conditions: renounce terrorism, recognize Israel, and accept all previous PLO-Israel agreements.

President Jacques Chirac's policy during the July-August 2006 Israel-Hezbollah war displayed the usual French desire to appear evenhanded. He criticized Israel's massive bombardment of Lebanese infrastructure as "completely disproportionate" to Hezbollah's provocation.

Thereafter, France again worked with the United States and other EU countries, plus the Russians, to create an enhanced UN interposition force (the UN Interim Force in Lebanon [UNIFIL]) on the Lebanese border, the original, weak UNIFIL having been created in 1982 after an earlier conflict. The new UNIFIL mandate included monitoring the cease-fire and acting as a buffer against a renewal of hostilities.

In a confusing series of events, President Chirac immediately offered a certain number of soldiers and to keep the standing French command of UNIFIL, a strong initiative soon contradicted by French backpeddling. The Italian government headed by Prime Minister Romano Prodi then unexpectedly offered a strong contingent and said it would take over the leadership of this more robust UNIFIL mandate from the UN.

Whatever France's embarrassment in establishing the new UNIFIL, the fact is that the Europeans have taken a serious step forward in assuming greater responsibilities in international crisis situations. In terms of military commitment, the enhanced UNIFIL mandate includes rules of engagement authorizing deadly force in self-defense, which implies a willingness to take casualties in the most explosive region in the world. Perhaps this is the beginning of Europe's reentry into Middle East peacemaking at a time when U.S. influence has been damaged by the Iraq situation.[25]

Conclusion

For better or worse, France still likes to go its own way. In terms of the organization of society, the French still believe that their quality of life trumps any other. They only reluctantly adopt foreign ways of doing things, especially when they come from what is considered to be an oppressive Anglo-Saxon political and economic model. On the other hand, the pervasiveness of an Americanized and globalized world culture creates constant conformist pressures that the French both love and hate.

At the level of foreign policy and international decisionmaking, French governments, both from the right and the left, would prefer a multipolar world if it were possible. As things are, the French want to be partners in their own way, at their own pace and time, in the most important international situations. They must accept U.S. supremacy, but they don't want to be taken for granted. De Gaulle's goal of a special French role in international relations has not entirely evaporated. But there was only one de Gaulle and the international framework has changed a great deal since the 1960s.

When French governments are self-confident, enlightened, and act in the right way at the right time, France's influence can be essential, as it has been in the case of historic Franco-German leadership in European integration. When in a state of flux and uncertainty domestically, as is the case as Jacques Chirac's twelve-year presidency ends, French governments have lacked the resolve and public support to innovate at the level of the country's difficulties. The basis for a strong foreign policy doesn't exist.

Globalization in particular haunts the French mood. Though many French companies have done well internationally, the French people, even more than other European societies, tend to fear globalization more than to see its positive side. For the French left, globalization is a constant temptation to demagogy.

Even European integration, long a French specialty, is now seen by many as yet another facet of the globalization phenomenon. This was a key motivation in French rejection of the proposed EU constitution in 2005. Americanization-globalization-Europeanization threatens to destroy the French social model and the French way of life that many cherish for understandable reasons. The future has become a source of anxiety rather than one of opportunity.

This needs to change. A renewed France is necessary to a reinvigorated Europe, itself necessary to face dangerous times in the world order. The time has come for a French New Deal.

Notes

1. In reality, young people torching cars (called "rodeo") was nothing new in France. It has been a kind of youth sport for fifteen years. According to an Interior Ministry report of August 14, 2006, in 2005 45,000 cars were burned, including 10,000 during the November 2005 riots. In the first six months of 2006 the number was 21,000.

2. Ronald Tiersky (ed.), *Europe Today: National Politics, European Integration and European Security*, Lanham, MD: Rowman & Littlefield, 2004, chapter 9, p. 251.

3. Mitterrand's controversial political career began in the Resistance movement in World War II. A soldier captured by the Germans during the blitzkrieg of June 1940, he was eighteen months in German POW camps before escaping back to France. Then—the controversial period—he was a civil servant in the Vichy regime for about a year, moving gradually during that time into the Resistance on French territory. (This metropolitan Resistance is to be distinguished from the better-known "external" Fighting France Resistance movement that was led by General Charles de Gaulle.) He became a notable Resistance leader, being appointed a junior minister in de Gaulle's first post-Liberation government. Mitterrand was born during World War I. See Ronald Tiersky, *François Mitterrand: A Very French President*, Lanham, MD: Rowman & Littlefield, 2003.

4. The best-selling French book on Jacques Chirac's presidency is Franz-Olivier Giesbert, *La tragédie du president: Scènes de la vie politique (1986–2006)*, Paris: Flammarion, 2006.

5. See Ronald Tiersky, "The Strategic Significance of Europe's Demographic Deficit," *American Foreign Policy Interests*, 26(4), August 2004.

6. Corinne Maier, *Bonjour paresse—De l'art et la nécessité d'en faire le moins possible en entreprise.* Paris: Editions Michalon, 2004; translated as *Hello Laziness! Why Hard Work Doesn't Pay*, New York: Random House, 2005. Maier is a part-time employee of the EDF, the French national electricity enterprise, working as an economist. She is also a practicing psychoanalyst who has written nine books.

7. *Le Monde*, June 6, 2006, p. 1.

8. Jean-Louis Borloo, minister of employment and social cohesion in the Villepin government, said that "job-seekers are the principal resource of this country." (On RTL radio, July 28, 2006, quoted in the *Canard Enchaîné*, France's weekly newspaper of informed political satire and gossip.) Favorable descriptions of the European Social Model can be found in Jeremy Rifkin, *The European Dream: How the European Vision of the Future Is Quietly Eclipsing the American Dream*, New York: Penguin Press, 2004, and T. R. Reid, *The United States of Europe: The New Superpower and the End of American Supremacy*, New York: Penguin Press, 2004.

9. *OECD Economic Survey, France 2005*, volume 2005/10, September 2005, p. 18.

10. These schools, in their prestige, might be compared to the John F. Kennedy School of Government at Harvard or the various elite U.S. business schools.

11. Nicolas Baverez, *La France qui tombe* (France Is Falling), Paris: Perrin, 2003, and *Nouveau monde, Vieille France* (New World, Old France), Paris: Perrin, 2005.

12. The quotation and succeeding points are from Alice Woodruff, *Wall Street Journal*, May 25, 2005, p. 16.

13. Jacques Julliard, *Le malheur français* (France's Misfortune), Paris: Flammarion, 2005, p. 54.

14. For a merciless account of the French left's fascination with the Soviet myth, see Tony Judt, *Past Imperfect: French Intellectuals, 1945–1957*, Berkeley: University of California Press, 1993.

15. Justin Vaisse, "Unrest in France, November 2005: Immigration, Islam and the Challenge of Integration," Congressional testimony, January 10, 2006 (www.brookings .edu). See the important new book by Jonathan Laurence and Justin Vaisse, *Integrating Islam: Political and Religious Challenges in Contemporary France*, Washington, DC: Brookings Institution Press, 2006.

16. Daniel DiSalvo and James W. Caeser, "Affirmative Action and Positive Discrimi-nation," *The Tocqueville Review*, XXV(1), 2004. But the controversial Nicolas Sarkozy in the 2007 presidential campaign called for outright hiring quotas for minority groups as the only way to social justice (balancing his hard-line policy as interior minister on ille-gal immigrants and his call for selective immigration).

17. "Muslims in Europe: Economic Worries Top Concerns About Religious and Cul-tural Identity," July 6, 2006, Pew Global Attitudes Project (www.pewglobal.org).

18. "Muslims in Europe," p. 6.

19. Martin Arnold, "French Immigration Data Show Rise Led by Africans and Asians," *Financial Times*, August 24, 2006, p. 3.

20. See Chapter 13 in this book on counterterrorism efforts, by Richard Aldrich and Wyn Rees.

21. France innovated globally in other ways, for example Unitaid, President Chirac's French-led international medicines organization to buy AIDS drugs from low-cost generic manufacturers, especially in India, to make "second-line" therapies for patients who have become resistant to the first generation drugs. France itself would contribute US$250 million of a $400 million budget with a tax on air travel tickets, ranging from Ucircle1 for an economy ticket within Europe to Ucircle40 for a long-distance business ticket. See the *Financial Times*, August 11, 2006.

22. See Chapter 12 by Jeffrey Simon and Sean Kay in this book.

23. Press conference text accessed at http://www.dangoor.com/74049.html.

24. A critique of European policy is found in Joseph Carmi and Arie Carmi, *The War of Western Europe Against Israel*, New York: Devora Press, 2003.

25. As of fall 2006, UNIFIL had been given 6,000 troops, including "heavily armed French marines in battle tanks, Italians in armored personnel carriers, and Spaniards in Humvees [that] have crowded into southern Lebanon, patrolling a space so small that troop convoys create constant traffic jams." Thanassis Cambanis, "UN Force Mobilizes Cautiously in Lebanon," *Boston Globe*, October 17, 2006, p. 4.

Suggested Readings

Cole, Alaistair, and Gino Raymond, *Redefining the French Republic*, New York: St. Mar-tin's Press, 2006.

Culpepper, Pepper D., and Peter A. Hall, *Changing France: The Politics That Markets Make*, New York: Palgrave Macmillan, 2006.

DiSalvo, Daniel, and James W. Caeser, "Affirmative Action and Positive Discrimina-tion," *The Tocqueville Review*, XXV(1), 2004.

Giry, Stéphanie, "France and Its Muslims," *Foreign Affairs*, September-October 2006, 87–104.

Gordon, Philip, and Jeremy Shapiro, *Allies at War: America, Europe, and the Crisis over Iraq*, New York: McGraw-Hill, 2004.

Hayward, Jack, and Vincent Wright (eds.), *Governing from the Center: Core Executive Coordination in France*, New York: Oxford University Press, 2002.

Hoffmann, Stanley, *France: Decline or Renewal?* New York: Viking Press, 1974.

Kramer, Steven Philip, "The End of French Europe?" *Foreign Affairs*, July-August 2006.

Laurence, Jonathan, and Justin Vaisse, *Integrating Islam: Political and Religious Challenges in Contemporary France*, Washington, DC: Brookings Institution Press, 2006.

Maier, Corinne, *Bonjour paresse—De l'art et la nécessité d'en faire le moins possible en entreprise*, Paris: Editions Michalon, 2004; translated as, *Bonjour Laziness: Jumping Off the Corporate Ladder*, New York: Pantheon Books, 2005.

Noiriel, Gérard, *The French Melting Pot: Immigration, Citizenship, and National Identity*, Minneapolis: University of Minnesota Press, 1996.

Sa'adah, Anne, *Contemporary France: A Democratic Education*, Lanham, MD: Rowman & Littlefield, 2003.

Tiersky, Ronald, *François Mitterrand: A Very French President*, Lanham, MD: Rowman & Littlefield, 2003.

Tiersky, Ronald, *France in the New Europe*, Belmont, CA: Wadsworth, 1994.

WEBSITES

The French foreign ministry site (in English) is *www.france.diplomatie.fr*. The president's site (in French) is *www.elysee.fr*. The prime minister's site (in English) is *www.premier-minitre.gouv.fr/en*. Major French newspaper sites are (in French) *www.lemonde.fr*, *www.lefigaro.fr*, *www.libération.fr*. The National Assembly site is (in French) *www.assemblee-internationale.fr*. The official EU website, with much information concerning France, is *www.europa.int.eu*.

CHAPTER 2

United Kingdom: New Labour, New Britain?

Jonathan Hopkin

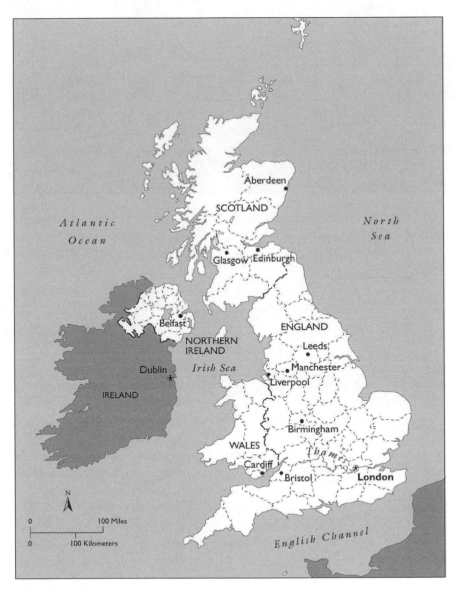

United Kingdom

Population (million):   60.1
Area in Square Miles: 94,548
Population Density per Square Mile: 635
GDP (in billion dollars, 2005): $1,941.9
GDP per capita (PPP, 2005): $32,265
Joined EC/EU: January 1, 1973

Performance of Key Political Parties in Parliamentary Elections of May 2005

Conservative and Unionist Party   32.3% (198 seats)
Democratic Unionist Party (DUP)   0.9% (9 seats)
Labour Party   35.2% (356 seats)
Liberal Democrats   22.1% (62 seats)
Party of Wales (Plaid Cymru)   0.7% (3 seats)
Scottish National Party (SNP)   1.5% (6 seats)
Sinn Fein   0.6 % (5 seats)
UK Independence Party (UKIP)   2.3% (0 seats)
Ulster Unionist Party (UUP)   0.5% (1 seat)

Main Office Holders: Prime Minister: Tony Blair—Labour (1997), Head of State: Queen Elizabeth II

On May 5, 2005, the Labour Party won a general election for the third time in a row, an unprecedented achievement for its leader Tony Blair, who had already presided over the longest period of Labour government in British history. Although not as decisive a victory as in 1997 or 2001, Labour had enough seats in the Westminster Parliament to govern comfortably for a third term of office. Blair himself had already announced that he would not stand for election a further time, so for him the result confirmed he would leave the party leadership undefeated. One might have expected scenes of jubilation at Labour Party headquarters, or at the very least quiet satisfaction at Blair's fulfillment of his ambition to turn Labour into the "natural party of government."

Instead, Tony Blair's election night involved one of the most embarrassing and humiliating scenes ever to involve a British prime minister. As tradition demands, on the evening of May 5 Blair was at his Sedgefield constituency in the northeast of England to hear the results of his own parliamentary election. As at every election since 1983, Blair stood alongside all the other candidates as the returning officer announced the results, confirming a comfortable victory for the Labour candidate. After the prime minister's rather solemn speech acknowledging victory, it was the turn of the losing candidates to speak, and by convention the winning candidate, even a prime minister, must hear them out. Blair stood rooted to the hustings as Reg Keys, the father of a British soldier killed in Iraq, took the microphone. Keys had stood for election against the prime minister in protest at the Iraq war, finishing in a respectable fourth place with 4,552 votes. The most successful Labour prime minister in history had no choice but stand in embarrassed silence as Keys remembered his son, Thomas, killed in Iraq four days before his twenty-first birthday: "I hope in my heart," he said, "that one day the Prime Minister may be able to say sorry . . . to the families of the bereaved, and that one day he might be able to visit wounded soldiers in hospital." A frowning Blair looked for a moment a defeated politician, the effect compounded by the bright yellow hat worn by another antiwar candidate who stood beside him, which bore the legend "BLIAR."

This extraordinary spectacle is revealing of the peculiar traditions of British politics, which combines the pomp and high theater of events such as the queen's speech, with the kind of earthy, street-level politics to which British politicians, however senior, must pay lip service. But it also suggests the paradoxical nature of Blair's political legacy as his period in office entered its final stages. On the face of it, Blair has not only enjoyed success as a party leader; his government has also presided over an unprecedented period of economic stability and growth, accompanied by falling crime, increased investment in schools, healthcare, and infrastructure, and a largely popular program of constitutional reforms. Yet at the same time public trust in the government and the prime minister has fallen precipitously, and Blair himself has become a hate figure for many on both left and right: for the former, because of his closeness to George

W. Bush and his enthusiasm for market reform; for the latter, because of increased taxes and business regulations. His election victory in 2005 was a qualified one: with only 35 percent of the vote on a reduced turnout, Blair's third government had received the active consent of only around a fifth of the electorate. By autumn 2006, Labour's support in the opinion polls had dropped to its lowest level for twenty years, and for the first time since Blair became prime minister, Labour began to contemplate the possibility of a return to opposition.

This chapter will trace the shifts in British politics since May 1, 1997, when almost two decades of continuous Conservative governments came to an end with a landslide election victory for the opposition Labour Party. This was a remarkable achievement for the party's youthful leader, Tony Blair, then forty-three years old, who had become party leader in 1994 after the sudden death of his predecessor, John Smith. Despite the unexpected nature of Blair's ascendancy to the leadership, he wasted no time in molding the party to his image, even to the point of informally renaming it "New Labour." This rebranding exercise, opposed by many party members, reflected Blair's determination to break with Labour's past and build bridges with disillusioned Conservative voters. The strategy was so successful that John Major's Conservative government suffered a historic defeat at the polls, with Labour winning a landslide majority on May 1. The following day, Blair followed tradition by addressing a crowd of Labour supporters assembled outside Number 10 Downing Street in bright spring sunshine. His words left no doubt that he saw the election victory as a vindication of his leadership: "I know well what this country has voted for today. It is a mandate for New Labour and I say to the people of this country—we ran for office as New Labour, we will govern as New Labour."[1]

Blair's Labour Party has had the time and political capital to do precisely that. Winning a further landslide in 2001, and a third, narrower, victory in 2005, Blair has governed longer than any previous Labour leader, in extraordinarily favorable circumstances. With a parliamentary majority even bigger than those enjoyed by Margaret Thatcher in her heyday of the 1980s, and a benign economic climate, the Labour government has had an unprecedented opportunity to make its mark on British society and politics. So has New Labour made a "New Britain"? After a decade in power, it has now become possible to provide a tentative answer to this question. This chapter will seek to draw a balance sheet on the Blair administration's achievements and failures, by analyzing the transformations brought about by this historically unprecedented period of left-of-center political dominance. It will look at three broad areas: the management of the British economy and welfare state, the important changes made to the British Constitution since 1997, and Blair's controversial foreign policy choices. The discussion will focus on the impact of New Labour, but in doing so will also provide a general overview of the main trends and developments in contemporary British politics.

New Labour and the British Economy

THE BACKGROUND: FROM "OLD LABOUR" TO "NEW LABOUR"

One of Tony Blair's key priorities on taking over as Labour leader in 1994 was to rid the party of its reputation for economic incompetence. Labour governments had presided over high-profile economic failures in the 1960s and 1970s, most notably the infamous "Winter of Discontent" in 1979 in which a series of strikes paralyzed the delivery of public services. Although the Conservative governments of Thatcher and Major also had their share of economic disasters to cope with, Blair perceived that Labour were not regarded as responsible custodians of the British economy. Moreover, it had become clear that a growing share of Labour's traditional working-class supporters felt that the Conservatives, with their stress on property ownership and low personal taxation, offered greater opportunities for improving their living standards. The new Labour leader spoke of meeting a self-employed electrician while on the campaign trail in 1992; the man used to be a Labour supporter, but since buying his own home and setting up his own business he had switched to the Conservatives. Blair felt that "his instincts were to get on in life. And he thought our instincts were to stop him."[2] In order to win an election Labour needed to convince such people that the party was on their side.

This strategy was a delicate balancing act. On the one hand, Labour needed to win over millions of voters who had supported Margaret Thatcher's harsh free-market reforms in the 1980s. On the other, the party needed to retain the support of millions of loyal Labour supporters for whom "Thatcherism" was anathema. Blair's first moves were to force through fundamental changes to the party's ideology. At his first party conference as leader he proposed rewriting Labour's historic "Clause Four"—a statement of the party's ideology and aims dating from 1918, which committed Labour to wholesale state control of economic activity. Party activists, disillusioned by four successive election defeats and confident Blair could return Labour to government, largely backed this change. The new statement of party aims was an early indication of Blair's broader political strategy. It replaced traditional socialist thinking with vaguer, generic ambitions to build a society where "power, wealth, and opportunity are in the hands of the many not the few."[3] This cleared the way for Labour to adopt a more pragmatic economic policy, steering a path between the excesses of Thatcherism and the now discredited pronationalization policies followed by Labour in the past. To drive the point home to voters, Blair stressed that "New Labour" was different from "Old Labour," and that there would be no return to failed policies of the past.

Box 2.1   From "Old" to "New" Labour:
The End of Socialism?

Clause IV of the Labour Party constitution approved in 1918:

> To secure for the workers by hand or by brain the full fruits of their indus-
> try and the most equitable distribution thereof that may be possible upon
> the basis of the common ownership of the means of production, distribu-
> tion and exchange, and the best obtainable system of popular administration
> and control of each industry or service.

Excerpt from Tony Blair's first speech to the Labour Party conference as leader,
October 4, 1994:

> Market forces cannot educate us or equip us for this world of rapid techno-
> logical and economic change. We must do it together. . . .
>   That is our insight: A belief in society. Working together. Solidarity.
> Cooperation. Partnership. These are our words. This is my socialism. And
> we should stop apologizing for using the word.
>   It is not the socialism of Marx or state control. It is rooted in a straight
> forward view of society. In the understanding that the individual does best
> in a strong and decent community of people with principles and standards
> and common aims and values.
>   We are the Party of the individual because we are the Party of commu-
> nity. Our task is to apply those values to the modern world.
>   It will change the traditional dividing lines between right and left. And it
> calls for a new politics.

(*Source: http://www.australianpolitics.com/uk/labour/941004blair-new-labour-speech.shtml*)

The "New" Clause IV approved by the Labour Party conference in 1995:

> The Labour Party is a democratic socialist party. It believes that by the
> strength of our common endeavor we achieve more than we achieve alone,
> so as to create for each of us the means to realize our true potential and for
> all of us a community in which power, wealth and opportunity are in the
> hands of the many, not the few. Where the rights we enjoy reflect the duties
> we owe. And where we live together, freely, in a spirit of solidarity, toler-
> ance and respect.

This new approach was elaborated in greater detail by one of Blair's close
advisors, sociologist Anthony Giddens, in a short book, *The Third Way.*[4] Giddens argued for a new approach to move beyond the statist policies of traditional social democracy, but also contrast the promarket doctrines of the new
right personified by Thatcher and Reagan. In the 1980s, Thatcher's policies had
led to a rapid increase in unemployment among blue-collar workers, accentu-

ated social inequalities, and dramatically reduced the power of trade unions. But her cuts in personal taxation and expansion of home ownership had won the Conservatives new support among sections of the working class that had been able to cope with economic change. Blair and Giddens perceived that a return to Labour's traditional pro-union, pro-welfare positions would be unpopular amongst centrist voters. The so-called Third Way was an approach that allowed Labour to safeguard perceived successes of the Thatcher-Major period, while addressing its failures.[5]

Labour's manifesto for the 1997 election spelled out what the Third Way meant in practical terms. Labour would be fiscally responsible, promising to follow clear fiscal rules to keep government borrowing low. There would be no increase in income tax rates, and the party would effectively freeze public spending for the first two years in office. At the same time, Labour promised to increase investment in key areas of the public sector, particularly the health service and the education systems. This greater spending would be paid for by a one-off "windfall" tax on excessive profits of utility companies privatized by the Conservatives, and through a program aimed at slashing long-term unemployment and its related social costs. Would this strategy shift power, wealth, and opportunity from the many to the few? After almost a decade of Labour government, we can start to provide an answer to this question.

THE CONSERVATIVE LEGACY:
FOR RICHER, FOR POORER

In many respects 1997 was a good time for Labour to win an election. From a short-term perspective, the British economy was in good shape by historical standards. After the pound's devaluation and dramatic exit from the European Exchange Rate Mechanism in September 1992, the British economy very quickly began to emerge from the deep recession that had begun in 1990. By 1997, unemployment had been falling continuously for five years, but without sparking inflation. The pound had stabilized at what was apparently a sustainable level. Britain appeared to be on the road to recovering from its postwar history of macroeconomic instability. Labour had hoped to win power in 1992, when an election was held in the middle of a recession, and the Conservatives appeared weak and divided. However, in retrospect Labour was fortunate to have lost the 1992 election: the Conservatives were left to sort out the crisis, and when Labour finally won they inherited a healthy economy.

But 1997 was also a good time for Labour to win for another reason. After almost two decades in power, the Conservatives had apparently exhausted their political agenda. Elected in 1979 after the Labour government had presided over five years of high inflation and balance-of-payments difficulties, the Conservative administration of Margaret Thatcher embarked on a radical program of reforms designed to transform the British economy. A restrictive monetary policy was adopted with the aim of killing off inflation, even at the expense of a sharp increase in unemployment from around 1.5 million in 1979 to over 3 million by 1982. Legislation was brought in to curb the power of the trade unions, with bans on secondary strikes, restrictions on unions' political donations, and compulsory ballots of members before strike action could be taken, with financial embargoes for unions that failed to comply. The Thatcher government also hoped to reduce social spending and address the "dependency culture" that some Conservatives believed the postwar welfare state had fostered. Unemployment benefits were frozen and state pensions indexed to price inflation rather than increases in average earnings, while government spending on healthcare and education was curbed. After winning a further parliamentary majority in 1983, the Conservatives set about reforming the tax system, cutting income and capital taxes, and privatizing state-owned industries. The battle against trade union power was concluded with the failure of the miners' strike in 1984–1985, provoked by the announcement of closures of unprofitable mines.

This program of reforms undoubtedly brought about a major shift in the structure and workings of the British economy, and had major social consequences. Faced with a world economic slowdown and a tight monetary and fiscal policy at home, many British companies, particularly in the industrial sector, were unable to survive, and unemployment soared. At the same time, the emphasis on defeating inflation favored the interests of the financial sector centered around the city of London, which thrived in the mid- to late 1980s. These changes led to a growing territorial divide between the prosperous southeast of England, which enjoyed high income growth and a housing boom, and the declining industrial north, which saw high unemployment, stagnation, and demographic decline. Loss of manufacturing jobs and the growing weakness of the trade unions led to a growth in income inequality that was exacerbated by fiscal reforms which rewarded high earners with income tax cuts while low earners were hit by increases in sales tax and other regressive taxes. On the whole, during the Thatcher years the rich became richer and the poor poorer.

The medium- to long-term effects of the Thatcher period began to be felt in the 1990s, under the governments of her successor, John Major. After the recession of 1990–1992, the British economy began what was to become a period of stable growth, attributed by many observers to the structural, market-oriented reforms of the Thatcher years. Middle-class incomes rose and many citizens, particularly in the south of England, enjoyed growing prosperity. At the same time, many Britons, including those who had benefited from higher living standards, were concerned that Thatcherism's harsh medicine had created an unequal and uncomfortable social environment, with growing numbers of alienated poor, a crumbling infrastructure, and failing health and education services. The unpopularity of the Major government after the devaluation of the pound in September 1992—an event known as "Black Wednesday"—suggested

Box 2.2   "There Is No Such Thing As Society": Thatcherism and the Welfare State

I think we have gone through a period when too many children and people have been given to understand "I have a problem, it is the Government's job to cope with it!" or "I have a problem, I will go and get a grant to cope with it!" "I am homeless, the Government must house me!" and so they are casting their problems on society and who is society? There is no such thing! There are individual men and women and there are families and no government can do anything except through people and people look to themselves first.

It is our duty to look after ourselves and then also to help look after our neighbor and life is a reciprocal business and people have got the entitlements too much in mind without the obligations, because there is no such thing as an entitlement unless someone has first met an obligation and it is, I think, one of the tragedies in which many of the benefits we give, which were meant to reassure people that if they were sick or ill there was a safety net and there was help, that many of the benefits which were meant to help people who were unfortunate—"It is all right. We joined together and we have these insurance schemes to look after it." That was the objective, but somehow there are some people who have been manipulating the system and so some of those help and benefits that were meant to say to people: "All right, if you cannot get a job, you shall have a basic standard of living!" but when people come and say: "But what is the point of working? I can get as much on the dole!" You say: "Look. It is not from the dole. It is your neighbor who is supplying it and if you can earn your own living then really you have a duty to do it and you will feel very much better!"

—Margaret Thatcher, speaking to *Women's Own* magazine, October 31, 1987.

(*Source: http://www.margaretthatcher.org/speeches/displaydocument.asp?docid=106689*)

that for British voters, improving economic conditions were not enough. This created an opportunity for the Labour Party, which had traditionally been strongly committed to the welfare state and the collective delivery of key services such as healthcare and schooling. But Labour had to convince voters that they could address their social issues without sacrificing economic stability. This balancing act was the essence of Blair's political strategy.

WINNING CREDIBILITY: BLAIR'S FIRST TERM

The initial priority of the Labour government was to win credibility as a competent manager of the economy. This was particularly important given the changes in the structure of the British economy over the period since Labour had last been in office. In a world of globalized capital flows, the financial services industry based in London had become undisputably the key strategic sector of the British economy, and the Conservatives had traditionally been the party closest to the city's interests. Labour's leaders felt that any lack of confidence among city institutions in the new Labour government could lead to capital flight and currency instability, which would derail their plans. In order to win over city elites, Blair and his economics spokesman, Gordon Brown, had embarked on a so-called prawn cocktail offensive, meeting key city figures over lunch to reassure them that Labour's economic plans would safeguard city interests. Once in office, Blair and Brown had a clear plan to consolidate this new relationship between the UK's financial elite and the party that had traditionally represented organized labor.

First, Labour had to address its reputation for fiscal irresponsibility. By signing up to the previous Conservative administration's budgetary plans for the first two years of the new Parliament, Labour were committing themselves to a tough approach to public spending; after all, the Conservatives were expecting to lose and felt free to make unrealistically restrictive plans about how much the government would need to spend. By sticking to these heroically frugal plans, Labour aimed to show the financial and business elite that it could be trusted to keep government borrowing low. It reinforced this approach with a so-called Golden Rule—a commitment that government would not borrow to fund current spending over the business cycle—and a further commitment to keep total government debt below 40 percent of gross domestic product. These policies were followed so strictly that the Labour government managed to run a budget surplus for every year of the 1997–2001 Parliament.[6]

A second fundamental reform was not tried before the election. In his first act after being named chancellor of the exchequer (treasury minister), Gordon Brown announced that the new government would no longer set interest rates, which would become the responsibility of the UK's central bank, the Bank of England. By putting monetary policy at arm's length, Labour hoped to enhance its credibility as a responsible manager of the UK macroeconomy. This policy also quickly appeared vindicated, as interest rates and inflation both dropped to historically low levels within Labour's first term of office. Remarkably for recent British economic history, unemployment also continued to fall without sparking price increases. The immediate success of these policy decisions was a boost to Labour's fortunes. First, they vindicated one of Labour's most prominent messages in their political campaigns—that they would put an end to the "boom and bust" of the Thatcher period and lay the foundations for more stable economic growth. Second, the success in reducing both inflation and unemployment at the same time allowed Brown to follow a cautious economic policy without having to demand too many sacrifices of Labour's traditional supporters.

Of course, Labour's success in managing the macroeconomy was hardly likely to be enough to satisfy the party's more left-wing supporters, who demanded action to reduce poverty and achieve a more equitable distribution of wealth. The government also proposed other, more traditionally social democratic, policies. The high levels of poverty among British pensioners were addressed by introducing a "minimum income guarantee" for the elderly, providing increased state pensions for those without private pension entitlements. The "New Deal" program, financed by a windfall tax on privatized utility companies, provided assistance to the long-term unemployed to encourage them back into the labor market. This formed part of a series of measures called "Welfare to Work," aimed at increasing employment as a way of reducing poverty without increasing the burden on the welfare state. The Labour chancellor Gordon Brown had identified low wages for unskilled workers as a "poverty trap" — many of the unemployed could not easily earn enough to move out of welfare. The government attacked this problem by establishing a minimum wage and by providing tax credits for low earners with family responsibilities, topping up low wages to encourage work over welfare. This was a classic example of Third Way thinking—a policy to reduce poverty and unemployment by neither pure market mechanisms, nor an exclusive reliance on welfare and redistribution. Although some observers remain skeptical about the specific impact of the New Deal on employment, the Labour government was able to point to a continued decline in joblessness through its first term in office as proof of its success.[7]

FINANCING THE WELFARE STATE: THE SECOND TERM

After almost a decade in power, few would question that Labour has managed to convince investors of its credentials as competent managers of the British economy. Indeed it is easy to lose sight of the fact that Labour was mistrusted by many in the business community until very recently. The very success of the Blair-Brown strategy for enhancing Labour's credibility led to criticism from within the party that the restrictive policies of the first term in office were, in fact, unnecessary, and that the government should instead have been focusing on rescuing the welfare state and key public services from decades of decline. The decision to effectively freeze public spending during the first two years of office was a good way of demonstrating Labour's commitment to balancing the government's books. However it also meant that key public services continued to be starved of cash well into Labour's period in office.

When the taps were finally opened after 1999, the main beneficiaries of increased spending were healthcare and education. Despite the Thatcher and Major governments' commitment to a healthy private market in health and education services, the vast majority of British citizens remained reliant on state provision in these two areas. Moreover, opinion polls had long shown that voters demanded higher spending on these services, and that many of them even claimed to be willing to pay higher taxes to achieve this. As regards spending, there is little question that Labour has met this demand for greater resources.

Education spending, for example, rose from £38 billion in 1997 to £73 billion in 2006, a spectacular increase in times of low inflation. Health spending, in turn, grew even faster, from £33 billion in 1997 to £96 billion in 2006.[8] Visible evidence of this greater largesse can be found in the new school and hospital buildings that sprung up around the country in the years after 2000. Evidence of increased performance in the delivery of services has been more controversial, however. Official government targets for cutting medical waiting times and achieving better school exam results have been met, but public skepticism over the effective improvement in services abounds. For some Labour opponents the prioritization of public health and education over private consumption has simply increased the pay of public-sector workers without any clear productivity gains.

The growth of government spending was the "big story" of Labour's second term as far as domestic politics were concerned. Much political debate therefore revolved around two related questions: how to pay for this higher spending, and how to ensure that this extra money was transformed into better services. The first question could be elided for some time thanks to the buoyant budgetary position built up during Labour's first term of office. However, as soon as the economic cycle began to turn downward, budget surpluses quickly turned to deficits in 2003 and by 2005 had breached the euro area's 3 percent limit. The problem of how to pay for higher spending was met in a combination of ways. First, Labour was obliged to allow some slippage in the observance of its own "fiscal rules," which required budgets to balance over the economic cycle. In 2005, Brown's Treasury recalculated the dates of the economic cycle in order to make the rules easier to meet, allowing higher borrowing to continue. Second, Labour responded by raising taxes. Although Brown stuck to Labour's promise not to increase income tax rates, he did increase revenues through fiscal drag, and also increased the British payroll tax—National Insurance—for high-end wage earners. Third, the government's budgetary position was helped by the consistent economic growth enjoyed from the mid-1990s, which reduced the costs of unemployment and brought increased tax receipts from property sales and consumption. In short, Labour seemed to have pulled off a difficult balancing act by significantly increasing public spending without a dramatic increase in personal taxation.

The issue of public-sector performance was if anything rather more difficult. Although Labour's natural supporters in the public sector were buoyed by increased spending and growing job opportunities, they were also hostile to the government plans to restructure public services in order to enhance productivity. Blair was convinced that the public sector was an ideal arena for Third Way politics. The government would increase spending—a classic social democratic policy—but insist on reforms to introduce the kinds of efficiency gains characteristic of private companies—a "new right" policy. This strategy ran into two obstacles. First, the public sector was the only sector of the British economy where trade unions remained strong, and the unions were generally unsympathetic to the reforms. Second, there was inadequate evidence that reforms such as the introduction of simulated markets in healthcare provision, or the publication of league tables of school exam performance, actually did anything to improve the delivery of services. As the Labour government moved into its third term, it faced the challenge of persuading a skeptical public that its higher taxes were in fact producing better services.

THE BALANCE SHEET

Tony Blair and Gordon Brown can point to several achievements in the fields of economic and social policy. Most obviously, Labour has presided over one of the longest periods of uninterrupted economic growth in British history, with high levels of employment, historically low inflation, and an average growth rate of 2.5 percent between 1997 and 2006, well above trend. Although this period of growth began earlier, after the 1992 devaluation, Labour can certainly take some credit for these benign economic conditions. The handing over of interest rate policy to the Bank of England helped bring inflation and interest rates down to unprecedented levels, while Labour's relatively cautious budgetary policy also contributed to low inflation. More controversially, a further factor appears to have made a significant contribution to this noninflationary growth. Record levels of immigration into the UK since the late 1990s have fuelled economic growth, particularly in services, while keeping a lid on wage increases. This growth in the labor force may not have been the result of deliberate government policy, but it has resolved the problem of capacity constraints in the booming personal-services sector in the overcrowded southeast of England. However, large-scale immigration has also created social tensions, while its contribution to containing wage growth has accentuated the unequal distribution of the fruits of economic growth.

Labour has perhaps been less successful in those areas that might have been expected to be a priority. Gordon Brown achieved what appeared to be an impossible task in dramatically increasing health and education spending without sparking a tax revolt. But the jury is still out on whether this investment will pay off in terms of better services. Perhaps more surprisingly, Labour has not been able to make serious inroads into one of Britain's more serious problems—its highly unequal distribution of income and wealth.[9] The Thatcher reforms had a dramatic effect on poverty rates, and by the 1990s Britain was the most economically unequal society in the European Union. Despite a number of flagship redistributive policies, such as the Welfare to Work program and higher pensions spending, income inequality remained stubbornly high, largely because of the increasingly large share of national income taken by the very top income groups. By increasing welfare allowances for children, Labour did succeed in moving many families out of poverty, but in the mid-2000s Britain remained a society with European-style tax rates and U.S.-style income inequality. This failure to make Britain a more integrated society must weigh heavily in the Blair government's "end of term report."

The British Constitution: A Modern Democracy?

The Third Way thinking that formed the basis of Tony Blair's governing strategy was not solely concerned with governing the economy and managing the social consequences of economic change. The Third Way also contemplated addressing the workings of democracy itself, in order to make the political system more open, transparent, and effective. Labour had developed a coherent and powerful critique of the failings of British democracy, which it saw as excessively centralized and elitist, and governed by an unaccountable metropolitan elite. The 1997 Labour manifesto therefore proposed a number of reforms in a bid to modernize and open up the UK political system.

THE BACKGROUND: THE UNITED KINGDOM'S "WESTMINSTER MODEL"

The United Kingdom is often described as the oldest democracy in the world. With the Magna Charta of 1215, the English king became subject to legal constraints, and the House of Commons—the lower house of the British Parliament—is the oldest legislative institution in the world, sitting continuously in the Palace of Westminster in central London since 1547. Unlike in many other countries, in Britain there has been no specific founding moment at which a democratic system became established. Instead, British democracy was the result of a centuries-long process whereby political power gradually passed from the monarch to the parliament, and the British Parliament itself won democratic legitimacy by progressively expanding voting rights until universal suffrage was finally attained in 1928. This conventional interpretation of a smooth transition from absolute monarchy to full democracy of course glosses over the political violence and social conflict that have marked several periods of British history, such as the religious tensions sparked by the Protestant Reformation in the sixteenth century, the civil war of 1642–1649, or the working-class mobilization of the nineteenth and early twentieth centuries, not to mention the frequently changing borders of the British state. However it does accurately reflect the remarkable institutional continuity the UK has enjoyed since at least the late seventeenth century, with a stable parliamentary monarchy that has managed to avoid the violent revolutions or foreign invasions suffered by many of its European neighbors.

This remarkable history has left the UK with a rather anomalous constitutional system. First of all, Britain does not even have a written constitution: there is no single text codifying and recording the rules regulating the political system. Instead the British constitution, such that it exists, consists of a mixture of legislation and conventions, many of which are only written down in academic texts. As a result, "much of the substance of the contemporary constitution remains shrouded in uncertainty."[10] Second, a number of features of Britain's "constitution" appear out of date and inappropriate for a modern, twenty-first-century democracy. For example, although the monarchy appears for the most part to play a purely symbolic role in British politics, a number of powers exercised by the British government, including the decision to engage British troops in combat, formally belong to the monarch through the so-called Royal Prerogative. This reflects the British political elite's reluctance to address the thorny issue of the constitution, rather than any particular enthusiasm for extending the powers of the queen. The anachronistic and sometimes dysfunctional nature of the British system of government can be best understood in terms of the British elites' preference for working around the constitution rather than openly and systematically updating it.[11]

This peculiar approach to defining the way government works has some advantages. The British constitution is inherently very flexible. When laws regulating the broader political system become obsolete, they can easily be changed. One of the defining principles of the British political system is "parliamentary sovereignty," which means that no Parliament can bind future Parliaments, and that legislation is not subject to judicial review. This gives the Parliament of the day unlimited freedom to legislate on any matter with a simple majority vote, making reform of the political system much more straightforward than in other democracies, where constitutional reforms often require enhanced majorities and often, popular referenda too. Parliamentary sovereignty explains in part why British governments have often preferred to leave the constitution alone: as long as a government enjoys a parliamentary majority, there are relatively few limits to its freedom of action.

This very flexibility is also a problem. Because there are few constitutional restraints on a parliamentary majority, a strong-willed government with sufficient parliamentary support can force through unpopular measures relatively easily. Moreover, through the Royal Prerogative many powers once belonging to the monarchy are now exercised by the head of the government, the prime minister, in the monarch's name. These powers, such as government appointments, are not subject to any consultation with parliament and imply a greater concentration of power around the head of the executive than is usual in parliamentary democracies. Parliamentary sovereignty, of course, also means that the executive is ultimately dependent on the majority support of the House of Commons in order to continue governing. British prime ministers, unlike U.S. presidents, can be forced to step down at short notice by a majority vote of censure, known as a

Table 2.1   Prime Ministers and Governing Parties in the United Kingdom 1945–2006

Dates	Prime Minister	Governing Party
1945–1951	Clement Attlee	Labour
1951–1955	Winston Churchill	Conservative
1955–1957	Anthony Eden	Conservative
1957–1963	Harold MacMillan	Conservative
1963–1964	Alec Douglas-Home	Conservative
1964–1970	Harold Wilson	Labour
1970–1974	Edward Heath	Conservative
1974–1976	Harold Wilson	Labour
1976–1979	James Callaghan	Labour
1979–1990	Margaret Thatcher	Conservative
1990–1997	John Major	Conservative
1997–	Tony Blair	Labour

"vote of no confidence." But provided the prime minister retains the support of a parliamentary majority, there are few limits on his or her power, since Parliament can pass any law and there is no higher judicial power to review legislation.

In practice, therefore, the British parliamentary system has tended to create strong governments subject to few checks and balances. British political parties tend to be fairly cohesive, and individual members of Parliament (M.P.s) are usually heavily dependent on their parties' support in their efforts to win reelection. As a result, governing majorities in Parliament are mostly disciplined in their support for the executive in general and the prime minister (who is also party leader) in particular. Moreover, members of the House of Commons are elected in small, single-member constituencies, which leads to a heavy overrepresentation of the winning party. Governments often enjoy very large majorities in the Commons that make their parliamentary position almost unassailable. The upper house of Parliament, the House of Lords, is traditionally an unelected body of nobility and party appointees, and therefore lacks the political legitimacy to challenge the power of the government. The Lords can return legislation to the Commons for redrafting, but ultimately must acquiesce in passing the legislation without amendment if the Commons stands firm. In the democratic era, the House of Lords, which until 1999 had a built-in Conservative majority due to the predominance of hereditary peers (nobles), has only used its delaying powers against Labour governments.

The Thatcher governments of the 1980s, for many of its opponents, epitomized the abuse of executive power made possible by the UK's constitutional vagueness and the distortions of its electoral system. With a little over 40 percent of the vote but a comfortable majority in the House of Commons, the Conservative administration forced a number of controversial and divisive measures through Parliament in the face of great popular unrest. Thatcher's own robust style was criticized as authoritarian, as she refused to consult with interest groups and trade unions, and even rode roughshod over Conservative opponents within her own government. In response, demands for constitutional reform grew, with the Electoral Reform Society arguing for the House of Commons to be elected by proportional representation, while a group named Charter 88 campaigned for a wholesale updating of Britain's constitutional arrangements, including the democratization of the House of Lords and greater transparency in government.

Ironically, Margaret Thatcher's own demise was a timely reminder that parliamentary sovereignty was not a blank check for the prime minister. Faced with an economic crisis and growing unpopularity over the reform of local taxes and her European policy, opposition mounted to Thatcher's leadership within the Conservative Party itself. At the end of 1990, a rival challenged Thatcher to a leadership election; although she won the election, the number of votes against her signaled that a substantial portion of her parliamentary party wanted a new leader. Persuaded by her own ministers that she was in an unsustainable position, she resigned, only three years after winning her third general election. But her long period in office, and Labour's own disillusionment at its inability to defeat Thatcher at the polls, had entrenched demand for constitutional change within the opposition party. When Tony Blair led Labour to victory in 1997, a reform of the British system of government was a key part of the party's program. This was consistent with Blair's "Third Way" thinking, which emphasized greater transparency and accountability in government as well as the importance of social reform. A more cynical interpretation would suggest that an ambitious program of constitutional reform was a good way of distracting Labour's more traditional supporters from Blair's lack of radical ambition in the field of economic and social policy.

Decentralizing Britain: Devolution and Northern Ireland

The most urgent item on Labour's reform agenda was "devolution"—the creation of new tiers of government in Scotland, Wales, and Northern Ireland, all part of the United Kingdom but culturally and politically distinct from England, where the bulk (around 85 percent) of the British population lives. Devolution addressed one of the most potent critiques of the British system of government: its intense centralization of power around the capital city, London, where the executive, civil service, and Parliament are based. Decentralization—bringing government closer to the people—was a prominent feature of Third Way discourse, and appeared to offer a response to citizens' growing sense of detachment from the political elite. Labour had long pushed for greater decentralization of power, unsuccessfully proposing devolution to Scotland and Wales in its previous period of government in the 1970s. Reviving this project in the 1990s was consistent with both Labour tradition and the New Labour image.

Understanding the devolution issue requires an understanding of the rather complex history of the United Kingdom.[12] It was argued earlier that the British state has enjoyed remarkable institutional continuity in the past three centuries, but the same cannot be said for the UK's borders. The core of the British state, England, has a long history as a unified nation, dating on some accounts from the tenth century. The history of Britain, however, is marked by a process of expansion, and then partial retreat. Wales was definitively annexed by England under King Henry VIII in 1536, and Scotland was absorbed into the British state by the Act of Union in 1707. The island of Ireland, long dominated by its larger neighbor, was integrated into the United Kingdom in 1800. This political unity of the British Isles did not last long. Discontent among the majority Catholic population of Ireland developed into a political movement for Irish independence, and the "Irish question" dominated British political life toward the end of the nineteenth century and the beginning of the twentieth. Faced with constant unrest, the London Parliament decided in 1921 to pull out of most of Ireland, but retained six counties with a large Protestant population (mostly descendants of Scottish settlers) in the north of the country. This act, known as "partition," allowed for the creation of an independent Irish Republic in the South, while the North remained part of the United Kingdom. Northern Ireland was governed by its own Parliament, based at Stormont Castle outside Belfast, which was dominated by Unionists—mostly Protestant supporters of the union with Britain. This arrangement was relatively stable until the 1960s, when the growing Catholic population of Ulster—largely of Irish Nationalist sympathies—began to protest against discrimination and denial of political rights. This movement, initially a peaceful protest, turned to violence as the Unionist-dominated security forces adopted a repressive line, and the British army was sent over to restore order. After thirteen Catholic protesters were shot by British troops on Bloody Sunday (1973), the situation developed into open conflict, between Nationalist paramilitaries (the Irish Republican Army—IRA) fighting for a united Ireland, Unionist paramilitaries defending the status quo, and the British army, which quickly became identified with the Unionist side. Two decades of sectarian violence followed, including terrorist attacks in London and other British cities.[13]

The situation in Scotland and Wales was very different. Although both countries had a distinctive national identity, expressed through culture, language, and political movements, Scottish and Welsh nationalisms were almost exclusively nonviolent. Political nationalism in the two countries had emerged with some force in the 1974 election, where both the Scottish National Party and Plaid Cymru (the Party of Wales) made spectacular electoral gains, winning substantial parliamentary representation at Westminster. Although the Labour government

of the late 1970s failed to push through devolution, Scottish and Welsh nationalism grew in strength in the 1980s and 1990s. This was in part a response to Margaret Thatcher's virulent English nationalism, and in part the result of Scotland
and Wales suffering disproportionately from the economic changes resulting
from her free-market reforms. Governed by an increasingly unpopular Conservative Party, despite voting overwhelmingly for the Labour opposition, both
Scotland and Wales saw big increases in support for more self-government, and
Labour adopted devolution as one of its priorities once elected.

Although devolution to Scotland, Wales, and Northern Ireland may have
appeared to form part of a coherent package of constitutional reform, there was
a clear difference between the Scottish and Welsh situations, on the one hand, and
Northern Ireland, on the other.[14] In Scotland and Wales, Labour was keen to
shore up its support base by delivering decentralized government. In Northern
Ireland, the aim was to resolve a historic problem facing the British state, taking
advantage of the shift in mood in Irish nationalism, increasingly favorable to a
negotiated solution. By dealing with these very different issues simultaneously,
Labour could also attempt to defuse the Northern Ireland situation by pointing
to the peaceful nature of territorial reform in the rest of the United Kingdom.

THE GOOD FRIDAY AGREEMENT

Although Labour can claim credit for addressing the Northern Ireland problem,
it also enjoyed favorable circumstances. Under John Major's Conservative government, the IRA had sent clear signals of a change in strategy, calling a cease-
fire in 1994 that held for two years. The Major government was unable to take
advantage of the opportunity, in part because of opposition to negotiations
among hard-line sectors of the Conservative Party, in part because his weak
government frequently sought the support of Unionist M.P.s in the House of
Commons to pass legislation. Shortly after the 1997 election the IRA called a
new cease-fire, and after several months of negotiations agreement was reached
between the Unionist and Nationalist leaderships in Northern Ireland, and the
British and Irish governments, with the U.S. administration playing an important mediating role.

The basis of this agreement was that the Northern Ireland Unionists would
share power with Nationalists in a new Northern Ireland Assembly and executive, rather than being governed directly from London, which most Unionists
preferred. In return, the Nationalists accepted the "principle of consent"—in
other words, that Northern Ireland would remain part of the United Kingdom
until a majority of its population decided otherwise. Given the Unionists'
majority status in the "Six Counties," this locked the province into the UK
for the foreseeable future, a major concession for the IRA, dedicated to the creation of a united, independent Ireland. The Irish Republic, as part of the deal,

removed its territorial claim on the Six Counties from its constitution. All of this was directed at reassuring the Protestant majority in the North that they would not be swallowed up into a united Ireland as a result of the agreement. Just as importantly, the agreement included a commitment, albeit vaguely worded, from the IRA to disarm and definitively renounce violence, while the British government undertook to reduce significantly its military presence in Northern Ireland.

The power-sharing agreement meant that the Nationalist community would gain a substantial role in the government of Northern Ireland, a role denied them under direct rule from Westminster. The Northern Ireland Assembly was to be elected by proportional representation in order to ensure each community was adequately represented. Moreover, its procedures were to be based on "cross-community consent": Assembly members would have to declare their "community identity"—Unionist, Nationalist, or "other"—and important decisions would require the support of either a majority of each community, or a 60 percent majority with at least 40 percent support in each community. This innovative arrangement forced the two sides into a close working relationship if the province was to be governed effectively, encouraging political leaders to overcome the suspicions of the previous decades. The outcome of the agreement remained uncertain even as the Blair government moved into its third term. On the positive side, an effective cease-fire of all the major paramilitary organizations had remained in place ever since the agreement, a remarkable achievement given the levels of bloodshed of the previous quarter century. Moreover, historical enemies had indeed been involved in joint decisionmaking, with Nationalist leaders for the first time taking on significant executive powers. On the negative side, the new devolved institutions had to be suspended four times and direct rule reestablished, due to the difficulties involved in verifying the IRA's adherence to the commitment to dismantle its paramilitary structure. Nevertheless, although the future of the agreement is in doubt, the achievement of a decade of effective peace has changed, perhaps irreversibly, the political atmosphere in Northern Ireland.

DEVOLUTION TO SCOTLAND AND WALES

In the context of resolving such a difficult issue as Northern Ireland, the creation of decentralized government institutions in Scotland and Wales appeared rather straightforward. Unlike Northern Ireland, where a majority of the population was at the very least skeptical, and in part openly hostile, to devolution, in Scotland and Wales there was broad support for institutions of self-government. Moreover, in the Scottish case, all the major parties with the exception of the Conservatives had been working together to plan devolution for some time. The vast majority of the Scottish political class was therefore broadly in agreement on the path to follow, and the Labour Party in Scotland, itself closely aligned with the national leadership in London, was an enthusiastic proponent. A referendum held in Scotland in September 1997, only four months after the Blair government was elected, showed overwhelming support for devolution, with 74 percent of Scots voting in favor.

The Scotland Act of 1998 established a Scottish Parliament in Edinburgh, which would elect a Scottish executive responsible for a range of policy areas, including education, healthcare, transport, and local government. The Parliament, elected by proportional representation, has legislative powers and can pass laws on any issue except those "reserved" to Westminster, the most important of which are foreign and defense policy, monetary and fiscal policy, and social security. The Wales Act of 1998 established devolved government for Wales, but with more limited powers. Only a bare majority (50.3 percent) voted in favor of devolution in the Welsh referendum, and the project came within a handful of votes of failing at the first hurdle. The Welsh Assembly, elected on similar principles to the Scottish Parliament, was granted only secondary legislative powers, meaning that it could only develop the detailed implementation of legislation emanating from the Westminster Parliament, rather than making law of its own. These secondary powers primarily related to education and health. However unlike Scotland, which had minor tax-raising powers, Wales was entirely dependent on the central government in London for its budget.

Devolution made an immediate political impact in these two territories. The first step toward devolution was the election of representatives to sit in the new institutions, and the elections in Scotland and Wales in 1999 suggested a major change in the workings of British politics.[15] First of all, the selection of candidates caused tensions in the governing Labour Party, as Tony Blair's national party leadership sought to block selection of popular local Labour figures, with only mixed success. Second, the elections took place under a form of proportional representation, making it difficult for Labour—the dominant party in both territories—to win sufficient support to govern alone. In Wales the party fell just short of a majority, forcing it to rely on the support first of the centrist Liberal Democrats, then of the Nationalist Plaid Cymru. The Labour administration's precarious position in the Assembly also helped dissident Labour members to assert their independence: after only a few months Blair's choice as first secretary in Wales was forced out of office and replaced by Rhodri Morgan, an opponent of the prime minister. In Scotland, Labour was far short of a majority, and therefore formed a coalition government with the Liberal Democrats. There, too, albeit for different reasons, there was instability in the leadership of the Scottish executive: the first Labour first minister, Donald Dewar, died suddenly after little over a year in charge, and his successor lasted no longer, before being forced out over a minor party-funding misdemeanor. Coalition government and initially frequent changes of executive leadership marked a departure from the patterns of government stability observed in Westminster.

Devolution, as might be expected, also led to Scotland and Wales adopting different policies to those followed in England. In Scotland, policy differences were partly the result of coalition government: although the Scottish Labour Party was close to the UK party leadership, the demands of coalition government with the Liberal Democrats led to policy decisions at odds with those taken at Westminster. The most notable examples of this were over university tuition fees, which were raised in England under Westminster legislation, but turned into a form of "graduate tax" on the future earnings of university graduates in Scotland. Controversial pro-market reforms to the running of the National Health Service and schools passed by the Blair government were adopted in neither Scotland nor Wales. Although devolution has not brought about dramatic change, it has opened up the possibility for the two countries to express their distinctiveness through their own institutions and through different patterns of policymaking. It has not been as successful as had been hoped in reversing the trend toward citizen disillusionment with democratic politics, and unedifying spectacles such as the spiraling cost of the new Scottish Parliament building in Edinburgh led to considerable skepticism over the benefits of devolution. However the popularity of the devolved institutions in their territories is relatively high, and even the initially unenthusiastic Welsh ultimately warmed to devolution, demanding powers comparable to those enjoyed by the Scottish Parliament.

DEMOCRATIZING WESTMINSTER AND WHITEHALL?

Although devolution and Northern Ireland had by far the highest profile, the Blair government also introduced other significant reforms to the British system of government. Perhaps most importantly, Labour was committed to reform of the upper house of the Westminster Parliament, the House of Lords. The House of Lords in 1999 was an extraordinarily anachronistic body, consisting of 759 hereditary peers, and 26 bishops and archbishops of the Church of England, as well as 510 "life peers"—political appointees, often former members of the House of Commons. In short, the House of Lords was not a democratic representative body, and contained a built-in majority of members of a centuries-old economic and social elite based around land ownership. Although the powers of the House of Lords had been gradually pared back throughout the twentieth century, it retained powers of revision and delay that could hinder, if not subvert, the implementation of the will of the people as expressed in the democratically elected House of Commons. Labour therefore stood for election in 1997 with a formal commitment to remove the voting rights of the hereditary peers. This was achieved in 1999, although 92 of the peers (voted by the other members of the Lords) were allowed to retain their voting rights. However, to the disappointment of more radical reformers, Blair's government refused to go further by introducing some kind of democratic legitimacy to the Lords, and the reform program stalled, leaving the second chamber populated largely by retired party politicians.

Labour also made a major commitment in its 1997 manifesto to the reform of the House of Commons, the pillar of the British system of government. Most radically, Blair promised an enquiry into the possibility of a reform of the electoral system for the Commons, followed by a referendum on a proposed reform. The enquiry, headed by former Labour chancellor Roy Jenkins, did take place, and recommended a form of proportional representation similar to that used in the Federal Republic of Germany.[16] However, this report was simply ignored, and no referendum took place. This outcome was perhaps predictable, in the light of the enormous difficulties involved in persuading members of an elected institution to change the system that elected them. The Blair government did introduce some changes to modernize the working practices of the Commons, including more family-friendly hours. But the basic workings of the Commons and its role in the constitution remained essentially the same.

The rest of the Labour reform project was largely successful on its own terms. The Human Rights Act of 1998 fulfilled the manifesto promise of incorporating the European Convention on Human Rights into UK law, resolving a major anomaly of Britain's unwritten constitution: the lack of any clear definition of individual rights. A Freedom of Information Act in 2000 also addressed another longstanding problem—the secrecy and lack of transparency in Britain's public administration (often referred to as Whitehall, the area of central London where most ministries are located). These reforms amount to significant progress in clarifying democratic rights and practices in Britain, and the Blair governments deserve recognition for this. However, after two terms of office there is little sign that British citizens feel closer to their political institutions than before 1997.

Britain in the World: Which Side of the Atlantic?

In 1997, the most pressing problem facing the United Kingdom in international affairs appeared to be its relationship with the European Union, marked by tensions and misunderstandings in the final years of the Thatcher-Major era. A decade later, a very different set of problems were posed, with the consequences of the September 11 attacks and the resultant changes to U.S. foreign policy. Although foreign and European policies were far from most voters' minds when Labour was elected to government in 1997, the tail end of the Blair premiership was dominated by Britain's international role, and particularly, its relationship with the United States.

THE BACKGROUND: ATLANTICISM
AND EURO-SKEPTICISM

At the end of World War II, the United Kingdom found itself in a contradictory position. On the one hand, it still retained a vast overseas empire and, by virtue of its successful defense of its borders against the Nazi military threat, was able to take its place at the postwar negotiations between the great powers at Yalta. On the other, Britain was exhausted by a conflict that had confirmed the extraordinary military and political weight of the two new superpowers, the United States and the Soviet Union. Its status was now clearly that of a "second-rate" world power, and its colonial interests were threatened by economic limitations and the growth of independence movements in various parts of the empire. It is often said that postwar British foreign policy has revolved around "managing decline"—retreating from colonial commitments and recalibrating its international role in recognition of its diminished resources. But this process of managing decline has thrown up a major dilemma. The UK, as a founder member of NATO boasting a "special relationship" with the United States, has seen a close transatlantic alliance as the key to maximizing its influence in the world. But this closeness to the United States, reinforced by a shared language and historical ties, has frequently been viewed with suspicion by Britain's partners in Western Europe, determined to enhance integration between the European democracies, in part to counterbalance U.S. power. British governments since the war have been pulled in different directions by the global perspective inherited from the country's imperial past, and the European imperative dictated by its geographical position and commercial priorities.

Britain's complex relationship with the rest of Europe began with the historic decision not to participate in the first phase of the process of European integration. Preoccupied with maintaining ties to the former colonies in the Commonwealth, and hoping to "punch above its weight" through the transatlantic "special relationship," the UK stayed out of the European Economic Community (EEC) established in 1957 by the Treaty of Rome. Very quickly, British foreign policymakers changed their mind, applying for membership in 1963, but the French president de Gaulle, suspicious of Britain's closeness to the United States, vetoed the application. When the UK finally entered the EEC in 1973, its essential characteristics were already entrenched, and the close alliance between the two largest founder members, France and West Germany, left Britain in a marginal position. Britain's ambiguous position was also illustrated by its close military cooperation with the United States, and the presence of significant U.S. military installations on British soil.[17]

Box 2.3   An Awkward Partner: Margaret Thatcher on Europe

. . . willing and active cooperation between independent sovereign states is the best way to build a successful European Community.

To try to suppress nationhood and concentrate power at the center of a European conglomerate would be highly damaging and would jeopardize the objectives we seek to achieve.

Europe will be stronger precisely because it has France as France, Spain as Spain, Britain as Britain, each with its own customs, traditions and identity. It would be folly to try to fit them into some sort of identikit European personality. . . .

I am the first to say that on many great issues the countries of Europe should try to speak with a single voice. I want to see us work more closely on the things we can do better together than alone. Europe is stronger when we do so, whether it be in trade, in defense, or in our relations with the rest of the world.

But working more closely together does not require power to be centralized in Brussels or decisions to be taken by an appointed bureaucracy.

Indeed, it is ironic that just when those countries such as the Soviet Union, which have tried to run everything from the center, are learning that success depends on dispersing power and decisions away from the center, some in the Community seem to want to move in the opposite direction.

We have not successfully rolled back the frontiers of the state in Britain, only to see them reimposed at a European level, with a European superstate exercising a new dominance from Brussels.

Certainly we want to see Europe more united and with a greater sense of common purpose. But it must be in a way which preserves the different traditions, parliamentary powers and sense of national pride in one's own country; for these have been the source of Europe's vitality through the centuries.

Excerpt from Margaret Thatcher's speech to the College
of Europe, Bruges, September 20, 1988

(*Source:* Reproduced at *http://www.brugesgroup.com/mediacentre/index.live?article=92*)

The essential tension between Atlanticism and Europeanism came to a head during the 1980s under the premiership of Margaret Thatcher. Thatcher was an instinctive Atlanticist, a great admirer of the United States and its economic dynamism, and supportive of the United States' tough approach to communism and the Soviet Union. Conversely, Thatcher was suspicious of France and Germany, and had little patience for the intricate negotiations that characterized European policymaking. Although a strong supporter of the European Community's deregulatory drive to create a Single European Market by 1992, she was generally unsympathetic to further integration. Her close personal friendship with Ronald Reagan, and poor relations with European leaders such as Mitterrand or Kohl, pushed her into increasingly Euro-skeptical attitudes at a time when other member states were planning to share sovereignty over an increasing range of policy areas, including monetary policy, and home and foreign affairs. The situation came to a head in 1990, when Thatcher marked her clear opposition to proposals made by European Commission president Jacques Delors in the House of Commons, declaring "no, no, no" to his vision of Europe.

Although Thatcher was forced out of office shortly afterwards, the situation under John Major improved little, and anti-European Conservative M.P.s forced Major to adopt a tough line toward the other member states. At one stage this went so far as to order British representatives to "boycott" all European decisionmaking processes, in protest against the European ban on British beef during the "mad cow disease" crisis. By the mid-1990s British relations with its European partners were at a low point, and one of Tony Blair's key promises during the 1997 election campaign was to place Britain "at the heart of Europe." This new pro-European policy included the controversial proposal for Britain to join the new euro currency agreed at the Maastricht summit of 1991.

BLAIR'S EUROPEAN POLICY

Tony Blair's relations with the other European Union (EU) member states got off to a promising start, in part because of the relief felt among other European leaders at no longer having to deal with an instinctively hostile Conservative administration. The honeymoon period in UK-Europe relations was extended because of the election of a number of center-left governments in the EU toward the end of the 1990s. Center-left leaders were eager to associate themselves with a leader who had won the 1997 election so decisively and was enjoying high levels of popularity in his own country. This led to the attempt by Blair and the German Social Democrat leader Gerhard Schröder to develop a close working relationship around Third Way principles, the German party having adopted a similar slogan, the "Neue Mitte" (New Center). However, the apparent conservatism of many of Blair's public statements, and the UK's refusal to commit to joining the euro zone, put a damper on cooperation.

The euro, launched in 1999, was a difficult issue for the Labour government to address. Opinion polls suggested that the British public was overwhelmingly opposed to membership, and the UK's relatively virtuous economic performance in the second half of the 1990s did little to predispose Euro-skeptic Britons toward a currency dominated by sluggish economies such as those in France, Germany, and Italy. Blair appeared strongly committed to membership, while his chancellor, the key figure in determining economic policymaking, was unenthusiastic. A "wait and see" approach was therefore adopted, with the government expressing its intention to join the euro "in principle," but only making a final decision in view of a complex set of five "economic tests," announced in 1997. These tests—such as, for instance, "Would joining the euro promote higher growth, stability, and a lasting increase in jobs?"—were sufficiently ambiguous as to allow the government to make a decision on the grounds of short-term realpolitik. The Blair government's failure to join the euro in the first wave has had stark consequences: given Britain's comparatively better economic performance since 1999 than the other large euro-zone countries, it would appear difficult in the extreme for it to join in the current circumstances. As of 2006, therefore, Britain remains a marginal force in European-level decision-making on macroeconomic issues.

However Blair's government did engage with European policymaking in other ways, most significantly by arguing strongly for structural reforms to liberalize European economies.[18] This pressure on relatively more regulated economies such as France and Germany to adopt an "Anglo-Saxon" model of economic governance was not always popular in European capitals, and reminded some Europeans a little too much of the overbearing style of his Conservative predecessors. However, Blair won sufficient support among some other reform-minded governments to launch the so-called Lisbon agenda for economic reform, at the European Council in the Portuguese capital in 2000. The aim of the Lisbon process, rather optimistically, was to turn the European Union into the world's foremost knowledge economy within ten years, an aim that half a decade later appeared laughable. However the Lisbon objective did amount to a coherent plan for reform, combining liberalization of markets with an emphasis on innovation and technology on the one hand, and sustainability and social justice on the other. Although the process has not been taken as seriously as Blair would have hoped, it certainly amounted to an important constructive British intervention in the debate on Europe's future.

More difficult for the Labour government was the constitutional issue arising from the expansion of the EU eastwards in 2005. Faced with a further ten member states, the EU's institutions clearly needed updating and reforming, but the proposal to combine this updating with the writing of a European Constitution created a serious dilemma for the UK. Britain's tendency toward Euro-skepticism, added to its tradition of constitutional ambiguity and flexibility, made a European Constitution an unwelcome proposal, and placed Labour in an uncomfortable position. Blair wanted to play an active, constructive role in the debate, but was wary of how the constitutional issue would play at home, and committed the government to holding a popular referendum. Although by most accounts Labour were successful in defending what the government perceived as UK interests in the proposed constitutional text, opinion polls continued to show unremitting hostility. Fortunately for Blair and his government, the "no" votes cast in the French and Dutch referenda on 2005 made the constitutional project unviable, allowing Britain to suspend its referendum and wait for the issue to disappear.

FOREIGN AND SECURITY POLICY: TONY BLAIR AND THE "WAR ON TERROR"

Although Blair quickly succeeded in overcoming much of the negative legacy of Euro-skepticism bequeathed by the Conservatives, his relationship with the other European member states was to run into trouble as a result of the dramatic events of September 11, 2001. The response to the challenge of Al-Qaeda terrorism drove a wedge between the United States and the most important continental European powers, Germany and France. Britain's difficult position as the transatlantic "bridge" was placed under acute strain by these developments, and the consequences of the choices made by the Labour government have defined the closing phases of Tony Blair's premiership.

Blair's emergence as an ambitious and activist world leader surprised many, as the Labour leader appeared to pay little attention to foreign affairs before his election in 1997.[19] Very quickly, however, he developed a distinctive approach to foreign affairs that contrasted with the flexible pragmatism that marked British policy toward international affairs in the postwar period. Very quickly the Blair government found itself involved in military action, first cooperating with the United States in air strikes on Iraq in 1998, then playing a visible role in the U.S.-led intervention in the Kosovo region of Serbia, where alleged ethnic cleansing was practiced against the Albanian majority population. Indeed, during the Kosovo conflict Blair made a major statement on foreign affairs in Chicago, in which he laid out an agenda for active commitment on the part of Western powers to intervene against dictatorships and use military action on humanitarian grounds. This speech demonstrates that the choices Blair made after September 11 were actually consistent with his thinking almost from the very beginning of his premiership. The British intervention in Kosovo was facilitated by Blair's close relationship with Bill Clinton, an enthusiast of Third Way thinking and fellow alumnus of Oxford University. What surprised many was Blair's keenness to continue such a close relationship with Clinton's successor, George W. Bush, a very different kind of political figure who appeared to have little in common with the British prime minister.

In the aftermath of September 11, Blair was quick to line up behind the U.S. administration in its response to the atrocities. The British government participated in the attack on Afghanistan, but perhaps most significantly, also backed the shift in strategy announced by the Bush administration soon after, which opened up the possibility of preemptive military action against potential threats to U.S. security. The Afghanistan operation received almost unanimous backing from shocked European governments, but the next phase of the U.S. "war on terror," military intervention in Iraq, divided the European powers to an unprecedented degree. Although opposition to the invasion of Iraq was weaker in Britain than in countries such as France, Italy, and Spain, public opinion could be described as at best skeptical, and there was deep unease within the Labour Party toward the plan. In these circumstances, Blair was able to exploit the powerful constitutional position of a British prime minister to push ahead with support of, and full participation in, the Iraq operation. Despite losing two members of his cabinet, who resigned in protest, and facing substantial parliamentary opposition from a large number of Labour M.P.s, Blair pressed ahead. The consequences were far-reaching.

As far as European politics were concerned, the Iraq issue divided the UK from the other major European actors on the international stage, with both France and Germany vehemently opposed. Blair was therefore forced to line up with conservative governments in Spain and Italy in supporting the Bush administration. This had consequences for Blair's European policy, with the initial attempts to form alliances with friendly center-left governments in France, and particularly Germany, being definitively shelved. The Lisbon agenda for economic reform was also tainted by association, as Blair's closeness to Bush on foreign policy discredited his center-left credentials on socioeconomic issues. More broadly, Blair's influence over European politics was affected by the increasing perception, especially in the founding member states of the European Community, that Britain was a mere proxy for U.S. power.

The consequences for Blair's domestic standing were if anything far more serious. Determined to roll back U.S. unilateralism, Blair was instrumental in persuading Colin Powell to seek a United Nations mandate for the invasion of Iraq, and regarded suspicions that Saddam Hussein was developing weapons of mass destruction (WMD) as the most effective rationale for a UN resolution. This move was insufficient to win broad international backing for the war, but did force Blair into exaggerating the available evidence of the WMD threat in a government document used to win over the British foreign policy community. The misleading suggestion that Iraq could launch WMD in forty-five minutes had devastating consequences for Blair's political credibility when, after the invasion, no such capacity could be found.

The political damage suffered by the Blair government over Iraq is difficult to calculate accurately, but appears substantial. First, even before the war massive demonstrations took place around Europe, with the turnout of up to 2 million protestors in London constituting perhaps the largest public protest in British history. Second, the war caused deep upset in Britain's large Muslim population. British Muslims, who are mostly of Pakistani or Bangladeshi origins and tend to be concentrated in the less prosperous areas of Britain's largest cities, had traditionally been strong supporters of the Labour Party, perceived as the most effective defender of ethnic minority rights. However, the Iraq war and its aftermath undermined this longstanding relationship. Muslim unease at Labour policy was exploited by George Galloway, a former dissident Labour M.P. expelled from the party for his close relations with the Saddam Hussein

Box 2.4   Blair on Iraq

"Saddam Hussein's regime is despicable, he is developing weapons of mass destruction, and we cannot leave him doing so unchecked. He is a threat to his own people and to the region and, if allowed to develop these weapons, a threat to us also.

"Doing nothing is not an option."

—House of Commons, April 10, 2002

"[Saddam's] weapons of mass destruction program is active, detailed and growing. The policy of containment is not working. The weapons of mass destruction program is not shut down. It is up and running. . . . The intelligence picture [the intelligence services] paint is one accumulated over the past four years. It is extensive, detailed and authoritative. It concludes that Iraq has chemical and biological weapons, that Saddam has continued to produce them, that he has existing and active military plans for the use of chemical and biological weapons, which could be activated within 45 minutes, including against his own Shia population; and that he is actively trying to acquire nuclear weapons capability."

—House of Commons, September 24, 2002

"We are asked now seriously to accept that in the last few years—contrary to all history, contrary to all intelligence—Saddam decided unilaterally to destroy those weapons. I say that such a claim is palpably absurd."

—House of Commons, March 18, 2003

"We expected, I expected to find actual usable, chemical or biological weapons after we entered Iraq. But I have to accept, as the months have passed, it seems increasingly clear that at the time of invasion, Saddam did not have stockpiles of chemical or biological weapons ready to deploy."

—House of Commons, 14 July 2004

(*Sources: http://news.bbc.co.uk/1/hi/uk_politics/2847197.stm; http://news.bbc.co.uk/1/hi/ uk_politics/2955632.stm; http://news.bbc.co.uk/1/hi/uk_politics/3893987.stm; also at http://www .publications.parliament.uk/pa/pahansard.htm*)

regime. Galloway founded a party called Respect, which mobilized around the Iraq issue and was able to win election in 2005, defeating a Labour M.P. in one of its safest London constituencies. Many Muslims also abstained, or supported the Liberal Democrats, who had opposed the war. The Iraq issue undoubtedly cost Labour in the 2005 election, which saw its majority cut in half and its vote share decline to just 35 percent.

Blair's decisions to back Bush's war in Iraq, and subsequent pro-U.S. positions over Israel and Palestine, including the Israeli attack on Lebanon in 2006, have become the defining features of the Blair premiership. Any British prime minister would have been placed in a difficult position by world events after September 11, 2001, given the UK's historically close relationship with the United States, and ambiguous relationship with the rest of the European Union. However Blair took a big risk in identifying himself so closely and so publicly with the Bush administration, which has become extremely unpopular in British and European public opinion. It is difficult to escape the conclusion that the Blair premiership will be remembered more for its foreign policy choices than for anything else.

Conclusion

In 2006, British politics was dominated by discussion of Tony Blair's political future. In 2004, Blair had already announced that the 2005 election would be the last he would fight as Labour leader. In the 2005 election, Labour won a third successive victory for the first time in its history, but the drop in its vote share to just 35 percent revealed the fragility of its support base. Although Labour still won a comfortable governing majority, this was purely an artifact of Britain's "first past the post" electoral system, which tends to overrepresent the largest parties in general, and Labour in particular. The Conservative Party's revival in 2006 after the emergence of a young and dynamic leader, David Cameron, also suggested that Labour's grip on power might soon loosen. In these circumstances, Blair soon came under pressure from nervous Labour M.P.s to give a clear indication of when he would resign from office.

Blair's near-decade in power has been a curious mix of unprecedented success and unexpected failure. The usual problems facing Labour governments in Britain in the past—economic problems, pressure from trade unions and other vested interests, small parliamentary majorities—have been conspicuous by their absence. Labour has presided over a remarkable period of consistent economic growth and rising living standards, and has won electoral success on an unprecedented scale, notwithstanding the losses in 2005. In many respects, Blair's government has been one of the most successful in recent British history, combining economic expansion with strong public investment in popular services such as education and healthcare. Despite persistent public fears over crime and disorder, official figures show a substantial and constant fall in reported offenses throughout the Labour decade in office. Power has been devolved to those countries that demanded more self-government, and the intractable problem of Northern Ireland is closer to a solution than at any time for decades. On most measures, the average Briton would appear to be far better off in 2006 than ten years earlier.

However, like almost all of his predecessors, Blair is to leave office as an unpopular prime minister. This is partly a pathology of the British system of government. Lacking any term limits, successful British prime ministers will tend to stay in office long enough for the public mood to change and voters to tire of familiar faces. But Blair's unpopularity is partly the result of the political consequences of his government's choices. The invasion of Iraq has proved a deeply unpopular decision. But there are other reasons for unpopularity: the increase in the tax burden, public impatience with the slow rate of improvement in public services, and the growing urgency of the environmental crisis. It is in the nature of a competitive two-party democracy such as the United Kingdom that political leaders do not receive gratitude for their achievements, but rather criticism for their failures. After a period of Labour dominance, the revival of the Conservative Party suggests that in the near future British politics will witness once again an alternation in power between its two major parties. However another possibility can be suggested: Labour's electoral decline, and the Conservative Party's persistent unpopularity in some sectors of society, could lead to a situation where no single party holds a parliamentary majority. The emergence of coalition governments in Scotland, Wales, and Northern Ireland offers a precedent for what may happen if the Westminster Parliament fails to deliver a governing majority. If this happens, it will represent a major change in the way Britain is governed.

Notes

1. http://www.number-10.gov.uk/output/Page8073.asp.

2. Stephen Fielding, *The Labour Party Since 1951: "Socialism" and Society*, Manchester: Manchester University Press, 1997, p. 25.

3. Labour Party constitution, at http://www.labour.org.uk/aboutlabour.

4. Anthony Giddens, *The Third Way*, Cambridge: Polity Press, 1998.

5. Robert Taylor, "Mr Blair's Business Model—Capital and Labour in Flexible Markets," in Anthony Seldon and Dennis Kavanagh (eds.), *The Blair Effect 2001–5*, Cambridge: Cambridge University Press, 2006, pp. 184–206.

6. Carl Emmerson et al., *The Government's Fiscal Rules*, Institute of Fiscal Studies Briefing Note 16, http://www.ifs.org.uk/bns/bn16.pdf#search=%22public%20borrowing%22.

7. Andrew Glyn and Stewart Wood, "New Labour's Economic Policy," in Andrew Glyn (ed.), *Social Democracy in Neoliberal Times*, Oxford: Oxford University Press, 2001, Ch. 8.

8. Jonathan Hopkin and Daniel Wincott. "New Labour, Economic Reform, and the European Social Model," *British Journal of Politics and International Relations*, 8(1), January 2006, 50–68.

9. See John Hills, *Inequality and the State*, Oxford: Oxford University Press, 2005, Chs. 9–11.

10. Hilaire Barnett, *Britain Unwrapped: Government and Constitution Explained*, London: Penguin, 2002, p. 52.

11. For a powerful denunciation of the risks inherent in this constitutional vagueness, see F. F. Ridley, "There Is No British Constitution: A Dangerous Case of the Emperor's Clothes," *Parliamentary Affairs,* 41(3), July 1988, 340–361.

12. For an extensive discussion of the history of the "territorial question" in modern British politics, see Vernon Bogdanor, *Devolution in the United Kingdom*, Oxford: Oxford University Press, 1998.

13. For an extensive account of the "Irish question," see John McGarry and Brendan O'Leary (eds.), *The Northern Ireland Conflict*, Oxford: Oxford University Press, 2005.

14. Charlie Jeffery, "Devolution and the Lopsided State," in Patrick Dunleavy, Richard Heffernan, Philip Cowley, and Colin Hay (eds.), *Developments in British Politics 8*, Basingstoke: Palgrave, 2006, pp. 138–158.

15. For an analysis of how the major British parties adapted to devolution, see Jonathan Hopkin and Jonathan Bradbury, "British Parties and Multilevel Politics," *Publius: The Journal of Federalism*, 36(1), January 2006, 135–152.

16. "Jenkins Commission" (Independent Commission on the Voting System), report presented to Parliament by the Secretary of State for the Home Department by command of Her Majesty, October 1998; available online at: http://www.archive.official-documents.co.uk/document/cm40/4090/4090.htm.

17. See Stephen George, *An Awkward Partner: Britain in the European Community*, Oxford: Oxford University Press, 1998.

18. See Jonathan Hopkin and Daniel Wincott, "New Labour, Economic Reform and the European Social Model," *British Journal of Politics and International Relations*, 8(1), January 2006, 50–68.

19. For an analysis of Blair's foreign policy thinking, see Michael Cox and Tim Oliver, "Security Policy in an Insecure World," in Patrick Dunleavy, Richard Heffernan, Philip Cowley, and Colin Hay (eds.), *Developments in British Politics 8*, Basingstoke: Palgrave, 2006, pp. 174–192.

Suggested Readings

Barnett, Hilaire, *Britain Unwrapped. Government and Constitution Explained*, London: Penguin, 2002.

Denver, David, *Elections and Voting Behaviour in Britain*, 3rd edition, Basingstoke: Palgrave, 2003.

Dunleavy, Patrick, Richard Heffernan, Philip Cowley, and Colin Hay (eds.), *Developments in British Politics 8*, Basingstoke: Palgrave, 2006.

Gamble, Andrew, *Between Europe and America: The Future of British Politics*, Basingstoke: Palgrave, 2003.

Geddes, Andrew, *The European Union and British Politics*, Basingstoke: Palgrave, 2003.

Heath, Anthony, Roger Jowell, and John Curtice, *The Rise of New Labour: Party Policies and Voter Choices*, Oxford: Oxford University Press, 2001.

Ludlam, Stephen, and Martin Smith (eds.), *Governing as New Labour: Politics and Policy Under Blair*, Basingstoke: Palgrave, 2003.

Seldon, Anthony, and Dennis Kavanagh (eds.), *The Blair Effect 2001–5*, Cambridge: Cambridge University Press, 2006.

Williams, Paul, *British Foreign Policy Under New Labour*, Basingstoke: Palgrave, 2006.

WEBSITES

Richard Kimber's Political Science Resources: *http://www.psr.keele.ac.uk/area/uk.htm*.
Constitution Unit, University College London: *http://www.ucl.ac.uk/constitution-unit/*.
Webpage of the prime minister: *http://www.number-10.gov.uk/output/Page1.asp*.
UK Parliament: *http://www.parliament.uk/*.
BBC British Politics Pages: *http://news.bbc.co.uk/1/hi/uk_politics/default.stm*.
Hansard Society: *http://www.hansardsociety.org.uk/*.
Conservative Party: *http://www.conservatives.com/*.
Labour Party: *http://www.labour.org.uk/home*.

CHAPTER 3

Germany: The Berlin Republic Still in Transition

Helga A. Welsh

Germany

Population (million):	82.5
Area in Square Miles:	137,830
Population Density per Square Mile:	598
GDP (in billion dollars, 2005):	$2,494.7
GDP per capita (PPP, 2005):	$30,253
Joined EC/EU:	January 1, 1958

Performance of Key Political Parties in Parliamentary Elections
of September 18, 2005

Christian Democratic Union (CDU)	29.3%
Christian Social Union (CSU)	7.5%
Free Democratic Party (FDP)	9.9%
Alliance 90/The Greens	8.3%
The Left (Die Linke)	8.8%
Social Democratic Party (SPD)	36.2%

Main Office Holders: Chancellor: Angela Merkel—CDU/CSU (2005); President: Horst Köhler—CDU/CSU (2004)

When I arrived in Munich in May 2006 for a summer of research, important changes had occurred in Germany since my stay the previous year. The national election in September 2005 had installed the first female chancellor and, two months later, a grand coalition government. Newspaper topics, however, sounded all too familiar: the government's urgency to pass long overdue reforms in various policy areas; Germany's evolving international status as exemplified by Chancellor Angela Merkel's upcoming visit to the People's Republic of China; the demographic crisis triggered by an aging population and low birth rates. The past was still present in daily reporting: for example, how the German pope Benedict XVI would be greeted in Poland, a country that suffered tremendously under Hitler's rule, and what words he would find in visiting the concentration camp at Auschwitz. The official motto of the imminent World Cup soccer championship, "A Time to Make Friends," reflected the host country's concern about its global image.

What is not or no longer mentioned in the media can be as telling as the headlines. The differences between democratic western and formerly communist eastern Germany were largely absent from front-page news and have been for some years. More important, lengthy editorials no longer address whether and to what extent the politics of the unified Germany will differ from that of the "old" Federal Republic (the former West Germany). After unification in 1990 and, to a lesser extent, the government's move from Bonn to Berlin in 1999, observers had wondered—some with trepidation, others with ambivalence—what this change might herald for domestic and foreign affairs.

In today's news, any reference to the Berlin Republic, as opposed to the Bonn Republic, is mostly factual and not weighed down by value judgments. Anxieties regarding, for example, waning commitment to European integration or a hegemonic role in Central and Eastern Europe have been laid to rest. The new capital of Berlin has reemerged as a cultural and scientific hub and, after architectural renovation of the city center, its past as a divided city has been erased; new traffic connections reconnect it with the world. At the same time, federalism engenders competition between Berlin and other major cities, such as Cologne, Frankfurt, Hamburg, Leipzig, and Munich. The sharing of competencies and power contrasts to unitary states such as the United Kingdom and France, where London and Paris clearly dominate the countries' cultural, economic, and financial life.

Although we think of history in terms of distinct time frames, such as the beginning and the end of the Cold War, developments are continuous. One period closes as another is already under way. Today, we recognize the characteristics of the Bonn Republic (1949–1990) with greater clarity; while gradual, and perhaps still too early to pin down, the departure to Berlin has entailed significant changes. How continuity has meshed with these changes—some anticipated, some unforeseen—will be the focus of this chapter.

Box 3.1   Berlin: City on the Move

Claudia Wahjudi (2005)

Viewed from the eleventh floor of a block of flats in the middle of the city, Berlin presents itself from its best side—in elegant gray. The plain of stone, asphalt, plaster, concrete, granite, steel and glass extends as far as the horizon, interspersed with the green of parks and the red brick of old factories. Rising up in the center, there are little towers, curved or straight, and a few skyscrapers, some functionally rectangular, others with the sharp angles familiar from computer games. Colors and forms tell of the discontinuities of the city's history: from industrialization, which suddenly made the little residence city a metropolis, to the pomp of the German Empire and the social reforms of the Weimar Republic; from the megalomania of the National Socialists to the bombs and firestorms of the Second World War; from the division of the city into an Eastern European half and a Western European half to the building boom that followed the fall of the Wall. But now you can only sense where the Wall, Berlin's most famous structure, once stood: somewhere over there between the round roof of the Sony Center and the new glass cupola of the Reichstag Building, the seat of the German parliament. . . .

Every time a political system collapses in Germany, its stone witnesses are disposed of in Berlin as an example to others. A practice that is not always free of contradictions. Some people would even like to have a section of the almost completely demolished Wall back: when a private museum recently built a mock-up, locals and tourists flocked to see it.

There is always building, demolition and rebuilding going on. The various currents of German society compete for visible representation in the capital, which in just 100 years has seen five German states and the end of the Second World War in Europe. Now it is like a patchwork quilt full of holes that someone is supposed to be mending. The architect Philipp Oswalt called his book about Berlin *Stadt ohne Form* (City without Form), a phrase that was certainly intended to have positive connotations: he believes all the city's discontinuities and lacunae offer freedoms—including intellectual freedoms. And the artist Erik Göngrich says, "I wouldn't have anything against the Schlossplatz staying empty for another 15 years. The people who are 20 today should also be able to create something later."

Berlin is a city of opposites. It has glittering new government buildings, embassies, shopping malls and sport arenas, but a few meters away plaster is peeling from a municipal building and cars are bouncing through potholes. The Love Parade, the famous street procession held to the sound of techno beats, was conceived in Berlin, which also hosts a Carnival of the Cultures, Christopher Street Day celebrations, the annual Berlinale film festival and a Biennale for contemporary art. The 2006 football World Cup final will kick off in its Olympic Stadium. The city has 19 universities and higher education institutions, three opera houses and about 300 galleries, you will hear Turkish, English, Polish and Russian being spoken, and some days more than 120 bands and orchestras perform there. Yet, to the amazement of guests from other major cities, Berlin seems pleasantly empty: such wide pavements, so much sky, so few traffic jams—it is almost as restful as a holiday resort.

History's Legacy

A TUMULTUOUS CENTURY

History is a combination of evidence and interpretation, which allows for both understanding and illusion. A country's history is particularly difficult to master when, as in Germany's case, the path toward a securely anchored liberal democracy was tortuous and marked by major ruptures. In one short century (1914–1991), to use Eric Hobsbawm's term, Germans experienced the collapse of three forms of dictatorship and one democratic political system. The first major transformation came in 1918–1919. As a result of defeat in World War I and the collapse of the Second Reich (1871–1918), an authoritarian monarchy was overturned and replaced with the democratic parliamentary system of the Weimar Republic. Its beginnings were inauspicious, associated with defeat and humiliation, widespread political violence, and severe economic and social problems. The constitution's optimistic assumptions about the balance of power among president, chancellor, and parliament were sorely tested by extreme party fragmentation and polarization, and economic deterioration after 1928 added to the sense of instability. Democracy was shallowly rooted in both the public and the elites and rather quickly abandoned. The National Socialist Party, one of many marginal radical groups in 1928, with 2.6 percent of the vote, received 37.8 percent in the 1932 elections. Once in power, Adolf Hitler ruthlessly and with amazing speed consolidated his leadership. Nazi Germany unleashed World War II to fulfill Hitler's geopolitical goal of building a "Thousand-Year Reich." Germany invaded most of Europe; Nazism's racist claim of "Aryan" superiority and anti-Semitic, homophobic, anticommunist, and eugenic views led to the murder, torture, and enslavement of millions of people across Europe and totalitarian rule in Germany itself.

By May 1945, Germans were confronted with utter defeat; to signify both an end and a new beginning, this moment is often referred to as "Zero Hour." Time, however, had not stopped; on the contrary, the past would shape German political institutions, policies, and political culture, yet the future was uncertain and open to different scenarios. The country's division into two states was central to, and an early by-product of, the emerging Cold War between East and West. Out of the ashes, in May 1949, the Federal Republic of Germany was created in the western part. The sleepy town of Bonn was chosen as the temporary capital and seat of government; similarly, the constitution was named the Basic Law to emphasize its transitory character, yet a stable democracy evolved. Soviet and eastern German communists founded the German Democratic Republic (GDR) in October 1949, where under Soviet tutelage, a communist dictatorship took hold. With the hope of eventual reunification and from a position of strength, Western allies and western Germans sought to secure democracy and to buffer against Soviet expansion. The West promulgated the Federal Republic as the official successor state of the defeated Germany; international recognition of the GDR was denied until the 1970s. The building of the Berlin Wall in August 1961 eliminated the last escape valve for eastern Germans; the ensuing diplomatic ice age between the two German states melted only gradually in the 1970s and 1980s.

Initially, both German states—supported by their respective allies—pursued unification. In response to West German chancellor Willy Brandt's 1969 pronouncement that there are two states but one German nation, eastern leaders developed a policy of strict demarcation and separate identity. For them, unification was no longer on the agenda. In the West, the practicality of the policy goal of unification was increasingly questioned. However, while apparently stable, the communist regime slowly regressed; in 1989 it suddenly collapsed. The promise of unification, kept alive in western Germany as a constitutional prerogative, finally and unexpectedly became reality after four decades of separation.

Article 23 of the Basic Law expeditiously allowed the former GDR to join the constitutional framework of the Federal Republic in October 1990. The more cumbersome approach of renegotiating a new constitution, based on Article 146, was never seriously considered. Unification was a jump into cold water, and its consequences have played out in many ways. Some of the goals associated with the merging of the two states have been fulfilled; for example, democratic stability was never in question. Others, in particular economic recovery of the eastern part, remain unfinished. Germans in east and west live in a democratic society whose fundamental beliefs are accepted, but "the growing together of what belongs together," to use the words of former chancellor Willy Brandt, has taken longer than anticipated.

At the time of unification, in Germany and abroad, questions were posed: How would the profound desire for stability, born out of the dramatic upheavals of the twentieth century, mesh with the need to adjust to new domestic and international circumstances? How would Germany find ways to live in peace, while self-consciously shadowed by its past?

A DIFFICULT FATHERLAND

The past may have made Germany, in the words of poet C. K. Williams, a symbolic nation;[1] Germans are usually defined not by what they are but what they represent. Germany is admired for its cultural and scientific achievements and reviled for horrible crimes. The first eighty years of its history as a nation-state were, in many ways, defined by authoritarianism, militarism, and nationalism.

The lessons of the Weimar Republic's democratic breakdown and the Nazis' smashing of constitutional parliamentary government influenced later politics. "Bonn is not Weimar"—the determination not to repeat the instability that led to Hitler's dictatorship informed the writing of the West German Constitution, the creation of its political parties, and its particular economic system after World War II. These steps aimed to avoid the mistakes of the past by defending democracy and establishing political, economic, and social conditions that would provide security for individuals and the country as a whole.

The horrors inflicted by the Third Reich forced Germans toward a critical and open confrontation with their past. This process started in 1945 as part of Allied denazification and democratization programs, but after the onset of the Cold War, swift political and economic consolidation took precedence. Although the future seemed more important then, the past would not go away. Challenged by a new generation, the hush muffling German involvement and collusion with Hitler's regime was shattered in the late 1950s and early 1960s, and, step by step, a historical consciousness emerged that informs the public discourse to this day. No interpretation of German history can avoid confronting the horrors of Auschwitz. The legacy of the concentration camps pervades debates ranging from abortion and political asylum to reparations of Nazi victims and foreign military involvement. It explains the heightened sensitivity at home and abroad to right-wing activities. After the fall of communism, how to address questions of justice and historical recollection in dealing with victims and perpetrators of the disposed communist regime added another layer of complexity. With the beginning of the twenty-first century, after a long silence, Germans also began once again to discuss their own suffering during and after World War II, including expulsions from their homes, mass rape, and the death and destruction wreaked by Allied bombing.

Predictably, how the past should be remembered often creates heated debates. While the discourse largely takes place among political and cultural elites, many of its arguments are reflected in newsprint, novels, popular movies, and television documentaries and trickle down into collective consciousness. Germany has joined the many Western European countries setting memories of the Holocaust quite literally "in stone."[2] The new capital of Berlin is home to the Jewish Museum and, after many years of controversy regarding its design and designation, the place of the Holocaust Memorial, officially named the Monument to the Murdered Jews of Europe. Berlin has also become the center of revival for Jewish culture in Germany. At the beginning of the 1930s, about 600,000 Jews lived in Germany; by 1950, the number had dwindled to 15,000 but rose to 25,000 by 1989. Today, the Jewish communities (Jüdische Gemeinden) in Germany represent more than 100,000 members, more than two-thirds of whom came from the former Soviet Union and arrived in Germany only after 1990. About 12,000 Jewish citizens live in Berlin. The large influx of Russian Jews has made the Jewish communities in Germany the third-largest in Europe and presented them the unique challenge of integrating the newcomers.[3]

The fall of communism ended Germany's division into two separate states, granted the country full sovereignty, and rendered obsolete its role as the front line between hostile ideological camps. The "German question" in the heart of

Europe finally had been resolved peacefully. Now, Germany's room for political maneuvering in the international arena increased. But have Germans reached the point where they can exhibit national interests and pride like other nationals without arousing fear? Not yet: their difficult past still undercuts the quest for normality. During the 2006 soccer World Cup, younger generations of Germans waved the German flag and sported the national colors, and reactions were mixed. Some felt that they were simply expressing loyalty and support for their national team, celebrating a joyous sporting event. Others saw the burst of red, black, and gold as one more step toward an enlightened or cosmopolitan patriotism that entails pride in one's country. Those who argued along these lines also felt that by using the colors in an identity-building but nonthreatening way, German soccer fans were preventing the radical right (neo-Nazis) from usurping them for their xenophobic purposes. Finally, some watched the display of national colors with unease. They recalled the dark sides of German history and preferred a *post-nationalistic* Germany. In their view, "normality" for Germany should and will forever remain elusive. Each interpretation has its merits; none is right or wrong. Rather, they are personal perspectives.

However, the responses do signal that new generations of postwar Germans are allowed greater leeway in balancing responsibility to history with political confidence.[4] The number of representatives in the lower house of parliament (Bundestag) who were born and/or socialized under the Third Reich has consistently declined. Today, only 15 of the 614 members were born before 1941, compared to almost one-third even a decade ago. In addition, with the advent of a coalition government between the Social Democratic Party of Germany (SPD) and the Greens in 1998, a new generation of political leaders came to the helm of the German government. In their youth, many of them had been active in critically examining Germany's past; as members or supporters of the "68ers," the rebellious student movement of the 1960s, their "antifascist" credentials were beyond dispute. In particular, the Green Party has its roots in the peace movement. Joschka Fischer, the respected foreign minister in both cabinets under Chancellor Gerhard Schröder, used his personal and his party's pacifist credentials to legitimize greater engagement in foreign and security policy. Pacifism and antifascism provided the basis for a new self-confidence; the role history plays in determining German interests remains a sine qua non in policymaking.

Untangling the Reform Gridlock

The German penchant for joining words and coining new ones is well known, and, since 1977, a new "word of the year" is chosen by a jury of experts. Without exception, the terms capture national issues of major significance. In 2005, the word of the year was *Bundeskanzlerin*, the feminine form of chancellor. The choice was more than a gesture toward the election of the first female head of government in Germany, Angela Merkel, but recognized the explicit change of women's place in society. One year earlier, *Hartz IV*, a reform package to overhaul the labor market, named after its main architect, made it to the top of the list; it signified the battles over, and the sensitivity toward, economic and social reform. In 2003, the term *das alte Europa* (old Europe), exclaimed by U.S. Secretary of Defense Donald Rumsfeld in frustration about countries such as Germany that were unwilling to join in the war against Iraq, proved the centrality of transatlantic relations and the ensuing debate regarding Germany's international identity. In 2002, price increases associated with the introduction of the new European currency, the euro, linked it to the German word *teuer* (expensive) to coin *Teuro*.

Some new words are of passing significance, while others become part of the vocabulary. Among the latter is the 1997 word of the year, *Reformstau*, or reform gridlock. Pressure for change in the areas of taxes, healthcare, pensions, labor market, and immigration built up in the 1980s but boiled over in the 1990s. Decisionmaking overload, political haggling, and resistance seemed to make reforms impossible. Hence, *Reformstau* was coined and was soon joined in the public discourse by such terms as "policy paralysis" and "stalled Republic" to describe the German malaise.

Economic globalization, with greater competition, outsourcing of jobs, spread of information technologies, and accelerated migration of ideas and people, has had profound effects on all Western economies. Germany has also had to deal with the economic and financial challenges associated with the transformation of the former East Germany from a polluted communist bankruptcy to a capitalist economy, albeit with a social face. The limits of the social and economic policies that promised "prosperity and welfare for all citizens" became obvious in an environment of shrinking, aging populations, declining economic growth rates, and competition for resources, including knowledge and education.

Although the costs of unification delayed and hobbled the initiation and implementation of important policy reforms, more fundamental problems were at work: the level or lack of elite and societal support and the role of political institutions. Like most Europeans, many Germans tend to turn to the government to address problems that affect their well-being. While direct state intervention is circumscribed, governmental institutions play important roles as mediators and set the legal framework for semipublic institutions, such as the Federal Agency for Labor. Economic and social systems, including the social welfare system, rely on a highly regulatory culture and transfer payments. These systems evolved after World War II and won out over competing ideas of socialism and pure capitalism. Germans prioritized economic and social stability. A high level of employment and social protection, extensive participatory rights for workers, collective bargaining, and close cooperation between labor unions and employer associations, both of which were given privileged access to, and roles in, managing the economy, became the criteria for the "model" Germany.

Praised as a social market economy, for many years this model worked extremely well. At least as important, the principles of social justice and social solidarity turned into important reference points in the political discourse and, to this day, find widespread public approval. In referring to the welfare state, German citizens use the term "social state" *(Sozialstaat)*; overall, the term "social" has a positive connotation. Germans are accustomed to measuring government performance by equality of outcomes. Any move toward replacing equal outcomes with equal opportunity requires both policy adjustments and a shift in citizens' expectations.

People in rich societies, then-chancellor Schröder said in 2002, are afraid that change will be detrimental to their personal situation.[5] Cuts in social benefits, especially when accompanied by increasingly unequal incomes, are unsettling to many. Persistent high unemployment and blasts from the media about the German malaise had the effect of darkening the mood and consumer confidence. Americans are often criticized for saving too little and spending too much. In 2004, Americans saved about 1 percent of their disposable income; Germans saved about 11 percent. While a high savings rate is good for individuals, the aggregate effect can, as in the case of Germany, depress domestic demand and economic recovery. Resistance to change has characterized the interconnected economic and political landscape.

In all democratic settings, politics is the art of getting things done and therefore requires bargaining and compromise. In the German "negotiation democracy," a complex system of checks, balances, and conflict-solving mechanisms emerged. Some features of consensual decisionmaking were intentional; others evolved through cultural preference and political stipulation. They may secure high levels of acceptance once new policies are formed, but they also slow down or even block policymaking processes. Thus, many observers have pointed to the institutional disincentives of the German political system, including the large number of veto players that block policy initiatives. The Federal Council, the second chamber of the national parliament, and the Federal Constitutional Court both have significant potential as tools of the opposition. Other veto players encompass powerful interest groups, in particular the labor unions.

Calls for leadership and decisive action to advance reforms increased after the 2002 election. In March 2003, Chancellor Schröder announced a widely heralded, comprehensive policy program, "Agenda 2010," to reform the welfare system and labor market policies. However, the cuts in social benefits associated with those policies aroused strong opposition, especially within the left wing of Schröder's party, the SPD, leading to widespread protests and the creation of a new party, the Labor and Social Justice Party, by former SPD members and trade union activists. The SPD suffered a series of devastating losses in regional elections, culminating in its stronghold of North-Rhine Westphalia in the spring of 2005. Immediately after the election in North-Rhine Westphalia and against conditions of stubbornly high unemployment, Chancellor Schröder declared

Box 3.2   Germany's Welfare State (excerpts)

Jan Valentin (April 2005)

Germany is "a democratic and social federal state." That is what it says in Art. 20 Paragraph 1 of the Basic Law, the German constitution. Other than that, the Basic Law largely leaves open the form to be taken by the economic and social system. Terms such as "social market economy," coined by the Federal Republic of Germany's first Minister of Economics, Ludwig Erhard, are not used in the Basic Law. Yet the welfare state is deeply anchored in German history. Already at the end of the nineteenth century, Reich Chancellor Otto von Bismarck initiated the first laws for a policy on workers and the poor. Today, the so-called "social security net" has been developed in detail in many sub-areas. A comprehensive system has been set up that does not only intervene in case of existential crises or "neediness."

Pensions insurance, statutory health insurance, insurance covering accidents at work and occupational illness, unemployment insurance and nursing care insurance are part of this system. In addition, there are payments to families, such as child allowance. This currently amounts to EUR 154 per month for each of the first three children and EUR 179 for each additional child. . . .

With 5.2 million out of work (March 2005 figures) Germany is seeing a postwar record. The high level of 12.6 per cent is placing a burden on the unemployment insurance system. Thus, it is also contributing to the high proportion of GDP spent on welfare payments, amounting to 27 per cent in 2004, according to the Federal Statistical Office in Wiesbaden; before German unity the figure was just under 16 per cent.

Welfare payments are defined as being all financial payments and payments in kind granted to private households or individuals by the state. They are largely financed by contributions by insured persons and employers, as well as by tax revenues and new government borrowing.

The fact that the proportion of people in society over 65 years of age will rise from 17 per cent today to approximately 28 per cent in the year 2050 is another factor placing demands on the welfare system. Today, under the so-called generation compact, there are still approximately three people in work paying for one pensioner. In the future, however, it seems likely that one person in work will have to pay for one pensioner, even if immigration exceeds emigration. A major problem in this context is Germany's low birth rate. On average, each woman in the economically weak eastern part of the country now has just 1.2 children. The figure for western Germany is 1.4. Thus, many potential pension fund contributors are not even born.

his intention to call early elections. His announcement set the stage for a controversial vote of no confidence in the German national parliament in July and a federal election in September 2005.

Using the 2005 election as background, I will highlight four aspects of German politics and policymaking: (1) the role of political parties; (2) the need for coalition governance; (3) the division of labor between the federal government and the individual states, or *Länder;* and (4) the policy of incrementalism.

Governance and Policymaking

THE PARTY STATE

Germany's political system is commonly called a party democracy or party state. Both expressions emphasize the central role of political parties. Functions and organizational principles for political parties are explicitly set out in Article 21 of the Basic Law, but the extent of party influence goes far beyond representing the will of the people in the legislature and executive. Over the years, representatives of the main parties have become an integral part of federal, state, and even public institutions, such as the public television stations; the staffing of leadership positions in many sectors of public life is characterized by power sharing among the main political parties.

Through its rulings, the Federal Constitutional Court has reinforced the central role of the main political parties and given meaning to the principle of "militant democracy" by banning two parties. In the early days of the Federal Republic, one party on the right, the Socialist Reich Party, and one party on the left, the Communist Party of Germany, were declared illegal on the basis of their antidemocratic ideologies. Since then, a more relaxed attitude toward questionable fringe parties has prevailed. Legal precautions have given way to trusting that the policy establishment and the electorate will reject extremism. While, as in other European countries, right-wing parties rear their heads, they have not achieved representation in the national parliament.

As for all parliamentary systems, the head of government—called chancellor in Austria and Germany; prime minister in other countries—is responsible to, and dependent on, his or her party. He/she is usually a member of parliament, is elected from its ranks, and can be removed by a vote of no confidence. In replacing chancellors, political parties and not the electorate are the prime movers and shakers; fixed term limits do not exist. Only Helmut Kohl's sixteen-year tenure ended with a clear verdict at the voting booth in 1998; in all other cases, the parties' political maneuvering determined the coalition partners that were able to form a new government. In Germany, the president, who acts as head of state, is chosen by an electoral college. The duties of the president are largely ceremonial, but presidents have used their "soft power" effectively to address questions of national significance, such as the reform gridlock or the disenchantment with politics.

The two major parties, Christian Democratic Union/Christian Social Union (CDU/CSU)[6] and SPD, vie for voters in the center of the political

Table 3.1   Federal Elections, Coalition Governments, and Chancellors (1949–2005)

Election Year	Coalition Parties	Chancellor
1949	CDU/CSU, FDP, and DP (German Party)	Konrad Adenauer (CDU)
1953	CDU/CSU, FDP, DP, and GB/BHE (All-German Bloc/Federation of Expellees and Displaced Persons)	Konrad Adenauer (CDU)
1957	CDU/CSU and DP	Konrad Adenauer (CDU)
1961	CDU/CSU and FDP	Konrad Adenauer (CDU) Oct. 1963: Ludwig Erhard (CDU)
1965	CDU/CSU and FDP Dec. 1966: CDU/CSU and SPD	Ludwig Erhard (CDU) Kurt Georg Kiesinger (CDU)
1969	SPD and FDP	Willy Brandt (SPD)
1972	SPD and FDP	Willy Brandt (SPD) May 1974: Helmut Schmidt (SPD)
1976	SPD and FDP	Helmut Schmidt (SPD)
1980	SPD and FDP Sept. 1982: SPD Oct. 1982: CDU/CSU and FDP	Helmut Schmidt (SPD) Helmut Schmidt (SPD) Helmut Kohl (CDU)
1983	CDU/CSU and FDP	Helmut Kohl (CDU)
1987	CDU/CSU and FDP	Helmut Kohl (CDU)
1990	CDU/CSU and FDP	Helmut Kohl (CDU)
1994	CDU/CSU and FDP	Helmut Kohl (CDU)
1998	SPD and Alliance 90/The Greens	Gerhard Schröder (SPD)
2002	SPD and Alliance 90/The Greens	Gerhard Schröder (SPD)
2005	CDU/CSU and SPD	Angela Merkel (CDU)

(*Source:* Adapted from Forschungsgruppe Wahlen e.V., *Bundestagswahl. Eine Analyse der Wahl vom 18. September 2005* [Berichte der Forschungsgruppe Wahlen e.V., 122], Mannheim: October 2005, p. 95.)

spectrum and portray themselves as catchall and social welfare parties; that is, as parties with wide appeal. After World War II, CDU/CSU and SPD represented clear ideological choices and strategies, ranging from economic to military policy. For many years, the strength of the SPD was based on a mass membership base, whereas the CDU was seen as the party with a built-in electoral majority. By the mid-1970s, the ideological positions of the major parties had converged in many areas, including foreign and security policy. The incremental narrowing of the ideological gap contributed to shifts in electoral strength and a growing number of voters who switched between parties. It also played a part in the neck-and-neck race between CDU/CSU and SPD in recent elections. In the September 2002 election, less than 7,000 votes separated the two parties. The SPD and the Greens, dubbed the Red-Green coalition, could continue to govern.

The 2005 election was supposed to be different. All signs pointed to a large margin of victory for the CDU/CSU; the election campaign focused almost exclusively on economic and social issues and the two major parties presented clear policy choices. The CDU/CSU advocated sweeping economic and social changes, whereas the SPD promoted more limited policy adaptations with greater attention to social justice. In the end, the CDU/CSU won 226 seats and its opponent, the SPD, 222 seats. For the first time in the history of the Federal Republic, the two major parties had garnered less than 70 percent of the vote; at the heights of two-party dominance in the 1970s, they won over 90 percent of the ballots.

The 2005 results indicated a divided electorate that, in turn, implied a greater polarization of society than Germans are accustomed to. Some favored comprehensive policy changes associated with globalization of the economy, the growing needs of a knowledge society, and the challenges associated with demographic change. Others felt that the proposed changes would lead to an unacceptable weakening of the social safety net, social decline for many, and future uncertainties. Politicians are challenged to introduce changes that are effective yet socially fair. This dilemma affects the people's or catchall parties, CDU/CSU and SPD, while such parties as the Free Democratic Party of Germany (FDP) and the Left Party use it to present distinct versions of the neoliberal versus socialist policy positions.

Table 3.2   2005 Parliamentary Election

Party	Second Vote[1]	No. of Seats	Difference 2005–2002 (in percentages)
SPD	34.2	222	−4.3
CDU/CSU	35.2	226	−3.3
Alliance 90/ The Greens	8.1	51	−0.4
FDP	9.8	61	+2.5
Left.PDS	8.7	54	+4.7
Other	4.0	0	+1.0

1. Germany uses a personalized proportional representation voting system. Each German casts two votes.The first vote elects one representative from a district, similar to the single-member district vote in the United States.The number of seats in the lower house of the parliament, however, is largely determined by a vote for a party list (second vote).

Only parties that receive at least 5 percent of all valid votes or three constituency mandates can be represented in the federal diet.

Voter turnout in the 2005 election was 77.7 percent.

(*Source:* Adapted from *Bundestagswahl. Eine Analyse der Wahl vom 18. September 2005* [Berichte der Forschungsgruppe Wahlen e.V., Mannheim, 122]. Mannheim: October 2005, p. 7.)

For most of the postwar period in West Germany, the FDP, rooted in classic European liberalism, had the luxury of choosing its coalition partner; a small party acted as the power broker. Traditionally, the FDP favors the CDU/CSU, although once, in 1969, it switched and aligned with the SPD. Since the 1980s, two additional parties have been elected to the national parliament. The Greens (officially, Alliance 90/The Greens after 1993) have brought "new politics" issues, such as gender, environment, peace, and grassroots participation, to the forefront. Ever since the Red-Green coalition of 1998–2005, the Green Party is seen as the SPD's most likely coalition partner.

Following the opening of the Berlin Wall in November 1989, the former ruling Socialist Unity Party changed program and leadership; it renamed itself the Party of Democratic Socialism (PDS). It has been highly successful in the eastern part of the country, but, due to its communist roots, its political representation in the federal diet, state parliaments, and local councils remains a point of contention. To complicate matters, disillusioned voters on the political left not only founded their own party, Labor and Social Justice, but, in 2005, also entered an electoral alliance with the PDS. Under the name of The Left.PDS (commonly referred to as the Left Party), this surprising marriage of political expedience aligned western and eastern voters to earn 8.7 percent of the national vote. At the national level, coalitions with the Left Party are ruled out by both CDU/CSU and SPD.

COALITION GOVERNMENTS

The need to form coalition governments is a recurring feature of German politics.[7] Only once, in 1957, was one party, the CDU/CSU, able to garner a majority of the votes, and even then it entered a coalition. In Germany and elsewhere in Europe, coalition governments most often form when one major party aligns itself with a minor party or parties to achieve a majority in the parliament. Under such arrangements, the profile and political clout of smaller parties are elevated.

The outcome of the 2005 election presented the major parties with a dilemma. None of the anticipated coalition arrangements worked. Neither an alliance between CDU/CSU and FDP or between the SPD and the Greens was able to muster the necessary parliamentary majority. The only viable solution turned out to be a grand coalition government; that is, a government led by the two major parties, CDU/CSU and SPD.

Grand coalition governments arouse quite different reactions. Supporters emphasize that coalitions can overcome political hurdles to move along the policy agenda from initiation to implementation since they garner sufficient votes in both houses of parliament. Some critics highlight the devaluation of democratic principles, lamenting that meaningful parliamentary opposition is limited to minor parties with no power to seriously challenge policy proposals. Other critics focus on whether such extreme majority coalitions can deliver promised policy changes. Far from innovative, they argue, grand coalitions promote policies that please the smallest common denominator since party competition continues; the partners can only agree to policy solutions that uphold their programmatic distinctiveness and thus do not alienate their voters. Critics and advocates agree that success is not guaranteed. It has to be supported by political will, and leadership is crucial. They also agree that grand coalitions should only be enacted for limited time periods in times of duress. Pressure to succeed is high, if added policy paralysis and public mistrust of politicians and political institutions are to be avoided.

The 2005 grand coalition government was not a novelty; a similar and, as regards policy outcomes, largely successful arrangement existed once before between 1966 and 1969. However, the election of a female chancellor, Angela Merkel, was. It was also the first time that a chancellor from the former East Germany has been chosen, although Merkel has carefully avoided making her eastern roots a matter of political significance. She holds a doctorate in physics and became politically active only in the final days of the GDR, when she joined one of the newly emerging parties. When it dissolved, she joined the CDU; her career under the tutelage of then-chancellor Helmut Kohl involved different posts in the cabinet and the party leadership. In 2000, Merkel became chair of the CDU. Her scientific background is often cited to explain her systematic approach to, and mastering of, complex policy issues as well as her nonideological approach to politics. Critics see the latter as reluctance to commit to clear policy positions; supporters see it as a desirable pragmatism committed to getting things done.

Having a woman at the helm of a major party and as head of government did cause a few headlines but no waves. The first female cabinet minister was appointed in 1961 and a practice of limiting women to one or two government positions and to "soft" areas, such as health, family, and youth, continued until the end of the 1980s. Viewed from this perspective, women in German politics have come a long way. Now, routinely, more than 30 percent of the members of the federal legislature are women, and women occupy leadership positions in parties and interest groups, including the powerful trade unions.

Many have argued that this grand coalition government merely formalized an informal political arrangement in place for years, since frequently divided majorities in the two houses of parliament have made the cooperation of CDU/CSU and SPD a necessity to pass legislation. Under divided majorities, the opposition party in the lower house has the majority in the upper house; thus, the upper chamber can be, and has been, used as an opposition party tool to prevent passage of legislation or to force significant changes. Indeed, the grand coalition government under Merkel could build on numerous reform proposals that have been batted back and forth between the two parties in parliament and in many rounds of informal talks. Cognizant of potential deadlocks,

Box 3.3   Excerpts of Policy Statement by Federal Chancellor Angela Merkel in the German Bundestag

Wednesday, November 30, 2005

I have christened the new coalition "a coalition of new possibilities." My hope is that it will open up new possibilities for our country, and for all Germans. And I hope that we will then seize this opportunity. Specifically, for me this means that the expectations the new Federal Government has of itself and of the country are by no means modest. We intend to create the conditions for Germany to return to the ranks of the top three in Europe in ten years.

The Basic Law, the social market economy, the dual system of vocational training—all these ideas were an inspiration for the whole world. The first car was built in Germany, the computer was invented and aspirin was developed here. We are still benefiting from these innovations today.

Why shouldn't we in the present day be able to recapture the sense of achievement we had in the founding years of the Federal Republic when Germany was in its infancy and usher in a second age of innovation?

Let us, then, surprise everyone with what we can do!

A grand coalition between two different mainstream parties provides us with the quite unexpected opportunity to ask ourselves what we can improve together, without being hampered by mutual accusations, without pointing a finger at the other side and asking who was responsible—solely responsible, of course!—for what mistake.

For one thing is clear: we all bear responsibility for the fact that we are not exploiting our possibilities to the full. . . .

The Vice-Chancellor of a previous grand coalition who subsequently became Chancellor [former Chancellor Willy Brandt (SPD)] once said, "We want to dare more democracy." I know that this statement triggered considerable debate, some of it extremely heated. But he undeniably struck a chord with people at that time. And speaking personally, I can say that it was music to the ears, particularly of those on the other side of the Wall.

Allow me today to amend this statement and sound the appeal, "Let us dare more freedom." Let us release the brakes that are holding back growth! Let us free ourselves from bureaucracy and outdated regulations. Many of our European neighbors are showing us what is possible. They are demonstrating that even prosperous countries can achieve high growth rates and bring down unemployment. I am convinced Germany can do the same! Let's prove that it is possible!

(Source: .http://www.bundesregierung.de/Content/EN/Regierungserklaerung/2005/11/2005–11-30-policy-statement-by-federal-chancellor-dr-angela-merkel-in-the-german-bundestag,layoutVariant=Druckansicht.html)

the formal coalition agreement between the two parties lays out a political agenda for domestic and foreign affairs. It also refers to specific procedural questions. The coalition parties agreed to meet at least once a month in a committee that "will discuss matters of fundamental importance requiring coordination between the coalition partners and bring about consensus in cases of conflict."[8] In its first months, the grand coalition hit the ground running and created plenty of reasons for the committee to meet frequently.

THE FEDERAL SYSTEM

Historically, regionalism in Germany has been strong and the impact of the regions and their state governments has manifested itself in, among other things, the *Länder*'s leadership role in asserting regional rights vis-à-vis the European Union; the training and recruitment of national leaders through state offices; the division of labor between the federal government and the individual *Länder*; the reciprocal influence of *Land* and national elections; and the eminent role of the Federal Council (Bundesrat) in policymaking. The writers of the Basic Law institutionalized regional participation and the creation of multiple checks and balances in policymaking. Decentralization is based on a complex division of power; the interests of the initially eleven and, after unification, sixteen *Länder* are represented in the second house of parliament, the Federal Council. Depending on the size of its population, each *Land* varies in its electoral weight from three to six votes. State governments select their regional representatives and instruct them how to vote; thus, each *Land* casts its vote as a unit. The interconnectedness of the federal and state levels has reinforced multilevel bargaining.

In recent decades, divided majorities in the two houses of parliament became more frequent: that is, from 1972 to 1982, 1991 to 1998, and again from 1999 to 2005. The passage of many bills could thus be blocked or subjected to lengthy negotiations in the mediation committee. A reform of the federal system was essential to get efficient decisionmaking back on track. Called the "mother of all reforms," the modernization of the federal system finally passed in July 2006. Discussed for decades, elaborated in more than two years in a special commission composed of members of both houses of parliament, the revision of the federal system has been hailed as the most comprehensive constitutional reform since the founding of the Federal Republic in 1949. It involves numerous changes in the Basic Law, the German Constitution, and federal laws.

One major goal of the reform was to clearly demarcate the responsibilities between the federal and regional governments. New boundaries are supposed to increase transparency and to reduce the number of bills requiring upper-house approval from more than 60 to 35–40 percent. In exchange for reduced power of the Federal Council—the body of the regional governments—the *Länder* achieved enhanced responsibility for certain policy areas, such as education and civil service matters. A separate goal was to limit the power of state governments in European matters. For a long time, critics felt that Germany's position in the EU was hampered by too many different actors—federal as well as state governments—that often spoke with different interests in mind. Under the new arrangement, state governments can only become active when their exclusive interests, such as education and culture, are involved. In negotiations with Brussels, one representative will act on behalf of all state governments.

German federalism is built on sharing the fiscal burden. To reduce economic inequities, funds are transferred from richer to poorer states. Although givers and takers have changed during the life of the Federal Republic, the West is more prosperous than the East, and, due to shifts in employment and industrial patterns, the South is now economically better off than the North. Up until 1994, uniformity (*Einheitlichkeit*) of living conditions in the different parts of Germany had been the constitutionally prescribed goal, but, as part of constitutional reform, the term was replaced with equality (*Gleichwertigkeit*). The political message is clear: the economic strains associated with unification have necessitated a rethinking of constitutional goals.

The superimposition of the East-West divide on the existing North-South gap has added new levels of competition and conflicts over the distribution of funds. Today, in the political struggle for influence, who is rich and who is poor matters more than ever. Financial strength and weakness have led to alliances between East and West and between the major political parties. In addition, the needs of the states have opened up new possibilities for the federal government to garner votes in the Federal Council in return for financial assistance. To expedite the revision of the federal system, restructuring financial relations between the federal government and the *Länder* was not addressed. It is targeted next.

INCREMENTAL REFORM

The lengthy reform impasse has disappeared: in recent years, new policies have been instituted regarding taxes, pensions, immigration, family allowances, healthcare, labor market, education, and the federal system, to name the most important. Looking back on the history of the Federal Republic, institutional and policy changes in Germany have been marked by a distinct preference for piecemeal approaches and consensual conflict-solving mechanisms rather than radical transformations. This tradition continues to this day; most recent reform acts have been incremental and, with few exceptions, refrain from altering the system's basic structures. Thus, no matter what reforms are passed, critics immediately point to their shortcomings and the need to complement them with further policy acts. All reforms have been a matter of heated debate. Lengthy discussions over many years raised expectations as well as anxieties regarding their outcomes. Media and other critics often fail to consider that new policies will take time to produce effects, and piecemeal approaches can alter the system in the long run.

Expert opinion is still ambivalent about whether Germany has weathered its reform crisis: Is the glass half-full or half-empty? The continued need for change is undisputed, yet what is open to discussion is the depth and transformative character of the reforms. Some argue that high long-term unemployment rates call for additional far-reaching measures in labor market policies; they point to low economic growth rates and high labor costs and advocate, among others things, deregulation and continued reforms in the labor and welfare sectors. When the move to the euro was negotiated in the 1990s, Germany was adamant about setting strict criteria as a precondition for participation in the program. Embarrassingly, from 2002 to 2005 its public deficit was so high that it did not fulfill those criteria. However, starting in 2006 Germany was back on track. Birth rates have consistently declined since the 1960s, while life expectancy has increased, jeopardizing the viability of the pension and healthcare systems. The immigration and integration act went into effect in 2005, but the practice of allowing immigrants to settle in Germany remains restricted, the immigration policies emotionally charged, and the migration surplus is decreasing.

However, others emphasize positive outcomes, beyond the fact that policies have actually changed. In 2003, Germany regained its role as export champion of the world next to the United States. Some tax rates have decreased. Relative to economic output, unit labor costs have fallen; labor unions and their workers have shown wage restraint; and working contracts have become more flexible. Consumer confidence has grown, and unemployment numbers have started to decline. For many years, it has been fashionable to portray a "sickly" German economy, yet some signs point to recovery.

The Merging of Old and New: Foreign and Security Policy

GERMANY'S EVOLVING INTERNATIONAL STATUS

Probably in no other policy area is the collective memory of Germany's past more persistent and relevant than in its foreign and security policy. After World War II, membership in international organizations provided an opportunity to reenter world affairs and to fend off potentially resurgent nationalism. The history of the Federal Republic is the history of a network of international cooperation.[9] Its integration into the European community began with the establishment of the European Coal and Steel Community in 1952. The Western allies' aspiration to control (West) Germany, while simultaneously integrating it into the international community of democratic nations, contributed to the creation of the North Atlantic Treaty Organization (NATO) in 1949, which, after a heated domestic debate regarding remilitarization, Germany joined in 1955. The notion that NATO was formed in order to keep the United States in Western Europe, the Russians out, and the Germans down captured the prevailing concerns.

Before unification, Germany was widely considered an economic giant but, due to its limited international role, a political dwarf. In 1990, the end of the Cold War allowed it to regain full sovereignty and to unify East and West. Since then, a process of ongoing change has enhanced its international status as a "middle power" but it still prefers to act in concert with other nations. An evaluation of German foreign and security policy depends on the source and the particular questions asked. Are we interested in Germany's influence on concrete foreign policy agendas and outcomes or its role in shaping specific policy environments? Are we concerned with Germany's role in Central and Eastern Europe or in international organizations, such as the European Union or the United Nations? Has Germany been staunchly multilateral in security and military affairs but more self-interested and aggressive in economic policies? Is it moving beyond the European theater to assert global influence?

Power—the ability to influence others to act in ways they otherwise would not—can be measured in terms of population, economic, and military strengths. Unified Germany, with its slightly more than 82 million people, clearly surpasses its powerful neighbor France (60.7 million) and the United Kingdom (60.1 million) in population. Despite some of its economic woes, it remains the largest economy in Europe and third-largest in the world. Its military is intentionally weak in certain areas. To this day, Germany renounces possession of nuclear, biological, and chemical weapons, and long-range combat aircraft and missiles. It has no general staff apart from NATO troops; its troop strength is down to around 250,000 soldiers. Its defense expenditures remain low in comparison to France and the United Kingdom, yet in recent years it has emerged as an important player in international peacekeeping and humanitarian efforts.

Power projection also depends on how a country is perceived by its international environment, which is the result of expectations that, in turn, are built on and influenced by long memories and conditioned by changes in that environment. Finally, to what extent power is translated into influence also depends on many variables, including the willingness to use economic and other resources, the preferences of domestic and international actors, and more intangible considerations, such as bargaining skills and institutional constraints and possibilities. No longer is Germany called a "political dwarf" or even a "reluctant power" but, more and more, the "central power in Europe," the "leading European power," a "global economic power," a "permanently reformed civilian power," or a "reemerging military power."[10] Expectations regarding its international engagement have been on the rise, although at times its position remains ambiguous. For example, the push by the Schröder government to claim a permanent seat on the United Nations Security Council was unsuccessful. It demonstrated Germany's new assertiveness to claim a secure role among the major powers as well as the limits of its power projection and bargaining skills.[11] On the other hand, in 2006, when the five permanent members of the Security Council worked on a set of proposals to engage Iran over its uranium policy, Germany was offered a seat at the negotiation table.

Despite a foreign and security policy that remains in flux, some characteristics of German foreign and security policy stand out. They are summarized here and taken up again in the following analysis.

- Germany's foreign and security policy continues to be shaped by the collective memory of the past and by interests and institutional arrangements that emphasize multilateral decisionmaking; that is, a team approach to solving international problems within the parameters of international organizations such as the European Union, NATO, and the United Nations. New leadership roles are almost always embedded in the framework of those organizations; Germany considers itself a partner in leadership.
- The strategic triangle—Berlin/Paris/Washington—remains the fulcrum of German foreign policy, even if the style of the discourse and the perception of influence have changed. European integration as a prerequisite for peace, France as Germany's most important ally in Europe, and the United States as a close partner are postulates that rely on stability in German foreign policy.
- Germany's evolving international status has been the result of ad hoc responses to changes in the international environment and not the outcome of strategic recalculations. Some observers, including members of the German foreign policy establishment, feel that the lack of strategy undermines the adequate allocation of resources to pursue national interests.
- Foreign and security policy remains a matter of broad consensus among German elites and the public. Thus, the change to a grand coalition government was not expected to produce any significant policy alterations, although differences in style and nuances can arise, even in continuity.

GERMANY AND EUROPE

European integration has extended from economic areas to include, among other things, foreign and defense policies, justice and home affairs, and the environment, and significantly changed the dynamics among European Union member states; the Europeanization of its members' national politics has evolved as a major postwar trend. Only a few policy areas remain outside the realm of European policymaking; as a result, an estimated 50 percent of all rules and regulations that are in force in Germany originated in the European Union.

European integration is widely seen as a success story, bringing peace and prosperity, yet headlines mostly announce various "crises." Those crises are instigated, first, by individual countries blocking policy proposals regarding, for example, the restructuring of the Common Agricultural Policy. Second, the unsuccessful ratification of new EU treaties through national referenda has repeatedly shaken the European policy establishment. The 2005 failed public referenda in France and the Netherlands for a European Union Constitution fall in this category. They have necessitated a "reflection phase" after a previous decade of multifarious activities that taxed politicians and citizens alike. Third, a "permanent crisis" relates to the openness of European integration with regard to both its final goal and territorial expansion.[12] Germany's role in these various crises has not been as instigator but problem solver and mediator. In overcoming national vetoes to facilitate passage of EU policy proposals, it has used diplomatic channels and, at times, was willing to accept additional financial costs. The German elite has reserved the right of approval of, and control over, aspects of treaty ratification; public referenda have not taken place. German politicians such as Joschka Fischer and public intellectuals such as philosopher Jürgen Habermas (at times together with French philosopher Jacques Derrida) have advanced European discussions on the role and future of Europe.[13]

The significance of membership in the European Union is undisputed for all countries but has special relevance for Germany. After World War II, German supporters of European integration saw membership as a way to assure reconciliation and lasting peace with rival and former enemy France; now and then, the two countries are considered the "motor" that drives the integration process. More broadly, "Project Europe" provided an avenue for peace, economic prosperity, and international recognition. The German Constitution explicitly authorizes the federation to "transfer sovereign powers to intergovernmental institutions," including a mutual collective security system and the European Union. Political elites recognize the interconnectedness of national and European politics; German and European interests are seen as compatible, if not identical. Commitment to Europe also reflects a strong attachment to multilateralism as an idea and a means to pursue national interests; according to Klaus Goetz, it has become part of the elites' "genetic code."[14] In contrast to many other countries in Europe, Germany's main parties do not contest European policies. They were hardly mentioned during recent electoral campaigns, and the changes, first from a CDU/CSU-FDP coalition government to a government led by the SPD and the Greens, and, most recently, to a CDU/CSU-SPD grand coalition, were marked by remarkable continuity in the policies toward the European Union.

At the same time, the political profiles and policy styles of chancellors vary and leave their imprint. Chancellor Helmut Kohl (1982–1998) considered German and European unity as two sides of the same coin; the promotion of European integration through close Franco-German relations was central to his European policy. Chancellor Gerhard Schröder (1998–2005) came to power with little foreign policy experience, yet he paved the way for a self-confident foreign policy style that paid greater attention to national concerns. Angela Merkel's impact on Europe is too early to assess, although she will lead the

Box 3.4   Chancellor Angela Merkel: Europe Needs a New Philosophy

(Summary of Speech given to the German Parliament)
Thursday, May 11, 2006

Europe understood as a community structured to ensure peace was an idea born out of the situation at the end of World War II and in the decades that followed this idea gradually became reality, Merkel noted at the beginning of her speech.

Despite its uncontestable successes, the peace ideal alone is no longer sufficient as a rationale for the European Union. The EU is not as popular with Europeans as its historical record might lead one to believe, Merkel observed.

During the Cold War the European Union was an alternative better than anything available on the other side of the Iron Curtain. The EU was able to define itself in terms of the ways in which it differed from communism.

The European Union today needs to base the reasoning that underlies its existence on factors within its own midst. The original motivation behind the establishment of the European Union needs to be superseded by a new philosophy.

Asserting European values in a globalized world

"Europe needs to show that it is capable of shaping policy in accordance with its own values in a world characterized by greater competition and globalization. This is the challenge we face," Merkel said.

People doubt that the European social market economy concept can be realized anymore. The question needs to be asked as to how this policy objective can still be achieved.

Merkel said people must be told the kinds of success Europe stands for, naming economic growth, social responsibility, and job security as examples.

Economic growth for a strong Europe

Europe will only be able to bring its weight to bear if it is economically strong and dynamic. This is why she supports the Lisbon Strategy for more growth and employment in Europe, Merkel said, adding that "Europe needs to be a leader in education, research, and innovation."

We need to keep asking ourselves where Europe has created obstacles to growth. The European Commission has come to the conclusion that bureaucracy reduction is an urgent priority.

National obligation

Merkel noted that Germany needs to live up to its own standards. It was Germany who insisted on the stability and growth pact with a view to giving the EU countries greater financial security. It is not acceptable for Germany to be in recurrent violation of the pact and out of compliance with its own demands.

Merkel indicated that she is aware of the added burden being placed on the public by tax increases. But the country's credibility is at stake and Germany must come back into compliance with the stability and growth pact as well as with its own constitution, she emphasized.

European foreign policy

Merkel underscored her commitment to stronger European cooperation in the foreign and security policy areas, saying that no one country can deal with the threat posed by terrorism on its own.

Europe also needs to defend its values. Experience in the Balkans has taught us that we need to intervene before it is too late. In Bosnia-Herzegovina, in Macedonia, and also as part of the Middle East Quartet the European Union has assumed responsibility with a view to promoting peace in the world.

Governability of Europe

To ensure the governability of the EU two problems need to be addressed. The first concerns the European constitution. "We need the constitutional treaty," Merkel stressed.

She noted that it contains a list of core European values, adding that a defined cultural identity is important in interacting with other cultures. It also clearly delineates institutional jurisdictions. "Blurred jurisdictions are a democracy deficit," Merkel said.

The second involves a clear definition of European limits: "An entity that does not have limits will not be able to act coherently." She said the promises made to candidate countries must be kept. However, it must be clear that the criteria for EU membership must be met: "Accession negotiations do not automatically lead to admission."

Merkel called upon the European Commission to clearly spell out candidate country deficits in its reports.

Added value for everyone

Europe should offer added value to all its citizens. We will succeed in convincing people of the advantages Europe holds out, based on the solid foundation provided by its successful history, Merkel concluded.

(*Source: http://www.bundesregierung.de/Content/EN/Artikel/2006/05/2006–05–11–europe-needs-a-new-philosophy,layoutVariant=Druckansicht.html.*)

European Union in the first half of 2007 as part of the routine six-month leadership rotation in the Council of the European Union. Expectations are high, not least because in the December 2005 Council summit meeting, she successfully brokered a compromise on the longstanding issue of the EU budget, earning accolades at home and abroad. She built on a previous negotiation pattern by first agreeing with France and then consulting Great Britain, yet departed from practice by including medium and smaller countries and, in particular, assured that the voices of Central and Eastern European countries were heard.

German citizens support European integration but somewhat less enthusiastically than their leaders; most see both advantages and disadvantages. Compared to other member countries, Germany is not as skeptical as the British or some of the Scandinavians, but not as supportive as some of the smaller countries, particularly the southern European countries. German citizens predominantly associate the common currency, free movement of people, cultural variety, peace, and greater world participation with EU membership. They widely endorse common security measures, defense policy, and foreign policy and predominantly approve of the proposed European Constitution. Divisive topics include EU enlargement, but nothing was more opposed by the German electorate than the introduction of the euro. A few months before euro coins and banknotes were officially introduced in January 2002, only 45 percent of western Germans and 27 percent of eastern Germans considered replacing the mark a good thing. This skepticism continues; the euro is "unloved but accepted."[15] In contrast, for the political elites, giving up the "sacred cow" of the national currency was unambiguously the price for unification: Germany had to sacrifice its lead financial role in Europe to compensate for its increased population and status. Neither one of the major political parties veered from completing the project.

To explain the unquestioned support for European integration, aspects of political culture, political structure, and policy style must be considered. Once again, history provides the starting point. After World War II, European integration provided a vehicle for international recognition; it was also widely seen as contributing to the economic miracle of the 1950s. Germany's complementary institutional structure has also been cited as facilitating its pro-European attitude. The highly decentralized political system, coalition governments, and the principle of delegation to semipublic institutions have made the interaction with European institutions, in the words of one observer, a "warm bath" instead of the "cold shower" that many British elites and citizens may feel.[16] Similarly, a bureaucratic culture of rules and regulations is part of both European and German policymaking. Finally, the lengthy negotiation and bargaining that allow package deals and aim at achieving consensus are key elements of both German and European policymaking. In other words, German politicians are at ease with the institutional and policymaking environment of the European Union.

Bargaining associated with the federal structure familiarizes German politicians with multilevel governance, but it has also hampered the effectiveness of German negotiating, since the *Länder,* which are represented with offices in Brussels, and the national government both clamor for attention and influence. Germany's relatively frequent infringement of European Union law can be partially attributed to the complicated power sharing implicit in German federalism. The 2006 Federalism Act intends to alleviate this longstanding problem. In the future, state governments will also be liable to shoulder the costs for noncompliance associated with EU sanctions.

Institutional features may also partially explain why a reluctant or negative attitude toward European integration has remained a "dark matter" in German politics. Charles Lees argues that through the expression of reservations about European Union policies and the election of small right-wing parties with an anti-European agenda, the *Länder* have given "soft Euro-skepticism" a limited outlet; it could be articulated and contained at the same time. In general, however, the adoption of an anti-European attitude by parties on the far right may have discredited Euro-skepticism "by association."[17] Despite pockets of anti-European attitudes, cross-party consensus in the EU's favor has remained stable.

No straightforward answer neatly delineates Germany's strengths and weaknesses in its interactions with the European Union; instead, a complicated network of institutional interactions and trajectories, depending on situation and interpretation, advance or hamper national influence. During his tenure, Chancellor Schröder became more outspoken about conditions that, in his view, no longer adequately reflected the changed European environment. Despite largely futile efforts to reduce its share, Germany is still the primary net contributor to the EU budget, although accession of the eastern *Länder* has also made it a noteworthy beneficiary of funds. Although with unification it has become by far the most populous country, Germany has only been marginally successful in elevating its voice in voting procedures. Its share of members in the European Parliament is higher than that of other member countries, but its votes in the much more important Council of Ministers have remained equal to those of other "large" countries.[18] On the other hand, Germany has been very successful in dictating the conditions under which countries can join the European currency and in setting the tone and pushing for expansion of the European Union into Central and Eastern Europe. Germany also played a crucial role in framing and implementing the 1999 Stability Pact for South Eastern Europe, which, to date, is one of the European Union's most important foreign and security policy initiatives.

For most of the postwar period, France and Germany set the timing according to which European integration moved or stalled. Cordial and close relations between French and German leaders covered up occasional bilateral conflicts of interest. The friendships between Konrad Adenauer and Charles de Gaulle, Helmut Schmidt and Valérie Giscard d'Estaing, and Helmut Kohl and François Mitterrand are legendary. The real and symbolic significance of the French-German relationship and its function as the engine of European initiatives and EU consensus builder was once again emphasized when Angela Merkel followed tradition and visited France one day after her inauguration as chancellor. In his welcoming speech, French president Jacques Chirac highlighted the role of Franco-German relations as an engine of European integration; in case the German-French axis would not function, he suggested, Europe would be like a vehicle from which an important part is missing.[19]

Not surprisingly, the relationship is closely watched and over the years observers have emphasized either ties that bind or degrees of separation. International developments since German unification have favored a more influential Germany and weakened the special position of France. France's national identity is closely tied to its prominent role in European and world affairs; thus, a shift in the balance of power between the two nations is an important reference point for French politicians. What remains undisputed, however, is that, after three German invasions of France between 1870 and 1940 alone, military conflict between the two has become unthinkable. Apart from official spats, they remain each other's most important trading partners, and thousands of educational exchanges and partnerships between towns and villages reinforce bonds at the grass-roots level.

Franco-German relations do not exist in a vacuum but are influenced by other international actors. For example, when British politicians are more engaged in continental affairs, France and Germany try to use them to strengthen their own position within Europe. If the British are more distant or play up the Anglo-American special relationship, then France and Germany tend to rely more on each other. The latter tendency emerged with force during the Iraqi conflict in 2002 and 2003. The deadlock in negotiations of the Common Agricultural Policy was resolved, bilateral initiatives in the area of the European Security and Defense Policy took off, and the two nations cooperated on controversial issues in order to bring the Draft Treaty establishing a constitution for Europe to a timely conclusion in June 2003. In addressing the Iraqi crisis and cooperating to strengthen Europe vis-à-vis the United States, France, and Germany catapulted common interests to the forefront but also unearthed frictions with other European countries.

In 2004, ten countries joined the European Union, eight of which are located in Central and Eastern Europe; Bulgaria and Romania became members in 2007, increasing the total number of EU member states to 27. Despite the German electorate's critical view, German politicians strongly supported Central and Eastern Europe's inclusion in the European Union and NATO, due in no small part to the wish to be surrounded by peaceful, democratic neighbors. Germany is the region's main foreign source for direct investment and maintains a multifaceted and high level of trading relations. More than any other EU member state, it provided substantial aid and assistance and a model for institutions, ranging from banking to electoral regulations. Incorporating Western institutions was a way for the Central and Eastern European countries to speed up the process of democratization and to compensate for the price they had to pay when Europe was divided after World War II.

Attention has now turned to further expansion, in particular the potential membership of Turkey. Turkish membership is a hotly debated and divisive issue in Europe, especially in Germany, where about 2 million Turks reside within its borders. A clear and consistent majority of German citizens disapprove of Turkish membership in the European Union. The question is one of the few to spark partisan differences. CDU/CSU politicians have long said that they prefer a "privileged partnership" to full membership, but Angela Merkel emphasized quickly after her election that she will adhere to previous agreements made between the European Union and Turkey. Accession negotiations, which were agreed upon in October 2005, continue.

The "return to Europe" for countries that used to be communist-governed and under Soviet influence also necessitated a reworked relationship with Russia. Germany was in a unique position to assist in the region's stabilization, since it could build on a longstanding close relationship. With the final withdrawal of Russian troops from eastern German territory in 1994, an important chapter in postwar history closed. In the tumultuous decade that followed, German policy was geared toward preventing a collapse of the Russian economy and its government. Since 2000, however, the Russian economy has boomed, fueled by rising energy prices. Under the leadership of President Vladimir Putin, domestic stability has replaced disorder; Russia has reemerged as a player in world politics, albeit one with increasing authoritarian tendencies.

Under Chancellor Gerhard Schröder, the German-Russian relationship was bolstered by his personal friendship with Putin and firmly anchored in protecting German economic interests in the region. Germany is by far the most important trade partner for Russia: In 2004, 14 percent of its imports were from Germany, followed by China's 6.3 percent; the United States lagged far behind with 4.2 percent. German imports from Russia center on energy resources: in 2004, 34 percent of oil imports and 42 percent of natural gas imports came from Russia.[20] The two countries have strong mutual economic interests, if not dependencies, but their relations are not exclusively based on economic expedience. As its closest partner in the West, Germany is uniquely positioned to help anchor Russia; yet, with other Western partners, it must find a way to engage Russia without ignoring the recent democratic backlash. The personal background of Germany's current chancellor may also suggest a more reserved relationship. After all, Merkel began her political career as an anticommunist in the former East Germany, while Putin was stationed in her home country as a foreign intelligence officer, working for the KGB.

TRANSATLANTIC RELATIONS

After the European Union, the relationship with the United States is the second major anchor of Germany's foreign policy. Integration with Europe and close cooperation with the United States have always been interrelated as part of Germany's strong commitment to Western alliances. With the advent of a European foreign and defense policy, they have become even more intertwined. Germany sees itself as the carrier of both national and European interests. Mutual trust between Europe and the United States, according to the coalition agreement signed by CDU/CSU and SPD, is essential for partnership and for a dialogue that, even when viewpoints differ, should be conducted in a "spirit of friendship." European security and defense policy should be viewed not as competition but as "strengthening the European pillar of the Atlantic security partnership. . . . German foreign policy will endeavor to help bring about positions coordinated between the European and transatlantic partners." Shared values, interests, and history are said to provide the foundation for future transatlantic relations.[21]

After World War II, West Germany in particular and Western Europe in general benefited greatly from U.S. support in military, economic, and political matters during the Cold War. U.S. leadership was crucial in bringing about German unification when the opportunity presented itself in 1989–1990. The network of cultural, economic, and political exchanges is dense and has reached a level that is normally reserved for countries that are members of regional integration schemes, such as the European Union. With record speed, the occupation power turned into a trusted friend and ally. Americans came to expect German leaders to emphasize friendship and appreciation and to criticize, if at all, subtly and behind closed doors.

The distinct downturn in relations during 2002 and 2003 created a shock and led to intense soul-searching among German elites and the public. To be sure, with joint responsibilities and tasks comes competition, and conflicts had emerged in the past as well, yet the level of disharmony and distrust evident during the Iraqi conflict revealed a new and different climate. The adage "all politics is local" may explain Chancellor Schröder's outspoken anti–Iraq war rhetoric during the 2002 electoral campaign. It led to emotional and tense exchanges between him and U.S. president George W. Bush. In explaining the deterioration of relations, the German government did not remain unscathed. Some criticized the unusual—and, by implication, unnecessarily harsh and undiplomatic—tone of SPD politicians during the electoral campaign and afterwards. Others point to the failure of Germany—and Europe more generally—to shoulder international responsibilities, including military, as one source of the U.S. administration's disillusionment.

Soon, the policy establishments on both sides of the Atlantic were working diligently at "normalization." There was wide agreement that emotional exchanges must become more businesslike but friendly, and instruments to deal with differences in the relationship must be created or redefined. Foreign policy is a matter of pursuing national interests in interaction with other countries. It cannot ignore the importance of personal relationships and policy styles of politicians at the helm. While good chemistry between leaders of different countries is no guarantee for the successful pursuit of interests, it can promote closer consultation and a cordial climate of cooperation. A significant step was taken with the election of Angela Merkel, although any replacement of Gerhard Schröder probably would have been perceived positively in Washington, D.C. Merkel's election also coincided with greater efforts by the Bush administration to consult with European leaders on matters of international concern. Early signs indicate that U.S.-German relations are back on track.

However, their normalization should not be thought of as a return to the previous status quo. The roles of both Germany and the United States have changed significantly since the end of the Cold War. The United States has advanced to the status of sole superpower whereas Germany—and Europe—claim greater involvement in global affairs. Recent strains in transatlantic relations reflect broader concerns about policy style and substance—for example, between unilateral and multilateral strategies and in the interpretation of security threats and environmental concerns. What has changed is that Germany has taken a more visible role in expressing those concerns than in the past. Like all other aspects of Germany's foreign policy, the reconfiguration of transatlantic relations is a "work in progress."

CIVILIAN POWER AND SECURITY POLICY

Maybe nowhere is the change in Germany's international role more apparent than in its security policy. Up until the 1990s, the preferred way to show international solidarity and responsibility was checkbook diplomacy. On the basis of Article 87a of the Basic Law, Germany shied away from direct involvement in military conflict in "out-of-area" operations and instead provided financial assistance to defray the costs. However, first the Gulf War in 1990–1991 and then the conflicts in the former Yugoslavia rendered this position increasingly untenable. Pressure mounted on the Kohl government to engage members of the armed forces in humanitarian and crisis management. The Federal Constitutional Court's 1994 ruling on Article 87a opened the door for possible out-of-area military deployment, provided that it was part of multilateral operations, had the blessing of the United Nations and the approval of the federal government. Burning villages and ethnic cleansing in Bosnia-Herzegovina and Kosovo catalyzed a moral policy of "never again" (Auschwitz) and reinforced the prevailing notion of "never alone."

In 1999, the postwar taboo on German military involvement was broken when the German air force engaged in the Kosovo conflict. Many have argued that the acceptance of Germany's increased role in foreign and security policies at home and abroad owes much to the Red-Green leadership of confirmed pacifists. Since then, Germany has rapidly widened its scope of military operations. In 1998, about 2,000 soldiers were engaged in humanitarian and peacekeeping operations abroad. At the beginning of the twenty-first century, the number had risen to over 8,000, making Germany one of the major sources of international troops. At the end of 2006, about 9,000 German soldiers were deployed in Africa, Asia, and Europe. In line with its security policy, military activities are pursued within the framework of international organizations, that is, NATO, the European Union, the United Nations, and the Organization for Security and Cooperation in Europe.

Germany has successfully shifted from territorial defense to international conflict prevention, including the fight against international terrorism, and crisis management. Its widening military engagement has been accompanied by ongoing reform of the armed forces, yet remains hampered by the reluctance to increase military spending to match goals. Personnel and materiel are stretched to their limits, but recent international developments have also driven home the need for action. Ironically, the Iraqi conflict has reinforced the conviction among major European powers, Germany included, that their role—in particular, their military role—has to be strengthened if the transatlantic alliance is to function better during international crises.

Transitioning Toward the New Germany

In the long view of history, the period of separation into a communist-governed eastern Germany and a democratic western Germany turned out to be no more than an interlude. German politics is most often analyzed as the continuous development of the Federal Republic of Germany. At first it seemed that the radical transformation of the former GDR was the price to pay for this continuity in the west. One part of the country was to change according to the parameters set out in the other. However, the sense of continuity was deceiving; new transitions, as I suggest in this chapter, caught up with the unified Germany. Unification, Europeanization, and globalization have affected policies, institutions, and identity.

Analysts of German politics are called upon to portray the simultaneous forces of continuity and change. Authors have tried to capture those potentially disparate dynamics by using such terms as "modified continuity" and "adaptation of existing policies." According to journalist Gunter Hofmann, Germans had to say farewell to the established party state, faith in economic growth, some aspects of the cherished social welfare state, and the model character of social partnership between unions and employer associations. But he also points to values that have survived unscathed: Western liberalism, Western principles of civilization, and the emancipation of citizens.[22]

If analysts strive to correctly weigh the balance between closures and new beginnings, politicians are asked to perform delicate balancing acts. Helga Haftendorn, a leading expert on German foreign and security policy, states in her recent book that in an environment of changing expectations and capabilities, Germany "walks a tightrope, balancing between the potential counteractions if it plays too dominant a role, or the reprimand that it is neglecting its interests and forfeiting its responsibility to help maintain security and stability."[23] Foreign and domestic policies are interwoven, since economic strength or weakness is invariably linked to Germany's status, particularly in European affairs, but also in its ability to fulfill international obligations. Economic reinvigoration, without neglecting social responsibility, remains a cornerstone of any domestic policy. For the German elites and citizens alike, the continuation of reform efforts in many aspects of their domestic policies remains the priority. The vision is to create a political, social, and economic environment that does not neglect the policy goal of social justice. Once again, the goal will be finding the right balance.

Finally, the impact of Germany's history will keep the question of normality in the political discourse. New generations of Germans continue to balance the responsibilities and constraints imposed by history with national consciousness and pride. However, the long journey toward normality has picked up speed.

Notes

1. C. K. Williams, "Das symbolische Volk der Täter," *Die Zeit* 46, 2002; http://www.zeit.de/2002/46/Symbol (accessed July 20, 2006).

2. Tony Judt, *Postwar: A History of Europe Since 1945*, New York: Penguin Press, 2005, p. 826.

3. For more detail see Jeffrey M. Peck, *Being Jewish in the New Germany*, New Brunswick, NJ: Rutgers University Press, 2006.

4. For a very readable account of Germany's road to normality, see Steve Crawshaw, *Easier Fatherland: Germany and the Twenty-First Century*, London: Continuum, 2004.

5. "Am Ende der ersten Halbzeit," *Die Zeit*, Politik 34, 2002; http://www.zeit .de/archiv/2002/34/200234_interview_schroe.xml (accessed July 20, 2006).

6. Various Christian-based political groups organized in 1945, but party consolidation across zones of occupation soon led to the emergence of the Christian Democratic Party of Germany (CDU). Political leaders of the Christian Social Union (CSU) in Bavaria decided to remain separate; the anomaly of two conservative parties with many programmatic similarities but regionally divided persists. The CDU is the main center-right party in all parts of Germany except Bavaria; its so-called sister party, the CSU, exists only as a Bavarian regional party. The two are being treated as one in this chapter, since they almost always act in unison at the federal level, occasional tensions notwithstanding.

7. Coalition governments are the norm at the state level as well; however, greater flexibility regarding the choice of partners prevails.

8. http://www.bundesregierung.de/nn_12890/Content/EN/StatischeSeiten/breg/ koalitionsvertrag-arbeitsweise-der-koalition.html (accessed July 20, 2006).

9. Beate Kohler-Koch, "Europäisierung: Plädoyer für eine Horizonterweiterung," in Michèle Knodt and Beate Kohler-Koch (eds.), *Deutschland zwischen Europäisierung und Selbstbehauptung*, Frankfurt and New York: Campus Verlag, 2000, p. 11.

10. The list is partially taken from Gunther Hellmann, "Precarious Power: Germany at the Dawn of the Twenty-First Century," in Wolf-Dieter Eberwein and Karl Kaiser (eds.), *Germany's New Foreign Policy: Decision-Making in an Interdependent World*, New York: Palgrave, 2001, p. 293.

11. Note that a clear majority of Germans supports a single European Union seat on the UN Security Council.

12. The typology of crises is taken from Andreas Maurer, "Die Europäische Union zwischen Dauerkrise und Dauerreform," *Ausblick: Deutsche Außenpolitik nach Christoph Bertram*, Berlin: Stiftung Wissenschaft und Politik, September 2005, pp. 26–29.

13. Speech by Joschka Fischer at the Humboldt University in Berlin, "From Confederacy to Federalism—Thoughts on the Finality of European Integration" (May 12, 2000), http://www.ena.lu?lang=2&doc=18824 (accessed July 30, 2006); on Habermas and Derrida see Daniel Levy et al., *Old Europe, New Europe, Core Europe: Transatlantic Relations After the Iraq War*, London and New York: Verso, 2005.

14. Quoted in Simon J. Bulmer, "Shaping the Rules? The Constitutive Politics of the European Union and German Power," in Peter J. Katzenstein (ed.), *Tamed Power: Germany in Europe*, Ithaca and London: Cornell University Press, 1997, p. 67.

15. Elisabeth Noelle-Neumann and Thomas Petersen, "Die Bürger in Deutschland," in Werner Weidenfels (ed.), *Europa-Handbuch*, vol. 2: *Die Staatenwelt Europas*, 3rd rev. ed., Gütersloh: Verlag Bertelsmann Stiftung, 2004, pp. 43–55.

16. Bulmer, "Shaping the Rules?" p. 50.

17. Charles Lees, "'Dark Matter': Institutional Constraints and the Failure of Party-Based Euroscepticism in Germany," *Political Studies*, 50(2), 2002, 244–267.

18. After November 2009 new voting procedures in the Council of Ministers will go into effect. However, the stipulation that decisions shall represent at least three-fifths of the population of the EU only slightly increases Germany's weight.

19. http://www.euractiv.com/de/agenda2004/antrittsbesuche-merkel-setzt-neue-akzente/article-149577 (accessed July 20, 2006).

20. Roland Götz, "Deutschland und Russland—'strategische Partner'?" *Aus Politik und Zeitgeschichte*, March 13, 2006, 14–23.

21. http://www.bundesregierung.de/nn_6538/Webs/Breg/EN/Federal- government/CoalitionAgreement/coalition-agreement.html (accessed July 21, 2006).

22. Gunter Hofmann, *Abschiede, Anfänge. Die Bundesrepublik. Eine Anatomie*, Munich: Verlag Antje Kunstmann, 2002.

23. Helga Haftendorn, *Coming of Age: German Foreign Policy Since 1945*, Lanham, MD: Rowman & Littlefield, 2006, p. 5.

Suggested Readings

Crawshaw, Steve, *Easier Fatherland: Germany and the Twenty-First Century*, London and New York: Continuum, 2004.

Green, Simon, and William E. Paterson, eds., *Governance in Contemporary Germany: The Semisovereign State Revisited*, Cambridge: Cambridge University Press, 2005.

Haftendorn, Helga, *Coming of Age: German Foreign Policy Since 1945*, Lanham, MD: Rowman & Littlefield, 2006.

Lees, Charles, *Party Politics in Germany: A Comparative Politics Approach*, Basingstoke, England and New York: Palgrave Macmillan, 2005.

Maier, Charles S., *Dissolution: The Crisis of Communism and the End of East Germany*, Princeton, NJ: Princeton University Press, 1997.

Markovits, Andrei S., and Simon Reich, *The German Predicament: Memory and Power in the New Europe*, Ithaca and London: Cornell University Press, 1997.

McAdams, A. James, *Judging the Past in Unified Germany*, Cambridge: Cambridge University Press, 2001.

Peck, Jeffrey M., *Being Jewish in the New Germany,* New Brunswick, NJ: Rutgers University Press, 2006.

Zelikow, Philip, and Condoleezza Rice, *Germany United and Europe Transformed: A Study in Statecraft,* Cambridge, MA: MIT University Press, 1995.

SPECIALIZED SCHOLARLY JOURNALS

German Politics (Routledge)

German Politics and Society (Berghahn Publishers)

Internationale Politik. Transatlantic Edition (in English; published by the German Council on Foreign Relations)

CHAPTER 4

Italy: A Troubled Democracy

Mark Gilbert

Italy

Population (million):	58.7
Area in Square Miles:	116,320
Population Density per Square Mile:	505
GDP (in billion dollars, 2005):	$1,661.9
GDP per capita (PPP, 2005):	$28,396
Joined EC/EU:	January 1, 1958

Performance of Key Political Parties in Parliamentary Elections of April 9–10, 2006

House of Freedoms, a coalition of:	49.5%
Forze Italia (FI)	23.6%
National Alliance (AN)	12%
Northern League (LN)	4.5%
Union of Christian Democrats and of the Centre (UDC-DC)	6.7%
The Union, a coalition of:	49.7%
Communist Refoundation	5.7%
Federation of Greens	2%
Italian Communists	2.3%
Italy of Values	2.3%
The Olive Tree	31.6%
The Rose in the Fist	2.5%

Main Office Holders: Prime Minister: Romano Prodi—The Union (2006); Head of State: Giorgio Napolitano—DS (2006)

I taly has been a divided democracy since liberation from the Nazis in 1945. Until the early 1990s, the split was along ideological lines. Italy was divided by the presence of the most successful communist party in Western Europe. The Italian Communist Party (PCI) led a permanent opposition to the governing coalitions headed by Christian Democracy (DC), but was never considered a legitimate party of government.

The uneasy relationship between the two "churches," Catholicism and communism, was moribund long before 1992, when the so-called Mani Pulite (Clean Hands) scandal broke. By proving numerous cases of corruption within the party system, Italian prosecutors destroyed the power base of the DC and its socialist allies. Earlier, the PCI had been compelled to reassess its atavistic attachment to the edifice of communist dogma by the fall of the Berlin Wall, by the collapse of the Soviet Empire in Eastern Europe, and by its own internal changes. These developments might have led to genuine renewal in Italian democracy. Instead, they have been followed by a stark polarization of the political system. This new divide is centered upon a single, highly controversial, individual: the billionaire media magnate Silvio Berlusconi, who in the wake of the corruption scandals formed a new political movement, Forza Italia, which proved capable, in company with the "post-Fascist" National Alliance and the Northern League, of winning both the 1994 and 2001 elections.

Berlusconi has also managed to unite the center-left. Opposition to Berlusconi has been the glue that has kept the rival Ulivo ("Olive Tree") coalition together. The Olive Tree is an unwieldy coalition of former communists, liberals, and Christian Democrats founded by Romano Prodi, a prominent academic economist and industrialist, in 1995. It is probably fair to say that without the populist challenge represented by Berlusconi and his allies, the center-left parties would not have found the will to coalesce into a single political force.

The Olive Tree governed the country between 1996 and 2001, with Prodi as premier for the first two years. In April 2006, Prodi once again became prime minister at the head of an even more ideologically heterogenous center-left coalition composed of the Olive Tree and the far-left Rifondazione Comunista (Communist Refoundation). Berlusconi and some of his allies shrilly insist that Prodi's government is a menace to democracy: the center-left has spent the five years since 2001 proclaiming that Berlusconi himself was a threat to democracy. There is no other country in Western Europe where such super-heated political rhetoric is a commonplace. In this respect, Italy is a disturbing exception to the rule in Western Europe.

The Little World

A key text for understanding postwar Italian politics is the short stories collectively known as *Il Piccolo Mondo di Don Camillo*, by the right-wing (but fiercely independent) humorist Giovanni Guareschi. Writing at the height of the Cold War, and at the height of the political struggle between the DC and the PCI, Guareschi personified the political debate of his time by recounting the battles between Don Camillo, a stubborn, impetuous Catholic priest from the Po River valley, and his rival, Peppone, the communist mayor of Don Camillo's little town. Guareschi's stories are a delightful read, but they also highlight some of the deep structural forces at work in postwar Italian democracy.[1]

The first, and most obvious, of these is the centrality of the conflict between communism and Catholicism. Many of the stories revolve around Don Camillo's attempts to undermine the political prestige of the local communists and to

Box 4.1   Cold War Propaganda

Both the DC and the PCI minced no words in their electoral posters. In a population where illiteracy was still widespread, and where general education levels were anyway low, striking images were crucial. The two posters reproduced below both date from 1953. Notice how both the DC and the PCI represent each other as insects.

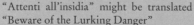

"Attenti all'insidia" might be translated "Beware of the Lurking Danger"

"Basta con la DC" means "No more DC"

(*Source:* The online data base Manifestipolitici.it, maintained by the Istituto Gramsci Emilia-Romagna, *http://www.manifestopolitici.it*).

strengthen the position of "God's party," even though his efforts in this direction often arouse the disapproval of the Christ on the cross in his church, which Guareschi, by a brilliant literary device, allows to speak and thus to act as the voice of conscience. A second force is the division between "lay" and Catholic, which appears in many of the stories. Italy was a rapidly modernizing society in the postwar period and society's traditional values were called into question by changes in social mores. Guareschi was openly reactionary on this question and in many of the stories he editorializes in favor of the beliefs of the dirt-poor, unmaterialistic, deeply religious (even superstitious) Italy that emerged from the war and against the tawdry values of the new prosperity. A third force is the gap between center and periphery. The political struggle between the DC and the PCI is much more abstract (and hence more bitter) at the national level. Don Camillo and Peppone more than once come to blows over political questions, but they always unite for the common good of the village when concrete issues need resolving. The national political parties, by contrast, appear in the stories as alien forces speaking divisive propaganda, and when their representatives appear in the village they are invariably humiliated in one way or another.

Guareschi regarded his stories as a good-humored quarrel with communism. It is one of the central facts of postwar Italian politics that the political divide caused by the presence of the PCI never blew up into all-out conflict. This was in part due to the caution of the national political leaderships of both the DC and the PCI, who knew just how far they could push their opposing numbers and who recognized one another's legitimacy as the voices of a large segment of the Italian population, but it was also due to the fact that Don Camillo and Peppone are instantly recognizable characters: people like them really did exist. Italians are often theatrical in their political rhetoric and extreme in their political views, but they are eminently pragmatic and deeply loyal to their own little corner of the world.

Politics 1946–1981: Christian Democracy in Power

From June 1946, when the first free postwar elections were held, until 1992, when the corruption investigations smashed its hold on power, the DC was the largest political party in Italy and the chief party of government. Nevertheless, by the 1980s, the party's hegemony over the political system was no longer unchallenged. It was reliant on the Socialist Party (PSI) for a parliamentary majority and the PSI drove a very hard bargain in exchange for its support: a harder bargain than Italy's economy and political system in fact were able to pay. The heyday of the DC's dominance is thus between the immediate postwar period and the early 1980s. Understanding the principal features of politics during the DC's years in power is thus essential for understanding the issues facing

Italian politics today. In a real sense, contemporary Italian politicians are dealing with the legacy of the decades of DC rule.

Three such features stand out. First, constitutional arrangements made a virtue out of consensus and placed the achievement of social justice through state action on a par with traditional liberal guarantees of individual rights. The first half of the 1948 Constitution, which lists the republic's fundamental principles, commands wide consent even today as an assertion of the values of the popular struggle against fascism. Second, a party system was determined by a highly proportional electoral law and by, in addition to the hegemony of the DC, the presence of two "excluded poles" (the PCI and the neofascist Italian Social Movement). And third, foreign policy was based upon the twin pillars of Italy's status as a founding member of both NATO and the European Community. Italy had few postwar illusions about her political standing (although she did hope against hope that the 1947 peace treaty with the wartime Allies would allow her to keep her colonies and became almost comically indignant when it unsurprisingly did not). Foreign policy, which during the Cold War was a matter of great domestic sensitivity, was kept in the hands of ministers the United States regarded as safe. During the years the DC was in power, Italy produced no figure comparable to Charles de Gaulle or Willy Brandt or Olof Palme; no individual was able to provide a persuasive vision of a future Europe outside of the Cold War straitjacket. This is true even of the greatest postwar DC statesman, Alcide De Gasperi, who was prime minister between December 1945 and July 1953.

THE INSTITUTIONS AND VALUES OF THE ITALIAN STATE

The 1948 Constitution was the product of the Constituent Assembly elected on June 2, 1946, the same day that the Italians voted narrowly to abolish the monarchy. It was a compromise agreement—inevitably, since the largest party in the Constituent Assembly, the DC, had obtained only 35 percent of the vote, less than the alliance of the PCI and the PSI, the two largest left-wing parties. Had the DC and the PCI not been willing to cooperate with each other to find mutually acceptable rules, Italy would have lapsed into political upheaval and perhaps even civil war. As a result, the constitution, despite much criticism since the early 1980s, has achieved iconic status in Italian political life as a symbol of national unity and has proved remarkably resistant to change.

The constitution is divided into two halves. The first part deals with the "fundamental principles" of the Italian state, while the second part details the competences of the various institutions composing the state. The constitution states that Italy is a republic "founded on labor" and gives precise guarantees of the right to work, to strike, to have paid holidays, and to receive a living wage. The rights of property, meanwhile, while they are indeed provided for, are made subject to their social utility and can be constrained by the state in pursuit of the other social goals advocated by the constitution.[2] Many influential figures in the DC actually shared the left's belief that the state should and would engineer social equality (it is a serious mistake dismissively to characterize the DC as a right-wing or outright reactionary party), but the DC also demanded two guarantees in return for allowing such "progressive" language to infuse the constitution: first, that the constitutional status of Catholicism as the official religion of the state, won by the Church from Mussolini in the so-called Lateran Pacts of 1929, should be preserved; second, that there should be powerful institutional safeguards to prevent the tyranny of the majority.

The DC obtained its goals. The PCI, with the exception of a single deputy, voted to keep the Church's constitutional role. The institutions established by the constitution, moreover, were designed to ensure that there were strong safeguards against the abuse of a popular majority. In addition to the establishment of a constitutional court and a judiciary whose independence is constitutionally guaranteed, the most important of these safeguards was the parliament. Italy's parliament, like the U.S. Congress, is an example of "perfect bicameralism." This means that it is composed of two popularly elected chambers, the Chamber of Deputies and the Senate, each of which has equal powers of scrutiny and assent over all legislation. The government, moreover, must command the confidence of both chambers to survive.

The comparison with the U.S. Congress is not a perfect one, however, since both chambers of the Italian parliament are elected concurrently and the Senate does not specifically represent the regions. On the other hand, the constitution provided that only voters over twenty-five years of age could vote in Senate elections, a provision that has remarkably remained unaltered to this day. In the Italy of the late 1940s, where people left school and married early, this provision had a clear conservative purpose. It effectively limited the suffrage for one chamber of parliament to working men and women with families. A second safeguard was the weakness of the executive. The constitution explicitly ensured that no single institution could take a dirigist role. The president of the republic was elected indirectly by an electoral college for a seven-year term, not by the popular vote, and while the president was given the power to call elections, to nominate ministers and members of the Constitutional Court and to delay legislation, and thus certainly was not a mere figurehead, he did not chair the Council of Ministers (cabinet) and had no power either to dismiss ministers or to set the policy agenda. Italian presidents have been mixed in quality: some, such as the political philosopher and economist Luigi Einaudi or the central banker Carlo Azeglio Ciampi, have been figures of high international reputation; more often, the choice fell upon mediocre powerbrokers within the DC's hierarchy.

The role of the president of the Council of Ministers, the formal head of the government, was very far removed from the role of a British prime minister or German chancellor. Crucially deprived of the power to hire and fire members of the cabinet, the president of the council's role became a sort of "mediator in chief" between the ministers in the government and the political leaders of the parties within the governing coalition—indeed, the constitution explicitly states that the president of the Council of Ministers "coordinates" the activity of the government rather than leads or directs it. The government's programs and priorities tended therefore to emerge only after broad consensus had been attained. When such consensus could not be found, governments formally instituted a government crisis. The party leaders trooped up to the Quirinale Palace in Rome to meet the president and plead their case. It is for this reason that postwar Italian governments were regarded abroad as notoriously unstable. But this was a mistake that it was very difficult for an Italian to make. At any rate until the 1970s, the government "crises" were for the most part really ritualized reshuffles of the cabinet that ended with the same old faces around the cabinet table being shifted from one job to another.

A third potential safeguard against the tyranny of the majority, though the enabling legislation permitting this device was not passed until 1970, was the abrogative referendum. Italy's Constitution permitted any group of concerned citizens that could obtain the valid signatures of 500,000 citizens to petition the Constitutional Court to hold a referendum to abrogate (i.e., cancel) laws that the group regarded as harmful. If the petition is approved by the court, a referendum is held and laws are struck off the books if two conditions are met. First, the referendum must attract the active participation of a majority of those having the right to vote; second, it must obtain a simple majority for change to the law. Parliament, however, has the right (and the duty) to draft new legislation to replace the abrogated law.

The electoral law, though not included in the constitution, was another important bulwark against the abuse of political power. Highly complex and nearly perfectly proportional, the law placed a high premium on representation at the expense of governability. In 1953, the DC, as largest party, passed an electoral law that would have given two-thirds of the seats in the Chamber of Deputies to any coalition that succeeded in getting more than 50 percent of the votes. Dubbed the *legge truffa* (swindle law), the law never came into effect. In the 1953 elections, thanks to a strong showing from the far-right monarchist and neofascist parties, the coalition of the DC and its liberal, republican, and social democratic allies obtained 49.85 percent of the vote and thus did not benefit from the "majority prize" in seats. The same parties had obtained 62 percent of the vote in the previous elections of 1948. The message was clear for Italy's politicians. The law was repealed, then president of the council Alcide De Gasperi retired from politics, and proportional representation (PR) remained the basis of Italian electoral law until 1993. But even the semi-majoritarian electoral law adopted in that year, in the wake of a massively supported referendum abolishing the electoral law for the Senate, was distorted in its effects by the insertion of a strong proportional "corrective." In 2005, Italy once again returned to a highly proportional electoral law for both the Senate and the Chamber of Deputies.

THE MAIN PHASES OF DC RULE

The electoral law constrained the DC to seek allies. In the tense elections of April 1948, just weeks after the Communist coup d'état in Prague and just weeks before the beginning of the Berlin blockade, the DC obtained 48 percent of the vote—the largest share it would ever attain. The DC's victory ushered in the period of so-called *centrismo*, whereby the DC, under De Gasperi and his immediate successors, governed the country with the parliamentary support of two small, anticommunist but nevertheless leftward-leaning parties, the Republicans (PRI) and the Social Democrats (PSDI), though after De Gasperi's death in 1954 most of the governments were entirely composed of DC ministers. Between February 1954 and May 1957, the politically conservative Liberals (PLI) were included in governments headed by two of the leading exponents of conservative opinion within the DC, Mario Scelba and Antonio Segni.

The DC, in fact, was split at the end of the 1950s over whether it should "open to the right" or "open to the left." In 1960, the DC, which had taken 42 percent of the vote during the parliamentary elections of 1958, relied briefly for its parliamentary majority on the support of the neofascist Italian Social Movement (MSI). This rehabilitation of the far right provoked riots across the country, particularly in bastions of antifascist sentiment such as the port city of Genoa, and the experiment ended abruptly. The DC therefore had to turn to the left, since there was nowhere else to go. Important leaders within the DC, notably Amintore Fanfani, who is a forgotten figure today but who was widely admired for his intellect and dynamism at the time by his peers around Europe, had been arguing for some years for a modernizing agenda that would include such progressive social measures as the nationalization of the electricity industry and improved welfare services. Fanfani formed the first government of the "opening to the left" in February 1962, when he governed in conjunction with the PSDI and the PRI with the external support of the Italian Socialist Party (PSI) in parliament.

In December 1963, the mediating skills of the most considerable DC leader after De Gasperi, Aldo Moro, brought the PSI into the government. The DC's "opening to the left" produced an electoral setback—in the 1963 general elections the party's popularity fell below 40 percent for the first time, while the PLI advanced to a postwar high of 7 percent—but Moro, thanks to the inclusion of the PSI (13.8 percent), enjoyed the luxury of being the first DC premier to have a large formal majority. His three governments accordingly endured for five years, but their achievement in the sphere of concrete reforms was far less than many socialist intellectuals had hoped. The failure of the center-left governments headed by Moro was the backdrop for the growing perception in English-language academic literature that Italy was a "republic without government," where conservative forces of immobilism could obstruct and erode attempts to achieve progressive change.[3]

More importantly, similar accusations were made by the radicals of the student and workers' movements that shook Italy from 1967 until the mid-1970s. The center-left experiment petered out in the face of this tumult, and the DC, which was also shaken by corruption scandals in these years, had no answer other than a confused return to *centrismo*. All the time, looming in the background was the growing strength of the PCI, whose electoral support had increased by small increments in every general election from 1948 to 1972, when it obtained over 27 percent of the vote. By 1973, a *sorpasso* (overtaking) of the DC by the PCI was no longer unthinkable. The PCI now had a moderate leader, Enrico Berlinguer, a Sardinian aristocrat whose personal integrity was respected even by his political opponents; its successful and democratic government of Tuscany, Umbria and Emilia-Romagna was regarded as a model for the rest of Italy by many foreign observers; the international climate, with détente and *Ostpolitik*, was more propitious; and many middle-class voters regarded the PCI as a force for moderation compared to the revolutionary left, a perception that Berlinguer reinforced by promising to stay in NATO and by setting the PCI firmly against the increasing violence of far-left groups such as Lotta Continua ("Unceasing Struggle") and the terrorist Red Brigades. Nevertheless, throughout the 1970s the United States left no doubt of its rooted aversion to PCI participation in the government. In this context of growing communist strength and comparative DC weakness, what was needed was what Berlinguer had called in 1973 a "historic compromise"—an accord between the two great mass parties whereby the DC, for the sake of appearances, would form the government, but would consult with the PCI on all aspects of its legislative program.

The mediating skills of Aldo Moro and the moderation of Berlinguer made such an accord possible, and after the elections of June 1976, in which the much-feared *sorpasso* did not occur, although the PCI did advance to over 34 percent of the vote, a government of "national solidarity" was formed by Giulio Andreotti, a shrewd, cynical power broker of impeccable pro-U.S. sympathies. The three governments headed by Andreotti over the next three years won the battle against terrorism, although there were many defeats along the way, the worst being the kidnapping and murder of Aldo Moro by the Red Brigades in March-April 1978; but those governments achieved (indeed, attempted) little in the field of social reforms. A frustrated PCI left the government in the spring of 1979.

In June 1979, the electoral performance of the PCI slipped (down 4 percent), while the DC held steady. The DC took advantage of the fact that the PSI, under the leadership of an ambitious Milanese, Benedetto (Bettino) Craxi, was ready to resume a role in government. The PSI entered the government in the spring of 1980. But the DC's hold on power was now seriously challenged for the first time. The then president, Sandro Pertini, a socialist, chose first a republican, Giovanni Spadolini, and then Craxi as president of the Council. The DC, to stay in power, was forced to "swallow the toad," to translate an Italian idiom, of losing the premiership. The DC's own level of support had remained remarkably stable, at just under 40 percent, for over two decades, but without the PSI it had no sufficient majority to govern. The tail, in the shape of a political party that in 1979 obtained just under 10 percent of the vote, would wag the DC dog for the next decade.

Able Diplomats

Italy has often been accused of not really possessing a foreign policy during the years of the DC's ascendancy. This is inaccurate, however. In the immediate postwar years, Italy, under the able leadership of De Gasperi, made a series of choices that would fix the direction of its foreign policy for the following decades. In the first place, Italy was a founding member of NATO, signing the Atlantic Treaty in 1949 in the face of fierce domestic opposition from the PCI and from many doubters within the DC, and joining the organization when it was established two years later.

The choice was a shrewd one. Italy needed to consolidate its democratic credentials in the eyes of the world and also needed to ensure that Marshall Plan aid flowed from the United States. Membership of the Atlantic Alliance served both purposes. Italy received over $1.4 billion from the United States between 1948 and 1952, and this money was a critical help during the austerity years of postwar reconstruction. There was a third reason for membership of NATO, though this is often forgotten outside Italy. Italy needed to bolster her defenses against a heavily armed communist neighbor (Yugoslavia) that had territorial claims against Italy and indeed had invaded the northeast of the country in the spring of 1945, withdrawing only after the threat of Allied intervention. When Italy joined NATO, the province of Trieste, on the Adriatic coast, was still a disputed territory, with the city being occupied by British and U.S. troops. The Trieste question was only resolved in 1954, when Italy and Yugoslavia reached a compromise that allowed Italy to keep the city itself but that ceded its hinterland to the communist state. The whole question of the future of Trieste was constantly on the minds of Italian statesmen during the first postwar decade.[4]

Italy subsequently became "NATO's Bulgaria" in the eyes of the domestic left: the most subservient of all the European countries to U.S. authority. Major NATO bases were established in Sicily and at Aviano, near Pordenone in the northeast; the Italian secret services were notoriously close to their U.S. counterparts; and U.S. ambassadors were an authentic power in domestic Italian politics and did not hesitate to intervene, notably at the time of the "opening to the left" and during the "historic compromise."

On the other hand, it is also true, and often forgotten, that Italy pursued her own low-key brand of détente with the Soviet bloc from the late-1950s onward. The Italian national oil company, ENI, guided by a controversial DC politician and policy entrepreneur, Enrico Mattei, broke the dominance of the U.S. energy majors by buying large quantities of cheap oil and gas from the USSR (and from the Third World) after 1960. In the mid-1960s, the Italian government provided generous credits to the USSR as part of the joint venture between the Soviet government and FIAT to build cars in what became the Togliatti car plant. Two Italian presidents (Giovanni Gronchi and Giuseppe Saragat) held formal summits with their Russian counterparts in the 1960s.[5]

Italy's main foreign policy achievement, however, was in the sphere of European integration. The writings of Italian intellectuals, notably those of President Einaudi and the liberal socialist thinker Altiero Spinelli, were important contributions to establishing the concept of European federalism. Italy was a founder member of the Council of Europe (1949), the European Convention on Human Rights (1950), and the European Coal and Steel Community (1951). Its political leaders, notably De Gasperi, pushed hard in the early 1950s for the creation of a federal union of the six countries—Belgium, France, Italy, the Netherlands, Luxembourg, and West Germany—that were engaged in building the (eventually stillborn) European Defense Community (1952). The process that led to the construction of the European Economic Community (EEC) was started in June 1955 in the Sicilian town of Messina, was pushed along at a Venice summit of foreign ministers in May 1956 and was signed in Rome in March 1957. Scholars of European integration, who typically read French, German, and English, but not Italian, have not unreasonably concentrated on the centrality of Franco-German relations for the creation of European institutions in the 1950s, but the Italian contribution was constant and far from negligible.

The "common market" created by the EEC treaty was an extremely useful stimulant to an Italian economy that was growing in leaps and bounds. The mental connection made by most Italians between "Europe" and prosperity is the most plausible explanation for the remarkable allegiance shown to the principle of supranationality by Italy's leaders and people since the 1950s. Between 1957 and the signing of the Single European Act (SEA) in 1986, Italy's leaders backed every attempt to deepen the powers of European institutions and to widen the numbers of countries involved in the European project—indeed, Italy was so angry when the SEA did not confer strong powers on the European Parliament that Italy symbolically refused to sign the treaty at the same time as most of the other member states.[6]

Moreover, when the European Community was in serious difficulty, Italian politicians used their considerable mediating skills to try to find workable solutions and to keep the Community from splitting apart. This occurred in 1961–1962, when Amintore Fanfani strove to find a compromise between Charles de Gaulle's concept of a "Union of States" with a strong and independent foreign policy identity, and the preferences of Atlanticist states such as Belgium and the Netherlands. In the early 1980s, at a time when both Great Britain and France seemed disenchanted with Europe, DC foreign minister Emilio Colombo, together with his German counterpart Hans-Dietrich Genscher, led a major diplomatic effort to identify areas of common ground shared by the member states. In the late 1980s, the treasury minister, Guido Carli, and officials from the Bank of Italy played a major role in the talks that eventually led to the agreement to establish monetary union.

While Italy's role in the development of European institutions has been less marked than that of France or Germany, or even Britain, one of the key legacies left by the DC is commitment to further European integration. Until very recently, "Europe" has been universally seen as an ideal worth making sacrifices for, as an essential economic instrument for Italy's development, and as a goal to aspire to. In Italy, evoking "European" standards is a useful rhetorical device for any politician intent on getting controversial measures through: Italians, betraying a chip on the national shoulder, cannot bear to think that they are at less than "European" levels in any sphere.

The DC in Power: A Balance Sheet

One has to look hard and long in the academic literature, at any rate in English, to find a positive word about the DC. And, indeed, the charge sheet that can be brought against the DC is long. The Italian state, as previous editions of this book have argued, was a "weak state" used instrumentally by the DC to distribute resources and buy consent.[7] Corruption, perhaps inevitably in a state ruled by a single party for four decades, was rife, as illustrated by a long series of scandals involving leading members of the DC in the early 1970s. The DC (and to a lesser extent the other parties in the DC constellation) can be accused of having "occupied" civil society and the economy. It was a positive asset to have a party card if one wanted to make a career in the civil service, the many nationalized industries, the banking sector, the media, or the universities. The DC was influenced by the hierarchy of the Catholic Church and as a result Italy's social legislation dragged far behind changes in social mores and habits. The DC turned a blind eye to the fact that its leading politicians colluded with the Mafia in Sicily and other parts of southern Italy: the Mafia, indeed, was transformed from a rural protection racket into a big business by the huge sums of money that the Italian state was spending, without too much care about who got the money, in southern Italy from the 1950s onward. The DC's anticommunism tipped over, in the case of some individuals, into distrust of democracy and willingness to contemplate authoritarian solutions on the Greek or Spanish model. Certainly, DC governments showed much less zeal in prosecuting exponents of "black" (neofascist) terrorism than they did in stamping out the terrorism of the undemocratic left, despite the string of appalling bomb blasts attributed to neofascist groups between the 1969 Piazza Fontana outrage in Milan and the 1980 bombing of Bologna station, in which over eighty people died.

Against these grave faults, however, it must be said that the DC managed to promote an "economic miracle" that left Italians with more money in their pockets than ever before, and to oversee the transition to a modernized society.

The first of these benefits was in part dumb luck. Italy benefited from the huge postwar expansion of the European economy. But since public opinion is quick to condemn them for economic failure, politicians have the right to claim the credit for economic success. Real gross domestic product (GDP) grew at a rate of over 5 percent a year between 1950 and the end of the 1960s, and reached almost 7 percent per year in the glory years of 1958–1963. Even in the 1970s, the recession year of 1975 aside, GDP growth all but maintained this heady rate of increase. The percentage of people working on the land fell from over 40 percent of the working population in the early 1950s to under 20 percent by 1970. Industrial production and exports of manufactures expanded rapidly: FIAT cars, Zanussi washing machines, and Piaggio scooters were sold all over Europe. Highly specialized industrial districts appeared, especially in what the sociologist Arnaldo Bagnasco has dubbed the "third Italy": the small family companies that thrived in these districts have been widely admired as a model for developing countries.[8] Italy's contemporaneous failure to develop world-beating big companies, however, remains something of a puzzle—and something of a handicap in the globalized economy that has emerged since the 1980s.

Such economic success came with a downside, however. Despite the constitutional provisions guaranteeing social equality, conditions of work for the *tute blu* (wearers of blue overalls, i.e., the industrial working class) were often grim. The reaction against sweatshop conditions led to the so-called "hot autumn" of 1969 and to a wave of strikes and permanent industrial unrest in the early 1970s. This unrest was placated only by passing a "Workers' Charter" in 1970, linking workers' pay to inflation and making burdensome concessions to the unions over pensions, job security and state-subsidized unemployment insurance. The service sector remained (and has remained to this day) hidebound in the extreme. Every profession, from taxi drivers to lawyers, had a gatekeeper in the form of a professional association that kept numbers low and tariffs high. The DC acquiesced in this illiberal state of affairs (and service sector businesses voted for them *en masse*). The Mezzogiorno (the south) lagged behind the north in terms of income per head and other indicators of individual and social well-being. The DC's attempts to solve this problem amounted to throwing money at it. The south was subsidized through the welfare system, through high levels of state employment, through high-profile state-financed industrial projects, and through cash handouts to local and regional bodies of all kinds. The result was the development of *assistenzialismo* (welfare-dependency) in the south and very little change in the overall patterns of wealth within the national economy.

The remorseless growth and rising personal prosperity brought by the economic miracle also brought serious environmental and social problems. All round Italy's industrial cities huge, ugly, cheapjack suburbs were thrown up to accommodate the flood of workers coming from the countryside. The Italian coast was partly "cementified" by speculative builders constructing illegal villas for the newly rich middle class—the "rape" of Sardinia being a particularly egregious example. Italian towns, most of which retain a medieval core, were soon clogged with traffic and begrimed with pollution. Italy's politicians closed their eyes (and opened their palms) to these environmental disasters.

The DC was also slow to come to grips with the social modernization that was a concomitant of economic growth. The explosion in Italy's universities in the 1960s and 1970s was due to the state's sloth in adjusting the universities' elitist practices and antiquated customs to the challenges posed by larger numbers of students from untraditional backgrounds. Pressed by the PSI, the DC reluctantly legalized divorce in 1969, but some of its more socially conservative members, led by Amintore Fanfani, launched a referendum attempt to abrogate this hated law. In what was widely regarded as an index of Italy's modernization, Fanfani's campaign failed dismally. On May 12, 1974, Italy voted by 59–41 percent to keep the divorce law.

Abortion was the next objective of the "Movement for Italian Women's Liberation": as late as the 1970s abortion was punishable by imprisonment. In May 1978, after the DC and the PCI had hammered out a compromise law that the radicals and the women's movement found too restrictive, abortion became legal. In a 1981 referendum, however, the abortion law was challenged by both pro-life Catholics and the radicals (who wanted a more liberal statute), but the electorate solidly voted to make no change. Over both divorce and abortion, the leaders of the DC had shown a shrewd grasp of just how far society wanted to go and had successfully introduced a more flexible legal framework for a society whose sexual customs and religious faith had become much looser since the start of the economic boom.[9]

All in all, the DC's record in domestic policy, if one looks at it with an unjaundiced eye, was far from a failure. The DC's longevity in power owed at least something to its skill in steering the ship of state, and not just to the passengers' suspicion of the alternative helmsman. The DC's record was mixed, to use a generous euphemism, but it had delivered peace, prosperity, and modernization and had anchored Italy in the core institutions of the democratic West. Few would have bet on such an outcome in 1948.

The 1990s: An Italian Revolution?

It is important to emphasize that the DC's record was mixed, but not entirely a failure, when one contemplates the enormous political upheaval of the early 1990s. Italy endured a dangerous crisis of domestic confidence in the early 1990s, and the traditional parties of government, with the exception of the PCI (which, however, had to change its name and political identity), were swept away. It is tempting to suggest that this upheaval was a rejection of forty years of DC hegemony: certainly, it is true that Italian public opinion rebelled against longstanding features of the DC regime. However, we should not make the mistake of thinking that the crisis was inevitable. The crisis of the early 1990s also owed a great deal to the breathtaking misgovernment Italy experienced in the 1980s as the DC- and PSI-led coalition engaged in reckless and unsustainable policies reminiscent of Latin America rather than Europe. In 1980, the Italy emerging from DC hegemony needed a period of gradual institutional and social reform and economic austerity, not least because the increasing pace of European integration—notably, after 1983, the stabilization of exchange rates in the European Monetary System (EMS)—required her to sort out her national accounts, modernize her infrastructure and address some of the structural causes holding back Italian competitiveness. What she got instead was a *sbornia* (binge). The Italian political élite, locked as they were in a conflict among themselves, threw caution to the winds. But Italy was not a healthy enough democracy to stand such treatment. Between 1991 and 1995, she fell into a political malaise that alarmed her neighbors and is still far from cured.

A CHAPTER OF MISDEEDS

In the 1980s, politics was characterized by a perpetual struggle for power between the DC and the PSI, and an equally interminable struggle within the DC itself. This constant politicking had negative effects. The long Craxi government (1983–1987), despite its theoretically large majority in parliament, was undermined by the willingness of DC parliamentarians to sabotage the government's program: the government crisis that brought Craxi down effectively lasted from February 1987 to the elections in June! Craxi had a personal reputation for being a *uomo forte*, but it is not just hindsight that suggests that this reputation was largely a carefully cultivated media myth. Craxi was more concerned with riding the "long wave" swelling PSI support to a position where he could cut himself loose from the DC and act as a true pivot in the Italian political system, able to treat with the DC and the PCI on equal terms and act as kingmaker. To this end, he was determined to control and use the state's resources in the same way as the DC. The PSI demanded its fair (or unfair) share of the top jobs in the state sector, and its nominees within the state promptly channeled illicit money to the PSI to finance the U.S.-style electoral campaigns (and personal extravagance) of the PSI's leaders. At the local level, the PSI's public officials became notorious for their venality; the PSI itself probably saw only a small fraction of the money that PSI officials demanded from businesses in exchange for public works contracts, changes to the zoning laws, and the like.

In electoral terms, Craxi's strategy had only mixed results. The transformation of the PSI into a hard-spending personal vehicle for its leader was appreciated by part of the electorate, notably yuppies and professionals, for whom membership in the PSI briefly became fashionable, but it undoubtedly soured many of the party's traditional voters. For all the razzmatazz of the PSI's electoral campaigns, the party never advanced beyond the 14.3 percent of the popular vote it obtained in the June 1987 elections, roughly the same level of support as it had enjoyed in the early 1960s.

The DC, meanwhile, was split between the desire for renewal and the traditional preference for keeping its hands on the levers of power. In 1982, the party elected a southerner, Ciriaco De Mita, as party leader. A stern critic of the DC's sprawling bureaucracy and a public advocate of modernizing the DC's heavy reliance upon using client networks and public spending to buy support (his own client networks were legendary), De Mita aroused great disquiet among the DC's barons. This disquiet intensified after the DC obtained its worst-ever result (under 33 percent) in the June 1983 elections.

Craxi was deposed as prime minister after the 1987 elections (at which the DC recovered slightly), but the political climate did not change. De Mita's hapless nominee as president of the Council, a youngish technocrat called Giovanni Goria, was paid back with interest for the DC's sabotage of the Craxi administration. By the time the Goria government collapsed in chaos in March 1988, it is fair to say that Italy had gone over a year without a stable majority in parliament and that political infighting had occupied practically all of the DC's leaders' time throughout that period. A cease-fire was urgently needed. The DC's chief power brokers accordingly made a pact with Craxi to give the PSI more power within the government, De Mita was forced out from the leadership of the DC, and the "eternal Giulio," as Andreotti is wryly nicknamed, formed a new cabinet in the summer of 1989. He would be president of the Council until the calamitous (for the DC) elections of April 1992.

This atmosphere of permanent political warfare did not bode well for good government. And, in fact, Italy was not well governed. The public finances collapsed as the government parties, intent on their own popularity contest, spent freely on pork barrel projects, on lavish pensions programs, and on (often useless) infrastructure. "Freely," in fact, is a tepid euphemism, as a quick look at the public accounts shows. In 1980, Italy's stock of public debt equaled 60 percent of GDP—too high, but far from unmanageable. By 1990, *despite* a decade of solid economic growth and *despite* a significant rise in the share of GDP taken annually in taxation (which went up by approximately 8 percent during the 1980s), the same figure had reached 97.8 percent: a rise of almost 38 percent in a single decade! Budget deficits were 10 percent or more of GDP every year from 1981 to 1991. A period of slow growth in the early 1990s, together with the 1992 election campaign, during which the public checkbook was used with a vengeance, only compounded the disaster. The debt stock reached a peak of 124.3 percent of GDP in 1994: a doubling of the national debt as a percentage of GDP in just fourteen years. Interest on the public debt alone took up 12 percent of GDP in 1993.[10] Management of the public finances is a strong argument in support of the thesis that the political crisis of the 1990s is rooted in the political behavior consequent upon the erosion of the DC's hegemony.

With the collapse of standards in public finance went a parallel collapse in public morality. Corruption became normal practice, as we have seen. Worse, the flood of money pouring from the state gave a huge stimulus to the Mafia, whose appetite for public contracts was huge and which had many political allies on their payroll. A single law, the notorious *legge 64* of 1986, distributed about $80 billion, at the then exchange rate, on a nine-year plan of "extraordinary aid" to the Mezzogiorno. Tens of billions of dollars more were spent on "relief" after the terrible Irpinia earthquake of 1980. Most of this money was never accounted for, but it certainly did not reach the earthquake victims, many of whom had to live in prefab houses for the next two decades. Gang warfare exploded in the Mezzogiorno from the early 1980s onwards as Mafia "clans" fought over the pickings. Certain small towns in Sicily (Gela being the most notorious) or Calabria (Taurianova) had murder rates that matched those of Bogotá or Medellin (Colombia) by the end of the 1980s.

The political parties' reaction to this challenge to law and order can most generously be described as equivocal. On the one hand, an FBI-like anti-Mafia force was set up under the command of a prosecutor, Giovanni Falcone, who had broken the Palermo Mafia in a series of trials in the early 1980s. On the other hand, they kept stoking the fires with public money, conducted no serious investigation into scarcely credible abuses of public spending by local political bosses, and ignored scandalous cases of evident Mafia involvement in politics. Certain political figures with known Mafia connections were honored colleagues in the Italian parliament. Yet so long as the Mafia delivered votes, many politicians were willing to turn a blind eye. Once again, we see a situation where the loss of the DC's hegemony over the political process *worsened* a system of collusion between the political class and the Mafia that is at least a century old. As the subtitle of a 1990 book on the south and its problems proclaimed: "For twenty million Italians democracy is in a coma and Europe is slipping away."[11]

THE REVOLT OF PUBLIC OPINION

By the mid-1980s, public unease with the political class had become more and more apparent. The political system was by now widely denounced as a *partitocrazia* (that is, a state run by and on behalf of the parties). Some leading Italian journalists went further and spoke openly of a "regime" and of a *nomenklatura*.[12] Revolt was inevitable in the absence of reform—but the parties showed no sign of wanting to reform. The revolt came from three main sources. First, in the south, civil society generated a vibrant anti-Mafia movement whose chief public face was the DC mayor of Palermo, Leoluca Orlando, but which soon evolved into a political party, La Rete (the Network), after Orlando was forced out of his job by the DC hierarchy in 1990 for collaborating with the PCI rather than the DC's official allies.

A second revolt was the growing demand for electoral reform. Proponents of electoral reform argued that one cause of *partitocrazia* was that voters were deprived of choosing a government by Italy's PR system of voting. The voters chose a party, but because no party ever got a majority, the decision as to who would be president of the Council was in the hands of the party bosses. Reformers proposed British-style "first-past-the-post" voting as a remedy. In addition, the electoral system allowed the voter to indicate the names of up to four candidates on the ballot slip. The candidates with the most preferences on each party list were the ones elected. This possibility was the source of much ballot fraud, and generated wasteful spending (and hence corruption) by candidates desperate to win office. In June 1991, a highly technical referendum eliminating the preference voting system was unwisely turned into a vote of confidence in the political system as a whole by the party hierarchies. Craxi, in particular, derided the referendum and actively tried to instigate absenteeism. The result of his activities was an electoral earthquake. Thousands of people were enthused to work for the abolition campaign and on June 9–10, 1991, the sovereign people dealt a massive slap in the face to their leaders. Over 60 percent of the adult population voted by a margin of 95.6 percent to 4.4 percent to get rid of the preference system.[13]

The third revolt was the most important of all. In the mid-1980s, voters in northern Italy increasingly began to turn to populist "leagues" demanding greater local autonomy. Between 1989 and February 1991, these leagues united into a single federal movement, the Lega Nord (Northern League), with a core goal of achieving the constitution of the "Republic of the North" within the context of a federal restructuring of the Italian state. The League's leader, a charismatic formal medical student called Umberto Bossi, vehemently attacked the waste and the corruption of Rome and portrayed the Italian South as a burden on the hardworking, prosperous northern regions. Northern League militants indulged in racist rhetoric against the Mezzogiorno and its inhabitants, and the movement also jumped on the bandwagon of opposing illegal immigration, which in the late 1980s was just beginning to be a problem in Italy, with an influx of people seeking work from the Maghreb countries and from Albania. Despite, or because of, this mix of policies, the League's electoral success was dramatic. In a country where electoral changes had previously been measured in fractions of a percentage point, suddenly a political force emerged whose electoral support grew exponentially from one election to the next. Bossi was first elected to the Italian Senate in 1987; his movement, the Lega Lombarda,

Box 4.2   The Northern League

The Northern League has the merit of making its ideas clear in plain language. Here are four passages summarizing its views:

> The Lega represents the North that has been squeezed beyond endurance for decades and is fed up—more than fed up—with this state of affairs. For this we are saying loud and clear: this state, and this method of managing public money is no longer acceptable to us. We want a change in direction and we want it now. We will no longer tolerate our hard work being wasted in this way. There are two alternatives. Either the political parties change the way they do things and get their claws off the public money that the North is transferring to the South . . . or the North will get up and go. Thirty million citizens have had enough of being made mugs of, of paying for everything and everybody. (Umberto Bossi, *Vento dal Nord. La mia Lega la mia vita*, Milan: Sperling & Kupfer, 1992, p. 136)

> The Lega Nord intends to represent the interests of small and medium-sized firms, not just for their mode of production, but also for the type of society which is behind these same firms. A society which is not multi-racial and therefore disintegrated, but which is instead characterized by a continuity of relations between citizens and institutions, so that the citizen feels part of society. It is this union which guarantees democracy. (*Lavoro e federalismo*, supplement to *Lombardia Autonomista*, no. 22, July 15, 1992)

> The real racist menace should be searched for in the theory and destructive practice of globalization, which, via a world-wide commercial subculture, is planning to construct a 'global village' which will be Anglo-Saxon in language and culture and totalitarian, upon the ruins of peoples. These globalizers are the true racists insofar as they deny the diversity of cultures and peoples. Patriotism is the last obstacle to the progress of the American and Islamic planetary empires. (*Padania, identità e società multirazziale*, pamphlet published by the Lega Nord, 1998)

> I believe that it is a moral obligation that must guide the actions of our political class, including those in government, to favor a policy that is seemingly now timidly starting to raise its head in recent documents of the European Commission, namely a policy of voluntary repatriation [*una politica di ritorno*]. This is the right road to follow, repatriation, the incentivization of a method that is the exact opposite of the filthy interests of the people traffickers who bring [immigrants] here without prospects, thus creating among young Muslims, the "beurs" as the French call them, a rage that is perhaps both justified and understandable. We need to back up the policy of stimulating repatriation with sacrifices on our part, because anything that we do to protect our identity and our social peace will be money well spent. I think, therefore, of the noble idea that our movement might launch of a Marshall Plan for north-west Africa. . . . There is an African elite that is in anguish as it sees (African) youth depart and hence deprive their countries of vital nutriment, of new generations. (Mario Borghezio, delegation chief of the LN to the European Parliament, from a speech given in Sestri Levanteto to the "federal political school" of the movement, November 19, 2005)

obtained 200,000 votes. By May 1990, the League could obtain 1.2 million votes in local elections in Lombardy, only fractionally less than the DC and more than both the PCI and the PSI. The League also scored well elsewhere in the north.[14]

The common factor uniting these three revolts against the party system was the malaise of Italian democracy. The anti-Mafia movements were making the unexceptionable point that a democracy that permitted local political bosses to exercise power in conjunction with gangsters was a deformation of democratic principles. The electoral reformers were saying that the structure of the electoral system was producing negative outcomes such as corruption and ballot fraud, and that Italian citizens had been robbed of their fundamental right to decide who should govern them. The League was saying that the state had broken its contract with the people of the north by wasting the money they had worked so hard to earn. Taken together, the three movements' positions constituted a powerful indictment of the turn Italian politics had taken in the 1980s.

Yet the political elite, with the eccentric exception of then president Francesco Cossiga, seemed not to take the ferment in civil society seriously. The League was routinely dismissed as a *fuoco di paglia* (straw fire) that would burn itself out quickly. Its positions seemed too extreme and its rhetoric too colorful to be taken seriously, and the DC did not believe that the League would permanently erode its vote.

The DC and the PSI also drew confidence from the internal troubles of the PCI. The collapse of the Berlin Wall caused the PCI to accelerate its slow transformation into a postcommunist but still leftist force. This transformation had begun late (Berlinguer, for all his personal dignity and his willingness to criticize the USSR, did not address the issue) and the question of whether or not to renounce communism bitterly divided the party after 1989. The party leader, Achille Occhetto, urged the creation of a party "new, even in name" in November 1989, as the Velvet Revolution highlighted the bankruptcy of the communist system. Yet many influential members asserted that the PCI had nothing to be ashamed of in its record: in their view, it had always stood for the parliamentary road to socialism and for political pluralism. The PCI spent more than a year debating the issue until, in February 1991, it transformed itself, amidst much polemic, into the Democratic Party of the Left (PDS) with a noticeably left-wing platform of policies.[15] A group of hard-liners, unable to digest the symbolism of the change, split from the party to form Communist Refoundation (PRC). The PSI fully expected the new party to be discredited by its historical ties to the Soviet bloc and to sink below the PSI in terms of electoral support.

Both the DC and the PSI mistook their calculations. The PDS threw itself into the June 1991 referendum campaign for greater democracy, a move that undoubtedly restored some of its credibility with the electorate. The League, energized by Bossi, impeccably organized, and working at the grassroots instead of in Rome TV studios, continued to make inroads into the DC's base electorate of small entrepreneurs and skilled artisans who, now free of their fear of the communist menace, could vote as their consciences dictated. The April

1992 general elections were thus a "landmark" in Italian electoral history.[16] The electorate, ignoring the avalanche of propaganda aired by the DC- and PSI-controlled national television networks, punished the DC and the PSI at the polls. The PSI lost votes and failed to overtake the PDS, which managed to poll 16 percent of the vote in elections to the Chamber. The DC slumped to just under 30 percent, down almost 5 percent from 1987. The League triumphed, getting nearly 9 percent of the popular vote and taking fifty-five seats in the Chamber. Bossi himself obtained 250,000 personal preferences. Even though the governing coalition retained a reduced majority of seats in the house—331 out of 630—nobody doubted that a major shift in the party system had occurred. The DC's and the PSI's hold on power was being retained by virtue of their patronage networks and from the inertia of some voters. They no longer had a national mandate.

In this moment of political weakness, the DC and the PSI were overtaken by events. Prosecutors in Milan and other cities in Italy intensified the corruption investigations they had initiated before the electoral campaign—by May 1992, it was already clear that the scandal would be of epic proportions. President Cossiga, striking a blow at the colleagues who had not heeded him, resigned, which meant that a new president had to be elected before a new government could be named. The DC and the PSI hoped to make the secretary of the DC, Arnaldo Forlani, the new president and to place Craxi as president of the Council. They no longer had the votes, however. While they were trying to find an alternative candidate to Forlani, the Mafia blew up Giovanni Falcone as he drove to Palermo airport. A wave of emotion swept the country. Falcone had been a symbol of all that was *right* with the Italian state. Aware that the public mood would tolerate no more delays, parliament elected Oscar Luigi Scalfaro, a senior member of the DC whose personal integrity was not in doubt, to the presidency at the end of May 1992. Scalfaro showed his independence at once by not nominating Craxi to the presidency of the Council. Instead, Giuliano Amato, a technocrat associated with the PSI, was appointed prime minister. His government spent the entire summer dealing with a huge currency crisis that eventually led, in September, to a 30 percent devaluation of the lira and its expulsion from the EMS. The devaluation was accompanied by draconian cutbacks in government spending and new taxation. These measures underlined that the days of open-handed state spending were over for good.

The following year saw the death of the DC and the PSI at the hands of prosecutors from all over Italy. Craxi was bombarded with investigations and was eventually placed on trial. Scarcely a day went by without new revelations of corruption. The word *tangenti* (bribes) became almost as well known outside Italy as pizza or spaghetti. Prosecutors in southern Italy homed in on links between DC politicians and organized crime. In March and May 1993, Andreotti was warned that he was under investigation for his alleged links to the Mafia and for having ordered the killing, in 1979, of an investigative journalist looking for skeletons in Andreotti's cupboard. A series of other prominent DC politicians in Naples were also warned that their alleged links to the Neapolitan Mafia, the Camorra, were being inspected.[17]

These investigations, which confirmed all the worst fears of most Italians about the nature of their political class, put the lid on the traditional party system. In June 1993, the League won 41 percent of the vote in municipal elections in Milan—double its already spectacular result in April 1992. But the League held no attraction for voters in central or southern Italy. There, the PDS, at the head of a left-wing coalition that included the Greens and Communist Refoundation, began to emerge as the largest political force, though the left's success in the south was being challenged by the neofascist MSI. The neofascists' leader, Gianfranco Fini, and Benito Mussolini's granddaughter, Alessandra, stood as mayoral candidates in Rome and Naples in November 1993, and though neither won, both did well. Flushed with this success, the MSI subsequently underwent a process of modernization, changing its name to the National Alliance (Alleanza Nazionale [AN]) and dropping some of the more overt fascist elements from the party program. This process was initially somewhat cosmetic, but rather like the PDS, which has become a social democrat party since the mid-1990s, it has been carried forward with seeming sincerity. By the end of the 1990s, AN, while still containing many individual members with a nostalgia for the black shirt, had become a recognized conservative party.[18]

In short, in 1993, the political center, dominated for so long by the DC, had fallen apart. A political vacuum had been created that looked as if it might be filled in elections scheduled for the spring of 1994 by extremist movements of the right and by a left that was ill-equipped ideologically for the Europe of the Maastricht Treaty and globalized capitalism. Did this development amount to a revolution? The answer to this question depends very much on whether one believes that Italy underwent a regime change or not. On the one hand, the constitution remained intact; President Scalfaro was a living symbol of the continuity of the Italian political system; the judiciary was, albeit with excessive zeal at times, cleaning up political life; and other institutions, such as the Bank of Italy, whose president, Carlo Azeglio Ciampi, became president of the Council in May 1993, were widely admired in the rest of the world. Indeed, there was an argument for stating that events in 1992–1993, like Watergate in the United States, had shown up the strength of Italy's regime, not its weaknesses.

On the other hand, the political revolution could not be gainsaid. The DC had been shattered; in December 1993, it was forced to change its name to the "Italian Popular Party" (Partito popolare italiano: PPI). The PSI and the other minor parties that orbited the DC had been all but wiped out. Most of the political old guard was under investigation. The former extremes were growing in political strength; the League, which had not even existed ten years before, was by far the largest party in most of northern Italy. If it was not a revolution, it felt like one.

Berlusconi's Italy

It was at this tense moment that the Milanese media entrepreneur Silvio Berlusconi decided in January 1994 to *scendere in campo* (take to the field) at the head of a political formation that he baptized "Come on Italy!" (Forza Italia). It is a measure of the uncertainty in Italian politics at this time that Forza Italia was able to take 21 percent of the vote and become the largest party in the country just three months later.

The soccer metaphor was natural for Berlusconi. The owner of AC Milan, at the time Europe's finest team, he exuded the image of a winner. The fact that his business empire was in the media was important. Berlusconi could not have created an election-winning party in a few months without owning a major corporation that possessed three national TV networks. The sales segment of the corporation, Publitalia, provided him with staff and plausible candidates. Berlusconi had glamour, that promise of wealth and beauty that hangs around people who are involved with TV.

Yet much more was involved. A close friend of Bettino Craxi, who had been involved in the P2 scandal, Berlusconi was an integral part of the old regime. Yet if this alienated many people, it may have reassured those who wanted continuity. Then, too, Berlusconi was a self-made businessman in a country that respects entrepreneurial talent. Berlusconi did not explain the problem of the public debt. Instead he set out to seduce the listener, to create the myth of an individual who incarnated "another" Italy, traditional in its emphasis on the family and anticommunism but new in its economic success. He showed, in short, the skill of a born marketer.

Since 1994, Berlusconi has been the dominant individual politician in Italy. But rather than seek to unite the country or to compromise with his opponents, he has polarized the political debate. With his strident anticommunist rhetoric, his populist attacks on the judiciary, his anomalous position as both a media baron and political leader, Berlusconi has turned up the rhetorical heat in Italian politics. His opponents have paid him back in the same coin. There is no other Western European country where the leaders of the main parties *routinely* accuse their rivals of being a menace to democracy. In this respect, the crisis atmosphere of 1993 has never been entirely superseded.[19]

Politics in the Age of Berlusconi

There is no space here to chart in detail all the twists and turns in Italian party politics since 1994. Accordingly, it is perhaps best simply to highlight some of the principal features of politics in the last twelve years.

First, party politics, in sharp discontinuity from the previous forty years, has been characterized by *alternation in government*. The parties of the center-right (Forza Italia, the Northern League, AN, Christian Democrats) have formed electoral alliances that have led to somewhat shaky right-wing governments between May and December 1994 and between April 2001 and April 2006. Berlusconi presided over both these governments, the first of which was brought down by the Northern League, and the second of which, the so-called "House of Freedoms," despite perpetual feuding between the coalition's component members, endured with only one major ministerial reshuffle. The left and the former DC were forced into an alliance by the 1994 elections, which illustrated that the left alone could not obtain more than just over 30 percent of the vote. Since 1995, the PDS (who changed their name again in 1998 to become the "Democrats of the Left") have allied themselves with the PPI and a lengthy list of minor parties in the Ulivo (Olive Tree).

The main architect of this coalition was Romano Prodi, a Bologna economics professor and former industrialist, whose political orientation had been on the left of the former DC. The Ulivo narrowly won the 1996 elections, but were forced to rely upon the Communist Refoundation's parliamentary support, which was withdrawn in October 1998. The Ulivo government was only saved by a group of Christian Democrats crossing the floor from Berlusconi's coalition to join the center-left. Three more center-left governments were formed between 1998 and 2001, and the first Ulivo government ended in some disarray. In April 2006, the voters chose to give the Ulivo a second chance by electing a Prodi-led coalition called "the Union," which unites the Ulivo and Communist Refoundation in a governmental alliance. It remains to be seen how stable this latest center-left government will be.

This alternation in government of highly heterogeneous coalitions is in part the result of the 1993 electoral law passed at the height of the political crisis after a second referendum on the electoral law, in April 1993, had sent a strong message that the electorate wanted to experiment with first-past-the-post voting. The electoral law attributed 75 percent of seats via elections in single member constituencies, but distributed the remaining seats by PR to parties able to get at least 4 percent of the national vote. The law left just enough wriggle room to allow the smaller parties to bargain with the bigger ones, rather than be forced to merge with them, and as a result Italy has remained a democracy with a bewildering, indeed excessive, number of small parties. However, there has been a constant hankering after a return to PR. In 2005, the "House of Freedoms" reintroduced PR for the elections held in April 2006.

It is also worth stressing that alternation in government has given great weight to two parties in particular: the Northern League and Communist Refoundation. As the 2006 election showed, Italy, like the United States, is split fifty-fifty between left and right. In 1996, Berlusconi lost only because the League chose to run alone. In 2001, the Ulivo's failure to make an electoral pact with the PRC cost it dearly; in 2006, despite the reintroduction of PR, the PRC was again decisive. The PRC is one of the most left-wing parties in Europe, with a strong anti-U.S. and antiglobalization platform. The League has flirted with far right ideology since 1994, and between 1996 and 1999 argued for the creation of "Padania"—a separate northern Italian state. Its advocacy of this policy was rewarded with its best-ever electoral result in the 1996 elections: a substantial 10 percent of the national vote—3.75 million votes—went to the League, and Bossi's movement even won thirty-nine electoral districts outright. The desire to break the domination of the extremes may yet lead, especially now there is a proportional electoral system, to the renewal, in minor key, of the DC. Catholic identity remains a strong factor in Italian politics, though whether an enlarged Catholic center party would collaborate with the center-left or the center-right is an open question.

Second, despite many claims that the political crisis of 1992–1993 had marked the end of the "first republic," *the institutions of the Italian state have remained largely unchanged*. There has been no significant constitutional reform despite an inordinate amount of time being spent on the issue. In 1998, the Ulivo launched a bicameral committee of parliament whose task was to find a bipartisan set of constitutional reforms. Its efforts in this regard were derided by professors of political science and constitutional law, but it did not matter anyway; after cooperating in drawing up a draft incorporating substantial changes to the second half of the constitution, Berlusconi decided not to back the changes in the decisive parliamentary vote. In 2000, the Ulivo introduced some minor increases in the powers of regional governments; it is widely agreed that this reform was too half-hearted and somewhat muddled. The 2001–2006 Berlusconi government, by contrast, introduced, without attempting to obtain bipartisan consent, a package of sweeping constitutional changes. These changes included "devolution" to the regions of powers over health care, education and the police (this was the price of the League for staying in government), the transformation of the Senate into a "chamber of the regions," a substantial strengthening of the powers of the president of the Council to make him or her an authentic prime minister able to hire and fire ministers, a reduction in the number of parliamentary deputies and senators, and an end to perfect bicameralism. The center-left, despite the fact that it had itself proposed several of these changes in the past, opposed the Berlusconi government's proposals in a constitutional referendum in June 2006. Berlusconi's package of reforms was soundly rejected by the electorate, which voted 62–38 percent against change.

Third, despite some painful austerity measures in the 1990s, Italy has *not succeeded in getting its public finances in order*. The legacy of the 1980s has proved a heavy one. During the 1990s, after the crisis of the first Berlusconi government in December 1994, President Scalfaro took the unprecedented step of appointing a government of non-party technocrats (jurists, professors, a general) that lasted until the elections of April 1996 with the parliamentary support of the left and the Northern League. This government was headed by a former central banker, Lamberto Dini. The main achievement of Dini's government was to rein in spending on welfare, especially pensions; thanks to the generosity of governments in the 1970s and 1980s, there was the threat of huge numbers of people born in the immediate postwar period being permitted to leave the workforce while they were still in their fifties. This would have imposed a crippling burden on the population of working age (and upon the public accounts). The 1996–1998 Prodi government was even tougher. It was faced with the task of qualifying Italy for membership of the euro in 1999. To this end, it had to get the annual deficit under 3 percent of GDP, which meant running a substantial surplus once payments on the accumulated debt were discounted. The 1997 budget imposed major cuts in public spending and introduced a "eurotax" on high incomes. Income was raised between 1994 and 2000 by an ambitious program of privatization (the motorway, gas and electricity networks, and several publicly owned banks were all sold off). Thanks to these measures, Italy was allowed to join the euro in 1999, with the other member states of the EU turning a blind eye to the fact that Italy's stock of public debt remained well over 100 percent of GDP. The success of Prodi in qualifying for the euro gave rise to a thriving academic literature lauding the power of the *vincolo esterno* (external constraint) of European unification as a force to induce Italy to modernize its state and undertake structural reforms.[20]

In fact, the experience since 1998 shows that the external constraint has been insufficient by itself to promote a virtuous cycle in Italian public spending. The national debt declined gradually from its 1994 peak of 124.3 percent of GDP to approximately 106 percent in 2004, but it has since begun to creep back upwards and is estimated to reach 108 percent in 2007. Under the 2001–2006 Berlusconi government, the budget surplus before interest payments was gradually eroded, and Italy, in 2006, risked returning to outright deficit spending despite the fact that the economy was expanding and the European growth outlook was good. This weakness in budgetary performance is due to the fact that the austerity measures of the 1990s were not accompanied by structural reforms to liberalize the economy and to promote growth—reforms that were all the more necessary because of the growth in competition from China in sectors (textiles, footwear, etc.) where Italy was a world leader. Italian growth has been anemic since the mid-1990s (the lowest in the EU) and this explains why the debt stock has remained stubbornly high.

Fourth, Italian politics has been dominated by the *Berlusconi question*. The center-left government that took power in 1996 surprisingly made no serious attempt to eliminate the evident conflict of interest that exists in Berlusconi's twin roles as media baron whose companies reach over 40 percent of the viewing public, and potential prime minister.[21] The latest Berlusconi government passed a media law in 2003 that, in the opinion of many experts—not all of them connected to the left—was designed to consolidate Berlusconi's already powerful position in the Italian media. A second conflict of interest lies in the fact that Berlusconi or his close advisors have been defendants in a series of high profile trials. Since 2001, Italy has been governed by a man who is facing serious charges of corruption, tax evasion, and money laundering. His close subordinates have been accused of bribing judges and collusion with the Mafia, among other crimes. In power, Berlusconi has dealt with this situation in two ways. First, Forza Italia deputies and the right-wing media have carried out a permanent campaign of denigration against the *toghe rosse*, supposedly communist judges who are alleged to be conducting a witch hunt against Berlusconi and his associates. Second, Berlusconi resorted to the simple expedient of retrospectively decriminalizing some of the laws he is alleged to have broken, and obtaining (a possibly unconstitutional) legal immunity from prosecution while in office. Months of parliamentary time were taken up after May 2001 with the passage of these so-called "made-to-measure laws."[22]

Berlusconi's behavior has personalized the political debate to a quite remarkable degree. There can be few contemporary instances (the second Nixon and Clinton presidencies are perhaps comparable) where political discourse has been so dominated by a single personality. Opposition to Berlusconi and what he represents is unquestionably the chief glue that keeps the Ulivo together; the right-wing parties, meanwhile, understand that without Berlusconi, and his media power and profile, they do not form a coherent alternative capable of governing. They have thus joined in the verbal battle on Berlusconi's side and voted in unison to keep him out of jail. Italian politics is today a cacophony of strident voices where politicians on both sides denigrate their opponents at will and seemingly without fear of the consequences. The effect of this constant verbal warfare has been to weaken still further Italians' never-high regard for the functioning of their democracy.

Italy in Europe and the World

During the last years of the DC, and in the period subsequent to the collapse of the party system in 1992–1993, the main principles of Italian foreign policy have remained the same: Italy has been pro-NATO in its international orientation and has worked to achieve greater levels of supranational integration in the European Union. The Berlusconi government of 2001–2006 was widely accused of being Euro-skeptic, but while members of the government did at times criticize the EU and its policies, the charge is somewhat overblown.

In policy toward European integration, Italy has backed all the most important evolutions in the political development of the EU since the SEA in 1986. Italy, in the person of Giulio Andreotti, played an important role in pushing ahead the talks for monetary union, and backed the Treaty on European Union

(1992). Italy was one of the keenest supporters throughout the 1990s of enlarging the EU to include the new democracies of Central and Eastern Europe, and has also persistently advocated the entry of Turkey, despite the fierce opposition of the Northern League and unease among public opinion over the question.

Italian politicians, notably Giuliano Amato and the leader of AN, Gianfranco Fini, played an important role in the convention that drew up a constitution for the EU between March 2002 and July 2003. It was to have been Italy's historic task, as president of the EU between July and December 2003, to supervise the intergovernmental conference (IGC) that amended the convention's draft and achieve agreement for a new Treaty of Rome. Unfortunately, events did not turn out as planned. Berlusconi's opening speech to the European Parliament in July 2003 ended in farce when the Italian premier lost his temper with hecklers on the Socialist benches of the parliament and compared a German member of the parliament to a concentration camp "Kapo." This scarcely credible gaffe provoked a major rift between Italy and Germany, and hindered Berlusconi's diplomatic efforts for the rest of Italy's presidential semester. Agreement on changes to the draft constitution was not reached until June 2004 under the Irish presidency of the EU. Berlusconi did obtain, however, the minor triumph of holding the formal signing ceremony in Rome in October 2004.

As the European Union evolves into a more closely integrated political unit with foreign policy ambitions, Italy, rather like Britain, has found its traditional foreign policy orientation being called into question. Italy, under any government, would hate to have to choose between the United States and the European Union. Its behavior during the Iraq crisis was symptomatic of its embarrassment over this issue. Berlusconi, like Tony Blair, Spanish premier Jose Maria Aznar, and several premiers from Central and Eastern Europe, backed the United States' hard line during the crisis. But unlike Britain, Italy did not commit fighting troops and immediately worked to mend fences with France, Germany, and Belgium in the aftermath of the crisis. Italy's behavior during the Iraq crisis was, in fact, paradigmatic. In every crisis of the 1990s, whatever the political orientation of the government of the day, Italy has backed the United States after a tormented domestic debate in which the anti-Americanism of large swaths of public opinion was very clearly heard. This was true of the first Gulf conflict in 1991, when the then Andreotti government supported Desert Storm and even made a token military contribution to the coalition; it was also true of the Kosovo crisis in 1999, when the government headed by Massimo D'Alema, the first former communist to become premier, was initially reluctant to use force and distinctly skeptical of the idea of an independent Kosovo. When NATO intervened militarily, however, Italy fell into line. Whether this pro-NATO orientation will survive in the current Prodi administration is anybody's guess. The "Union" coalition contains at least three parties (Communist Refoundation, the Communists of Italy, and the Greens) that make Michael Moore seem like an apologist for the neoconservative foreign policy followed by the United States since 9/11.

Box 4.3   Thoughts About Europe and the United States

The relationship between the United States and the European Union has been a subject of lively debate in recent years in Italy. Here are two opposing views on the significance of the United States in the world today.

The West
Unity Between Europe and the United States
Let us work to unite, not divide, the peoples and states of Europe. Let us work to unite, not divide, Europe from the United States. The West is a single unit. The old continent and the new share an invisible charter of values that founds the natural order of life on the freedom of the individual. Let us work so that the European Union grows as coherent political force, as a protagonist on the international stage. . . . We are for a Union with its own defence and security policy. But such a policy should not be seen as an instrument for returning to a world of "competitive bipolarism" where the object of our rivalry is the United States. We see such a policy as a means to be able to take on, in partnership with the US, autonomous military and political burdens that hitherto Europe has not been able to shoulder. In our vision of the world Europe and the United States are bound to the same destiny.

(*Source:* Forza Italia, Carta dei valori. Le idee-chiave del nostro progetto.)

We have always distinguished between the American people and its government, between America and its administrations . . . you will not find a single writing, nor a transcription of a speech, a harangue, that is directed against America as a people, or a nation. . . . Only hagiographers of the Reagan-Bush era can accuse the left in Italy of congenital anti-Americanism. . . . But now we are living in an era of new capitalist globalization. This has had, and still has, its center in the United States. The U.S.'s military and economic role is overwhelming, and this gives it a guiding function in the process of globalization, even when this process is enduring a long period of economic crisis and consent like the present one. The United States is the promoter and agent of war on international scale. They are one side of the coin that has terrorism on the other side. The United States with its economic policy condemns millions of people to misery on our planet. With its policy toward energy consumption, and its refusal to sign the Kyoto protocol, it makes a determining contribution to the destruction of the national resources of the planet, to the point of calling the earth's very survival into question. With its refusal to adhere to tribunals of international justice, it excludes itself from any kind of judgment upon its actions and asserts the right to be a world police force free from any legitimate control over its actions.

(*Source:* Fausto Bertinotti, President of the Italian Chamber of Deputies, in *Liberazione europea*, May 30, 2004.)

In the 1990s, Italy achieved a high reputation for its skills in peacekeeping missions. Italian peacekeepers were active in southern Iraq until December 2006; this is just the latest of a series of missions in Afghanistan, Somalia, and elsewhere that have occupied thousands of Italian troops every year throughout the 1990s. After the United States and the United Kingdom, Italy is the third-largest contributor to UN-sponsored peacekeeping operations. In the spring of 1997, when Albania collapsed in the wake of a financial scandal and a wave of Albanian migration threatened to spill over into Italy, Italy initiated and led an EU "coalition of the willing" that restored order in Albania and brought about some measure of economic and political reconstruction.

As this book went to press, Italy was playing a similar role in supporting the UN-backed peacekeeping force in Lebanon. Italy sees peacekeeping in the Balkans and the Mediterranean as the essential task for a common European foreign policy, and believes that the EU could become an active regional player without jeopardizing its relations with the United States.

Last but not least, at any rate for the Italians, Italy has argued that its high profile in peacekeeping actions, together with its obvious economic importance, justifies its being included as a permanent member of the UN Security Council. Britain and France's possession of permanent seats at the UN rankles Germany, Japan, Brazil, and India as well as Italy, but there is no sign that Britain and France will decide to relinquish their places in favor of a single EU seat. In 1998, Italy successfully opposed a plan to enlarge the Security Council by including Germany, Japan, and three other places assigned permanently to Africa, Asia, and Latin America, and has since continued to press its own claims for a permanent seat.[23]

Italy's ambitions for a greater world role for herself and for Europe, however, only underscore the central theme of this chapter: the troubled nature of Italian democracy. Italy's economic achievements have been undeniable in the postwar years; its diplomacy is inventive and talented; and it has shown a tremendous and durable commitment to European integration. Nevertheless, it does not command the automatic respect that Britain, France, Germany, or even the Netherlands, Spain, and Sweden do. Why not? The answer surely is that Italy's political class and the Italian state inspire little confidence, either within Italy or without. Moreover, it appears that the collapse of the political system based upon Christian Democracy, far from being a new beginning for Italian democracy, has merely ushered in a new era in which political conflict has taken a new and dangerous path of mutual denigration and delegitimization. It is a telling fact about Italian democracy in 2007 that it seems quite unimaginable that a new Guareschi will appear to satirize both sides in the conflict and conduct an ironic quarrel either with the values and political style propagated by Berlusconi or with the antediluvian attitudes of some of the parties on the Italian left.

Notes

1. See Giovanni Guareschi, *The Don Camillo Omnibus*, London: Gollancz, 1974 for a comprehensive introduction in English to the *piccolo mondo*.

2. It should be noted, however, that the Court of Cassation (the High Court of Appeal) decreed in February 1948 that a distinction should be drawn between norms subject to immediate enforcement (*norme precettizie*) and those that were merely "programmatic." The more progressive norms of the constitution were ruled to fall into this latter category. See Martin J. Bull and James N. Newell, *Italian Politics: Adjustment Under Duress*, Cambridge: Polity, 2005, pp. 7–8.

3. Percy Allum, *Italy—Republic Without Government*, New York: Norton, 1973.

4. Works on Italy and foreign policy in English include: E. T. Smith, *The United States, Italy and NATO, 1947–1952*, London: Macmillan, 1992; G. Rabel, *Between East and West: Trieste, the United States and the Cold War*, Durham, NC: Duke University Press, 1988.

5. See John Van Oudenaran, *Détente in Europe: The Soviet Union in the West Since 1953*, Durham, NC: Duke University Press, 1991, pp. 260–268.

6. On Italy and European integration, see: Antonio Varsori, "Italy's Policy Towards European Integration 1947–1958," in Christopher Duggan and Christopher Wagstaff (eds.), *Italy in the Cold War: Politics, Culture and Society*, Oxford: Berg, 1995; F. Roy Willis, *Italy Chooses Europe*, Oxford: Oxford University Press, 1971; Francesca Fauri, *L'Italia e l'integrazione economica europea 1947–2000*, Bologna: Il Mulino, 2001.

7. In the earlier editions of this book, Patrick McCarthy brilliantly used the story of Pinocchio to illustrate this point. *Pinocchio*, as McCarthy points out, is more than a children's tale. It is also a parable about Italians' struggle to obtain social justice from the state and to create the instruments of citizenship.

8. The reference is to Arnaldo Bagnasco, *Tre Italie: la problematica territoriale dello sviluppo italiano*, Bologna: Il Mulino, 1977.

9. For the role of referenda in contemporary Italian political history, see Anna Chimenti, *Storia dei referendum*, Bari: Laterza, 1993.

10. For the full figures, see the excellent survey in Martin Bull and James N. Newell, *Italian Politics: Adjustment Under Duress*, Cambridge: Polity Press, pp. 28–35.

11. Giorgio Bocca, *La Disunità d'Italia*, Milan: Garzanti, 1990.

12. Giampaolo Pansa, *Il Regime*, Milan: Sperling & Kupfer, 1990; Sebastiano Messina, *Nomenklatura: come sopravvive in Italia la specie politica più antica nel mondo*, Milan: Mondatori, 1992.

13. For a detailed account in English of the June 9, 1991, referendum, see Mark Gilbert, *The Italian Revolution: The End of Politics, Italian Style*, Boulder, CO: Westview Press, 1995), chap. 6, pp. 87–105.

14. For the early days of the Lega Nord, see Anna Cento Bull and Mark Gilbert, *The Lega Nord and the Northern Question in Italian Politics*, London: Palgrave, 2001, pp. 9–41.

15. The literature on the end of the PCI is vast, even in English. However, David Kertzer, *Politics and Symbols: The Italian Communist Party and the Fall of Communism*, New Haven, CT: Yale University Press, 1996; and Leonard Weinberg, *The Transformation of*

Italian Communism, New Brunswick, NJ: Transaction Publishers, 1995, are both extremely useful. In Italian, Piero Ignazi, *Dal PCI al PDS*, Bologna: Il Mulino, 1992, is remarkable.

16. The fullest account of the 1992 elections is in Patrick McCarthy and Gianfranco Pasquino (eds.), *The End of Postwar Politics in Italy: The Landmark Elections of 1992*, Boulder, CO: Westview, 1993.

17. The accusations were the start of a ten-year legal odyssey for Andreotti. In November 2002, he was sentenced to twenty-four years' imprisonment for the murder of the journalist in question, Mino Pecorelli. This conviction was overturned on appeal in October 2003. In the same year, he was exonerated of having had links with the so-called new Mafia in the 1980s. The court nevertheless made clear its belief that Andreotti had used the Mafia to further his earlier political career. It did not have jurisdiction over this offense, however, since the statute of limitations had expired. Andreotti is today a regular guest on Italian TV and was the preferred candidate of the "House of Freedoms" for the presidency of the Senate in 2006.

18. For the transformation of the AN, see Piero Ignazi, *Extreme Right Parties in Europe*, Oxford: Oxford University Press, 2003, chap. 3, pp. 35–61.

19. These introductory paragraphs on Berlusconi contain material written by Patrick McCarthy in the second edition of this volume. Two books on Berlusconi have recently been published in English: Paul Ginsborg, *Silvio Berlusconi: Television, Power and Patrimony*, New York: Verso, 2005; and Alexander Stille, *Sack of Rome*, New York: Penguin, 2006.

20. See, in particular, Kenneth Dyson and Kevin Featherstone, "Italy and EMU as a 'vincolo esterno': Empowering the Technocrats, Transforming the State," *South European Society and Politics* 2, 1996, 272–299; Sergio Fabbrini (ed.), *L'europeizzazione d'Italia: L'impatto dell'Unione europea sulle istituzioni e le politiche italiane*, Bari: Laterza, 2003; Maurizio Ferrara and Elisabetta Gualmini, *Salvati dall'Europa?* Bologna: Il Mulino, 1999; Michele Salvati, "Moneta unica, rivoluzione copernicana," *Il Mulino*, January 1997, 5–23.

21. David Hine, "Silvio Berlusconi, i media e il conflitto di interesse," in Paolo Bellucci and Martin Bull (eds.), *Politica in Italia Edizione 2002*, Bologna: Il Mulino, 2002, pp. 291–307.

22. Berlusconi's legal difficulties are the subject of an interesting book in English: David Lane, *Berlusconi's Shadow: Crime, Justice and the Pursuit of Power*, London: Allen Lane, 2005.

23. For a useful survey of recent Italian foreign policy, see Osvaldo Croce, "Italian Security Policy after the Cold War," *Journal of Modern Italian Studies*, 8(2), summer 2003, 266–283.

Suggested Readings

Andrews, Geoff, *Not a Normal Country: Italy After Berlusconi*, Ann Arbor: Pluto Press, 2005.

Arlacchi, Pino, *Mafia Business: The Mafia Ethic and the Spirit of Capitalism*, Oxford: Oxford University Press, 1995.

Bufacchi, Vittorio, and V. Burgess, *Italy Since 1989: Events and Interpretations*, London: Palgrave, 2001.

Bull, Martin, and James N. Newell, *Italian Politics: Adjustment Under Duress*, Cambridge: Polity Press, 2005.

Cento Bull, Anna, and Mark Gilbert, *The Lega Nord and the Northern Question in Italian Politics*, London: Palgrave, 2001.

De Grand, Alexander, *The Italian Left in the Twentieth Century: A History of the Socialist and Communist Parties*, Bloomington: Indiana University Press, 1989.

Ferrera, Maurizio, and Elisabetta Gualmini, *Rescued by Europe? Social and Labour Market Reforms in Italy from Maastricht to Berlusconi*, Amsterdam: Amsterdam University Press, 2004.

Gilbert, Mark, *The Italian Revolution: The End of Politics, Italian Style?* Boulder, CO: Westview, 1995.

Ginsborg, Paul, *A History of Contemporary Italy: Society and Politics 1943–1988*, London: Penguin Books, 1990.

Ginsborg, Paul, *Italy and Its Discontents 1980–2001*, London: Allen Lane, 2001.

Gundle, Stephen, *Between Hollywood and Moscow: The Italian Communists and the Rise of Mass Culture*, Cambridge: Cambridge University Press, 1995.

Hellman, Stephen, *Italian Communism in Transition: The Rise and Fall of the Historic Compromise in Turin*, Oxford: Oxford University Press, 1989.

Hine, David, *Governing Italy: The Politics of Bargained Pluralism*, Oxford: Oxford University Press, 1993.

McCarthy, Patrick, *The Crisis of the Italian State*, New York: St. Martin's, 2001.

McCarthy, Patrick (ed.), *Italy Since 1945*, Oxford: Oxford University Press, 2000.

Pasquino, Gianfranco, "Italy: A Democratic Regime Under Reform," in Josep M. Colomer (ed.), *Political Institutions in Europe*, London: Routledge, 1996.

Pasquino, Gianfranco, and Patrick McCarthy (eds.), *The End of Postwar Politics: The Italian Elections of 1992*, Boulder, CO: Westview, 1993.

Sassoon, Donald, *Contemporary Italy: Politics, Economy and Society Since 1945*, London: Longman, 1997.

Zamagni, Vera, *The Economic History of Italy 1860–1990: Recovery After Decline*, Oxford: Clarendon Press, 1993.

CHAPTER 5

Scandinavia: Still the Middle Way?

Eric S. Einhorn and John Logue

SCANDINAVIA

Norway

Population (million):	4.6
Area in Square Miles:	125,050
Population Density per Square Mile:	37
GDP (in billion dollars, 2005):	$210.3
GDP per capita (PPP, 2005):	$45,512
Not a member of EC/EU; joined European Economic Area	1992

Performance of Key Political Parties in Parliamentary Elections of September 12, 2005

Centre [agrarian] Party (SP)	6.5%
Christian People's Party (KrF)	6.8%
Coast Party (Kyst)	0.8%
Conservative Party (H)	14.1%
Labour Party (DNA)	32.7%
Left Party (V)	5.9%
Progress Party (FrP)	22.1%
Socialist Left Party (SV)	8.7%

Main Office Holders: Prime Minister: Jens Stoltenberg—DNA (2005); Head of State: King Harald V

Sweden

Population (million):	9.0
Area in Square Miles:	173,730
Population Density per Square Mile:	52
GDP (in billion dollars, 2005):	$286.1
GDP per capita (PPP, 2005):	$31,691
Joined EC/EU	January 1, 1995

Performance of Key Political Parties in Parliamentary Elections of September 17, 2006

Centre [agrarian] Party (C)	7.9%
Christian Democrats (KD)	6.6%
Green Party (MP)	5.2%
Left Party (V)	5.8%
Liberal People's Party (FP)	7.5%
Moderates (M)	26.2%
Social Democrats (SD)	35.0%

Main Office Holders: Prime Minister: Fredrik Reinfeldt—M (2006); Head of State: King Carl XVI Gustaf

Denmark

Population (million):	5.4
Area in Square Miles:	16,637
Population Density per Square Mile:	326
GDP (in billion dollars, 2005):	$186.2
GDP per capita (PPP, 2005):	$34,367
Joined EC/EU	January 1, 1973

Performance of Key Political Parties in Parliamentary Elections of February 8, 2005

Danish People's Party (DF)	13.2%
Unity List—The Red Greens (ERG)	3.4%
Conservative People's Party (KF)	10.3%
Christian People's Party (KrF)	1.7%
Radical Liberal (RV)	9.2%
Social Democracy in Denmark (SD)	25.9%
Socialist People's Party (SF)	6%
Liberal [agrarian] Party of Denmark (VD)	29.1%

Main Office Holders: Prime Minister: Anders Fogh Rasmussen—VD (2001); Head of State: Queen Margrethe II

Finland

Population (million):	5.2
Area in Square Miles:	130,560
Population Density per Square Mile:	40
GDP (in billion dollars, 2005):	$164.5
GDP per capita (PPP, 2005):	$31,367
Joined EC/EU	January 1, 1995

Performance of Key Political Parties in Parliamentary Elections of March 16, 2003

Christian Democrats (KD)	5.3%
Finnish Centre [agrarian] Party (Kesk)	24.7%
Finnish Social Democratic Party (SD)	24.5%
Green Party (Vihr)	8.0%
Left Wing Alliance (Vas)	9.9%
Conservative Party (Kok)	18.5%
Swedish People's Party (RKP/SFP)	4.6%
True Finns Party (PS)	1.6%

Main Office Holders: Prime Minister: Matti Vanhanen—Kesk (2003); President: Tarja Halonen—SD (2000)

The Rise and Fall of the Scandinavian "Middle Way"

The Scandinavian "middle way" first attracted international attention in the 1930s at the depths of the Great Depression, coinciding with an era when the fragile foundations of democracy were crumbling across Europe. Industrial capitalism based on "free markets," as well as the still-shallow roots of political democracy, were threatened by a rising fascist tide on the right and a brutal but, for many on the left, attractive communist model in the Soviet Union. President Franklin D. Roosevelt's 1933 perception of "a third of the nation, ill-clothed, ill-fed, and ill-housed" described most of the industrialized world. Out of this chaos came a unique welfare-state model in Denmark, Norway, and Sweden, offering a "middle way" between these extremes. It developed over time and out of an accumulation of experience. But if you have to pick a "birthday," January 30, 1933, is our choice.

Copenhagen was cold and foggy in its mid-winter gloom. The political and economic situation was as bleak as the weather. Fully 40 percent of Danish wage earners—two out of five—were out of work in this gray third winter of the Great Depression.

The Danish Employers Federation had announced that it would lock out all union members still working on February 1 to enforce its demand on the unions for a 20 percent wage reduction. Farm mortgage foreclosures, following a general collapse of agricultural prices, cast a long shadow in the countryside. The Danish Social Democratic prime minister, Thorvald Stauning—a former cigar worker who had led the government briefly in the 1920s and formed another government with the center-left Radical Liberals in 1929 on the eve of the Depression—called an extraordinary Sunday-morning parliamentary session. The agenda was legislation to extend the national labor contract under which the unions worked, thus to stave off economic disaster. Behind closed doors, the government negotiated with the Agrarians and Radical Liberals to provide the necessary votes on the bill's third reading the following day. When an acceptable compromise could not be reached, Prime Minister Stauning invited the negotiators home for what turned out to be a historic bargaining session.

The agreement that emerged in the predawn hours of January 30 in Stauning's modest apartment in a city-owned housing block on Kanslergade called for four major actions:

1. an extension of the existing labor agreements without wage reductions;
2. a massive public works program to put the unemployed back to work and to provide winter relief for their families;
3. a devaluation of the currency to stimulate farm exports and agricultural price supports to stabilize farm incomes; and

4. a fundamental restructuring of the Danish patchwork of social insurance and poverty relief measures into a comprehensive program.

The exhausted cabinet members and Agrarian Liberal Party leadership announced the agreement to parliament and struggled through Monday evening to finish putting the deal together. Without realizing it, these Danish politicians were founding what would become known as the Scandinavian middle way.

This was, however, not the only portentous political event of January 30. South of the Danish border that same Monday, the German president, Paul von Hindenburg, facing the Weimar Republic's collapse into economic depression and political extremism, summoned a controversial, untried party leader to form a new government. The recipient of von Hindenburg's confidence was Adolf Hitler.

THE MEANING OF THE MIDDLE WAY

Hitler's Third Reich engulfed Europe in flames during the next decade, but it collapsed finally under its own aggressive and self-destructive impulses. The hard-won Danish "Kanslergade Compromise," by contrast, set the pattern for the modern Scandinavian welfare states that have far outlasted Nazism.

The Kanslergade Compromise called for wide-ranging state intervention to manage the market economy. The government became involved in setting wages and agricultural prices, establishing credit and exchange policy, and putting the unemployed back to work. It created a comprehensive economic security net for the unemployed and for all those out of the labor market. And, as a compromise between Social Democrats, Radical Liberals, and Agrarians, it broadened and cemented the center of the political spectrum.

In a way, events in Germany that day changed the very complexion of democratic politics in Scandinavia. Before Hitler's assumption of power, the Scandinavian Social Democrats—by far the largest party in Denmark, Norway, and Sweden—could reasonably strive to win a majority on their own to enact a socialist program, with the political polarization that would ensue. In Finland the Social Democrats had emerged from a civil war in a tie with the Agrarians for the largest percentage of the vote. But with Hitler's rise to power in the Weimar Republic, the handwriting was on the wall: compromise among democratic parties was vital.

As Hitler consolidated his power by crushing the German Social Democrats, the Communist Party, and the independent trade unions, in Sweden a new Social Democratic government quickly followed the Danish example by agreeing with center parties on minimum farm prices and a public works program to create jobs for the unemployed. The Norwegian Labor Party struck a similar deal with its Agrarian Party in 1935.

A compromise across the dividing line between socialist and "bourgeois" parties was a kind of defeat for the Scandinavian socialist and social democratic parties because it postponed indefinitely the achievement of true socialism. But cooperation did solidify democratic politics in a situation that threatened the very existence of social democracy.

Thereafter, Scandinavian compromise became much more than a tactic; it grew to be seen as virtuous in itself because it solidified a broad national consensus around democracy. The social democratic welfare state, interventionist and protective of the people, became a surrogate for socialism. Its principle was to achieve redistribution and broadly shared prosperity through compromises acceptable to the nonsocialist center parties. Moreover, compromise worked: state intervention in the collapsing market economy began to stabilize farm income, put the unemployed back to work, reduce conflict in the labor market, and offer hope to the Scandinavian peoples in despair over the Depression and the threat of German aggression.

Right and left faced off despite the Nazi threat in countries such as France. But in Scandinavia, a "national democratic compromise" started building what the Swedish Social Democratic prime minister, Per Albin Hansson, called "the people's home": a society that took care of all its citizens.

This Scandinavian model—an interventionist state managing the market economy toward a combination of growth, full employment, and large-scale welfare programs supported by agreement between employers and unions—was widely followed subsequently in Western Europe. In fact, it was the precursor of the Western European "postwar Keynesian consensus" after World War II. In the 1930s the U.S. journalist Marquis Childs (*Sweden: The Middle Way* [1936]) dubbed the Scandinavian accord "the middle way"—meaning a middle or third way between "savage" capitalism—i.e., the failed capitalism of the Depression era in the West—and Stalinist communism, the totalitarian regime then reigning in Russia.

After the war, the Scandinavian democracies continued to constitute a middle way in the Cold War ideological and geopolitical conflict, both in domestic and foreign policy terms. For many in the West (including the United States) the Scandinavian middle way was extremely attractive. A leading U.S. journalist, William L. Shirer, for example, in *The Challenge of Scandinavia* (1955), updated Childs's account to describe the region's blend of capitalism with a social conscience; private production would support full employment and an expanding social welfare network, and it would reduce social and economic inequalities.

In domestic policy, Denmark, Norway, and Sweden built advanced capitalist market economies in which the state played both a regulatory and a redistributive role. Under predominantly Social Democratic governments, the state's role for a generation was far greater than in almost all of the other Western, capitalist democracies, although policy innovations in Scandinavia often set the pattern for policies elsewhere on the Continent ten or twenty years later.

During the Cold War, the Scandinavians sought a middle way in foreign policy as well. Although strong supporters of the United Nations, they recognized quickly its limitations. Efforts to fashion a Scandinavian defense union that would provide a viable military foundation for neutrality broke down in 1949, and on Scandinavia's western fringes, Denmark, Norway, and Iceland joined the North Atlantic Treaty Organization (NATO), although they often seemed reluctant members. Finland, which had fought World War II on the German side, signed a separate peace agreement with the Soviet Union in 1944; its neutrality was guaranteed by treaty. Sweden continued to pursue a neutrality policy that had kept it out of war since 1815. Defense strategists wrote of a "Nordic balance," in which Swedish neutrality between NATO in the west and the Warsaw Pact in the east guaranteed Finnish neutrality and independence vis-à-vis the Soviet Union and permitted Denmark and Norway to pursue a strategy of lowering tensions on the northern flank of NATO by refusing to allow foreign troops or nuclear weapons on their territory.

In international economic affairs, there was balance as well. Denmark joined the European Community (now the European Union) when Britain did in 1973, albeit reluctantly; the Norwegians, even more reluctant, voted narrowly against joining Europe. Sweden and Finland held that joining the European Community would compromise their neutrality. All four distinguished themselves by supporting international cooperation that reached across the dividing lines between east and west and between north and south.

Finland developed differently between World War I and World War II— primarily because of the bitter civil war between the "Whites" and the "Reds" in 1917–1918 that the conservative Whites won. Yet in the post–World War II period, Finland came increasingly to resemble the rest of the Scandinavian area in the realm of domestic politics, as it caught up in terms of industrialization, welfare, and living standards. Even its peculiar international position gradually assumed a more Scandinavian "balance."

All this changed at the end of the 1980s. With the end of Soviet dominance of Eastern Europe and the collapse of the USSR itself in 1991, the Scandinavian countries found their middle way questioned anew. What was it a middle way between?

The middle way that had served the Scandinavian countries so well domestically and internationally from the 1930s into the 1980s became confused amid economic crises and globalization, along with political discord at home. Sweden and Finland opted for EU membership and closer ties to Europe in 1995. The middle way's extensive public services, high taxes, and state regulation of the market economy were challenged as well by international economic integration and the growing predominance of free-market thinking. New interest groups and social changes, including new roles for women, an aging population, and significant non-European immigration, challenged the consensus.

The rest of this chapter analyzes the rise and fall of the Scandinavian model in domestic politics, in European integration policy, and in foreign policy generally.

A Social Laboratory

The Nordic countries are idiosyncratic in many ways. They are small in terms of population (see the data on pages 162–163). With the exception of Iceland (with a quarter of a million inhabitants), they are roughly comparable to medium-sized U.S. states. When compared to other members of the European Union, Sweden is about the size of Greece or Portugal; only Ireland and Luxembourg are smaller than Denmark and Finland.

Denmark, Iceland, Norway, and Sweden share common roots ethnically, linguistically, and culturally; and Finland—despite its distinct ethnic and linguistic origins—shares a common Nordic history and religion with them. Further, Denmark, Iceland, Norway, and Sweden also were distinguished by remarkable internal ethnic, racial, religious, and linguistic homogeneity. This aspect of Scandinavian societies, more than any other, made the development of the solidaristic Scandinavian model possible.

Until they began to receive a substantial flow of immigrants in the 1960s, 97 to 99 percent of the population of each country shared the same cultural, linguistic, and racial roots. About 95 percent of the populations were Lutheran and belonged to the state church. As a consequence, politics and policy in all three countries focused for decades to a unique degree on economic and class issues rather than the religious, linguistic, and ethnic conflicts that often dominate other societies. However, a generation of immigration, much of it from non-European countries, has literally changed the face of Denmark, Norway, and Sweden. Today, more than one in ten Swedish residents were born abroad. For the first time in more than a century, "ethnic" and immigration issues have become a source of political conflict.

Historically, Finland has been substantially more divided domestically than its Scandinavian neighbors. The legacy of Swedish settlement and rule until 1809 and of Russian rule from 1809 to 1917 left a significant Swedish-speaking population on the southwest coast of Finland and a considerable Russian Orthodox religious minority. Moreover, Finland was torn by a bitter civil war in 1917–1918 between Reds and Whites. The former were radical socialists who sought to emulate Lenin's Bolshevik revolution; the latter were a coalition of primarily antiradical nationalists. The Finnish Whites, backed by German troops, won the war and interned their opponents in concentration camps for a number of years. Half a century later, how Finns voted in national elections still was closely tied to which side of the civil war their grandfathers had fought on. Unlike Denmark, Norway, and Sweden—where the communists played a major role only immediately after World War I and World War II—the Finnish labor movement was split down the middle between communists and social democrats by the civil war and its aftermath. This division prevented the social democratic dominance in Finland that Denmark, Norway, and Sweden witnessed in the 1930s.

Box 5.1   Why Do the Scandinavian Welfare States Survive?

One mystery to Americans is how political support for the Scandinavian welfare states survives when ordinary working people have to pay 50 percent to 60 percent of their earnings in income and other taxes. When their taxes come due, why don't they rise up in anger and overthrow the government? After all, American taxpayers have rebelled at far lower rates.

The answer is, first, that the Scandinavian welfare states rest on the principle of *solidarity*. By contrast, welfare programs in the United States rest on the principle of social insurance (Social Security, Medicare, workers' compensation, unemployment insurance) or altruism (charity to the poor). The limit of social insurance is that we agree to insure ourselves against only those risks that we cannot afford, and altruism is even more circumscribed, limited to keeping the bodies and souls of the poor together. But solidarity—defined as "reciprocal responsibility and mutual obligation"—has permitted the Scandinavians to build far more elaborate structures of mutual support on a consensual basis.

Second, Scandinavian welfare measures are generally *universal* in scope, rather than means-tested. Thus both transfer payments (such as pensions, sick pay, maternity pay, family allowances) and social services (such as medical and dental care, home assistance for the elderly, free education through college, and day care and after-school care for children) are available to everyone in the category, whether they are poor, working class, or middle class. Transfer payments are usually taxed, so the post-tax benefit to the best-off is much less than the benefit to the worst-off. Fees for some social services, such as day care, also rise with income. But generally speaking everyone is in the same system and receives the same benefits. Every year, almost every family receives some benefits. As a witty phrase describes the situation, "the richest 90 percent help support the poorest 90 percent."

Such universal programs are costly. Scandinavian public spending on social security transfer payments is 20 percent to 40 percent higher than elsewhere in Europe.[1] Rising take-up rates for social services such as day care and after-school care have continued to push up social welfare spending despite the financial constraints on public-sector spending. More disturbing, the self-restraint of the older generation about utilizing the welfare net is giving way to a culture of "entitlement" among the younger generation. Thus in Denmark, for example, statistics indicate that the young are sicker than the old, even taking into account legitimate reasons, such as taking care of ill children. Still, universal public provision of social services generally provides a higher standard and is cheaper than provision through employer-funded, private insurance schemes. The classic case is medical care, which is both far more costly (by about 70 percent) in the United States as a proportion of gross domestic product and less adequately distributed than in Scandinavia. Consequently, the Scandinavian countries' health statistics (infant mortality, life span, etc.) beat the United States by a wide margin. Likewise the "top 1 percent" in Scandinavia earn three or four times the median income, and not ten or more times as in the United States. Typical middle-class incomes are very similar to the U.S. level, while low-income groups in Scandinavia have a substantially higher living standard than in the United States: after-tax, after-benefit poverty rates in Scandinavia are only about a quarter of the U.S. rate.

Everyone pays, but everyone also benefits.

---

1. Accounting definitions make exact comparison difficult. Overall social expenditures in Germany, Belgium, and the Netherlands are roughly comparable to Scandinavia, with France not far behind. See William Adema and Maxime Ladaique, "Net Social Expenditure," 2005 ed., *OECD Social, Employment and Migration Working Papers No. 29* (OECD, 2005).

Geopolitical proximity to "big brother" Russia shaped the Finns' national political agenda. Finland by itself fought a brave but doomed war against Russia in the winter of 1939–1940. Then, after Germany invaded the Soviet Union in June 1941, Finland reentered the war on the German side, exiting with a separate peace treaty in 1944. Russia held a major naval base on Finnish soil covering the approaches to Helsinki until 1956.

In the postwar period, the decline in the Swedish minority through assimilation and emigration to Sweden has diminished traditional ethnic and linguistic divisions, and memories of the Finnish civil war have gradually faded. Migration into Finland has been much less than that seen in most Western European countries. And, of course, Finland's dangerous situation vis-à-vis Russia changed dramatically with the Soviet Union's collapse. In the last thirty years, Finnish politics has converged increasingly with the general Scandinavian social democratic model.[1]

DOMESTIC POLITICS: HOW DIFFERENT IS SCANDINAVIA?

Its location on the geographical fringe of Europe has meant that the Scandinavian countries have escaped some European developments entirely, while lagging behind on others.

Throughout most of the nineteenth century, the Scandinavians trailed western Europe in both industrial and political development. Industrialization came late, beginning only about 1855 in Denmark, 1890 in Sweden, and 1905 in Norway—a full century after England, Germany, Belgium, and France. Viewing nineteenth-century European political development in terms of three central themes—constitutionalism, nationalism, and democracy—the Scandinavians lagged behind in all but the first, with Sweden's strong state and well-established constitutional traditions and Norway's 1814 Constitution remaining the oldest written European constitution still in force. Nationalism first became a major impulse in Denmark following its confrontations with German nationalism along its southern boundary after 1848 and the loss of Denmark's German duchies in 1864.[2] Norway enjoyed a national cultural revival in the 1880s, and its confrontation with Sweden over full independence in 1905 sharpened national feelings in both countries. Political democracy (parliamentary supremacy) came even more slowly: 1884 in Norway, 1901 in Denmark, and 1917 in Sweden and Finland.

Late development in these spheres meant that the economic basis for liberalism developed late. The agrarian and labor movements, which began in Scandinavia as elsewhere in Europe in the latter half of the nineteenth century, swept through the countryside and the new industrial towns like a prairie fire. Organizing in a virtual vacuum, the "popular movements" of family farmers and industrial workers built their own economic and political organizations, which claimed the high ground of an egalitarian response to industrialization and political democracy. Thanks to the high literacy levels encouraged by Lutheranism and by state educational policies in the eighteenth and early nineteenth centuries, the democratic popular movements were led from below, and the tie between the leaders and the led remains close even today.[3]

Even as the Scandinavians lagged behind Europe in many areas in the eighteenth and nineteenth centuries, they led in one: the strong state. The Swedes developed in the sixteenth and seventeenth centuries what was probably the most modern state in Europe in terms of its capacity to govern, and Swedish military prowess from the Thirty Years War through Charles XII's misadventures in Russia reflected both the state's strength and the success of state-sponsored development of military industries. By the time of the establishment of modern political organizations and democratic institutions in the last part of the nineteenth century, the Scandinavians had a well-established tradition of a strong state and a professional civil service. The right saw the strong state as good in itself; the left, as a tool for reform.

These three factors—relative isolation, powerful popular movements, and a strong state—created the conditions for the Scandinavian middle way in the twentieth century.

Social Democracy and European Development: Success, Then Crisis

More than any other single factor, what set Scandinavian politics and policy apart was the predominant role played by the "popular movements"—farmers and labor—that represent the economically disenfranchised. Organizing from below in a virtual political vacuum in the latter half of the nineteenth century, farm and labor organizations swept the countryside, towns, and cities in an evangelical wave. In addition to the creation of the agrarian and labor parties, which came to be the great bearers of the democratic tradition, they created an immense economic and cultural infrastructure.

For the agrarian movement, the economic infrastructure was in the form of purchasing, processing, and marketing cooperatives that created the economies of scale that enabled family farmers to compete with the great estates. The cultural side was provided by the "folk colleges" that educated generation after generation of farm youth between the harvest in the fall and planting in the spring, the community centers in the countryside that offered everything from weekly dances to study circles and political debates, and the agrarian newspapers that preached egalitarianism in a class-bound society.

For labor, it was the trade unions in the crafts and industries; consumer cooperatives for everything from food to clothing to housing to funerals; every

kind of cultural group from chess clubs and marching bands to scouts, kinder-
gartens, and adult education; and social democratic newspapers, which were the
first Scandinavian mass-circulation papers.

Both agrarian and labor movements shared certain central values. These
included egalitarianism, a belief in democracy, and a strong commitment to
building their own institutions. Allied in the struggle for political democracy,
farmers and workers had much that united them even when ideology—private
property versus socialization of the means of production—divided them. It is
not inconsequential that the Danish Social Democrats adopted land reform and
support for small farmers as their agrarian policy in the 1890s, much to the cha-
grin of the more orthodox German Social Democrats who were otherwise the
Danes' mentors.

This massive political organization preceded the establishment of parliamentary democracy everywhere except Norway, where it coincided with the
democratic breakthrough. Because numbers had not counted previously in politics, the conservatives had never taken the trouble to organize. Consequently,
they found themselves playing catch-up after the agrarian radicals' and labor
movement's ideas had already won adherents from their tenants in the countryside and servants in the cities.

Scandinavian popular movements were most remarkable in the degree to
which they drew their leadership from the ranks of the movement itself, rather
than from the educated elite. The liberal agrarian parties were led predominantly by farmers and the labor parties by workers—not lawyers, teachers, civil
servants, or priests. This kept them honest. Government for the people works
best when it is by the people and of the people.

The combination of democracy from below—of leaders sprung from and
tied to the organizations of those they lead—with relative ethnic and religious
homogeneity, overarching agreement of basic values, and relatively small communities, offers powerful drivers for a cohesive, solidaristic welfare state based,
as one turn-of-the-century trade union tract put it, on the principle of "reciprocal obligation or mutual responsibility."

Despite such advantages, nineteenth-century Scandinavia was a poor, class-
ridden, and static region, as reflected in the waves of immigration to North America that also contributed to rapid social changes. Millions of Swedes and
Norwegians as well as many Danes and Finns simply left for new opportunities.
At first this removed considerable political and economic pressure, but later it
stimulated interest in social, economic, and political reforms even among national
conservatives. Knowledge of better economic opportunities abroad and the success of democratic government in North America and later Britain encouraged
domestic reformers in both the labor and agrarian movements. Nationalists
recoiled at the loss of youthful and energetic citizens.

Out of these conflicts emerged a civil society of the strongest sort. Citizens
in the popular movements connected in a myriad of voluntary associations that

mediated between them and the state and also provided direct economic, cultural, and social benefits. Organizing successfully around these associations, popular movements ultimately also captured state power. The state was transformed, beginning in the 1930s, to offer many of the benefits that the voluntary organizations had themselves previously provided. In the last thirty years, the welfare, educational, and regulatory functions of the popular-movement organizations were transferred to public administration, and many of the social and cultural functions previously provided by the popular-movement organizations were taken over by local and national government and provided by public employees instead of movement members. This generalized those social services to all the people, but it removed them from control from below. This also left the popular movements—especially the social democratic labor movement—dependent on control of the state to achieve their objectives.

For a half century, this approach was remarkably successful. The existence of a strong state and the tradition of an honest and professional civil service offered the mechanism for building a more egalitarian society. Principles of Keynesian economics advocating job-creating public programs were independently developed by Scandinavian economists during the Depression. Cautiously applied, they offered a route to use the state to improve the performance of capitalist market economies. The combination of the two provided the means to solve the classic problem of industrial capitalism—great and pervasive poverty amid great wealth—without revolution, by a lasting commitment to spread growth more equally than the existing distribution of wealth and income. That commitment lay at the core of the Kanslergade Compromise and the subsequent, similar national compromises in Norway and Sweden. It was driven forward politically by the Social Democrats with what proved to be a virtually unparalleled grasp on power in democratic elections.

Within the lifetime of a single generation, this commitment transformed Scandinavia from a region of great poverty—characterized by the immigrants' "flight to America"—into societies of widely shared affluence. The image of "the fortified poorhouse," as the title of Zeth Höglund's book characterized the Sweden of 1913, gave way to Per Albin Hansson's view of Sweden as "the people's home" in the 1930s as class struggle gave way to national construction under social democratic government. By the 1960s, Sweden and Norway, which had been among the poorest European countries some fifty years earlier, were among the most affluent. The slums and poverty were gone.

The Scandinavian success relied on the use of the state to achieve broad economic goals, and that rested on the assumption that the nation-state was the relevant unit for economic policy. That certainly was true following the collapse of the international trading system in the 1930s, which was anomalous given Scandinavia's long global trading history. It was equally true in the reconstruction after World War II. But by the 1960s and 1970s, as growing national affluence transformed the lives of the working class, the Scandinavian countries once again become fully enmeshed in an interdependent global trading system. This development accelerated prosperity but brought vulnerability to the oil crises of the 1970s and the ever more invasive global business cycle.[4]

Political Democracy Scandinavian Style

Denmark, Norway, and Sweden share a great deal in terms of political structures and political actors. Finland is different historically, but it has converged on the other three countries in the postwar period.[5] Much of what they have in common stems from their similarities in terms of cohesion, as discussed earlier. Some of it stems from their close ties in the Nordic Council and various European organizations, which facilitated diffusion of political ideas. The Scandinavian labor movements and the Social Democratic Parties have interacted especially closely over the years.

POLITICAL INSTITUTIONS

All four countries are parliamentary democracies. All are clearly democratic in the sense that regular elections determine who holds political office and what policies are made. All are parliamentary systems in the sense that parliament—the legislative body—is the most important branch of government.

Denmark and Sweden are pure parliamentary systems. The legislative majority selects the executive (the prime minister and the cabinet) and can force the executive out by a vote of "no confidence." In both cases, parliament is the ultimate arbiter of the constitutionality of its own legislation, although a variety of checks are imposed on parliamentary abuses of power, as we will discuss. In neither country do courts review the constitutionality of parliamentary legislation, as the U.S. Supreme Court does, but their membership in the EU has injected substantial portions of EU law into their national legal systems. National courts enforce these European laws.

Norway also is a parliamentary democracy, but it has a modest tradition of judicial review, and the Norwegian Constitution, dating back to 1814, prevents calling early elections, which is otherwise a standard characteristic of parliamentary government.

Finland has a mixed presidential-parliamentary form of government, not unlike that of France in the Fifth Republic. The president, who heads the executive branch, is directly elected by a popular vote (prior to 1994, Finnish law provided for indirect election) for a six-year term and directs foreign policy, commands the armed forces, and can dissolve parliament. A new constitution entered into force in 2000, and it clarified and strengthened the primacy of the prime minister and the cabinet, which are selected by the parliament. Together the executive cabinet, led by the prime minister, and parliament share primary responsibility for domestic and EU affairs. Parliament can force the cabinet from office by a vote of "no confidence." In practice this division has made the prime minister the most important part of the executive branch in terms of policymaking, but there certainly were times during the Cold War when the president's role overshadowed that of his prime minister. There is no national judicial review of the constitutionality of legislation, but again national courts frequently enforce the supremacy of EU law.

Despite the multiparty system—today seven to ten or more parties are represented in the national parliaments—and the rarity of single-party majorities, the Scandinavians have had stable and effective government because they practice what Dankwart Rustow called "the politics of compromise" in his 1955 classic of that name (*The Politics of Compromise: A Study of Parties and Cabinet Government in Sweden*). Scandinavian government is coalition government, sometimes through multiparty governments and at other times through bargains worked out in parliament between a minority government and other parties whose agreement has been attained on an issue-by-issue basis.

Although Denmark and Sweden maintained an upper house of parliament until 1953 and 1970, respectively, all four now elect a unicameral—single-house—parliament. The Norwegian parliament (Stortinget), divides into two bodies to consider certain types of legislation, although most proceedings take place in the plenary parliament. In all parliaments, much of the detailed legislative and oversight work and most of the necessary multiparty compromises are worked out in standing committees. There are usually parliamentary committees for each governmental ministry, plus some with special competency (constitutional affairs or relations with the European Union). Parties are represented on committees in proportion to their overall strength, but coalitions are usually required for any significant actions. Most proceedings are in secret, precisely to encourage interparty compromises, but occasional hearings are held publicly and there are increasing demands to "open up" the parliamentary processes to greater media scrutiny.

In all four countries, a proportional representation system is used in electing parliament. Thus, all parties of significant size are represented in parliament with approximately the same proportion of seats as they have support among voters. Although proportional representation was introduced in an existing multiparty system and stabilized it for a number of decades, as new lines of division—including those over the European Union, the environment, and immigration—have come to the fore in recent years, this election system has permitted growing fragmentation in parliament.

The basic principle of parliamentary democracy—that the prime minister and the executive branch are responsible to the majority in the house of parliament with the broadest suffrage—was established in 1884 in Norway, while the country was still under Swedish rule; in 1901 in Denmark; and in 1917 in Sweden. Finland established the same principle in 1917 with independence from Russia, but the losing side in the civil war was pretty much excluded from politics during the 1920s.

Denmark, Norway, and Sweden remain *constitutional monarchies*. Scandinavian monarchs took office within constitutional limits (Karl Johan in Sweden in 1809 and Norway in 1815; Haakon VII in Norway in 1905) or accepted them with relative grace (Frederik VII in Denmark in 1849). They proved more resistant to yielding the power to choose the prime minister to the elected parliamentary majority (1884 in Norway, 1901 in Denmark, and 1917 in Sweden), but here, too, they bowed to the winds of change. Although the governmental power of the Scandinavian monarchs is virtually nil today, they remain important symbols of national unity, above the lines of party or division by interest. In times of crisis, this symbolic role has had real political significance.

In Finland, the president has the symbolic role played by the monarchs as well as a more practical role in foreign policy. Although elected with a partisan affiliation, the Finnish president stands above party lines while in office. For more than fifty years (1939–1991) the presidents assumed a special role in managing relations with the USSR. This also enhanced presidential internal political powers.

All four countries have *unitary*, rather than federal, governments in the sense that all sovereignty resides in the national government, and the powers of the provinces and other subunits of government are derived from the national government. However, Finland provides far-reaching local autonomy for the Swedish-speaking Åland Islands, and Denmark provides even greater autonomy for Greenland and the Faeroe Islands, which have been granted the status of near independence. The Faeroes never joined the European Community, and Greenland, which acquired autonomy in 1979, quickly used its independence to withdraw from the European Community—the only territory to date to do so. In the past decade both have grown increasingly impatient with their ties to Denmark, but with no substitute in sight for the large budgetary subsidies that are sent from Copenhagen, the status quo will continue for a while longer.

Although power is clearly concentrated in the hands of the national government, many governmental services have been delegated to municipal and county government. Thus, most social services, including education, medical care, hospitals, and services for children, families, and the elderly, are provided by municipalities. Indeed, a higher proportion of governmental spending occurs at the local level in Scandinavia than at the state and local levels in the United States. Thus, within unitary states, the Scandinavians have thoroughly decentralized the provision of governmental services.

In order to make this decentralization effective, Denmark, Norway, and Sweden undertook similar consolidations of local government in the late 1960s and early 1970s. The consequence was to cut the number of local governments by half in Norway, three-fourths in Sweden, and four-fifths in Denmark. (In Finland, a similar consolidation was blocked, and the number of local administrations was reduced only by about a sixth in this period.) Generally speaking these reforms were successful in establishing the capacity to expand social services in smaller towns and rural areas, but they undercut the relationship between citizens and their government in rural districts. Although the density of elected officials remains high in Scandinavia by comparison to most other democracies, it is much diminished in comparison to the past.

Local and regional governments enjoy substantial taxing powers, but their dependence on budgetary transfers from the central government and the standardization of social, educational, and other local services has constrained their autonomy. Another major consolidation of local and regional governments is scheduled for 2007 in Denmark and under discussion in Norway.

One striking aspect of Scandinavian politics is the degree to which government and the civil service are seen as national resources. This is a result of a convergence of causes. Scandinavian conservatives have traditionally supported a strong state as an instrument of national development. Popular movements, including especially the social democratic labor movement, have seen the government as a mechanism to generalize their egalitarian goals to the entire society. General antigovernment or antistate movements have always been weak. The distrust of government that we see across the political spectrum in the United States has generally been absent in Scandinavia. Furthermore, Scandinavian public administration generally has been deserving of citizen respect: its bureaucrats have been self-effacing, efficient, and honest.

However, that popular belief in the benevolence of public administration does not extend to the transnational public-policy dimension. The European Union's multitudinous rules and regulations frequently strike most Scandinavians as downright arcane. For example, the European Union promulgated measures regulating the size of strawberries and curvature of cucumbers shortly before the 1992 Danish referendum on the Maastricht Treaty; an effort to harmonize the dimensions of condoms, however, foundered on Italian opposition. One acerbic Danish placard during this referendum put it succinctly: "If you think there are already enough idiots running your life, vote no!" As EU regulations become targets for public ridicule and additional policy responsibilities shift from national capitals to distant EU institutions, the problem of the "democratic deficit" will become more acute.

POLITICAL ACTORS

Scandinavian democracy historically has been based on strong, disciplined, mass-membership parties, which organize hundreds of thousands of voters as dues-paying party members. Parties have structured political competition at the local as well as the national level. They provided channels for recruiting political leaders; the career pattern was to start by running for the local municipal council. Municipal office or parliament followed for those who proved themselves. Regular local party meetings ensured close contacts between the elected officials and their party constituency. Because the parties offered different policy choices in the election campaigns, they allowed citizens a means to control not just the people in government but also the policies of government. Problematic for democratic participation has been an accelerating decline in party memberships. Social Democratic Parties, which no longer automatically enroll union members, account for much of this decline, but all traditional parties have been hit.

The parties have been complemented by equally strong interest groups that organize workers, farmers, and employers. These groups, which we will look at, have typically been closely linked to individual parties. The unions have traditionally been Social Democratic (except in Finland, where they were hotly contested by the Communists), the farmer organizations have been the mainstays of the agrarian parties, and the employers have typically had a looser association with the Conservatives. Unlike many Western countries, Scandinavian labor unions have maintained their remarkably high memberships (often over 80 percent of blue- and white-collar employees). While most are rather passive members, organized labor remains a strong political actor.

PARTIES AND PARTY SYSTEMS

From the origins of parliamentary democracy at the turn of the century to the 1970s, the predominant pattern in all four countries was the five- or six-party system. On the right was the Conservative Party, which had been late to organize a mass base because it had wielded the levers of power on behalf of the elites and propertied classes before the democratic breakthrough. In the center were the nineteenth-century proponents of democracy: the Liberals and the Agrarians. To the left of center were the Social Democrats, their junior allies in the nineteenth-century push for democracy. The Social Democrats outgrew the coalition by the mid-1920s and typically polled about 40 to 45 percent of the vote from the 1930s through the 1970s. On the extreme left were the radical socialists—Communists from the 1920s through the late 1950s—and the Socialist People's Parties, which displaced the Communists in the late 1950s and early 1960s in Denmark and Norway. The remaining communists in Sweden and Finland became increasingly independent of the Soviet Union after 1960 and evolved into "radical socialist" parties by the 1980s.

There were also some variants on this general theme, especially in the center of the political spectrum. The accommodating proportional representation system allowed small parties to gain parliamentary seats on issues such as prohibition, land taxation, and cultural distinctions. The Finns had a Swedish People's Party to represent the Swedish-speaking minority. The Norwegians supported a strong Christian People's Party, which was culturally and religiously conservative but centrist in economic terms. It gradually grew into a major force in Norwegian politics. Over the past forty years similar parties have appeared in the other Nordic countries.

From the 1920s through the 1970s, the voters were roughly split between the parties of the right and center (the "bourgeois parties") on the one hand and the left (the "labor" or "socialist" parties) on the other. Although those with bourgeois leanings divided their votes among three or four parties of approximately equal size, the Social Democrats typically captured the lion's share of the labor vote—40 to 45 percent of the total—with the Communists/Socialist People's Party getting 5 to 10 percent. Numerically this gave the Social Democrats an obvious edge. Furthermore, because of the deep historical division during the struggle for parliamentary democracy between the Conservatives on the one hand and the Agrarians and Liberals on the other through the 1930s, the Social Democrats were able to form coalitions with the parties of the center once they put socialization of the means of production on the back burner after 1933.

Thus, the Social Democrats achieved a degree of hegemony in Denmark, Norway, and Sweden that was unparalleled in democratic elections. Social Democrats led the government of Denmark from 1929 to 1968 with only two breaks totaling four years (and two more during the German occupation); of Norway from 1935 to 1965 with a break of two weeks in 1963 and of five years during the German occupation; and of Sweden from 1932 to 1976 with a break only of a couple of months in the summer of 1936. They were able to use these extraordinary periods in government to reshape society through building an exceptionally strong public sector.

Finland constituted something of an exception. The Finnish labor vote (and trade unions as well) were roughly evenly split between the Communist Party and the Social Democrats, and they were direct political competitors. Consequently, the fulcrum of Finnish party politics was in the center, especially with the well-led agrarian Center Party. After 1960 the Communist-led electoral alliance vote declined, and it has taken a course similar to that of the radical socialists in the other countries and has been integrated into the parliamentary give-and-take.

The culmination of this period of Social Democratic construction of the Scandinavian welfare state was the reforms of the late 1960s and early 1970s, which expanded social services into rural areas and raised income replacement rates for the unemployed, sick, injured, and disabled from 40 to 50 percent of their market income to 70 to 90 percent. These reforms came on line just about the time the oil price shock of 1973–1974 set off a period of economic adjustment and economic globalization throughout the West. Social democratic ideas and their carefully constructed tools of public economic management, as we will discuss, offered fewer answers in a global economy.

This relatively stable party system changed dramatically in the 1970s and 1980s. New protest parties arose on the right in protest against high taxes, growing immigrant populations, and the fact that the bourgeois parties that finally took governmental power in the late 1960s and 1970s administered the social democratic system rather than abolishing it; these were the so-called Progress Parties in Denmark and Norway and the New Democracy Party in Sweden. Finland had the somewhat similar but weaker protest parties, including the Rural Party (now known as the "True Finns"). There was further subdivision in the center. Denmark saw the development of a Christian People's Party and a Center Democrat split from the right wing of the Social Democrats. In Sweden, the Christian Democrats also broke into parliament. Environmentalist parties won seats in both Sweden and Finland, and the Danes and Norwegians both sent a few members to parliament from groups to the left of the Socialist People's Parties.

The consequence was that the relatively stable five- or six-party model of the 1920–1970 period has given way to a seven- or eight-party model in which the Christian Democrats in the center and a protest party on the right seem to be a permanent part of the parliamentary constellation today. The Scandinavian Christian Democrats have more of a "Sermon on the Mount" orientation than the rightist orientation of U.S. fundamentalists. Although socially conservative (especially on the issues of abortion, drugs, pornography, and alcohol), they are strong supporters of the welfare state, foreign aid, and restrained materialism. They show a remarkable streak of religious tolerance as well: although Christian Democratic voters are overwhelmingly devout, evangelical Lutherans, the Danish party was led for some years by a Catholic, and the Swedish party included a prominent immigrant Jewish physician among its leaders and members of parliament. (They have not yet taken ecumenicalism to the point of inclusion of Muslims, however.) Consequently, they have accommodated themselves easily to the give-and-take of parliamentary compromise.

The protest parties of the right have not, however, and they were initially kept outside the patterns of parliamentary coalitions. Driven originally by opposition to taxes and bureaucracy, they have in recent years become increasingly strident in their opposition to immigrants, particularly those racially or culturally distinguishable, such as Africans, Asians, and Muslims. For a long time they were "heard" but not "listened to." This began to change in the late 1990s as their electoral advances made them too large to be ignored. Nonsocialist governments in Norway and most recently in Denmark have counted on parliamentary votes from the "New Right." In local government the pattern is similar; once radical parties draw 10 to 20 percent of the vote, their political influence grows.

Although the division of the voters between the blocs long remained relatively even, there has been an increasing tilt to the right, especially when the rightist protest parties gained a growing share of working-class votes. Further, the Social Democrats were weakened by a seepage of voters to their left, especially over the issue of European Community membership in the 1970s in Denmark and Norway and European Union membership in 1995 in Sweden. For the current division of parliamentary seats among the parties, see Table 5.1.

The cumulative loss of Social Democratic votes since the 1980s has been 5 to 15 percentage points compared to the 1940s–1970s; even with proportional representation, this produces a significant shift in the parliamentary balance. The forty years of Social Democratic hegemony that began during the Depression came to an end. However, despite the increased party fragmentation, loss of part of their voting base, and a certain poverty of ideas, the Social Democrats remained the largest party in parliament in Denmark (until 2001), Norway, and Sweden. The Finnish Social Democrats have also been the largest parliamentary party for most of the post-1945 period. Although the Social Democrats have ceased to be the normal party of government, it was hard to govern against them, and they were perfectly capable of savaging governments of the right that tried to cut the welfare state.

One of the major consequences of the fragmented party system and declining Social Democratic hegemony has been the growing prevalence of minority cabinets. If we split the post–World War II period at the 1972 mark—the Danish and Norwegian European Community referendums—the Danes managed majority governments for 25 percent of the period prior to 1972 and 3 percent of the period since. The Norwegians had majority governments for 80 percent of the pre-1972 period and 10 percent of the period since. The Swedes mustered majority governments for 40 percent of the first period and only 11 percent of the most recent period. Finland remains committed to broad majority coalitions, which have accounted for nearly all its governments over the past thirty years. While one might think that this would produce political paralysis, the governments seem to function about as effectively as in the past.

There are three reasons for this. The first is the value, already discussed, placed on compromise, which makes minority government much less frustrating than it otherwise would be. The second is that various "radical" and "protest" parties on the political left and, more tentatively, on the right have become substantially less radical and more interested in participating in shaping legislation through compromise; Social Democratic minority governments can turn to their left as well as to the center for votes, while nonsocialists look to their right. The third is that, by and large, Scandinavian governments of the last twenty years have only undertaken major domestic reforms with broad parliamentary support extending well beyond the governing coalition.

Table 5.1   Party Parliament Strength in November 2006

Country/Party	Seats
Denmark	179
Social Democrats	47
Liberals*	52
Danish People's (rightist)	24
Conservatives*	18
Socialist People's	11
Radical Liberals	17
Leftists	6
Greenland and Faeroe Islands	4
Finland	200
Social Democrats*	53
Center (agrarian)*	55
Conservatives	40
Left Alliance	19
Swedish People's*	9
Greens	14
Christian Democrats	7
True Finns	3
Norway	169
Labor (Social Democrats)*	61
Conservatives	23
Progress (rightist)	38
Socialist Left*	15
Christian People's	11
Center (agrarian)*	11
Liberals	10
Sweden	349
Social Democrats	130
Moderates (conservatives)*	97
Liberals*	28
Christian Democrats*	24
Leftists	22
Center (agrarian)*	29
Greens	19

* In government as of November 2006

INTEREST GROUPS

The Scandinavian countries are the most thoroughly organized in the world. Practically everybody belongs to his or her economic interest organization. Manufacturers, shopkeepers, renters, farmers, workers, and students are all organized. Overall, 75 to 90 percent of all wage and salaried workers are union members, and farmer and employer organizational percentages are equally impressive. Schoolchildren, university students, priests, and military personnel each have their usually well-ordered group.

As this list suggests, Scandinavian interest organizations are divided primarily along economic lines. This mirrors the lines of political division in these societies. Moreover, the larger of the interest organizations, including both the trade union federation and the employers' organization, are sufficiently inclusive that they have to take broader, societal interests into consideration. Furthermore, until recently they were highly centralized: labor agreements were negotiated nationally between the national employers' organization and the national trade union organization. Recently collective bargaining has been decentralized by economic sector (e.g., metal industry, public-sector employees, etc.). In practice, unions and employers keep a close eye across the labor market, and contract provisions tend to move across it in similar directions. Thus, areas of conflict and cooperation spread across the economy and have immediate societal consequences.

As a result, the Scandinavian countries remain models of a peculiar kind of social democratic *corporatism*, in which interest organizations as a matter of course are integrated in making and implementing public policy. Some prefer to call the process "the negotiated economy." Interest organizations have highly professional staffs and constantly are encompassed in governmental commissions in designing policy, including the Swedish "remiss" system of formal consultation on major initiatives with all relevant interest organizations. It is a process of interest representation very different from Washington lobbying.

Not only are Scandinavian interest organizations involved in drafting policy, they implement it. Consider the national labor agreement, for example, in the years that a single overarching national contract for the private sector is negotiated: the unions and the employers, with the government as a third party, hammer out the contract, since the contract essentially determines wage formation for the period. The primary aim of the government, in terms of management of the economy, is to ensure that wage increases are noninflationary.

The practice of corporatism is eased by the small scale of the national political class in the Scandinavian countries. One faces the same people across the table. Working together becomes second nature. Economic globalization, neoliberalism, and, perhaps, European integration may create stress for this cozy but flexible structure. Structural economic changes, the relative decline of the industrial sector, and the rise in small enterprises also challenge the Scandinavian corporatist model. However, the current international interest in the Scandinavian "flexicurity" (flexible labor markets, active public retraining, and generous social security systems) shows that corporatism has not been static.

RESTRAINING THE GOVERNORS

The concentration of power in unicameral parliaments and the presence of strong, disciplined parties not only permit effective and responsive policymaking but also raise the specter of majority tyranny. What prevents a unified parliamentary majority from running roughshod over all opposition? What prevents systematic abuses of citizen rights? In the United States, the system of government has been carefully designed to avert majority tyranny by the division of powers between the three branches of government—legislative, executive, and judicial—and between the federal and state governments. The court system is engaged in a continual review of governmental acts. The Scandinavians do not have those mechanical checks and balances built into their government institutions. They have developed a different set of checks on abuse of power and majority tyranny.

First, the ombudsman—a Scandinavian concept that has entered the English language and U.S. practice—serves as a standing, independent check on abuses of executive power. This position was created in the Swedish Constitution of 1809 as a parliamentary restraint on abuse of royal executive power; today it serves as a more general check on abuses throughout the executive branch. The Swedish ombudsman is elected by parliament for a four-year term and is empowered both to respond to formal citizen complaints and to initiate investigations on, for example, the basis of press reports. In recent years, the Swedish ombudsman has handled about three thousand cases a year; about 90 percent are citizen-initiated. Less prominent but even older is the institution of the chancellor of justice (Justitiekanslern) created in 1713 by King Charles XII. In March 2006 the chancellor's office pressured Foreign Minister Freivalds to resign after she lied about her efforts to censor an anti-Muslim website. The modern media are also watchdogs: just after the change of government in Sweden in October 2006, two new conservative ministers were forced to resign when the press revealed unpaid taxes and radio/TV license fees.

The Finns added an ombudsman in 1919 at the birth of the republic on the Swedish model. The Danes added a parliamentary ombudsman in the Constitution of 1953, and the Norwegians established a similar office in 1962. The formal powers of ombudsmen are amplified by a strong tradition of parliamentary inquiry (both questions to the government and committee hearings) and investigative journalism.

Second, voter referenda have periodically checked parliamentary majorities. This is most formalized in Denmark, which has held nineteen referenda since 1915; Denmark is second only to Switzerland in direct citizen votes on key legislation, but there are no "initiatives" (citizen-proposed legislation). All constitutional changes go to a citizen vote (after having been approved by two sessions of parliament with an intervening election), any legislation except finance and tax measures can be sent to a vote by one-third of parliament, and any surrender of national sovereignty can be sent to a vote by one-sixth of parliament. Such provisions strengthen the hands of the minority vis-à-vis the majority. While Finland and Norway lack constitutional sanction for binding referenda (and Sweden limits it to constitutional changes), governments have always abided by voter decision except in the case of the Swedish referendum concerning which side of the road they should drive on (in 1955, despite the government's recommendation and common sense, Swedes voted to continue driving on the left; in 1967 the government shifted without a referendum). Increasingly, highly divisive issues such as nuclear power (Sweden, 1980) and European Community/European Union membership (Denmark 1972, Norway 1972 and 1994, Sweden and Finland, 1994) and further EU integration (Denmark 1986, 1992, 1993, 1998, and 2000; Sweden 2003) have been decided by the people directly.

Third, two aspects of Scandinavian political culture tend to check parliamentary majorities. One is that facts count in Scandinavian politics. The policy debate, both in the media and the parliament, is couched in empirical terms. Demagoguery discredits the user, except, possibly, on the immigration issue. The other is that a value is placed on broader compromise. Part of the reason for this is purely practical: parties involved in the compromise will not reverse the policy when they are in government. But another part is the concept that legislation passed by narrow majorities is less legitimate than that passed by broad majorities. Thus there is a tendency to seek broader majorities than are necessary simply to pass legislation.

Finally, Scandinavian corporatism provides an open door in policymaking. Major legislative initiatives generally are preceded by governmental commissions that involve not only the political parties but all the relevant interest groups. Trade unions, employers, and farmers' organizations are involved in practically all of these, and more specialized interest organizations take part in commissions in their spheres of interest. Such political transparency is reinforced by an active and diverse media and supplemented nowadays by the Internet. Thus major legislation on, for example, changing higher education involves teacher unions and student organizations as well as primary economic interest groups.

The Welfare State and Economic Stability

The Scandinavian responses to the economic crises of the 1930s marked a sea change in the role of the state. The old "night watchman state" provided national defense, justice, police protection, roads, and elementary education. The new "welfare state" was to regulate the market economy to ensure full employment and growth and to provide social and economic security for those out of the labor market because of old age, sickness, unemployment, and disability and for families whose market income was small and number of children large.[6] This is what political scientists have come to call the "postwar consensus," but in Scandinavia it started before World War II, driven primarily by the predominant popular movements with more of an egalitarian perspective.

Scandinavian welfare states, like those in Europe generally, are not for the poor alone. They are a method of providing universal social services and economic security for the middle class as well as the working class and the marginalized poor. Practically all social welfare expenses are in the public sector. This includes family allowances, day care and after-school care, unemployment, healthcare, maternity and sick pay, pensions, disability, housing subsidies, and social assistance. In the United States, by contrast, a number of these, including medical and dental care, maternity and sick pay, and the bulk of our pensions, are handled privately through employers. Unlike the U.S. provision of these services, which varies tremendously between occupational groups and among employers, Scandinavians universally receive about the same benefits.

In the postwar period, Scandinavian governments worked to achieve broadly shared affluence by two mechanisms. First, they sought to manage the economy to limit cyclical unemployment and to bring up the standards of the worst-off in the labor market by channeling capital investment and labor from the least efficient firms to the most efficient firms. The trade unions' "solidaristic wage policy" was the most effective mechanism for this purpose. Over time, it raised the wages of the unskilled relative to the skilled and of women relative to men at the same time as it increased the overall efficiency of the economy.

Second, they sought to spread the dividends of economic growth more equally than the existing system distributed income and wealth. Those outside the labor market or in low-income groups gained, but no one lost absolutely. As a result, the policy enjoyed widespread political support, and social expenditures expanded rapidly.

Between 1960 and 1974, social spending as a share of GDP nearly doubled in the Scandinavian countries. The growth really was a product of substantial improvements in the social security net that included raising income-replacement ratios for the unemployed and the disabled, raising pension levels, and expanding some social services from urban areas to include rural areas. With unemployment at a minimal 2 percent level, it cost little to raise the income replacement ratio to 80 or even 90 percent of market wages. All this occurred during a period of prolonged economic growth and, generally speaking, shared the affluence of those in the labor market with those outside and those with low-income families in the labor market with numerous children. (See Table 5.2.)

By contrast, the 1974 to 1984 period was characterized by the two oil crises and the unpredicted combination of economic stagnation and inflation ("stagfla-

Table 5.2   Public Social Security Transfers as a Percentage of GDP, 1960–2004.
Average for Period

	1960–1973	1974–1979	1980–1989	1990–1999	2004
Denmark	9.5	14.0	17.1	19.1	16.9
Finland	6.6	11.2	13.9	20.3	16.8
Norway	10.3	12.9	12.7	15.9	15.0
Sweden	10.0	15.9	18.3	20.9	18.0
EU (15) average	11.4	12.3	16.5	17.3	
United States	6.4	10.2	11.0	12.6*	12.0

Source: Organization for Economic Cooperation and Development, *Historical Statistics, 1960–97; Historical Statistics, 1970–99; OECD in Figures 2005* (Paris: OECD, 1999, 2000, and 2005, respectively).

Note: *average 1990–1996.

tion") in most Western economies. In Denmark, new social expenditures from the end of the good years finished coming on line, and there was also a rapid expansion of countercyclical social expenditures because of the bad times that saw unemployment rise from the frictional level of about 2 percent to 8 percent. Sweden continued to grow the national economy and hold down unemployment by expanding the public sector; this kept unemployment at 3 percent and restrained social spending for countercyclical programs but pushed some economic problems forward. Norway, blessed with North Sea oil, escaped the hard times. Finland's economy benefited from continuing modernization and substantial trade with Soviet Russia and other eastern European states.

Rising social expenditures in a low-growth economy began to squeeze the tax base, private consumption, and capital investment. Increasingly since the 1970s, the Scandinavian countries have struggled with maintaining economic balance. Generous unemployment benefits protected living standards when the economy turned bad, but how long can you sustain using 4 to 5 percent of GDP for that purpose? Denmark did so for two decades (1975–1995), but the cost forced unemployment policy reforms that, like Sweden's longstanding policy, emphasized "activation"—emergency employment or training—rather than passive support. Rising income tax levels yielded increasing tax avoidance strategies until tax reform broadened the tax base by reducing deductions and bringing down marginal rates in the 1980s and early 1990s. All of the Scandinavians except the oil-rich Norwegians repeatedly sought to trim welfare programs at the margins. But despite their best efforts to hold down costs, the secular trends pushing costs up combined with growth in unemployment (particularly long-term unemployment) continued to push spending and taxes up. Governmental expenditures rose roughly 15 percent of GDP between 1974 and 1996 in all Nordic countries except Norway (unchanged thanks to petroleum-fueled prosperity). However, structural economic changes finally reversed this negative trend after 1995, and social expenditures have declined over the past decade as unemployment fell and economic growth accelerated. The Scandinavian states have once again become models of effective adjustment to the global economy.

While the welfare state was being constructed—from the 1930s through the early 1970s—increased expenditures were closely correlated with real gains in living standards. Unemployment compensation was enhanced, maternity and paternity leaves were introduced, pensions went up, housing was improved, day-care centers built, etc. In recent years, however, expenditures have continued to rise without such clear improvements in welfare.

Today, the cost of social programs is being pushed up in Scandinavia by three other forces: demography, technology, and rising take-up rates. Aging populations—and Scandinavians top the list internationally in terms of life expectancy—require longer pensions and more services. To deal with the former, national pension-funding reforms have raised pension savings and cut unfunded liabilities. The latter is more troublesome. Improved (and expensive) medical technology continues to drive the costs of the healthcare system higher; despite the comprehensive and efficient national health systems in the four countries, a healthcare cost crisis looms. And take-up rates for social programs have continued to rise among the young, who shape their behavior to conform to the mold of the social-benefit system. The result is that increasing expenditures do not necessarily increase welfare. Medical technology certainly extends life, but much of the costs of that new technology are incurred in the last few months of life, when the quality of life is low.

Scandinavian social programs' costs burden national economic competitiveness, but strong public sectors can also be a competitive advantage. Global capital mobility means that investment in high-wage areas, such as the Nordic countries, will lag unless productivity (and applied research), or currency devaluations, maintain competitiveness. Fortunately, innovative firms, rising education levels and labor force skills, and cost containment in both the public and private sectors have been successful over the past decade. Some Scandinavian policies, such as the active labor market policy and the solidaristic wage policy, address the competitiveness issue directly. Others, such as national health insurance, spread medical costs generally across society, rather than burdening particular employers.[7] The economic protections provided to families through the social welfare system encourage employees to accept technological innovation. The term "flexicurity"—a flexible economy resting on a secure social security system—has been coined to describe twenty-first-century Scandinavia.

A different—and troubling—issue in Scandinavia is the rapid increase in a noticeable immigrant population. Today about 5 percent of the population of Sweden, Denmark, and Norway carry foreign passports, as do 2 percent of the population of Finland, and the percentage of the foreign-born is higher, especially in Sweden, where more than 10 percent were born somewhere else. They and their immediate descendents are now citizens, but integration into the social mainstream has been very uneven. To a considerable extent, support for the solidaristic social welfare system rested on the fact that those who benefited and those who paid were very similar. They spoke the same language, worshiped in the same church (at least at Christmas), shared the same culture, and looked very much alike. Under these circumstances, solidarity was easy. It is far from clear that the same solidarity will pertain as immigrant populations grow. Successful integration of non–Western European immigrants has so far eluded the Nordic countries. The result has been higher social costs and the rise of explicitly anti-immigrant parties in Denmark and Norway.

Box 5.2   Cartoons and Immigrants: No Laughing Matter

Early in 2006 Denmark faced one of its worst foreign policy crises since World War II. The country's largest newspaper, the liberal *Jyllands-Posten*, published the previous September a dozen caricatures of the Prophet Muhammad, or other drawings about contemporary Danish perceptions of Islam. For some religious Muslims, any portrayal of their holiest prophet is sacrilegious, and the humorous, derogatory, or satirical drawings offended many, including some non-Muslims. Without imagining the possible global consequences, several editors at the paper had invited numerous Danish cartoonists to submit such drawings to prove that they would not be intimidated by the threat some artists felt at drawing even positive images of the Prophet. For weeks the issue simmered; Danish prime minister Fogh Rasmussen refused a request by Arab ambassadors to discuss the issue even though he specifically addressed issues of tolerance and mutual respect in his annual New Year address.

Several radical Islamist activists were not content to let the issue fade. Traveling through the Middle East, they complained to several Arab governments about the intolerable insult directed at their faith. To embellish the case, several especially insulting pictures—neither drawn nor published in Denmark—were added to the "collection." Within days Arab and foreign media spread the "news" and riots erupted in dozens of cities throughout the Muslim world. Danish embassies were attacked and in some cases destroyed (usually with the passive assistance of the "protecting" local government). Danish firms and products faced widespread boycotts. Other Scandinavian and European papers published the caricatures in support of the right to publish freely. Soon talk of a "clash of civilizations" and the threats to freedom filled the debate.

Underlying this crisis is the challenge of integrating tens of thousands of recent immigrants into the once homogeneous Scandinavian countries. Accommodating differences has always been a challenge to societies, even when the migrants came from distant Scandinavian regions: Finns moving to Sweden in 1950s and 1960s or Greenlanders moving to Denmark a decade later often received less than enthusiastic

(continued)

Box 5.2   *(Continued)*

welcomes. The real challenge was adjusting to non-European immigrants who were a trickle in the 1960s but became the majority of immigrants twenty years later. Now even Scandinavian-born children of the immigrants face significant lags in educational and vocational progress. Some social housing estates have largely immigrant populations with "natives" fleeing the surrounding areas and schools.

Sweden and Iceland have relied on the labor market supplemented by language and other support to promote integration. When immigrants work and become self-supporting, they are more likely to adjust to the culture. Denmark faced its largest wave of immigrants and refugees during a time of high unemployment and tended to support the new residents through generous social benefits. It was not a successful program, and over the past decade the emphasis has been on rapid movement into the labor market, compulsory language and cultural instruction, and reduced social benefits. Norway and Finland have tended more toward the Danish model. In both Norway and Denmark, rightist populist parties have attracted growing political support from voters who fear and distrust the new multiethnic society in which they live. In response, the mainstream political parties have shed their reluctance to discuss the problem and have reaffirmed the supremacy of traditional Scandinavian values, particularly against violence and in favor of women's rights.

More positively, moderates among the immigrant groups have entered the political process through the traditional political parties and are represented from city councils to national parliaments. A willingness to discuss the problems openly—still a challenge in Sweden—but respectfully may have received a boost from the "cartoon crisis," but the immigration and cultural diversity issues will figure prominently in Scandinavian politics for many years to come.

In the long run, Scandinavian prosperity in the global economy depends on sustaining the currently successful pattern of high wages and high performance. That requires action in Brussels and Frankfurt, where full employment has not been part of the prevailing ideology of the European Union and especially the European Central Bank. And it requires both anchoring domestic, and attracting foreign, capital. And so pension and tax reforms have encouraged a high rate of savings bringing mass investment (under professional management) even to Sweden, which in the past has prospered with perhaps the most concentrated ownership of any capitalist country under social democratic economic management.

The past thirty years have been a watershed. The great social democratic project—the comprehensive welfare state supported by state economic intervention to manage the market economy—was completed with the able assistance of the center parties. There was no new, equivalent central thrust for reform. Minority governments of the center-right and center-left could administer this system, but it came under increasing pressure. Accelerating demographic changes—an aging and increasingly "multicultural" population—as well as relentless changes in the European Union and in the global economy ensure that the pressure will continue.

And so the question becomes whether and how the Scandinavian model can continue to be reshaped to meet the challenges of economic globalization while retaining its comprehensive, solidaristic, and humane structure. That is the challenge for the first decades of the new millennium.

The Roads to Europe

Europe, including Scandinavia, faced four vital questions in the wake of World War II. Two continental conflicts within a quarter century had threatened to extinguish European civilization. Armed struggle for control of Europe could not be allowed to occur again. At issue was, first, whether cooperation should be regional or global. A closely related second question was whether states should seek to build intensive integrated communities with like-minded states or whether cooperation should be restrained so as to include the largest number of participating countries (so-called "depth" versus "breadth," or "deepening" versus "widening" arguments). Third, should collaboration focus narrowly on specific economic or other policy problems (i.e., functional issues) or should it seek broad federal arrangements in which states would yield sovereignty over a range of policy matters? Finally, should this new international regime reinforce intergovernmental cooperation or should it carefully construct new international organizations with supranational responsibilities?

The Scandinavian states responded cautiously to these questions. Domestic issues were primary, but defensive isolation had failed between 1939 and 1945. The collapse of world trade in the 1930s had hurt their economies. Sweden had narrowly preserved its traditional neutrality during World War II, but only by accommodating the dominant belligerents. Denmark, Norway, and Finland had been invaded and found traditional nonalignment and neutrality largely discredited at the end of war. All had supported the League of Nations after World War I, only to see ruthless power politics and fanatical nationalism return. After 1945 they hoped that the emerging United Nations organization would allow them to preserve their independence while participating in the global community and a revitalized collective security system. Finland's position as a defeated power made its position especially precarious. Hard-liners in the Soviet Union believed that Finland had been a willing ally of Nazi Germany; instead, Finland's "continuation war" against the Soviet Union had been retaliation for Stalin's attack on Finland in 1939 (which had been encouraged by the Nazi-Soviet pact of August 1939 that established spheres of domination over Eastern Europe).

Scandinavia sought security and prosperity through broad European cooperation. All wished to avoid new divisions despite the obvious differences between the Western democracies and Stalin's Soviet Union. The term applied to this policy of reconciliation and constructive diplomacy was "bridge building." Bridges are built over chasms; the Scandinavian states recognized the fundamental conflicts that threatened the postwar order.

It is useful to view Scandinavian foreign policies from five perspectives: Nordic, West European, Atlantic, East European, and global. Such geopolitical shorthand is, admittedly, not precise, especially given the many changes since the Cold War.

The Nordic perspective reflects history and culture, but it also implies deliberate choices. We have mentioned the common roots of the Scandinavian states, which are traceable to a loose dynastic entity known as the Kalmar Union (1397–1523).[8] The next four hundred years saw frequent and often bitter rivalry in the Nordic region until the current five independent states emerged in the twentieth century. Sweden and Denmark competed for hegemony throughout the Baltic: first against the Hanseatic League and later against the emerging Slavic powers of Poland-Lithuania and finally Russia. The dominance of Russia from the eighteenth century onward and later the growth of German power forced the Scandinavians into an increasingly defensive position. Not until the collapse of the Soviet Union and its sphere of influence after 1990 would the Nordic states take a proactive role (now based on cooperation) in the Baltic.

Yet even as nationalism was shaping five distinct sovereign countries, there were calls for regional cooperation. They followed two lines: a romantic "pan-Scandinavianism" that argued for a federation of the increasingly democratic societies of the north, and pragmatic functional proposals covering a range of public policies common to the industrializing economies of the five states. Although "Scandinavianism" ended historic rivalries, it did not prevent the further division of the region into the five modern nations. The practical policy approach proved most fruitful, starting with a monetary union at the end of the nineteenth century (which collapsed following World War I), an "interparliamentary union" in 1907, and regular meetings between political leaders.

After World War II, the more ambitious goals of advocates for Nordic integration repeatedly ran into two obstacles. First, the interests of the Scandinavian countries were often different and not infrequently competitive. This strengthened historical and nationalist desires in Norway, Finland, and Iceland to maintain full independence from the older Scandinavian states. Second, outside political and economic ties outweighed Scandinavian alternatives. This would be seen most dramatically in security policy after 1948, when Denmark, Norway, and Iceland chose the Atlantic alliance led by the United States; Finland accommodated its foreign relations within the narrow limits demanded by the Soviet Union; and Sweden reaffirmed its historical and successful nonalignment.

Later, economic cooperation followed a similar path with broader European opportunities outweighing the potential of narrower Nordic proposals.

Although intra-Scandinavian trade expanded significantly after 1950, access to European and global markets remained the higher priority. Despite these setbacks, in 1952 the Nordic countries established the Nordic Council—essentially an extension of the interparliamentary union—that would coordinate legislation and encourage Nordic initiatives whenever consensus could be reached. Underlying the development of Nordic policy cooperation was the primacy of Social Democratic and Labor parties during much of the 1945 to 1975 period. Even in Iceland and Finland, where this was not the case, centrist governments adopted much of the Social Democratic agenda on labor, social, and economic issues. This paved the way for regional cooperation.

Nordic cooperation continues on three levels—parliamentary, ministerial, and nongovernmental—but most efforts are now channeled through the European Union. The annual meetings of parliamentary delegations from the five countries (plus the three autonomous regions: Åland, Greenland, and the Faeroes) encourage pragmatic cooperation and foster personal contacts across the region as well as a comparative perspective on policy issues. Ministerial contacts are more intense and continuous. In addition, there are regular ministerial "summits," since 1971 routinized through the Nordic Council of Ministers, which bring together the top political and administrative people for detailed discussions and planning. A common Nordic political culture that emphasizes consensus, fact-finding, pragmatism, and responsibility helps this process. Common positions on European and international questions can multiply the weight of these small states. Finally, there are the various nongovernmental organizations in the educational, cultural, and scientific area that bring Scandinavians together on specific projects and interests. Again, this invigorates Nordic cooperation at the grass roots but also mobilizes important interests in support of these activities.

"Western Europe" was at first a Cold War concept, but it increasingly gained real political and economic significance. The Nordic countries chose not to be part of the evolving European community that started with the Brussels Pact of 1948, the Schuman Plan of 1950 for a coal and steel community, and especially the Treaty of Rome in 1957, which sparked the development of a European common market. Yet all but Finland participated in the European Recovery Program (the Marshall Plan) and became part of looser institutional structures that were also favored by Great Britain. Likewise, Denmark and Norway found that NATO membership brought them closer to the Western European democracies and expedited reconciliation with the Federal Republic of Germany. By the 1960s relationships with expanding Western European institutions (notably the Common Market) became a permanent issue on the Scandinavian political agenda.

The Atlantic dimension overlaps considerably with the Western European, but it has three distinctive facets. After 1940 the Scandinavian states developed sustained and intensive relations with the United States (and to a lesser extent Canada), with which they had previously had important ethnic ties but no intensive diplomatic history. Further, the Atlantic dimension brought particularly the three Scandinavian NATO members into a much wider community in Europe (especially with the Mediterranean NATO members). Finally, it evolved into a broader western community exemplified by the Organization for Economic Cooperation and Development (OECD), which emerged in 1960 out of the narrower Marshall Plan structure. Even after the end of the Cold War, the Scandinavian states have sought to keep the United States immersed in European affairs and have encouraged NATO's enlargement eastward. Interestingly, neither Sweden nor Finland considered NATO membership but they were satisfied with the Partnership for Peace.

Relations with Eastern Europe and the former parts of the Soviet Union represent the legacy of the Cold War, which also dominated Scandinavia for more than forty years. For the past two centuries, Scandinavia's relations with Eastern Europe have been distant, and Russia was most often seen as a threat. After a period of "bridge building" between 1944 and 1948, the Scandinavian countries chose different options to cope with the east-west struggle. Common to each was a desire to maintain relatively low tensions in the Nordic region and to develop autonomous Nordic relations. Since 1990, Scandinavia's "eastern question" has become far more complex. At present three developments have emerged from the former eastern bloc. First is the renewed independence of the Baltic states of Estonia, Latvia, and Lithuania. The Scandinavian countries have greeted this unexpected development with sustained economic and political involvement. Second, Russia's instability and uncertain steps toward democracy represent a continuing challenge for the Nordic states. The norm had been an authoritarian, powerful, but often conservative Russia. Finally, as the expanding EU encompasses Central and Eastern Europe, the Nordic countries must adjust to changing institutional and political arrangements while maintaining their influence and independence.

Finally, there is a global perspective that includes Scandinavia's historic commitment to the United Nations and other forms of international cooperation. Scandinavian military units have played a role in many of the UN peacekeeping missions. The Nordic countries have global economic interests and collectively represent a substantial global economic power. They are among the most generous and steadfast contributors to international economic assistance efforts and often champion the less-developed countries in international organizations. Yet they are far from major actors whose decisions can affect global affairs. Here, too, a strategy of bridge building can be constructive, as illustrated by the role of Norway and its late foreign minister, Johann Jørgen Holst, in facilitating the 1993 Israeli-Palestinian Oslo Accords. More recently, Norwegian diplomats have brokered peace talks in Sri Lanka and western Sudan (Darfur), alas with scant success to date.

POST–WORLD WAR II SECURITY OPTIONS

Initially the Nordic countries placed their trust mainly in the new United Nations and its promise of "collective security" and broad global cooperation. The disappointments of the 1930s were balanced by the lessons of appeasement and the leadership promised by the United States, along with hopes for Soviet cooperation in the postwar order. As a defeated power, Finland was initially denied membership in the UN, but the other four Nordic nations were in from the start. Scandinavians could see that their best foreign policy option was continuing great-power cooperation in the UN. The appointment of Norwegian statesman Trygve Lie as the first secretary general of the UN augured well for Scandinavian engagement.

Denmark and Norway were accepted as victorious powers while Sweden's wartime neutrality was discreetly ignored. Small Danish and Norwegian contingents were part of the Allied occupation forces in Germany. Likewise, temptations to exact retribution against defeated Germany were resisted. Reconciliation would be the goal.

After 1945, there were two new factors in European and Scandinavian geopolitics: the dominant position of the Soviet Union in Eastern Europe and the Baltic and the global stature of the United States. Soviet forces occupied Finland, but their behavior there had been tolerable. Soviet forces had liberated northern Norway and assisted the desperate civilian population as much as they could. They withdrew shortly after the war, and despite some Soviet security claims in the Arctic territories of Svalbard, Soviet-Norwegian relations were cordial. Likewise, Soviet forces liberated the Danish Baltic island of Bornholm from the Germans in May 1945, but withdrew a year later without incident.

With the apparent breakdown of east-west cooperation in 1946–1947, the Scandinavian states sought to play a mediating role. The term "bridge building" was applied to diplomatic efforts to reconcile the two blocs. Had the focus been northern Europe, such pains might have borne results, but Scandinavia was distant from the conflict's center in Central and Eastern Europe. The "iron curtain" identified by Winston Churchill in 1946 did not run through Scandinavia, although Finland was vulnerable. Precise fulfillment of the terms of the onerous peace treaty and delicate negotiations by veteran diplomat and later president Juho Paasikivi preserved Finnish sovereignty. Sweden provided the Soviet Union with generous postwar economic credits to atone for its wartime neutrality and to stimulate its postwar economy. All of the Scandinavian countries were handicapped by the weakness of their two main trading partners: Germany and Britain. Hence the Nordic countries were enthusiastic when U.S. Secretary of State George Marshall announced a European Recovery Program in June 1947.

Tensions continued to rise over the next eighteen months. Danish and Norwegian communist parties enjoyed an initial surge of support because of their role in the anti-Nazi resistance, but their strength quickly dissipated. Only in

Finland did communists remain a factor as a result of the Soviet support. When the Soviet government rejected participation in the Marshall Plan, the door also slammed for Finland (although the United States found other channels to assist Finland). The February 1948 coup that ousted the democratic Masaryk government in Czechoslovakia was a severe psychological shock. Like Scandinavia, postwar democratic Czechoslovakia had sought to be a bridge builder between east and west. Yet its regard for Soviet interests had not prevented Stalin from overthrowing a democratic coalition government, installing a ruthless communist regime, and isolating Czechoslovakia from its Western European neighbors.

At about the same time Moscow sent a threatening letter to the Finnish government that demanded reassessment of Soviet-Finnish ties. Given the strength of the Finnish communists, the peace terms already imposed a year earlier and the proximity of Soviet troops to Helsinki, many feared a repetition of the Prague coup. Finnish leaders kept their nerve. Discreetly, Finnish communists were removed from sensitive governmental positions, while Finnish leaders assured Moscow of their understanding of Soviet security needs. A treaty of "friendship, cooperation, and mutual assistance" was negotiated and became the basis of the next forty years of Finnish-Soviet relations. It required Finland to obtain Moscow's approval for political and economic ties with the West and basically gave Moscow a so-called *droit de regard* (veto right) to scrutinize Finnish foreign policy and in practice, for more than twenty years, Soviet veto power over certain Finnish politicians. Crucially, however, it did not end Finland's recovering parliamentary democracy and capitalist economy.

Soviet-Nordic relations eventually stabilized, especially following the marked improvement during the post-Stalin "thaw" when the Russians unilaterally withdrew from their Finnish base in Porkkala in 1956, but in 1948 pessimism prevailed. In the Scandinavian capitals, fear of Soviet intentions and recognition of the limits to the UN as a basis for future security inspired a reappraisal of their security situation.

Neither the United States nor Great Britain had focused on Scandinavia after 1945. The United States had northern strategic concerns, but these were mainly the air bases in Iceland and, to a lesser extent, Greenland. Both were essential for U.S. military operations in Europe, and their strategic importance would grow significantly during the Cold War. There was sympathy for the Finns and their resistance to Soviet pressure; Finnish repayment of earlier U.S. loans had a remarkable impact even on isolationists. While Finnish options were sharply limited, the other Scandinavian states agreed to reassess their collective security in 1948–1949. Isolated neutrality was discredited in Denmark and Norway, and even the Swedes seemed willing to consider a regional security arrangement.

The effort to create a nonaligned Scandinavian Defense Union failed basically because Norway sought closer ties with the emerging Western defense alliance that evolved into NATO. As one Norwegian politician put it, "We want to be defended, not liberated." Western (in practice, U.S.) military assistance would be directed at the broader alliance and not at peripheral blocs, and without such assistance Scandinavian military potential would remain at a level characterized by one contemporary observer as a "0+0+0=0" equation. After Norway's choice, Sweden was uninterested in a bilateral arrangement, and Denmark followed Norway into the North Atlantic Treaty Organization in April 1949. Sweden would preserve its nonalignment in peace and hope for neutrality in war.

For the next forty years, this arrangement prevailed with only marginal adjustments. Norway became initially the most enthusiastic Scandinavian NATO member, although the Norwegians adopted a policy of nonprovocation toward the Soviet Union, with which they shared a border in the far north. Denmark also refused to allow permanent foreign bases on its territory in time of peace, although NATO staff and periodic military exercises were accommodated. Denmark also accepted U.S. bases in Greenland without inquiring too closely about their military activities. Norway made a substantial effort to build up its armed forces; in Denmark, defense expenditures were controversial. Nevertheless, both countries developed and maintained military forces and alliance ties that were without historical precedent.

Sweden's nonalignment initially stimulated a considerable defense effort. Swedes believed that their successful neutrality during World War II came from achieving enough military strength to make invasion too costly. That became their defense policy in the Cold War, although we now know that Sweden cooperated secretly with NATO in the 1950s and 1960s in coordinating a defense against the Soviet Union.

THE NORDIC BALANCE

By the 1960s, Nordic foreign policies had established patterns that, with occasional variations, were maintained until the end of the Cold War in 1990. Each Nordic country had, of course, its own interests and priorities. Despite the lack of a formal common Nordic foreign policy, each country has assessed the impact its foreign policy might have on an overall "Nordic balance." In addition, as the Norwegian analyst Arne O. Brundtland and others noted, each Nordic country generally has assumed that the success of one Nordic country's foreign policy would benefit the entire region and minimize regional tensions. Nordic regional cooperation avoided defense and security policy, although a *de facto* Nordic bloc emerged in the 1960s in the United Nations and other international organizations. Nordic political leaders continued their tradition of regular informal consultation on issues of common interest.

Traditional small-state discretion gradually gave way to activism; indeed Finland's expansive president, Urho Kekkonen, pursued "active nonalignment" for twenty-five years in order to maximize his country's options and assure the Soviet Union of Finland's friendly intentions. His preemptive anticipation of

Soviet requests elicited domestic and foreign criticism, including the notorious concept of "Finlandization." Coined by West German politicians but broadly used by Western conservatives and critics of détente, it implied a passive regard for Soviet interests in lieu of Western cooperation.

Swedish leader Olof Palme also rejected the discretion of his predecessors and tried to shape a Swedish profile of active nonalignment in international affairs. A prominent global figure, Palme increasingly challenged the superpowers and promoted the development agenda for the so-called Third World until his assassination in 1986. He pushed a distinctive Swedish policy that gave the country international visibility that it had not had before and has not had since. He became the symbol of a strident criticism of U.S. foreign policy in the wake of the Vietnam War. Both Finland and Sweden put pressure on Denmark and Norway to minimize their engagement in NATO and to reconsider a more active Nordic security commitment. There were many in these countries who were tempted to follow such a line, but the choice of 1949—to rely primarily on broader Western defense cooperation—prevailed.

The Nordic balance remained deliberately vague and flexible throughout the Cold War. NATO and particularly the U.S. guarantee to Western Europe formed the foundation of national security policy in Denmark, Iceland, and Norway, and both Finland and Sweden counted on that ultimate source of assistance should things go wrong. All sought to reinforce the reality that northern Europe was not the main axis of east-west tensions.

Despite the different Nordic responses to the Cold War, each country sought to combine credible national security, conflict-avoidance with the Soviet Union, and cautious steps toward relaxation of tensions between east and west. From the outset, few Scandinavians believed that the Soviet Union had a timetable for war with the West. War was more likely to occur because of miscalculation or the escalation of conflicts outside of Europe. Hence a policy of "reassurance" and conflict resolution won broad support, although there were genuine arguments about how to carry it out. This was not a policy of "appeasement"; Nordic criticism of Soviet human rights violations and imperialism in Eastern Europe became louder through the 1970s and 1980s. As noted earlier, both the Nordic and global dimensions of foreign policy allowed considerable diplomatic opportunities. Not all were successful, but such negotiations would at least communicate to the superpowers (especially the USSR) that the Nordic countries believed in "peaceful coexistence" combined with full respect for national independence.

While successfully restraining most Cold War tensions in their region, the Nordic countries never succeeded in creating a region truly distinct from the larger European context. In the security sphere they had insufficient power; in economic matters their ties to Europe remained supreme. By 1961, however, the dynamic Common Market was a serious issue in Scandinavia. West Germany had become again a vital market for the Scandinavian states, soon surpassing Britain.

As security issues waned, economic questions demanded difficult choices: first between competing blocs and models (the European Economic Community [EEC] versus the looser European Free Trade Association [EFTA]), and then over the extent of integration and its political consequences.

AN END AND A BEGINNING FOR THE NORDIC BALANCE

Nearly twenty years after the sudden collapse of communism in Europe and the end of the Cold War, it is hard to recall the passions and tensions of its final phase. First, the failure of east-west détente at the end of the 1970s—despite the Helsinki Accords of 1975, which recognized the geopolitical status quo of the Cold War as well as the legitimacy of human rights issues in Europe—was a severe disappointment to all of the Scandinavian countries. The renewed strategic arms race and military rivalry, competition in the Third World, and a general global atmosphere of political confrontation in the 1980s threatened the Nordic region. The development of new Soviet intermediate-range missiles and their deployment increased the threat of nuclear war in Europe. The Western response, the so-called dual track strategy of deploying U.S. intermediate-range ballistic and cruise missiles in Europe while preparing for an arms-control agreement in Europe, sharpened the confrontation. Antinuclear movements, which had appeared in the early 1960s and waned with détente in the 1970s, quickly sprang up again across Western Europe, not least in Scandinavia.[9]

Second, the steady buildup of the Soviet northern fleet (based mainly on the Kola Peninsula close to northern Scandinavia) brought about a Western naval rearmament. Although Scandinavia had been peripheral to the central European arms race, the naval and missile competition intruded into the entire region. This was compounded by a global militarization that saw regional struggles in Central America, Africa, the Middle East, and Asia. Europe seemed to be free of direct military adventures, but it was easy to imagine "horizontal escalation" (the geographic spreading of armed conflict) into the Continent. NATO's call for increased military spending was accepted by Norway but not Denmark.

Third, the collapse of reformist movements in several communist countries, most notably Poland in 1981, gave little hope of evolution toward democracy and human rights. The ideological war between east and west returned to a depth of bitterness not seen for twenty years. There seemed to be little that small states could do to bridge the chasm.

Then, and almost without warning, the political winds shifted. The accession of Mikhail Gorbachev to leadership in the Soviet Union in 1985 was the key element, but both U.S. president Reagan and especially Britain's Margaret Thatcher were quick to sense an opening with the new regime in the Kremlin. The spontaneous summit meeting in Reykjavik, Iceland, between Reagan and Gorbachev in November 1986 failed to produce a conclusive Euro-missile agreement, but unlike previous diplomatic disappointments, this meeting seemed to intensify negotiations and the spirit of compromise. The Soviet regime proclaimed "new thinking" in both domestic and foreign policy. Washington, London, and Bonn were prepared to give the Gorbachev proposals a full hearing.

In 1989–1991 Scandinavians, along with Europeans and Americans, watched with amazement as forty years of east-west competition ended, a dozen Marxist-Leninist regimes collapsed, and the Soviet Union split into its component republics. More proactively, the Nordic states gave diplomatic and economic support to the emerging independence movements in the Baltic republics (Estonia, Latvia, and Lithuania), which had been forcibly annexed by the Soviet Union fifty years earlier. As in 1918–1920 and 1945–1949, Nordic leaders had to rethink their international position and foreign policy priorities. The challenge would be to balance traditional interests and perspectives with the new opportunities and threats of a changed world. The Nordic balance soon became the "Northern Dimension" to the European Union.

Scandinavia and the European Union

Scandinavia, as noted earlier, remained on the periphery of the European integration project for nearly twenty-five years after World War II. Three factors have repeatedly deterred the Scandinavian states from aggressively pursuing European integration and unity. First was the alternative attraction of Nordic economic cooperation. Although initial attempts to form a Nordic customs union in the 1950s failed, the project was resurrected in new versions until 1970, when Denmark and Norway declared definitively for the European alternative. However, only Denmark joined the EEC in 1973, while Norwegian voters rejected membership and Sweden and Finland never applied. Denmark would preserve its Nordic links and would even promote regional interests in Brussels, but the limits of Nordic cooperation seemed clear. Second, the ultimate goal of a united Europe enjoyed only modest support among the political leadership and the public in these small states, historically unaligned and mistrustful of larger neighbors. Third, with broader free-trade ambitions, the Nordic countries have resisted having to choose sides in economic communities. Until 1973 Britain and Germany belonged to different European trading blocs, while the attractions of global trade (especially with North America and Japan, and even with the socialist countries such as the Soviet Union, China, and Eastern Europe) deterred commitment to the European project.

The Scandinavian states favored European cooperation over unity. Cooperation aimed at removing barriers to free trade and investment as well as policy collaboration in areas of common concerns (e.g., environment, refugees, human rights, defense) have come to be regarded as "Europe à la carte." States can pick and choose the collection of projects in which they will participate. The alternative they rejected was more grandiose: a "United States of Europe" with genuinely federal institutions that would move significant portions of public policy into a European entity. National governments would still have residual powers through the principle of "subsidiarity," but like other federal systems, the whole would be more than the sum of its parts. Ancient cultures and states would be unlikely to disappear or become mere provinces, but the four-hundred-year tradition of state sovereignty largely would be ended in principle as well as practice. This second vision has little support in Scandinavia and has met much vigorous resistance.

ECONOMIC COOPERATION

As trading states, the Scandinavian countries have long been wary of economic isolationism. All suffered from the economic nationalism and mercantilism of the interwar period. In response, domestic protectionism gained a foothold in the agricultural and other primary economic sectors.

The Scandinavian countries did not participate significantly in any of the meetings between 1955 and 1957 that led to the Rome treaty establishing the EEC. Likewise they had not been involved in the precursors of the Schuman Plan and the European Coal and Steel Community of 1952. The broader trade bloc did raise concerns, especially in Denmark and Sweden, which had important economic ties to the rapidly growing West German economy. British refusal to consider participation and its establishment of an alternative European Free Trade Association (EFTA) in 1959 confirmed the division of Europe into "sixes and sevens." Generally the Scandinavians favored free trade for industrial goods and international services (e.g., shipping), but only Denmark accepted similar liberalization for the agricultural sector. None of them believed that integration of all economic sectors, as had begun with the European Coal and Steel Community, was relevant for their economic situation. This distinction between free trade and harmonization would continue.

By 1961 it was clear that the EEC would progress and that EFTA would be less significant. The ambiguous British decision to apply for EEC membership forced the Scandinavian countries to reconsider their position. French president Charles de Gaulle delayed British entry for a decade, but when in 1969 the issue again became germane, it was clear that the EEC was an economic and political success and that there would be no other significant European alternative. As the European option again appeared promising, the Nordic countries (now including Finland) commenced negotiations on a wider Nordic economic community that would possibly lead to a common Nordic entry into the EEC. This possibility threatened Finland's special regard for Soviet sensibilities, but Sweden too was concerned about its "nonaligned" status (a point already raised in

1963). In short, whenever a wider European option became promising, the Nordic countries found they each had different perspectives.

The result would be four Scandinavian roads to Europe, with Denmark's entry into the EEC in 1973, Sweden and Finland in 1995, and Norway's twice (1972 and 1994) failed entry attempts. Just to complicate matters, the two Danish autonomous North Atlantic territories of Greenland and the Faeroe Islands remained outside of the EEC, with Greenland actually withdrawing in 1982.

It is notable that joining Europe has been a divisive issue in domestic politics everywhere, even including Finland, where the European Union seemed to offer guarantees against renewed Russian pressure in the future. The referenda results in Table 5.3 suggest just how disputed this key decision in fact was. Ironically, the strength of domestic opposition has not slowed Danish integration into European structures in those areas approved by the voters; Denmark has typically ranked among the top countries in the European Union in actually adapting national legislation and regulation to fit European requirements. As late entrants, Sweden and Finland had to accept the developing European Union in 1995, including its extensive rules and regulation (the so-called *acquis communitaire*). The ongoing EU debates and, in the case of Denmark, repeated referenda on Europe disrupted the normal patterns of partisan allegiance in domestic politics.

RELUCTANT EUROPEANS

As the European integration project pursues union in the wake of the Maastricht Treaty of 1991 (as amended in Edinburgh [1992] and further in Amsterdam [1997] and Nice [2001]), the Nordic countries remain skeptical participants. Norway is linked through the agreement on a European Economic Area (EEA), which was negotiated in 1990, took effect in 1993, and essentially gives these countries access to the "Single European Market" in all areas excepting agriculture, natural resources, and other issues of vital national interest. This is the "outer ring" of the European orbit, and although EEA countries (there are only three: Iceland, Norway, and Liechtenstein) have essentially full access to European markets, they have no direct influence on the development of the European Union.

Denmark, along with Britain, circles the EU more closely. Both are signatories to the Maastricht Treaty but have significant, though different, reservations. Denmark has rejected monetary union, although its economy is among the strongest in the EU and its currency has been closely tied to the German mark and now the euro since 1982. It has been cautious about harmonization of police and judicial affairs and participation in key elements of the common foreign and security policy. Every significant change in European policy has sparked a bitter fight in Denmark and resulting national referendums. The 1997 Amsterdam

Table 5.3   European Community/European Union Referenda

	Denmark						Norway		Sweden		Finland
	1972	1986	1992	1993	1998	2000	1972	1994	1994	2003	1994
Yes	63.3	56.2	49.3	56.7	55.1	46.8	46.5	47.8	52.3	41.8	57.0
No	36.7	43.8	50.7	43.5	44.9	53.2	53.5	52.2	46.8	56.1	43.0
Turnout	90.1	75.4	83.1	86.5	74.8	86.7	79.2	88.8	82.4	81.2	70.8

Sources: Danish Folketinget Website: www.ft.dk; Nordic Council, *Norden i Tal, 2002.* Swedish Riksdag website: www.riksdagen.se.

Note: The referenda were as follows: Denmark 1972: Joining the EC;

     1986: EC single market;

     1992: Maastricht Treaty;

     1993: Edinburgh agreement modifying Maastricht;

     1998: Amsterdam treaty;

     2000: adopting the euro;

     Norway 1972 and 1994, Sweden 1994, Finland 1994: Joining the EC/EU.

     Sweden 2003: common European currency.

revision of the union treaty was approved by the Danish voters, but in September 2000 they rejected the euro as their national currency. The Danish government accepted the Nice treaty of 2001, which prepared the EU for a significant expansion to include eastern and southern European states. Although domestic opponents of the EU have railed against opening the union to hordes of poor eastern Europeans, others see the expansion as postponing "federalism" for an indefinite period. Anti-EU parties (on the extreme right and left) are well represented in parliament, and a quarter of the delegates elected by the Danes to the European Parliament are anti-EU activists.

Norway has debated the EU issue for more than forty years, and twice its voters vetoed membership that had been approved by wide parliamentary majorities. As elsewhere in the region, Norwegian "Euro-skeptics" have bundled political, cultural, and economic issues into their program, but economic factors seem salient. Although the 1972 rejection predated Norway's current petroleum-fueled prosperity, the continuing boost of oil and gas exports has shielded the country from most of the economic strains of the past thirty years. Most oil revenues are now shunted into a massive "Government Pension Fund—International," which invests globally and whose assets approached $ 270 billion in fall 2006. Protection of Norway's heavily subsidized agricultural sector and regionally significant coastal fisheries has also been a factor weighing against membership. As a member of the European Economic Area since the early 1990s, the Norwegian industrial, labor, and service sectors are fully integrated with the EU. Policy cooperation extends to justice, education, and other sectors. The main drawback of this "junior membership" is absence from most of the EU policy-making process.

Sweden and Finland became EU members in 1995 after vigorous national debates and referenda. As new members they were forced to swallow the whole EU system, but not without protest and regret. Their EU parliamentary delegations have strong anti-EU contingents, and opinion at home is no less skeptical of the EU project than that of the doubting Danes. Neither is firmly committed to a common European security policy or to federalism. Like the Danes, they have encouraged eastward expansion, especially to the Baltic states and Poland. During their EU presidencies they have pushed the social and labor agenda as well as budgetary and administrative reforms of EU institutions. Only Finland has fully joined the Economic and Monetary Union, with the euro replacing the Finnish *markka* as the national currency in 2002, while Sweden rejected the common currency in 2003.

Today the Scandinavian countries still see the EU mainly in pragmatic economic terms. They have been especially cautious about expanded cooperation on foreign and security policy matters despite the turmoil in the Balkans after 1990, the "war on terrorism" after September 2001, and a host of continuing crises in Africa, the Middle East, and elsewhere that suggest that world politics is not only the global economy. They accepted without significant debate the expansion of the EU to include twelve Central, Mediterranean, and Eastern European countries, including the Baltic states and near-neighbor Poland, but maintain various restrictions on labor migration. EU countries with full employment (the Nordic countries, Ireland, and the UK) are actually warming to eastern and central European workers as greatly preferable to non-Europeans. The proposed European constitutional treaty promised vigorous debate and referendums in the Scandinavian countries, but its rejection by voters in France and the Netherlands in 2005 postponed that confrontation. The EU's current "period of reflection" suits the mood of most Scandinavians quite well.

All of the Nordic countries supported the U.S. response to the terrorist attack of 9/11. Danish and Norwegian troops serve with the UN-sanctioned but NATO-led International Security Assistance Force in Afghanistan. The reluctant "multilateralism" of the Bush administration and its willingness to work within the UN and NATO seemed a hopeful sign to those suspicious of the previous raw unilateralism of the U.S. administration. Unfortunately the invasion and occupation of Iraq in 2003 by U.S. and British troops deepened Nordic concerns and divisions. The Danish government gave wholehearted support to military action against the Saddam Hussein regime and provided a military contingent for the occupation, while the Swedes, Finns, and Norwegians were critical of the U.S. and British response. It was yet another reminder of the different national perspectives across Scandinavia. The differences were purely governmental; public opinion throughout Scandinavia is very much in line with the general European public distaste for the Bush administration's unilateralist nationalism.

For the Scandinavian Social Democrats in particular, the European Union and economic globalization more generally pose some ironic dilemmas. Although they have always been rhetorically internationalist—and have lived up to the rhetoric in development aid and in direct support for foreign trade unions and labor parties in the Third World and Eastern Europe—their success at home has been premised on the relevance of the nation-state as the unit for making economic policy. The generous and humane provisions of the social democratic welfare states in Scandinavia yielded a truly decent society for all, but they were dependent on strong, carefully managed economies and full employment. It is far from clear that those are at the top of the European Union's economic agenda. If the welfare state was the surrogate for socialism for the Scandinavian Social Democrats from the 1930s through the 1980s, what is to be the surrogate for the welfare state?

The habits of nonalignment and independence of all Nordic states, along with their still vigorous sense of nationhood and self-confidence, color their view of Europe. They are also a factor in the continuing debate about non-European immigration and the challenges of multiculturalism. Once again a Nordic "middle way" has emerged toward the regional and global challenges of the new century. Scandinavians are pragmatic skeptics, seeking "just enough Europeanization" to respond to economic, social, and political challenges. As successful states and just societies, they see no need to bury themselves in a federal Europe. The successful reform and reinvigoration of the "Scandinavian model" since 1990 have given them renewed confidence at home and relevance for larger EU countries seeking new ideas. But they are not isolationists; the past century taught them that their fates are intimately tied to their continent and to global developments. The Nordic EU bloc of three is likely to support a "social Europe" in which the principles of "subsidiarity" and pragmatism will make the Scandinavians more comfortable in the European home. Through reforms and innovation—such as "flexicurity"—the Scandinavian countries will challenge their European neighbors to do better.

Notes

1. For an excellent survey of Scandinavian history, see Derry 1979; more concise and up-to-date is Nordstrom 2000. For full citations, see "Suggested Readings" below.

2. Until the war of 1864, the German-speaking duchies of Schleswig, Holstein, and Lauenburg were part of the Danish realm under an exceedingly complex constitutional arrangement. Schleswig had a substantial Danish population that was denied rights under German rule between 1864 and 1918. Following the German defeat in 1918, the Allies supervised a referendum that returned the northern third of Schleswig (Slesvig) to Denmark. Since 1920, the Danish-German border has been fixed, and since the 1950s, the two nationalities have seen greatly improved local relations.

3. Denmark and Norway were under the same monarch from 1380 to 1814. Starting in 1737 in rural Norway, the country was the first in the world to institute universal,

compulsory education, culminating in the Danish education act of 1814. Sweden followed with a similar law in 1842. By the second half of the nineteenth century, literacy was nearly universal in Scandinavia, and secondary and adult education was advanced by the "folk colleges" and workers' education movements.

4. There are many excellent studies of the global economy. See especially Robert O. Keohane and Joseph S. Nye, *Power and Interdependence,* 3rd ed., Boston: Addison-Wesley, 2000; and for the smaller European states, Peter J. Katzenstein, *Small States in World Markets: Industrial Policy in Europe,* Ithaca, NY: Cornell University Press, 1985.

5. There is a rich literature on Scandinavian political institutions and political actors. For good surveys with copious bibliographies, see the volumes by Olof Petersson and by Eric S. Einhorn and John Logue in "Suggested Readings."

6. For a more comprehensive discussion of the Scandinavian welfare programs and their impact, see Einhorn and Logue, chapters 6–10.

7. Economic policy issues in the Nordic countries are discussed in detail in the economic surveys published every year or two by the Organization of Economic Cooperation and Development as *Economic Surveys: Denmark,* etc. Sweden's economic problems and especially its welfare have received much international attention in the 1990s. The harshest critique may be found in the writings of Assar Lindbeck, most recently in "The Swedish Experiment," *Journal of Economic Literature* 35, September 1997, 1273–1319. A more technical and less pessimistic survey is Richard B. Freeman, Robert Topel, and Brigitta Swedenburg, *The Welfare State in Transition: Reforming the Swedish Model,* Chicago: University of Chicago Press, 1997. Both the *Financial Times* and *The Economist* regularly survey the Nordic economies, the latter most recently in June 2003.

8. At the end of the fourteenth century, all three Scandinavian crowns passed to Danish queen Margrethe I. In 1397, this union was formalized by a treaty drafted in Kalmar, Sweden. Although the Kalmar Union survived until 1523, it was constantly challenged. Norway remained united with Denmark until 1814 and then with Sweden until 1905. Iceland was part of the Danish realm until 1944. The Swedish province of Finland became a Russian Grand Duchy in 1809 and declared its independence in 1917.

9. A concise summary of the Nordic region during the Cold War may be found in "The Nordic Region: Changing Perspectives in International Relations," *The Annals of the American Academy of Political and Social Science,* Martin O. Heisler, special ed., vol. 512, November 1990; and in the books by Stephen J. Blank, *Finnish Security and European Security Policy,* Carlisle Barracks, PA: U.S. Army War College, 1996, and by Don Snidal and Arne Brundtland, *Nordic-Baltic Security,* Washington, DC: Center for Strategic and International Studies, 1993.

Suggested Readings

Derry, T. K., *A History of Scandinavia: Norway, Sweden, Denmark, Finland, and Iceland,* Minneapolis: University of Minnesota Press, 1979.

Einhorn, Eric S., and John Logue, "Can the Scandinavian Model Adapt to Globalization?" *Scandinavian Studies* 76(4), winter 2004, 501–534.

Einhorn, Eric S., and John Logue, *Modern Welfare States: Scandinavian Politics and Policy in the Global Age,* New York: Praeger, 2003.

Heidar, Knut, *Norway: Elites on Trial,* Boulder, CO: Westview, 2001.

Ingebritsen, Christine, *The Nordic States and European Union: From Economic Interdependence to Political Integration,* Ithaca, NY: Cornell University Press, 1998.

Ingebritsen, Christine, *Scandinavia in World Politics,* Boulder, CO: Rowman & Littlefield, 2006.

Jussila, Osmo, Seppo Hentilä, and Jukka Nevakivi, *From Grand Duchy to a Modern State: A Political History of Finland Since 1809,* London: Hurst, 1999.

Nordstrom, Byron J., *Dictionary of Scandinavian History,* Westport, CT: Greenwood, 1986.

Nordstrom, Byron J., *Scandinavia Since 1500,* Minneapolis: University of Minnesota Press, 2000.

Petersson, Olof, *The Government and Politics of the Nordic Countries,* Stockholm: Fritzes, 1994.

Thakur, Subhash, et al., *Sweden's Welfare State: Can the Bumblebee Keep Flying?* Washington, DC: International Monetary Fund, 2003.

CHAPTER 6

Russia: European or Not?

Bruce Parrott

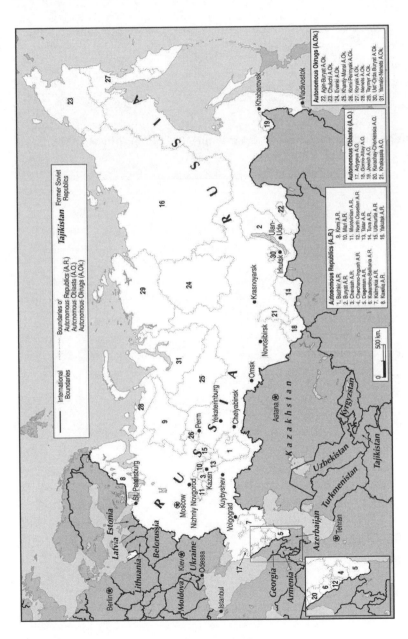

Russian Federation

Population (million):	143
Area in Square Miles:	6,592,819
Population Density per Square Mile:	22
GDP (in billion dollars, 2005):	$1,546.0
GDP per capita (PPP, 2005):	$10,801
Joined EC/EU:	n/a

Performance of Key Political Parties in Parliamentary Elections
of December 7, 2003

Communist Party	12.8%
Homeland Union	9.2%
Liberal Democratic Party	11.7%
United Russia	38.0%

Main Office Holders: President: Vladimir Putin (1999); Prime Minister: Mikhail Fradkov (2004)

Is Russia part of Europe? For almost three centuries observers have debated this question, and their answers have been shaped by the specific conditions in Europe as well as in Russia. During the eighteenth-century era of enlightened despotism, Russia's dominant elites regarded it as part of Europe, and prominent Europeans agreed. Near the start of the eighteenth century, Peter the Great, one of the most important monarchs in Russian history, traveled extensively in Europe and based his sweeping administrative and economic reforms on the models he found there. A half century later Voltaire, a leading thinker of the French Enlightenment, wrote an admiring history of Tsarist Russia and corresponded with Catherine the Great, another of Russia's modernizing autocrats.[1] Russia's acquisition of a colonial empire outside Europe strengthened its resemblance to other European imperial states. In the case of countries such as Britain and France, these empires lay overseas. In the Tsarist case, the empire grew primarily through overland expansion into adjacent territories such as the Caucasus and Central Asia. Despite this difference, the Tsars regarded their empire building as a manifestation of their country's "civilizing" European role, and so did many European observers.

However, several changes during the nineteenth and twentieth centuries raised new questions about Russia's relationship to Europe. First, the spread of heterodox political ideas in Europe aroused Russian anxiety and ambivalence about links with the West. Although the Tsars wanted to strengthen Russia through closer economic relations with Europe, they feared that nineteenth-century Europe's increasingly volatile mixture of democratic, nationalist, and Marxist ideas would infect Tsarist society. Fear of such infection nourished the mid-nineteenth-century debate between the "Westernizers," a group of political and cultural figures who believed that Russia should emulate trends in the West, and the "Slavophiles," a cultural and political group that believed Russia should follow a distinctive non-Western path of development.

In a certain sense, Tsarist fears of ideological "infection" from Europe came true when the communists seized power in Russia under Lenin's leadership near the end of World War I. However, Lenin and his successors did not intend to remake Russia along conventional Western lines. They sought to transform it according to a communist vision that existed only in the world of Marxist social theory. They viewed Europe as a theater for communist revolution rather than a model to be imitated, and they expected that communism would ultimately spread to all of Europe and beyond. In other words, they believed that the non-communist world would increasingly be modeled on the Soviet Union, not the other way around.

Rather than bridge the differences between Russia and Europe at large, the victory of a communist vanguard in Russia deepened them. For seven decades Russia, as the geographic and demographic core of the Soviet state, was the focus of the Marxist-Leninist drive to create a novel communist order. Launched under the ruthless tyranny of Joseph Stalin, this all-out drive for socioeconomic transformation not only created the world's first planned industrial economy but also killed millions of Soviet citizens through the violent collectivization of agriculture, the creation of a vast network of prison labor camps, and blood purges that decimated the ranks of the Soviet elite itself.

The communist system profoundly altered Russia's social and economic structure, but it did not spread to Europe—at least not to the Western European countries beyond the reach of Stalin's army at the end of World War II. Instead Western Europe, anchored by the strategic power of the United States, gradually evolved toward a common liberal order antithetical to communism. Due partly to the exhausting effects of World War II, the major European states were also steadily compelled to give up their colonial empires—one of the main features they had earlier shared with Tsarist Russia. In contrast to the USSR, the states of Western Europe no longer had the global ambitions and global reach they had previously possessed.

Toward the end of the twentieth century the prospects for a new convergence between Europe and Russia improved dramatically. In the mid-1980s Mikhail Gorbachev, the last Soviet leader, introduced unprecedented internal changes designed to humanize the repressive Soviet political order. These sweeping changes ultimately triggered the collapse of Soviet communism and reversed the vectors of international influence that Soviet officials had long tried to promote. After taking power in Russia and helping enact the final dissolution of the Soviet Union, President Boris Yeltsin and his political allies launched a campaign to make Russia a "normal" state based on liberal-democratic and capitalist principles borrowed from the West. In contrast to a long line of Soviet leaders, they sought to rejoin Europe rather than remake it. However, the workability of their program for westernizing the country was untested. Moreover, it was unclear whether Russia was ready to disavow the USSR's global role and operate as a regional European power.

The hallmark of this monumental effort to transform Russia has been acute uncertainty for elites and ordinary citizens alike. During the Soviet era the communist leadership tirelessly promoted the political myth that Marxism-Leninism enabled it to forecast the future. If Soviet citizens learned to discount this claim during the final decades of Soviet power, at least they experienced a large measure of predictability in their personal lives. The form of authoritarianism that evolved after Stalin's death in 1953 offered citizens a substantial measure of socioeconomic security despite heavy restrictions on political freedom. The collapse of the Soviet Union, however, exploded the predictability of daily life along with the ruling myth of communist infallibility. For some Russians the end of the Soviet system brought freedom and economic opportunity; for others, it brought political disappointment and severe economic hardship. For virtually everyone it brought great uncertainty.

The Soviet collapse also left ordinary Russians unsure of their country's international role. Would Russia establish strong links with Europe, thereby

Box 6.1   From a Speech by Deputy Head of the Presidential Administration Vladislav Surkov to Workers of the United Russia Political Party

Moscow, February 7, 2006

[A]s President [Vladimir Putin] has indicated in his speeches, on the whole we have followed the same path as other European countries. . . . [A]bsolutism reached its apogee in Russia at about the same time as in France. . . . Russia abolished "dealing in people" [serfdom and slavery] . . . even earlier than . . . the United States of America. Our parliamentarism isn't much younger than that of other countries. As for the fact that we had quite a strange totalitarian state in the twentieth century, it's necessary to remember that we weren't alone, that Nazi Germany, Fascist Italy, and Francoist Spain existed in the same Europe . . . .

The big [Soviet] problem was . . . that such a closed society . . . produced an ineffective elite. . . . [A]t a time when people of the stature of Peter the Great were needed, a group of poorly educated and irresponsible comrades came to power. . . . [Former U.S.] Secretary of State Shultz writes in his memoirs that he was shocked by the incompetence of the Soviet leaders. . . . Rejection of such a society was unavoidable. . . .

[However,] the mass of the country was not prepared . . . for life in conditions of contemporary democracy. . . . [R]ather than move toward democracy, we got . . . an oligarchy. . . . In place of public discussion we got continual court intrigue. Instead of representation we got manipulation. . . . Competition was replaced by corruption. . . . If what I've described is democracy and a free and just society, then what is Sodom and what is Gomorrah? . . . [W]hen people try to convince us that someone [in Russia] is dismantling democracy, that is an absolute distortion. . . . The president is returning the real meaning of the word "democracy" to all democratic institutions. . . .

Russia, without a doubt, must remain in the ranks of the powers that make decisions about . . . the world order. . . . [F]or 500 years ethnic Russians and Russian citizens have been a state-bearing people . . . in contrast to many of our friends from the Soviet Union and many other countries. . . . It's clear that some countries that proclaim entry into the European Union to be their national idea are very happy countries; it is not necessary for them to think much. For them everything is very simple. The "Muscovites" . . . are guilty of everything, now we're running to Brussels and everything there will be all right. It's necessary to remember that these nations were not sovereign for one day of their history. . . . This is normal. They were the province of one country and will become the province of another. . . .

[In Russia] a psychology called "offshore aristocracy" has been established. . . . [Members of this group] see their future and the future of their children as outside Russia. . . . [S]uch people will not stand up for [Russia] or be concerned about it. . . . If our business community is not transformed into a national bourgeoisie, then, of course, we have no future. . . .

(continued)

> ## Box 6.1   *(Continued)*
>
> A second line of political restorationism . . . is . . . the isolationists. . . .
> These people are almost Nazis, people who spread the idea that the terrible
> West is threatening us, that . . . China is stepping on us, . . . that Russia is for
> Russians, Tatarstan, apparently, is for Tatars, Yakutia is for Yakuts. . . . [I]f
> the national-isolationists come to power . . . [this] will lead the nation to a
> demographic catastrophe and a political crash. . . . [T]o provoke interethnic
> conflicts in our country is very dangerous. . . . [W]e must strongly oppose
> this. We stand for a Russia that is for ethnic Russians, Tatars, Mordovians,
> Ossetians, Chechens, for all of our peoples, for the entire Russia-wide nation.

expanding Europe's geographical extent and international influence? Or would it
withdraw from Europe and "face east," seeking closer ties with Asian powers
such as China in a bid to counterbalance the ascendancy of the United States and
U.S. allies in Europe? And what of its relations with the fourteen other former
republics of the USSR? Would Moscow accept their adherence to western groupings such as the European Union and NATO, or would it resist these trends?

Dimensions of Postcommunist Change

To succeed, the reform program for joining the West required fundamental
changes in the traditional Soviet order. These included establishing a new territorial state in the heart of the former USSR, creating a democratic political system for
choosing leaders and making policy, building a capitalist economy based on private ownership and competitive markets, stimulating civic activism, and creating a
system of public administration that could uphold the rule of law in public life.

Considered individually, each of these objectives was daunting. Taken
together, they represented a mammoth undertaking. Like individuals, governments have trouble dealing with more than one or two major problems at the
same time, due to the limits on their resources and decisionmaking capacity. In
the past two decades, for instance, the U.S. government has been unable to enact
effective healthcare reforms—but this is a modest task compared to the sweeping political agenda that has confronted Russian leaders and citizens. The
attempt to recast Russia's national identity, political structure, economic order,
social life, and system of public administration—*all at the same time*—was
bound to produce many unforeseeable consequences.

In deciding how to approach this complex political agenda, Russian leaders
and officials have faced perplexing choices about which political tools to use.

The consolidation of democracy is sometimes said to depend on a national consensus that "elections are the only game in town"—in other words, that no one can become a major government leader without winning a democratic election. Established democracies rest on the assumption that it is illegitimate to influence the outcome of an election by, for example, urging the armed forces to intervene or using government intelligence agencies to collect confidential information about opposition candidates. Mature democracies allow the leading candidates unfettered access to the news media. To a lesser extent, they also limit the electoral use of economic resources by, for example, buying votes or diverting government funds to favor some candidates over others. In postcommunist Russia, elections have indeed acquired heightened importance as a mechanism of elite selection and elite legitimation. However, Russia has inherited many undemocratic tools of coercion and manipulation from the Soviet era, and the competitors for power have frequently resorted to them—sometimes in order to preempt similar action by their political rivals.

The tumultuous attempt to democratize and marketize public life has imposed severe strains on Russian society. Successful cases of capitalist democracy depend on the existence of a vigorous civil society able to foster participatory values in the citizenry and articulate the social interests that feed into government decisionmaking. As used here, the term "civil society" denotes an extensive network of voluntary associations that are active, autonomous from the government, and allow individuals to join or leave on their own initiative. The fact that these civic associations accept the legitimacy of one another's interests, even when those interests diverge, is conducive to social pluralism and political compromise.[2]

In the USSR the ruling elite, guided by a fundamental hostility to social pluralism, suppressed any tendency toward the development of a civil society. The elite forced society into a straitjacket, extending the party-state apparatus into every corner of daily life and creating a façade of monolithic popular support for communist rule. This Marxist-Leninist formula for state-society relations was boldly rejected by Gorbachev after he became the leader of the USSR. Seeking to tap the population's suppressed initiative and energy, Gorbachev slashed the power of the party-state apparatus and unleashed a surge of spontaneous sociopolitical activism that initially strengthened his campaign to revitalize the Soviet system. The vast upheaval he set in motion has continued in various guises for some two decades, but its long-term social consequences remain uncertain. Has this torrent of change created the basis of a genuine civil society, or is society destined once again to become a handmaiden of the state?

Knowing a bit about the key turning points in Russia's recent development makes it easier to understand the interaction among these factors. One turning point, of course, was the dissolution of the USSR. The process of political liberalization launched by Gorbachev ultimately escaped his control and generated increasing polarization between anti-Marxist liberals and Leninist conservatives. In 1991 a radical democratic challenge from opponents of the Soviet regime and an unsuccessful last-ditch coup attempt by its supporters intensified the centrifugal forces undermining the Soviet Federation.[3] The outcome was Russia's emergence as an independent state with Boris Yeltsin as president, the promulgation of a program of radical economic reform known as "shock therapy," and a temporary ban on the Communist Party.

Another turning point came in 1993, when President Yeltsin's increasingly bitter political conflict with the Russian parliament finally prompted him to disband the parliament and use the army to crush the opponents who resisted. One result of this confrontation was the adoption of a new Russian constitution with government powers heavily skewed toward the presidency at the expense of the parliament.

A third turning point came in 1995–1996, when the severe economic hardships resulting from shock therapy made it seem likely that Yeltsin would be defeated by a communist candidate in the impending presidential election. Yeltsin seriously considered delaying the election, but in the end a group of new business tycoons who had acquired enormous wealth from the first stages of economic reform rallied around him, enabling him to mount an effective campaign and win the election. These tycoons, commonly known as "oligarchs," deeply feared a possible restoration of communist power.

A fourth turning point came in 1999–2000, when Yeltsin unexpectedly resigned a few months before the end of his term to smooth the way for Vladimir Putin, the politically untested prime minister, to become his successor. Feverish maneuvering in the run-up to the election enabled Putin to defeat better-known presidential candidates who might have prosecuted Yeltsin and his close associates for corruption. Putin, who had spent most of his career in the Soviet security service, began to place security service "alumni" in other state agencies and took steps to rein in the most aggressive oligarchs.

A fifth turning point came in 2003–2005, when Putin's campaign to establish political order and tame the oligarchs culminated in the targeted destruction of Yukos, the country's largest and most efficient oil company. The Yukos affair redefined the relationship between wealth and power in Russia. It marked the ascendancy of political elites determined to reestablish the dominance of the Russian state, and it paved the way for further reductions of electoral competition and freedom in the political arena. These changes were manifested in Putin's landslide victory in the 2004 presidential election against a field of minor political personalities.

National Identity and Statehood

Russia's postcommunist experience highlights the complex interaction among national identity, statehood, and democratization. Today the view that every nation should have its own territorial state, or sovereign political structure, is widely accepted. However, the fit between existing nations and established states is anything but automatic. Most contemporary observers agree that nations are social groupings whose distinguishing characteristics can change over time; they also agree that in the absence of a common understanding about who belongs to a nation—and therefore to the corresponding state—democratization is extremely difficult. Democratic theory rests on the proposition that a nation or a people (the *demos* in the word democracy) must govern itself.

But what if there is widespread disagreement about which individuals and territories belong to the nation? Democratic theory cannot answer this fundamental question. The problem cannot be resolved by invoking the principle of national self-determination, because conducting a national plebiscite or convening a representative national assembly requires prior agreement on which individuals are entitled to vote or be represented—the very question that the procedure is supposed to solve. Without a shared understanding of national identity, the inhabitants of a territory are likely to clash over whether they should have a single state or separate states. So any historical situation that requires recasting a nation's identity or a state structure to make them compatible hobbles the attempt to build democracy.

The Soviet breakup posed the question of which persons and lands belong to the Russian nation. This conundrum was somewhat mitigated by the fact that the Russian republic had been one of the constituent elements of the now-defunct Soviet Federation. Provisional Russian boundaries and a set of rudimentary political institutions already existed; indeed, these institutions were the mechanisms Yeltsin and his allies used to build up power on the eve of the Soviet collapse. Still, independent Russia's emergence from a larger state hampered the construction of a new political system. Many inhabitants of Russia remained ambivalent about the diminution of the state and the apparent shrinkage of the Russian nation.

One problem was whether to "unmix" the multinational populations inherited from the USSR—and if so, how. Many ethnic Russians lived in other former Soviet republics, and many non-ethnic Russians (such as Ukrainians or Georgians) lived in Russia. Should all of these people become citizens of their "ethnic homeland" and "return" to it, even if they were born in another republic and had always lived there? Like most former Soviet republics, Russia dealt with this question by offering national citizenship to all its inhabitants (as well as to the inhabitants of other republics who requested it). Nevertheless, the issue of ethnic Russians living abroad has remained a sore point in Russian domestic politics and foreign policy. This is especially true of Russia's relations with Estonia and Latvia, two former Soviet republics that have refused to grant citizenship automatically to the ethnic Russians who put down roots there during the Soviet era. These countries have established stringent criteria for naturalization to emphasize that they were forcibly incorporated into the USSR under Stalin and to fend off any new efforts by Moscow to control them through the local ethnic Russian population. For most ethnic Balts, as well as the citizens of some other former Soviet republics, the end of Moscow's domination represents a deeply satisfying national achievement that must be carefully preserved.

Most inhabitants of Russia view the Soviet collapse through a different lens. For many of them the breakup of the Soviet state came to be perceived as a national loss. Even though the USSR was not a purely Russian state, Russian culture and language enjoyed a privileged position within it, and many Russians regarded the whole of the USSR as their homeland. Hence they regretted the independence of the other constituent republics, especially Belarus and Ukraine, whose main national groups have East Slavic origins in common with ethnic Russians.[4]

Although Moscow has gradually negotiated border agreements with most other former Soviet republics, the problem of ethnically mixed populations remains a source of political anxiety. This is especially true because contemporary Russia itself is a federation consisting partly of regional units that are the nominal homelands of non-Russian ethnic minorities such as the Tatars. The resulting fear that Russia might disintegrate just as the USSR did helps explain why during the past dozen years Moscow has waged two brutal local wars to prevent Chechnya, a small region in Russia's southwest inhabited primarily by the Chechen ethnic minority, from becoming independent. The brutality of Moscow's military forces has been paralleled by numerous acts of terrorism that Chechen insurgents have committed in southern Russia and in Moscow.

Constitutions and Elections

Building reliable political institutions on these uncertain national-territorial foundations has been difficult. In the late 1980s Gorbachev introduced media freedoms and contested elections as part of his campaign to democratize the Soviet system. But no stable set of democratic institutions crystallized across the USSR, and Russia's achievement of independence at the end of 1991 sharpened the basic contradictions among its own government organs. According to Russia's Soviet-era constitution, the Russian republic's government was parliamentary in form. However, as part of his struggle against Gorbachev, Yeltsin had used a popular referendum to create a new Russian presidency and had won the ensuing election. When the USSR disintegrated soon afterward, independent Russia emerged as an awkward political hybrid. The parliamentary powers enshrined in the constitution conflicted with the powers exercised by the president.

During the brief surge of national enthusiasm following the failed conservative coup and Russia's achievement of independence, the parliament granted Yeltsin authority to make a wide range of decisions by presidential decree, but tensions soon escalated as Yeltsin and his parliamentary critics argued over drafts of a new constitution and traded accusations over the mounting human price of shock therapy. Convinced that Yeltsin was driving the economy to ruin, these critics adopted increasingly confrontational tactics, including a serious threat to impeach the president. Yeltsin finally decided to dissolve the parliament; many of his parliamentary opponents barricaded themselves inside the parliament building and designated their own national president and minister of defense. Yeltsin ended the standoff by ordering the military to shell the parliament building and arrest his parliamentary opponents. Although he reneged on his promise to make early presidential elections part of a crisis settlement, suspicions that he harbored dictatorial ambitions were somewhat allayed by his decision to hold early elections for a new parliament and conduct a referendum on his proposed new constitution.

The 1993 crisis has exercised a lasting influence on Russia's political development. Successful democratization requires the establishment of a constitutional structure that limits the government's capacity for arbitrary action, and the revamped constitutional structure that emerged from Yeltsin's victory over parliament gives too much power to the presidency. Under the Yeltsin constitution, the parliament lacks the authority to approve the president's selection of ministers for the government cabinet; it can reject his nominee for prime minister, but if it does so three times consecutively he can dissolve the parliament and call new parliamentary elections. This situation has made it very difficult for the legislature to exercise effective oversight over ministerial behavior and the performance of government agencies, since cabinet ministers are beholden for their posts to the president rather than to the prime minister and other parliamentarians. With one brief exception, none of the prime ministers Yeltsin appointed during his eight years as president came from the party with the largest representation in the parliament.

Almost as serious has been the problem of creating an autonomous judiciary that can interpret the laws dispassionately and ensure that officials and citizens obey them. In 1993 the Constitutional Court was caught in the political cross fire between Yeltsin and the parliament, and Yeltsin showed his displeasure over the court's role by reducing its powers under the new constitution. The Soviet legacy of disdain for courts and the legal rights of individuals has made courts at the lower levels of the judicial system especially weak and susceptible to political pressures. Burdened with many judges selected during the Soviet era for their subservience, the courts must also contend with powerful government investigators and prosecutors who are used to overriding legal safeguards and giving breaks to well-connected individuals. As a result, the judicial branch has generally been unable to counter corruption and other dysfunctional official behavior, including widespread jurisdictional conflicts between the central government and regional governments.

Together with a constitutional structure based on checks and balances, competitive elections are the bedrock of a functioning democracy. Although

Russia has held national parliamentary and presidential elections at regular intervals since 1993, the conduct of these elections has frequently fallen short of fully democratic standards. This is especially true of elections to the presidency, the most powerful institution in the political system.

On the eve of the 1996 presidential campaign, Yeltsin's single-digit public approval ratings seemed to guarantee that he would be defeated, perhaps by the candidate of the refurbished Communist Party of the Russian Federation (CPRF). Faced with this prospect, Yeltsin made preparations to declare a state of emergency and postpone the election, and some oligarchs signaled that they would favor this step. Significantly, Yeltsin's presidential campaign committee included the head of the Federal Security Service, Russia's main institutional successor of the Soviet Committee for State Security (KGB). It also included the head of the Presidential Security Service, part of a twenty-thousand-strong leadership-protection force that possessed substantial intelligence-gathering capabilities of its own.[5] The chief of the Presidential Security Service, a long-time Yeltsin confidant, repeatedly urged that the election be postponed, and only after he lost a political struggle with other campaign advisors did Yeltsin decide to hold it on time.

Measured by one key yardstick, the election marked the democratic high point of Russia's long political history. The intensity of contestation among the candidates and the closeness of the vote totals were unprecedented.[6] But the election also suffered from serious shortcomings. The media, which were dominated by a handful of new business tycoons who favored Yeltsin's reelection and journalists with a strong aversion to communism, devoted disproportionately large coverage to Yeltsin's campaign and very little to that of his CPRF opponent. Moreover, the media failed to reveal that between the two rounds of voting Yeltsin suffered a heart attack that raised serious questions about his capacity to fulfill the duties of the presidency.

Four years later the transfer of presidential power from Yeltsin to Putin was marred by much more serious political machinations. In parliamentary elections held shortly before the presidential election was to occur, government-owned media outlets launched vicious personal attacks on the two prospective presidential candidates who had the greatest chance of winning the presidency. Deterred by their shrinking popularity ratings, these two candidates ultimately decided not to run, although the CPRF candidate and a few other nationally known politicians stayed in the race. Yeltsin then resigned a few months early, paving the way for Prime Minister Putin, his chosen successor, to become acting president and defeat this less threatening assortment of opponents in early presidential balloting. During the abbreviated electoral contest Putin did not deign to present a campaign platform; his victory was already virtually certain. On taking office, his first public act was to issue a decree granting Yeltsin, as a former president, immunity from arrest, prosecution, and interrogation.

The 2004 presidential contest marked the post-Soviet low for presidential elections. Thanks to the Kremlin's tight control of the media, Putin's high public approval ratings, and the possibility of provoking personal retaliation, no national politician with a serious political following was willing to enter the race. Instead, Putin faced a small group of second-rank candidates; the contest was like a series of Ralph Naders challenging an incumbent U.S. president.[7] Under these conditions, even prospective Russian voters who told interviewers they were dissatisfied had trouble naming a candidate they supported. Putin won a landslide victory, racking up more than 70 percent of the vote.

In addition to fair elections, successful democratization hinges on the creation of a system of political parties that enables voters to hold government leaders responsible for the government's conduct. Russian parties, however, make little contribution to this democratic objective. For most of the postcommunist period they have been weak and, with a few exceptions, short-lived. The most important exception is the CPRF, which inherited the grass-roots structure and die-hard adherents who previously belonged to the Communist Party of the Soviet Union. Another is the relatively liberal Yabloko party, whose political fortunes have declined sharply in recent years.

Many parties have sprung up or disappeared, dividing and uniting with new political factions, making it almost impossible for voters to hold party politicians responsible for government actions. For example, in 1999 three of the biggest party contenders—Fatherland–All Russia, the Union of Right Forces, and Unity—were all created between two and four months before the parliamentary election. In both the 1999 and 2003 parliamentary elections 60 percent of the votes for the national party-list seats were cast for parties that had not competed in the previous election. Moreover, most parties are centered in Moscow and lack solid regional roots.[8]

During Putin's first presidential term, the government adopted a new party law and an electoral law designed to strengthen parties, but its effects have been mixed at best. In 2003 United Russia, a new umbrella party, won slightly less than two-fifths of the party-list vote in the parliamentary elections, but ultimately obtained control of more than two-thirds of the seats in the lower house of parliament when members elected as independents aligned themselves with the party. Although this outcome enhanced Putin's dominance of the legislature, vertical party links between the top of the political system and politics at the regional and grass-roots levels have actually weakened. In 2003 an opinion survey revealed that the proportion of respondents who said that none of the existing parties represented their interests had climbed to almost 50 percent.[9]

The weakness of the party system can be traced to several causes. To begin with, well-connected electoral candidates can turn to the media as a powerful alternative mechanism for mobilizing voters. In the United States the media have been an important long-term factor weakening political parties; the parallel effects in Russia have been much more pronounced because of the absence of preexisting party structures and traditions. In addition, well-endowed interest groups may find lobbying the executive branch and bribing bureaucrats more effective ways of achieving preferential treatment on some particular issue than pursuing general changes in the law through legislative parties. Moreover, most presidential candidates have not affiliated themselves with a particular party. Rather than treat the creation of a durable political party as a major leadership task, both Yeltsin and Putin chose to run for office and to govern in a "nonpartisan" fashion that gives the appearance of putting them above the partisan political fray.

At the grass-roots level, party formation has been hampered by widespread public suspicion that anyone who joins a political party invites the kind of compulsory political participation and restrictions on personal autonomy that membership in the CPSU imposed. As in other postcommunist countries, this aversion to organizational membership has also undercut public willingness to participate in the civil-society organizations that ordinarily feed into the activities of political parties.

Paths Toward Capitalism

The trauma of shock therapy starkly dramatized the complex relationship between democratization and capitalist economic reform. Although free markets are necessary for the survival of democracy, democracy is not always necessary for the creation of an effective market economy, and the relationship between the *processes* of democratization and marketization is especially problematic.

In Russia, where the government had controlled all enterprises as part of a centrally administered command economy, building capitalism required that reformers carry out three broad types of change: liberalization (paring back government intervention in price-setting, distribution, foreign trade, and so forth); stabilization (balancing government budgets and limiting the growth of the money supply to prevent runaway inflation); and privatization (distributing most state property to private owners subject to the economic discipline of competitive markets). In the Soviet era, attempts to introduce much more limited economic reforms in a gradual fashion had been defeated by the foot-dragging tactics of political and bureaucratic opponents. Together with the severity of the economic problems carried over from the final Soviet years, this may be one reason the Yeltsin government tried to introduce its market reforms in a single "big bang."

The political consequences of attempting shock therapy turned out to be different from what many observers expected. The most enthusiastic proponents prophesied that rapid marketization under the auspices of a democratic government would create many "winners"—economic and social groups committed to institutionalizing capitalism and democratic political practices. By contrast, some pessimistic opponents warned that rapid marketization would create so many losers and so much suffering among ordinary citizens that it would trigger an authoritarian popular backlash against democratization as well as economic reform. The outcome fell midway between these forecasts. Attempts to implement shock therapy turned out to be far more difficult and painful than its proponents had anticipated, but the short-term effects were less damaging to electoral democracy than many of the opponents had feared. Nonetheless, shock therapy did damage the quality of Russian political life in ways that became clearer with the passage of time.

Although some reformers tried to ensure that privatization would give ordinary Russians a material stake in shock therapy, the main beneficiaries were officials carried over from the Soviet elite and a significant number of ambitious newcomers willing to seize economic opportunities and exploit them ruthlessly. Bear in mind that the volume of economic resources waiting to be privatized was huge, and that there was no tested body of law and administrative procedure to regulate the scramble for ownership. It is as if the U.S. government owned hundreds of corporations such as Microsoft, Exxon Mobil, du Pont, US Steel, United Airlines, and General Motors, and suddenly had to decide how to distribute them to the public in the midst of a paralyzing constitutional crisis over executive-legislative relations and relations between the federal government and the states. With economic stakes like these up for grabs, Russia's shaky governmental structures came under enormous pressure. To capture and hold these large new sources of wealth, ambitious individuals had compelling motives to manipulate the loose government privatization guidelines and, when necessary, to subvert basic democratic processes.

Paradoxically, the size of the economic stakes also made it harder to carry out shock therapy completely. Some aspiring members of the new economic elite had an interest in freezing economic reform at the halfway point—i.e., at a stage where they had become owners but could exploit their personal connections with government officials and the loopholes in the many remaining forms of regulation to reap spectacular gains.[10] For the same reason, government officials in a position to extract bribes had little incentive to reduce or streamline the regulations. Take the example of oil exports. Attempting to avoid a further inflation spike, the government kept energy prices much lower at home than they were on the world market. This in turn required that it limit oil exports to keep adequate supplies inside the country. Hence any businessman able to wangle a government license to export oil was guaranteed an extravagant profit, and any official with the power to grant a license—a power soon acquired by Yeltsin's Presidential Security Service—was in a position to obtain a handsome bribe.

Because privatization was slanted toward individuals with inside connections, it created an economy with an exceptionally high concentration of ownership and a disproportionately large number of rich capitalists by international standards. Today Russia ranks between tenth and fifteenth in the world by size of GDP. This puts it in the economic neighborhood of Spain, Brazil, and Mexico. However, Russia ranks fourth worldwide in the number of billionaires, all of them created in no more than a decade and a half. Only the United States,

Germany, and Japan have more billionaires. Russia's new rich have benefited from once-in-a-lifetime economic opportunities offered by the cut-rate privatization of state assets and other methods of manipulating government policies. Highly profitable export sectors, such as the oil and gas industries and aluminum production, have become the focus of an especially bitter struggle for ownership and control among business and government elites.

The struggle to acquire valuable properties and economic favors from the state has been ruthless and sometimes deadly. The economic opportunities created by shock therapy were enormous, but so were the risks. Criminal gangs quickly became involved in the quest for property and state favors, and the disputes were often settled by violence. In the "mob war" of the early 1990s, dozens of bankers were assassinated, mostly in Moscow.[11] The career of Boris Berezovsky exemplifies the dangers and opportunities of these years. During the 1990s Berezovsky became one of the country's most powerful tycoons and wielded great influence over the policies and even the electoral survival of the Yeltsin government. However, achieving this status nearly cost him his life. In 1993 Berezovsky, still a minor economic player with ties to organized crime, fled for several months to Israel to avoid physical threats. The next year, after returning to Russia, he narrowly escaped being killed by a car bomb planted by rivals for control of the bourgeoning automobile market.

Faced with such physical dangers, the oligarchs sought to protect themselves by creating their own security forces. The Yeltsin government's continuing budgetary crisis led to drastic reductions in the funding of government agencies, including the military and the security police, and to sharp reductions in personnel. Under these conditions, the oligarchs used their new wealth to buy the services of individuals skilled in the arts of intelligence gathering and physical coercion. These individuals were recruited from the ranks of security agencies, the armed forces, and sports clubs.

Consider the example of the holding company founded by Vladimir Gusinsky, a rising media tycoon during the early Yeltsin years. To protect its property and enforce its agreements with other firms, Gusinsky's company established a one-thousand-man private security force. The force was headed by Filip Bobkov, a former deputy chairman of the KGB who had led the KGB department responsible for monitoring and repressing dissenters critical of the Soviet regime. Many free-standing private security concerns were set up by former government officials with similar backgrounds. By one count, half of these private firms were headed by retired KGB officers, one-quarter by retired officers from the Ministry of Internal Affairs, and the rest by retired officers from military intelligence and other agencies.[12] These trends show that the oligarchs' new wealth gave them the capacity to purchase coercive and intelligence resources that had previously been the sole prerogative of the state. They reflect the oligarchs' search for personal security and commercial advantage in the chaotic political and economic conditions of the 1990s.

During the Yeltsin era, security was much easier for rich businessmen to buy than for entrepreneurs of modest means. In the first two or three years of economic reform many new businesses were started. Soon, however, the reported growth in the number of small businesses flattened out. There were two main causes for this change. One was a surge in the activities of organized crime, which saw small businesses as easy targets for the extortion of "protection" payments. Another was the growth of predatory behavior by government officials, especially tax officials, who used their posts to squeeze bribes out of small business owners in exchange for allowing them to operate with fewer hindrances. To reduce such harassment, many small entrepreneurs switched their activities to the underground economy; in the late 1990s government estimates indicated that at least one-quarter of the country's economic activity was in the unofficial sector. Although some of the reported slowdown in establishing new businesses was due to such evasive behavior, much of it was undoubtedly real. The Russian statistics present a striking contrast to other postcommunist countries such as Poland and Hungary, where new businesses were about eight times as numerous in per capita terms and accounted for a substantial share of GDP.[13]

The obstacles to the creation and expansion of small businesses had political implications as well as economic ones. In most countries, the owners of small businesses are an important element of the middle class and one of its main economic underpinnings. In Russia, however, the conditions of shock therapy impeded the growth of this socioeconomic group. The Russian middle class has grown in the post-Soviet period, but it contains disproportionately large numbers of white-collar workers employed at various levels of government. Some evidence suggests that in Russia, small-enterprise owners are the business group most favorably disposed toward the election of political leaders and the rule of law, probably because they lack the connections and resources used by big business owners to get special favors from the government.[14] On the other hand, white-collar government employees lack independent sources of legitimate income but do have opportunities for graft that predispose them against reform. The stunted development of the small business sector has therefore narrowed the social foundation for the growth of democracy in Russia.

During the Putin years the forms of elite competition over property have changed significantly. The recourse to physical violence to settle business disputes has declined markedly, but this does not signify that Russian business practices are converging with those of the advanced capitalist countries. By undercutting the resources of some oligarchs, the severe financial crisis of 1998 triggered a new round of struggle in which aggressive new claimants manipulated bankruptcy laws and local "pocket" jurisdictions to wrest holdings from their financially weakened competitors. In other words, a bitter struggle among business magnates continued even after a large amount of property had been transferred from state ownership to private hands. This raised the question of whether privatization had prompted Russian tycoons to put a new emphasis on productive entrepreneurship or had simply perpetuated their past preoccupation with amassing greater quantities of assets, and whether government reformers could promote such a shift by strengthening the curbs on illicit economic activities.[15] Although the answer remained uncertain, in 2006 the gangland-style murder of the deputy chairman of the Russian Central Bank, the leader of a government campaign to eliminate corruption from the commercial banking sector, sharpened doubts that reformers could tame the all-out struggle for economic advantage.

Public Administration and Federalism

Successful democratization and marketization both depend on basic changes in the operation of government agencies. Recent U.S. observers have tended to regard good public administration as a natural by-product of political and economic liberalization, but in fact effective bureaucracies are an unusual modern achievement that should not be taken for granted. Under certain conditions, liberalization can actually worsen the functioning of government bureaucracies and heighten the administrative obstacles to successful reform. To achieve a transition to capitalist democracy, government agencies must give up many previous powers connected with the centralized control of society while taking on many new tasks connected with the operation of a market economy. Bureaucrats frequently have a strong incentive not to give up their old prerogatives, especially when these can be used to extract bribes. Moreover, they often lack the capacity to carry out their new responsibilities due to a shortage of the necessary technical skills or guidance from up-to-date laws.

These problems become especially severe when the territorial state is being recast. In the modern world, states are the master institutions of social life. The stability of nearly all other institutions—the worth of the national currency, the rules of property ownership and inheritance, business contracts, court verdicts, the validity of marriages, the certification of professional credentials, and the allocation of the electronic broadcast spectrum, to name just a few—hinges on the integrity of the state. When the state is weakened, other institutions are called into question and effective governance becomes much more difficult.

Take, for example, the early efforts of the Yeltsin government to establish a modern central bank and manage the national currency (the ruble). When Russia declared independence it had a central bank of sorts, but the bank had not yet established some key financial tools, such as a market in government bonds, that are available to central bankers in developed capitalist countries. Moreover, the man who headed the bank in the mid-1990s believed that its main purpose was to keep industrial firms afloat with heavily subsidized loans, rather than to protect the value of the currency against inflation. This situation was compounded by the nature of the Soviet breakup, which gave the central banks of all the other former republics the authority to issue ruble credits—thereby preventing the Russian Central Bank from controlling the growth of the money supply. Within two or three years the government solved this problem by abolishing the "ruble zone" that united most of the former Soviet republics, but not before great economic and human damage had been done in Russia.

Similar and longer-lasting problems plagued the government's effort to collect taxes and balance the budget. During the final stage of Yeltsin's political duel with Gorbachev, the government of the Russian republic waged an economic war against the Soviet central government for the control of fiscal resources and industrial enterprises. The aim was to cripple the central government by encouraging Russian banks and regional administrations to refuse to pay their customary taxes into the federal budget while continuing to draw their regular subsidies from the same budget. In addition, Yeltsin and his allies undermined the central government's control over enterprises located in Russia by offering the enterprise managers lower tax rates and enlarged subsidies if they would shift their allegiance to the Russian government. One effect of this political tactic was to show regional administrators and economic managers that they could avoid or reduce tax burdens by negotiating with higher-level overseers and playing them off against each other.[16] This lesson, which persisted long after the Soviet breakup, contributed to the plunge in the Russian government's own tax receipts, which fell from about one-sixth of GDP in 1992 to less than one-tenth of GDP in 1996.

Russia's problems with public administration have been intensified by the country's geographic immensity and cultural diversity. Even without the rest of the USSR, the territory of the Russian Federation still encompasses eleven time zones and an ethnically diverse population. About one-quarter of Russia's eighty-eight territorial units are so-called autonomous republics formally designated as the homelands of particular ethnic minorities such as the Tatars. This feature of Russia's federal structure bears a limited resemblance to the ethnofederal structure of the USSR (where all the constituent republics were designated as the homelands of particular ethnonational groups). As mentioned above, this structural resemblance has contributed to the fears of some observers and government officials that Russia, too, might disintegrate, and has played a role in Moscow's policies toward the breakaway region of Chechnya.

During the Yeltsin years relations between the federal government and the regions were marked by a dramatic "power deflation." Like the USSR as a whole, Soviet Russia had been a federation in name but a unitary state in fact, and during the 1990s a large amount of administrative and economic power shifted from Moscow toward various regions. The specific allocation of power between Moscow and individual regions was decided through horse-trading and bilateral power-sharing deals whose terms were generally kept secret. As a result, Russia had no consistent national pattern of center-region relations arrived at through public discussion and legislative action—one of the key features of a genuine federation.[17] Playing on divisions and disorganization inside the federal government, the most assertive regions managed to wrest a great deal of power from Moscow and often ignored its wishes.

For its part, the Yeltsin government needed regional governments to support it, especially by using their so-called administrative resources to mobilize the pro-Yeltsin vote during federal election campaigns. During the 1996 presidential campaign, for example, Yeltsin offered about a dozen regions new agreements that expanded their control over regional natural resources and finances. These circumstances spawned many legal and policy contradictions between the federal and regional governments. One analysis at the end of Yeltsin's presidency found that about one-quarter of regional laws and regulations were incompatible with the federal constitution.[18]

Putin has worked hard to eliminate such inconsistencies and reclaim power for the central government. Putin's consolidation of personal power in the presidency has made it much harder for the regions to gain concessions by playing off political actors in Moscow against each other, especially during elections. In addition, soon after taking office Putin established seven administrative "super regions" headed by presidential appointees. The leader of each super region is supposed to supervise about a dozen regional governments and ensure that their policies mesh with those approved in Moscow. Along with a tightening of Moscow's control over appointments, these presidential overseers have curbed regional influence over the regional offices of various federal agencies, such as tax collection and law enforcement.

Although this step has eliminated many contradictions between regional and federal laws, the subsequent adoption of new regional laws has generated fresh contradictions that will be difficult to eliminate in the absence of an effective court system with the power to resolve jurisdictional conflicts. This is probably one reason that in 2004–2005 Putin pushed through a federal law replacing the popular election of regional executives with appointment by the president (and pro forma approval by the regional legislature). Although rationalized as a response to a bloody school seizure by Chechen terrorists, the measure was actually an additional attempt to strengthen the leverage of the federal government in the country's far-flung regions. It further undermined the elements of federalism in Russia, and it posed a serious risk of overcentralization of power in the presidency.

The Depletion of Society

The past two decades of upheaval have taken Russian citizens on a dizzying roller-coaster ride from the heights of optimism to the depths of despair and part way back. Public optimism and political involvement peaked during Gorbachev's campaign for *glasnost* (uncensored public discussion) and *perestroika* (restructuring and reform). At the height of the campaign, the number of subscriptions to liberal newspapers containing real news skyrocketed, while subscriptions to orthodox newspapers stagnated or declined. There was a logical connection between *glasnost* and this surge in popular attention to political affairs, since open news media are a key mechanism through which potential members of civil-society groups learn about one another and articulate their common interests.

The level of direct public participation in politics also soared, even at moments when physical repression was a real danger. Near the climax of the struggle for political liberalization in the spring of 1991, pro-Yeltsin forces staged several Moscow protests that drew as many as 200,000 demonstrators. When Gorbachev declared a ban on public demonstrations and mobilized 50,000 troops to enforce it, Yeltsin countered by calling for another demonstration. Faced with a massive protest turnout on the streets of Moscow, Gorbachev pulled back from ordering a military assault, and Yeltsin and the demonstrators prevailed.

Since this high point of public enthusiasm and involvement, Russian society has undergone a marked political demobilization. In part this demobilization was caused by shock therapy. The decision to free many prices caused a huge spike in inflation that wiped out the savings of many ordinary Russians. Although the depositors had banked these savings during the Soviet years partly because they could not find any goods they wanted to buy, slashing the apparent buying power of the accounts had a devastating emotional impact—especially because it was followed by a plunge in the real standard of living for many citizens. In the first three years of shock therapy, Russia's GDP fell by between one-third and one-half, and continued to contract for most of the decade. Sustained growth did not resume for almost eight years, and then only after a severe new financial crisis that drove down real wages by one-third between 1997 and 1998. The plunge impoverished many white-collar employees, technical specialists, and skilled workers, especially those employed in the state sector—in other words, many people who had substantial educational and professional credentials.[19] This dire economic situation was compounded by mounting wage arrears, as cash-starved employers tried to bridge the financial gap by holding back the wages they owed their employees.

These socioeconomic shocks coincided with a broader demographic crisis in Russian society. Since independence Russia's reported population has declined by about 4 percent, to about 143 million persons. Male life expectancy has dropped from 62 years to 58.6 years, and female life expectancy from 73.8 to 72.1 years.[20] The origins of the crisis can be traced back to the final three or four decades of Soviet power, but the trauma of shock therapy has made it worse, and Russia's rate of population loss is likely to accelerate under the influence of high levels of environmental pollution and other severe public health problems.[21]

Although Putin has identified the demographic crisis as the most acute problem facing Russia, the government's response to it has been weak, especially with

respect to the mounting danger of an AIDS epidemic that could sharply accelerate the population decline. Demographers project a total population of about 134
million inhabitants in 2020; the median estimate for 2050 is around 111 million.
Some observers predict that the economy will soon be hamstrung by a severe
shortage of workers and that the declining number of able-bodied men of draft
age may cut the military to less than half its current size. As in other countries,
the demand for labor has contributed to high levels of immigration, much of it
illegal, from Third World regions such as Central Asia. The influx of these non-
Slavic immigrants has been large enough to spark vigorous public controversy,
but not large enough to eliminate the negative economic consequences of the
population decline.

The country's ethnic diversity has increasingly become a source of social
tensions. About 80 percent of the population consists of ethnic Russians.
Although this is a much higher level of ethnic homogeneity than the USSR had,
some parts of Russia, such as the Northern Caucasus and the Middle Volga
regions, have large concentrations of ethnic minorities. The marked increase in
friction between ethnic Russians and ethnic groups from the Northern Caucasus has been reflected in a growing Russian tendency to view all inhabitants
from the Caucasus as members of a single racial category of untrustworthy
"blacks." Ethnic Russians are especially hostile to the Chechens—an attitude
that has been reinforced by the wars in Chechnya and dramatic acts of terrorism
by Chechen rebels. During Putin's presidency Russian hate crimes directed
against minorities have received widespread publicity, and popular sentiment
favoring "Russia for the Russians" has gained ground. This outlook has received
support from the highly conservative clerics who dominate the Russian Orthodox Church. Some of these churchmen contend that to be a Russian an individual must have an Orthodox background—a narrow view that relegates the
members of non-Orthodox minorities to second-class status.

These trends pose the question of whether Russia is becoming a society that
is predominantly "uncivil." In any society, the uncivil and civil sectors have
some features in common: both consist of active voluntary associations, and
both are autonomous from the state. The key difference is that uncivil groups
refuse to acknowledge that other groups' interests are legitimate and deal with
them by illicit means that may include violence. Organized crime, networks of
corruption, and terrorist groups are all examples of uncivil social elements in
Russia. Of course, even solidly democratic countries are home to some uncivil
groups. The United States, for instance, has a long tradition of organized crime
in big cities such as Chicago and New York, as well as a history of hate groups
such as the Ku Klux Klan. The key issue is the relative weight of civil and uncivil
groups in a given country.

In Russia, the balance between civil and uncivil groups is unfavorable. The
level of citizen membership in voluntary associations is very low. In postcom-

munist countries the level of associational membership is generally lower than in countries emerging from non-communist authoritarian systems. But Russia's level is low even by comparison with most other postcommunist countries, and the professional and entrepreneurial elements of society have taken few steps to organize themselves and protect their interests as groups.[22] The level of membership in trade unions is a partial exception, but most unions have been carried over from the Soviet era and have retained members largely because they still exercise control over social welfare benefits.

Much as in the Soviet era, trust plays a major part in the life of ordinary Russians, but they place their trust in individuals with whom they have long-standing personal ties, not in impersonal civic organizations. Although a substantial number of nongovernmental organizations (NGOs) have been created, most lack broad-based support and rely heavily on foreign donors for funding. The pursuit of outside funding distracts NGOs from developing strong grass-roots connections and focusing on the issues that most concern ordinary Russians; it also makes them vulnerable to the charge that they are the tools of foreign governments. On the "uncivil" side of the ledger, the level of criminal activity remains high, and corruption continues to expand. Opinion surveys conducted during Putin's second term showed that more than 60 percent of the public believed the governing authorities to be corrupt, up substantially from the level of public skepticism when Putin became president.[23]

The attitudes of the Russian public combine a positive disposition toward democracy with persisting cynicism and ambivalence. Russians recognize and prize the new personal freedoms they have gained as a result of the end of Soviet power. However, they regard the Russian government as just as unresponsive to public opinion as the Soviet government was, despite the introduction of multi-candidate elections. In fact, survey respondents believe the Russian government is less likely than the USSR was to treat them fairly, in part because they see it as far more corrupt. Although Russians have an unusually high regard for Putin as a leader, they have very low opinions of the national parliament, the cabinet, the courts, and political parties—levels far lower than those typical of EU citizens.[24]

Surveys show that most Russians are opposed to major changes of political structure—such as a military dictatorship—that would amount to a formal repudiation of democratic principles. However, they are much less ready to condemn arbitrary official acts, including violations of human rights and press freedoms that citizens in most European countries would regard as undemocratic. A minority of respondents, young as well as old, also have ambivalent or positive feelings about Stalin as a leader.[25] Overall, much of this rather pessimistic world view might be regarded as rational, given Russia's recent history. However, without a positive disposition toward civic and political action, ordinary Russians cannot be expected to exert a significant influence on the evolution of the political system.

The Quest for a "Strong State"

When Putin became president in 2000, most Russians greeted him as a welcome change from the ailing and erratic Yeltsin. Methodical and low-key, the new president spoke frankly about the country's problems and seemed determined to address them. He put a special emphasis on establishing order in Russian public life and strengthening the faltering economy. Putin promised to establish the "dictatorship of law" by requiring consistent compliance from the oligarchs as well as ordinary citizens and by working to make the laws and administrative decisions of various state organs consistent with one another.

Among Putin's early achievements were the introduction of simplified tax laws, which increased the government's revenues and helped it pay down foreign debts, and an impressive economic revival sustained in large measure by a dramatic rise in the price of Russian oil on global markets. The enthusiastic public response to these changes was easy to understand. Between 2000 and 2005 the average real income of Russians increased by about 75 percent, halving the number of people below the official poverty line. Putin's public approval ratings consistently ranked above 70 percent and sometimes climbed to the low 80s.[26]

Although Putin regularly paid lip service to the goal of further democratization as well as economic liberalization, his acts increasingly belied his words. One straw in the wind was his heavy reliance on personnel with security service backgrounds to fill governmental posts having nothing to do with security issues. Putin had risen rapidly from relative political obscurity during the 1990s and lacked a wide circle of politicians he could trust. A belief that this narrow political base would limit his freedom of action may have been Yeltsin's main motive for choosing him to become the next president.

Putin coped with this paucity of tested political acquaintances by turning to individuals with backgrounds in the security police and the armed forces—the so-called *siloviki* or "force wielders." Individuals with these backgrounds made up about a third of the ministers and deputy ministers appointed in Putin's early years as president, plus about 70 percent of the staffs of the new super regions.[27] Within this pool, former members of the security services were politically more significant than ex-military men because the security services had traditionally penetrated all parts of Russian society and possessed an assortment of manipulative tools that extended well beyond the threat or use of violence.

These staffing decisions bolstered the tendency of the state to play an increasingly assertive role. The initial targets of state pressure were Berezovsky and Gusinsky, the two tycoons who had acquired dominant positions in the media and had used their media clout to advance their own narrow objectives. Under Kremlin-orchestrated harassment from the tax police, the courts, and compliant creditors such as the giant Gazprom energy corporation, the two were stripped of their media empires and driven into foreign exile.

The most important watershed in the Kremlin's relations with the oligarchs was the Khodorkovsky affair of 2003–2005. Mikhail Khodorkovsky, head of Yukos, the richest and best-managed Russian oil company, rejected indirect signals from the government that he should follow these other oligarchs into exile. Instead he plunged deeper into politics and began to underwrite opposition parties in the run-up to the 2003 parliamentary elections. He also worked to reduce the taxation of energy companies—taxation that was essential to maintaining Russia's new-found fiscal health—and challenged the government monopoly on the shipment of energy to foreign buyers.

The trial and imprisonment of Khodorkovsky and his business partners on charges of embezzlement and tax evasion were politically motivated. In the course of privatization the defendants had undoubtedly engaged in many illegal and corrupt acts, but so had other tycoons who were not put on trial. Moreover, Khodorkovsky had recently taken his company in a new direction, upgrading its corporate governance and transparency in order to attract foreign investment. His real offense was to challenge the Kremlin's growing political dominance. The arrest was well-timed to appeal to Russian voters, who had bitter memories of privatization and would soon have an opportunity to vote in the parliamentary and presidential elections. Around this time, one survey revealed that about 90 percent of the population felt all large fortunes had been built up illegally, nearly 80 percent favored reviewing or revoking the results of the privatization process, and almost 60 percent advocated opening criminal investigations of the rich.[28]

Putin's policy toward civil society is more active and restrictive than Yeltsin's was. Under Putin, harassment of civil-society activists by the police and tax authorities has increased, and the government has begun to sponsor its own "in-house" organizations to compete against genuinely autonomous civil-society groups.[29] For example, it founded a youth group called *Nashi* ("Our Own") to channel the activities of young people into politically acceptable forms. Suspended above this assortment of sponsored organizations is a new, quasi-autonomous "Public Chamber" created by the government. It was supposedly set up to facilitate government consultations with society, but its main purpose is to bleed off genuine grass-roots energy and initiatives. These measures bear more than a passing resemblance to the Soviet approach to society during the post-Stalin era. Although far less comprehensive and repressive than the Soviet approach, Putin's policy reveals a similar distrust of autonomous social activity and the unregulated expression of social interests.

Russia and Europe

In the post-Soviet period, Russians who favor close ties with Europe have faced two fundamental problems that both stem from changes in Europe itself. First, the strategic imperatives that linked Russia to Europe at certain points in the past have disappeared. As long as the major European powers posed military threats to one another, they had a strong security motive to draw Russia into Europe as a counterweight, even when they found its internal politics distasteful. This is what motivated France and Britain to conclude a military alliance with Russia against Germany before World War I and to pursue a similar alliance with the USSR on the eve of World War II. After World War II, however, the European powers laid aside their historic military rivalries, partly in order to counter the geopolitical threat from the USSR. Although post-Soviet Russia has changed dramatically and is far weaker militarily than the USSR, some Western observers continue to doubt that the changes have permanently altered Russia's international objectives. This is especially true of observers from Poland and other new EU members that were long trapped inside the Soviet Bloc. Thus, to the degree that strategic calculations shape contemporary European attitudes toward Moscow, they make Russian integration into Europe less likely, not more.

Closely related changes within the European states have also made integration a far bigger challenge for Russia than in the past. Two decades ago, Gorbachev evoked an enthusiastic response from Western Europe by proclaiming that the USSR was part of a "Common European Home" that bridged the continent's Cold War divide. Today, however, postcommunist Russia seeks acceptance by a different Europe—one which has reached an unprecedented level of political and economic integration and therefore judges Russia by more exacting criteria. Candidates for EU membership must satisfy demanding EU standards for democratic governance, and under Putin Russia has moved farther from those standards, not closer to them. The gap separating Russian capitalism from EU economic practices is just as large. To become a realistic EU candidate, Russia would first have to undergo a protracted process of internal change, and even then the EU, whose appetite for enlargement seems nearly exhausted, would probably refuse at the end of the day.

On the Russian side, disenchantment with the idea of joining the West has also grown for several reasons. The Yeltsin government carried out shock therapy under the banner of westernizing the Russian system. Since the reform effort was actively promoted by the United States and the European Union, the severe socioeconomic hardships that resulted gave many Russians second thoughts about the wisdom of westernization. For a significant minority of Russians the word "democracy" became identified with hardship, disorder, and extreme economic inequality. A small proportion of the population even came to believe that the Yeltsin reforms were part of a Western conspiracy to weaken Russia. These sentiments have increased some Russians' receptiveness to the idea that Russian cultural values are fundamentally different from those of the West.

Foreign policy disagreements have contributed to the more distrustful Russian outlook. NATO's decision to extend membership to several of Moscow's

Box 6.2   Excerpts from Mikhail Gorbachev, *Perestroika: New Thinking for Our Country and the World* (1988), pp. 180–183, 190–191

This metaphor [of a common European home] came to my mind in one of my discussions. . . . It did not come to me all of a sudden but after much thought and, notably, after meetings with many European leaders. . . . I could no longer accept in the old way the multi-colored, patchwork-quilt-like political map of Europe. The continent has known more than its share of wars and tears. It has had enough. Scanning the panorama of this long suffering land and pondering the common roots of such a multi-form but essentially common European civilization, I felt with growing acuteness the artificiality and temporariness of the bloc-to-bloc confrontation and the archaic nature of the "iron curtain." . . .

Now, about the opportunities the Europeans have . . . to be able to live as dwellers in a "common home."

1. The nations of Europe have the most painful and bitter experience of the two world wars. The awareness of the inadmissibility of a new war has left the deepest of imprints on their historical memory. It is no coincidence that Europe has the largest and the most authoritative antiwar movement. . . .

2. European political tradition as regards the level of conduct in international affairs is the richest in the world. European states' notions of each other are more realistic than in any other region. Their political "acquaintance" is broader, longer, and hence closer.

3. No other continent taken as a whole has such a ramified system of bilateral and multilateral negotiations, consultations, treaties, and contacts at virtually every level. It has to its credit such a unique accomplishment in the history of international relations as the Helsinki process [the Conference on Security and Cooperation in Europe, subsequently renamed the Organization for Security and Cooperation in Europe]. . . . Then the torch was taken up by [an international conference in] Vienna where, we hope, a new step in the development of the Helsinki process will be made. So, the blueprints for the construction of a common European home are all but ready.

4. The economic, scientific, and technical potential of Europe is tremendous. It is dispersed, and the force of repulsion between the East and the West of the continent is greater than that of attraction. However, the . . . prospects are such as to enable some modus to be found for a combination of economic processes in both parts of Europe to the benefit of all . . . .

Europe "from the Atlantic to the Urals" [Russia's Ural Mountains] is a cultural-historical entity united by the common heritage of the Renaissance and the Enlightenment, of the great philosophical and social teachings of the nineteenth and twentieth centuries. . . . A tremendous potential for a policy of peace and neighborliness is inherent in the European cultural heritage. . . .

(*continued*)

Box 6.2   (Continued)

The building of the "European home" requires a material foundation—constructive cooperation in many different areas. We, in the Soviet Union, are prepared for . . . new forms of cooperation, such as the launching of joint ventures, the implementation of joint projects in third countries, etc. . . .

True, all of this would increase the European states' mutual interdependence, but this would be to the advantage of everyone and would make for greater responsibility and self restraint.

Acting in the spirit of cooperation, a great deal could be done in that vast area which is called "humanitarian" [and includes human rights]. A major landmark on this road would be an international conference on cooperation in the humanitarian field which the Soviet Union proposes for Moscow. At such a conference the sides could discuss all aspects of problems which are of concern to both East and West, including the intricate issue of human rights. That would give a strong new impetus to the Helsinki process.

---

former allies in Eastern Europe upset members of the Russian foreign policy establishment, and a further round of NATO enlargement that included the Baltic States vexed them even more. In the interim, NATO's decision to use force against Serbia over Kosovo without UN authorization made the alliance look like a potential threat to Russia, which feared secessionism inside its own borders, especially in Chechnya. Europe and the United States treated Moscow's first war in Chechnya with considerable diplomatic restraint, but they voiced stronger criticism when Moscow renewed the military conflict in the late 1990s and allowed its forces to commit rampant human rights violations against the local population. Many Russians, however, viewed the conflict quite differently. Moscow launched the war following a series of terrorist explosions in the heart of Russia that took several hundred lives and that the government blamed on the Chechens. In these circumstances, a significant proportion of Russians felt the new war was justified—in contrast to widespread public condemnation of the earlier one.

In addition, under Putin Russia has become involved in an intensifying competition with the West to influence the direction of change in several other former Soviet republics located on Russia's borders. Two prominent cases are the disputed presidential elections in Ukraine, where the "Orange Revolution" of 2004–2005 sidetracked Moscow's favored candidate, and in Belarus, where Russia successfully backed the fraudulent reelection of the incumbent president. Russian policymakers seem especially determined to block the U.S.-led campaign to win NATO membership for Ukraine, and in recent years their efforts appear to have achieved some success.

These disagreements reflect a broader divergence of outlooks between Russia and the West. In the Yeltsin and early Putin eras, many Western and Russian leaders appeared to share the assumption that Russia and other former Soviet republics were converging with Western political and economic patterns. There was, in other words, broad-gauged agreement about what progress in the Soviet successor states should look like. Thanks to this shared outlook, leaders from across the continent declared their commitment to the political and human-rights standards established under the auspices of the Organization for Security and Cooperation in Europe (OSCE).

However, after several years of Putin's presidency, a "values gap" has started to appear between Russia and the West. In particular, the Russian government has begun to champion its own definitions of democracy and democratic practice. It has emphasized the theme of "sovereign democracy," by which it means that outside states should not try to tell Russia or nearby countries how to organize themselves internally or how to behave abroad. And it has worked to make these definitions stick—for example, by sending Russian observers who proclaimed that elections in neighboring countries such as Belarus were free and fair even when OSCE observers condemned them.

These controversies have spilled over into Russia's economic relations with Europe. By a wide margin, Europe is Russia's largest trade partner and biggest source of direct investment, but European-Russian energy relations have become a focus of tension. Toward the end of the Soviet era, Moscow gradually expanded trade with Europe and built a controversial pipeline to transport natural gas from Russia to Western Europe. The Soviet government took great pains to calm suspicions that it would manipulate the supply of natural gas for political purposes. Since that time European dependence on Russian gas has grown dramatically, but Moscow's missteps have once again made the energy relationship a matter of Western political debate. In 2006 Russia, attempting to manipulate Ukraine's internal political alignments to suit its own preferences, reduced gas shipments to Ukraine. Because the same pipeline carries gas to Western Europe, this measure caused economic disruptions there and provoked a public outcry, even though Russia quickly resumed full gas shipments.

This episode raised larger questions about the acceptable level of increased Russian investment in European energy-distribution systems and the acceptability of Russian curbs on Western investment in energy production and pipelines inside Russia. These issues seem sure to become entangled with the concurrent European debate over the terms of ownership and competition among the EU members' own national energy corporations. Given the scope of Europe's energy needs and the importance of energy sales for Russia's economic prosperity, the Russo-European disagreements are likely to be resolved through

Box 6.3   From the Declaration on Human Rights and Dignity of the Tenth World Council of The Russian People

Convened by the Russian Orthodox Church, Moscow, April 6, 2006

Aware that the world . . . is facing a threat of conflict between the civilizations with their different understanding of the human being and the human being's calling—the World Russian People's Council, on behalf of the unique Russian civilization, adopts this declaration:

Each person as image of God has singular unalienable worth, which must be respected by every one of us, the society and state. . . .

Rights and liberties are inseparable from human obligations and responsibilities. The individual in pursuit of personal interests is called to relate them to those of the neighbor, family, community, nation and all humanity.

There are values no smaller than human rights. These are faith, morality, the sacred, [and the] motherland. Whenever these values come into conflict with the implementation of human rights, the task of the society, state and law is to bring both to harmony. It is unacceptable, in pursuit of human rights, to oppress faith and moral tradition, insult religious and national feelings, cause harm to revered holy objects and sites, jeopardize the motherland. . . .

We reject the policy of double standards with regard to human rights, as well as attempts to use them for political, ideological, military and economic purposes, for imposition of a particular socio-political system.

We are willing to cooperate with the state and all benevolent forces in ensuring human rights. Particularly important for this cooperation are such endeavors as preserving the rights of nations and ethnic groups to their religion, language and culture, defending the freedom of conscience and the right of believers to their own way of life, combating ethnically and religiously motivated crime, [and] protecting against arbitrary actions by the authorities and employers. . . .

We seek dialog with people of diverse faiths and views on human rights and their place in the hierarchy of values. Like nothing else, this dialogue today will help avoid the conflict of civilizations and attain a *peaceful diversity of worldviews, cultures, legal and political systems on the globe.*

compromises of some kind. But they show that even limited integration within one key economic sector faces significant obstacles.

Although Russia is highly unlikely to be integrated with Europe, it is more likely to remain engaged with Europe than with any other major country or group of countries outside the boundaries of the former USSR. At the elite level, Russian liberal reformers continue to be interested in Europe. Within the citizenry as a whole, Europe enjoys a more favorable reputation and exercises a much stronger attraction than any other region, including the United States and China. A sizable proportion of Russians regard themselves as Europeans; none, of course, regard themselves as North Americans, and few see themselves as East Asians. Moscow's leaders may make common diplomatic cause with China to check U.S. geopolitical ventures in the Middle East or Central Asia, and they may threaten to export their energy supplies to Asian markets as a gambit in their energy negotiations with European countries, but Russia's demographic and economic center of gravity remains west of the Ural Mountains, in European Russia. Together with Moscow's apprehensions about the long-term security implications of Asia's unprecedented economic dynamism in recent decades, this structural factor nearly guarantees that Russia will not "turn" geopolitically from Europe to Asia.

Conclusion: Russia's Futures

Russia's steady shift toward hypercentralization has given Putin unparalleled preeminence. The key question is whether the political structure he has built can deal with the grave problems of economic development and human welfare facing Russia. Historically, Russian leaders have often attempted to overcome crises by concentrating power and multiplying the state's administrative controls over society. Under Putin, memories of the severe political conflicts and predatory economic behavior during the Yeltsin era have strengthened the impulse to follow this path.

Putin has worked hard to strengthen the Russian state and has achieved some significant successes. However, it remains unclear whether his formula of state-centered rule can revive Russia socially and economically. In a domestic context "state strength" can refer to quite different things. One is the negative capacity of state leaders to defeat actions by social actors they oppose. Another is the positive capacity of leaders to achieve their substantive socioeconomic objectives for the country. A state that is powerful in the negative sense may be quite weak in the positive sense, especially if it attempts to control a wide range of social and economic activities.

To succeed in the modern world, states need high levels of active cooperation from their citizens and high levels of information about the internal workings of society. By relying increasingly on direct administrative control, the Russian government will almost certainly thwart essential socioeconomic initiative and shrink both the quality and quantity of information reaching policymakers. The typical result of such restrictive tactics is a state that claims a monopoly on political initiative but that also lacks the capacity to deal effectively with real societal issues—in other words, a state that combines the appearance of great power with the reality of substantive weakness.

Several factors will shape Russia's political course during the next few years. The first is what happens to the vast executive powers that Putin has concentrated in the presidency. If Putin leaves office in 2008 according to the established constitutional deadline, how destabilizing will that change of executive leadership be? Putin has groomed two potential successors for the presidency, but whether presidential power can be smoothly transferred to either of them remains uncertain. It is unclear whether Putin's unusual level of popularity, which has been a major source of both his personal dominance and the overall stability of the political system, can be transmitted to a successor. Given the high level of insecurity that still shadows the country's economic elite, control of the state remains extraordinarily important, which increases the chances of a divisive elite conflict. If Putin chooses to postpone the election or revise the constitution so as to stay in power after 2008, this will defer a succession struggle but might ultimately make the transfer of power more turbulent.

Although the competition among the rivals for executive power may receive electoral legitimation, the succession process is nearly certain to be pseudo-democratic rather than genuinely democratic. In Russia, democratic elections have failed to become the "only game in town" for choosing leaders, but competitors for power cannot dispense with elections entirely. Rather, the electoral process is one important political arena that aspirants for power must seek to control. In key instances, the decisive variable is the preelection struggle over who will get onto the ballot, not who will win when citizens go to the polls. Under certain conditions the existing electoral procedures might again become the object of real electoral competition, as happened with Soviet elections in the Gorbachev years. But this could occur only if political and economic circumstances inside Russia change fundamentally.

Global economic conditions and the national economy's performance will have a major effect on Russia's political evolution. If the energy sector continues to grow rapidly and foreign demand for Russian energy remains strong, this will contribute to domestic political stability. On the other hand, if Russia's special brand of state-dominated capitalism causes energy output to falter, this will create new political tensions. Above all, a sharp drop in energy prices due to a global recession or other factors would generate severe economic stresses and could lead to major alterations in the political system. One likely scenario would be a renewed effort by the ruling elite to revive growth through liberal authoritarianism—that is, an attempt to build autonomous competitive markets under the auspices of an authoritarian state committed to more consistent legal rules and government administration. If this policy recipe were tried and failed, a shift toward political as well as economic liberalization might become more likely.

In any case, the country's political development will be influenced by the changing preferences of key social groups. If members of the economic elite choose to pursue greater political and economic security by acting in concert to limit government power, Russia could move in a liberal political direction. If they continue to vie with one another for special favors from the state, as has often occurred in the past, an authoritarian political outcome is more probable. The expansion and political orientation of the middle class will also be important. Sustained pressure from an enlarged middle class could facilitate reform of the government bureaucracy and help strengthen the integrity of the judicial system. On the other hand, if the middle class fails to generate this kind of "demand for law," serious reform of the government apparatus is unlikely to succeed. Whether a shrinking society wracked by a severe health crisis can generate this kind of political pressure is uncertain. A dramatic increase in immigration might alleviate the demographic decline, but it could easily heighten frictions between ethnic Russians and non-Russians.

Even if Russia ultimately follows a liberal political path, many years are likely to pass before a qualitatively new form of engagement with Europe becomes possible. Closer integration of energy networks is quite probable, but socioeconomic integration along a broader front is not. For many years to come, an ambivalent Russia is likely to remain on the periphery of an ambivalent Europe. Internationally as well as domestically, the uncertainty that has pervaded Russia's recent past is likely to shadow its future as well.

Notes

1. Martin E. Malia, *Russia Under Western Eyes: From the Bronze Horseman to the Lenin Mausoleum*, Cambridge, MA: Belknap Press of Harvard University Press, 1999, pp. 4–12, 43–60.

2. Ernest Gellner, *Conditions of Liberty: Civil Society and Its Rivals*, New York: Allen Lane Penguin Press, 1994, pp. 1–12, 88–96; Richard Rose, "Toward a Civil Economy," *Journal of Democracy*, 3(2), April 1992, 13–26.

3. The coup plotters were conservative leaders from the political police (KGB), the military, and the central organs of the Communist Party and the government. The state of emergency they declared soon collapsed due to their lack of political determination and paralyzing splits inside the military and police agencies. By discrediting the conservatives, the failed coup attempt boosted the centrifugal forces in the country. Equally important, it enabled Boris Yeltsin to eclipse Gorbachev. Yeltsin led public opposition to the coup, while the plotters held Gorbachev in seclusion until the attempt collapsed.

4. Vera Tolz, "Conflicting 'Homeland Myths' and Nation-State Building in Post-Communist Russia," *Slavic Review*, 57(2), summer 1998, pp. 267–294.

5. Amy Knight, *The Security Services and the Decline of Democracy in Russia, 1996–1999*, Donald W. Treadgold Papers, 23, Seattle, WA: University of Washington, 1999, pp. 14–16.

6. Timothy J. Colton, "Putin and the Attenuation of Russian Democracy," in Alex Pravda (ed.), *Leading Russia: Putin in Perspective. Essays in Honour of Archie Brown*, New York: Oxford University Press, 2005, pp. 103–118.

7. This analogy is taken from Colton, "Putin and the Attenuation of Russian Democracy."

8. In 1999, Unity fielded candidates in only one-sixth of the regional single-member districts, and the Union of Right Forces in less than one-third of them. Richard Rose,

"How Floating Parties Frustrate Democratic Accountability: A Supply-Side View of Russia's Elections," in Archie Brown (ed.), *Contemporary Russian Politics: A Reader*, New York: Oxford University Press, 2001, p. 217.

9. Stephen White, "The Political Parties," in Stephen White, Zvi Gitelman, and Richard Sakwa (eds.), *Developments in Russian Politics*, 6th edition, Durham, NC: Duke University Press, 2005, p. 90.

10. Joel S. Hellman, "Winners Take All: The Politics of Partial Reform in Postcommunist Transitions," *World Politics,* 50(2), January 1998, 203–234.

11. Paul Klebnikov, *Godfather of the Kremlin: Boris Berezovsky and the Looting of Russia*, New York: Harcourt, 2000, pp. 21, 31–32.

12. Vadim Volkov, *Violent Entrepreneurs: The Use of Force in the Making of Russian Capitalism*, Ithaca, NY: Cornell University Press, 2002, pp. 77, 133.

13. Calculated from Harley Balzer, "Routinization of the New Russians?" *Russian Review*, 62(1), January 2003, 23.

14. Timothy Frye, "Markets, Democracy, and New Private Business in Russia," *Post-Soviet Affairs,* 19(1), January-March 2003, 24–45.

15. Andrew Barnes, *Owning Russia: The Struggle over Factories, Farms, and Power*, Ithaca, NY: Cornell University Press, 2006, pp. 1–10.

16. Piroska Mohacsi Nagy, *The Meltdown of the Russian State: The Deformation and Collapse of the State in Russia*, Northampton, MA: Edward Elgar, 2000, pp. 64–66.

17. Alfred Stepan, "Russian Federalism in Comparative Perspective," *Post-Soviet Affairs,* 16(2), April-June 2000, 144.

18. Cameron Ross, "Putin's Federal Reforms," in Cameron Ross (ed.), *Russian Politics Under Putin*, New York: Manchester University Press, 2004, p. 166.

19. Bertram Silverman and Murray Yanowitch, *New Rich, New Poor, New Russia: Winners and Losers on the Russian Road to Capitalism*, expanded edition, Armonk, NY: M. E. Sharpe, 2000, pp. 51–54, 153.

20. The demographic data in this paragraph are from the Population Reference Bureau, *http://www.prb.org/Template.cfm?Section=PRB&template=/ContentManagement/ContentDisplay.cfm&ContentID=6506*, accessed July 10, 2006; and the U.S. Census Bureau, *http://www.census.gov/cgi-bin/ipc/idbsum.pl?cty=RS*, accessed July 10, 2006.

21. Murray Feshbach, "Russia's Population Meltdown," *The Wilson Quarterly,* 25(1), winter 2001, 12–21; Nicholas Eberstadt, "The Future of AIDS: Grim Toll in Russia, China, and India," *Foreign Affairs,* 81(6), 2002, 22–45.

22. Marc Morje Howard, *The Weakness of Civil Society in Postcommunist Europe*, New York: Cambridge University Press, 2003; Michael McFaul and Elina Treyger, "Civil Society," in Michael McFaul, Nikolai Petrov, and Andrei Ryabov (eds.), *Between Dictatorship and Democracy: Russian Post-Communist Political Reform*, Washington, DC: Carnegie Endowment for International Peace, 2004, pp. 140–141; Balzer, "Routinization of the New Russians?" p. 25.

23. The Levada Center (Russian-language version), *http://www.levada.ru/files/1142009322.doc*, accessed July 11, 2006.

24. Stephen White, "Russia's Disempowered Electorate," in Cameron Ross (ed.), *Russian Politics Under Putin*, New York: Manchester University Press, 2004, pp. 76–78.

25. Vladimir Petukhov and Andrei Ryabov, "Public Attitudes Toward Democracy," in Michael McFaul, Nikolai Petrov, and Andrei Ryabov (eds.), *Between Dictatorship and*

Democracy: Russian Post-Communist Political Reform, Washington, DC: Carnegie Endowment for International Peace, 2004, pp. 269, 290; Sarah E. Mendelson and Theodore P. Gerber, "Soviet Nostalgia: An Impediment to Democratization," *Washington Quarterly,* 29(1), winter 2005–2006, 83–96.

26. The Levada Center (Russian-language version), *http://www.levada.ru/prezident.html,* accessed July 11, 2006.

27. Julie Anderson, "The Chekist Takeover of the Russian State," *International Journal of Intelligence and Counter Intelligence,* 19(2), summer 2006, 239–240; Stephen White and Olga Kryshtanovskaya, "Putin's Militocracy," *Post-Soviet Affairs,* 19(4), 2003, 294.

28. Sergei Guriev and Andrei Rachinsky, "The Role of Oligarchs in Russian Capitalism," *Economic Perspectives,* 19(1), 2005, 140.

29. McFaul and Treyger, "Civil Society," pp. 159–166.

Suggested Readings

Barnes, Andrew, *Owning Russia: The Struggle over Factories, Farms, and Power,* Ithaca, NY: Cornell University Press, 2006.

Brown, Archie, *The Gorbachev Factor,* New York: Oxford University Press, 1996.

Brown, Archie (ed.), *Contemporary Russian Politics: A Reader,* New York: Oxford University Press, 2001.

Fish, M. Steven, *Democracy Derailed in Russia: The Failure of Open Politics,* New York: Cambridge University Press, 2005.

Gustafson, Thane, *Capitalism Russian-Style,* New York: Cambridge University Press, 1999.

Hoffman, David E., *The Oligarchs: Wealth and Power in the New Russia,* New York: Public Affairs, 2001.

Knight, Amy W., *Spies Without Cloaks: The KGB's Successors,* Princeton, NJ: Princeton University Press, 1996.

Lieven, Anatol, and Dmitrii Trenin (eds.), *Ambivalent Neighbors: The EU, NATO and the Price of Membership,* Washington, DC: Carnegie Endowment for International Peace, 2003.

McFaul, Michael, *Russia's Unfinished Revolution: Political Change from Gorbachev to Putin,* Ithaca, NY: Cornell University Press, 2001.

McFaul, Michael, Nikolai Petrov, and Andrei Ryabov (eds.), *Between Dictatorship and Democracy: Russian Postcommunist Political Reform,* Washington, DC: Carnegie Endowment for International Peace, 2004.

Reddaway, Peter, and Dmitri Glinski, *The Tragedy of Russia's Reforms: Market Bolshevism Against Democracy,* Washington, DC: United States Institute of Peace Press, 2001.

Taubman, William, *Khrushchev: The Man and His Era,* New York: W. W. Norton, 2003.

Tolz, Vera, *Russia: Inventing the Nation,* New York: Oxford University Press, 2001.

Volkov, Vadim, *Violent Entrepreneurs: The Use of Force in the Making of Russian Capitalism,* Ithaca, NY: Cornell University Press, 2002.

PART TWO

EUROPEAN INTEGRATION AND THE EUROPEAN UNION

CHAPTER 7

The European Union: From Community to Constitution?

John Van Oudenaren

Philosophers have dreamed about a united Europe for centuries, but it was not until World War II that a serious movement toward European integration began. Postwar leaders, many of them veterans of the anti-Nazi resistance, believed that if Europe was to achieve a durable peace and economic prosperity after the war, it needed to overcome the nationalism and economic autarky that characterized the 1930s and that had reached their epitome in Hitler's Germany and Mussolini's Italy. The question was how to begin the process of building a more united Europe, especially in the aftermath of a six-year conflict that had left deep hatreds and widespread economic destruction.

In the immediate postwar period, the Western European countries took some initial steps toward integration. France and Britain concluded an alliance in the 1947 Treaty of Dunkirk. In March 1948, these two powers and the three Benelux countries—Belgium, the Netherlands, and Luxembourg—concluded the Brussels treaty, establishing the organization that later became the Western European Union. The five signatories pledged to come to each other's defense in the event of external attack; hold regular consultations among their foreign ministers; and to cooperate in the economic, social, and cultural spheres.

The United States also played an important role in encouraging the Europeans to work together. By early 1947, the Truman administration had concluded that the Soviet Union was not prepared to cooperate with the Western powers in establishing a stable European order. In Eastern Europe, communist regimes were consolidating their grip on power. In Western Europe, people were still suffering the aftereffects of war, including shortages of food and fuel, unemployment, and hopelessness about the future.

In a speech at Harvard University in June 1947, U.S. Secretary of State George C. Marshall proposed a program of aid designed to pull Europe to its feet. The United States offered to provide Europe with money and goods, but only if the Europeans themselves came up with a plan for using aid effectively, and only if the plan was designed as a joint effort rather than a hodgepodge of national requests. After a series of preliminary meetings, in April 1948 sixteen European states founded the Organization for European Economic Cooperation

(OEEC). Based in Paris, this organization helped to administer Marshall Plan aid and provided a forum in which the member states negotiated arrangements to lower intra-European trade and currency barriers. The European Recovery Program, as the Marshall Plan formally was known, thus provided a powerful external stimulus to intra-European cooperation.

The conclusion of the Brussels pact and the founding of the OEEC were important first steps on the road to integration, but they fell short of meeting the aspirations of those in Europe who wanted a complete break with the past and whose objective was nothing less than the establishment of a "United States of Europe." Known as federalists, they believed that integration should not be a matter just for governments, but that it should be based directly on the will of the people. In 1947, the federalists launched a campaign to convene a European assembly, whose members would not be chosen by or under the control of the national governments, that would undertake the task of constituting a new organization to unite the peoples of Europe. The federalists succeeded in convincing the five signatories of the Brussels pact to convene a ten-power conference in London in early 1949 to discuss their ideas.

The conference quickly revealed a split, however, between Britain and the Scandinavian countries, who wanted integration to proceed on the basis of agreements among states, and those on the Continent who favored more radical forms of integration. The London conference led to the creation of the Council of Europe, a Strasbourg-based organization that works to harmonize laws and promote human rights in Europe. Although useful in its own way, the Council of Europe fell short of becoming a truly federal institution for Europe. The elected governments in key countries had proven unwilling to cede sovereign powers to a supranational body, such as the federalists were proposing. Integration was endorsed, but largely on the basis of intergovernmental agreement. As will be seen, the tension between supranationalism and intergovernmentalism has been a permanent feature of the integration process that persists to the present day.

The other major development of the late 1940s was the creation of the North Atlantic Alliance. The United States had emerged from World War II committed to promoting economic and political stability in Europe, but it did not intend to conclude a military alliance with Western European states, which went against the U.S. tradition of "no entangling alliances." However, the communist takeovers in Eastern Europe and the onset of the Cold War led to a shift in attitudes. In April 1949 the United States, Canada, the five Brussels powers, and four other European states signed the North Atlantic Treaty, in which they pledged to come to each other's assistance in the event of external attack. The signing of the treaty was followed by the creation of the North Atlantic Treaty Organization (NATO) and the establishment of an integrated military command. Like the Marshall Plan, NATO was an important U.S. contribution to the postwar revival of Europe and to the fledgling process of building a united Europe. It allowed the

European countries to concentrate on economic cooperation, leaving sensitive and contentious matters of defense to the transatlantic organization.

Establishing the Community

THE EUROPEAN COAL AND STEEL COMMUNITY

The accomplishments and disappointments of the late 1940s began the process that led, in the 1950s, to the creation of the three sister institutions known as the European Communities and that became the basis for today's European Union: the European Coal and Steel Community (ECSC), the European Economic Community (EEC), and the European Atomic Energy Community (Euratom). The first of these institutions, the ECSC, was the inspiration of Jean Monnet, a French businessman who had spent the war years in the United States and who had devoted much thought to the problem of bringing about a European union.

Like the federalists, Monnet was convinced that integration had to be based on something more than intergovernmental agreement. Europe needed institutions and laws of its own—a pooling of sovereignty that could survive the vagaries of national politics. But Monnet also believed that the federalists had been naïve in thinking that a united Europe could be brought about through a constitutive assembly that directly challenged the powers of the nation-states. In his view it was essential to start the process of integration on a different basis. Geographically, the key to building a new Europe was reconciliation between France and Germany. He thus was willing to go ahead, if necessary, without the British and the Scandinavians. He also believed that it was more important to achieve practical results in a few sectors than to make broad commitments to economic, political, cultural, and defense cooperation that were impossible to implement. While proposing to narrow the geographic and sectoral scope of the European integration process, he was convinced that integration had to be far-reaching and irreversible, with real powers transferred to a supranational body whose decisions would be binding on the countries forming the Community.

Working behind the scenes, Monnet managed to convince the French and West German governments to embrace his ideas. On May 9, 1950, French foreign minister Robert Schuman formally proposed to the French cabinet Monnet's plan for France and Germany to combine their coal and steel industries under a joint authority. This authority was to be independent of the governments of the two countries and would guarantee each country full and equal access to a common pool of resources. The significance of this proposal was as much political as economic. With the production of coal and steel—the very sinews of modern military capability—subject to a joint authority, war among Western European states would become unthinkable.

The Schuman Declaration, as the proposal became known, was enthusiastically welcomed by the West German chancellor, Konrad Adenauer. Belgium, Luxembourg, the Netherlands, and Italy also expressed interest in joining the new Community. The Benelux countries already had established an economic union among themselves and were eager to cooperate on a new basis with their larger neighbors. For Italy, joining the ECSC reflected a decision by its postwar leaders to "scale the Alps"—to turn Italy's energies toward northern Europe and away from the disastrous African and Balkan ambitions of the former dictator, Benito Mussolini.

The treaty establishing the ECSC was negotiated in the months following Schuman's dramatic declaration and signed in Paris in April 1951. The ECSC became operational in July 1952. For the commodities covered—coal, coke, iron ore, steel, and scrap—the ECSC created a common market in which all tariff barriers and restrictions on trade among the six member countries were banned. To ensure the operation of this common market, the ECSC treaty provided for the establishment of four institutions, roughly corresponding to the executive, legislative, and judicial branches of government, with extensive legal and administrative powers in the coal and steel sectors.

The High Authority was established as a nine-member commission with executive powers to administer the workings of the common market. The members of the authority (two each from France, Germany and Italy; one each from Belgium, Luxembourg, and the Netherlands) were to be "completely independent in the performance of their duties." They were to decide what was best for the ECSC as a whole, rather than to represent the views of the member countries. The High Authority was empowered to issue decisions, recommendations, and opinions prohibiting subsidies and aids to industry that distorted trade, to block mergers and acquisitions and other types of agreements among firms, and under certain circumstances to control prices. It could impose fines to ensure compliance with its decisions. Monnet was named the first head of the High Authority, and for several years lent his energies and reputation to building its powers.

The Council of Ministers was established as a counterweight to excessive power in the hands of the High Authority. It consisted of ministers from the national governments of the member states, with each state represented by one minister. For some policy actions, the Council of Ministers had to endorse the decisions of the High Authority. Some decisions were taken by unanimity, others by majority voting. Thus, even within the Council of Ministers member states could not always exercise a veto over collective decisionmaking. This was quite different from organizations such as NATO, where decisions were taken only by consensus and where a single state could always block adoption of a decision to which it was opposed.

The Common Assembly was designed to introduce an element of legislative participation in the work of the ECSC. Its members were not directly elected by the people but were chosen by the national legislatures. Its power, moreover, was to advise rather than to pass legislation. Still, the principle of parliamentary participation was established, and the powers of what later was to become the European Parliament were to expand greatly in subsequent decades.

The other institution of the ECSC was the European Court of Justice, which was set up to settle conflicts between the member states of the Community, between member states and the institutions of the Community (e.g., the High Authority), or between the institutions of the Community itself.

These institutions were the first genuinely supranational bodies in Europe. They could exercise authority—in their limited areas of competence—over the national governments of the member states. Establishment of the ECSC thus entailed a transfer of sovereignty from the national level to the central institutions, which were to be located in Luxembourg.

The ECSC was an immediate success. Along with steps already under way in the OEEC, the elimination of barriers to trade in the coal and steel sectors contributed to the European economic renaissance of the early 1950s. Politically, the Community began the process of reconciliation between France and West Germany. At the same time, however, ECSC's scope of activity was by definition quite limited. It dealt with a single economic sector, and it lacked an external profile. It could not, for example, negotiate tariffs with foreign countries. It therefore was understandable that the ECSC members should try to build upon their success and look for ways to broaden the scope of integration. Initially, they turned to defense. In May 1952, the six ECSC countries signed a treaty establishing a European Defense Community (EDC) in which decisions over defense and a jointly commanded European army were to be made by supranational EDC institutions patterned on those of the ECSC. However, in August 1954, the French National Assembly rejected the EDC treaty, rendering the process of European integration a severe albeit temporary setback. Whereas national governments and parliaments were willing to surrender sovereignty in some key economic areas, the EDC experience showed that defense was too sensitive—too close to core issues of national identity—to be treated the same way. The emphasis thus shifted back to economics.

THE EUROPEAN ECONOMIC COMMUNITY

Following the EDC setback, the foreign ministers of the six ECSC states met in Messina, Italy, in June 1955 to consider ways to energize the integration process. At the time, two potential courses of action were widely discussed: a further stage of *sectoral* integration based on a proposed atomic energy community, and a plan for *market* integration through the elimination of barriers to trade and the eventual creation of a common market. Those in Europe, including Monnet and many in France, who saw integration primarily as a process of building up shared institutions and accomplishing common projects, tended to stress the importance of the atomic energy community. Others, especially in West Germany, who saw European integration more as a process of tearing down intra-European barriers, emphasized the common market. These two approaches came to be known as "positive" and "negative" integration, and both have played a role in the development of Europe.

At Messina, the ministers agreed to establish a committee charged to study these options and to formulate concrete proposals. The Spaak Committee (named for its chairman, Belgian foreign minister Paul-Henri Spaak) presented its report to the May 1956 Venice meeting of foreign ministers. It struck a balance between the two approaches to integration and proposed that the ECSC states create both a European Atomic Energy Community (Euratom) and a European Economic Community (EEC). Following detailed and arduous negotiations, in Rome on March 25, 1957, the six signed two treaties creating these new entities.

Like the European Coal and Steel Community, Euratom subsequently came to play an important role in a single sector of the economy. It promoted the development of nuclear power and established a common pool of radioactive fuels for use in the member states. Of the two institutions created in 1957, however, the EEC—or Common Market as it was widely known—was by far the more important. The agreement establishing the EEC became known as the Treaty of Rome and remains in many ways the core constitutional document of today's European Union.

The basic objective of the EEC was simple in principle, albeit sweeping in its implications: to create an internal market characterized by the free movement of goods, services, persons, and capital. Initially, the overwhelming emphasis was on eliminating obstacles to trade in goods. The Treaty of Rome provided for the phasing out, in stages, of all tariffs and quantitative restrictions on trade among the member states. The creation of a common internal market also necessitated the establishment of a common external tariff and a common commercial policy. Since goods that entered one member state could travel freely to other EEC countries, it was desirable for these countries to adopt the same tariffs toward third countries, lest goods simply be diverted to ports in countries with the lowest tariff for a given import. The EEC thus was empowered to speak with one voice in international negotiations conducted within the framework of the General Agreement on Tariffs and Trade.

The Treaty of Rome used the basic institutional framework established for the ECSC. The High Authority for the EEC was called simply the European Commission, a less grandiose name that reflected the desire on the part of the founding member states to cut back somewhat the powers of the supranational authority. Nonetheless, the Commission was endowed with broad executive powers, including the sole right to initiate Community legislation. The member states were responsible for selecting the commissioners, who were chosen for four-year terms (five-year since 1979). The Commission president, also provided for under the treaty and selected by the member states, quickly emerged as the most visible champion of and spokesperson for the Community.

A Council of Ministers was to be the main decisionmaking body of the EEC, in which representatives of the member states would vote on proposals put forward by the European Commission. Votes could be made on the basis of unanimity or by qualified majority—a weighted system that assigns votes in rough proportion to the population sizes of the member states and that requires a certain critical mass of votes to pass a measure. France, Italy, and West Germany each had four votes, Belgium and the Netherlands two, and Luxembourg one. Twelve of the seventeen votes were considered a qualified majority. In practice, qualified majority voting (QMV) was disliked by some member-state political leaders, especially in France, as too supranational and was little used until the 1980s. As in the ECSC, the chairmanship of the Council rotated, with each member state serving as Council president for a six-month period. In addition, the member states agreed that the three communities—the ECSC, Euratom, and the EEC—all could share the same Common Assembly and Court of Justice. The ECSC High Authority remained in Luxembourg, but the new European Commission was established in Brussels, which became the de facto capital of uniting Europe. The Common Assembly was situated in Strasbourg, France. The treaty also provided for the establishment of two other institutions, the Economic and Social Committee and the European Investment Bank, that were to play much lesser roles in Community decisionmaking.

As in the case of the ECSC, the impetus to creating the EEC was as much political as economic. Operating under a concept that became known as "functionalism," promoters of European federalism believed that the gradual expansion of economic ties and of cooperation in various practical spheres such as atomic energy eventually would "spill over" into the political realm, as governments, parliaments, and national electorates yielded sovereignty in small but politically manageable steps. This aspiration to go beyond economic cooperation was expressed in the very first sentence of the Treaty of Rome, in which the signatories declared their determination "to lay the foundations of an ever closer union among the peoples of Europe."[1]

Although the focus of the EEC was on the creation of a common market through the elimination of barriers, the Treaty of Rome also provided for the establishment of common policies in other areas. Agriculture was the most important, but others included transport, competition (antitrust), and policy toward colonies and former colonies in Africa and the Caribbean. Over time, the EEC was to assume a role in a growing range of policy areas, some, such as telecommunications and industry, closely linked to the internal market, but others, such as the environment, much broader in scope.

Completion of the common market for goods took place between 1958 and 1968, a period of rapid economic growth and rising prosperity. Businesses became more efficient and productive as they were able to sell to a larger market and were forced to invest to meet competition from firms in other countries.

Notwithstanding these successes, there were many gaps in the integration process, and a number of unresolved economic and political problems would come back to haunt Europe in the more difficult economic climate of the 1970s. The elimination of barriers and the expansion of trade in the EEC were mainly confined to goods. Of the "four freedoms"—free movement of goods, services, persons, and capital—the last three existed mainly on paper. Transportation, telecommunications, banking, insurance, and other service businesses still were organized along national lines, with little competition across borders. Most European governments maintained controls on the cross-border flow of capital. And free movement of labor within the EEC was mainly limited to the large number of workers from southern Italy who went to work in the factories of northern Europe to meet the growing labor shortages of the 1960s.

The Common Agricultural Policy (CAP) was established in 1962 in accordance with the general goals laid down in the Treaty of Rome. Its design was based on the assumption that agricultural production had unique characteristics that required rules for farmers different from those for industry. Because European farms were smaller and less efficient than those in certain other parts of the world, European agricultural products generally were more expensive than imports. To protect European farmers and ensure them a stable or rising standard of living, the CAP relied on tariffs and subsidies. Importers of food from non-EEC markets paid a variable levy (tariff) intended to raise the price of imported food to that of domestic production. The Community also established a common fund to finance purchases of farm products on the European market in order to bolster domestic prices. This system worked in sustaining farmers' incomes and ensuring stability of supplies, but it also led to higher food prices for consumers, overproduction (the famous "wine lakes" and "butter mountains"), and disputes with trading partners who were being progressively squeezed out of the protected EEC market. Indeed, the first serious trade dispute between the United States and the Community was the "chicken war" of 1963, which resulted from U.S. loss of access to the large West German poultry market as a result of the CAP.

DE GAULLE AND THE "EMPTY CHAIR"

As the EEC developed in the 1960s and proved its economic value, it somewhat paradoxically faced a growing political challenge within its own ranks. The source of this challenge was French president Charles de Gaulle, a leader of the French Resistance in World War II who had retired from an active role in politics in 1946. He returned to power in 1958 amid the crisis caused by France's colonial war in Algeria and pushed through a new constitution that created a strong presidency, a post he himself occupied for the next decade.

The French leader broke with his European partners on two major issues: the powers and responsibilities of the EEC's institutions and the question of British membership in the Community. De Gaulle's approach to both reflected his nationalism and his questioning of the path down which Europe was headed. He believed that France needed to be strong and independent—to recover the national greatness that it had lost in World War II. He thus instituted economic and political reforms aimed at modernizing French industry and society and making France more competitive with Germany. These measures indirectly benefited the cause of integration by helping to create the rough balance of power between France and Germany that was the basis for the EEC's development. At the same time, however, de Gaulle was extremely wary of surrendering French sovereignty to the newly created supranational bodies in Brussels.

The issue of supranationalism came to a head in mid-1965 over the question of CAP financing. With the phasing in of the common market running ahead of schedule, in the spring of 1965 European Commission president Walter Hallstein proposed that the EEC acquire its "own resources" (i.e., revenue raised directly by the EEC, rather than contributed to the EEC budget by the member states) by July 1967, some three years ahead of schedule. Hallstein further proposed a new budgetary mechanism in which the Commission and the European Parliament would have enhanced powers, while those of the member states in the Council of Ministers would diminish through the introduction of qualified majority voting in place of unanimity for certain issues. De Gaulle saw these proposals as a grab for power by a nascent European superstate in Brussels and as an attack on French sovereignty. He responded by announcing the policy of the "empty chair." Throughout the second half of 1965 France boycotted all meetings of the Council of Ministers.

The crisis was resolved in January 1966 with the adoption by the six of what became known, after the site of the meeting, as the Luxembourg Compromise. The "compromise" was little more than an agreement to disagree. The six pledged that when issues very important to one or more states were to be decided, the Council of Ministers would try to reach decisions by unanimity. France registered its view—not endorsed by others—that when important issues were at stake unanimity *had* to be reached to take a decision. While noting the disagreement on this constitutional point, the six concluded that there was no need to prolong the impasse in EEC decisionmaking. Hallstein retreated from his proposals, France took its place in the Council of Ministers, and normal business resumed.

The effect of the 1965 crisis on the Community was profound. Although the other five members would not yield to de Gaulle's attempt to reinterpret the Treaty of Rome by imposing the unanimity requirement, they had no wish to provoke another crisis. They thus tended to make decisions by consensus—a practice that lasted until well into the 1980s. The powers of the European Commission were cut back, as it was widely blamed for provoking the crisis by reaching prematurely for more authority. These developments all tended to slow decisionmaking in the EEC and helped to reverse the momentum toward a federal Europe that had built up in the late 1950s and early 1960s.

Britain had been active in the early postwar moves toward European integration, but it had declined to join the original six in forming the ECSC and the Common Market. The British economy at that time was still considerably larger than those of the continental European powers, and Britain retained strong links with its colonies, the Commonwealth, and the United States, with which it had a "special relationship" growing out of World War II. It thus was unwilling to surrender sovereignty to a fledgling enterprise based in Brussels. Instead, Britain took the lead in founding the European Free Trade Association, a looser grouping of states whose other founding members were Austria, Denmark, Norway, Portugal, Sweden, and Switzerland. By the 1960s, however, the empire was dissolving, and Britain's ties with the Commonwealth and the United States were diminishing in importance. British economic growth was lagging that in continental Europe, where British industry saw new and growing markets. Thus in the summer of 1961, Britain, joined by Denmark and Ireland, applied to become an EEC member.[2]

The British government received a rude shock when, at a news conference in January 1963, de Gaulle announced that he would veto Britain's application. This decision was rooted in de Gaulle's distrust of the "Anglo-Saxon powers" and his view that Britain would be a stalking horse in the Community for the United States, whose influence in Europe he wanted to diminish. This view made the other Community countries, and especially the West Germans, uncomfortable, but it was not something they could change, given the requirement for unanimity in key Community decisions. The same three countries subsequently reapplied for membership in May 1967, but de Gaulle would not lift his opposition to British membership.

Despite these many problems, by the end of the 1960s European leaders could be satisfied with the progress of integration since the early 1950s. The Common Market largely was completed, and the economic results were positive. Franco-German reconciliation was a reality. Moreover, de Gaulle relinquished his post in April 1969 and his successor, Georges Pompidou, although adhering to the basic Gaullist line, was less suspicious of European integration than his predecessor. He announced, in July of the same year, that France no longer would oppose Britain's admission to the EEC. The time thus seemed right for bold new initiatives. At the Hague summit in December 1969 the leaders of the six agreed to explore ways to strengthen the EEC's institutions, to establish an "economic and monetary union" by 1980, and to begin cooperation in the foreign policy sphere. As will be seen, however, many of these initiatives were soon put on hold or implemented very slowly, as the EEC entered a more difficult phase under worsening international circumstances.

DEVELOPMENTS IN THE 1970s

The 1970s saw a number of milestones in the process of European integration. Cooperation in the field of foreign policy, or European Political Cooperation (EPC), was launched in 1970. The member states agreed to "consult on all questions of foreign policy" and where possible to undertake "common actions" on international problems. However, EPC was to take place outside the federal structures and institutions of the EEC. The European Commission and the European Court of Justice thus did not have competence or jurisdiction in foreign policy matters, making EPC a much weaker form of cooperation than that established in the economic sphere by the Treaty of Rome.

On January 1, 1973, the first enlargement of the Community took place, as Denmark, Ireland, and Britain became members. This was the first of six enlargements (see Table 7.1), each of which has required complex negotiations on such matters as payments into and from the Community budget, transition periods for phasing in Community rules, and the weight of each member state in the Community's institutions.

Despite these achievements, the optimistic expectations of the late 1950s and the 1960s were deflated in the 1970s, as the integration process was slowed by unfavorable external economic and political conditions. Economic policymakers worldwide became preoccupied with the problems of the U.S. dollar and the breakdown of the Bretton Woods monetary system. In August 1971, the United States suspended the convertibility of dollars into gold. This was followed by devaluation of the dollar and a worldwide shift to floating exchange rates. EEC finance ministers and central bankers tried to maintain a "joint float" of their currencies against the dollar, but in the absence of a stable and predictable global monetary system European plans to achieve economic and monetary union by 1980 were put on hold.[3]

Table 7.1 Membership and Enlargements of the EC/EU

Belgium, France, Germany, Italy, Luxembourg, the Netherlands	Founding Members, 1958
Denmark, Britain, Ireland	1973
Greece	1981
Portugal, Spain	1986
Austria, Finland, Sweden	1995
Cyprus, Czech Republic, Estonia, Hungary, Latvia, Lithuania, Malta, Poland, Slovakia, Slovenia	2004
Bulgaria, Romania	2007
Turkey, Croatia	No date set

The oil crisis of 1973–1974 delivered another external shock to the integration process. When war broke out in October 1973 between Israel and its Arab neighbors, the Arab countries cut back the export of oil. Importing countries scrambled to find supplies to keep their economies going. In Europe, divergent national responses to the embargo strained the new EPC. Even after the embargo ended, oil prices had shot up to four times their 1970 level. One result was the economic recession of 1974–1975, the most severe since the 1930s.

Governments tended to look to national solutions to combat rising unemployment. The Treaty of Rome prohibited the reimposition of tariffs and import quotas, but governments increased many open and hidden subsidies to industry, and in some cases imposed new nontariff barriers to trade that undermined the single market. The European economies eventually recovered from the recession, but for the remainder of the decade the industrialized world in general was plagued by "stagflation," the devastating combination of low growth and high inflation.

Among the few positive developments of the 1970s was the strengthening of the Franco-German relationship under French president Valéry Giscard d'Estaing and German chancellor Helmut Schmidt and the founding, at their urging, of the European Council. At the December 1974 Paris summit the leaders of the member states agreed to hold such meetings three times (later changed to twice) each year. These regular gatherings constituted a new institution, the European Council.

Unlike the Council of Ministers, which was assigned extensive legislative responsibilities under the Treaty of Rome, the European Council was to operate more informally. It was a forum in which leaders could get together behind closed doors for discussion and bargaining. It became the preferred means by which European leaders reached compromises on deadlocked issues and launched new initiatives relating to the future of the EEC. Actual policy implementation still took place in and through the existing treaty-based institutions — the Commission, the Council of Ministers, and the European Parliament — but the European Council became the "motor" behind the integration process.

Along with Commission president Roy Jenkins, Giscard and Schmidt also were instrumental in founding, in March 1979, the European Monetary System (EMS). All three individuals were former finance ministers who had been involved in the global financial upheavals of the early 1970s. Under the old Bretton Woods system, the value of most currencies was fixed against the dollar, which in turn was set relative to gold. With the breakdown of this system, the value of currencies relative to each other was set by the markets, and wild swings over periods of weeks and months frequently occurred. EMS was designed to eliminate sharp changes in the value of the European currencies against each other. These changes were a deterrent to cross-border trade and investment, which thrive on stable and predictable prices, and tended to weaken the single market (since a change in the relative value of currencies easily could swamp the trade-promoting effects of tariff elimination).

The EMS was a system of fixed but adjustable currency rates built around a central unit of account, the European Currency Unit (ECU). The latter was an artificial currency whose value was set by a weighted basket of EEC member-country currencies. In the EMS, each national currency had a fixed rate against the ECU. The central rates in ECUs then were used to establish a grid of bilateral exchange rates. Authorities in both countries were responsible for ensuring that this rate fluctuated by no more than 2.25 percent (6 percent in the case of Italy). The central rates were not intended to be set for all time, but they could only be changed with the consent of the other members of the EMS. The EMS thus provided a high degree of at least intra-European monetary stability in the 1980s and paved the way for a still more ambitious project, economic and monetary union (EMU), at the end of the decade.

The first direct elections to the European Parliament took place in June 1979, bringing to Strasbourg a popularly elected body of men and women who could claim to speak for "Europe" on behalf of the electorate. The EEC also began accession negotiations with the three Mediterranean countries, Greece, Portugal, and Spain. These countries were much poorer than the EEC average, and all three were emerging from authoritarian rule and attempting to establish democratic systems. While many in Europe questioned whether the Community could afford to absorb these applicants, European leaders saw an overriding political imperative for Mediterranean enlargement. The Community thus began accession negotiations in 1976–1979, although membership was only achieved for Greece in 1981 and Portugal and Spain in 1986.

The Single European Act

CRISIS IN THE EARLY 1980s

The EMS, direct elections to the European Parliament, and the start of enlargement negotiations with the Mediterranean countries were all stirrings of a new dynamism in European integration that was to take hold in the mid-1980s. Throughout the early 1980s, however, the EEC remained bogged down by a myriad of economic and political problems. The 1979 revolution in Iran produced a second oil shock and another deep recession. The terms "Europessimism" and "Eurosclerosis" were coined to sum up a widespread sense that Europe's internal structures—businesses, the welfare state, the educational system—were resistant to change and unable to respond to increased competition from Japan, the United States, and the newly industrializing countries.

This was also a time of extensive leadership change in Europe. Already in 1979, in Britain the Labor government was replaced by Conservative prime minister Margaret Thatcher, a forceful leader known for her skepticism about

European integration.[4] In France, the center-right coalition led by Giscard was replaced in 1981 by a Socialist-Communist alliance led by François Mitterrand, and in Germany the following year Social Democrat Helmut Schmidt was succeeded by a more conservative leader, Christian Democrat Helmut Kohl. At least for a while these new governments headed off in radically different directions. In Britain, for example, the free-enterprise-oriented Thatcher was busy privatizing state-owned firms such as British Steel and British Airways, while in France Mitterrand was carrying out a program of nationalizing many industrial and financial firms that previously had been in private hands.

Within the EEC, Thatcher presented a particular challenge in that she was committed to redressing an imbalance in Britain's budgetary contribution to the Community. This imbalance resulted from the fact that Britain imported large amounts of food and industrial goods from outside the EEC on which it paid customs duties and agricultural levies to Brussels, while it received far less back from the CAP, owing to the small size of its farming sector relative to those in other Community countries. By 1979, this imbalance was well over $1 billion per year and growing. For five years, Thatcher pressed her counterparts in the European Council for a rebate, all but crippling political decisionmaking in the Community. The British budgetary question finally was resolved at the Fontainebleau summit in June 1984, where the heads of government agreed to cut Britain's contribution as well as to undertake a wider budgetary reform.

The Fontainebleau summit was a turning point in other respects as well. Responding to growing concerns in the European Parliament and the business community about the seeming drift in the Community, the leaders agreed to a proposal by Mitterrand to establish a committee to explore ways to improve the functioning of the EEC and of EPC. This committee consisted of one high-level representative from each member state, and became known as the Dooge Committee, after its chairman, former Irish foreign minister James Dooge. One month after Fontainebleau, the EEC governments took another important step by agreeing that French finance minister Jacques Delors would become president of the European Commission when a new term began on January 1, 1985. Delors's leadership and the willingness of European leaders, including Thatcher, to consider major changes in the working of the EEC helped revive it in the second half of the 1980s.

THE SINGLE-MARKET PROGRAM

Discussion about the internal market had intensified in the late 1970s and early 1980s, both among government officials and the leaders of large European corporations, who were increasingly concerned about Europe's lackluster economic performance. The Treaty of Rome stated that the EEC was *supposed* to become an internal market characterized by the free flow of goods, services, persons, and capital. As a practical matter, only a free market in goods had been established, and even this was riddled with exceptions and had been undermined to some extent in recent years by the erection of new nontariff barriers. Differing national standards and technical regulations hindered the import of products from other EEC countries. Paperwork at the borders and disparate national policies on taxation, health and safety, company law, and subsidies to industry all tended to fragment the European market.

The situation with regard to services, capital, and persons was even worse. Service industries remained largely national, controls on capital were in place and in fact served as important instruments of national economic policy (central banks, for example, could lower interest rates and be confident that savers would not be able to take their money and invest it in a neighboring country where banks might be offering a higher rate of return), and the ability of Europeans to work or set up businesses in other Community countries was strictly limited by rules on residency, working permits, and nationally oriented pension and insurance schemes.

Shortly after taking office, Delors announced that the European Commission would introduce a program to eliminate all barriers to the internal market by the end of 1992. This program of action with a firm date for completion was to capture the imagination and win the support of business, government, and ordinary citizens and workers, as "1992" became the slogan of the late 1980s and early 1990s.

Delors entrusted implementation of the 1992 program to Lord Cockfield, the British commissioner responsible for the internal market. Cockfield and his staff produced, in the first half of 1985, a detailed plan that was presented in the form of a white paper to the European Council. The Commission listed approximately three hundred proposals that needed to be turned into Community law to complete the internal market. Each proposal was assigned a target date, so that the whole program would be implemented by December 31, 1992.

The report identified three kinds of barriers to the operation of the internal market—physical, technical, and fiscal—all of which it proposed to dismantle. Physical barriers included customs posts and paperwork and inspections at borders. Technical barriers included national standards and regulations that did not always have the intent of impeding commerce among EEC member states, but that in practice had this effect. They included rules on the content and labeling of foods, chemicals, and pharmaceuticals; car safety standards; different procedures for public procurement; different banking and insurance regulations; national rules on air, rail, road and water transport; and different rules on copyright and trademark protection. Fiscal barriers related both to types and levels of taxation, including value-added and excise taxes, which varied widely across Europe.

While the single-market program generated enthusiasm throughout the Community, Delors and his advisers realized from the beginning that many of its specific measures would be difficult to turn into law. Much Community legislation takes the form of directives, which lay out general guidelines as to "the result to be achieved," but leave it to the member states to enact appropriate national legislation. Governments were reluctant to pass directives that might affect adversely domestic interests or that could be controversial to implement at the national level. With each of several hundred proposed measures requiring unanimous approval by twelve governments, there was little chance that the ambitious single-market program could be implemented. Institutional reform, meaning change in the way the Community took decisions, thus was needed.

RELAUNCHING THE COMMUNITY

In his July 1985 speech to the European Parliament, Delors noted that a new treaty would be needed if the member states were to complete an ambitious single-market program. Dooge's Ad Hoc Committee on Institutional Reform presented its final report to the Brussels summit, in which it called for both a broadening of the EEC's objectives and areas of responsibility and for selected institutional reforms that would strengthen the Community and speed decisionmaking. To achieve these objectives, it recommended convening an Intergovernmental Conference (IGC) among the member states that would draw up a new treaty of European Union. The report did not command universal support for all of its points. The British, Danish, and Greek members declined to endorse its central recommendation for an IGC, and other members dissented on lesser points. But the general thrust of the report was toward significant changes in the Treaty of Rome as a way of restarting the integration process and ensuring that the single-market program would be implemented.

The European Council took up the Dooge Report at its June 1985 session in Milan, the same meeting at which it endorsed the Commission's white paper on the internal market. Italy, a founding member and traditionally a strong proponent of European integration, occupied the European Council presidency, and Prime Minister Bettino Craxi was determined to move the EEC forward. Under the Treaty of Rome, the member states were empowered to call at any time, by simple majority vote, an IGC to negotiate treaty revisions. This provision never had been invoked, however, in part because there was limited interest in such revisions but also because, following the Luxembourg Compromise, governments invariably made major decisions by consensus, even when the treaties allowed for majority or qualified majority voting. After hours of discussion in which Thatcher argued against convening an IGC, Craxi forced a vote on whether to call an IGC. The result was seven to three, with Britain, Denmark, and Greece opposed.

Thatcher was furious at what she saw as an unprecedented disregard of the rule of consensus within the European Council and concerned that the more integration-minded states would use the IGC to push forward a strengthening of the EEC's supranational powers. But Britain also supported the single-market program, the substance of which by then was closely intertwined with the perceived need for procedural reform. Thus Britain as well as the other dissenters approached the IGC ready to play a constructive role, although determined to block the most ambitious reform proposals.

The IGC began in September 1985, and culminated in an intense round of bargaining among the Community leaders at the December 1985 Luxembourg summit. The result was a new treaty, called the Single European Act (SEA), that was formally signed in Luxembourg on February 17, 1986. The treaty came into effect on July 1, 1987, after all of the member states had ratified it.

The SEA broadened the Community's areas of responsibility and, as had long been suggested by proponents of institutional reform, made changes in Community decisionmaking processes. New policy areas not mentioned in the Treaty of Rome but added to Community competence included environment, research and technology, and "economic and social cohesion" (meaning regional policy aimed at narrowing income disparities between different parts of the Community). The SEA also inserted a new article in the Treaty of Rome that specified completion of the internal market by the end of 1992.

The SEA specified that for certain policy areas the Council of Ministers was empowered to take decisions by qualified majority vote. These areas included some social-policy matters, implementation of decisions relating to regional funds and Community research and development programs, and, most important, most measures "which have as their object the establishment and functioning of the internal market." This last amendment, expressed in a new article inserted in the Treaty of Rome, was the crucial change that Delors and others saw as essential to allowing the completion of the single-market program by the end-of-1992 deadline.

The SEA also increased the power of the European Parliament, largely at the urging of its members, who since 1979 could claim with some justification to be the only popularly elected "European" politicians. Whereas the Treaty of Rome required only that the Parliament be consulted on a piece of legislation (proposed by the European Commission) before its adoption or rejection by the Council of Ministers, the SEA introduced a cooperation procedure under which the Parliament could demand from the Council of Ministers an explanation as to why its proposed amendments had not been adopted. The treaty also introduced an assent procedure under which the Parliament was required to approve certain key legislative actions, including the Community budget and association agreements with countries outside the EEC. These changes expanded the power of the European Parliament and marked a further stage in its transition from a consultative to a genuinely legislative body. In the judicial sphere, the SEA made one important change by providing for the establishment of a new Court of First Instance. In the decades since the establishment of the ECSC, the importance of the European Court of Justice had steadily increased, as the Court interpreted Community law and adjudicated legal disputes between the Community and its member states, among institutions of the Community, and between private firms and citizens and member-state governments. One effect of the growing importance of the European Court of Justice, however, was a rising workload. To address this problem, the SEA empowered the Council of Ministers to found a new Court of First Instance to hear many lesser cases.

Finally, the Single European Act introduced an important change in the foreign policy sphere by creating a legal basis for European Political Cooperation. Under the terms of the act, the signatories henceforth were bound by legal agreement, rather than just a political commitment, to consult and cooperate with each other in the foreign policy sphere. However, the EPC itself was not (unlike, for example, such new policy areas as environment or regional policy) incorporated into the Treaty of Rome. There thus was no such thing as a Community foreign policy, but only an agreement among the member states that they would forge a common foreign policy. This meant that foreign policy would remain a matter for intergovernmental cooperation rather than supranational coordination. Community institutions such as the Commission would not have a role in European Political Cooperation, and foreign policy decisions would not be subject to the jurisdiction of the European Court of Justice.

The SEA was an uneasy compromise between those in Europe who wanted progress toward political union and those, like the British and the Danes, who would have preferred not to convene an IGC at all. It introduced important reforms in the Community's founding treaty and demonstrated that the member states could use the mechanism of an intergovernmental conference to push the integration process forward. Above all, it elevated to the level of a legal principle the key goal—a single market by the end of 1992—that was to preoccupy the Community in the late 1980s and become all but synonymous with the "relaunch" that Delors had sought to achieve. It also provided added means to achieve that goal through expanded use of qualified majority voting and created the basis for a stronger external profile on the eve of what was to become an extraordinary period of international change.

The late 1980s was a period of dynamism in Europe. Economic growth improved and the rate of unemployment fell, as millions of new jobs were created. Good economic performance was partly attributable to favorable trends worldwide, but the enthusiasm generated by the 1992 program also contributed. European and non-European firms alike increased their investments in the Community to prepare for the intensified competition and expanded opportunities of the single market. The late 1980s also were marked by favorable international political trends. Mikhail Gorbachev took power in the Soviet Union in March 1985 and gradually steered the Soviet Union on a path of reform. Change in the East provided new vistas for the Community's foreign economic policy and for the member states through EPC. Virtually no one in the Community was prepared, however, for the dramatic events of 1989, which were to lead to new intergovernmental conferences and yet another treaty revision.

The Treaty on European Union

The Treaty on European Union, or the Maastricht Treaty, as it was commonly known after the Dutch city in which it was signed, was by far the most extensive revision of EEC treaties ever attempted. Many of the changes wrought by Maastricht had been under discussion for decades, and some likely would have come about under any circumstances. But there can be little doubt that the sweeping changes in Central and Eastern Europe—the fall of the Berlin Wall, the reunification of Germany, and the collapse of communism—gave a powerful external push to reform.

Economic and Monetary Union (EMU) had been on the Community agenda since 1969, but was all but forgotten in the 1970s and only slowly revived as an issue in the 1980s. Despite Thatcher's distaste for the idea and the skepticism of others, including in the powerful central banking community, by 1988 talk of EMU again was becoming fashionable. The EMS had been operating for nearly a decade, and had been quite successful in its original goal of insulating intra-European trade from turbulence in global currency markets and from the wild swings in the value of the dollar that marked the Reagan years. As the EMS evolved toward a de facto fixed-rate regime, a growing number of economists and political leaders argued that Europe should take the next logical step and move to full EMU.

The single-market program also strengthened the case for EMU. Proponents argued that there was an inconsistency between the creation of a single internal market and the maintenance of separate currencies, since changes in the value of these currencies affected the prices of goods and services traded in the internal market and thus constituted a barrier to trade. National currencies also imposed transaction costs on businesses and consumers. A second factor strengthening the case for EMU was the elimination, under the single-market program, of all national controls on capital. In 1988 the twelve agreed, as part of the single-market program, to remove all such controls by 1990. Economists warned that it would be very difficult to sustain the EMS—a system that retained different national currencies but that tightly regulated variations in the value of these currencies relative to each other—in circumstances in which investors had complete freedom to move money across borders to seek the highest rate of return.

Responding to the growing interest in EMU, at the June 1988 Hanover summit the European Council agreed to establish, under the chairmanship of Delors, a committee to propose concrete steps leading to economic and monetary union. Composed mainly of the central-bank heads from the member states, the Delors Committee developed a detailed three-stage plan for the establishment of EMU. It proposed that in stage three, exchange rate parities be "irrevocably fixed" and full authority for determining economic and monetary policy be transferred to EEC institutions. The report stressed that with the expected completion of the single market (including for capital), and the establishment of competition and regional policies, the Community already had accomplished much of the work toward EMU.

At the June 1989 summit the European Council approved the Delors Committee's three-stage approach, and declared that stage one of EMU should begin on July 1, 1990, with the closer coordination of member-state economic policies and completion of plans to free the movement of capital. The European leaders further agreed that another IGC would be held to consider moving to stages two and three, which unlike stage one, required extensive amendment of the EEC treaty. Before these plans could be implemented, however, developments in Central and Eastern Europe radically changed the international context in which the Community approached its future development.

The EEC had evolved primarily as an economic institution, but it had been profoundly shaped by the political and ideological conflict on the continent. Strengthening Western Europe against Soviet pressures always had been an important motivation for supporters of the Community. The division of Germany had helped to further integration by making France and West Germany roughly equal in size and ensuring that the latter would look to its western neighbors for economic and political partnership. This was a major change from earlier periods, in which Germany had always had strong economic and political links with Eastern Europe.

The unexpectedly rapid collapse of communism in 1989–1991 thus raised questions about the future of European integration. The opening of the Berlin Wall in November 1989 and the fall of the East German regime raised the question of German reunification. After elections in East Germany and a set of fast-moving two-plus-four negotiations involving the governments of the two German states and the Soviet Union, Britain, France, and the United Kingdom (the four victor powers of World War II), Germany was reunited in October 1990. The five states of the former East Germany, with some 16 million inhabitants, automatically became part of the Community.

Although leaders such as Mitterrand had come around to accepting German reunification as inevitable, they were concerned that creation of a larger and more eastward-oriented Germany could damage the process of European integration. The Community was a child of the Cold War, and the latter's end inevitably raised questions about the EEC's future. Mitterrand was determined to push forward with plans to "deepen" the Community, and thereby to ensure that the new Germany would remain firmly anchored in the West. He was supported in this by the Germans themselves, especially Helmut Kohl.

EMU most likely would have gone ahead in any case, but developments in Eastern and Central Europe lent new urgency to this project. In December 1989, at the Strasbourg summit, the European Council agreed to convene an IGC on EMU by the end of 1990. The leaders also agreed to adopt a social charter—a Community-wide agreement on labor standards that the trade unions had pressed for as a concomitant to the single European market. Britain did not sign the social charter and it opposed the ICG, but on both issues it was unable to dissuade the other member states from moving forward.

Alongside these developments in the economic sphere, the changing international situation gave new momentum to the old project for European Political Union (EPU). In April 1990, Kohl and Mitterrand jointly called for new and concrete steps to realize the aspirations to EPU already expressed in the Single European Act. The Kohl-Mitterrand proposal set the agenda for an extraordinary session of the European Council in Dublin in April 1990, at which the twelve leaders reaffirmed their commitment to political union. Meeting in the same city two months later, the European Council agreed to convene an IGC on political union to begin at the same time as the IGC on EMU and to run in parallel with it. Both IGCs formally opened at the Rome summit in December 1990. Thus, after not holding a single such conference in the three decades after 1955, the Community was to have three IGCs in five years, two of which would run concurrently. This extraordinary situation reflected the extent to which, as Delors had phrased it, history was "accelerating," forcing the Community to respond.

NEGOTIATING THE MAASTRICHT TREATY

The IGCs were conducted as formal diplomatic conferences involving regular meetings at the ministerial and working levels. Their focus was on strengthening the decisionmaking process in areas in which the EEC already had competence and on extending the range of issues subject to common policymaking. If these were the general goals, there was little agreement among the twelve about how they were to be accomplished. Italy and the Benelux countries were the strongest supporters of European integration and pressed for the most sweeping revisions. Britain and Denmark were leery of change, and sought to block many of the most extensive reforms. France wanted a strong Europe, but was skeptical of the transfer of supranational powers to Brussels. It thus favored expanded use of intergovernmental cooperation along the lines already established in EPC. Germany tended to align its positions with those of France, but on foreign policy and defense matters it was wary of endangering NATO by building up a European defense alternative. On EMU, it wanted strong safeguards to ensure that the future European currency would be as stable as the German mark.

The negotiations lasted a year, and concluded at the December 1991 Maastricht European Council with agreement on the Treaty on European Union, which extensively amended the Treaty of Rome and added new provisions on matters beyond the scope of the latter treaty. The text was agreed only after last-minute negotiations in which Britain and Denmark secured the right to "opt out" of certain of the treaty's provisions. Agreement to disagree was in some cases the most that could be achieved. Still, the reforms were substantial, and went far beyond anything that had been accomplished in the previous thirty-five years of the Community's existence. As the name indicated, the treaty brought into being a new entity called the European Union, which was defined in the treaty as "mark[ing] a new stage in the process of creating an ever-closer union among the peoples of Europe." The Union itself was set up as a complicated structure of three "pillars" dealing with different and partially overlapping policy areas using different decisionmaking processes. The first pillar would consist of the three existing communities—the EEC (renamed the European Community [EC] to reflect its broadened and no longer strictly economic areas of responsibility), the ECSC, and Euratom—in which the member states have pooled sovereignty and transferred decisionmaking powers to the European Commission, the Council of Ministers, the European Parliament, and the European Court of Justice, with a powerful guiding role also assigned to the European Council.

The second pillar, Common Foreign and Security Policy (CFSP), replaced and was based upon EPC. Decisions in the second pillar were to remain largely intergovernmental in character, with only a limited role for Community institutions. Such decisions would not be subject to the jurisdiction of the Court of Justice. The European Commission could suggest actions under CFSP, but it was not given the sole right of initiative in this area (the member states also could initiate policy actions under CFSP). The Maastricht Treaty specified certain foreign policy goals that were to be pursued under CFSP, such as safeguarding the common values, fundamental interests, and independence of the Union, strengthening its security, and promoting peace and respect for human rights. These objectives were to be pursued through "common positions" and "joint actions" by the member states, with decisions on these matters taken primarily by unanimity. CFSP also provided for the "eventual framing of a common defense policy" and assigned implementation of EU defense decisions to an existing body, the Western European Union, previously not linked to the structures of the European Communities.

The third pillar consisted of cooperation in the fields of Justice and Home Affairs, including asylum policy, control of external borders and immigration from outside the Union, and combating drug addiction and international crime. The completion of the single European market and the abolition of controls on the movement of people and capital had made EU-level cooperation in these areas increasingly necessary. Proponents of cooperation often stressed that international crime syndicates had adjusted to the single market, while the police and judges still were very national in their outlook. At the same time, the member states with their very different legal traditions and approaches to such sensitive internal matters were reluctant to surrender sovereignty to Brussels in these areas. The twelve thus agreed to establish the third pillar on an intergovernmental basis, with decisionmaking procedures similar to those used in CFSP. Nonetheless, the members made a commitment to collaborate with each other, and there were provisions in the treaty for strengthening this collaboration over time by establishing new bodies such as the European Police Office (Europol).

The Maastricht Treaty established the principle of "subsidiarity," a concept that attempts to define which decisions are to be taken at which levels. Issues of primarily local importance are to be taken as close to the citizen as possible. Subsidiarity was introduced in part as a response to fears of excessive centralization of powers in Brussels. The treaty also established a European citizenship, to exist alongside and in addition to national citizenship, that brings with it certain rights, such as the right of an EU citizen to be represented by the consulate of a another member state while overseas or to vote in local elections while resident in another member state.

Continuing the pattern established in the SEA, the Maastricht Treaty strengthened the European Parliament by adding a new procedure, called "co-decision," under which the EP for the first time could block legislation introduced by the European Commission and passed by the Council of Ministers. Co-decision was prescribed only for a limited number of policy areas, although one of these—the internal market—was quite important. The Parliament also was given a say in the appointment of the Commission and the Commission president, hitherto a matter of exclusive concern for the Council of Ministers. The treaty also established a new institution, the Committee of the Regions, to provide a means whereby regional entities in Europe—states and provinces—can give direct input to policymaking in Brussels.

Perhaps the most significant achievement of the Maastricht Treaty was the establishment of the EMU. Building upon the Delors Committee report and the experience of the EMS, the treaty established a detailed timetable and institutional provisions for the phasing-out of national currencies and the introduction of a European money, initially called the ECU and later renamed the euro. Stage two of EMU was to begin on January 1, 1994, and bring about increased economic coordination and preparations for the single currency. In stage two, the member states were to meet certain economic convergence criteria relating to inflation, national debt and deficits, currency stability in the EMS, and long-term interest rates designed to ensure that the economies entering the Economic and Monetary Union would have broadly similar economic performance. The emphasis in the convergence criteria was on price stability and the continued fight against inflation.

The treaty stipulated that stage three would begin no later than January 1, 1999, and would entail the "irrevocable locking" of the value of the European currencies against each other and their eventual phasing out by July 2002. The treaty provided for the establishment of a European Central Bank and a European System of Central Banks that would be responsible for conducting monetary policy at the EU level. Britain and Denmark, both traditional skeptics of EMU, secured "opt-outs" from the main provisions of EMU, and were not required to surrender their national currencies in 1999–2002 if they chose not to do so.

Britain also achieved an opt-out from one other Maastricht innovation, the Social Protocol. Eleven of the member states were strongly committed to incorporating, in the EU's first pillar, extensive new provisions on worker health and safety, working conditions, social security, and related matters. Britain was opposed to this change, which it saw as an encroachment by Brussels on traditional member-state responsibilities. Although opposition of a single state normally is sufficient to block treaty revision on any matter, on this issue it was agreed that the eleven states would adopt a European Community social policy in a separate protocol, which Britain would not be bound to observe. This, along with the British and Danish opt-outs from EMU, was the first time in the history of the Community that a member state was granted a major derogation from a treaty provision. Along with the other complexities of the Maastricht Treaty, notably the three-pillar structure and the vagueness surrounding the subsidiarity concept, these derogations reflected the degree to which Maastricht itself was a compromise among widely different perspectives on European integration. It permitted the more integration-minded states to move ahead in sensitive areas, while allowing the skeptics to preserve cherished national prerogatives.

BEYOND MAASTRICHT: AMSTERDAM AND NICE

After nearly a decade of rapid change, it was perhaps inevitable that the pace would slow and that a reaction to further integration would set in. With Western Europe racing toward union and the old order in Eastern Europe rapidly disintegrating, people needed time to digest these changes. After a short-lived economic boom, the costs of German reunification helped to precipitate another recession in Europe, bringing to an end the job growth of the late 1980s. War in the Persian Gulf and the outbreak of civil war in the former Yugoslavia caused added uncertainty. The mood in Europe became introspective, more focused on national concerns such as crime, immigration, and unemployment and more skeptical of the headlong rush to union.

The first highly visible sign that sentiments had changed occurred in June 1992, when voters in Denmark narrowly rejected the Maastricht Treaty in the national referendum that was required under the Danish Constitution. Since all twelve signatories had to ratify the treaty for it to go into effect, the EEC was thrown into crisis. By September 1992, the political crisis had spilled over into the financial markets, threatening the integrity of the EMS, one of the key building blocks of the planned EMU. In the same month the French electorate approved the Maastricht Treaty, but only by the narrow margin of 51 to 49 percent. In Germany, the treaty was challenged in the supreme court, where opponents argued that it contravened the German Constitution by transferring powers of the German states to Brussels.

In the end the Maastricht Treaty was ratified. The European Council negotiated additional opt-outs for Denmark, and in May 1993 the Danish voters approved the treaty by a healthy margin in a second referendum. Legislatures in the other countries approved the treaty, as did the German federal court. Thus Maastricht went into effect on November 1, 1993, some ten months later than originally planned. The European Union was born, even though many voters were confused about the new name and uncertain what it meant for them.

The inadequacies of the Maastricht Treaty were recognized by its creators even before the difficulties with ratification arose. In many areas, disagreements among the member states had led to vague compromises and statements of intent that could be interpreted in different ways. For example, the article that introduced defense into the EU structure stated: "The common foreign and security policy shall include all questions related to the security of the Union, including the eventual framing of a common defense policy, which might in time lead to a common defense." But how were terms like "eventual" and "might in time" to be interpreted and translated into action? Recognizing that such vagueness could not be tolerated indefinitely, the twelve agreed in the Maastricht Treaty to hold another conference in 1996 to review the workings of the treaty and to introduce such amendments as were deemed necessary.

As 1996 approached, the impending IGC became ever more closely associated with enlargement. On January 1, 1995, the membership of the Union expanded to fifteen, with the accession of Austria, Finland, and Sweden. These were neutral countries that previously had declined to join an organization of NATO member states (Ireland being the only non-NATO member of the Community), but that had revised their position with the end of the Cold War. Even more important for the Union was the prospect of membership for the former communist countries of Central and Eastern Europe. When the Maastricht Treaty was signed, it was still unclear whether these countries would become full members, or whether they would settle for a looser form of association based on free trade and cooperation in other spheres. Increasingly, however, the leaders of these countries pressed for full EU (and NATO) membership, motivated by a strong desire to be fully integrated into the West, to buffer themselves against instability in the former Soviet Union and a possible resurgence of Russian power, and to have influence over the institutions shaping the development of Europe. After a period of debate about the wisdom of committing to absorb a relatively poor region with over 100 million inhabitants, the EU leaders concluded that they had no choice. At the June 1993 Copenhagen summit, the European Council agreed that these countries could become members, but only after a period of transition in which they prepared their economies and established working democracies.

The prospect of adding ten or more members lent new urgency to calls for the reform of EU institutions. At fifteen, the Union already was too large to function with essentially the same set of institutions that had been devised in the 1950s for a community of six. With twenty members, the European Commission had lost its collegial character. The European Parliament was already larger than most national parliaments. Under the rotating system of presidencies, member states could expect to chair the European Council and the Council of Ministers only once every seven-and-a-half years.

The IGC convened in Turin in March 1996. In addition to streamlining decisionmaking in advance of enlargement, its goals were to strengthen a CFSP that was widely seen as having been ineffectual in the face of the wars in the former Yugoslavia, and to develop the Union's third pillar, which had made little progress in forging common EU policies on immigration, asylum, and combating cross-border crime. After more than a year of intense negotiations among the member states, the IGC concluded in June 1997 with the approval of a new treaty amending Maastricht and the other founding treaties. Called the Treaty of Amsterdam after the city in which it was signed, the agreement provided for some strengthening of the Union's CFSP, for example by creating the post of High Representative for CFSP and by developing "common strategies" toward third countries and regions as a new policy instrument. It also mandated closer cooperation in third-pillar matters such as immigration and asylum policies, in large part through a phased shift of these responsibilities from the third to the first pillars. As in past revisions, the powers of the European Parliament were expanded somewhat. In addition, Britain under newly elected Prime Minister Tony Blair joined the Social Protocol.

On balance, however, the changes in the Treaty of Amsterdam were modest compared to those agreed at Maastricht. Because enlargement was not imminent and because national governments were preoccupied with making the painful adjustments to be ready for EMU, the member states largely postponed to a future IGC extensive reforms of the Union's decisionmaking apparatus. Instead, they adopted a legally binding protocol to the treaty that stipulated that at least one year before the membership of the Union reached twenty, a new IGC would be convened to carry out a review of the institutions and to examine in particular three questions: the size and composition of the Commission, the weighting of votes in the Council of Ministers, and the possible extension of qualified majority voting in the Council. Dubbed by the press the Amsterdam "leftovers," these seemingly technical questions related to the fundamental character of the Union and to such matters as the balance of power between small and large states and the relative mix of supranationalism and intergovernmentalism in the makeup of the Union.

The third and decisive stage of EMU began on January 1, 1999. The euro was introduced as scheduled, with eleven EU members (all but the United Kingdom, Denmark, Sweden, and Greece) adopting the common currency and forming their own grouping of economic and financial ministers to coordinate euro-related policy matters. The technical switchover to the euro over the long

New Year's holiday went surprisingly well, without computer crashes or increased volatility on financial markets. Nonetheless, broader questions continued to hang over the future of the common currency. Governments committed to creating jobs and cutting rates of unemployment pressed the newly formed European Central Bank to adopt more expansionary monetary policies, raising anew old questions about the balance between political control and central-bank independence. The member states also differed over the future of the EU budget, with Germany and the Netherlands insisting that their large net contributions be trimmed and Spain and the other Mediterranean countries holding out for continued large regional aid payments from Brussels.

The enlargement process also inched forward. In July 1997, the Commission issued a detailed plan called *Agenda 2000* for bringing an initial round of candidate countries into the Union early in the twenty-first century and for reforming the Union's own budgetary and agricultural policies to cope with enlargement. Based upon the recommendations in *Agenda 2000*, the European Council decided that accession negotiations with six leading candidate countries—the Czech Republic, Cyprus, Estonia, Hungary, Poland, and Slovenia—could begin in March 1998. At Helsinki in December 1999, the member states further declared that all of the central and East European candidate countries and Malta (although not yet Turkey) had made sufficient progress in bringing their political and economic situations up to EU levels to begin accession negotiations. The EU thus was on track for a "big bang" enlargement, probably in 2004–2006, that could bring as many as twelve new countries into the Union.

Progress toward enlargement focused attention once again on the problem of institutional reform that Amsterdam was supposed to resolve but that it had merely deferred to the future. The Amsterdam Treaty managed to survive another hard-fought Danish referendum and, following approval by the national parliaments, went into effect in May 1999. However, in March 2000 the member states launched yet another IGC, the fourth to take place in less than a decade, to deal with the Amsterdam leftovers. Throughout the remainder of 2000, the member states engaged in tough bargaining over the future of the Union. Some member states favored capping or reducing the size of the European Commission to preserve its effectiveness. This would mean, however, that in an enlarged Union every member state would not always have one of its citizens as a member of the Commission—an innovation that was strongly resisted by the smaller countries. The Commission and some of the more federalist member states favored extension of qualified majority voting to policy areas still subject to decision by unanimity. These pressures were resisted by Britain, which still wanted to retain a veto over tax policy; France, which wanted to maintain control over its national cultural policies as they related to foreign trade; and various other member states on issues of particular national concern.

The most sensitive issue was the reweighting of votes in the Council of Ministers. The system of qualified majority voting was designed to ensure efficiency through use of majority voting but to preserve some of the safeguards associated with the unanimity procedure. Legislation could not be blocked by one or two recalcitrant member states, but neither could it be passed, as in most national parliamentary systems, by a narrow numerical majority. This system generally had worked quite well. However, as many more small countries joined the Union, France and the other large member states were increasingly concerned about the declining relative weight of the bigger countries. Whereas the original Community of the 1950s had had three large and three small member states, an enlarged Union would have only six large member states (France, Germany, Italy, Poland, Spain, and the UK) and eventually more than twenty smaller members. Concerned about the diminution of its relative influence, France pressed for a reweighting of votes in favor of the large member countries (although not, somewhat inconsistently, an increase in Germany's weight relative to France to reflect its increased post-reunification population!).

In the end the fifteen approved, at the December 2000 European Council, a new agreement that became known as the Treaty of Nice. As shown in Table 7.2, the treaty decided how many seats in the European Parliament and weighted votes in the Council of Ministers each current and projected member would have after enlargement. To reduce the size and thereby preserve the cohesion and effectiveness of the Commission, the "big five" gave up their second commissioner. The treaty further stipulated that after membership reached twenty-seven, the EU would shift to a rotation system in which the number of commissioners would be less than the number of member states. For the foreseeable future, however, each member could still have its "own" commissioner. The relative weighting of the big states was increased, but France (along with Italy and the UK) continued to have the same number of votes in the Council of Ministers as Germany. To give somewhat greater weight to population and to defuse German complaints of unfairness, a complex "triple majority" was put in place, under which a qualified majority vote had to have not only the required number of Council votes, but also be formed by countries representing at least 62 percent of the Union's population.

Although Nice technically cleared the way to enlargement by deciding the distribution of decisionmaking power in an enlarged Union, the treaty was hardly the simplification and streamlining that many European commentators thought was essential. Its provisions were more complicated than ever, leaving plenty of scope for determined minorities to block legislation. At the insistence of the member states, policy decisions in such key areas as taxation, social policy, cohesion policy, asylum and immigration, and above all such constitutional issues as reform of the treaties remained subject to unanimity rather than qualified majority voting. Most tellingly, the treaty was long, complicated, and difficult for the average citizen to understand and support, a circumstance that was underscored dramatically in June 2001 when the traditionally pro-Europe Irish electorate voted down the treaty. Nice finally went into effect after the Irish voters approved the treaty in a second referendum in October 2002.

Table 7.2   Member State Representation in the EU Instiututions

	Votes in the Council of Ministers	Representatives Elected to the European Parliament
Austria	10	18
Belgium	12	24
Bulgaria	10	18
Cyprus	4	6
Czech Republic	12	24
Denmark	7	14
Estonia	4	6
Finland	7	14
France	29	78
Germany	29	99
Greece	12	24
Hungary	12	24
Ireland	7	13
Italy	29	78
Latvia	4	9
Lithuania	7	13
Luxembourg	4	6
Malta	3	5
Netherlands	13	27
Poland	27	54
Portugal	12	24
Romania	14	35
Slovakia	7	14
Slovenia	4	7
Spain	27	54
Sweden	10	19
United Kingdom	29	78
Majority	255 votes, representing a majority of the member states, comprising states accounting for at least 62% of the EU population	
Total	345	785

At the same time that it wrestled with these internal questions, the EU was beginning to assert itself more on the international scene. Euro notes and coins came into circulation in January 2002, successfully completing the transition to EMU and giving the Union tangible proof of its cohesion and its ability to accomplish ambitious, long-term goals. After the debacle in the former Yugoslavia in the early 1990s, the Europeans moved to strengthen CFSP and to add to it a defense dimension that would cooperate with NATO but could act autonomously if necessary. At the December 1999 Helsinki summit the EU adopted a decision to establish a 50,000–60,000-person military force that would be capable of taking on the full range of peacekeeping and peace enforcement tasks, either in cooperation with NATO and the United States or, if need be, acting alone. Member states were slow to approve the added defense spending that was needed to turn these plans into reality, but the EU clearly was intent on building a defense and defense industrial identity apart from NATO and the United States.

While U.S. policymakers generally applauded the EU's efforts to become a more active player in international politics, tensions between the EU and the United States increased over a range of economic, political, and security issues. European politicians spoke openly about building a new European identity by distinguishing Europe from the United States. Differences between the EU and the United States arose over policy toward the Middle East, the International Criminal Court, the Kyoto Protocol on global warming, and other issues. These strains were already evident in the late 1990s under the Clinton administration, but they became particularly acute after the arrival of the Bush administration in Washington in January 2001 and, even more so, after the September 11, 2001, terrorist attacks on the United States.

ENLARGEMENT AND THE CONSTITUTION

The perceived shortcomings of the Nice treaty led to renewed efforts at institutional reform. Even before the treaty had been concluded, political leaders such as German foreign minister Joschka Fischer, British prime minister Tony Blair, and French president Jacques Chirac had given speeches calling for more vigorous and imaginative debate about the envisioned endpoint of the integration process ("finality") and the need for radical reforms going beyond institutional tinkering. Among the ideas suggested in the debate were creating an elected post of EU president, scrapping the Commission altogether to create an executive of member-state government representatives, and setting up an additional legislative chamber parallel to the European Parliament that would be composed of members of national legislatures.[5]

To thrash out these ideas, the European Council agreed, at the December 2001 Laeken summit, to launch a European Convention composed of representatives of member-state governments, members of national parliaments, Commission representatives, and representatives of the European Parliament. Even though they were not yet members of the Union, the candidate countries were invited to participate. Chaired by former French president Giscard d'Estaing, the Convention was charged with drawing up proposals for a European constitution. These proposals then could be presented to the member states for discussion at an

IGC to be convened in late 2003 or early 2004. This approach reflected the emerging sense in Europe that after more than fifty years of integration, the EU needed a basic set of rules that would not be subject to change at frequent IGCs and that could be understood by and serve as a rallying point for the European citizenry. Whether a written constitution could resolve all of the internal dis-agreements and uncertainties about power sharing and Europe's "finality" remained unclear. Nonetheless, the convention began work in March 2002 with great enthusiasm, its members conscious that they were embarking on a constitu-tion-building exercise that in some ways paralleled (although in others was very different from) the one that had taken place in the United States in the 1780s.

After sixteen months of intense work and deliberation, the convention adopted a draft constitutional treaty and forwarded it to the European Council for further consideration by the member states. If adopted by the member states, the treaty would supersede the 1957 Treaty of Rome and all subsequent amendments and additions (the Single European Act, Maastricht, Amsterdam, and Nice) to the EU's founding treaties. The three-pillar structure was to be abolished and replaced by a single European Union that would have legal per-sonality and the ability to conclude binding agreements with other countries and international organizations. The treaty would preserve the five key EU institutions, but make changes in how they operated, including the establish-ment of a Council president to be elected by the member states for a two-and-a-half-year term (to replace the rotating six-month presidency in chairing Council meetings), the establishment of the post of an EU foreign minister, and new roles for the national parliaments in ensuring the proper application of the subsidiarity principle in EU legislation. The powers of the European Parliament were to be extended to new (although still not all) policy areas, and the compli-cated triple-majority system enshrined in the Nice treaty was to be abolished. In place of the system of national weights used since QMV was established in the Treaty of Rome, the new system would require that for legislation to be adopted it must be supported by a majority of member states representing at least 60 per-cent of the EU population.

When the IGC convened in Rome in October 2003 to consider the draft constitutional treaty, key member states led by France and Germany, the Euro-pean Commission, and of course Giscard hoped for its rapid approval, without significant amendment. This did not happen, however. Spain and Poland (the latter already participating in the IGC as a prospective member state) were unhappy with the diminution from the Nice formula of their relative voting power in the new treaty and blocked its adoption at the European Council. The member states finally approved the treaty in June 2004, after adjustments were made in the formula for QMV to satisfy the two holdouts. Under the new com-promise, passage of legislation would require the support of at least 55 percent of the member states representing 65 percent of the EU's population; in cases where states representing 35 percent or more of EU population chose to block legislation, at least four member states had to comprise the blocking group. Ratification by the member states was to take place in 2004 and 2005, and the treaty to go into effect by 2006.

Meanwhile, the long pre-accession process for the candidate countries moved toward conclusion. At the December 2002 Copenhagen summit, final agreement was reached on admitting ten new member states on May 1, 2004. Two countries, Bulgaria and Romania, were making slower progress, but were expected to be ready for membership by 2007. The leaders of the ten accession countries met in Athens on April 16, 2003, with their member-state counterparts to sign the accession treaty. Enlargement went ahead as scheduled in May of the following year, after the fifteen member states and each of the acceding countries had ratified the accession treaties.

Under the provisions of the Treaty of Nice, ten new commissioners from the new member states took their place in an expanded European Commission. Voters in the new member states elected their representatives to an enlarged European Parliament, and the voting formula in the Council of Ministers was adjusted, in accordance with the Treaty of Nice, to give the new and old member states their assigned weights. In a few areas, transitional arrangements remained in effect, causing a certain degree of resentment in the new member states about the possible emergence of two classes of members. The old member states were allowed to keep restrictions on the free movement of labor from the acceding countries, and the new member states were not expected to adopt the euro for periods of five years or more, or until they had further strengthened their economies. For the most part, however, the new member states were full participants in all of the policies and programs of the Union, beginning, most prominently with the single market (apart from the restrictions on movement of labor).

CRISIS AND DRIFT

The wrangling over the provisions of the constitutional treaty in late 2003 and early 2004 reflected the difficult political environment in Europe in the first decade of the twenty-first century. Enlargement was a clear success, but voters were worried about further expansion to the east and south, and especially to Turkey, which was pressing to become an EU member state. At the Lisbon summit in March 2000, the European Council had set the goal of making Europe the world's most dynamic economy by 2010, but member-state governments generally had not implemented the reforms—increases in research and development spending, revamping of antiquated pensions and healthcare systems, and the filling of gaps in the single market, for example—that would be required to achieve such a grandiose goal. Far from closing the gap, Europe's economic growth continued to lag behind that of other regions of the world. In foreign affairs, the 2003 Iraq war badly split the EU, as France and Germany took the lead in opposing the U.S. effort to topple Saddam Hussein, while leaders in other member states—especially Britain but also Spain, Italy, and the accession countries—were more supportive of U.S. policy. Europe itself was caught up in the post–September 11 conflict between Islamic radicalism and the West, as was seen most dramatically in the March 2004 bombings in Madrid that killed almost two hundred people.

In this complex political, economic, and security environment, the EU suddenly but in retrospect perhaps not surprisingly was thrown into crisis over ratification of the constitutional treaty. In March 2005, voters in Spain approved the treaty by an overwhelming margin. Parliaments in a number of member countries that decided not to hold referenda also swiftly ratified the treaty. On May 29, however, voters in France rejected the treaty by a stunning margin of 55 percent "no" and 45 percent "yes." A few days later, voters in the Netherlands delivered a similar verdict.

The rejection of the treaty in two founding member states of the EU came as a shock to political leaders across the continent, and reflected the degree to which public perceptions of the integration project had diverged from the views of the pro-integration elites in politics, business, and the media. Where the latter saw a larger and more cohesive EU as the key to enhancing Europe's role in the world and to solving the economic and political challenges raised by globalization, the former were no longer so sure about the benefits that integration offered to the average citizen. In France, anti-treaty campaigners made effective use of "the Polish plumber"—a hypothetical immigrant from a new member state who comes to France and competes with local workers by undercutting the prevailing wage rates—to link enlargement with economic insecurity. In the Netherlands, people shocked by the murder of Dutch film maker Theo van Gogh in November 2004 by an Islamist radical in an Amsterdam park in effect voted against enlargement, globalization, and open borders by rejecting the treaty.

The leaders of the twenty-five member states responded to the votes in France and the Netherlands by declaring, at the June 2005 European Council, a "pause for reflection" in which they would not press for ratification of the treaty. Experts and politicians put forward various ideas for how all or parts of the treaty might be salvaged, including new referenda, revisions of the Nice treaty that would put into effect parts of the constitutional treaty, or action by the European Council on reforms that might not require treaty amendment. Political leaders and Euro-skeptic campaigners were cool to these ideas, however, on the grounds that the voters *had* spoken and that it was time, for a change, for the leaders to listen to the people and to slow or at least redirect the elite-driven process of integration.

At its session in Brussels in June 2006, the European Council completed its first assessment of the "reflection period," but took no decisions about how to proceed with ratification of the existing or even a modified constitutional treaty. Rather, the leaders struck a pragmatic note and stressed the importance of the EU taking concrete actions in areas of particular concern to the citizens. These areas included promoting economic growth and the creation of new jobs, dealing with the challenges of illegal immigration and terrorism, and promoting, as the European Council phrased it, "the European way of life in the face of globalization and demographic trends."[6]

Whether the EU could register successes in these areas in a way that would regenerate popular enthusiasm for integration remained unclear, however. Citizens, especially younger ones, tended to take for granted many of the hard-won achievements of the EU—free movement across borders, the single currency, and the stabilization of Central and Eastern Europe, for example—and to focus their attention on the perceived flaws in the integration process or the risks of extending the Union to poorer and unstable regions to the east and south. Under these conditions, the fate of the constitutional treaty remained very much up in the air. While few predicted that the EU would break up or that Europe would revert to the nationalist rivalries of the 1930s and 1940s, steady progress toward a stronger, more coherent, and more unified Europe as envisioned in the constitutional treaty was not a sure bet. At least for the next few years, the EU seemed destined to muddle along. Whether this would be an adequate response to a world marked by such developments as the economic and political rise of China and India and the ongoing challenges of terrorism, global warming, and instability in the developing world remained a concern for thoughtful people in Europe and beyond.

Notes

1. For the texts of the treaties, see European Commission, *European Union: Selected Instruments from the Treaties,* Luxembourg: Office for Official Publications of the European Communities, 1995. The treaties also can be found on *http://europa.eu.int.*

2. For the UK's complex relationship to the EU, see Hugo Young, *This Blessed Plot: Britain and Europe from Churchill to Blair,* Woodstock, NY: Overlook Press, 1999.

3. For the monetary turmoil of the 1970s, see Paul Volcker and Toyoo Gyohten, *Changing Fortunes: The World's Money and the Threat to American Leadership,* New York: Times Books, 1992.

4. For Thatcher's views on Europe, see her memoirs, *Downing Street Years,* New York: HarperCollins, 1993.

5. For a more detailed analysis of the issues, see Youri Devuyst, *The European Union at the Crossroads: An Introduction to the EU's Institutional Evolution,* Brussels: PIE-Peter Lang, 2002.

6. *Brussels European Council, June 15–16, 2006: Presidency Conclusions,* Brussels: Council of the European Union, June 16, 2006.

Suggested Readings

Dinan, Desmond, *Ever Closer Union: An Introduction to European Integration*, 3rd edition, Boulder, CO: Lynne Rienner, 2005.

Grant, Charles, *Delors: Inside the House That Jacques Built*, London: Nicholas Brealey, 1994.

Kenen, Peter B., *Economic and Monetary Union in Europe: Moving Beyond Maastricht*, New York: Cambridge University Press, 1995.

Monnet, Jean, *Memoirs*, Garden City: Doubleday, 1978.

Moravcsik, Andrew, *The Choice for Europe: Social Purpose and State Power from Messina to Maastricht*, Ithaca, NY: Cornell University Press, 1998.

Nugent, Neill, *The Government and Politics of the European Union*, 5th edition, Durham: Duke University Press, 2003.

Tsoukalis, Loukas, *The New European Economy Revisited*, New York: Oxford University Press, 1997.

Van Oudenaren, John, *Uniting Europe: An Introduction to the European Union*, Lanham, MD: Rowman & Littlefield, 2004.

CHAPTER 8

The European Economy and Economic Governance

Erik Jones

For most economists, economic governance is the heart of European integration, if not the soul.[1] The politicians who forged the European Union (EU) may have thought about war and peace, nationalism and supranationalism, but the institutions they constructed were economic and the challenges that they faced centered on problems of economic governance. Moreover, while it is true that the EU's Common Foreign and Security Policy (CFSP) and its policies related to Justice and Home Affairs (JHA) have gained prominence in recent years, such gains have done little to diminish the significance of economic governance for the European project. When European voters go to the polls to elect members of the European Parliament, they think about job security and employment prospects. When politicians worry about declining popular support for European integration, they talk about globalization, fiscal austerity, and welfare state reform. And when European leaders want to reconnect Europe to the people, they focus on jobs, growth, and competitiveness.

Of course there is more to European integration than economics. Still, economic matters are of central importance. They are also fiendishly hard for policymakers to explain to the general public—particularly in terms of why things happen and who should be held to account. If unemployment increases in Germany, for example, is the German government responsible or should blame fall on the European Central Bank (ECB)? Is German unemployment an unavoidable consequence of economic linkages at the world-market level (globalization) or is it an unintended consequence of political and institutional arrangements at the national and regional level within Germany (federalism and the welfare state)? How does economic performance in Germany fit together with economic performance elsewhere? Is Germany growing slowly because Ireland and Spain are growing too quickly? Is slow growth in Germany pulling down performance in Belgium, France, Italy, and the Netherlands? Has construction of the single currency made things better or worse? These questions defy easy answers because the national economies of Europe are so interdependent. What happens in any one country can have a profound influence on all the rest.

Worse, the effect of one country's performance on the others can easily rebound against the first country itself.

Economists labor hard to develop ever more sophisticated answers to questions about how Europe's economies fit together and how they can be managed best. In turn, much of this sophisticated economic advice has been built into the institutions and policies of the European Union. The single European currency, the euro, and the European Central Bank are good examples. The euro exists for many reasons, but economically it serves to fix exchange rates between national currencies in order to facilitate trade while at the same time eliminating dangerous market speculation. The ECB exists for one reason—to manage the euro. The primary goal of the ECB is to preserve price stability in those countries that have adopted the euro—called, collectively, the "euro zone" or "euro area." It does this without political interference using a two-pillar strategy that focuses on both the expected rate of inflation and the historic rate of monetary growth. As it has evolved, the ECB has developed complex models for forecasting how prices in the euro zone will develop, for testing different policy responses, and for estimating what will be the result. It even has its own coded language for communicating policy moves before they take place and for justifying them after the fact. Finally, there is a technical economic argument that can be made to support each of these many facets of the ECB's design and operation. Not all economists buy into the arguments of the ECB and some, such as the Belgian economist Paul De Grauwe, have lodged important critiques.[2] Even so, the economists at the ECB are clever enough to support their views and sophisticated enough to hold their own in academic debate.

Unfortunately, however, technical sophistication is only part of what economic governance is all about. Political scientists talk about "governance" as opposed to "government" whenever it is clear that the active participation of actors outside the state is necessary for public policy to be effective. Politicians can vote to raise their own salaries or to put a man on the moon without depending too much on how the rest of society responds. But when they want to tackle complex problems such as slow growth or high unemployment, they need to pay close attention to the behavior of firms, trade unions, consumers, and the like. This is as true for the ECB as for any other policymaking institution. Central banks do not make price inflation.[3] Prices are set by producers, suppliers, retailers, and consumers, just as wage decisions are made by employers, workers, and trade unions. Economists use strong assumptions about the behavior of these nonstate actors in setting up their models, talking about "perfect competition" when they think that market forces will work themselves out, or introducing specific patterns of strategic interaction when they fear markets might fail. However, politicians are less able than economists to take behavior—even bad behavior—for granted. If at all possible, they need to lock in good behavior from the start. At a minimum, politicians need to convince the people to keep them in office until the good effects of their policies can come about.

Hence, building popular support is at least as important for economic governance as sophisticated analysis, if not more so.

Popular support requires information. The people of Europe cannot be expected to take the "great promise" of the European economy on trust. They have to be persuaded to support European policies and then reassured that they have made the right choice. In this sense European economic governance is no different from economic governance elsewhere. By implication, European politicians have a double responsibility: they have to explain why things are happening and what is being done in response. This is not as easy as it sounds. In part the difficulty lies in the fact that sophistication and communication are at loggerheads. Just because there are good reasons to believe that a particular policy is "right" does not make that policy any easier to understand or appreciate. On the contrary, the more complicated the arguments in favor of the "right" policy, the more likely people are to opt for something that is simpler even if "wrong." This is what the British economist John Maynard Keynes meant when he talked about "practical men" being the "slaves of some defunct economist."[4] Economic analysis can help explain what is happening and why. Economists can also give some insight into what should be done and by whom. But there is more to the problem of European economic governance than that.

The purpose of this chapter is to explain how European economic governance is organized and why. In this way it is a useful complement to any reading on the problems facing the European economy. It is also a useful corrective for those who believe that solving economic problems through sophisticated technical analysis is what European integration is all about. The explanation builds on five contentions:

- First, the European economy exists on many levels at once. It is European, but it is also national, regional, and local.
- Second, the most prominent of these levels is the national level, and not the European, regional, or local ones. Moreover, this is true no matter whether we measure "prominence" in terms of economics or politics.
- Third, the national economies of Europe are very different, even distinctive. Although it is often useful to generalize about a European model or models, such models work best when they are sketched in broad terms and do not hold up well under closer scrutiny.
- Fourth, national differences in Europe are political as well as economic, and they are institutional as well as accidental.
- Fifth, the process of European integration has both challenged and reinforced national differences. There has been a progressive "Europeanization" of the different member states to be sure. But European integration has also contributed to the preservation of national distinctiveness.

This chapter has four sections. The first looks at the performance of the European economy as a way to explain why questions of governance are so important. The second develops the notion of multilevel economic governance. The third deals with the contentions about member-state predominance and national distinctiveness. The fourth focuses on the impact of European economic integration on the member states and considers what we should expect from a Europe that is organized in this way.

European Economic Performance

Governance issues only arise when people think that things are not going well, and economic governance is no exception. For many Europeans, the concern is that their economy is falling behind the global competition—particularly when compared with the United States but also when confronted with rising powers such as China, India, or Brazil. A good example of such concern can be found in a recent book by Italian economists Alberto Alesina and Francesco Giavazzi called *Europe's Future* in the U.S. edition or, more tellingly, *Goodbye Europa* when published in Italian. Alesina and Giavazzi argue that Europeans do not work enough, that their productivity is low, that they do not invest enough in research and development, that they have antiquated educational institutions, and that they are too dependent upon the welfare state. As a result, Europe's economy is growing much more slowly than that in the United States, Europeans are getting poorer relative to Americans, and the prospects for Europe's children are getting worse rather than better.[5]

If we look at the macroeconomic data, there is a lot for Europeans to worry about. Although the European Union and the United States are roughly the same size economically, GDP per capita is much higher in the United States than in Europe—even if we only focus on the fifteen west European countries that were member states before the enlargement to Central and Eastern Europe on May 1, 2004 (the EU15). Measured in dollars corrected for relative purchasing power, GDP per capita was just under $29,000 in the EU15 in 2004 while it was almost $40,000 in the United States. Moreover, the gap is getting wider and not narrower over time. Real GDP growth in the United States outpaced growth in the euro zone for nine of the ten years starting in 1995. As a result, the gap in GDP per capita between Europe and the United States has increased from just over $7,000 in 1995 to almost $11,000 in 2004.[6]

The comparison between Europe and the United States looks even worse when the focus is on unemployment and employment. The standardized unemployment rate in the EU15 was 7.9 percent of the active labor population in 2005, while it was only 5.1 percent of the active labor population in the United States. And while the unemployment rate was higher, the labor force participation rate was lower—only 71.3 percent of the working-age population in the EU15 compared to 75.4 percent in the United States. Put these numbers together and the result is a wide difference in employment-to-population ratios, with just over 65 percent of working-age people in Europe having a job compared to between 71 and 72 percent in the United States. Moreover the contrasts are even sharper when you look at the younger (fifteen–twenty-four) or older (fifty-five–sixty-four) segments of the population. In 2005, the employment-to-population ratio for youths in the EU15 was only 36.4 percent compared to 52.6 percent in the United States; the same statistic for older workers was 35 percent in the EU15 and 55 percent in the United States.[7]

The relatively low rate of employment in Europe augurs badly for the future. If young people do not start working until later in life, they lose the opportunity to acquire important skills and to build up capital (say, to buy a house). If older workers are forced out of employment, they have to make their pension savings last longer or suffer a dramatic fall in personal income. Finally, society as a whole suffers because labor is a resource that is simply too valuable to waste so extravagantly. And it will suffer even more as Europeans grow older and have fewer children. At the moment, women between the ages of fifteen and forty-nine have many fewer children in Europe than in the United States. Of the larger countries in Europe, France is at the high end of the range, with women having 1.9 children on average in 2003. Italy and Germany are on the other end of the scale, with either just under or just over 1.3 children on average. Meanwhile women of child-bearing age in the United States have just over 2 children.

Without children, Europe's population growth has slowed down and the cost of European welfare states has increased. The only way to square the circle is either to get Europeans to work more hours or to produce more per hour worked. Unfortunately neither seems to be happening. On the contrary, Europeans are working less and European productivity growth is slowing down. In 2004, for example, workers in the United States each put in about 1,824 hours of labor, while workers in Britain put in 1,669 hours, workers in France put in 1,520, and workers in Germany put in only 1,443. That year, labor productivity growth (measured in terms of output per hour) was 3.16 percent in the United States compared to only 1.49 percent across the EU15. It is small wonder, then, that economists such as Alesina and Giavazzi are worried.

But what is to be done? The easy implication is that Europe should accept that they need to be more like the United States. Nevertheless it would be wrong to jump to that conclusion for at least two reasons. First, the news from the United States is not all good. The obvious point is about income inequality. Simply, the distribution of income across society in the United States is more unequal than in any large European country apart from Poland—and the gap between the United States and similarly wealthy countries (such as Germany or France) is considerable. And if the United States appears inequitable, it also appears inefficient. The United States spends almost twice as much on healthcare per capita as any of the large European countries. Nevertheless, life expectancy in the United States is lower and infant mortality is higher. Europeans are expected to live between two and four years longer than Americans and U.S. infants die at between 1.5 and 2 times the rate of European infants.

The second reason for not asking Europe to become more like the United States is that the aggregate data for U.S. economic performance reveal important differences from one part of the country to the next. Hence while it is true that U.S. income has increased significantly over the past years, much of that increase can be localized to the states of New England. Income performance in the southeast of the United States—states such as Mississippi or Alabama—has been stagnant by comparison; income performance in the southwest has fallen sharply.[8] A similar point can be made about the number of hours Americans work from one sector of industry to the next. In manufacturing it is true that working hours have remained relatively constant on a weekly basis. But they have fallen sharply across U.S. workers viewed as a whole. According to the U.S. Bureau of Labor Statistics, the average working American put in just under thirty-four hours a week in 2005 compared to a thirty-nine-hour workweek in 1964.[9] These current figures do no look so different from what we see in Europe—particularly in the poorer countries around the Mediterranean. Indeed, recently revised data from the Organization for Economic Cooperation and Development show that the average working American put in just thirteen hours more than the average working Italian in 2005 and almost 250 hours less than the average working Greek.[10]

The reality is that the more we look into the data, the less clear any comparison between Europe and the United States actually becomes. The question of income equality is a good example. Although U.S. incomes are more inequitable across society as a whole, they are not more inequitable across regions—indeed, regional income inequality in Europe and the United States is much the same. Moreover, the share of population living in regions below the national average is much less in a broadly dispersed country such as the United States (at just 58 percent) than it is in countries with more easily identifiable population centers such as Great Britain (64 percent), Sweden (79 percent), or France (at 82 percent!).

Of course it is still relevant to ask how Europe can be made to perform better economically. But before doing so it is necessary to consider how European countries work together in the first place. The problem of economic governance is prior to the problem of economic performance. And the significance of any performance comparison with the United States is best considered last.

Multilevel Economic Governance

Economic governance within the European Union takes place at many levels: European, national, regional, and local. So, for example, monetary policy decisions are taken by the European Central Bank, fiscal policy is decided by the member states, employment policy may be a purview of regional governments (where these exist), and the actual measures used to connect workers to jobs, to regulate shop openings, and to zone commercial space are implemented at the local level. This "multilevel governance" is hardly a surprising state of affairs. Anyone who visits the United States encounters a similar situation. There you find a similarly broad array of federal, state, and local actors each with their own responsibilities, rules, and constituencies. Germany, Italy, and Belgium are much the same. Indeed, it would be exceptional to find a country that did not engage in economic governance on multiple levels at the same time.

What is unique about the European situation is that the national level is not the highest level of aggregation. Instead, the Europeans have created a set of institutions for economic governance that operate above the national level (called "supranational") to which they have increasingly subscribed at all levels. This point is both subtle and important. The European Union is more than just a separate layer of bureaucracy that the member states have added on top of their own political and economic institutions. The EU is also much less than (and should not be expected to become) some larger replacement for the bureaucracy that European countries have at the level of the national state. Rather the European Union has evolved as an intrinsic feature of the multilevel systems of governance that already existed within different European countries. In each of the member states, the EU is as much a force on its own as it is a factor at the national, regional, and local levels.[11]

This European state of affairs is interesting for two reasons. First, it is historically unprecedented. Although groups of countries have created international organizations in the past, contact with these organizations has been dominated by national governments. Individual U.S. states have little or no contact with the United Nations while, by contrast, most regions within EU member states have dealings with the EU (and many even maintain representatives in Brussels). While there may be some exceptions to this rule that national governments monopolize relations with international organizations, never has there been a group of countries that has willingly created a set of institutions as intrusive and omnipresent as those of the European Union.

The second reason that the European state of affairs is interesting is that the European Union constitutes an explicit attempt to strengthen the economic rationality underlying the political organization of European countries. The European economies were not doing as well as they might when the various steps in European integration were taken, and the proponents of European integration intended (among other goals, perhaps) to help them do better. Indeed, whether or not other issues came into play in motivating the proponents of Europe is less important than the simple observation that economic rationality played a prominent role.

To understand this point, it is first necessary to accept that most political organizations—nations, regions, even cities—are arbitrary from an economic perspective. They may compete in economic terms and the economically stronger units may win in many of these competitions, but that does not mean they were created for economic reasons. There is no real economic logic to France, for example. Instead, France exists and so the French must figure out how to make the most of what they inherited as an economy. The same is true of Germany, Italy, and the United Kingdom—not to mention the United States. It is even more true for smaller countries such as Norway, Sweden, Denmark, Belgium, or the Netherlands. None of these countries is "optimal" in terms of economic criteria we might draw up to benchmark market functioning, self-sufficiency, and geographic or demographic scale. Moreover, none of these countries is unique in being "suboptimal."

In contrast with the nation building that gave rise to its own member states, the European Union was created with explicit considerations of economic "optimality" in mind. Would the customs union at the heart of the European Economic Community give rise to more trade creation than trade diversion? Would the common market result in efficient movements of capital and labor? What are the costs of not completing the internal market, and what are the benefits of doing so? How can a European Monetary System be designed to broaden the zone of monetary stability in Europe? Does the European Union constitute an optimum currency area? What are the criteria that Great Britain should use in deciding whether or not to join the euro? It is not even necessary to understand these questions fully in order to accept that they played a much more important role in debates about the creation of "Europe" than they did in the national integration of France, Germany, Italy, or the United Kingdom. The EU has an essential economic rationality that the member states do not (and arguably do not need).

The economic rationality underlying European integration plays an important role in how the EU functions as a whole. The political (cultural, historical) rationality behind the member states influences how the EU functions as well. Hence, for example, the 1992 Maastricht Treaty introduced a doctrine of subsidiarity according to which the EU would act "in areas which do not fall within its exclusive competence . . . only if and in so far as the objectives of the proposed action cannot be sufficiently achieved by the Member States and can therefore, by reason of the scale or effects of the proposed action, be better achieved by the Community."[12] What the treaty does not make clear is who determines what is sufficient and what is better.

This is where the European experience of multilevel economic governance differs from the type of multilevel governance that you might run into in a single country or member state. EU institutions do not do things because they "can," they do them because they can win acceptance that they can do them better or that the other levels of governance cannot do them well enough. By the same token, when the EU does things poorly or politicians in the member states feel their actions are sufficient, then the EU institutions are unable to act (and their actions are unwanted).

WHAT IS CHOCOLATE? THE ISSUE
OF COMMON STANDARDS

Voluntary industrial standards provide a good example. These standards set out in precise detail what things are, how they look, what they are made of, and how they work. They can describe anything from the height of a table to the thickness of a pencil to the length of a piece of paper, and they define the difference between mineral water and tap water, orange juice and orange drink. These standards are industrial—particularly insofar as they describe how things are made. They are also voluntary. By and large, firms use internationally agreed voluntary industrial standards because it makes good economic sense to do so. Imagine trying to fill the photocopier if every paper company decided to cut paper to different dimensions.

The problem with voluntary industrial standards is getting everyone to agree on a specific common template. Those who get to set the standard have the advantage that all of their machines are calibrated in the right way. Meanwhile, those who have to take the standard as given must pay whatever it costs to adjust. This is true particularly when the "voluntary" standard is backed by law once it is established—like the juice-drink or mineral-tap distinctions suggested above. Worse, sometimes it is impossible to make the adjustment. When the European Union proposed in 1994 to define a "chocolate" bar as having at least 50 percent cacao, the British candymaker Cadbury risked having to re-brand some of its most popular confections as being something other than chocolate. In all likelihood, that would have led to the collapse in demand for these sweets. Because Cadbury is a major company in the United Kingdom, the British government complained and the EU agreed to call just about anything chocolate (provided it has at least 1 percent cacao).

This example is a good one because for much of its history the European Community and now the European Union was very bad at writing voluntary industrial standards. Although everyone in Europe could agree that having such standards is important and having only one European standard would be better still, no one was willing to pay the cost of adjusting to a European norm that they did not pick themselves. Nevertheless, the European Union has turned out to be very good at writing the broad frameworks within which different national industrial standards can compete. Continuing with the chocolate example, while the EU conceded that just about everything is chocolate it also asked that confectioners print the percentage of cacao on the packaging. This way consumers can decide what they prefer and all markets can be open to the different types of treats.

The example of voluntary industrial standards is also useful because it illustrates the broader problem of governance (compared to the narrow problem of government). Most industrial standards are too sophisticated for policymakers to write and so instead they rely on technical expertise provided by business and, in many cases, not-for-profit organizations concerned with environmental or consumer welfare. Moreover, since many industrial standards are purely voluntary, the groups that set them usually organize outside the formal institutions of the state—as quasi-public or even wholly private-sector standards-setting agencies. These groups do not need the European Union to provide expertise, institutional support, or even financial resources. However, they do need help in coordinating their actions from one country to the next—so that standards set in Germany do not conflict with those set in the United Kingdom in a way that serves no one's real interest and yet proves very costly in terms of trade. The potential costs of not having such coordination should be evident to anyone who has tried to plug in a British hair dryer while traveling in Germany (the plugs do not fit), who has brought any electrical appliances from the United States to Europe (the current is different), or who has driven their car from France to the UK (where they drive on the right side of the car as well as on the left side of the road).

Of course no one should expect the EU to fix these well-entrenched differences between national standards. As much as it may be worth to get everyone in Europe to agree on the same way of doing things, the costs of getting there from here are prohibitive. Still, the EU can have a positive effect where the costs of transition are much lower, where the problems of compatibility can be resolved at the margins through market competition (rather than starting over from scratch), and where national differences have not yet become too entrenched (and therefore too costly to change).

The potential for European influence in standard setting is limited and yet still very important. Indeed, the idea that the European Union sets the broad guidelines for acceptable competition between different national and firm-specific standards was the genius behind the completion of the single European market in the 1980s and early 1990s that most observers regard as the "relaunching" of European integration. National governments could not eliminate the effect of differing voluntary industrial standards as nontariff barriers to trade on their own. They needed the European Community to help.

MOTIVES AND MONEY: THE EUROPEAN MONETARY SYSTEM AND THE EURO

A similar story could be told about the creation of the euro as the single European currency. The two goals that national policymakers wanted to achieve were low inflation and stable exchange rates. The European Monetary System (EMS) provided a convenient intergovernmental solution—which is to say, one where only national governments needed to be involved. Originally, it should be noted, the EMS was created outside of the formal institutions of the European Economic Community, and the exchange rate mechanism (ERM) at the heart of the EMS focused on bilateral currency relations between participating countries rather than on relations between individual countries and some European whole. Over time, however, it became clear that the EMS was insufficient. Although the ERM did help to underwrite price stability across participating countries, it could not guarantee that exchange rates would remain stable across diverging national economic conditions, in response to widespread currency speculation, and when confronted with unexpected shocks.

The EMS faced all three of these challenges in the early 1990s and effectively broke down as a result. Market speculators noted a growing divergence between economic performance in the United Kingdom (then a member of the ERM) and the rest of Europe and so began speculating that the British government would have to devalue the pound sterling. This speculation coincided with the economic aftershocks of German unification: the German government increased spending to cover the cost of adding five new *Länder* (regions) with a combined population of around 16 million citizens. In turn, the German central bank (the Bundesbank) raised interest rates to ward off the price inflation that this new spending threatened to bring with it. The other EMS countries had to follow the tightening of German monetary policy in order to stay in the ERM. Yet for many of these countries—and Britain in particular—higher interest rates made no sense. In 1992, British policymakers were much more worried about unemployment than inflation, and higher interest rates would make unemployment worse and not better. Market speculators seized on this crucial difference and increased their pressure on the British pound. In the end, the British government buckled and withdrew the pound from the ERM.

The EMS survived the exchange rate crisis of 1992 but its reputation as a means for providing Europe's twin goals of low inflation and stable exchange rates did not. Subsequent currency crises in 1993 and 1995 made it clear that the EMS was at best a transitional arrangement, coaxing and coaching the member states from a system of separate bilateral exchange rates to a fully fledged Economic and Monetary Union (EMU). The question in the mid-1990s was whether EMU would come about or whether governments would look to some other solution altogether. That the EMS was no longer functioning was hardly in doubt.

In the end, most EU member states opted to secure low inflation and stable exchange rates through EMU. The difference between EMU and the EMS is the difference between multilevel governance and an intergovernmental agreement. The EMS was an agreement between countries that survived only so long as governments chose to put participation in the ERM above other economic objectives. Europe's EMU is different because it includes action at all different levels—European, national, regional, and local. At the European level, EMU provides for low inflation through a common monetary policy implemented by a European Central Bank, which is itself mandated to focus on achieving the goal of price stability (as mentioned above). Meanwhile, EMU addresses the problem of exchange rate stability first by locking in an agreement to fix bilateral exchange rates "irrevocably" between participating countries, and then by replacing national currencies with a European one. This European action can go a long way toward achieving the twin goals of low inflation and price stability. Nevertheless, EMU is one area where Europe cannot succeed by itself.

The national role within EMU is a supporting one. All EU member states (including those outside EMU) are obliged to conduct their economic policies in the common interest and to ensure that their actions do not disrupt the smooth functioning of the monetary union or impede the achievement of price stability within those countries that have adopted the single currency—referred to collectively as the euro zone. This obligation plays out in three different ways. First and most obviously, the obligation to act in the common interest can be seen in the "stability and growth pact," through which all EU member states have agreed to set their medium-term government financial accounts to be close to balance or in surplus. The obligation to set economic policy in the common interest also operates through the "excessive deficits procedure," wherein most member states (apart from the United Kingdom) have committed to avoid running fiscal deficits that are greater than 3 percent of gross domestic product (GDP) or public debts that are greater than 60 percent of GDP. The third manifestation of the commitment to act in the common interest can be found in the "broad economic policy guidelines" that are set by the member states at the European Union level to provide both general and country-specific guidance as to how economic policies should be designed and implemented. Of course such commitments have not always been honored (about which more later). The point remains, however, that they are an important part of the function of Europe's EMU.

Even with a strong ECB and committed national governments (or binding fiscal rules) it is still possible that EMU will not achieve its dual objectives of low inflation and stable exchange rates. Economists have warned all along that action also needs to be taken at the regional and local levels—by trade unions, employers, and government officials charged with aiding and retraining the unemployed. In the early discussions of EMU, policymakers accepted a convenient assumption from the economics literature: that local actors could be assumed to behave much like a perfectly flexible marketplace. This "competitive local factor markets" assumption made it easy to ignore the need for action below the level of the national state.[13]

Politicians could not maintain such an unrealistic assumption forever. As it turned out, they soon abandoned the assumption of competitive local factor markets and began to take action to bring such competitive markets into being. Shortly before EMU started in 1999, the member-state governments introduced a series of complementary reform processes:

- In 1997, they called for national governments to encourage the adoption of more-active labor market policies at the national, regional, and local levels;

- In 1998, they pushed for more aggressive liberalization of both product markets (the markets for goods and services) and factor markets (the markets for labor and capital); and
- In 1999, they called for a macroeconomic dialogue between policymakers, trade unions, and employers—both to ensure that the interests of wage negotiators were represented in macroeconomic policy decisionmaking and, more important, to underscore the role of wage bargaining in facilitating stable prices while also making it possible for different regions to adjust without the benefit of flexible exchange rates.

These efforts to encourage action at all levels culminated in the so-called Lisbon strategy, announced in March 2000. It was clear from the start that the Lisbon strategy would subsume and add onto the various efforts to tackle unemployment, market inefficiency, and broader social coordination that had come before it. However, rather than simply offering a modest improvement in European economic performance, the explicit objective of that strategy was to transform Europe into the world's most competitive and dynamic knowledge-based economy (see box, "Presidency Conclusions"). The inflated rhetoric of this objective drew immediate attention (and belated ridicule, once it became clear that the goal of building a world-beating economy would not be met). What was less evident, was that the success of the Lisbon strategy was instrumental to the success of the single currency itself. Even before the euro notes and coins were introduced in January 2002, the ECB president began cajoling the member states about the need to tackle unemployment, to make markets more flexible, and to convince wage negotiators of their responsibility for the economy as a whole.[14] Such comments became a consistent refrain at the ECB that assumed only more stridence over time. While most outside observers emphasized the supranational character of the ECB, the ECB itself retreated into the logic of multilevel governance.

This retreat of the ECB reflects the high degree of interdependence across the European economy. With the creation of Europe's single currency—indeed, with the creation of the EU itself—Europe developed a multilevel economy as well as a multilevel system of governance. Within that economy different levels and different statistical aggregates became important for different reasons. Policymakers have to focus on monetary data at the European level, fiscal data at the national level, unemployment data in regions, and so on. In a similar way, European firms have learned to develop different strategies for European competition and at the domestic or local levels. Trade unions have adapted to suit as well—with local or firm unions participating in sectoral or national federations that in turn join into transnational or even larger European arrangements. Within this melee, the challenge has been to figure out which level is the most important for any given problem and how the different levels of the European economy interact. European economic governance has become more sophisticated and the problems it faces have become more complicated.

Box 8.1   Presidency Conclusions

Lisbon European Council
March 23–24, 2000

The European Council held a special meeting on March 23–24, 2000, in Lisbon to agree on a new strategic goal for the Union in order to strengthen employment, economic reform and social cohesion as part of a knowledge-based economy. . . .

The new challenge

1. The European Union is confronted with a quantum shift resulting from globalization and the challenges of a new knowledge-driven economy. These changes are affecting every aspect of people's lives and require a radical transformation of the European economy. The Union must shape these changes in a manner consistent with its values and concepts of society and also with a view to the forthcoming enlargement.

2. The rapid and accelerating pace of change means it is urgent for the Union to act now to harness the full benefits of the opportunities presented. Hence the need for the Union to set a clear strategic goal and agree on a challenging program for building knowledge infrastructures, enhancing innovation and economic reform, and modernizing social welfare and education systems.

The Union's strengths and weaknesses

3. The Union is experiencing its best macro-economic outlook for a generation. As a result of stability-oriented monetary policy supported by sound fiscal policies in a context of wage moderation, inflation and interest rates are low, public sector deficits have been reduced remarkably and the EU's balance of payments is healthy. The euro has been successfully introduced and is delivering the expected benefits for the European economy. The internal market is largely complete and is yielding tangible benefits for consumers and businesses alike. The forthcoming enlargement will create new opportunities for growth and employment. The Union possesses a generally well-educated workforce as well as social protection systems able to provide, beyond their intrinsic value, the stable framework required for managing the structural changes involved in moving towards a knowledge-based society. Growth and job creation have resumed.

4. These strengths should not distract our attention from a number of weaknesses. More than 15 million Europeans are still out of work. The employment rate is too low and is characterized by insufficient participation in the labor market by women and older workers. Long-term structural unemployment and marked regional unemployment imbalances remain endemic in parts of the Union. The services sector is underdeveloped, particularly in the areas of telecommunications and the Internet. There is a widening skills gap, especially in information technology where increasing numbers of jobs remain unfilled. With the current improved economic situation, the time is right to undertake both economic and social reforms as part of a positive strategy which combines competitiveness and social cohesion.

The way forward

5. The Union has today set itself a new strategic goal for the next decade: to become the most competitive and dynamic knowledge-based economy in the world, capable of sustainable economic growth with more and better jobs and greater social cohesion. Achieving this goal requires an overall strategy aimed at:

— preparing the transition to a knowledge-based economy and society by better policies for the information society and R&D, as well as by stepping up the process of structural reform for competitiveness and innovation and by completing the internal market;
— modernizing the European social model, investing in people and combating social exclusion;
— sustaining the healthy economic outlook and favorable growth prospects by applying an appropriate macro-economic policy mix.

6. This strategy is designed to enable the Union to regain the conditions for full employment, and to strengthen regional cohesion in the European Union. The European Council needs to set a goal for full employment in Europe in an emerging new society which is more adapted to the personal choices of women and men. If the measures set out below are implemented against a sound macro-economic background, an average economic growth rate of around 3% should be a realistic prospect for the coming years.

7. Implementing this strategy will be achieved by improving the existing processes, introducing a new open method of coordination at all levels, coupled with a stronger guiding and coordinating role for the European Council to ensure more coherent strategic direction and effective monitoring of progress. A meeting of the European Council to be held every Spring will define the relevant mandates and ensure that they are followed up.

(*Source:* The full text of these Presidency Conclusions can be downloaded from: *http://www .consilium.europa.eu/ueDocs/cms_Data/docs/pressData/en/ec/00100-r1.en0.htm*)

Member States Matter

Within the complicated multilevel system of European economic governance, most of the most capable institutions are at the national level. In general, national institutions have more personnel, greater expertise, longer experience, and more financial resources (deeper pockets) than their European or EU counterparts. As a consequence, the European Union relies on national institutions even in those areas where its authority is clearly established. Indeed, EU reliance on national institutions takes place both where national-level institutions have a long history of policy competence, as with national central banks, and where they do not, as with national competition authorities.

CENTRAL BANKING AND THE UNIQUENESS OF THE ECB

The case of monetary policy is interesting because of the ECB's widespread reputation for being a uniquely powerful supranational institution. In many ways it is both uniquely powerful and uniquely supranational. No international organization has ever assumed such direct control over a traditional national competence as the ECB has over monetary policy within the euro zone. The International Monetary Fund (IMF) is intrusive in those countries that require its assistance, but IMF conditionality pales into insignificance when compared with the direct impact of the ECB's common monetary policy. By the same token, few if any monetary unions have ever succeeded in creating a truly supranational central bank.[15] Instead they have tended to rely on the bank of the strongest participant to set monetary policy for the union as whole. For example, the monetary union that existed for more than seventy years between Belgium and Luxembourg maintained separate national monetary authorities (albeit the Belgian National Bank was the more powerful of the two). Even the monetary union between England, Scotland, and Northern Ireland is built on national banks, led by the Bank of England.

The European Central Bank is uniquely powerful and uniquely supranational. As central banks go, however, it is also very decentralized. Monetary policy decisions are not made by the ECB acting alone, but by the Governing Council of the European System of Central Banks (ESCB) (see box, "Membership and Monetary Policymaking"). The ESCB includes the ECB and the national central banks of all EU member states. Only those countries that participate in the single currency are allowed to vote on the Governing Council—meaning that with twelve countries participating in the euro zone, there are twelve representatives of national central banks who vote on the monetary policies decisions of the euro zone. By implication, there are two national central bank representatives for each of the six representatives from the ECB. Moreover, this preponderance of national votes will only increase with successive enlargements of the euro zone—Slovenia is set to join in 2007. Once the total membership of the Governing Council reaches twenty-one (with fifteen national representatives and six from the ECB), the ESCB will have to break with the principle of one country, one vote. Nevertheless, that change will hardly alter the relative balance of power between national and European representatives to the Governing Council and so monetary policy decisionmaking should be expected to reflect the decentralized character of the ESCB well into the future.

The alleged "decentralization" of decisionmaking in the Governing Council is hotly refuted by the ECB—which maintains that all decisions are made by consensus in the interests of the euro zone as a whole. Even so, there is some statistical evidence to suggest that monetary policy decisions are best explained by looking at national and not European-level performance. The national central

Box 8.2   Membership and Monetary Policymaking in the Euro Zone

As of January 1, 2007, there are thirteen countries that have chosen to adopt the euro: Austria, Belgium, Finland, France, Germany, Greece, Ireland, Italy, Luxembourg, Netherlands, Portugal, Slovenia, Spain. There are fourteen other EU member states that have not. Of these, three have shown great reluctance to participate in the single currency: Britain, Denmark, and Sweden. The remaining eleven are preparing to join: Bulgaria, Cyprus, Czech Republic, Estonia, Hungary, Latvia, Lithuania, Malta, Poland, Romania, and Slovakia. These countries must meet the five convergence criteria set out in the 1992 Maastricht Treaty in order to join. Specifically, they must:

- Have passed legislation to ensure the political independence of their national central banks;
- Participate in the exchange rate mechanism of the European Monetary System without realignment or unusual volatility for a period of two years;
- Ensure that their fiscal deficits are below (or declining toward) 3 percent of gross domestic product and that their public debts are below (or declining toward) 60 percent of gross domestic product;
- Have an inflation rate that is within 1.5 percentage points of the three best performers in terms of price inflation; and,
- Have long-term interest rates that are within 2 percentage points of the three best performers in terms of price inflation.

In practice, the inflation target is the most difficult to achieve for most of the countries in Central and Eastern Europe. As formerly communist countries, they are experiencing very high rates of economic growth while they catch up to West European standards of living. In turn, this growth is pushing up rates of inflation. You might argue that these relatively high inflation rates are the price for such high growth. But the implication is that these countries will not be able to join without slowing down their economies—in which case it is worth wondering whether the costs of participating in the single currency do not outweigh the benefits.

The economics of joining the euro are complicated but the politics are not. All EU member states participate in the European System of Central Banks, but only those countries that join the single currency can send their central bank representative to the Governing Council of the ESCB. Since the Governing Council of the ESCB is responsible for making decisions about monetary policy for the euro zone, having a representative on the Governing Council is an important symbol of being at the heart of European decisionmaking.

bank governors have also shown a bad tendency to speak their minds in public about where monetary policy should be going—and to send mixed and confusing signals to financial markets by doing so.

Nevertheless, it may be true that the Governing Council is more supranational than its institutional makeup would suggest. What the ECB does not deny, is that any supranational character in its decisionmaking is very fragile—that is why it does not publish how different representatives voted on the Governing Council, why ECB presidents usually hold off decisionmaking until the Governing Council can act out of consensus and without a formal vote, and why the ECB had such difficulty preparing the decisionmaking procedures of the Governing Council for enlargement. As the ECB itself has acknowledged, if the votes were published then national representatives could be held to account for their separate national interests. Hence, by making decisions without voting formally, the ECB president hopes to lower the pressure for published voting records. He has been only partly successful. Voices in the European Parliament regularly call for greater transparency in the ESCB Governing Council procedures—specifically, published voting records. Meanwhile, it is clear that the member states regard their own central bank governors as "national" representatives to the ESCB. Indeed, the very tenacity of the more powerful member states in their insistence on maintaining voting positions in the Governing Council is what led to the complicated proposals that the ESCB ultimately adopted to reform its institutions in anticipation of further enlargement of the euro zone (see box, "European Central Bank").

Decisionmaking is not the only area where the member states play a prominent role in the common monetary policy. Three other areas stand out as well: research, implementation, and supervision. In terms of research, the ECB has invested a great deal in developing a reputation for its Europe-wide analysis. Nevertheless, the national central banks collectively have many more researchers (and research resources) at their disposal, they have much better access to national-level data, and they have long-established procedures for providing monetary policy advice. So while it is true that the ECB has made substantial progress in developing its own reputation for research, it is also true that the common monetary policy draws upon a much deeper pool of research resources via the member-state central banks than the ECB alone can provide.

Implementation is another area where the ECB draws upon national-level resources. When monetary policy decisions are announced at the ECB in Frankfurt, that is only the first step in changing monetary conditions in the European economy. The next step is for monetary authorities to intervene in the markets—either buying or selling public securities to lower or raise the amount of currency in circulation. These "open-market operations" are undertaken by the national central banks and not by the ECB itself, because the national central banks have better access to the markets, because they can trade in a wider array of national public securities with near-equal liquidity, and because they have both the per-

Box 8.3   European Central Bank

Recommendation, under Article 10.6 of the Statute
of the European System of Central Banks
and of the European Central Bank, for a Council Decision
on an amendment to Article 10.2 of the
Statute of the European System of Central Banks
and of the European Central Bank
(ECB/2003/1)
(2003/C 29/07)
(Submitted by the European Central Bank on 3 February 2003)

To maintain the Governing Council's capacity for efficient and timely decision making in an enlarged euro area, the number of governors having voting rights has to be smaller than the overall number of governors in the Governing Council. A rotation system is an equitable, efficient and acceptable way of assigning voting rights among the governors. The six members of the Executive Board maintain permanent voting rights. Any change to this would be difficult to reconcile with their special status as laid down in the EC Treaty and the Statute. They are the only members of the Governing Council who are appointed at the European level by a Treaty procedure and who operate solely in the euro area context and for the ECB, the competence of which spans the whole euro area. Finally, it has to be taken into account that the President, a member of the Executive Board, also has the casting vote in the event of a tie in the Governing Council.

The design of the rotation system should be guided by five fundamental principles, i.e. "one member one vote;" "ad personam participation;" "representativeness;" "automaticity/ robustness" and "transparency."

First, the "one member one vote" principle, which is the core principle of the ECB/Eurosystem's decision making, has to be retained for members having a voting right. However, a rotation system necessarily implies that there will no longer be permanent voting rights for all the members of the Governing Council as the number of governors increases.

Second, all members of the Governing Council will continue to participate in its meetings, irrespective of whether they have the voting right or not, in a personal and independent capacity. EN C 29/6 Official Journal of the European Union 7.2.2003

Third, since the introduction of a rotation system could theoretically lead to situations in which the members of the Governing Council having voting rights were from Member States which, taken together, might be perceived as not being sufficiently representative of the euro area economy as a whole, it should be designed in a manner which excludes such outcomes. In order to achieve representativeness, the rotation system has to differentiate between governors with respect to the frequency with which they have voting rights, with governors from larger Member States enjoying more frequent periods with voting rights than those from smaller Member States. Although the introduction of considerations of representativeness marks a departure from the existing provisions for voting in the Governing Council, this is exclusively motivated by the need to accommodate the impact of enlargement on the Governing Council's decision-making. This ex ante differentiation between governors should apply exclusively to the prior determination of the frequency with

(continued)

Box 8.3   (Continued)

which each governor has the voting right. For all governors having voting rights at any point in time, the "one member one vote" principle would continue to apply. Consequently, this differentiation should not impact on actual substantive decision-making, but is only relevant in the process of determining who votes when.

Fourth, the rotation system has to be devised in a manner whereby the system itself, any rule on the allocation of governors to different groups, and any rule on the assignment of voting rights to such groups, allow the system to adjust automatically to the process of euro area enlargement. In addition, it has to be capable of accommodating up to 27 Member States, i.e. the current EU Member States and the 12 accession countries listed in the Declaration on the enlargement of the European Union which is annexed to the Treaty of Nice. This "robustness" principle implies, in particular, the avoidance of situations in which, as a result of the workings of the rotation system, the members of a group of smaller Member States enjoy higher voting frequencies than the members of a group of relatively larger Member States.

Fifth, the design of the rotation system has to be transparent. Consequently, the language of the revised Article 10.2 of the Statute has to be reasonably accessible and meet the requirements of primary Community law.

[. . . the actual proposal is . . .]
"Each member of the Governing Council shall have one vote. As from the date on which the number of members of the Governing Council exceeds 21, each member of the Executive Board shall have one vote and the number of governors with a voting right shall be 15. The latter voting rights shall be assigned and shall rotate as follows:

- *as from the date on which the number of governors exceeds 15, until it reaches 22, the governors shall be allocated to two groups, according to a ranking of the size of the share of their national central bank's Member State in the aggregate gross domestic product at market prices and in the total aggregated balance sheet of the monetary financial institutions of the Member States without a derogation. The shares in the aggregate gross domestic product at market prices and in the total aggregated balance sheet of the monetary financial institutions shall be assigned weights of 5/6 and 1/6, respectively. The first group shall be composed of five governors and the second group of the remaining governors. The frequency of voting rights of the governors allocated to the first group shall not be lower than the frequency of voting rights of those of the second group. Subject to the previous sentence, the first group shall be assigned four voting rights and the second group 11 voting rights;
- *as from the date on which the number of governors reaches 22, the governors shall be allocated to three groups according to a ranking based on the above criteria. The first group shall be composed of five governors and shall be assigned four voting rights. The second group shall be composed of half of the total number of governors, with any fraction rounded up to the nearest integer, and shall be assigned eight voting rights. The third group shall be composed of the remaining governors and shall be assigned three voting rights."

sonnel and the expertise to make sure that open-market operations have the desired effect in terms of raising or lowering euro-zone interest rates.

A final area is financial supervision or what economists refer to as "prudential oversight." This supervision is necessary to ensure that the banking system remains stable, that banks do not assume excessive risks, and that bank depositors are protected from potential losses due to bad management. The ECB has the legal competence to assume responsibility for conducting prudential oversight across the EU banking system as a whole, but so far has chosen not to do so. Instead, the ECB maintains that prudential oversight is best conducted by national regulators and not European ones. This view stands to reason. Just because the ECB can do something does not mean that it should. And given the larger personnel and deeper knowledge of domestic banking institutions held by national regulators, it is better to leave the job to them. Of course better is not always best. In the summer of 2005, the Italian central bank governor, Antonio Fazio, used his authority for prudential oversight to block the takeover of an Italian bank, Antonveneto, by a Dutch one, ABN-Amro. During the course of the summer, the Italian press released mobile-telephone intercepts between Fazio and another Italian banker who also sought to gain control over Antonveneto. From the intercepts, it appeared that Fazio favored the Italian bid for reasons that had little to do with the stability of the Italian banking system. Even so, the ECB was reluctant to interfere. In successive press conferences, journalists pressed the ECB president about whether he would sanction Fazio for actions unbecoming a member of the Governing Council (where Fazio represented Italy). Here too the ECB president deferred to national authorities. The crisis only ended when the Italian government forced Fazio to stand down and the acquisition of Antonveneto by ABN-Amro was allowed to go through.

The Fazio case illustrates the drawbacks of relying on national-level institutions, particularly where such institutions are deeply embedded in national political, economic, and social life. Before and during Fazio's tenure as governor of the Bank of Italy, the Italian central bank was one of the most highly trusted and respected institutions in Italy. Indeed, during the country's political revolution of 1992–1993, the bank was a unique source of stability for Italians. Fazio appears not only to have abused the popular trust, but also to have underestimated the extent to which his seemingly arbitrary and autocratic behavior had compromised the Bank of Italy and jeopardized relations within the wider ESCB. Now the Bank of Italy has to work hard to rebuild its reputation and to restore its good relations with Europe.

COMPETITION AND FAIR TRADE

The case of competition policy is very different. When the process of European integration started, few of the participating countries had separate institutions to regulate and protect market competition. Arguably, only one country, West Germany, had institutions that worked well. Therefore, it would be a mistake to argue that the European Union should rely on national competition authorities to support European competition policy because national authorities have more expertise and experience than European institutions do. In fact the reverse is more likely to be the case. Nevertheless, the European Union has devolved much of the responsibility for competition policy onto national authorities—many of which were expressly created for this job. In doing so, the EU has accepted that these national authorities will apply the rules differently from one country to the next. The role of the EU in this new system is to target those cases that require European-level attention and to police the system as a whole to make sure that the differences between national competition authorities do not grow too large.[16]

To understand why the European Union would make this kind of delegation, it is first necessary to consider what competition policy is all about. The basic idea is to create and enforce rules to prevent powerful firms or other actors (usually governments) from using their economic resources to distort competition in the marketplace.[17] Firms can do this by colluding with their competitors to set prices or divide markets (horizontal collusion); by colluding with their suppliers, distributors, and customers to freeze out the competition (vertical collusion); by fusing together to create a predominant market position (mergers); or by extracting subsidies or other favors from national, regional, or local governments (state aids)—usually in exchange for commitments about where they will make investments or create jobs. Such actions reduce the competitiveness of the marketplace and, as a result, they tend to raise prices, restrict choices, lower innovation, and remove many of the advantages that made European economic integration worthwhile in the first place.

Unfortunately, while the goal of European integration is to increase market competition, the effect is often the opposite. By lowering barriers to trade between national markets, European integration creates new opportunities for collusion between firms in different countries (to carve up the new larger market) and new incentives for collusion between firms in particular countries (to freeze out new competitors coming from abroad). By lowering the barriers to cross-border investment, European integration makes it possible that national firms will fall under foreign control or move their production to other countries. These things are not bad in the abstract, but they are frightening to politicians who have to explain why foreigners are "buying up the national patrimony" and why firms are "sending jobs abroad." Hence European integration increases the incentive for governments to give state aids to domestic firms—and it strengthens the arguments that domestic firms can make when demanding state aids from governments. Finally, European integration makes it possible for cross-border mergers to give rise to firms that could dominate in any given national market. Not only would such European powerhouses have the potential to act as monopolies within specific member states, but they could threaten the survival of one-time "national champions" as well.

The European Union has a clear interest in protecting European market competition and a clear competence to do so. The powers of the European Commission to deal with horizontal and vertical collusion date back to the start of the European Economic Community in the late 1950s. The power to regulate mergers and to prohibit state aids came during the completion of the internal market in the late 1980s. And, over the years, the Commission has developed considerable expertise in evaluating and assessing the economic consequences of potentially anticompetitive behavior. Here it should be admitted that while it is easy to outline what competition policy should do in theory, it is very difficult to describe what constitutes anticompetitive behavior in practice. When does collusive behavior between firms distort markets and when does it make them more efficient—as with the adoption of voluntary industrial standards above? When do mergers create market-predominant firms and when do they just give rise to greater economies of scale? When are state aids unfair subsidies and when are they rational state investments? There are no easy answers to these questions. Instead there are only case-specific ones. As the European Commission developed its own expertise, it also developed a reputation for good judgment. Both—expertise and judgment—are essential for the success of European competition policy. So why would the European Union choose to delegate this clear competence of the European Commission back to the member states?

Three reasons stand out. First, the volume of economic activity became too large for the European Commission to hope to keep up with vis-à-vis its responsibility for regulating competition in the European marketplace. The success of European integration can be seen in the torrent of cross-border relationships, mergers, and investments—not just among Europe's giant multinational corporations, but among the medium-sized and smaller companies as well. If the European Commission tried to approve each and every transaction (and for a while, it did), then its own approval process could become a drag on the efficiency of the European marketplace. Monopoly or collusive practices are not the only threat to market competition. Inefficient regulation and bureaucratic "red tape" are problems as well. European competition authorities recognized that they risked losing both the ability to do their job well and their hard-won reputation for judgment and expertise, and so looked to national competition authorities to reduce their work load.

The second reason is that national governments recognized the importance of protecting market competition in this new, integrated Europe and so invested increasing public resources in building national authorities to do so. Although there is repeated press speculation about national efforts to use industrial policy (state aids) to create and sustain national champions, the heyday of state-directed industrial development (called *dirigisme*) ended in the 1970s and early 1980s. By that time, even those countries such as France, which had a solid reputation for using state money to build industrial powerhouses, discovered that the pace of technological innovation and economic change was simply too great for the state to play a successful guiding role. Instead, firms would have to pick their own investments and they would have to work hard to make sure that these investments paid off. The state could help by supporting precompetitive research and by policing anticompetitive practices, but it could no longer lead the economy as a whole. Of course this is not to say that national governments no longer give subsidies or provide other protection to politically important firms. Obviously, they do. In 2005 and 2006, there were a number of state interventions to protect national industries from competitive threats, both real and imaginary. Italy's Antonio Fazio was hardly unique in playing that role (although his motives may have been more troubling). The French government made similar efforts to block foreign takeovers of Arcelor (a steel company), Danone (a yogurt maker), and Suez (an energy conglomerate). The point is that such state aids and other forms of political interference now work at the margins of the economy rather than providing its central impetus. Meanwhile, the development of competent national competition authorities has assumed ever greater importance.

The third reason for European competition authorities to delegate responsibility back to the national level is that context matters in the complex economic arguments about whether collusive behavior, mergers and acquisitions, or state aids can have market-distorting (read anticompetitive) effects. When competition authorities want to understand the impact of a particular firm, action, or policy, they have to look at the structure of the local market, to unpack any other complex cross-share holdings or working relationships, they have to analyze distribution patterns and consumer choices, and then they have to make a judgment about whether anticompetitive behavior can or could exist. These judgments have real financial consequences for investors, workers, and consumers. Therefore it is important not only that the judgments be right, but also that they are accepted as "just" given the circumstances. National competition authorities have an advantage over the European Commission in this regard because their actions are more focused on one marketplace and because they work closely and consistently with the same market actors.

The delegation of competition policy from the European Commission to national competition authorities brings a number of clear advantages. The most important among these is that the European Commission can focus its energies where they can make a difference. The current complaint against U.S. software giant Microsoft is a case in point. European competition authorities maintain that Microsoft is distorting market competition by withholding interface protocols necessary for Microsoft applications to work with other server software and by bundling its software so that an operating system includes a web browser, media player, and so on. Microsoft counters that interface protocols are proprietary software and that media components are integrated features of the operating system itself. The arguments on both sides are very complicated and very technical. Microsoft has huge expertise and financial resources, and it is determined to win—not the first battle, perhaps, but certainly the last. For European regulators to succeed in their position, they have to bring huge resources of their own to bear. This would not be possible if all European Commission personnel responsible for competition policy were tied down vetting routine mergers and acquisitions among medium-sized or larger enterprises in each of the twenty-five member states. Having shed much of this day-to-day responsibility, the Commission is better able to focus on dealing with Microsoft as a European-level concern.

THE NATIONAL DEFAULT

Monetary policy and competition policy are two of the hard cases for European delegation to national institutions because European competence in these matters is so clearly established. Nevertheless, such delegation takes place as if by default: national institutions do things that European institutions cannot and they liberate European institutions to focus attention on matters of European concern. This default functions much like the principle of subsidiarity, where the European Union is enjoined to take action only where it can perform better than the member states or where member-state action is insufficient. However, the European default to national institutions is more practical than theoretical. The European Union delegates to national institutions not out of specific ideological concern, but because such delegation makes sense in the complicated multilevel economic governance of Europe.

This default to national institutions is not without problems, however. First, it raises the specter that national institutions will work in the national interest and not the wider European one. The Fazio case is not a good example of this problem because it centers more on political or perhaps personal self-interest. The French government's defense of the Suez energy group is a better example. When the Italian energy group Enel threatened to buy out Suez, the French government responded by engineering a merger between Suez and the publicly controlled French utility Gaz de France. This merger not only promised to keep Suez in French hands but also to help the French government reduce its stake in Gaz de France. From a European perspective, the outcome is less than wholesome for at least three reasons. First, French government actions smack of a sort of economic nationalism that is at odds with European market liberalization (particularly if you are Italian). Second, French policy reinforces the national character of European energy markets at a time when the liberalization of so-called "network industries" (electricity, gas, telephone) is a priority. Third, the combination of Suez and Gaz de France has implications for market competition both within France and elsewhere—particularly Belgium, where much of the gas distribution network is controlled by companies that are at least partly owned or operated by either Suez or Gas de France. Hence in June 2006, the European Commission announced that it would have to investigate the merger to determine whether anticompetitive practices could be the result.

The second problem with the default to national institutions is that they may not work well either individually or taken as a group. This problem is not so great in the context of either central banks or competition authorities. Central banks tend to work well together because most central bankers use the same economic models and share a common economic philosophy or world view. Central banks also have precisely defined roles that translate consistently from one country to the next. The same is true for national competition authorities in Europe, although the reason for similarity across competition authorities has less to do with the generic nature of competition policy than with their historical development during the process of European integration. There was a time when those competition authorities that existed saw themselves playing very different roles even in close neighboring countries—so, for example, the German authorities fought to break up cartels while the Dutch did not. Within the context of a European competition policy, however, national understandings of what can and should be done have become more alike. Hence, national competition authorities work well together in Europe because they were designed to do so.

The problem of poorly functioning or incompatible national institutions is more generic than policy-specific. It crops up at the interface between national markets and in comparisons across national performance. Here it is useful to return to the Lisbon strategy and to the notion of perfectly competitive local-factor markets that was introduced in the context of the single currency (above). In the late 1990s, national politicians in Europe worried that their economies were not doing well individually and that these individual failings were bringing down the process of European integration as a whole. The efforts to promote employment, liberalize product and factor markets, and engage in a broader macroeconomic dialogue with employers and workers were only part of the solution. And it was recognized that a more comprehensive approach was required. Hence the March 2000 Lisbon strategy did more than just harness past efforts to a new and ambitious strategic objective. It also introduced a new "open method of coordination" to help the member states work more effectively together.

The open method (as it is called) is a new pattern for European integration. Rather than focusing on the establishment of common rules or principles that all member states can accept or abide by (the "community method"), the open method focuses on helping national governments tailor national policies to national needs. There are common benchmarks and targets built into the process, to be sure. Nevertheless, the emphasis is on helping member states manage their differences rather than on forcing them to be more the same.

Neither the Lisbon strategy nor the open method proved to be much of a success. The recession that set in from 2001 to 2003 slowed national reform efforts even as it raised unemployment. The modest growth that followed in 2004–2006 offered little respite. Meanwhile, the inflated rhetoric about building a world-beating knowledge-based economy by 2010 only made matters worse. When the European Commission began preparing its mid-term review of the Lisbon strategy in 2004, many were quick to say the whole enterprise was a failure. The March 2004 European Council called for the creation of a high-level working group to be chaired by former Dutch prime minister Wim Kok in order to map out how the Lisbon strategy could be reformed. Kok's report (published in November) was a damning indictment. Although the high-level group underscored the need for some coordination of national reform efforts, it admitted that the open method was ill-equipped for the task. It had too many targets, too many priorities, too many meetings, and too few results. Nevertheless the Kok report insisted that some effort had to be maintained. The Lisbon strategy cannot be abandoned because the problem it addresses—the poor individual and collective functioning of national institutions—cannot be ignored. If anything, the integration of the European economy into the wider global competition has made matters worse. Hence the report concluded that national reform efforts must be redoubled. Indeed, the performance of the European "model" is at stake (see box, "Facing the Challenge").

Box 8.4   Facing the Challenge

The Lisbon Strategy for Growth and Employment
Report from the High Level Group
chaired by Wim Kok
November 2004

Conclusion

Europe's leaders need to instill hope that tomorrow will be better than today. Europe has considerable economic and social strengths, as the High Level Group has identified. The program of reform outlined in this report is eminently deliverable and will bring improvement. It needs to be clearly understood and explained, and then delivered. The act of delivery, along with the associated improvement, will start to put Europe on a virtuous circle of better economic performance, rising confidence and expectations, and improved trust.

Changes such as the opening up of markets, the modernization of social policy, pensions and healthcare systems, promoting the adaptability of the labor market or even education systems have an immediate impact on people's daily lives. Many of these changes are positive, despite the common portrayal of them. For example, more competition empowers consumers, improved care for children and the elderly enhances the lives of carers, typically women, while access to lifelong education offers workers the chance of mobility, self-improvement and greater

(continued)

Box 8.4   *(Continued)*

opportunity. However, unless the program is understood as a comprehensive package, each component will not be given the chance to prove it can work and contribute to generalized improvement. The chance of moving on to a virtuous circle of improved performance and trust will be greatly reduced.

The need for reform has to be explained especially to citizens who are not always aware of the urgency and scale of the situation. "Competitiveness" is not just some dry economic indicator that is often unintelligible to the man in the street; rather, it provides a diagnosis of the state of economic health of a country or a region. In the present circumstances, the clear message must be: if we want to preserve and improve our social model we have to adapt: it is not too late to change. In any event the status quo is not an option. Engaging and involving citizens in the process has two mutually reinforcing attractions: it in effect seeks public support by giving people elements for debate and it leverages that support to put pressure on governments to pursue these goals.

The High Level Group is not calling for indiscriminate action; reform packages should be balanced, well thought through and properly designed. Equally, there should be a strengthening and modernization of the distinctive European approach to organizing the economy and society, so embedding core European values that all Europeans care about. The issue is delivering on the promises and undertakings that have been made, and that will entail significant change.

The promotion of growth and employment in Europe is the next great European project. Its execution will require political leadership and commitment of the highest order, along with that of the social partners whose role the High Level Group wishes to sustain. However, the privilege of voice and participation is accompanied by responsibility which we urge all to accept. The citizens of Europe deserve no less.

The measures we propose require—in our European democratic system—sustained political determination. In the end, much of the Lisbon strategy depends on the progress made in national capitals: no European procedure or method can change this simple truth. Governments and especially their leaders must not duck their crucial responsibilities. Nothing less than the future prosperity of the European model is at stake.

(*Source:* Luxembourg: Office for Official Publications of the European Communities, 2004).

MODEL OR MODELS?

The Kok report's reference to the European "model" tapped into an old debate about the political and economic organization of European countries: Is there one European model or several? Are European countries converging on some common model, or do they remain persistently different? If they remain different, then what does it mean to be "European"? These questions border on a level of philosophical abstraction that is not often at the center of policy discussions. Nevertheless, the answers to these questions contain a practical element that challenges fundamentally what integration is all about.

The Belgian economist André Sapir put his finger on this practical dimension in a briefing paper he wrote for the informal September 2005 meeting of the Council of Economic and Finance Ministers held in Manchester, the United Kingdom.[18] In essence, Sapir argued that there is not one European social model, but four. The difference between them is how they handle questions of efficiency and equity. In this context, efficiency relates to how easily people can change jobs, how quickly employers can let go of employees, and how long it takes unemployed workers to find new employment. Efficient markets are fast and easy on all counts while inefficient ones are slow and difficult. Equity, by contrast, refers to the distribution of income across social classes and the level of poverty across society as a whole. Equitable societies have an equal distribution of income and a low level of poverty and inequitable ones do not.

Framed this way, it is tempting to imagine a trade-off between equity and efficiency, particularly if you believe that equity can only be provided by those types of labor market institutions that protect jobs, support wages, and redistribute income from rich to poor. However, what Sapir finds is that no such trade-off exists, at least not necessarily. There are some countries, such as the Nordic ones (Denmark, Finland, Norway, and Sweden), that somehow manage to combine high levels of equity with equally high levels of efficiency. There are others, such as the Mediterranean ones (Greece, Italy, Portugal, and Spain), that suffer from the worst of both worlds—low equity and low efficiency. Therefore, if there is any evidence of a trade-off, it is only between the Anglo-Saxon countries (such as the United Kingdom) that do well on efficiency but poorly on equity, and the Continentals (namely France and Germany) that are more equitable than efficient.

So what are we to make of Sapir's analysis? He offers two conclusions. First, it is clear that some countries need reform more than others and that different countries need to change themselves in different ways: The Mediterranean countries need to act across the board and with urgency; the Continentals need to free up their markets; the Anglo-Saxons need to focus on income inequality; and the Nordics need to make sure they do not lose their favorable combination of factors. The second conclusion is that national reform efforts need coordination and support from the European level—both because there are some problems that only the European Union can address and because coordination is necessary to make sure that what counts as a solution in one country does not turn out to be a problem for all the rest. Put another way, European institutions are necessary precisely because national economic models are different and if the Lisbon strategy has failed as a solution then it must either be fixed or replaced. Doing away with European assistance is not an option in the multilevel European economy.

These conclusions are sensible but they leave open the question about why countries are different in the first place. Here we must rejoin the more abstract debate about the nature of national distinctiveness or what many academics working in comparative political economy have come to refer to as "Varieties of Capitalism" after the book edited by Peter Hall and David Soskice.[19] Hall and Soskice have a specific argument that national differences can be traced back to the coordination strategies of firms, but they have a more general claim about the development of institutions and what they call "institutional complementarities." The more general claim is what really matters in assessing the durability of national differences and the problem of coordinating national institutional reforms.

Essentially Hall and Soskice argue that economic and political institutions develop according to a logic of appropriateness or "fit." Policy recommendations do not make sense in the abstract; they only make sense in a particular national context. Hence no matter what economists may recommend about which institutions would be best at providing market efficiency or social equity, the problem confronting policymakers is how to make the best out of the institutions they already have. Moreover, policymakers cannot focus on what is best while holding everything else constant. Rather they have to take into account the impact of any changes in one institution on all the rest. What is "best" is best for the economic and political system as a whole and not just for the particular institution in question.

The point here is abstract but it is also important. Consider, for example, recommendations to get rid of employment protection laws. Economists argue that employment protection laws—rules that make it difficult for employers to fire workers—have the perverse effect of lowering employment and lengthening unemployment. Firms will not risk hiring workers that they may not need (and cannot get rid of later) and they will be more reluctant to rehire workers or fill vacancies after they finally manage to let an employee go. If this economic analysis is correct, and there is much statistical evidence to suggest that it is, then why do all countries not work to get rid of employment protection legislation? Certainly the experience of Denmark would suggest that they should. The Danish government has reduced most obstacles to firing workers and focused instead on making it easier for the unemployed to retrain themselves to find new jobs. This formula (called "flexicurity") seems an obvious solution to combining the need for market efficiency with the desire for social equity. Even better, Danish flexicurity appears to work; employment in Denmark is high, the distribution of income is equitable, and the poverty rate is very low. So the question about employment protection legislation could be rephrased as why do other countries not follow the Danish model?

If we follow the institutional logic of Hall and Soskice, the answer is straightforward. Other countries do not follow the Danish model because they do not have the wider institutional and cultural environment within which Danish flexicurity is possible. They do not have the high tax base, the readily available adult-education programs, the strong social support networks, the balanced double-income households, the high-quality public infrastructure, and the efficient benefits administrators that are all necessary to ensure that unemployed workers can find new employment. In other words, countries do not follow the Danish model because to do so they would have to *be* Denmark. Moreover, once we begin to unpack the institutional preconditions for Danish success, it becomes easier to determine whether the good macroeconomic performance is really due to policies to promote flexicurity or whether it should be attributed to a range of other possible factors—which Herman Schwartz has grouped in terms of "luck, pluck, or stuck."[20] Is Danish economic performance the result of favorable circumstances (luck), smart policy innovation (pluck), or just muddling through (stuck). The answer, Schwartz finds, is very mixed and highly contingent. And while Schwartz admires many of the policy innovations introduced by the Danes, he concludes that they have very little to offer as a model to others.

So what are other countries to do? Continuing the example of employment protection legislation, they should look to see whether it is possible to remove such protections without imposing unnecessary or insupportable hardships. They should consider whether doing so will alienate important political or economic groups (such as trade unions) in a way likely to cause problems elsewhere. They should ensure that worker retraining is available and effective. They should improve the matching of people looking for work and firms trying to hire. And they should provide the necessary financial resources both to government agencies and to the people most likely to be affected. This is only a partial list of the factors that must be considered. Nevertheless, it is enough to make it clear both that domestic context matters and that domestic differences across European countries are unlikely to wither away either quickly or easily. If Italy is reluctant to adopt the Danish model it is because Italy is not Denmark (and because Italians do not want it to become Denmark, either). If Italy is doing poorly in terms of both equity and efficiency, the Italians will have to find their own path to reform.

Europeanization and the Rescue of the Nation-State

Different countries are different and they should be expected to remain so. This is true despite the fact that some countries perform better on all counts, some have strengths and weaknesses, and others are in desperate need for reform. Moreover, what is good for one country may not be possible for another. And the very existence of these national differences not only makes it essential that EU member states engage in some type of European-level coordination but also makes it more likely that European-level institutions will come to depend upon their counterparts within the member states. European integration does not exist to eliminate national differences. Rather, in many ways, it exists because of national differences.

This is a strong contention to end with but it ties together this discussion of European economic governance around a pair of open questions: What kind of Europe is being created? What are the implications for European member states?

The answer to the first question is less programmatic than most "pro-Europeans" or European federalists would like. The Europe that is emerging is not a clear-cut federalist ideal type or even a close approximation of an existing federal state such as the United States. Rather it is a complicated beast, centering on the member states and yet also including important elements at other levels. Moreover, the multiple levels of governance in Europe are increasingly interdependent: the European Union needs the member states at least as much as the member states need the EU.

The answer to the second question is ambiguous. In many areas it is clear that the process of integration has changed the member states, both as they adapt to the requirements for dealing with each other and with European institutions on a regular basis, and as they pursue common strategies and goals.[21] In other areas, however, the result of integration has been to help the member states retain their national distinctiveness by facilitating reforms that would have to take place in any event, by solving problems that no state alone can address, and by creating a European buffer between the member states and the outside world.[22] In this way, European economic governance continues to function on many levels at once and the member states remain different even as they become more alike.

Notes

1. See, for example, Loukas Tsoukalis, *What Kind of Europe?* Oxford: Oxford University Press, 2005.

2. Paul De Grauwe's textbook on European monetary integration has become the canonical work in the field. See Paul De Grauwe, *Economics of Monetary Union*, Sixth Edition, Oxford: Oxford University Press, 2005.

3. According to the now-predominant quantity theory of money, central bankers do indeed make price inflation by changing the quantity of money in circulation. There is much that is useful in this view, at least when looking at the long run. Over the short run, however, even the most mainstream economists admit that price- and wage-setting behavior is controlled by private agents and not central bankers. See, for example, N. Gregory Mankiw, *Macroeconomics*, Sixth Edition, New York: Worth Publishers, 2006, Chapter 9.

4. See John Maynard Keynes, *The General Theory of Employment Interest and Money*, New York: Harcourt, Brace and Company, 1936, p. 383.

5. My comments are based on the Italian edition: Alberto Alesina and Francesco Giavazzi, *Goodbye Europa: Cronache di un Declino Economico e Politico*, Milano: Rizzoli, 2006. The English edition is published by MIT Press.

6. Unless otherwise indicated, the data in this subsection are taken from the 2006 edition of the *OECD Factbook*, which is available online to subscribers at http://www.oecd.org.

7. These data for employment and unemployment are taken from the statistical annex to *OECD Employment Outlook: Boosting Jobs and Incomes, 2006*, Paris: OECD, 2006.

8. These data are from the United States Bureau of Economic Analysis and can be found at http://www.bea.gov.

9. The Bureau of Labor Statistics is part of the U.S. Department of Labor. These data are available from http://www.bls.gov.

10. See *OECD Employment Outlook: Boosting Jobs and Incomes, 2006*, Paris: OECD, 2006, p. 265.

11. On multilevel governance, see Gary Marks and Liesbet Hooghe, *Multi-Level Governance and European Integration*, Lanham, MD: Rowman & Littlefield, 2001.

12. This language is quoted directly from Article G, Paragraph 5 of the Treaty on European Union. See http://europa.eu/eur-lex/en/treaties/dat/EU_treaty.html.

13. For an analysis of this "competitive local factor markets" assumption, see Erik Jones, "Economic and Monetary Union: Playing for Money," in Andrew Moravcsik (ed.), *Centralization or Fragmentation? Europe Before the Challenges of Deepening, Diversity, and Democracy*, Washington, DC: Brookings Press for the Council on Foreign Relations, 1998, pp. 59–93.

14. See Erik Jones, "European Monetary Union and the Problem of Macroeconomic Governance," in Ronald Tiersky (ed.), *Europe Today: National Politics, Integration, and European Security*, Second Edition, Lanham, MD: Rowman & Littlefield, 2004, pp. 59–87; "European Macroeconomic Governance," in Jeremy Richardson (ed.), *European Union Power and Policymaking*, Third Edition, London: Routledge, 2006, pp. 329–349.

15. The exception here is probably the Soviet Union—which would be an uncomfortable benchmark for the EU to measure itself against.

16. For a recent analysis, see Imelda Maher, "The Rule of Law and Agency: The Case of Competition Policy," *IEP Working Paper 06/01*, London: Chatham House, March 2006.

17. In the United States, competition policies are referred to as "antitrust" policies because they were launched as part of President Theodore Roosevelt's efforts to break the influence of big business "trusts" (or holding companies) in U.S. political life.

18. The paper was later published as André Sapir, "Globalization and the Reform of European Social Models," *Journal of Common Market Studies*, 44(2), June 2006, 369–390.

19. The seminal work in this area is Peter A. Hall and David Soskice (eds.), *Varieties of Capitalism: The Institutional Foundations of Comparative Advantage*, Oxford: Oxford University Press, 2001.

20. See Herman M. Schwartz, "'The Danish Miracle': Luck, Pluck, or Stuck?" *Comparative Political Studies*, 34(2), March 2001, 131–155; and Uwe Becker and Herman Schwartz (eds.), *Employment Miracles: A Critical Comparison of the Dutch, Scandinavian, Swiss, Australian and Irish Cases Versus Germany and the United States*, Amsterdam: Amsterdam University Press, 2005.

21. For a survey of this influence, see Simon Bulmer and Christian Lequesne (eds.), *Member States and the European Union*, Oxford: Oxford University Press, 2005.

22. This line of argument is borrowed from Alan Milward, *The European Rescue of the Nation-State*, London: Routledge, 1992.

Suggested Readings

Becker, Uwe, and Herman Schwartz (eds.), *Employment Miracles: A Critical Comparison of the Dutch, Scandinavian, Swiss, Australian and Irish Cases Versus Germany and the United States,* Amsterdam: Amsterdam University Press, 2005.

Bulmer, Simon, and Christian Lequesne (eds.), *Member States and the European Union,* Oxford: Oxford University Press, 2005.

De Grauwe, Paul, *Economics of Monetary Union,* Sixth Edition, Oxford: Oxford University Press, 2005.

Jones, Erik, *The Politics of Economic and Monetary Union: Integration and Idiosyncrasy,* Lanham, MD: Rowman & Littlefield, 2002.

Maher, Imelda, "The Rule of Law and Agency: The Case of Competition Policy," *IEP Working Paper 06/01,* London: Chatham House, March 2006.

Marks, Gary, and Liesbet Hooghe, *Multi-Level Governance and European Integration,* Lanham, MD: Rowman & Littlefield, 2001.

Milward, Alan S., *The European Rescue of the Nation-State,* London: Routledge, 1992.

Pelkmans, Jacques, *European Integration: Methods and Economic Analysis,* Second Edition, London: Prentice Hall, 2001.

Sapir, André, "Globalization and the Reform of European Social Models," *Journal of Common Market Studies,* 44(2), June 2006, 369–390.

Tsoukalis, Loukas, *What Kind of Europe?* Oxford: Oxford University Press, 2005.

CHAPTER 9

EU Law

Imelda Maher

The EU as a legal system is unique.[1] There is no precedent for it. At the same time, it enjoys characteristics of long-existing national legal orders in that it aspires to uphold the rule of law. It is difficult to classify and poses great challenges for existing orthodoxies in legal scholarship, for judges both in national courts of the member states and in the European Court of Justice (ECJ). Despite being in existence for over fifty years, the debate as to its nature and in particular as to whether or not it can be said to be constitutionalized remains unresolved. Given the negative votes in the French and Dutch referenda that have stalled the adoption of the proposed EU constitution, the short answer is "no" but there is a long-established body of law and of scholarship that embraces the notion of the constitutionalization of the EU. The extent that it has already been constitutionalized is difficult to assess given that another characteristic of EU law is that it is in a constant process of change. As such, it is entirely consistent with other legal regimes where the nature of law is that it embodies a contradiction: it offers continuity and predictability while also allowing for flexibility, adaptation, and change both through judicial interpretation in case law and through statutory reform.

It is this combination of continuity and change that is one of the most important characteristics of EU law. Just as there is no legal concept "Europe," so it is unhelpful to think of EU law as one big unchanging and immutable monolith. The rhetoric of the law is one of uniformity and a certain level of consistency is vital for the effective operation of any legal order. However, by critically exploring the law, the notion of uniformity may become only one of several characteristics for EU law. Other features—a sort of bounded diversity—also become apparent such that EU law is seen as being different at different times, in different contexts and for different actors. This idea of change coexists with that of continuity and consistency. There is a single body of EU law but that does not come exclusively from a top-down enforced hierarchy of rules and decisions. Its (sometimes qualified) acceptance by the "peoples of Europe" and especially by the national courts of Europe despite differences in legal traditions, legal cultures, language, political needs, and practical disputes is also central to the emergence and constitutionalization of EU law.

The ECJ as the primary court in the EU is the main driver of the constitutionalization of EU law. It has been the focus of much attention in law and political-science literature—albeit in very different ways. Traditional doctrinal legal scholarship that dominates much of the literature focuses on the decision-making of the Court (and of its junior partner, the Court of First Instance) and engages in detailed analysis of the legal reasoning of the Court and the significance of decisions for the development of the law. Political-science scholarship, on the other hand, provides an institutional analysis of the Court as a strategic rational actor examining its capacity for shaping the EU and its position vis-à-vis other institutions and the member states. This chapter, drawing on both approaches, adopts a broad systems perspective that sees EU law and the EU political system as social systems operating separately but also inextricably linked.

EU law is primarily concerned with legality underpinned by the rule of law and its inherent values of procedural fairness, equality, and ultimately preventing the abuse of power. The discourse is one of legality or illegality.[2] The exercise of power in the political sphere when viewed through the lens of law is not concerned with whether that was the best way to achieve a particular policy outcome or what side-bargains or interests might have been accommodated in securing a particular agreement. Instead, the fundamental question is whether or not the activity in question was legal or illegal as defined by EU law and interpreted by the Court. Law is distinct from politics and has its own often very technical discourse that can make it opaque at times. As a separate social system, it has a purpose (upholding the rule of law) and perspective (seeking to ensure legality) that ideally will lead (however imperfectly) to justice. As such it does not just have the functional role of articulating policies through the enactment of rules, or their interpretation and implementation. It is this concern with legality that ensures some sort of balance is maintained between the need for consistency and legal certainty on the one hand and change and diversity, on the other, that ensures enough flexibility so the law can be sufficiently responsive to its social, political, and economic environments.

In this chapter I discuss four different dimensions of EU law as a means of understanding what is distinctive about it, its centrality for the EU, and how the balance between continuity and change is achieved and negotiated, focusing on the relationship between the ECJ and national courts. These dimensions are: (1) European law; (2) EU law: supranational or international law? (3) EU law and national law and (4) EU law as a tool of integration. In doing so, the chapter draws on both law and political-science literature. It uses systemic and institutional perspectives to introduce the multifaceted and complex nature of EU law so it is not viewed as a set of unproblematic and uniform rules. It explores the nature of EU law, its uncertain, incomplete but relatively entrenched constitutionalization, and the legal doctrines that underpin that process.

European Law

EU law is informed by the different legal traditions of the member states. Thus there is a sense of commonality underpinning some aspects of EU law, most notably in the field of human rights. The ECJ explicitly draws on the common traditions of the member states and the European Convention of Human Rights (1948), of which all member states are signatories, to identify and develop a human rights law for the EU.[3] This is codified within the Human Rights Charter.[4] The Charter is currently declaratory only, i.e., it is not legally binding. If the draft constitution were adopted, it would be fully incorporated into EU law. In the meantime, the case law of the various European courts is binding on the EU institutions and on the states when carrying out or failing to carry out their obligations under EU law. There is also a general human rights provision in the Treaty on European Union (or Maastricht Treaty).[5] Nonetheless to talk of a common legal tradition is misleading even in the field of human rights where, for example, Ireland has a constitutional right to life that has the effect of precluding abortion while abortion is available in all other member states.

There are two main legal traditions represented in the EU: civil law and common law. In simple terms, the civil law is seen as having been especially influenced by Roman law and later by the Napoleonic Code introduced in 1804.[6] Codification places an emphasis on the written law codes with less emphasis on the role of judges. The other main legal tradition is the common law, which places greater emphasis on case law. There is less codification and, in the United Kingdom, no single written constitutional document. With the accession of the UK and Ireland to what was then the European Economic Community (EEC), the common law became part of the European legal tradition that informs EU law. The fact that it was a late-comer means the institutional framework of the EU reflects the civil law tradition. This is particularly pronounced in the design of the ECJ. Its rules of procedure were modeled on those of the International Court of Justice in The Hague[7] and reflect civil law procedure with pleadings mostly written with short oral hearings. A single judgment only is given in each case. There are twenty-seven judges and the Court meets in chambers of three, five, and thirteen and, for extremely important cases, fifteen judges. Thus, in marked contrast to common law courts, there is never a dissenting opinion. Instead, the advocate general (of which there are eight in total) is an officer of the Court who provides a learned opinion after the pleadings and prior to the Court's own secret deliberations, giving an overview of the relevant law and indicating how s/he thinks the case should be decided. The Court follows this advisory opinion in about 80 percent of cases.

The substance of EU law is also informed by national law and practice. For example, the British experience of liberalization under the Thatcher government

Box 9.1

The ECJ has twenty-seven judges and eight advocates general. It is the supreme court of the EU.[1] Following the Single European Act, the Court of First Instance was set up in 1989.[2] It has twenty-seven judges and no advocates general, although in rare cases where the issue is deemed particularly difficult, one of the judges will act as advocate general. It also sits in chambers and in rare cases can sit as a single judge. There is an appeal on a point of law from its decisions (within two months) to the ECJ.

Under the Treaty of Nice, judicial panels may be created. There is currently one panel, the Civil Service Tribunal, which in effect is the employment tribunal for EU institutions and their employees.[3]

---

1. Article 220–245 EC. Statute of the Court of Justice, November 2005, available at http://www.curia.europa.eu/en/instit/txtdocfr/txtsenvigueur/statut.pdf. Rules of Procedure of the Court of Justice as amended, available at http://www.curia.europa.eu/en/instit/txtdocfr/txtsenvigueur/txt5.pdf.

2. Article 224 EC and Decision 88/591 [1988] OJ L 319/1. Rules of Procedure of the Court of First Instance available at http://www.curia.europa.eu/en/instit/txtdocfr/txtsenvigueur/txt7.pdf.

3. Article 220 EC; Decision 2004.752/EC establishing the European Union Civil Service Tribunal, [2004] OJ L 333/7.

---

in the 1980s was influential in the way market liberalization was developed in the EU. In this sense, EU law can be seen as a European amalgam of national laws and legal institutions, but this would underestimate the unique nature of EU law and the extent to which it transcends national European traditions.

EU law is the only law in the world that has authoritative versions of its law in (currently) twenty-three languages. This Europeanizes EU law more than any other characteristic. It renders the law more complex. The Court can cross-refer to different language versions when deciding how to interpret a particular provision. It has also encouraged national courts to use different language versions when deciding whether or not the meaning of a particular provision is clear or not.

It also means that the Court may opt for a unique EU law definition in order to avoid negotiating between multiple national legal doctrines. Thus even though every national legal system necessarily has a legal definition of what constitutes a "worker," for example, the ECJ gave the word a new definition in EU law, thus securing a level of uniformity that transcends national diversity and minimizes differences born of language.

Technically, there is no such thing as European law because "Europe," however understood, is not a legal entity. In addition, while the concept of "Europe" may be all-embracing geopolitically, culturally, and as the embodiment of a myriad set of ideals and values, the scope (jurisdiction) of EU law is not, for two reasons. Geographically, there are some European states (e.g., Norway and

> ## Box 9.2   Excerpt from Case 283/81
> ## Srl CILFIT (1982) ECR 3415
>
> "18. To begin with, it must be borne in mind that Community legislation is drafted in several languages and that the different language versions are equally authentic. An interpretation of a provision of Community law thus involves a comparison of the different language versions.
>
> 19. It must also be borne in mind, even where the different language versions are entirely in accord with one another, that Community law uses terminology which is peculiar to it. Furthermore, it must be emphasized that legal concepts do not necessarily have the same meaning in Community law and in the law of the various member states.
>
> 20. Finally, every provision of Community law must be placed in its context and interpreted in the light of the provisions of Community law as a whole, regard being had to the objectives thereof and to its state of evolution at the date on which the provision in question is to be applied."

Switzerland) that remain outside of the EU and are not looking to become members, while some other European states (e.g., Croatia) are not yet members. From a substantive legal perspective, EU law does not govern all aspects of society. Instead, like any federal law its powers (competence) are limited to those fields identified in the Maastricht Treaty. Those competences are either exclusive to itself, shared with the member states, or allow the EU to support, coordinate, or complement member-state actions. Should EU law be enacted where there is a lack of competence, then the measure can be declared void by the ECJ.[8]

Treaty reform often contains a paradox. On the one hand, reform often confers new competencies on the EU. On the other, reform often tried to constrain the ever-expanding scope of EU competence given ever-present concerns about the EU democratic deficit. This tension can be seen, for example, in the debate surrounding the Maastricht Treaty, which introduced both Economic and Monetary Union—arguably the biggest development in the EU since its foundation—and the principle of subsidiarity, which seeks to limit (however imperfectly) EU legislative action by requiring it to be taken only where the legislative objectives cannot be achieved at national level and are better achieved at the EU level.[9]

The difficulty for those concerned about the expanding scope of EU law is that Article 95EC empowers the European Council to adopt harmonizing internal market measures and Article 308EC empowers it to adopt legislation necessary to achieve a treaty objective for which there are no explicit treaty powers. The ECJ has only twice struck down measures enacted under these catchall provisions.[10] Significantly, both provisions are functional in nature—they are concerned with achieving treaty objectives and do not and are not designed to

---

**Box 9.3   From Damian Chalmers,
Christos Hadjiemmanuil, Giorgio Monti and Adam
Tomkins, *European Union Law* (Cambridge:
Cambridge University Press, 2006), p. 167**

The question of democratic legitimacy, the "democratic deficit" in Euro-speak, has dominated debate surrounding the Community legislative processes. Such debate critiques the democracy of Community law making in three ways. First, there are concerns about the quality of representative democracy. Such concerns focus both on the parliamentary input in the processes and the extent to which Community law making undermines parliamentary democracy at a national and regional level. Secondly, there are concerns about the quality of participatory democracy. Community law making has been accused of being insufficiently plural, of not listening to enough interested parties and of giving too great weight to some interests. Finally, concerns have been expressed about the quality of deliberative democracy—the quality of public debate that surrounds and informs the law-making processes. Concerns have been expressed that Community law is too much characterized by negotiation between interests rather than public debate between citizens.

---

address constitutional questions of democratic accountability and legitimacy of EU action.

Thus the thorny political issue of the relationship between the exercise of national and EU power is problematic for three reasons (at least). First, the conferral of legal competence in the treaty is poorly articulated with no list of competences. The draft constitution does contain such a list, thus potentially curbing their unchecked expansion.[11] Second, the two catchall provisions that allow the EU to act are functional and take no explicit account of wider issues of accountability and legitimacy. Third, the subsidiarity principle is seen as generally ineffective at limiting EU action.[12]

To conclude, EU law is unique and yet can be described as European law in that it is informed by and draws on the different national legal traditions both substantively and institutionally. Jurisdictionally, it is limited in that some European states are not members, and substantively, its competence is limited. Finally, in European terms, the EU is a very new legal order and as such does not have the strong historical roots that the concept of Europe can claim.

EU Law: Supranational or International Law?

The EU, as a treaty-based entity, is a creature of international law but has a constitutionalizing quality that sets it apart from international law. It can bind member states, subject them to sanctions (in the form of fines),[13] and can create rights for their citizens. Hence it is referred to as supranational in nature. Where the EU legal order lies on the spectrum between international and supranational law has and does change over time. In some fields it remains largely intergovernmental in nature and hence akin to international law, e.g., in cultural policy, where harmonization of laws is expressly excluded.[14] This reflects the limited competence of the EU. In other fields, e.g., competition law, member states are subject to the full force of EU law.[15] The extent to which EU law is supra- or international is determined by many different factors, including political factors, legal principles of subsidiarity and competence, functional concerns of integration and better regulation, and by considerations of legitimacy—the democratic deficit acting at times as a powerful constraint.

EU law develops in a haphazard and often uncertain way. While there are path dependencies in the sense that precedent exerts a powerful but not overwhelming influence on the ECJ, the logic of the law can be overestimated. For example, on a very practical level the Court now meets in chambers, rendering the idea of a single voice to a legal fiction, save in cases recognized in advance as very significant, wherein a plenary court meets and even then only fifteen judges will sit out of a total of twenty-seven. On an institutional level, the character of EU law can differ, as was most apparent in the EU in the 1960s when the Council acted primarily as an intergovernmental entity operating through consensus while the ECJ was forging a unique set of constitutionalizing principles for a supranational EU law.

The EU treaties were entered into by sovereign states voluntarily and, while the principle of qualified majority voting was in the treaties from the outset, the practice of consensus for law making was quickly established in the Council and ultimately articulated in the Luxembourg Accords, a political agreement by the states, the effect of which was to make unanimity a requirement for any legislation, slowing down the pace of adoption such that it could take years for some measures to become law—e.g., it took sixteen years before a Merger Regulation was adopted in 1989.[16] This "Eurosclerosis" was only broken with the adoption of the Single European Act (SEA) in 1985, which reformed the treaty and broke the deadlock in the Council. Thus EU law making had a distinctly international law flavor to it up until the SEA, due to the principle of consensus. A very different vision was advocated by the ECJ at the same time. It saw the EU as a unique legal entity that differs from international law in two fundamental respects: first, it binds member states such that EU law is supreme over national law, and second, unlike international law where the subjects of that law are only states and international bodies, the subjects of EU law are also individuals. This means that EU law can confer rights on them that are enforceable against member states who in most policy fields are responsible for the implementation and enforcement of EU measures. This radical vision of EU law coexisted with the de facto unanimity requirement in the Council of Ministers, where the interests of the states were paramount right through the 1960s and 1970s. This paradox can be explained in several different ways.[17]

First, it is useful to take an evolutionary perspective of EU law, with the supranational nature of the law developing over time. Thus, while initially it may have been conceived and may have looked much like international law, this view is now outdated (for European Community [EC] law at any rate) given the way EU law has been interpreted by the ECJ and the extent to which that vision of EU law has been accepted by the national constitutional courts.

Second, because the judgments of the Court are necessarily cloaked in dry, formal language, the long-term impact of these early cases was not always apparent. To put it baldly, who would have thought that a case concerning the classification of urea formaldehyde for the purposes of customs duty would be one of the most important building blocks of EU law?[18]

Third, member states retain the power of treaty revision, so even if the Court could incrementally develop EU law, if it were seen as encroaching too much on state interests, the treaties could be revised to reflect this. Thus while the scope of the preliminary reference procedure—an important procedural basis on which the ECJ hears cases from national courts—has itself never been limited; when variations of it have been introduced in new parts of the treaty, it has always been modified in order to curtail the power of the Court.[19] On the other hand, the treaty could also be revised to incorporate the case law of the Court, e.g., the introduction of Article 6 TEU on fundamental rights. Indeed, case law can act as a springboard for more radical treaty revision. The entire single-market project can be seen in this light.[20] In other words, the Court has a zone of activity within which it can interpret the law in a manner consistent with the integration agenda, but there are some limitations on this given the

---

Box 9.4   Eric Stein, "Lawyers, Judges, and the Making of a Transnational Constitution" (1981) 75 Am. J. I. L. 1–27, at 1.

Tucked away in the fairyland Duchy of Luxembourg and blessed, until recently, with benign neglect by the powers that be and the mass media, the Court of Justice of the European Communities has fashioned a constitutional framework for a federal-type structure in Europe. From its inception a mere quarter of a century ago, the Court has construed the European Community Treaties in a constitutional mode rather than employing the traditional international law methodology. Proceeding from its fragile jurisdictional base, the court has arrogated to itself the ultimate authority to draw the line between Community law and national law. Moreover, it has established and obtained acceptance of the broad principle of direct integration of Community law into the national legal orders of the member states and of the supremacy of Community law within its limited but expanding area of competence over any conflicting national law.

wider political context within which it operates, and this helps to explain why a radical jurisprudence coincided with inertia in relation to law making.

Fourth, up until the 1990s, the means of enforcing EU law were weak. There was no judicially enforced sanction against a state that failed to meet their legal obligations, even if they were brought before the ECJ by the Commission. States' sovereignty and interests were not unduly affected by the jurisprudence of the Court, and they could claim to be keen supporters of the integration agenda knowing there was little or no redress for those obligations they failed to carry out.[21]

Finally, the Court could claim supremacy of EU law when states were adopting legislation by consensus, as it could confidently point to the unconditional and irrevocable assumption of the relevant EU obligations. Such unanimity also minimized any concerns about the democratic legitimacy of EU law at the time that the Court was crafting these principles. This would change with the shift to qualified majority voting under the SEA.

The paradox of a radical jurisprudence and sclerotic legislative process was challenged when the SEA reinvigorated the market integration agenda. It removed the presumption of unanimity, allowed a greater role for the European Parliament, and increased the use of qualified majority voting. This shift was due in part to the Cassis de Dijon case, which introduced the principle of mutual recognition of national standards. It required states to accept lawfully produced goods from other member states without the imposition of any additional requirements, save in narrowly drawn circumstances.[22] By publishing a notice on the judgment, the Commission ensured that its potential impact was brought firmly into the political arena and to the attention of the Council of Ministers.[23] The SEA can in part be seen as the states reasserting control over the integration agenda. The effect of the case was deregulatory (negative integration). Goods only had to comply with the regulatory standards of the exporting member state, rendering redundant vast swathes of national standards. The single-market program broke the log jam in the Council and led to the introduction of EU legislation establishing common EU standards or a system for the recognition of equivalent national standards. Thus there was re-regulation—a form of positive integration—at the EU level.[24] This regulatory shift can be seen as a key moment when the supranational character of the EU was asserted.

The supranational character of EU law was further affirmed in the Maastricht Treaty but only for the largest and oldest part, i.e., the European Community (EC). Economic and Monetary Union (EMU) was set out and the law-making role of the Parliament (through the cooperation procedure) was enhanced. The ECJ was given the power to impose fines on member states that failed to comply with a judgment that they were in breach of their EU obligations.[25] Thus the bindingness of EU law—a fundamental feature of its supranational character—was underlined. At the same time, Maastricht redefined the nature of EU law by creating a three-pillar structure, of which the EC pillar is the largest and the most supranational. The other two flanking pillars, dealing with justice and home affairs (now Police and Judicial Cooperation in Criminal Matters) and foreign and security policy, operate much closer to an international law model, with the consensus principle the primary basis for legitimate action.

The uneven development of EU law continues. Most recently, this can be seen in how the introduction of EMU in 1999 with its uniform and centralized monetary policy implemented by a very independent European Central Bank, was rapidly followed in 2000 by the Lisbon process, with its emphasis on new governance methods that are much closer to practices in classic international bodies such as the Organization for Economic Cooperation and Development and the International Monetary Fund, rather than those found in the EU.[26] This simultaneous shift toward high levels of integration and bindingness is allied in other policy fields with an emphasis on soft law (nonbinding but nonetheless influential norms),[27] which is a key characteristic of international law. This hybridity is indicative of the complexity of EU law, with change and flexibility coexisting with continuity and consistency.

EU Law and National Law

How EU law is classified can help clarify but does not define the relationship between EU and national law. By defining this relationship hierarchically, the ECJ emphasizes the unique nature of EU law. *Costa v. ENEL* was the first case where the Court asserted that EU law was supreme. The issue in the case was what law should a national court apply when faced with relevant but conflicting EU law and national laws? The clear answer provided by the ECJ was that EU law was supreme over national law. Where there was a conflict between the national and EU rules, the EU rules applied. The ECJ did not—and indeed does not have the power to—declare national law void. Instead, it is simply not applied when it conflicts with EU law. There is a clear logic behind this so-called supremacy principle: if there are common EU rules, they should apply equally throughout the entire EU. The EU would disintegrate if EU law did not in general apply consistently throughout the Union. All the member states had agreed to the objectives of the EU, so in principle there was little to object to when the ECJ set out this choice-of-law rule, especially as the national law is simply disapplied and not declared void.

This explanation addresses the issue in fairly narrow technical legal terms. In fact the ECJ had gone much further than simply creating a choice-of-law rule; it defined the nature of the EU legal order in a radical and dynamic way—and created a principle that is not referred to anywhere in the governing treaties. It is a classic example of judicial law making facilitated by treaty silence on the relationship between national law and EU law. The extract in Box 9.5 occurs

Box 9.5   Case 6/64 Costa v. ENEL (1964) ECR 1[1]

By contrast with ordinary international treaties, the EEC Treaty has created its own legal system which, on the entry into force of the Treaty, became an integral part of the legal systems of the member states and which their courts are bound to apply.

By creating a Community of unlimited duration, having its own institutions, its own personality, its own legal capacity and capacity of representation on the international plane and, more particularly, real powers stemming from a limitation of sovereignty or a transfer of powers from the States to the Community, the Member States have limited their sovereign rights, albeit within limited fields, and have thus created a body of law which binds both their nationals and themselves.

The integration into the laws of each Member State of provisions which derive from the Community, and more generally the terms and the spirit of the treaty, make it impossible for the States, as a corollary, to accord precedence to a unilateral and subsequent measure over a legal system accepted by them on a basis of reciprocity. Such a measure cannot therefore be inconsistent with that legal system. The executive force of Community law cannot vary from one state to another in deference to subsequent domestic laws, without jeopardizing the attainment of the objectives of the Treaty set out in Article [10(2)] and giving rise to the discrimination prohibited by Article [12]. . . .

It follows from all these observations that the law stemming from the Treaty, an independent source of law, could not, because of its special and original nature, be overridden by domestic legal provisions, however framed, without being deprived of its character as Community law and without the legal basis of the Community itself being called into question.

---

1. The Court used the Article numbers that were relevant at that time. The new numbering is inserted in this quotation for ease of reference. The principle of supremacy applies to the EC treaty pillar.

---

right at the start of the *Costa* judgment with the Court making the fundamental point that the treaty has created its own legal system that is an integral part of the legal systems of the member states and that the states in creating such a legal system have limited their sovereign rights and created a body of law that binds both themselves and their nationals.

The explicit declaration of a new legal order in *Costa* was not surprising given the radical step already taken the previous February in Van Gend en Loos where the ECJ stated that "the Community constitutes a new legal order of international law for the benefit of which the states have limited their sovereign rights, albeit within limited fields, and the subjects of which comprise not only member states but also their nationals."[28] In reaching this conclusion it considered the spirit, the general scheme, and the wording of the treaty. The conclusion of the judgment is nonetheless more than the sum of its parts, as nothing in the treaty suggested that individuals could receive rights and have obligations imposed on them by the then EEC law nor that it was a new legal order. Despite the weakness of the legal argument of the Court, these two cases have formed the basis for the emergence of the two key constitutional principles of EU law: supremacy and direct effect (of which more below), with the ECJ time and time again reasserting in particular the principle of supremacy.

The judgments in these cases combine strong declaratory and aspirational statements as to the new legal order with a rationale of efficacy. This left many questions unanswered, the most important of which was how could the EEC, as it then was called, constitute a supreme legal order creating obligations for individuals when it was silent on the protection of fundamental rights? This question became all the more acute when the Court extended the principle by holding that EEC law was supreme even over national constitutions. The validity of EEC law could not be called into question by any national constitutional law—even one pertaining to fundamental rights. Two rationales for this were put forward: first, it would undermine the uniformity and the efficacy of EEC law; and second, more fundamentally, the very character of EEC law and the legal basis of the EEC itself would be called into question. Thus there is a shift in the reasoning of the Court—from making a positive statement as to the nature of EEC law as a new legal order to seeing any incursion on the validity or uniformity of EEC law by a conflicting national law as a threat to its very nature. The ECJ, adopting strongly defensive language, saw any encroachment by national law on EEC law as imperiling "the very foundations of the Treaty."[29]

THE SUPREMACY DOCTRINE AND NATIONAL CONSTITUTIONAL COURTS

The ratcheting up of the rhetoric of the Court and its defense of the supremacy principle arose in the context of the reluctance of some constitutional courts to accept it. At this time there were six member states. For Luxembourg and the Netherlands the principle of supremacy for international treaties was already part of domestic law so the issue was unproblematic. The Belgian courts also accepted it with alacrity, Belgian law being silent on the point. France, Italy and Germany were reluctant to accept the principle. This is a reflection of three different factors.[30]

First, for these states the idea of an international treaty having automatic priority over domestic law and especially the constitution was novel. The ECJ tried to get around this by separating EU law out from ordinary international law. Nonetheless, while the French Cour de Cassation accepted the principle in 1975 for all French ordinary courts, it was 1989 before the Conseil d'Etat, the supreme administrative court, accepted it.[31] This was despite the fact that there was a provision in the French constitution giving priority to international treaties even over later French laws.

Second, there were (rightly) serious concerns about what was then essentially a trade treaty being able to override the strong rights in the German (and Italian) constitutions.

Third, in terms of institutional "fit" and from a procedural position, the introduction of the supremacy principle required national courts to disapply national law—something most of them did not have power to do under domestic law. This power marked a big departure which they were reluctant to undertake without the endorsement of their own constitutional courts. This was true of the German and the Italian courts.

The more intractable issue however has been that of the protection of fundamental rights with both the German and Italian constitutional courts retaining the power under their own laws to rule on the application of EU law should it impinge on fundamental rights.[32] What we see is a standoff between these courts and the ECJ. They accept the functional concern that EU law does need to be supreme in order to be effective but that this is the case only where it is appropriate. Where an EU law breaches a fundamental constitutional right then these constitutional courts have indicated that they may not recognize the supremacy principle.

For those states that joined after the early supremacy cases in the 1970s, the importance of the principle was obfuscated by the consensus model operating at the Council level. For the English courts there was the well-established principle of parliamentary sovereignty that in essence does not allow any earlier Parliament to bind any later Parliament and UK accession was predicated on no more than an Act of Parliament. The acceptance of the principle did not occur until 1989 and even now, if Parliament were to expressly and unequivocally choose to derogate from its EU law obligations it is not clear which law the national courts would recognize.[33] The Irish constitution was modified so as not to cause difficulty with the principle but the Supreme Court held that any additional transfer of sovereignty to the EU requires a change of the constitution that can only be achieved through popular referendum.[34]

States that acceded later to the Union where the impact of supremacy was more apparent could ensure that their constitutions addressed the supremacy issue directly although this creates the position that the supremacy of EU law is accepted by the national courts because of what national law says. The EU law principle is mediated through national law. But even with later accessions, the issue can be unresolved as can be most clearly seen in the Polish constitutional court decision which sets out a clear statement of national constitutional sovereignty.

Thus there are competing visions of EU law. The ECJ has identified it as a new legal order to which the states have transferred their sovereignty. On the

Box 9.6   Polish Membership of the European Union (Accession Treaty) (Polish Constitutional Court), judgment K18/04 of May 11, 2005

12. The concept and model of European law created a new situation, where, within each Member State, autonomous legal orders co-exist and are simultaneously operative. . . . The existence of the relative autonomy of both, national and Community, legal orders in no way signifies an absence of interaction between them. Furthermore, it does not exclude the possibility of a collision between regulations of Community law and the Constitution.

13. Such a collision would occur in the event that an irreconcilable inconsistency appeared between a constitutional norm and a Community norm, such as could not be eliminated by means of applying an interpretation which respects the mutual autonomy of European law and national law. Such a collision may in no event be resolved by assuming the supremacy of a Community norm over a constitutional norm. Furthermore, it may not lead to the situation where a constitutional norm loses its binding force and is substituted by a Community norm, nor may it lead to an application of the constitutional norm restricted to areas beyond the scope of Community law regulation. In such an event the Nation as the sovereign, or a State authority organ authorized by the Constitution to represent the Nation, would need to decide on: amending the Constitution; or causing modifications within the Community provisions; or, ultimately, on Poland's withdrawal from the European Union.

14. In particular, the norms of the Constitution within the field of individual rights and freedoms indicate a minimum and unsurpassable threshold which may not be lowered or questioned as a result of the introduction of Community provisions.

(*Source: http://www.trybunal.gov.pl/eng/summaries/documents/K_18_04_GB.pdf*)

other hand, some constitutional courts including the German, Italian, Danish,[35] Irish and Polish courts accept the principle only to the degree that that transfer of sovereignty is consistent with their constitutions and the fundamental rights protected thereunder. What we are left with is a form of legal pluralism with two parallel and equally valid legal orders (national law and EU law), mutually dependent and coexistent but framed by and responding to different norms (the treaty and national constitutions) and at the same time predicated on a shared vision of the rule of law, and increasingly, fundamental rights.[36] While the principle of supremacy is at last written into the draft constitution, which would also render binding the Charter of Fundamental Rights, the tensions, compromises and parallelism between national constitutions and EU law are likely to continue with a zone of indeterminacy—despite the clear and unequivocal language of the ECJ—between it and national constitutional courts.[37]

EU Law as a Tool for Integration

THE DOCTRINE OF DIRECT EFFECT

In conjunction with the development of the supremacy principle, the ECJ also set out the doctrine of direct effect. This is the twin constitutionalizing principle of the EU. Under this doctrine, EU law confers rights and imposes obligations on the citizens of the EU as well as the member states, and this feature fundamentally distinguishes it from international law.

Under this doctrine, provided a measure is sufficiently clear, it can be relied on by an individual in a national court, i.e., it is directly effective within the national legal order. Unlike the principle of supremacy, which is conceptually straightforward, this doctrine is more problematic. There is a tension between the instrumentality of the law as a tool for integration and the rule of law. EU law is a tool of integration but that can never be its sole purpose as conceived by the ECJ. It is also concerned with principles of procedural fairness, consistency, and equality as embodied in the rule of law.

This tension between efficacy and doctrinal coherence arises in part out of the multilevel nature of EU law (and governance) and is apparent in the debate surrounding the direct effect of directives. Directives are EU legal measures that are binding on member states only as to the result to be achieved—it is for the states to decide what means to adopt to achieve that objective.[38] Given this split, there is generally a two-year implementation period between enactment at the EU level and implementation at the national level. This can be contrasted with regulations, which apply directly, uniformly, and in their entirety without the need for any

---

Box 9.7   Case 26/62 Van Gend en Loos v Nederlandse Administratie der Belastingen (1963) ECR 1

The conclusion to be drawn from this is that the Community constitutes a new legal order of international law for the benefit of which the states have limited their sovereign rights, albeit within limited fields, and the subjects of which comprise not only Member States but also their nationals. Independently of the legislation of Member States, Community law therefore not only imposes obligations on individuals but is also intended to confer upon them rights which become part of their legal heritage. These rights arise not only where they are expressly granted by the Treaty, but also by reason of obligations which the Treaty imposes in a clearly defined way upon individuals as well as upon the Member States and upon the institutions of the Community.

national implementing legislation. The ECJ has placed considerable weight on this distinction given the discretion states have under directives. If the two-year period for the implementation of a directive has expired and a member state has not implemented it correctly, then an individual may rely on the directive against that state before a court. A state cannot rely on its own wrong-doing (in this instance, the failure to meet its obligations under the directive) as a defense.[39]

Directives are addressed only to states and impose no obligations on individuals; thus in the eyes of the Court it is not possible to rely on a directive against another individual.[40] Hence directives are directly effective only vertically against the state but not horizontally against other individuals. The Court maintains this position even though it creates unevenness in the application of the law. It is possible to rely on the directive (after the expiration of the time limit for implementation) only if an individual is lucky enough to be able to frame their case so the state is the defendant.

The ECJ emphasizes the efficacy of EU law in its case law on direct effect. Yet that efficacy is undermined by the limited direct effect of directives. The Court has instead developed alternative means of improving efficacy. First, it has defined what constitutes "the state" very widely, thus extending the scope of EU law.[41] The problem with this is that agencies that may be sued under a non-implemented directive may have no responsibility or ability to ensure its implementation.

Second, national courts are required to interpret national law as far as possible in a manner consistent with EU laws introduced both before and after the national law in issue in order to avoid inconsistency between the two sets of laws.[42]

Finally, there are a small number of cases giving rise to what is termed "incidental direct effect," where one particular directive can be relied on even in a dispute between two private parties. The context for this underlines the efficacy considerations of the Court. Member states are required to notify the Commission of their draft measures implementing directives so the Commission can ensure they meet EU law requirements. The measures do not become operative unless notified. In this case law, where a private party sought to rely on a national technical measure that was not notified to the Commission, the ECJ held that the failure of the state to notify means that the national measure cannot be relied on in court. This means the unnotified national regulation is unenforceable. The net effect is that this particular directive can be relied on in a dispute against another private party, but the ECJ refuses to see this as allowing direct effect of directives against private parties. The distinction is doctrinally possible to see but is very fine for such an important doctrine.[43] These cases can be seen as specific to ensuring that member states notify implementing measures so the Commission can monitor their compliance and hence the effectiveness of EU law at the national level, but the effect of the cases is the same as horizontal direct effect. The instrumentality of the law in this instance and the weakness of the legal analysis are such as to underline the normative frailty of the law in this important constitutional context of the overarching effect of EU law for individuals.

STATE LIABILITY

The doctrine of state liability for breach of EU law has been developed also by the ECJ to improve effectiveness. The synergy between the instrumental and the normative here is also important, and in the *Köbler v. Austria* case the ECJ provides a radical vision of the scope of state responsibility and liability and, in doing so, redefines the relationship between the ECJ and national courts.[44] This relationship is pivotal in the development of the EU legal order, and the role of national courts is of critical importance.

Individuals can claim damages against a state where it breaches EU law provided certain conditions are met. The measure relied on does not have to be directly effective, but it must have been intended to confer rights on individuals. Two other conditions must also be met: the breach must be sufficiently serious, and there must be a direct causal link between the breach of the obligation on the state and the loss or damage sustained by the injured parties.[45] The breach is sufficiently serious where the measure was imprecisely worded, was reasonably capable of having the erroneous construction in fact given to it, and there was no case law available for guidance.[46] This condition addresses the fact that whether a measure is correctly implemented or not may not be apparent where the law is complex. The final condition of causation is standard—damages are only available where the losses suffered were due to the legal wrong.

There are two controversial dimensions to this doctrine. First, it is debatable whether it does advance the efficacy of EU law in the longer term to have coercive sanctions available against member states at the national level in addition to the declaratory judgments at the EU level that can ultimately lead to fines. The relationship between EU and national law is, as we have seen, a complex one—the condition of the imposition of liability itself makes that clear by requiring a sufficiently serious breach of EU law. This complexity is not limited to interpretation of legal measures, but is about the alignment and operation of what are parallel but interdependent legal orders at the national and supranational levels. If there are problems of "fit" with states failing to comply then the issue may involve difficult issues that extend well beyond law and that might be more appropriately addressed in the wider context of political accountability at the subnational, national, and supranational levels.[47] In other words, it is questionable whether the national courts are the appropriate institutions within which to tackle the maverick state failing to live up to its obligations under EU law. This may be better addressed through the Council and, in some cases, by the Commission bringing the state before the ECJ.

The counterargument is that EU law must be rendered effective and it is important for individuals to have redress when they suffer loss. This places the emphasis on individual rights and their relationship with EU law over and above the wider debate as to state accountability and the balance between legal orders, favoring a response embedded in the courts and the legal order rather than a political response.

The second controversial element of this debate is that a member state can now be liable for damages where an individual has suffered loss due to a national court of last instance (i.e., from whose decision there is no appeal) having manifestly infringed EU law in the way it applied it.

Box 9.8   C-224/01 Köbler v. Austria (2003) ECR I-10239

33. In the light of the essential role played by the judiciary in the protection of the rights derived by individuals from Community rules, the full effectiveness of those rules would be called in question and the protection of those rights would be weakened if individuals were precluded from being able, under certain conditions, to obtain reparation when their rights are affected by an infringement of Community law attributable to a decision of a court of a Member State adjudicating at last instance.

34. It must be stressed, in that context, that a court adjudicating at last instance is by definition the last judicial body before which individuals may assert the rights conferred on them by Community law. Since an infringement of those rights by a final decision of such a court cannot thereafter normally be corrected, individuals cannot be deprived of the possibility of rendering the State liable in order in that way to obtain legal protection of their rights.

35. Moreover, it is, in particular, in order to prevent rights conferred on individuals by Community law from being infringed that under the third paragraph of Article 234 EC a court against whose decisions there is no judicial remedy under national law is required to make a reference to the Court of Justice.

36. Consequently, it follows from the requirements inherent in the protection of the rights of individuals relying on Community law that they must have the possibility of obtaining redress in the national courts for the damage caused by the infringement of those rights owing to a decision of a court adjudicating at last instance. . . .

51. As to the conditions to be satisfied for a Member State to be required to make reparation for loss and damage caused to individuals as a result of breaches of Community law for which the State is responsible, the Court has held that these are threefold: the rule of law infringed must be intended to confer rights on individuals; the breach must be sufficiently serious; and there must be a direct causal link between the breach of the obligation incumbent on the State and the loss or damage sustained by the injured parties . . .

52. State liability for loss or damage caused by a decision of a national court adjudicating at last instance which infringes a rule of Community law is governed by the same conditions.

53. With regard more particularly to the second of those conditions and its application with a view to establishing possible State liability owing to a decision of a national court adjudicating at last instance, regard must be had to the specific nature of the judicial function and to the legitimate requirements of legal certainty. . . . State liability for an infringement of Community law by a decision of a national court adjudicating at last instance can be incurred only in the exceptional case where the court has manifestly infringed the applicable law.

54. In order to determine whether that condition is satisfied, the national court hearing a claim for reparation must take account of all the factors which characterize the situation put before it.

55. Those factors include, in particular, the degree of clarity and precision of the rule infringed, whether the infringement was intentional, whether the error of law was excusable or inexcusable, the position taken, where applicable, by a Community institution and non-compliance by the court in question with its obligation to make a reference for a preliminary ruling under the third paragraph of Article 234 EC.

56. In any event, an infringement of Community law will be sufficiently serious where the decision concerned was made in manifest breach of the case-law of the Court in the matter.

This decision highlights two particular problems with the state liability doctrine. First, as with the supremacy doctrine, the ECJ takes no account of how national courts can apply the doctrine and whether or not the national legal order is designed to accommodate doctrines such as this. It inverts the hierarchy of national courts such that a lower court can now review the judgment of the highest court in the land in order to establish whether or not it has manifestly infringed EU law. It undermines legal certainty and, from a judicial politics perspective, creates an element of coercion between the ECJ and the highest national courts. In the light of the supremacy debates, we see national constitutional courts marking a limit to the supremacy doctrine predicated either on human rights or the extent to which national governments can hand over sovereignty to the EU. Now, in the doctrine of state liability, we see the ECJ setting a limit on those same courts and underlining their obligations in the way they apply EU law. Granted the threshold set is high—the error on the part of the national court has to be obvious before liability for damages is considered. In *Köbler* itself, the error was not deemed manifest and it is unlikely that the issue is one that is likely to arise very often, but it constitutes another important marker in the dynamic relationship between EU law and national law and between the ECJ and national courts that defines the constitutionalizing process of EU law.

NATIONAL COURTS AS EU COURTS:
THE PRELIMINARY REFERENCE PROCEDURE

EU law could not have become a tool of integration without the national courts. The ECJ may define and interpret EU law, but it is the national courts that give effect to it and breathe life into its sometimes Delphic pronouncements. The higher national courts, as we have seen, enter into a dialogue with the ECJ as to the nature of EU law through their judgments. Lower courts have had their role and position within the national legal order redefined by the ECJ. All national courts are now constitutional courts in that (1) they can disapply national laws inconsistent with EU law; (2) can award damages against the state where it is found to have breached EU law, and (3) most radically, they can even review a judgment of their own highest courts where a party claims damages for a manifest error in relation to EU law.

The importance of the role of the national courts can be best seen where their capacity to deal with the EU responsibilities thrust upon them do not fit within their judicial systems. This happened most spectacularly in relation to the rather mundane issue of Sunday trading hours. When parties claimed that English Sunday trading restrictions breached free-movement rules by restricting the scope for sales of imported goods from other member states, the ECJ initially gave a decision leaving much discretion to national courts. The effect was to cause considerable disarray in the lowest-level courts in England, where the issue was addressed. Court diaries were completely overwhelmed as parties sought to argue the niceties of EU internal market rules in courts where judges are part-time and not legally trained. Eventually, the ECJ reversed its position and sought to bring an end to the legal uncertainty.[48] Without engaging in the substantive rules, the Sunday trading debacle shows the need for some consistency between the obligations of national courts and their role, resources, and status within their own legal systems.

The relationship between the ECJ and national courts is centered on the key legal tool of the preliminary reference procedure in Article 234EC.

This provision allows the ECJ to answer questions sent to it by national courts as to the validity and interpretation of EU law. The mechanism is centered on a court/court dynamic with individuals having no right to a reference. It is for the national court to decide whether or not to make one. It suspends proceedings while it is pending and applies the ruling to the case when the ECJ has given its answer. In theory, it is the ECJ who interprets and the national court that applies the law, but in practice the distinction between interpretation and application is blurred, with the decision of the ECJ often leaving little room for doubt as to the final outcome of the case.

National courts generally are compliant with rulings, although this is difficult to measure because indirect means of avoiding a ruling may be possible given the complexity of litigation.[49] About 45 percent of cases before the ECJ

Box 9.9   A234EC

The Court of Justice of the European Union shall have jurisdiction to give preliminary rulings concerning:

  (a) the interpretation of this treaty;
  (b) the validity and interpretation of acts of the institutions of the Community and of the ECB. . . .

When such a question is raised before a court or tribunal of a Member State, that court or tribunal may, if it considers that a decision on the question is necessary to enable it to give judgment, request the Court of Justice to give a ruling thereon.

When any such question is raised in a case pending before a court or tribunal of a Member State against whose decisions there is no judicial remedy under national law that court or tribunal shall bring the matter before the Court of Justice.

are preliminary references.[50] It is the primary legal tool for ensuring a uniform interpretation of EU law in national courts. This allows the ECJ to participate in judicial decisions anywhere in the EU in any tribunal that decides to refer questions to it. The willingness of national courts to avail themselves of this interpretative tool, combined with the creative use of it by the ECJ, has underpinned the twin doctrines of direct effect and supremacy.

The procedure treats courts of last resort (which necessarily includes the highest courts) differently from other courts. If there is no appeal from a decision, then the national court has no discretion and must refer the matter to the ECJ. This mandatory rule has been softened by the ECJ itself—no reference is needed if the matter is so obvious as to leave no room for reasonable doubt.[51] Senior national courts are thus able, and indeed arguably encouraged, to interpret EU law for themselves. This can be seen as accepting the absence of references from some constitutional courts or as strategically availing itself of the expertise of the most senior courts in the EU to limit the overwhelming number of cases coming before it.[52] Courts from whose decision there is an appeal have discretion as to whether to make a reference or not. In all cases, the reference must be necessary for the outcome of the case.

National courts have been transformed into European courts by the constitutionalization of EU law and their acceptance of that role is the key to the transformation of EU law. The interesting question is why and to what extent they have been willing to accept this role, and there is an extensive literature on this question. Acceptance is not straightforward, as the following factors (which are by no means exhaustive) indicate.

The nature of judicial identity as nonpolitical is one that is shared between courts—including all courts in the EU—and is an important factor in the acceptance and use of the procedure driven by a commitment to the rule of law, a shared discourse, and institutional autonomy embedded in liberal democracies.[53] This sense of identity is important. At the same time, a distinction can be drawn between courts, such as those between lower and higher courts.[54] Lower courts, through their acceptance of the EU court mantle, acquire additional jurisdiction and power as well as enhanced status and the sense of belonging to an international judiciary. For higher courts that enjoy considerable powers and status, acceptance of EU law may mark a limitation on their powers and may lead to a review of their decision where none previously existed. Their powers may also be enhanced vis-à-vis national legislatures and governments where EU law confers additional powers on national courts to review national laws and government decisions.[55]

The substantive law being considered is also relevant. Some fields may pose particular difficulties for some judiciaries, e.g., abortion in Ireland, where references are likely to be avoided. In other fields, the ECJ can be seen as a resource to assist in the interpretation of difficult legal concepts or as a decoy in politically difficult decisions where the outcome may provoke strong political or popular reaction. It is also important to distinguish acceptance of EU law in the day-to-day operation of the courts in trade, tax, and other matters from the larger constitutionalizing questions of the supremacy of EU law over national constitutions. Much of the case law where the impact of EU law is raised does not raise constitutional issues but instead relates to more mundane issues. For example, regulation and taxation are the main substantive areas in case law in the UK.[56]

Procedural and institutional issues are also important. How standing—the right to bring a particular case—is acquired may have an impact on prevalence of cases. For example, sex-discrimination issues are raised in the English courts partly because of the strong government agency that has standing to bring the matter before the national courts.[57] The extent to which judicial activism is possible or envisaged within the national legal order may impact on whether or not references are made.

Inside the (uncertain) boundaries of the supremacy doctrine, national courts have generally accepted EU law—at least sufficiently to allow the system to operate and become embedded over time. Even outside the contentious issue of the supremacy of EU law over national constitutions, acceptance is a complex issue shaped by multiple procedural, institutional, and substantive factors.

Conclusion

EU law is distinct both from the political system within which it operates and from other legal orders. It is, as the ECJ has reminded us so many times, a new legal order. Yet even as a new legal order it shares characteristics common to national law, such as its commitment to the rule of law and respect for fundamental rights. Its genesis in an international treaty gives it a strong international-law "flavor," while it also is influenced by the two legal traditions found in the member states: common law and civil law. A primary fault line, common to all legal orders but perhaps more pronounced in the EU law context, is that between ensuring the efficacy of the law and meeting the requirements of the rule of law. Thus debates about the scope of EU competence will continue, with a balance constantly needing to be struck between the perceived need for EU action and the corresponding issue of the democratic legitimacy of that action. The fault line is apparent in the limited direct effect of directives and in the standoff between national constitutional courts and the ECJ over the precise scope of the supremacy principle. The resulting legal pluralism and judicial dialogue through intermittent case law will remain dynamic even if the supremacy principle is incorporated in future treaty revisions. The engagement of national courts at all levels in the more mundane aspects of EU law legitimates what is perhaps now best described as a "new-ish" legal order. National courts, having shown that they take EU law seriously, will assume increased responsibility for it. Such fragmentation will require a more pronounced hierarchy between them and the ECJ. Such hierarchy is relatively unproblematic, as between the ECJ and lower national courts, but, despite *Köbler*, national constitutional courts will continue to act as judicial equals. Thus legal pluralism will remain a hallmark of EU law, which is generally accepted despite the diversity of legal cultures and political needs within which it operates. The EU legal order thus remains a, if not *the*, primary example of "unity in diversity" within Europe.

Notes

1. For ease of reference, the term "EU law" is used throughout even though historically, early judgments refer to European Economic Community law and much of the doctrine discussed applies only to the EC treaty, the largest and most important part of the EU treaties.

2. On autopoiesis, see Günter Teubner, *Law as an Autopoietic System*, Oxford: Blackwell, 1993; Imelda Maher, "Community Law in the National Legal Order: A Systems Analysis," *Journal of Common Market Studies*, 36(2), 1993, 237–254.

3. See, for example, paragraph 35 of case C-540/03 *European Parliament v. Council* June 27, 2006, not yet reported. Available at: http://curia.eu.int/jurisp/cgi-bin/form.pl?lang=en&Submit=Submit&alldocs=alldocs&docj=docj&docop=docop&docor=docor&docjo=docjo&numaff=&datefs=&datefe=&nomusuel=&domaine=&mots=human+rights&resmax=100.

4. [2000] OJ C 364/1.

5. Article 6 TEU.

6. See generally Konrad Zweigert and Hein Kötz, *Introduction to Comparative Law*, 3rd ed., Oxford: Clardendon, 1998.

7. Nigel Foster, *EU Law*, Oxford: Oxford University Press, 2006, p. 70.

8. See Article 230 EC.

9. Article 5 EC.

10. Case C-377/98 *Netherlands v. European Parliament and Council* (Biotechnology Directive) [2001] *European Court Reports* (ECR) I-70789, and case C-491/01 *R v. Secretary of State for Health ex parte British American Tobacco* [2002] ECR I-11453.

11. Article I-12–Article I-17 of the draft constitutional treaty.

12. See, for example, N. W. Barber, "The Limited Modesty of Subsidiarity," *European Law Journal*, 11(3), 2005, 308–325.

13. Article 228 EC.

14. Article 151 EC.

15. Articles 85–90 EC.

16. The first draft appeared in 1973; see D. G. Goyder, *EC Competition Law*, 3rd ed., Oxford: Clarendon, 1998, p. 383.

17. See generally Karen J. Alter, *Establishing the Supremacy of European Law: The Making of an International Rule of Law in Europe*, Oxford, Oxford University Press, 2001.

18. Case 26/62 *Van Gend en Loos v Nederlandse Administratie der Belastingen* [1963] ECR 1.

19. Article 234 EC and the modified provisions are Article 68 EC and Article 35 TEU.

20. Karen J. Alter and Sophie Meunier-Aitsahalia, "Judicial Politics in the European Community: European Integration and the Path-Breaking Cassis de Dijon Decision," *Comparative Political Studies*, 24(4), 1994, 535–561.

21. Alter, *Establishing the Supremacy*, ch. 6.

22. Case 120/78 *Rewe-Zentral Ag v. Bundesmonopolverwaltung für Branntwein* (Cassis de Dijon) [1979] ECR 649; [1979] 3 Common Market Law Reports (CMLR) 494.

23. Communication from the Commission of October 3, 1980, concerning the consequences of the judgment given by the Court of Justice on February 20, 1979, in Case 120/78 OJ 1980 C 256/2.

24. See generally Fritz Scharpf, *Governing in Europe: Effective and Democratic?* Oxford: Oxford University Press, 1999; and Alter and Meunier-Aitsahalia, "Judicial Politics in the European Community" above n. 20.

25. Article 228 EC.

26. Armin Schäfer, "A New Form of Governance? Comparing the Open Method of Coordination to Multilateral Surveillance by the IMF and the OECD," *Journal of European Public Policy*, 13(1), 2006, 70–88. Dermot Hodson and Imelda Maher, "The Open Method as a New Mode of Governance: The Case of Soft Economic Policy Co-ordination," *Journal of Common Market Studies*, 39(4), 2001, 719–745.

27. K. W. Abbott, R. O. Keohane, A. Moravcsik, A-M Slaughter, and D. Snidel, "The Concept of Legalization," *International Organization*, 54(3), 2000, 401–419; Francis Snyder, "The Effectiveness of European Community Law: Institutions, Processes, Tools and Techniques," in T. Daintith (ed.), *Implementing EC Law in the United Kingdom: Structures for Indirect Rule*, Chichester: Wiley, 1995; David Trubek and Louise Trubek, "Hard and Soft Law in the Construction of Social Europe: The Role of the Open Method of Co-ordination," *European Law Journal*, 11(3), 2005, 343–364.

28. Case 26/62, above at note 18.

29. Case 11/70 Internationale Handelsgesellschaft [1970] ECR 1125; [1972] CMLR 255. Case 106/77 Simmenthal [1978] ECR 263; [1978] 3 CMLR 263 paragraph 18.

30. Bruno de Witte, "Direct Effect, Supremacy and the Nature of the Legal Order," in Paul Craig and Gráinne de Búrca (eds.), *The Evolution of EU Law,* Oxford: Oxford University Press, 1999.

31. Cour de Cassation, Decision of 24 May 1975 in *Administration de Douanes v. Société 'Café Jacques Vabre'* et SARL Weigel et Cie [1975] 2 CMLR 336; Conseil d'Etat, Decision of 20 Oct. 1989 Nicolo [1990] 1 CMLR 173.

32. For Germany, see *Brunner v. The European Union Treaty* [1994] 1 CMLR 57. For Italy, see *Frontini v. Ministero delle Finanze* [1974] 2 CMLR 372.

33. Paul Craig, "Britain in the European Union," in Jeffrey Jowell and Dawn Oliver (eds.), *The Changing Constitution,* 4th ed., Oxford: Oxford University Press, 2000.

34. *Crotty v. An Taoiseach* [1987] IR 713.

35. *Carlsen v. Prime Minister,* judgment of the Højesteret, 6 April 1998 [1999] 3 CMLR 854.

36. Neil McCormick, *Questioning Sovereignty,* Oxford: Oxford University Press, 1999.

37. Article I-5a: "The Constitution, and law adopted by the Union's Institutions in exercising competences conferred on it, shall have primacy over the law of the Member States." Per Cramér, "Does the Codification of the Principle of Supremacy Matter?" *Cambridge Yearbook of European Legal Studies,* 7, 2004–2005, 189–211.

38. Article 249 EC. The Treaty expressly excludes Framework Directives in the third pillar from the doctrine of direct effect; see Article 34 TEU.

39. Case 148/78 Ratti [1979] ECR 1629.

40. C-91/92 *Faccini Dori v. Recreb* [1994] ECR I-3325.

41. C-188/89 *Foster v. British Gas* [1990] ECR I-3133.

42. This is called indirect direct effect. See case C-106/89 *Marleasing v. La Comercial* [1990] ECR I-4135, [1992] 1 CMLR 305. Even though Article 34 TEU excludes framework directives from having direct effect, this interpretative obligation on national courts applies even to those directives; see case C-105/03 *Pupino,* June 16, 2005 available at curia.eu.

43. See Stephen Weatherill, "Breach of Directives and Breach of Contract," *European Law Review,* 26(2), 2001, 177–186. The relevant directive is 98/34, laying down a procedure for the provision of information in the field of technical standards and regulations [1998] OJ L204/37. The leading case is C-443/98 *Unilever Italia SpA v. Central Food SpA* [2000] ECR I-7535.

44. C-224/01 *Köbler v. Austria* [2003] ECR I-10239. See also case C-173/03 *Traghetti del Mediterraneo SpA v. Italy,* 13 June 2006, available at curia.eu.

45. C-46 and 48/93 *Brasserie du Pêcheur v. Germany* and *R v. Secretary of State for Transport ex parte Factortame (No. 3)* [1996] ECR I-1029.

46. C-392/93 *R. v. HM Treasury, ex p. BT* [1996] ECR I-1631.

47. See generally Carol Harlow, "Francovich and the Problem of the Disobedient State," *European Law Journal,* 2(3), 1996, 199–225.

48. Richard Rawlings, "The Eurolaw Game: Some Deductions from a Saga," *Journal of Law and Society,* 20(3), 1993, 309–340. See case 145/88 *Torfaen* [1989] ECR 3851 and the definitive resolution in C-169/91 *Council of the City of Stoke-on-Trent* [1992] ECR I-6635.

49. See Damian Chalmers, Christos Hadjiemmanuil, Giorgio Monti, and Adam Tomkins, *European Union Law*, Cambridge: Cambridge University Press, 2006, p. 280.

50. Chalmers, Hadjiemmanuil, Monti, and Tomkins, *European Union Law*, p. 281.

51. Case 283/81 Srl CILFIT [1982] ECR 3415.

52. Chalmers, Hadjiemmanuil, Monti, and Tomkins, *European Union Law*, p. 300.

53. See generally Damian Chalmers, "Judicial Preferences and the Community Legal Order," *Modern Law Review*, 60(2), 1997, 164–199.

54. Karen Alter, "The European Court's Political Power," *West European Politics*, 19(3), 1996, 458–487.

55. Walter Mattli and Anne-Marie Slaughter, "The Role of National Courts in the Process of European Integration: Accounting for Judicial Preferences and Constraints," in Anne-Marie Slaughter, Alec Stone Sweet, and J.H.H. Weiler (eds.), *The European Courts and National Courts: Doctrine and Jurisprudence*, Oxford: Hart, 1998.

56. Damian Chalmers, "The Much Ado About Judicial Politics in the United Kingdom: A Statistical Analysis of Reported Decisions of United Kingdom Courts Invoking EU Law 1973–1998," Jean Monnet Paper 2000/1 (2000).

57. Catherine Barnard, "A European Litigation Strategy: The Case of the Equal Opportunities Commission," in Jo Shaw and Gillian More (eds.), *New Legal Dynamics of European Union*, Clarendon: Oxford University Press, 1995.

Suggested Readings

Alter, Karen J., *Establishing the Supremacy of European Law: The Making of an International Rule of Law in Europe*, Oxford: Oxford University Press, 2001.

Bermann, George, Rodger Goebel, William Davey, and Eleanor Fox, *Casebook: Cases and Materials on European Community Law*, 2nd ed., St. Paul, Minn.: West Publishing, 2002, with 2002 and 2004 supplements.

de Búrca, Gráinne, and Joanne Scott (eds.), *Law and New Approaches to Governance in the European Union and the United States*, Oxford: Hart, 2006.

Chalmers, Damian, Christos Hadjiemmanuil, Giorgio Monti, and Adam Tomkins, *European Union Law*, Cambridge: Cambridge University Press, 2006.

Craig, Paul, and Gráinne de Búrca, *EU Law: Text, Cases and Materials*, 3rd ed., Oxford: Oxford University Press, 2003.

Craig, Paul, and Gráinne de Búrca (eds.), *The Evolution of EU Law*, Oxford: Oxford University Press, 1999.

Douglas-Scott, Sionnaidh, *Constitutional Law of the European Union*, Harlow: Longmans, 2002.

Hartley, Trevor C., *European Union Law in a Global Context: Text, Cases and Materials*, Cambridge: Cambridge University Press, 2004.

Weiler, J.H.H., *The Constitution of Europe—Do the New Clothes Have an Emperor?* Cambridge: Cambridge University Press, 1998.

Weiler, J.H.H., "The Transformation of Europe," *100 Yale Law Journal*, 2403–2483, 1991.

CHAPTER 10

EU Enlargement:
The Return to Europe

John Van Oudenaren

The collapse of communism caught the European Community (EC) by surprise. At the time of its third enlargement in January 1986, few politicians in Brussels or the national capitals would have predicted that within five years they would be debating membership for ten candidate countries from Central and Eastern Europe, three of which were then still part of the Soviet Union. It was assumed that with the accession of Portugal and Spain, the Community more or less had reached the limits of its expansion in Western Europe and that the challenge of the future was to "deepen" cooperation among existing members rather than "widen" to new members. The outlook changed dramatically as Soviet power withdrew from Europe and the newly democratic countries of Central and Eastern Europe looked westward for help in bolstering their political systems and their newly established market economies.

Change in the region began in the late 1980s, after the coming to power in the Soviet Union of the reformist Mikhail Gorbachev in March 1985. Preoccupied with his own country's internal economic problems, Gorbachev made clear that he would not interfere with changes that fellow "socialist" countries might undertake to revive economic growth and close the widening technology and productivity gaps with the West. Gorbachev was a reformer, not a revolutionary. He intended to improve and streamline the communist system, not dismantle it. However, by 1989 the process he had helped to unleash had largely spun out of his control, as popular movements in the countries of Central and Eastern Europe rose up against their communist leaders.

Partially free elections took place in Poland in June 1989, resulting in a resounding victory for the opposition Solidarity movement. In the same month, roundtable talks between government and opposition began in Hungary, aimed at fundamental change in the political system. By mid-1989, there was reason to hope that at least these two countries were on a path that would lead to the establishment of market economies and pluralist political systems.

Western governments felt a strong need to respond to these signs of change and to support them with external aid. At the July 1989 Paris summit of the seven largest industrialized democracies (the G-7), the leaders of the West and Japan

343

issued a declaration of support for economic and political reform in Eastern Europe and called for an international conference to coordinate Western aid to Poland and Hungary. In December 1989, the EC Council of Ministers approved PHARE (Pologne Hongrie: Actions pour la Reconversion Economique), a Community-funded program of technical assistance to encourage the development of private enterprise and the building of market-oriented economies.

By the fall of 1989 the reform process was accelerating, turning into a full-fledged, albeit largely peaceful, revolution against the communist order. In September, Hungary opened its border with Austria, allowing thousands of East German citizens to travel through Czechoslovakia and Hungary to West Germany. After months of mass demonstrations in Leipzig, Dresden, and other cities, on November 9 the Berlin Wall was thrown open by an East German government that could no longer control its borders. In November and December, opposition rallies led to the ouster of the communist regime in Czechoslovakia. In December, roundtable talks between government and opposition began in Bulgaria. For the most part these revolutions were peaceful, but they culminated in late December with bloody fighting in Romania between opposition and security forces, and the execution, on Christmas Day, of former dictator Nicolae Ceaucescu and his wife, Elena.

The most immediate political challenge facing Western governments was German unification. West German chancellor Helmut Kohl quickly seized the initiative on this issue, putting forward, in November 1989, a ten-point plan for creation of a German confederation. The United States supported unification, but Britain and France were skeptical. The Soviet Union had taken a hands-off attitude toward the changes in Eastern Europe, but it vigorously opposed unification. The Soviet Union still had several hundred thousand troops in the German Democratic Republic (GDR), and as a World War II victor power it had certain legal rights in Germany. In the GDR itself, it initially was unclear whether the voters would opt for rapid absorption by West Germany or whether they would seek to maintain some kind of separate identity within a German confederation.

By the fall of 1990, these uncertainties were resolved. In July, Kohl and Gorbachev met at a Soviet retreat in the Caucasus and reached agreement on the external aspects of German unity. Germany would remain in NATO, Soviet troops would be withdrawn, and a special bilateral treaty of friendship and cooperation between Germany and the Soviet Union would be signed. On August 31 the two German states signed a treaty on unification, and on September 12 the four victor powers concluded a treaty on the "final settlement with regard to Germany." On October 3, less than a year after the breaching of the Berlin Wall, Germany was united.

Unification had major implications for the EC. Most directly, it entailed the enlargement of the Community through the addition of the five states of the former GDR. By becoming a part of the Federal Republic, these states automatically joined the Community without the complex, formal accession process other new members faced. With the addition of sixteen million new citizens, Germany became by far the largest EC member state, but one that was less affluent, on a per capita basis, than it had been before unification. The eastern states immediately became eligible for EC regional aid funds traditionally earmarked for southern Europe and depressed regions of the Community. Indirectly, the challenge of anchoring a larger Germany in the west encouraged France and Germany to work together to reform and strengthen the EC, culminating in the conclusion, in February 1992, of the Treaty of Maastricht. The treaty established a new entity, the European Union (EU), that incorporated the existing Community along with new mechanisms for cooperation in foreign and security policy, justice, and home affairs.

The Europe Agreements

While focusing on the immediate question of Germany, the Community and its member states took up the broader challenge of stabilization in Central and Eastern Europe as a whole. Grant aid, loans, expanded trade, political dialogue, and support for selective admission to Western organizations all became elements in the Community's approach. At an extraordinary session of the European Council in November 1989, French president François Mitterrand proposed the establishment of a special bank to help finance economic transition in the Central and East European countries. The other member states embraced Mitterrand's idea, which led to the founding of the European Bank for Reconstruction and Development the following year. In July 1990, the Community extended its PHARE program to Bulgaria, Czechoslovakia, and Yugoslavia. Assistance to Romania was temporarily delayed, owing to the post-Ceausescu government's suppression of student demonstrations in the spring of 1990, but in 1991 Bucharest became eligible for PHARE grants.

Responding to requests for increased access to West European markets, the Community also set about negotiating new trade arrangements to replace those that had been concluded in the 1980s with the then still communist countries with their centrally planned economies. In August 1990, the European Commission proposed the conclusion of what it called "Europe Agreements" among the Community, its member states, and Hungary, Poland, and Czechoslovakia. The name was chosen to underline the difference between these agreements and the Community's association agreements with many countries outside Europe, notably in North Africa and the Middle East.

These agreements provided a legal framework to facilitate the expanding economic, commercial, and human contacts between the Community and countries that were rapidly emerging from communism. In addition, they offered an interim response to the requests from many of the countries of Central and Eastern Europe for rapid admission to the Community as full members. The EU was neither economically nor politically prepared to admit new members at this time, and few experts believed that the fragile Central and East European economies were ready to cope with the competitive pressures and demanding regulations that would come with full membership. The Europe Agreements thus were intended to establish a form of association that would help to prepare the Central and East European countries for membership, as well as provide concrete and symbolically important links to the Community that, while falling short of membership, reflected a commitment on the part of Western Europe's major economic bloc to take responsibility for its eastern neighbors. The preambles to the agreements noted the aspirations of the Central and East European signatories to join the Community, but they stopped short of guaranteeing that membership was assured.

The key economic provision of the Europe Agreements was the establishment, within a ten-year period, of free-trade arrangements between the Community and the associated countries. Expanded market access was controversial in some member states, where protectionist lobbies sought to maintain tight quotas on the import of iron and steel, textiles, and agricultural goods—the very items these countries had to sell. At one point Hungary and Poland threatened to suspend the negotiations unless they received a better offer from the Community negotiators. The deal was improved, and in December 1991 these two countries and Czechoslovakia concluded the first of the Europe Agreements. (The agreement with Czechoslovakia was later replaced, following the breakup of that country in 1993, by separate agreements with the Czech Republic and Slovakia.) Europe Agreements also were reached with Romania (February 1993), Bulgaria (March 1993), Estonia, Latvia, and Lithuania (June 1995), and Slovenia (June 1996).

Under the terms of the agreements, the Central and East European states were required to align their laws with those of the EU countries and to adopt EU rules on competition and many technical standards. In the forty years since the founding of the European Steel and Coal Community, the EU had passed some 100,000 pages of legislation. These laws in turn often required national legislation or rules to ensure their implementation. For the Central and East European states to cooperate successfully with their western neighbors, and especially to aspire to eventual membership, they had to undertake the arduous task of replacing communist (or nonexistent) laws with legislation compatible with that developed over the course of decades in the rest of Europe.

Under the provisions on financial cooperation, the Europe Agreements reaffirmed the availability of grant assistance under the PHARE program and made the Central and East European states eligible for loans from the European Investment Bank, the EC's Luxembourg-based bank that supports infrastructure projects in the Community itself. Reflecting the concern in Western Europe about possible surges of immigrants from the economically distressed east, the agreements were cautious with regard to the movement of workers. Their liberalizing effect in this sensitive area was rather modest, as they improved the lot of Central and East European workers already in EU countries rather than facilitating new flows of people.

Outside the economic sphere, the Europe Agreements provided for expanded political dialogue and cultural cooperation. High officials were to meet at regular intervals to discuss topics of common interest and to aim at achieving convergence in the foreign policy positions of the Central and East European states and the Union. Many cultural and educational exchange programs funded by the Community were extended to Central and Eastern Europe. To monitor implementation, each Europe Agreement provided for the establishment of an association council consisting of representatives of the EU, the member states, and the associated state. These councils were to meet at the ministerial level at least once each year to review progress and to take decisions regarding further action.

The Debate on Enlargement

The negotiation and early implementation of the Europe Agreements proceeded in parallel with a vigorous debate on enlargement throughout the continent. Almost immediately after assuming power, the postcommunist leaders of Central and Eastern Europe began to push for admission, as quickly as possible, to the EU and to other Western institutions such as NATO. This approach evoked an ambivalent response in Western Europe. On the one hand, political leaders were concerned about instability: the spread of ethnic conflict such as had erupted in the former Yugoslavia, surges of refugees and migrants, environmental disasters, and political extremism. Membership in a strengthened EU was probably the only way to ensure, over the long term, that upheaval and reversion to dictatorship were banished from the region. In addition, many in Western Europe felt a strong sense of obligation to their neighbors in Central and Eastern Europe—especially to those who had led the fight against communism. Welcoming these people into the European family was clearly the right thing to do.

On the other hand, the costs and complications of enlargement promised to be enormous and could well derail the ambitious plans of the 1980s to create a Union with a single currency, a common foreign and security policy, and increased powers for its central institutions. There also was the difficult question of where to draw the line—even if the decision in principle to admit former communist countries was taken, it still was necessary to decide which countries, how many, and according to what criteria. It was not too difficult to envision Germany's eastern neighbors, Poland and the Czech Republic, becoming members, but what about the countries in the unstable Balkans? The question of membership became even more acute when, at the end of 1991, the Soviet Union dissolved into fifteen constituent states, raising the prospect that the Baltic countries or Ukraine or even Russia might apply.

Moreover, the former communist states were not the only candidates for membership. In May 1992, the EU and the European Free Trade Association (EFTA), a grouping that included Austria, Finland, Norway, Sweden, and Switzerland, agreed to create a European Economic Area in which nearly all EU-EFTA barriers to trade were eliminated. Although the EFTA states were affluent democracies with market economies, most had refrained from joining the EU out of concern that doing so would compromise their political neutrality and antagonize the Soviet Union. However, with the Cold War ending, this reason was no longer valid and most of the major EFTA states decided to apply for Union membership. In addition, two smaller Mediterranean states, Cyprus and Malta, had applied already in 1990. Finally, there was the problem of Turkey: it had an association agreement with the Union that dated back to the 1960s and also had applied for membership. Many political leaders in Western Europe were doubtful that Turkey, with its size, relative poverty, and cultural distance from Europe, would ever become a member, but it was important not to reject it out of hand, given Turkey's strategic importance and longstanding record as a loyal member of NATO.

In the debate on enlargement, British prime minister Margaret Thatcher and her successor, John Major, were among the most enthusiastic proponents of enlargement. They tended to favor the earliest and broadest possible expansion. As Thatcher later wrote, "Having democratic states with market economies, which were just as 'European' as those of the existing Community, lining up as potential EC members made my vision of a looser, more open Community seem timely rather than backward."[1] At the other pole of the debate were the federalists, such as Commission president Jacques Delors, who although they recognized that something had to be done for Central and Eastern Europe, were concerned that a broader and more diverse membership would undermine progress toward a more cohesive Union. Delors was skeptical about the admission of even the EFTA countries, and warned that it would take fifteen to twenty years before the Central and East European countries were ready for membership.[2]

The most decisive voice in the debate was probably that of Kohl, who favored enlargement to Central, Eastern, and Southeastern Europe—including the three Baltic states—but ruled out membership for Russia, Ukraine, and other states of the former Soviet Union. Kohl's position was somewhere between that of the British, who were accused by many of favoring indiscriminate and hasty enlargement, and that of Delors and many in the southern European countries, who sometimes were suspected of wanting to postpone enlargement indefinitely. The German view therefore tended to emerge as the compromise position.

The June 1993 Copenhagen meeting of the European Council was the first occasion on which the EU member states formally declared enlargement to the

Central and East European countries as an explicit goal. Although they did not set a timetable, the EU leaders stated that accession would "take place as soon as an associated country is able to assume the obligations of membership by satisfying the economic and political conditions required."[3] The associated countries were those countries with which the Union had concluded or planned to conclude Europe Agreements. Poland, Hungary, Czechoslovakia, Romania, and Bulgaria already had signed such agreements, and the European Council had signaled its intention to negotiate Europe Agreements with the three Baltic states and Slovenia. Negotiations aimed at concluding Partnership and Cooperation Agreements with Russia and the non-Baltic states of the former Soviet Union were under way or planned, but these agreements were not intended as a prelude to membership, which was not mentioned in their preambles. Thus by the time of the Copenhagen Council, the future shape of the European Union had been decided: it would include ten or more states in the Baltic to Black Sea region, but it most likely would not include Russia, Ukraine, or other countries in the former Soviet Union.

The European Council further specified four criteria for determining whether an associated country was ready for membership: first, stability of institutions guaranteeing democracy, the rule of law, human rights, and respect for and protection of minorities; second, existence of a functioning market economy; third, capacity to cope with competitive pressures and market forces within the Union; and fourth, the ability to take on the obligations of membership, including adherence to the aims of political, economic and monetary union. The "obligations of membership" meant acceptance of what in the EU lexicon was known as the *acquis communautaire*, a term used to denote the sum total of the Community's achievements in harmonizing legislation, creating a single market, and forging common policies.

Membership had to be comprehensive; there could be no "a la carte" acceptance of some areas of integration and rejection of others. Recognizing that the *acquis* itself was expanding as the EU became involved in new policy areas, the European Council did not insist that the new members meet all EU standards and participate fully in all areas of integration from day one of membership. They were not, for example, expected or required to adopt immediately the Union's single currency. But they had to commit to eventual participation in monetary union. Similarly, they were expected to participate in the Union's Common Foreign and Security Policy, and to cooperate in the development of a European security and defense identity.

Although it was up to the Central and East European applicants to meet these political and economic criteria, the European Council established one condition for the EU itself to meet, stipulating that "the Union's capacity to absorb new members, while maintaining the momentum of European integration, is also an important consideration in the general interest of both the Union and the candidate countries."[4] This condition later was interpreted to mean that negotiations regarding the admission of additional candidates—apart from the EFTA countries, three of which were admitted in January 1995—would not begin until at least six months after the completion of the Intergovernmental Conference (IGC) that was scheduled to convene in 1996 and that would take up the question of institutional reform of the Union.

With the Copenhagen decision, the EU committed itself to admitting ten countries with a combined population of 105 million. Measured at purchasing power standards, per capita gross domestic product (GDP) in the region was less than one-third the EU average. In addition to its relative poverty, Central and Eastern Europe was highly diverse, with different languages, religions, and historical traditions. The magnitude of the enlargement challenge facing the Union thus called for an effective pre-accession strategy to prepare these countries for membership, and also for an overhaul of the Union's own policies and institutions to enable it to function with a larger and more diverse group of members.

Pre-Accession Strategy

THE INTERNAL MARKET

Joining the Union entails a process of market integration that is deeper and more intrusive than that necessitated by other kinds of free-trade arrangements. As defined by the Treaty of Rome, the internal market is "an area without internal frontiers in which the free movement of goods, persons, services and capital is ensured."[5] Other provisions in the EU treaties prescribe certain social and employment standards that members are expected to maintain as they operate the single market, and place strict limits on state aid to industry and on cartels and monopolies that hinder competition.

At the request of the European Council, in 1995 the Commission issued a white paper that spelled out the demands of participation in the internal market-places on the member states: "An internal market without frontiers relies on a high level of mutual confidence and on equivalence of regulatory approach. Any substantial failure to apply the common rule in any part of the internal market puts the rest of the system at risk and undermines its integrity."[6] It went on to note that "any systematic checks and controls that are necessary to ensure compliance with the rules take place within the market and not when national borders are crossed." To operate in the internal market, a member state must adhere to the general principles contained in the EU's founding treaties and to a large body of secondary legislation, most of which takes the form of directives that are passed by the Council of Ministers (with the co-decision of the European

Parliament); these directives are then transposed into national laws and regulations that vary from country to country, depending upon legal and administrative traditions and other circumstances. Compliance with EU directives and with other sources of Community law is monitored by the Commission and is subject to the jurisdiction of the European Court of Justice.

In addition to the translating of directives into national legislation, the internal market relies heavily on the principle of mutual recognition. Beginning with the famous "Cassis de Dijon" ruling of 1979, the European Court of Justice has held that any good circulating legally in one member state also must be free to circulate in any other part of the Union, except in certain special circumstances in which a member state can prove that some danger to health or safety might result. In the single European market program of the late 1980s and early 1990s, the member states made a virtue of necessity by using mutual recognition—rather than the more time-consuming and politically difficult harmonization of national law—to complete the single market program.

Under the mutual recognition principle, any product that Poles lawfully produce or import must be available to Germans, Spaniards, Belgians, and everyone else in the Union. Belgian consumers thus want to be assured that Polish-made products are safe and reliable. This system places a heavy premium on establishing adequate standards and effective regulatory and inspection bodies in the acceding countries. Similarly, Belgian companies that compete with Polish producers in the same single market must be confident that they are competing on a level playing field—that Polish firms, particularly state-owned firms left over from socialism, are not benefiting from hidden or open subsidies, tax concessions, and other advantages that contravene EU norms.

POLICY INTEGRATION

In addition to market integration, joining the Union entails extensive policy integration in such areas as transport, the environment, and, most important for the countries of Central and Eastern Europe, agricultural and cohesion policies. Policy integration is in some respects even more challenging than market integration, if only because of the large costs involved, notably in the Common Agricultural Policy (CAP) and in the Structural Funds.

Agriculture has long been a problem area for the EU. Originally intended to ensure food security for Europe and an adequate standard of living for its farmers, the CAP accomplished this objective by maintaining EU agricultural prices above world market levels and buying surplus products from farmers that then were stored or dumped on world markets. The result was a huge burden on the EU budget, high food costs for European consumers, and disputes with many of the EU's leading trading partners, including the United States and

Canada. Governments and outside experts were concerned that extension of the CAP to new countries in Central and Eastern Europe, all with large agricultural sectors and many small, inefficient farms, would overburden the EU budget and lead to new international trade frictions.

The Commission attempted to allay these concerns, stressing that agriculture would be a problem for enlargement only if the Union failed to carry through with planned reforms of the CAP. Launched in 1992, CAP reform's key element was a phased decoupling of income support for farmers from price support in the markets. Instead of maintaining farm incomes through the ruinous policy of maintaining high overall price levels, after 1992 the CAP allowed prices to move toward world levels while giving farmers direct compensatory payments to maintain their incomes. The Commission calculated that because pre-accession agricultural prices and farm incomes in Central and Eastern Europe were by EU standards already low, the CAP funds that would flow to farmers in these countries would be much less than often was predicted. The Commission also noted that there was scope in these countries for integrated rural development—for new economic activity in rural communities (e.g., food processing and packaging, tourism, national parks and forests, and handicrafts) that would not result in added production of unneeded milk, grain, and meat. Demographic factors also were expected to ease the burden of integrating Central and East European agriculture into the CAP, as the children of farmers nearing retirement age chose not to continue farming and took up other jobs in the industrial and service sectors of the economy.

Structural or cohesion funds were another sensitive area of policy integration addressed by the Commission. As part of a long-term effort to narrow income disparities in the Union, the EU provides these funds to poorer countries and regions for infrastructure and other economic development projects. Relatively wealthy countries such as Sweden and the Netherlands are net contributors to the cohesion funds, while Greece, Ireland, Portugal, and Spain historically have been the main beneficiaries. It was obvious that if the same formulas that were used for disadvantaged regions in the existing Union were applied to the much poorer countries of Central and Eastern Europe, the demands on the EU budget would be unsustainable. The Mediterranean countries made clear that they would resist attempts to divert regional aid from the south to the east to underwrite enlargement. The candidate countries thus were advised to have realistic expectations of how much direct assistance they would receive as members from the EU budget. For their part, the European Commission and the EU member states recognized that, as with agriculture, enlargement provided a strong rationale for the EU to improve the efficiency of its cohesion policies and to adopt measures to ensure that funds were provided only to those countries and regions that really needed and could effectively use such assistance.

The Accession Process

Admission of new member states is governed by the Treaty on European Union, which stipulates that any European state that respects the principles of "liberty, democracy, respect for human rights and fundamental freedoms, and the rule of law" may apply to become a member of the Union. According to the procedure set forth in the treaty, applications are addressed to the Council of Ministers. The Council then asks the Commission to prepare an opinion on the candidate's suitability for membership, after which the Council must decide unanimously on whether to open accession negotiations. Negotiations are carried out by the Commission and the presidency of the Council and are aimed at producing draft treaties of accession between the applicant countries and the members of the Union. Once the negotiations are completed, a draft treaty is submitted to the Council and the European Parliament for approval. The Council must approve the treaty unanimously, and the Parliament by an absolute majority. The member states and the applicant country then formally sign the accession treaty, which is submitted for ratification by all parties in accordance with national constitutional provisions. In most cases this means a simple vote by parliament, but it also can involve a national referendum. (In 2003, the candidate countries held referenda on joining the Union, while the current member states did not do so.)

Between March 1994, when Hungary became the first Central and East European state to apply formally for membership, and June 1996, when Slovenia filed its application, all ten associated countries completed this step in the process. The Commission began working on its opinions shortly after receiving the membership applications from the candidate countries, relying upon experts from its own bureaucracy and on information gathered from the applicant countries. The prospective members were asked to complete long and detailed questionnaires to determine how much convergence with EU norms and legislation had been achieved and to identify remaining problem areas. At its December 1995 Madrid session, the European Council asked the Commission to prepare a "composite paper" that would include opinions on all ten Central and East European countries. As already decided shortly after Copenhagen, negotiations on enlargement would not begin until six months after the completion of the post-Maastricht IGC. With the conference expected to conclude during the Dutch EU presidency in the first half of 1997, the summer of that year became the target date for the Commission to complete its opinions on all of the applicant countries.

As expected, the Commission delivered its long-awaited report in July 1997, a little less than a month after the Amsterdam summit closing the IGC. Entitled *Agenda 2000*, it gave a detailed assessment of each of the eleven candidate countries—the associated countries and Cyprus.[7] It also recommended steps that the Union needed to take to be ready for enlargement. In judging the preparedness of the candidate countries for membership, the Commission referred explicitly to the political and economic criteria established by the European Council at Copenhagen. As measured against these criteria, it recommended that five Central and East European states were ready to begin accession negotiations: the Czech Republic, Estonia, Hungary, Poland, and Slovenia. In addition, it reiterated an earlier opinion that Cyprus was ready to start accession talks. It rejected one applicant—Slovakia—for political reasons, namely the lack of democracy and respect for human rights under Prime Minister Vladimir Meciar. It concluded that four other countries—Bulgaria, Latvia, Lithuania, and Romania—needed to make greater progress with economic transformation before accession negotiations could begin.

At the December 1997 European Council in Luxembourg the EU heads of government endorsed the Commission's recommendation in favor of Cyprus and five Central and East European countries, but they also put in place certain mechanisms intended to minimize any sense of exclusion on the part of the other five Central and East European candidates. They announced that the accession process would begin on March 30, 1998, at a twenty-six member meeting in London. The participants would be the fifteen EU member states, the ten associated states, and Cyprus. This meeting would set the overall framework for accession talks with the candidates and symbolically underline that all eleven had the same status and the same theoretical chance to achieve membership. Within this framework, the EU proposed to establish an "enhanced preaccession strategy" based on a new mechanism, the "accession partnership," and to begin the first accession negotiations. The EU stressed that those countries not asked to begin negotiations in 1998 were not necessarily being left permanently behind: they could catch up by improving their economic and, in the case of Slovakia, political performance. The Commission was asked to make annual reports to the Council and to recommend when additional countries were ready to begin accession negotiations.[8] Following a positive report on progress issued by the Commission in the fall of 1999, at the December 1999 Helsinki summit the European Council backed the start of accession negotiations with six additional countries: Bulgaria, Latvia, Lithuania, Malta, Romania, and Slovakia. Negotiations with these countries thus began in early 2000.

The Accession Negotiations

In principle, a country joining the EU is asked to accept the *acquis communautaire*. There thus would not seem to be all that much to settle in the accession negotiations. In practice, however, candidate countries often try to negotiate transition periods for the phasing in of Union rules and policies on their territory, or even to secure permanent derogations from certain EU policies or legal provisions. In such negotiations, the current EU member states and the Commission generally try to minimize all such derogations and to keep transition phases relatively short, so as to preserve the unity and coherence of the Union and especially its single market. The acceding countries, on the other hand, may have incentives to delay the adoption of certain costly standards or to seek other exceptions to the *acquis* in response to particular domestic economic or political circumstances. The negotiations also deal with budgetary, policy, and institutional questions: how much each new member state will pay into and receive back from the EU budget, production quotas and subsidy levels under the CAP, how many seats it will receive in the European Parliament, how many votes in the Council of Ministers, and so forth.

As was predicted by many in the early 1990s, agriculture was the most difficult issue in the enlargement negotiations. The basic framework for the negotiations was set at the Berlin European Council in March 1999 where the fifteen, generally following the guidelines established in *Agenda 2000*, adopted a budgetary framework for the period 2000–2006 based on the assumption that as many as six new member states could join the Union in 2002. In the agreement, CAP spending in the current member states in the first post-enlargement year was set at €39.4 billion, while comparable spending for six new member states was set at €1.6 billion. There was no provision for direct income support for farmers in the new member states, a decision taken on the grounds that such payments were a replacement for earlier indirect supports that farmers in the new member states had never received.[9]

When negotiations on the agricultural chapter opened in June 2000, the Berlin framework quickly became a sticking point. In their opening positions, all of the candidate countries requested that direct payments be granted to their farmers at the same level provided to farmers in current member states. The 1999 Berlin budget agreement did not provide for such payments, which some member states argued were not part of the *acquis* and should not be extended to new members. Reacting to the strong political response in Poland and other candidate countries to its position on direct payments, in early 2002 the Commission revised its initial approach and proposed that direct payments to farmers in the new member states be set at 25 percent of EU levels upon enlargement and rise to 100 percent over a ten year period, a stance that the candidate countries still argued was unacceptable and would put their farmers at a competitive disadvantage.[10]

After agriculture, the item in the accession negotiations with the greatest financial implications was the structural and cohesion funds. The Commission outlined its proposed approach to the negotiation of the structural funds chapter in January 2002, staying roughly within the Berlin framework (after allowing for adjustments in the enlargement scenario).[11] It proposed that structural operations funds be phased in over a three year period from 2004 to 2006 to take account of the absorption capacity of the new members. Aid would be capped at 4 percent of GDP, considerably below the levels received by Portugal and Ireland in the 1990s. The ten new member countries would receive some €25.567 billion in 2004–2006. EU aid per capita in the new member countries would reach €137 in 2006, compared with €231 in the four current member state cohesion countries. Additional structural funds would be allocated for nuclear safety projects (closing Soviet-built plants in Slovakia and Lithuania), northern Cyprus, and a special fund for institutional capacity building in the new member states.

Another difficult issue in the accession negotiations was the free movement of people. Movement of labor within the EU is one of the four freedoms (along with free movement of goods, services, and capital) guaranteed in the Treaty of Rome and made the centerpiece of the program in the late 1980s to early 1990s to complete the Union's internal market. But free movement of labor to and from Central and Eastern Europe also has been highly controversial in the current member states, provoking widespread fear, particularly in Germany and Austria, about waves of cheap labor moving westward and exacerbating unemployment and depressing wages. In view of the sensitivity of the free movement of labor issue, this was an area in which the Union itself, departing from its usual stance that the *acquis* should be kept intact and that transition periods and exemptions be as limited as possible, insisted upon an extensive transition regime and a delay in the full application of the *acquis* for at least five years.

Another important issue in the accession negotiations was the Schengen system of border controls. Begun in 1985 as an intergovernmental arrangement among five member states of the then EC, Schengen was incorporated into the *acquis* with the 1997 Treaty of Amsterdam and was expected to be implemented in full by the candidate countries from day one of membership (even though Britain and Ireland have opt-outs and do not participate in Schengen). The need to tighten the external borders of the Union is seen in Brussels and the national capitals as an inevitable counterpart to the removal of barriers to the flow of goods and people within the Union. With internal border controls dismantled, crossing the external borders of the Union to enter one member state means in effect legal entry into all member states of the Union. Governments in EU capitals thus insisted that the new EU members control their external borders. To comply with Schengen, the candidate countries were required to impose visa restrictions on visitors from Russia, Ukraine, Belarus, Moldova, and other countries of the former Soviet Union, a move that caused tension with some of these countries, particularly with Russia over access to Kaliningrad, an exclave of Russia that after enlargement would be surrounded by EU member states (Lithuania and Poland). They also were required to take practical measures to improve the control of their external borders, including hiring additional and more professional border guards, building additional fences and watchtowers, and improving surveillance by aircraft and helicopter.

Although at times difficult, the negotiations on these and the other enlargement-related issues proceeded relatively smoothly. Beginning with the easiest and least controversial areas, the negotiators "closed" successive chapters with the candidate countries, as the latter continued to make progress in adapting their economic and political systems to EU norms. In the crucial area of the single market, the Commission largely prevailed in its insistence on acceptance of an undiluted *acquis*. With the important exception of free movement of labor, remarkably few transitional arrangements were granted in the relevant chapters.

The one area in which the single market *acquis* was affected by transition arrangements is the free movement of labor, which was done largely at the insistence of the current member states. Under the terms of the free movement of persons provisions to be included in the accession treaties, for two years following accession each of the member states in the existing Union was allowed to apply national measures to limit access to their labor markets from the new member states. Following this period, there would be reviews of new member state labor market access to the old member states, and the latter would be allowed to keep transition arrangements in place for another three years. These provisions were intended to limit the flow of labor from east to west, but they were also a political gesture, aimed at assuaging concerns in countries such as Austria and Germany about unemployment and competition for jobs from workers in the new member states.

In view of the steady progress being made in the accession negotiations, at the European Council meeting in Göteborg in June 2001 the fifteen set the end of 2002 as the target date for concluding accession treaties with those countries judged ready for membership, a timetable that would allow these countries to join the Union in 2004 and to take part as members in the elections to the European Parliament set for June of that year.[12] At the Laeken European Council in December 2001, the fifteen confirmed this timetable and named the ten countries that they regarded as on track for membership in 2004: the Czech Republic, Cyprus, Estonia, Hungary, Latvia, Lithuania, Malta, Poland, Slovakia, and Slovenia. The stage thus was set for a "big bang" enlargement that, among the negotiating candidate countries, would leave out only Bulgaria and Romania, whose economic performance and progress in adopting the *acquis* still lagged that of the other candidate countries.[13]

However, as 2002 began there still were many unresolved issues relating to agricultural payments and production levels, the EU budget, and certain rules and regulations for which various candidate countries sought exceptions or transitional arrangements. Because the negotiations with the candidate countries on agriculture were linked to the EU's own internal discussions on the reform of the CAP, finalization of this issue was deferred from the initial target date of the spring of 2002 to the fall of that year, after the scheduled national elections in France and Germany. The stage thus was set for an intense round of negotiations during the Danish presidency in the second half of 2002, aiming at a finalization of the accession terms at a December summit in Copenhagen.

End Game

In October 2002 the European Commission delivered its long-awaited recommendations on which countries were ready to finalize accession negotiations by the end of the year. It reaffirmed the choice of the "Laeken 10" and stated that Bulgaria and Romania were not ready for membership, but that they could join the main group by 2007.[14] Meeting in Brussels in late October, the heads of state and government of the fifteen made the final decisions about the financial terms to be offered to the new member states upon accession. In the compromise final offer on agriculture to the candidate countries, the fifteen agreed to start direct payments at the 25 percent level and not raise them to full Union levels until 2013—an arrangement that was not essentially different from the deal on offer in the spring and that was criticized by candidate country governments as unfair and possibly endangering prospects for approval of the accession treaty in national referenda. The October European Council also settled on the amount of aid under the structural and cohesion funds to be given to the new member states in 2004–2006, cutting assistance from the €25.567 level agreed at Berlin to €23 billion.

These decisions paved the way to an intense final round of negotiations with the ten lead candidate countries, aiming toward conclusion at the December Copenhagen summit. Acting on its own initiative, in late November the Danish presidency put forward a supplementary package intended to win final acceptance of the deal by the accession countries. The package called for additional spending of €2.45 billion beyond the levels agreed by the European Council in October, to be devoted to agriculture, improving border security, and, for Slovakia and Lithuania, nuclear dismantling. Following continued hard bargaining in the days leading up to the Copenhagen summit, the Danish package became the basis for the final accession deal. It was agreed that some €40.4 billion would be paid by the Union to the accession countries in 2004–2006, half of it to Poland. This was a gross figure, not counting payments into the EU coffers from the accession countries. Total net transfers to the new members in the remainder of the budget period were projected to be about €12 billion. The EU stuck to its original position that direct payments to farmers in the new member states would be set at 25 percent of EU levels, but the accession countries won the right to transfer money from long-term EU aid funds and their own national budgets to direct payments, with the effect that such payments could already reach 60 percent of EU levels by 2004. These terms ultimately were accepted by all ten of the candidate countries in the days leading up to the summit, resulting in a triumphant outcome in Copenhagen.

From Fifteen to Twenty-Five

The conclusion of the accession negotiations took place amid deepening intra-European and transatlantic tensions over the post–September 11 international situation and in particular over the U.S. project to drive Iraqi dictator Saddam Hussein from power on the grounds that his alleged possession of weapons of mass destruction posed a grave threat to regional and global security. France and Germany led the opposition to the United States, backed by Belgium and several other smaller European countries and the overwhelming majority of European public opinion, while Britain, Spain, and Italy were more supportive of U.S. policy. The divisions among the EU member states and across the Atlantic placed the candidate countries in an awkward position, forcing them to choose between solidarity with the United States or with key European countries.

The crisis came to a head in January 2003, as France took the lead in opposing the United States in the UN Security Council. Asked to comment on the growing opposition to U.S. policy in Europe, U.S. Secretary of Defense Donald Rumsfeld provoked a storm of controversy by claiming that the opposition was centered in "old Europe" and that the "center of gravity is moving east." A week later, the leaders of Spain, Portugal, Italy, the UK, Denmark and three accession countries—Hungary, Poland, and the Czech Republic—published an open letter in the European edition of the *Wall Street Journal* in which they declared their commitment to solidarity with the United States. The "Letter of Eight," as it became known, was followed by a declaration by the Vilnius 10—the Baltic countries, Albania, Bulgaria, Croatia, Macedonia, Romania, Slovakia, and Slovenia—offering their support for Washington. French president Jacques Chirac was furious at these apparent breaches of intra-European solidarity and claimed that the Central and East European countries had "missed a good opportunity to keep quiet." This remark in turn caused deep offense in the accession countries and raised questions about whether "old" member states such as France in fact were prepared to welcome the new member states as equals.

Although these developments severely strained political relations in Europe, they did not derail the enlargement process, which went ahead as planned. Under the auspices of the Greek presidency, the leaders of the ten accession countries met in Athens on April 16, 2003 with their member state counterparts to sign the accession treaty. Despite the earlier controversies over agriculture and finance, voters in the acceding countries overwhelmingly approved the accession treaty: 84 percent for and 16 percent against in Hungary, 93–6 in Slovakia, 77–23 in Poland, 77–23 in the Czech Republic, 54–46 in traditionally Euro-skeptic Malta, 90–10 in Slovenia, and 91–9 in Lithuania. In most of these countries, the only shadow over the referenda was low turnout: only 46 percent of eligible voters cast their ballots in Hungary, and 52 percent in Slovakia, numbers that suggested more indifference and ignorance than outright opposition.

With ratification complete, accession of the ten new member states went ahead as planned on May 1, 2004. Ten new commissioners, one from each of the acceding countries, took their places in a European Commission expanded to twenty-five members. Voting in the Council of Ministers took place in accordance with the weights assigned in the Treaty of Nice (see Chapter 7). In some areas, e.g., with regard to support for aid to poorer regions, the new member states functioned as a bloc, but in most respects they were quickly integrated into the "normal" politics of the EU, forming coalitions with small and large states from the old Union and differentiating themselves from fellow new member states as their national interests and their domestic political situations required.

In a few areas, transitional arrangements remained in effect. Free movement of labor from the old to new member states was deferred for up to five years, and the new member states were not expected to adopt the euro in place of their national currencies for a number of years. (In June 2006, the European Council announced that Slovenia was the first of the new member states to meet the criteria set by the 2002 Maastricht Treaty for adoption of the euro, and would do so on January 1, 2007.) For the most part, however, the transition from candidate to membership status went remarkably smoothly. The surest sign of the success of enlargement was, ironically, the decline in popular enthusiasm for the EU in the new member states, as membership increasingly was taken as part of the status quo, rather than a dream to be fulfilled, as it had been in the years immediately following the fall of communism.

Perhaps more important for the future of the EU were the growing signs of "enlargement fatigue" in the older member states, where enthusiasm for further expansion was muted by concerns about cost, fear of immigration from the east and south, and resentment that the political leaders had not adequately consulted with the voters over enlargement. Such feelings about enlargement were one of the factors in the growing backlash against European integration that was seen in 2005, and help to explain the rejection by French and Dutch voters in the spring of that year of the proposed EU constitutional treaty (see Chapter 7).

The Future of Enlargement

For both the old and new member states, a key question was how fast and how much further expansion to the east and south would proceed. Bulgaria and Romania were part of the original group of countries provisionally offered membership at Copenhagen in 2003, and their candidacies were relatively uncontroversial. Both were on track to join in 2007, provided they continued to make progress on essential reforms highlighted in the Commission's pre-accession reports, notably judicial reform, strengthening their administrative capacities, and dealing with corruption. This in fact was accomplished, after the

Commission issued a favorable report concluding that both countries had made substantial progress in tackling areas of lagging performance.

Three other countries or groups of countries presented greater challenges: Turkey, the Western Balkans, and the remaining European countries, including Ukraine, Moldova, and Belarus, that generally were not regarded as near- or even medium-term candidates for EU membership, but that are neighbors of the expanded Union and part of "wider Europe."

TURKEY

Turkey and the EC signed an association agreement in September 1963, similar to the 1962 agreement between the Community and Greece that helped to pave the way to eventual membership of that country. The 1963 agreement referred to "the accession of Turkey to the Community at a later date."[15] It was followed in 1970 by the conclusion of an additional protocol to the 1963 agreement that came into effect in January 1973 and that stipulated that the two sides were to establish a customs union within a twenty-two-year period, or no later than the end of 1995. In April 1987 Turkey formally applied for EC membership, but its candidacy was not taken very seriously in Brussels or the member state capitals, given Turkey's poverty and such complicating issues as Turkey's relatively poor record on democracy and human rights, and the Turkish military presence in the northern part of Cyprus, which Turkey had invaded in 1974 in a dispute with Greece over the island.

Despite deteriorating political relations between the two sides over human rights and other issues, Turkey and the EU concluded the long-awaited customs union in March 1995, along with an accompanying package of financial aid. The European Parliament threatened to reject ratification of the agreement over Turkey's human rights record, but under heavy prodding from the Commission and member state governments, finally approved it in December 1995, allowing the customs union to begin on January 1 of the following year. Many in Western Europe saw the 1995 agreement as a substitute for EU membership. Turkey, in contrast, regarded the customs union as a step toward EU membership, which remained a key objective.

In *Agenda 2000*, the European Commission affirmed Turkey's eligibility for membership, but it drew attention to the many economic, political, human rights, and foreign policy problems that came with Turkey's candidacy. In the December 1997 Luxembourg decisions, Turkey was not invited to begin accession negotiations along with the six leading candidate countries, nor was it given the prospect of rapidly catching up with the other candidate countries, as were the second wave Central and East European countries. This decision in effect placed Turkey in a separate category and provoked a severe crisis in Turkish-EU relations. The fact that Western Europe seemed to be backing away from earlier pledges regarding membership contributed to a deep sense of betrayal in Turkey.

Relations between the two sides finally took a turn for the better in December 1999, when the Helsinki European Council, endorsing the recommendation in the Commission's October 1999 progress report, formally upgraded the status of Turkey to candidate member. The heads of state and government declared that "Turkey is a candidate state destined to join the Union on the basis of the same criteria as applied to the other candidate states."[16] To lend substance to this claim, the EU agreed to develop a pre-accession strategy for Turkey and to conclude an accession partnership agreement on the same basis as those negotiated with the other candidate countries. Turkey also was granted the right to participate in certain EU programs and in multilateral meetings among the EU member states and the candidates for membership.

Turkey continued to make steady progress in aligning its norms with those of the EU—by, for example, abolishing the death penalty and strengthening civilian control of the military. On the basis of these improvements, Turkey was invited to begin accession negotiations with the EU in October 2005, starting with the elaborate screening process used in all such negotiations. The European Council emphasized that Turkey was a legitimate candidate for membership whose fate was largely in its own hands. If it met the Copenhagen criteria and showed that it shared "the values, objectives and the legal order set out in the [EU] treaties," it would become a member. In reality, the picture was more complex. Membership for Turkey was deeply unpopular in most of the EU member states, and leading politicians in Germany and elsewhere called for the negotiation of a "privileged partnership" between the EU and Turkey that would confer on the latter many of the benefits of membership, but that would not extend to full participation in EU decisionmaking or allow for the free movement of people between Turkey and the Union.

Turks generally rejected such suggestions as insulting and reflective of a European bias against a historically Islamic albeit secular country. But it remained unclear whether Turkey would be willing, over a period of a decade or more, to make all of the reforms requested of it in a way that would negate the arguments of those in Europe skeptical about its candidacy. A particularly important sticking point between Turkey and the EU has been Cyprus. Turkey has refused to recognize the Greek Cypriote-controlled government in Nicosia, and opposed the entry of Cyprus into the EU, arguing that Cypriote government did not legitimately represent the ethnic Turkish minority on the island. The EU has rejected this position, and has stressed that it is unthinkable that Turkey can get very far in the accession process as long as it does not have normal relations with one of the member states of the Union.

Beyond this political issue, Turkey faces huge challenges in aligning its legislation with EU norms, raising the economic level of its backward rural regions, and finding peaceful solutions to the desires of its large Kurdish minority for more autonomy, before it will be ready for membership. At best, dealing with these challenges will take a decade or more. Should Turkey succeed in meeting the Copenhagen criteria, however, the EU would have a difficult time in *not* fulfilling promises that have been made by so many governments and political leaders over so many decades. In this sense, Turkey's bid for future EU membership is indeed largely—although perhaps not entirely—in its own hands.

THE WESTERN BALKANS

After the wars of the 1990s that followed the breakup of communist Yugoslavia, the EU took the lead in working to stabilize the group of countries known as the Western Balkans—Albania, Bosnia-Herzegovina, Croatia, Macedonia, and Serbia and Montenegro (the loose federation that replaced Yugoslavia in 2003, and that technically included the ethnic Albanian province of Kosovo). As these countries are surrounded by present and future EU member states, geography virtually dictates that they at some point will become members of the Union.

In June 1999, following the conclusion of the war between NATO and Serbia over Kosovo, the EU launched the regional Stability Pact for Southeastern Europe and offered to negotiate bilateral Stabilization and Association Agreements with each of the Southeast European countries that participated in the pact. The latter agreements are very similar to the Europe Agreements in that they provide for the establishment of free-trade areas with the EU as well as cooperation across a wide range of policy areas. Macedonia signed such an agreement with the EU in April 2001 and Croatia in October of the same year. Collectively these agreements comprise what the EU terms the Stability and Association Process for the region.

At the Feira European Council in June 2000 the EU leaders declared the countries of the Western Balkans "potential" future members of the Union. As in the case of the Europe Agreement countries, the prospect of membership will accelerate the process of economic integration between these countries and the EU, although this inevitably will take longer in the more economically backward and politically troubled parts of the region. At the European Council session in Thessaloniki in June 2003, the fifteen adopted the *Thessaloniki Agenda for the Western Balkans: Moving Towards European Integration,* which reaffirmed the membership perspective for these countries and outlined steps needed to move them from their current pre-candidate status to the formal start of preparations for membership.

Croatia formally submitted its application to join the EU in February 2003 and, after receiving a favorable opinion of its candidacy by the European Commission, was invited by the Council of Ministers to begin accession negotiations in October 2005, at the same time as Turkey. With a relatively prosperous economy and direct borders on two EU member states (Hungary and Slovenia), the

Croats were hoping for a relatively quick accession process. EU officials warned, however, that while Croatia most likely was "next in line," further enlargements after Bulgaria and Romania most likely would take place in 2010 at the earliest. The timing has less to do with the qualifications of Croatia itself than with concerns about the EU's own ability to absorb additional members, given the backlash against enlargement in the older member states.

Elsewhere in the Western Balkans the outlook for early EU accession is less promising. All of these countries have weak economies and suffer from high levels of corruption and organized crime, including smuggling and trafficking in arms and human beings. Serbia, the largest state in the region, is still dealing with the aftereffects of war, the Slobodan Milosevic dictatorship of the 1990s, and the loss of two former provinces, Kosovo and Montenegro. Kosovo has been patrolled by NATO peacekeepers and under UN administration since 1999, when NATO stepped in to stop the "ethnic cleansing" of the Albanian population by Serbian military and paramilitary forces. It is destined to join the EU at some point as an independent state, but will have to find ways of dealing with its own non-Albanian minorities, including a number of ethnic Serbs who remain loyal to Serbia proper, in order to gain European acceptance.

Montenegro declared its independence in June 2006, following a referendum in which 55.5 percent of the electorate voted in favor of a break with Serbia. It now faces the task of building an independent state that, like Kosovo, will aspire to join the EU on its own. Bosnia remains an uneasy federation of ethnic Bosnians, Croats, and Serbs, where EU military and police forces are stationed to maintain the peace. Macedonia, a former Yugoslav republic that borders on Greece, is economically backward and internally divided between ethnic Macedonians and a large and assertive Albanian minority. Albania, a separate country that was never part of Yugoslavia, is politically more unified than most of the countries in the Western Balkans, but faces the same economic and social problems left over from the communist era.

Working within the general framework of the Stability and Association Process, the EU is now using various tools aimed at improving economic and political conditions in these countries in order to prepare them for eventual membership. In December 2000, the Union established the Community Assistance for Reconstruction, Development, and Stabilization (CARDS) program as the primary means to implement the objectives of the Stabilization and Association Process. In the 2000–2006 period, CARDS made available €4.650 billion in grant aid for investment, institution building, and other measures aimed at achieving four objectives: reconstruction, democratic stabilization, and the return of refugees; institutional and legislative development, including harmonization with EU norms and approaches; structural reform and sustainable economic and social development; and promotion of closer regional cooperation among these countries and between them and the current and other prospective members of the EU. The Union also has granted preferential access to its internal markets for the countries of the Western Balkans, and seeks to coordinate with them on foreign policy matters and other areas of cooperation.

The road to actual membership is likely to be long and difficult, however. While the relatively small size of the countries of the Western Balkans makes them relatively easy to absorb economically, the eventual addition of a number of what are in effect micro-states (Montenegro's population, for example, is just over 600,000) will compound the governance problems of the Union by raising the number of delegations in the European Parliament, further complicating voting formulas in the Council of Ministers, and adding further twists to the old dilemma of balancing the interests of the small and large member states in a vastly expanded EU (see Chapter 7). Despite these problems, however, political leaders in Brussels and the EU member states are committed to eventual membership for the countries of the Western Balkans, as this is seen as the only enduring solution to what otherwise would become a source of permanent political and economic instability inside the very heart of the EU itself.

WIDER EUROPE

In contrast to its policy toward the Western Balkans, the EU has never declared that the countries of the former Soviet Union necessarily will become members of the Union. Russia is seen as far too large ever to be absorbed by the EU, and in any case has not expressed an interest in membership, which effectively would mean the end of Russia's cherished role as an autonomous great power in the international system. In contrast, Ukraine, Moldova, and even countries further afield such as Georgia have declared their aspirations to join the Union.

While there is some support in the EU for membership for these countries—notably in Poland, which borders on and has close political ties to Ukraine—Brussels and most national capitals are skeptical about whether the EU has the capacity to absorb, at least in the near to medium term, a region that is this large, that has so many internal problems, and that historically has had only limited ties with Western Europe. In an effort to head off a premature discussion of membership, as well as to help these countries deal with the same kinds of economic and political problems that plague the Western Balkans, the EU has launched a "new neighborhood policy" aimed at achieving integration and stabilization short of full membership. The object of the policy is to stabilize the EU's immediate periphery by creating something of a middle ground between membership and exclusion.

At their November 2002 session, the EU foreign ministers declared the "need for the EU to formulate an ambitious, long-term, and integrated approach toward each of these countries, with the objective of promoting democratic and economic reforms, sustainable development and trade, thus helping to ensure greater stability and prosperity at and beyond the new borders of the Union."[17]

In March 2003 the Commission issued its *Wider Europe—Neighbourhood: A New Framework for Relations with Our Eastern and Southern Neighbours. Communication from the Commission to the Council and the European Parliament*, which proposed that the EU "should aim to develop a zone of prosperity and a friendly neighbourhood—a 'ring of friends'—with whom the EU enjoys close, peaceful and co-operative relations."[18] To implement this policy, the Commission proposed using many of the same instruments employed in the pre-accession process for Central and Eastern Europe and the Western Balkans: grant aid, technical assistance, economic development loans, harmonization of laws and technical standards, enhanced political dialogue, and the eventual establishment of preferential trading links between the EU and the "neighborhood" countries.

It is doubtful, however, whether the new neighborhood policy will represent anything like a permanent solution to the EU's challenge of dealing with wider Europe. Two problems are likely to undercut the effectiveness of the policy. The first is resources. While the EU has declared stabilization of its periphery to be a priority, the Union also has other, even higher, priorities, such as completing the accession of Bulgaria and Romania, preparing the Western Balkans for membership, and dealing with the challenge of Turkey. How much money and political attention will be left over for Ukraine and the other neighborhood countries is thus uncertain. Second, there is little reason to expect that countries such as Ukraine will be permanently satisfied to remain on the periphery of the EU. They are likely to continue their quest for full membership, if only to be a part of the "club" that increasingly sets the rules for Europe as a whole.

Conclusion

Enlargement has been the great success story for the EU over the last fifteen years. By providing aid, technical assistance, and increased opportunities for trade and economic integration, all under the firm but reasonable conditions embodied in the 1993 Copenhagen criteria, the EU has succeeded in moving a dozen or more relatively poor, undemocratic countries to higher levels of prosperity under conditions of political democracy and the rule of law.

The very success of this process, however, raises two huge questions for the future. First, can the EU itself cope with the "enlargement fatigue" that has set in among the voters in the existing Union as they worry about the economic competition, the dilution of their identities and of their countries' relative power in the EU, and the import of problems that have come to be identified with vast and seemingly open-ended enlargement to the east and south? Second, can the EU eventually settle on a "final" set of borders? This will require developing friendly and cooperative relationships with neighboring countries that will *not* become members of the Union. Common sense suggests that the EU cannot expand indefinitely—that it must have ultimate borders. But few politicians have been willing to give a definitive answer to the question of which country or countries will be the last to be brought in, and which will be the first to be left out. Until this question is answered, however, voters are likely to be cautious in giving their full support to a Union whose future character and identity will be impossible to judge.

Notes

1. Margaret Thatcher, *The Downing Street Years,* New York: HarperCollins, 1993, p. 769.

2. Charles Grant, *Delors: Inside the House That Jacques Built,* London: Nicholas Brealey, 1994, p. 143.

3. *The European Councils: Conclusions of the Presidency 1992–1994,* Luxembourg: Office for Official Publications of the European Communities, 1995, p. 86.

4. *The European Councils: Conclusions of the Presidency 1992–1994,* p. 86.

5. *European Union: Selected Instruments Taken from the Treaties,* Luxembourg: EC Office for Official Publications, 1995, vol. 1.

6. Commission of the European Communities [hereinafter, CEC], white paper: "Preparation of the Associated Countries of Central and Eastern Europe for Integration into the Internal Market of the Union," COM(95), 163, May 3, 1995, p. 8.

7. CEC, *Agenda 2000,* 3 vols., Strasbourg, DOC/97/6–8, July 1997.

8. "Luxembourg European Council, 12 and 13 December 1997: Presidency Conclusions," SN 400/97, p. 4.

9. "Presidency Conclusions: Berlin European Council, 24 and 25 March 1999," Doc/99/1.

10. CEC, *Enlargement and Agriculture: Successfully Integrating the New Member States into the CAP: Issues Paper,* SEC (2002) 95 final, Brussels, January 30, 2002.

11. CEC, *Communication from the Commission: Information Note—Common Financial Framework 2004–2006 for the Accession Negotiations,* Brussels, SEC (2002) 102 final, January 30, 2002.

12. "Presidency Conclusions: Göteborg European Council, 15 and 16 June 2001," SN 200/1/01.

13. "Presidency Conclusions: European Council Meeting in Laeken, 14 and 15 December 2001," SN 300/1/01.

14. CEC, *Towards the Enlarged Union: Strategy Paper and Report of the European Commission on the Progress Towards Accession by Each of the Candidate Countries,* Brussels, COM (2002) 700 final, October 9, 2002.

15. Agreement establishing an association between the European Economic Community and Turkey, Ankara, September 12, 1963, *Official Journal of the European Communities,* 3687 (1964).

16. "Presidency Conclusions: Helsinki European Council, 10 and 11 December 1999," SN 300/99.

17. General Affairs Council, 2463rd Council meeting, Brussels, November 18, 2002, 14183/02.

18. European Commission, COM, 2003, 104 final, March 11, 2003, p. 4.

Selected Readings

Much information is available on the website of the European Union, http://europa
.eu.int, and in particular the home page of the Directorate-General for Enlargement
of the European Commission, http://europa.eu.int/comm/enlargement/index_en
.html.

Avery, Graham, and Fraser Cameron, *The Enlargement of the European Union*,
Sheffield: Sheffield Academic Press, 1998.

Baun, Michael, *A Wider Europe: The Process and Politics of European Union Enlargement*, Lanham, MD: Rowman & Littlefield, 2000.

European Commission, *Towards the Enlarged Union: Strategy Paper and Report of
the European Commission on the Progress Towards Accession by Each of the Candidate Countries*, Brussels, COM(2002) 700 final, October 2002 (available at
http://europa.eu.int).

Van Oudenaren, John, *The Changing Face of Europe: EU Enlargement and Implications
for Transatlantic Relations*, Washington, DC: American Institute for Contemporary
German Studies, 2003.

CHAPTER 11

The New Central and Eastern European Member States in 2004

Graham Bowley

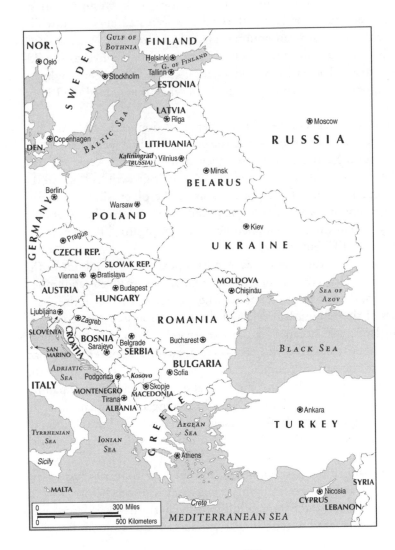

In August 2005, standing on Toompeah Hill and looking out over Tallinn, the ancient capital of Estonia, I could see yellow evening light settling on the Baltic Sea. It was the end of a long journey that over the past year had taken me, as a journalist for the *International Herald Tribune* reporting on the European Union, across much of the map of Western and Eastern Europe. Now, I had come to this northernmost tip of the group of young, former communist nations that just fifteen months earlier had become the latest wave of countries to join the European Union.

From Toompeah Hill, the economic benefits that membership of the EU had brought Estonia were tangible. Ferries were busily entering the docks from Finland. Daring shapes of modern buildings—Radisson Hotel, Union Bank—punctured the once drab skyline, while newer constructions still clad in scaffolding were rising beside them. Below the rooftops, rich Western tourists thronged the cobbled squares and sat in the Old Town's restaurants. Meanwhile, further south across the Estonian countryside, I had seen new Western-style business parks booming around cities such as Tartu, and foreign investors building factories and roads. The past year and a half, it seemed, had been bright for those Eastern nations that had embraced the West when they joined the EU on May 1, 2004.

But there had also been a darker side to their accession to the EU. As I had taken my road across the continent during the past year, I had seen the mood of the people of Western Europe turn against their new neighbors. Over the past few months, the easterners' dynamism and fast economic growth had earned the resentment of large portions of the populations of the older, slower-growing Western nations. In countries such as Germany and France, where the economies were blighted by high unemployment, people no longer regarded the new countries as partners in the EU, but as rivals.

The result had been a tumultuous year in European politics and one of the deepest crises in the fifty-year history of the EU. In national referendums in May and June 2005, the voters of France and the Netherlands, two of the original six founders of the Union, had rejected the EU's proposed new constitutional treaty in large part because of the easterners' presence in the Union. Recently, despite their own powerful economic growth, the sourer mood had begun to creep into the eastern countries. There was disappointment about the western lack of welcome as well as growing impatience that the fruits of painful economic reforms in some countries were slow in coming and unequally shared. A month after visiting Estonia, I flew to Poland where I watched the election of a new nationalist government that exploited disaffection with reform and hostility to the EU.

The EU had changed the new countries, and the new countries had transformed the EU in ways that could hardly have been foreseen before May 1, 2004. As I stared out from the Estonian hill into the dark that was descending over the Baltic, Europe faced questions that would continue to loom large for years to come: Would the West open its arms and accept fully the dynamic young eastern nations of the EU, or would it keep in place restrictions to competition and freedoms that not only harmed their own economies but which the countries of the east viewed as a betrayal? Would the easterners in turn seek deeper integration with the West or would they retreat into angry nationalism? Were the problems caused by enlargement merely temporary indigestion, or did the eastern borders of the accession countries mark the boundaries of what Europe ultimately could be? Did it therefore throw doubt on the EU membership aspirations of nations such as Ukraine and Turkey?

The Road to Accession

To understand how Europe had reached this point, it is important to know what had happened over the past decade and a half since the countries of Central and Eastern Europe had emerged from the broken shards of the communist world. The dark questioning of 2005 seemed a world away from the heady celebrations that took place when the countries of Central and Eastern Europe joined the EU on May 1, 2004. The EU's latest enlargement marked the historic reunification of Europe, the removal of barriers erected by the Cold War. It added ten new countries to the EU's existing fifteen, including eight former communist nations—Poland, Hungary, the Czech Republic, Slovakia, Slovenia, Estonia, Lithuania, and Latvia—alongside Malta and Cyprus. It expanded the EU's landmass by around a third and increased its population to 450 million. It was reunion on a personal as well as a continental scale, especially for those who had lived for the past five decades on the borderlands between the opposing systems of Western capitalism and communism. In April 2004, on the eve of enlargement, I went to Trieste, the northern Italian port city, where I met Emma Vatta, a lively, laughing woman of seventy, who for decades had been separated from her family by the nearby border with Yugoslavia. Now, as Slovenia prepared to join Italy in the EU, and the borders that had disfigured Europe and divided the Trieste region and its people were being redrawn, she would finally be reunited properly with her cousins. "It will be like it was before the war, with no borders and no obstacles," Vatta told me, tearfully, sitting in her kitchen as she raised a glass of Istrian wine.[1]

For others in the West, enlargement was the inevitable next stage of the historical development of the EU. What would become in March 1957 the European Economic Community, and eventually the European Union, had begun in 1951 as a system for sharing Europe's coal and steel resources between six members and had gradually expanded to take in almost all of the western part of the European continent. When communism collapsed and the Iron Curtain fell in 1989, the EU pledged to take in the countries of the east. Germany, which along with France was the EU's chief integrationist motor, felt a particular moral obligation, especially toward Poland, the biggest of the eight former communist states, to help the victims of Nazism and communism.

But there was also strategic and economic advantage for the West. Bringing the young countries into the bosom of the EU would help foster stability in the Union's own backyard, just as Spain and Portugal put their authoritarian pasts far behind them when they joined the community in an earlier enlargement in 1986 and spread the zone of openness and democracy to the continent's south. Openness also meant open markets, and the Western countries saw economic opportunity for their companies in the new populous markets in the east for exports and as a low-cost manufacturing base, since wages and other costs were a fraction of those further west.

For the easterners, accession offered no less of an opportunity. It was a chance for economic growth, a chance to catch up with the living standards of the West. The EU for them would be an anchor in the West's prosperous stability, allowing them to turn their backs on the chaos and poverty of the East. They had witnessed the earlier phenomenal success of once backward nations such as Northern Ireland, which had grown rapidly and become one of the wealthiest countries in Europe after it had joined the EU. They wanted to emulate Ireland's experience. The EU also represented protection from Russia, and, because the multilateral EU gives equal votes on many issues to all countries large or small, protection from big countries of Western Europe such as Germany, too. As the crowds cheered in the squares of Bratislava, Prague, and Tallinn on May 1, 2004, they were cheering a guarantee of future security, economic well-being, and a final break with the communist past.

THE ASPIRANT NATIONS MADE TOUGH CHANGES

By then they had had to make many painful changes. All of the former communist countries applied for EU membership soon after emerging from the shadow of the Soviet Union. Estonia, one of the smallest new nations with a population of 1.5 million, presented its application for membership on November 24, 1995. Before membership negotiations could even begin, the first test the aspirant countries had to meet was the EU's political criteria, called the Copenhagen criteria, by demonstrating "democracy, rule of law, human rights, and the respect for and protection of minorities."[2] At the EU summit in Luxembourg at the end of 1997, the European Council—the heads of state or government from the existing EU states—agreed that Estonia had met these criteria and decided to start accession negotiations with Estonia, along with five other countries—Poland, Hungary, Slovenia, Czech Republic, and Cyprus. The remaining four countries, plus Bulgaria and Romania, were given the go-ahead at the Helsinki EU summit in December 1999.

As soon as the decision to admit them was taken, the EU began twelve sets of simultaneous bilateral negotiations. The EU's body of law, the 80,000-page *acquis communitaire,* had to be painstakingly transferred onto the countries' own statute books. The *acquis* is divided into thirty-one chapters covering everything from agriculture and the environment to the free movement of labor. The aspiring countries had to complete all thirty-one chapters one by one, slowly, painfully, and exactly. To conform, they instigated reforms such as slashing tariffs, selling off state-owned companies, overhauling their banking sectors, cutting state subsidies, opening their telecommunications and energy markets to competition, and clamping down on corruption.

They harmonized regulatory regimes such as customs procedures and met Brussels standards in everything from aviation to zoos. To help them to change, the EU granted them early financial assistance, such as that distributed under the PHARE program, which stood for "Poland and Hungary: Aid for Economic Restructuring," and which initially focused on food aid but became broader. In the mid-1990s, the applicant countries also struck free-trade agreements with the EU, which covered increasingly large portions of their economies.

The countries freed prices, cut government spending and subsidies, and indulged in an orgy of deregulation and free trade. Estonia, for example, was one of the few countries in the world to remove subsidies from agriculture completely (but these had to be reintroduced later in line with EU subsidy levels). In their lust to emulate the market economies of the West, some of the new countries surpassed their western neighbors. Estonia introduced a strict macroeconomic framework that was more rigorously anti-inflationary and fiscally conservative than many in the West. In the early 1990s, it had suffered rapid inflation as raw-material prices jumped following the breakup of the Soviet Union. In 1992, inflation was running at an annual rate of 1,076 percent. In the same year, Estonia became the first country to break away from the free-falling ruble zone. In its monetary reform, it introduced the Estonian *kroon,* which it fixed via a currency-board system to the German deutsche mark at a rate of 1DM to 8 *kroons.* It allowed unrestricted exchange. In January 1999, it transferred this peg to the euro.

While it made these advances in monetary policy, in the fiscal sphere it was a pioneer in introducing the system of a "flat tax" rate, a low and standard rate for all levels of personal and corporate income, set in 2006 at 24 percent. It started a low tax trend that spread throughout Europe. (Four of the new members had adopted flat taxes by 2006.) Slovakia has so far gone furthest, with a 19 percent flat tax on income, capital, and consumption. Hungary plans a reform that would extend its low income tax rate to more income levels. Poland said it was considering a tax reform (as of early 2006) that from 2009 would mean that all but the richest Poles would pay a flat rate of income tax of around 18 percent. These rates compare to the much higher corporation tax rates of around 34 to 38 percent in Germany, Italy, and France, and they played an important role in attracting new inward investment made by foreign companies.

THE CHANGES TRIGGER AN ECONOMIC BOOM

The progress the nations made toward the Union delivered enormous economic benefits. As soon as they were announced as official candidates for EU membership, the prospect of EU entry unleashed a boom in foreign direct investment, as foreign companies were reassured that they would be operating in a stable Western-style business environment in the years ahead. "The EU is the guarantee to investors that stability is going to continue in the same way," Ilmar Lepik, head of economics at the Bank of Estonia, the central bank, in Tallinn, told me in 2005. "It is a matter of trust. That is the difference the EU has made since last year. It is important if you are very small and very alone."[3]

Then there were the low wages, cheap land prices, and a dynamic youthful population eager to make up for their lost years under communism. The free-trade agreements with the EU meant that by locating in the new states these companies could then sell their goods in the rich western markets without incurring tariffs every time they crossed the border. EU aid, paid to both domestic and foreign entrepreneurs, was an added benefit.

I witnessed all of these factors at work when I spent three days in Estonia with a group of British farmers who had invested in land near Turi, a town about an hour south of Tallinn, and near the southern city of Tartu. They were part of a small vanguard of farmers from Western Europe that I came across who had sought opportunity in the new, formerly communist, eastern reaches of the EU. Their presence reflected the advantages offered by Estonian agriculture over costlier Britain: In the green countryside around Turi and Tartu, dilapidated Soviet barns and lines of pine forests, home to storks and wild boar, punctuated vast stretches of land, most of it still untouched since the collapse of the old planned Soviet economy. The newcomers found that if they cleared the soil and worked it, the local government gave it to them more or less for free. The land was so plentiful and cheap that many of the foreigners could not always tell me exactly how much real estate they owned.

As well as cheap land, the farmers got cheap labor. The big collectivized farms brought with them work forces of hundreds. The soil was poorer quality than in England. The local workers, too, were sometimes hard to motivate and easy to offend. They were used to a slower precapitalist life, Clifton Lampard, one of the British farmers, told me. He had to spend weeks persuading some of his workers not to kill the farm's best cows (with a hammer blow to the head) to eat when they felt hungry, while I saw one of his workers falling down drunk. When Lampard stopped villagers from entering the dairy where they had traditionally helped themselves to milk, he was lambasted in the local town newspaper. But once the Westerners had installed modern equipment, added hundreds of cows to the herds, and introduced new working practices, production costs came down to just over half those in the West. In Lampard's brightly lighted barn near Turi, Vivi Norma, fifty-five, a tough woman with a mouth full of dirty teeth, and two other women milked a hundred cows an hour compared with twelve an hour under the Soviet system. Lampard had a barn full of shiny tractors and he told me that EU development aid from Brussels paid for around two-thirds of the farmers' new machinery. "Our farm in England is not nearly as profitable," he said.[4]

Overall, the farmers seemed content with their investments. Land prices were rising, and they had begun to rejuvenate a native agricultural industry in which employment had shrunk from 115,000 jobs in 1992 to 32,000 by 2000.

Between the early 1990s and 2004, more than €150 billion of foreign direct investment flowed into the ten accession countries. Investment was by no means limited to Estonia, nor was it confined to agriculture. It flowed into the car sector and into electronics, furniture manufacture, pharmaceuticals, and into modern services sectors such as banking and retail. I witnessed the effects of the investment boom in Plzen in the Czech Republic, a city a few hours' drive west from Prague, where the city's famous, centuries-old brewery had been bought—and polished up—by SAB Miller, a multinational brewing company. The car park was full of cars with German number plates; many Germans regularly drove across the nearby border to enjoy the cheap beer.

The evidence of the new money was everywhere. On the outskirts of Plzen, big foreign stores with brand names such as Tesco, Britain's homegrown version of Wal-Mart, lined the highway approaching the city, and an Audi and Porsche car showroom, a Carrefour superstore, and a Panasonic factory crowded a 120-hectare, or 300-acre, industrial park near the university; nearby, a Mercedes-Benz research center occupied a former Soviet airfield barrack. Petr Osvald, Plzen council's director of European affairs, showed me around and told me that the city planned a science and technology park, valued at 200 million Czech *koruny*, or US$8 million, to be built among the decrepit aircraft hangars of the military airfield, and supported financially by EU financial aid and more outside private investment.

Elsewhere in the Czech Republic, car manufacturing had boomed, largely reflecting investment by German car companies. Volkswagen had invested more than €3 billion in Skoda in the Czech Republic, so that by 2006 Skoda was the country's largest employer, with 90,000 employees. After Spain and China, the Czech Republic had become the third-largest location for the German car industry. Car industry growth had been even more marked in Slovakia, which some have described as the Detroit of Eastern Europe. By 2007, according to some estimates, Slovakia was due to produce more cars per 1,000 inhabitants than any other country in the world.[5]

Further north in Estonia, the investment boom had been in tourism, construction, shipping, and electronics. Elcoteq, the large Finnish electronics manufacturer, used Estonia to assemble mobile phones for Nokia and Ericsson. Tallinn was home to one of the main offices of Skype, the Internet phone company owned by eBay. Hungary had become another popular location for high-tech manufacturing of mobile phones and computers. Overall, in the decade between

1992 and 2002, the accession countries had increased their share of the global market of information and communications technology manufacturing fourfold from 1 percent to 4 percent.[6]

This investment boom was accompanied by acceleration in cross-border trade. By 2001, the Central and East European countries had no more tariffs or quotas for industrial goods, although restrictions remained for trade in services and farm goods. As a result, in the ten years before accession, Hungarian exports increased by 380 percent (in dollar terms) and Czech exports by 280 percent. Most were sold to markets in countries in the EU. By 2000, the big Central and East European nations were selling 60–75 percent of their exports to the EU.

In Estonia's case, a large proportion of its export trade was with Finland and Sweden, its EU neighbors in the Baltic Sea region. This trend continued after accession in 2004, leading to a boom in shipping industries in the area. EU membership might have been expected to turn all eyes to Brussels, but in fact the lowering of borders, and the quickening of trade between the Baltic neighbors, meant that increasingly the Baltic became a region with its own character and its own center of gravity. Finland and Sweden were Estonia's biggest investors, and these countries cared more and more for each other's well-being and security. There were other examples of different regions coalescing into various groupings. The Visegrad Group, a loose alliance of Poland, Hungary, the Czech Republic, and Slovakia, together began to lobby for their own interests within the EU. In this way, it made less and less sense to talk about the Central and East European nations as a uniform bloc.

The robust growth of foreign investment and trade fuelled rapid expansion of the accession countries' young market economies after they emerged from communism. Poland and Hungary, the two biggest accession countries, grew by around 4.4 percent a year and 3.6 percent a year respectively between 1995 and 2004. This compared to growth in Germany between 1995 and 2004 of 1.3 percent annually and France's 2.2 percent. In 2005, even the slowest-growing new economy, Hungary, grew faster than the euro-zone average, while the Baltic countries grew at four times the euro zone's pace.[7]

Among the Baltic nations, Estonia, helped by its extreme economic reforms, experienced one of the fastest growth rates among the new accession states. This growth followed a deep recession between 1990 and 1994 brought about by the breakup of the Soviet Union when the Estonian economy diminished by around a third. It began to grow again in 1995 when gross domestic product expanded by 4.5 percent. By 1997 it was growing at a rate of more than 10 percent. There was a setback in 1999, when the Russian financial crisis severed trading lines into what was still one of Estonia's biggest markets. This experience underlined the extent to which the former Soviet republics were still dependent on their former master.

In Estonia, the biggest effect was felt in those industries whose export target was Russia, such as the food industries, including farming. As a result, GDP fell by around 1 percent in 1999 and unemployment rose to 15 percent. But the economy recovered in 2000, albeit with a somewhat altered structure as industries such as transport and services became more prominent, while the share of traditional manufacturing and agriculture fell. In the years around accession, GDP grew annually by 6 to 7 percent, and in the final months of 2005, GDP was growing by an outstanding annual rate of 11.1 percent.

ACCESSION BROUGHT NEW POLITICAL CONFIDENCE

As well as economic benefits, accession to the EU had created important political advantages for the new countries. Being in the EU secured powerful allies among nations such as Britain, France, and Germany. As a result, their standing on the world stage became heftier and this gave them greater confidence, particularly in their relations with Russia, their former hegemon.

During Ukraine's "Orange Revolution" in 2004, Aleksander Kwasniewski, Polish president, and Valdas Adamkus, his Lithuanian counterpart, felt secure enough to intervene in the aftermath of the disputed presidential elections as they secured victory for Viktor Yushchenko. They engineered robust European backing—despite reservations by some leaders in France and Germany—for Yushchenko, persuading Leonid Kuchma, the outgoing Ukrainian president, and Viktor Yanukovych, the successor preferred by Kuchma and Moscow, to accept defeat. There is no doubt that the crowds of prodemocracy protestors gathering in Kiev's Independence Square drew encouragement from the knowledge of the EU's broader support. Their strident people power helped eventually to secure Kuchma's concession.

After 2004, Poland used its position as the largest new member within the EU to argue for a stronger eastern dimension to the Union's foreign policy. This meant promoting deeper ties between the EU and Ukraine and even Moldova and Belarus. Poland hoped these nations could eventually join the EU, thus expanding the region of stable accessible democracies and giving Warsaw a further bulwark between it and Russia.

In the small Baltic nations, membership conferred some sense of greater security even at a time when many saw Russia as a renewed danger. They viewed the Russia of President Vladimir Putin as an increasingly authoritarian state that desired to reassert some of the influence it lost after the Soviet Union's demise. This time, their concern was not so much about military attack and occupation as about overbearing political and economic pressures and disruption from Moscow. For example, one fear was that Russia, the source of more than three-quarters of Eastern Europe's oil and gas, could disrupt energy supplies or exploit that threat to exert influence on its western neighbors. This fear was realized temporarily in January 2006. In what many saw as a political swipe at its former satellite, Russia cut supplies of natural gas to Ukraine, alleging that the government in Kiev was siphoning off gas from Russia's pipelines and not paying its energy bills. In the ensuing knock-on effect, gas supplies fell in countries across eastern, central, and western Europe until Moscow turned the gas back on.

This event occurred at a time when world oil prices were climbing above $60 a barrel, a development that lent energy-rich Russia added heft in world politics. Nevertheless, despite Russia's stronger bargaining power, in 2005 Estonia still felt secure enough to confront Russia in a long-running dispute about their shared border. In May 2005, Estonia and Russia signed a treaty defining the border, but when the Estonian parliament later ratified the treaty, it included a reference to Soviet occupation and, according to the government in Moscow, a clause that could one day allow Tallinn to claim more land from Russia. Moscow reacted by pulling out of the treaty.[8]

Following the election of a new nationalist government in Poland in late 2005, Warsaw demonstrated an even more marked and willing muscularity toward Russia and Germany, its two large neighbors.

In particular, ire focused on a plan, sponsored by Putin and Gerhard Schröder, who until 2005 was German chancellor, to build a gas pipeline between Russia and Germany, bringing Siberian gas west that would bypass Poland and the Baltic countries, following a route instead beneath the Baltic Sea.

Radek Sikorski, Poland's defense minister, underlined the new government's confrontational attitude toward Moscow, which at times bordered on outright taunting, when, in November 2005, he opened up previously sealed Warsaw Pact military archives, including a 1979 map that apparently showed Soviet plans to sacrifice Poland in the event of nuclear war with the West. The map showed hypothetical plans in the event of a NATO attack on Warsaw Pact countries. "It is crucial to educating the public in the way that Poland was kept as an unwilling ally in the Cold War," Sikorski said at a press conference, which seemed timed to coincide with the visit of a number of Western journalists, including myself. "It is important for people to know who was the hero and who was the villain." This tactic was just one example of the new Polish government playing to its more conservative, anti-Russian supporters and emphasizing Poland's break with its communist past.[9]

The Western Backlash Against the East

While accession brought undoubted advantages for the East, in the West it was greeted with increasing sourness in the months after May 2004. Some of the big Western countries that had dominated the EU in the past resented the fact that the newcomers wanted to pursue policies that clashed with their own interests or wishes. This had begun on the eve of enlargement in 2003 when Poland, in particular, threw itself behind the U.S.-led invasion of Iraq, but France and Germany opposed it. Poland sent around 2,500 troops in a peacekeeping role to southern Iraq, and the Czech Republic, Estonia, Latvia, Lithuania, and Slovakia also committed troops. The new countries were caught between the ties to their new allies in the EU and their loyalty to the United States, which had stood by them during the Cold War and helped deliver them from the Soviet Union. The easterners' staunch backing of the United States earned a rebuke from President Jacques Chirac of France, who said the new eastern EU members should know when it was better to keep quiet in world affairs. "They missed a good opportunity to keep quiet," he said at an EU summit that was called to discuss the war, in Brussels in February 2003.

It was in France that public opinion began to turn most bitterly against the newcomers. In the run-up to enlargement, some in France had feared that expansion of the union eastwards would create a new German-dominated sphere of influence. The new countries would look to Berlin for leadership, paving the way to growing German dominance within the EU. In fact, after enlargement, as Poland allied itself with Britain and the United States on foreign policy in Iraq, and at home most of the new countries pursued neoliberal, Anglo-Saxon economic policies, it seemed that a London-Warsaw axis was a more real threat to French interests.[10]

France was discovering, as were all the original EU countries, that a union of twenty-five countries was very different from an EU of fifteen, and, whatever the ideological battle, each nation's voice was heard less clearly among the new multilingual throng. Throughout 2004 and 2005, Turkey was in negotiations to begin membership talks with the Union, and French public opinion was inflamed by the worry that European identity and French influence would be swamped even further if Turkey, a large Muslim nation of 70 million people, joined the EU. A further snub for France was that the new member countries mostly preferred to speak English in Brussels, which meant that English was supplanting French as the lingua franca of the Brussels bureaucracy. It was getting harder and harder for France to play its traditional leading role, and this was a severe blow for a nation that had been among the Union's founding six and which, for fifty years, had seen the EU as a means of projecting French power on a continent-wide scale. The Union had been conceived as "a big France," as one European commissioner, Pascal Lamy, described it. But now, suddenly, France was no longer the main player in Brussels.

WESTERN COUNTRIES BECOME ALARMED AT THE EASTERNERS' ASSERTIVENESS

The concerns among the EU's old guard were intensified when the new countries began to fight more intensely in Brussels for their own interests, even beyond foreign policy in Iraq or toward Russia. In the long drafting of the proposed EU constitutional treaty, which was to be the next major step in EU integration, Roman Catholic Poland argued strongly for a reference to Europe's Christian heritage, refusing to back the treaty until it secured an amendment in the preamble to the treaty; it failed.

In the fall of 2004, Poland also played a key role in the furor surrounding Rocco Buttiglione, which deprived the EU of a governing executive body for a month. Buttiglione was a conservative Roman Catholic politician from Italy who was proposed as the EU's justice and home affairs commissioner. When, in his appointment hearings in the European Parliament, Buttiglione described homosexuality as a sin and said marriage existed to allow women to have children, his opinions drew the opprobrium of liberals in the Parliament, who blocked Buttiglione's selection, and delayed the installation of the entire new twenty-five-member Commission. Poland joined the side that lobbied hard for Buttiglione to be appointed, but Buttiglione eventually stepped down and Italy proposed an alternative commissioner.[11]

A further illustration of the new countries' assertiveness was the tough line they took in the EU budget negotiations in 2005. As the EU countries tried to calculate how much each nation would contribute to the Union's budget for the next financial period, which spanned 2007–2013, and how the billions of euros in new funds would be spent, the relatively poor newcomers faced a stiff push by the rich countries in the west—countries such as Britain, Germany, the Netherlands, and France—which were traditionally the EU's paymasters, to scale back the size of EU payments and spending. They said that their own economic problems, as well as waste and bureaucracy in the EU, meant they could not be as generous as they had been in the past.

This scaling back would have meant a large reduction in the transfer of billions of euros of development aid to the poor new countries compared with what they had expected—and, to a certain extent, had been promised—when they joined the EU. But at a European summit meeting in Brussels in December 2005, Poland held out for a better deal, and especially canny negotiating by Poland's then prime minister Kazimierz Marcinkiewicz and his team helped secure funding that was less than originally expected but still a good deal for Poland. Another incident that boosted Warsaw's growing reputation for being "awkward" came a month later. In January 2006, Poland, the Czech Republic and Cyprus held up a decision on value-added tax (VAT) rates when they demanded that they be allowed to charge lower rates on some economic sectors, such as home renovations. This was a wider range of exemptions than was being proposed by the EU's other members. Poland's insistence led to frantic meetings in Brussels and at one point threatened to endanger Europe's entire VAT regime and lead to a general rise in sales taxes across the continent.

To some, Poland's behavior was reminiscent of that of Spain, a similar-sized country, which also was relatively poor and relied on aid from the west after it joined the European Community in 1986 and began to fight hard for its own self-interests. It was the natural behavior of a new, big country testing the waters and trying to find its place in the Union. But in some ways, Poland seemed even more "awkward" than Spain, a perception that grew following the election of the new Polish government in fall 2005.

With the arrival of this government, Poland seemed to make an even more odd fit with the rest of the EU. The new Polish president, Lech Kaczynski, was a conservative defender of family values and a critic of abortion and homosexuality. As mayor of Warsaw, he had banned the city's annual gay pride march, and in the days immediately following the election, the European Commission in Brussels expressed deepening unease at the new government's apparent support for the death penalty. The new government's values, it seemed, were in many ways the opposite of what the EU stood for.

The cultural clash became vivid in the corridors of the European Parliament in Strasbourg, France, where members from the Western countries mixed uneasily with some of their counterparts from Poland. In December 2005, Polish members of the Parliament placed an anti-abortion display in a corridor. Showing children in a concentration camp, it was meant to link abortion and Nazi crimes, and prompted a scuffle with Western liberal members to the EP who tried to take it down. The fracas was seen by some as the latest skirmish in an incipient culture war in the heart of Europe that could only get worse as Poland tried to stretch its muscles. "New groups have come in from Poland, the Czech Republic, Latvia, and Catholicism is certainly becoming a very angry voice against what it sees as a liberal EU," Michael Cashman, then fifty-four and an EP member from Britain who had campaigned for gay rights, told me as we sat in his office in Brussels. Cashman looked disillusioned. "On women's rights and gay equality, we are fighting battles that we thought we had won years ago."[12]

Poland's battles over the EU budget and the sales tax were legitimate attempts to defend its interests, but in other cases Poland began to smart at the EU's strictures and even threatened to break some of the Union's rules. In a step in January 2006 that drew fierce protests from the European Commission in Brussels, Poland tried to prevent a banking takeover by UniCredit, an Italian banking group, of HVB, a German rival, because it involved the merger of two of the groups' Polish subsidiaries, UniCredit's Pekao and HVB's BPH. Together the two subsidiaries would have formed a new number-one bank in Poland, and this prompted public concern in Poland that consolidation would lead to job losses and could undermine the viability of the country's last state-owned bank. However, the Commission said that Poland's stance was an attack on one of the central principles of the EU, the free movement of capital. Many of the EU's older members regularly infringed EU law and often drew the frowning condemnation of the Commission, but the surprise in Poland's case was that Warsaw had chosen to contest the Union's rules so early after enlargement. The Polish government and UniCredit eventually struck a compromise under which UniCredit would be allowed to take over BPH but would have to sell almost half the bank's branches and the bank's brand name.

THE EASTERN COUNTRIES' ECONOMIC GROWTH ECLIPSES THE WEST'S

For all these reasons, the western nations began to treat their new eastern neighbors more warily. But probably the most important reason for the west's change of sentiment toward the east was the easterners' sparkling economic performance during this period. This shamed most countries in the west whose economies were stuck in or close to recession, and where growth rates barely nudged above 1 or 2 percent annually. In Germany in 2005, unemployment stood at 5 million, its highest level since World War II. Amid painful restructuring, some leaders and voters in the west began to blame the easterners for contributing to the west's malaise. In particular, one fear was that low taxes of nations such as Estonia and Slovakia were luring away investment and thus also jobs from the western economies.

One way out was for the big western countries to cut taxes, but this implied parallel cuts in government spending, which would jeopardize the west's generous welfare systems. A nightmare prospect opened up, played out in western public debate, of a downward spiral in spending and taxes as governments engaged in what was called "social dumping"—cutting taxes and slashing welfare programs, which would spell the end of the European social model, a route western voters didn't want to follow. Instead, France and Germany accused the newcomers of unfair tax competition and promoted the idea of a minimum rate of corporation tax for the whole of the union. Nicolas Sarkozy, then French finance minister, threatened the new eastern countries by suggesting that the rich countries would cut the development aid they gave to the easterners via the EU budget if they refused to raise their taxes.

A second fear felt strongly by voters in the west was that not only were western companies exporting jobs to cheaper locations in the east, but tens of thousands of immigrants from the eastern countries were moving to the west and taking many of the jobs that still remained at home. There was outrage in Germany in the fall of 2004 when around 25,000 slaughterhouse workers lost their jobs to Polish and Czech immigrants willing to work for 5 euros an hour or less. This was a pittance by German standards, but good money in some of the eastern countries where annual incomes were low. In 2003, for example, the average income in Germany was more than $27,000, compared with around $5,000 in Poland, according to some estimates.

Another nightmare prospect opened up, this time of a "race to the bottom" in wages and spiraling unemployment among native workers. It was a debate familiar in the United States, where immigration from Mexico has been equally controversial. But whereas in 2006, the U.S. economy was booming, the threatened influx from Europe's east came at a time when unemployment in Germany, for example, was already at postwar record levels and fears about the future were easily exacerbated. In a survey published by *Der Speigel* magazine in 2004,

Box 11.1   Battle of the Models: The European Social Model Versus Anglo-Saxon Capitalism[1]

Much of the debate about the immediate effects of the entry of the central and east European countries into the European Union focused on the supposed clash between Anglo-Saxon capitalism and the European social model. This became known as the "battle of the models."

European Social Model

Sometimes called "Rhineland capitalism," it features heavy regulation of markets, a comprehensive system of social and job security, and widespread consultation among governments, employers, and labor unions. Underlying this style of capitalism is a preference for stability to encourage growth and the avoidance of risk and turbulence.

The problem is that Europe's aging population means it is becoming increasingly difficult to sustain and finance such a system when there are fewer people of working age who are paying taxes. The desire for consensus also makes it difficult to keep up with nimbler rivals in today's world, which is characterized by rapid technological change and robust global competition.

Anglo-Saxon Model

Practiced in Britain and Northern Ireland, and adopted in varying forms by some of the Central and Eastern European EU member states, it is heavily influenced by U.S.-style capitalism. It emphasizes less regulation, focusing instead on the openness of markets, competition, and risk taking. State intervention is frowned upon, taxes are lower, and welfare payments are more restricted. There is a big role for the private sector, and people's lives are assumed to be improved by the maximization of corporate profits. It has generated high growth rates and low unemployment in recent years, but critics say it also has led to a woeful deterioration in public services, such as the transport infrastructure in Britain, long working hours, and wide wage disparities.

Nordic Model

This combines elements of the other two: strong social protection but also a willingness to integrate fully into the global economy, including flexible labor markets. It is marked by a sense of cooperation between workers and employers, and it emphasizes investment in research and development by outward-looking businesses. Taxes are high but generally accepted in return for good public services, including education, child care, and retraining.

With productivity high, Finland, Sweden, and Norway are among the most competitive countries in the world and their economies among the fastest-growing in Europe. But some say the Nordic model's lessons cannot be applied to bigger, more diversified countries such as Germany or France.

---

1. From Graham Bowley, *International Herald Tribune*, October 23, 2005.

on the eve of enlargement, 73 percent of Germans said they expected that enlargement would threaten their jobs. At the same time, some studies suggested that 80 percent of German companies in 2005 expected to increase their investments in the new member states in the coming years.

In fact, the actual transfer of jobs from west to east as a result of enlargement was probably muted. According to research by the Osteuropa Institut, only around 70,000 jobs were transferred east by companies relocating. In a survey, 60 percent of businesses said their investments in the east had in fact preserved jobs at home by strengthening their companies.[13]

As for migration, a report published by the European Commission in February 2006 dismissed fears of a flood of eastern migrant workers—dubbed "Polish plumbers" in the European press—when it found that migrants from these countries did not take domestic workers' jobs, but instead filled skills gaps in the labor market. They contributed positively to economic growth and to state finances. The report also found that East European workers sought out employment and did not abuse social security payments when they moved to Western countries, which had been a common fear.[14]

ACCESS TO WESTERN JOBS RESTRICTED

Despite these findings, the perception remained that the eastern states were a threat, and as a result, in 2004, twelve of the fifteen existing EU members chose to keep their labor markets closed to workers from the new eastern nations for up to seven years. Only three countries—Ireland, Sweden, and the UK—removed restrictions so that from May 1, 2004, Central and Eastern European people could apply freely for jobs in these western economies. In the other twelve states, foreign workers were still required to apply for permits to work legally in the west. (In 2006, some of the western nations such as Spain, Finland, and even France signaled that they would begin to lift some or all of the restrictions, but Germany retained its labor barriers.)

WESTERN GOVERNMENTS WATER DOWN THE EU SERVICES DIRECTIVE

The strength of public feeling against immigrants was underlined when, in February 2005, thousands of protesters from Belgium, France, and other countries across Western Europe marched through Brussels to protest against a new EU law proposed by the European Commission called the "services directive."

In its original form, the law was intended to complete the EU's so-called single market by giving all companies that provided services the freedom to work in all countries and move across national borders. The labor market safe-

> ## Box 11.2   Immigrants from the East: Where Did They Go?
>
> Free movement of persons is one of the most fundamental freedoms guaranteed by Community law. It includes the right for EU nationals to move to another EU member state to take up employment and to establish themselves in the host state with their family members. EU member states are precluded from directly or indirectly discriminating against migrant workers and their families on the basis of their nationality. EU migrant workers and their families are entitled to equal treatment not only in employment related matters, but also as regards public housing, tax advantages and social advantages.
>
> The percentage of EU10 nationals in the resident population of each EU15 Member State was relatively stable before and after enlargement, with increases in the UK and, more conspicuously, in Austria and in Ireland.
>
> (*Source:* From the European Commission's "Report on the Functioning of the Transitional Arrangements Set Out in the 2003 Accession Treaty (May 1, 2004—April 2006)," February 2006.)

guards that countries had put in place would still stop individual workers. But businesses that sold services—from consultants and accountants to builders, plumbers, and hairdressers—would be able to compete freely in all countries across the Union on equal terms with domestic service companies. The proposed law, which was debated fiercely in Europe throughout 2005, became another touchstone for western popular misgivings in countries with strong social democratic traditions such as Germany and France about Anglo-Saxon economic liberalization and the threat of cheap and unregulated labor flooding across the continent from the east.

In Brussels, the demonstrators wore stickers and carried banners proclaiming the need to protect "Social Europe" and "No to Social Dumping." The law became an especially sensitive issue in French politics, and in the French media José Manuel Barroso, president of the European Commission, was vilified for moving the EU in a liberal direction. This was an abrupt and surprising reversal in how the Commission was traditionally perceived. In the past, the Commission was a close ally of France and had been seen as a bastion of social and environmental protection. But now it was suddenly seen, at least in France, as spearheading eastern-influenced, free-market capitalism. Barroso tried to defend himself, but in the run-up to a key summit meeting of EU leaders in Brussels in March 2005, Jacques Chirac told Barroso to stay off French media because he was only making the Commission and Europe more unpopular, at least in France.

The EU summit in March 2005 became a showdown between those countries, such as Britain and Poland, that supported the services law in its most liberalizing form and the nations grouped around France, which wanted to water it down. In the end, the proposed directive was gutted: by the end of the two-day summit, France and Germany succeeded in including broad exemptions to the law that protected many areas of domestic service sectors from cross-border competition, such as healthcare, social services, and education.[15]

TENSE EU BUDGET NEGOTIATIONS

The negotiations for the EU's 2007–2013 budget were a further illustration of the west's waning enthusiasm for enlargement, in essence showing that the rich countries of Western Europe were no longer willing to pay extra billions in EU aid to update the easterners' infrastructure or extend the west's generous agricultural subsidies to the east. The EU's new 2007–2013 budget, the first since the new countries had joined the EU, was billed as the one that would pay for enlargement and the full integration of the poor former-communist east into the richer west. In 2004, the commission proposed a generous settlement of around €1 trillion over seven years, or around 1.2 percent of EU GDP. The implication of this number was that those countries that were traditionally the biggest contributors would have to increase their payments further, while the poorer members among the western states such as Spain and Greece would see a lot of their aid diverted to the new eastern countries. I saw the desperate need for this aid in the east in Plzen, where there were blocks of decaying high-rise apartment buildings and the city's suburbs lacked modern water treatment.[16]

In 2004, the group of six countries that contributed the most per capita to the EU budget—Sweden, the Netherlands, Britain, Germany, Austria, and France—said that spending had to be kept at 1 percent of EU GDP. At a summit of EU leaders in Brussels in June 2005, discussions degenerated about who should pay what, and there was an unsightly standoff between Prime Minister Tony Blair of Britain and President Jacques Chirac of France and Gerhard Schröder, chancellor of Germany. Chirac urged Blair to pay more into the EU's coffers. Blair said Britain would only increase spending if France cut its own generous EU farming subsidies, which Chirac refused to do.

The meeting was one of the most ill-tempered in living memory, according to diplomats who sat in on the discussions. It was a measure of how the ten new countries had utterly changed the dynamics of the Union. At one point during the summit, the new members, which were eager to get agreement so money from the budget could start flowing eastward, grouped together and offered to compensate Britain for an increase in spending. However, final agreement, setting the budget at €862.4 billion, or 1.045 percent of EU GDP, had to wait until the next EU summit in December. At the end of negotiations, all the rich countries agreed to pay slightly more, but not as much as originally foreseen. "There will be a very large shift of resources and that money will go to the new member states," Tony Blair, looking bleary-eyed, said at a 3 a.m. press conference at the close of the negotiations, which he had chaired.

Europe's New Constitution Stumbles

But even more than the controversy over the budget and the services directive, the clearest signal of the western public's rising antipathy toward the east, and their general discontent with the Union, was the rejection of the EU's new constitutional treaty in referendums in France and the Netherlands in the summer of 2005.

The treaty had been drawn up over two years of consultation and argument, and was finally signed on October 29, 2004, when EU leaders, plus the leaders of four EU candidate countries (Bulgaria, Romania, Turkey, and Croatia), met on the Capitoline Hill in Rome in the same hall where nearly fifty years earlier the original founding members had established the European Economic Community. Amid the frescoes and statues, and surrounded by the scent of olive groves, they celebrated the fact that the Union at last had a single legal document that could help it work efficiently with the new Central and East European members. Without it, some feared, a union of twenty-five or more members could grind to a halt. But before the treaty could become law it had to be ratified in each member state, either by parliamentary vote or by national referendum. Nearly ten countries, generally those with the most ambivalent attitude toward the new treaty, decided to hold referendums, including France, the Netherlands, Poland, the Czech Republic, and Britain.

France held its referendum on May 29, 2005. In the debate ahead of the vote, the treaty document itself became largely irrelevant as opinion instead focused on disapproval of President Jacques Chirac's government, complaints about the effects of the last EU enlargement, and hostility toward Turkey joining the EU. The prospect of Turkish EU membership was so unpopular in France that to defuse domestic unrest Chirac had promised that, even if talks about membership began with Turkey, France would hold a referendum before Turkey could officially join the Union. Nevertheless, as opinion polls showed, by rejecting the treaty, voters in France felt they could deliver an uncompromising verdict on the 2004 enlargement as well as the possible future accession of Muslim Turkey, which was even poorer and, they felt, represented an even greater threat to Western Europe's economies and welfare state. In the end, France's electorate voted by 55 percent to 45 percent against the treaty.

The result transformed the political landscape of both France and the EU overnight. "The European process does not come to an end today," Jean-Claude Juncker, prime minister of Luxembourg and holder of the European Union's rotating presidency at the time, told a press conference in Brussels after the results of the vote came through. Juncker said the treaty was "not dead" and that the ratification had to continue. The treaty's next test, however, was even harder than it had been in France.

The referendum in the Netherlands three days later on June 1, 2005, took place against a particularly hostile atmosphere toward immigrants. In 2004, in Amsterdam, a Muslim extremist had murdered Theo van Gogh, an outspoken critic of Islamist law. This death had followed the earlier rise of Pim Fortuyn, a Dutch politician who had built enormous popularity by criticizing the Netherlands' traditional openness to immigrants. Dutch society was in convulsions as its people reexamined their traditionally liberal society and asked whether they were doing enough to make immigrants assimilate. This combined with enlargement to fuel hostility toward the new countries of the east.

When I walked out on to the streets of The Hague, the Dutch capital, one morning two weeks before the referendum, people complained to me that the EU, a project that had begun as a customs union and had brought huge economic benefits for this small trading nation, was now veering dangerously toward a social and political integration that represented an unprecedented attack on Dutch sovereignty, identity, and way of life. People complained of a lack of democracy in the EU and that they had had no say in the direction the Union was taking. As in France, one prominent concern was that the entry into the EU of the Eastern European countries, and the possible entry of Turkey in a few years' time, was helping cheaper foreign workers fill Dutch jobs and adding to the Netherlands' acute immigration problems.

Standing outside the Dutch parliament, Lobi van der Gragt, a woman visiting the Hague from a flower-growing region in northwest Holland, told me that she wasn't happy with the EU, so why vote for a constitution that cemented it? "We see our money going abroad," she said, waving her finger at me.

The "no" camp had been bolstered by high-level supporters such as Geert Wilders, a populist politician who urged rejection of the treaty so as to keep Turkey out of the EU. "The Dutch were never asked about the introduction of the euro, enlargement, Turkey," Rob Boudewegm, senior fellow at the Clingendael Institute of International Relations in The Hague, told me. "This is the first time they can give their opinion and it is no."

The Dutch rejected the treaty by an even larger margin than the French—by 62 percent to 38 percent. Again, Jean-Claude Juncker stood up on a stage in Brussels and said that ratification of the treaty had to go on. But in the wake of the French and Dutch "no" votes, countries across the continent saw that the treaty politically was dead, for now at least, and one by one called off their referendums.

Nine countries had ratified it before the French went to the polls, including, in the east, Hungary, Lithuania, Slovakia, and Slovenia. After the rejections, the Czech Republic postponed its proposed referendum until the end of 2006, and Poland delayed its vote indefinitely.[17]

Box 11.3   Excerpts from the Proposed EU Constitutional Treaty

Establishment of the Union

"Reflecting the will of the citizens and States of Europe to build a common future, this Constitution establishes the European Union, on which the Member States confer competences to attain objectives they have in common.

"The Union shall be open to all European States which respect its values and are committed to promoting them together."

The Union's Values

"The Union is founded on the values of respect for human dignity, freedom, democracy, equality, the rule of law and respect for human rights, including the rights of persons belonging to minorities. These values are common to the Member States in a society in which pluralism, non-discrimination, tolerance, justice, solidarity and equality between women and men prevail."

The Union's Objectives

"The Union's aim is to promote peace, its values and the well-being of its peoples.

"The Union shall offer its citizens an area of freedom, security and justice without internal frontiers, and an internal market where competition is free and undistorted."

Solidarity Clause

"The Union and its Member States shall act jointly in a spirit of solidarity if a Member State is the object of a terrorist attack or the victim of a natural or man-made disaster. The Union shall mobilise all the instruments at its disposal, including the military resources made available by the Member States."

The Union and Its Neighbors

"The Union shall develop a special relationship with neighbouring countries, aiming to establish an area of prosperity and good neighbourliness, founded on the values of the Union and characterised by close and peaceful relations based on cooperation."

Eastern Disillusionment

Given such antagonism from their new neighbors and allies in the west, it is perhaps unsurprising that some in the east also began to view EU membership with a creeping disillusionment. This had set in even before enlargement. Initially, in the 1990s, the new countries had been enthusiastic in their embrace of the prospect of EU accession. The accession process dominated domestic politics, and governments were judged on their ability to deliver the reforms that nudged the nation gradually toward membership. In Slovakia, Prime Minister Vladimir Meciar was ousted as the country's leader when his rule was seen as obstacle to EU membership, and Mikulas Dzurinda, a more pro-EU leader, was elected in 1998.

Yet as accession neared, fatigue at the quick pace of reforms set in. This combined with the years of economic struggle since the fall of communism and frustration at the delays in securing EU membership. There was also impatience that living standards, although improving dramatically, were taking so long to catch up with those in the west. (Incomes in accession countries were less than half the EU average in 2006.) After the countries had closed all of their thirty-one chapters with the EU negotiators, each had to approve final accession to the EU, and nine chose to do so in national referendums; the tenth, Cyprus, held a parliamentary vote. On the eve of the referendums, the gripes about the approaching EU membership turned into full-blown fears about what accession would finally mean. In many cases, these involved worries about loss of identity and surrendering national sovereignty so soon after gaining hard-won independence from the Soviet Union. This was one of the fears raised in the Czech Republic by the country's president, Vaclav Klaus, an outspoken Euro-sceptic, who tried to weaken the "yes" vote. In Estonia, people feared the reimposition of cumbersome and costly rules and regulations, and higher prices, especially of sugar, which was expected to rise in cost as cheap imports were restricted. The future price of sugar became one of the central topics of debate on the streets of Tallinn.[18]

THE ASPIRANT COUNTRIES VOTE IN REFERENDUMS

Despite these concerns, on June 14, 2003, the Czech people approved accession by 77 percent, on a low turnout of 55 percent. The Czech prime minister Vladimir Spidla said that this "vote puts an end to the results of the Second World War. We have come back to where we are strong and have great opportunities." In Poland, which held its referendum a few weeks later on June 8, 2003, 77 percent voted in favor, on a turnout of 59 percent. On September 14, 2003, Estonia voted two-thirds in favor of accession on a turnout of 64 percent.

All ten countries approved accession but the votes were hardly unequivocal backing for the EU. They were a "yes" but a diffident "yes" to the Union, a sense that persisted into 2004 and past the accession date of May 1. Just over a month later, only one in five eligible voters bothered to turn out to vote in the European parliamentary elections, the first for the new countries.

Despite the fears that accession could spark economic catastrophe for the new states, enlargement triggered a further economic spurt as inward investment and growth surged. Foreign direct investment rose from €7 billion in 2003 to around €13.8 billion in 2004. In Poland, it rose from below €4 billion in 2003 to €7 billion in the following year. Exports rose by around a fifth.[19]

Box 11.4   New EU Members: Referendums on EU Membership

Country	Population (mn)	Referendum date	Turnout %	% in favor
Poland	38.6	June 2003	59	77
Czech Republic	10.2	June 2003	55	77
Hungary	10.0	April 2003	46	84
Slovak Republic	5.4	May 2003	52	93
Slovenia	2.0	March 2003	60	90
Latvia	2.3	Sept 2003	73	67
Estonia	1.4	Sept 2003	64	67
Lithuania	3.6	May 2003	63	91
Cyprus	0.8	Parliamentary approval		
Malta	0.4	March 2003	91	54

The new countries had feared they would be swamped by German exports. Instead, in the year after enlargement they were overrun by German buyers. As a result, GDP in the new member states accelerated from an annual rate of 3.7 percent to 5 percent in 2004. The first traches of EU farm aid also began to be dispersed in the months after enlargement, and farmers' incomes rose by a half in the new member states in 2004—doubling in the Czech Republic, and increasing by nearly three-quarters in Poland. According to the European Commission's "Eurobarometer" opinion survey, in 2004 attitudes among easterners rose to their most positive levels since the mid-1990s.

TURBULENT POLITICS

Despite the opinion polls, in the years following accession the new member states still managed to elect parties that stood on anti-EU platforms. These parties drew support from sections of the population that were not taking part in the economic boom. By no means was everybody sharing in the fruits of economic growth, a fact that was perhaps most clearly illustrated in Poland, which had some of the richest regions of the EU's new east and the poorest, and where unemployment in 2006 was around 18 percent and youth joblessness stood around 40 percent of the work force on average—in some areas it was much higher.

The general trend was that while urban areas such as Warsaw had prospered, rural regions had stagnated. Rural incomes had fallen way behind those in some of Poland's cities. The beneficiaries of EU integration had been the young and well-educated, while the old, the sick, and the jobless had generally not kept up. In Warsaw and a handful of other cities, a well-defined professional entrepreneurial middle-class grew up who could afford cars, foreign holidays, and consumer electronics. But in the small towns and villages there was poverty and, sometimes, real hopelessness.

It was this disenfranchised constituency that Poland's Law and Justice Party appealed to in the September 2005 general elections. In the run-up to the elections, it seemed that Law and Justice would most likely be the junior partner in a coalition government with the Civic Platform Party. Both were young parties that had grown out of Poland's Solidarity movement of the 1990s. Both defined themselves against the previous government of former communists, the Democratic Left Alliance, which had become embroiled in sleaze and corruption allegations. Both parties were conservative and broadly pro-market. But Civic Platform was more outward-looking and pro-European than Law and Justice. It promised continued economic reform, perhaps even more extreme than in the past, including a flat tax, and wanted Poland to adopt the euro quickly.

In contrast, Law and Justice said that it wanted to focus on cleansing Poland of the sleaze and corruption of the past. On election day in Warsaw, outside a polling station in the towering communist-era Palace of Culture and Science, one voter, a pensioner named Jerzy Cymanski, who had worked for forty years in railway construction, expressed a view that was widespread when he told me that the country's previous leaders "were not socialist, but people who just wanted to make quick money. The same can happen again." Law and Justice was more pro-U.S. and less European than Civic Platform. In the run-up to the election, it swung further to the protectionist left, opposing more rapid free-market reforms and favoring the retention of social welfare programs and a high level of state benefits for the poor. It also emphasized a return to Christian values and moral change. It played to a common feeling that the west was forgetting its obligations to the Poles, who had suffered so much under Nazism and communism.

In the September elections, Law and Justice, which was led by twin brothers Lech and Jaroslaw Kaczynski, defied expectations and won 155 of the 460 seats in the Sejm, the lower house of parliament. Its partner-cum-rival Civic Platform won 133 seats. In the presidential election that followed two months later, Law and Justice again defeated Civic Platform, as Lech Kaczynski triumphed over Donald Tusk. It was a clear signal that Poles had grown tired of relentless economic and social transformation and yearned for a period of stability. Poland's longing for the supposed certainties of the past meant Law and Justice turned to some unlikely allies in the ensuing coalition negotiations for government. It spurned Civic Platform, and in spring 2006 formed an uneasy ruling coalition with two extremist parties—Samoobrona, or Self-Defense, a populist, rural party led by Andrzej Lepper, and the League of Polish Families, a right-wing Catholic nationalist group, both hostile to the EU.

Since enlargement, the politics of the new EU countries had, if anything, become slightly more unstable than they had been in the run-up to accession. Politics in these still-young former communist countries had always tended to be a seesaw, as the populations oscillated between a yearning for change and, as the pain of the reforms hit home, a nostalgia for the imagined securities of the communist past. Countries in the region changed their government every twenty months on average in the first decade after communism. Poland was first to vote its own communists back into power in 1993. The communists lost in 1997, won again in 2001, and lost again in 2005. Hungary too followed a similar pattern: postcommunists won office in 1994, lost it in 1998, and regained power in 2002.[20] When Slovakia returned Mikulas Dzurinda in 2003, it was the first time a prime minister in one of the Visograd countries had won two elections in a row, but Dzurinda was voted out in elections in June 2006 in favor of a left-wing rival.

The parties in these nations were still in their infancy and lacked deep roots. They tended to have small memberships, and personalities tended to matter more than ideologies. Whereas in the years up to 2004, accession provided a focus, this focus disappeared after 2004.

Instability was a feature of Czech politics. As in most countries in the EU's new east, the Czech Republic was dogged by repeated scandals about corruption, which seemed to be another feature of the political and public life of these young countries that were trying fitfully to put their communist pasts behind them and construct a new society. Vaclav Klaus, who became prime minister in 1992, and was probably the single most successful politician in Central and Eastern Europe in the postcommunist era, was forced to relinquish power in 1997 following a controversy over party funding. In 2003, he became the country's second president, succeeding Vaclav Havel, and was openly critical of the Brussels bureaucracy and the "unification of Europe." The political turmoil has continued since enlargement. Vladimir Spidla resigned following disastrous results in the European parliamentary elections only a month after accession. In April 2005, weeks of crisis ended with the resignation of Prime Minister Stanislav Gross amid a scandal over the financing of a luxury apartment, and Jiri Paroubek became the country's third prime minister since July 2004. Paroubek, however, lost power in bitterly fought general elections in June 2006. The apparent victor, Mirek Topolanek of the conservative Civic Democrat Party, a former businessman, won only 100 seats in the 200-seat chamber and suggested he would rely on two small centrist parties for support, but was unable to form a stable coalition government. The Czech Republic entered a further period of weak government. Slovakia, too, appeared to take a step backwards after elections in 2006 returned a weak populist and antireform government.

ECONOMIC MODERNIZATION IN QUESTION

The Baltic nations were not spared the political turbulence. They saw many governments following independence. By 2006, Estonia's current prime minister, Andrus Ansip, leader of the center-right Reform Party, headed the country's eighth administration in twelve years. But Estonia at least was spared another prominent feature of the post-enlargement era, a relaxation in economic reform. The Estonian government promised to continue strict pro-market modernization measures such as cutting social spending and taxes, and encouraging foreign investment. But in many other countries, accession was followed by a slowdown in the pace of economic modernization.

This may have been because the first reforms were the easiest and now countries had to tackle more difficult challenges, which took longer. But the slowdown may also have been because countries were relaxing after securing entry into the Union. For example, the European Bank for Reconstruction and Development's "Transition Report" reports a slowdown after 2004.[21]

This by no means happened in all countries. According to the World Bank's "Doing Business" report, Slovakia and Latvia were among the world's fastest-reforming countries in 2004. Estonia and Lithuania too were ahead of Germany, France, and Italy.

But Hungary and Poland were rated poorly in the same survey; in Hungary and the Czech Republic, the business environment was deteriorating. In the Czech Republic, infrastructure constraints, skill shortages, labor market regulations, and the tax burden were getting worse, not better. Companies in Poland were reporting worries about economic stability.[22]

The result is that many of the Central and East European economies continued to have serious weaknesses, such as high unemployment and weak public finances, which acted as a drag on balanced, widespread growth.

Countries were struggling to control welfare spending and budget deficits, especially Hungary, the Czech Republic, and Poland. In 2004, for example, Hungary suffered a foreign exchange crisis when financial markets took fright at mounting fiscal and current-account deficits. In June 2006, the Organization for Economic Cooperation and Development warned that the Czech Republic still had much to do in reducing its public deficit and debt levels, and called for reform of the state-funded pension system. One of Poland's chief problems remained its stodgy and bureaucratic state sector, which consumed a large proportion of the economy and which successive governments had found tough to rein back. Its high taxes and social charges made labor expensive and contributed to unemployment. They were one of the reasons why hundreds of thousands of young Poles had gone abroad since enlargement. Heavy social transfers to pensioners and others, including some of the developed world's most generous disability payment schemes, weighed down spending. In Poland, electricity privatization was being held up by pressure from trade unions; there were also deep sensitivities about transferring the country's petrochemical industry, the post office, and railway infrastructure to the private sector. Poland still had an unwieldy and inefficient farming sector.

EURO MEMBERSHIP

The economic backsliding put back some of the eastern countries' plans for joining the euro, the European single currency.

In what was seen as the inevitable next step in their ever-increasing integration into Europe, most of the new countries had declared when they acceded to the Union that their next goal was to give up their own currencies and embrace the euro as soon as possible. All new EU members in fact have an obligation to join the euro at some point, though no time scale is stipulated and, in order to adopt the currency, they first have to pass the strict entry tests, called the Maastricht criteria, which ensure that no new member threatens the stability of the currency. These economic tests include having an inflation rate of no more than 1.5 percentage points above the average in the three EU countries with the lowest rates, a budget deficit of no more than 3 percent of gross domestic product, and debt of no more than 60 percent of GDP. They also have to be members of the European exchange rate mechanism for at least two years.

Following accession, some of the new countries remained on track, mainly the smaller nations that had more vulnerable currencies than the larger members and for whom the rewards of the euro—financial stability, the removal of exchange rate risk for foreign investors, and higher inward investment and thus faster growth—were greater. Estonia, for example, kept strict control of spending, and ran a budget surplus. It joined the exchange rate mechanism in 2004. But others have gone astray. In May 2006, the European Commission gave its first judgment since enlargement on which of the new countries could join the euro. It ruled that only Slovenia had met the entry criteria, paving the way for Slovenia to join the euro currency bloc in 2007. Estonia and Lithuania had both seemed likely to join Slovenia in the euro, but they both failed. Estonia's problem was its rapid economic growth, which had translated into high inflation. Poland and the Czech Republic were disqualified because of their excessive fiscal deficits, but both countries' governments had already said that joining the currency was not a priority, a reflection of the increasingly Euro-sceptical nature of their populations.

The EU Becomes Less Welcoming to Countries on the Outside

While the EU was a colder place for the new Central and East European nations that joined in 2004, it was also less welcoming for the countries still outside the

EU who hoped one day to follow them into the Union. Western European leaders had taken note of voters' rejection of the constitutional treaty, and of opinion polls that pointed to continued suspicion in the west of poorer countries from the east, and slowed down, for the time being at least, the pace of EU enlargement. This "enlargement fatigue" was bad news for the long queue of poor, aspirant countries waiting to join the EU.

In May 2006, the European Commission delayed a decision about whether Bulgaria and Romania, the first in line, could accede in 2007 or 2008, urging Bulgaria in particular to take steps to address corruption, organized crime, human trafficking, and money laundering. Both nations, which together have a combined population of 30 million, were much poorer than the ten that joined on May 1, 2004. Later in 2006, the Commission agreed that both countries could join the EU in 2007, but only under strict conditions such as tight controls on migration.

The Commission also took a firm line against Serbia. It suspended Serbia's accession talks until Serbia cooperated more in finding and handing over Radko Mladic, a war crimes suspect, to the International Criminal Tribunal for the former Yugoslavia in The Hague.

Another nation from the former Yugoslavia, Croatia, was preparing to join the Union at the earliest by 2009 or 2010. Beyond these countries, the EU had acknowledged Macedonia as a candidate country, and had signaled that Bosnia-Herzegovina, Montenegro, and Albania were on track to join the EU as well. Ukraine had made plain its ambitions to build stronger ties to the Union and one day perhaps to join it. But the political reality of Western Europe hindered its ambitions. In the fifteen western nations that made up the EU before 2004, little more than a third of the people supported the entry of the western Balkans, for example.

Some of the fiercest opposition was reserved for Ukraine and Turkey, both larger than the biggest country that had joined in the last round of enlargement, Poland. Turkey, especially, could arouse strong antipathy among some Western Europeans. They said that Turkey, a mainly Muslim nation of 70 million, is not in fact in Europe. These critics said that the borders of the EU should be defined by what they said were its Christian roots. In 2006, around three-quarters of the people in France and in Austria opposed Turkish membership in the EU. France was already home to one of Europe's biggest Muslim populations—about 6 million, or 10 percent of the total population—while Austria sat on the border with the new Central and Eastern European nations and therefore was among those countries that had felt the economic effects of their arrival in the Union the hardest.

I saw the strength of this opposition in October 2005 when I visited the Victor Adler Market in a working-class district of Vienna, where amid the venison and cheese and wine stalls, local people expressed deep fears about the immigration and competition for jobs that they said Turkish membership of the EU would unleash. "We will be overrun," Gottfried Piswanger, forty-nine, a butcher, told me, as he shook his head. "We are already too full. And when they come, they do not adjust."

Piswanger's reservations were reflected in the heated negotiations between EU governments in Luxembourg later the same month when the Austrian government insisted that the EU offer Turkey a second-class status rather than full membership.

After two days of dramatic bargaining, the European foreign ministers agreed to offer Turkey the prospect of full membership. It was a momentous step in Turkey's four-decade quest to join the EU. It had first applied for associate membership status in 1959. "This is a truly historic day for Europe and for the whole of the international community," said Jack Straw, the British foreign minister who was chairing the talks. Turkey's entry into the EU, Straw said, "will bring a strong secular state that happens to have a Muslim majority into the EU, proof that we can live, work and prosper together." But Austria won assurances that the EU could halt Turkey's membership process if the Union was not ready to absorb another country.

In addition, the framework for membership comprised all sorts of safeguards, including long-term powers for western countries to help them stop Turkish immigrants drifting westwards, along the lines of the barriers put in the way of workers from Central and Eastern Europe. The west's reservations meant that the discussions with Turkey were likely to be long and tough and would probably last until 2014 at the earliest. Even then the talks could fail and membership might never be granted to Turkey.

A Brighter Future as the EU Develops?

The EU of 2014, however, may be a place very different from the EU that existed in the first few years following the accession of the countries from Central and Eastern Europe in 2004. By then, the new members, powered by continued economic reform, may be islands of renewed prosperity and stability that sit more comfortably alongside the western nations. The western countries, in turn, may have overcome their initial suspicion of the newcomers. They may be ready to embrace their cousins in the east, and even other members beyond their borders.

Notes

1. Graham Bowley, "Under One Flag: Trieste's Hopes Reawaken as Borders Open," *International Herald Tribune*, April 28, 2004.

2. Europa, European Union website: http://europa.eu/scadplus/glossary/accession _criteria_copenhague_en.htm.

3. Graham Bowley, "Letter from Estonia: Changed by Joining EU, and Changing It, as Well," *International Herald Tribune*, August 17, 2005.

4. Graham Bowley, "British Farmers Grow Roots in Estonia," *International Herald Tribune*, August 26, 2005.

5. Katinka Barysch, "Enlargement Two Years On: Economic Success or Political Failure?" *Centre for European Reform*, April 2006, p. 15.

6. Barysch, "Enlargement Two Years On," p. 16.

7. Barysch, "Enlargement Two Years On," p. 6.

8. BBC website, "Russia Spurns Estonia Border Deal, " BBC News, June 27, 2005: http://news.bbc.co.uk/2/hi/europe/4626141.stm.

9. Graham Bowley, "Russian Sacrifice: Poland," *International Herald Tribune*, November 25, 2005.

10. George Parker, "The British Star Is Rising but Only the French See That," *Financial Times*, October 9, 2004.

11. Graham Bowley, "The EU's Growing Pains: East Europeans Are Forcing a Reappraisal," *International Herald Tribune*, March 9, 2005.

12. Graham Bowley, "Conservative Poland Roils European Union," *New York Times*, December 4, 2005.

13. Quoted in Barysch, "Enlargement Two Years On," p. 15.

14. European Commission, "Report on the Functioning of the Transitional Arrangements Set Out in the 2003 Accession Treaty (period 1 May 2004—April 2006)," February 2006: http://ec.europa.eu/employment_social/news/2006/feb/report_en.pdf.

15. Graham Bowley and James Kanter, "Chirac Urges French to Back EU Charter," *International Herald Tribune*, March 24, 2005.

16. Graham Bowley, "EU Turns Its Attention and Resources to East," *International Herald Tribune*, July 18, 2005.

17. See Europa, the EU's website, "Ratification and State of Play": http://europa.eu/constitution/ratification_en.htm.

18. Nicholas George and Stefan Wagstyl, "Soviet Union to European Union," *Financial Times*, September 13, 2003.

19. Stefan Wagstyl, "Accession States Reap Rewards of EU Membership," *Financial Times*, April 26, 2005.

20. *The Economist*, "Freedom to Choose in the Visegrad Countries: But to Choose What?" November 20, 2003.

21. Quoted in Barysch, "Enlargement Two Years On," p. 9.

22. Barysch, "Enlargement Two Years On," p. 9.

Suggested Readings

Europa, the website of the European Union, www.europa.com.

Bainbridge, Timothy, *The Penguin Companion to the European Union*, London: Penguin, 2003.

Barysch, Katinka, *One Year After Enlargement*, London: Centre for European Reform, 2006.

Cooper, Robert, *The Breaking of Nations: Order and Chaos in the Twenty-First Century*, London: Atlantic Books, 2004.

Leonard, Dick, *The Economist Guide to the European Union*, London: The Economist, 2005.

Leonard, Mark, *Why Europe Will Run the 21st Century*, London: Fourth Estate, 2005.

Zielonka, Jan, *Europe as Empire: The Nature of the Enlarged European Union*, London: Oxford University Press, 2006.

Statistics: Central and Eastern Europe

Czech Republic

Population (million):	10.2
Area in Square Miles:	30,448
Population Density per Square Mile:	335
GDP (in billion dollars, 2005):	$208.9
GDP per capita (PPP, 2005):	$20,417
Joined EC/EU	May 1, 2004

Performance of Key Political Parties in Parliamentary Elections of June 2–3, 2006

Czech Social Democratic Party (CSSD)	32.3%
Christian and Democratic Union—Czechoslovak People's Party (KDU-CSL)	7.2%
Czech and Moravian Communist Party (KSCM)	12.8%
Civic Democratic Party (ODS)	35.4%
Green Party (SZ)	6.3%

Main office holders: Prime Minister: Mirek Topolánek—ODS (2006); President: Václav Klaus—ODS (2003)

Hungary

Population (million):	10.1
Area per Square Mile:	35,919
Population Density in Square Miles:	281
GDP (in billion dollars, 2005):	$171.4
GDP per capita (PPP, 2005):	$16,994
Joined EC/EU	May 1, 2004

Performance of Key Political Parties in Parliamentary Elections of April 2006

Alliance of Free Democrats (SzDSz)	6.5%
Alliance of Young Democrats–Hungarian Democratic Forum (FIDESz-MPS)	42.0%
Hungarian Socialist Party (MSzP)	43.2%

Main office holders: Prime Minister: Ferenc Gyurcsány—MSzP (2004); President: László Sólyom (2005)

Poland

Population (million)	38.2
Area in Square Miles:	124,807
Population Density per Square Mile:	306
GDP (in billion dollars, 2005)	$526.2
GDP per capita (PPP, 2005):	$13,791
Joined EC/EU	May 1, 2004

Performance of Key Political Parties in Parliamentary Elections of September 25, 2005

Citizens' Platform (PO)	24.1%
Democratic Left Alliance (SLD)	11.3%
Law and Justice (PiS)	27.0%
League of Polish Families (LPR)	8.0%
Polish People's Party (PSL)	7.0%
Self-Defence of the Polish Republic (SRP)	11.4%

Main office holders: President: Lech Kaczynski—PiS (2005); Prime Minister: Jaroslaw Kaczynski—PiS (2006)

Slovak Republic

Population (million):	5.4
Area in Square Miles:	18,923
Population Density per Square Mile:	284
GDP (in billion dollars, 2005):	$81.9
GDP per capita (PPP, 2005):	$15,241
Joined EC/EU	May 1, 2004

Performance of Key Political Parties in Parliamentary Elections of June 17, 2006

Christian Democratic Alliance (KDH)	8.3%
Communist Party of Slovakia (KSS)	3.9%
Direction—Social Democracy (Smer)	29.1%
Hungarian Coalition Party (SMK)	11.7%
New Civic Alliance (ANO)	1.4%
People's Party—Movement for a Democratic Slovakia (LS-HDS)	8.8%
Slovak Christian Democratic Union (SDKU)	18.4%
Slovakian National Party (SNS)	11.7%

Main office holders: Prime Minister: Robert Fico—Smer (2006); President: Ivan Gascaronparovic (2004)

Slovenia

Population (million):	2.0
Area in Square Miles:	7,819
Population Density per Square Mile:	256
GDP (in billion dollars, 2005):	$44.6
GDP per capita (PPP, 2005):	$22,293
Joined EC/EU	May 1, 2004

Performance of Key Political Parties in Parliamentary Elections of October 3, 2004

Democratic Party of Retired People of Slovenia (DeSUS)	4%
Liberal Democracy of Slovenia (LDS)	22.8%
New Slovenia—Christian People's Party (NSI)	9.0%
Slovenian Democratic Party (SDS)	29.1%
Slovenian People's Party (SLS)	6.8%
Slovenian National Party (SNS)	6.3%
United List of Social Democrats (ZLSD)	10.2%

Main office holders: President: Janez Drnovscaronek (2002); Prime Minister: Janez Janscarona—SDS (2004)

Estonia

Population (million):	1.3
Area in Square Miles:	17,413
Population Density per Square Mile:	77
GDP (in billion dollars, 2005):	$22.4
GDP per capita (PPP, 2005):	$16,635
Joined EC/EU	May 1, 2004

Performance of Key Political Parties in Parliamentary Elections of March 2, 2003

Centre Party (K)	25.4%
Estonian People's Union (R)	13.0%
Fatherland Union (I)	7.3%
Moderates (M)	7.0%
Reform Party (RE)	17.7%
Res Publica (RP)	24.6%
United People's Party (EURP)	2.2%

Main Office Holders: Prime Minister: Andrus Ansip—RE (2005); President: Toomas Hendrik Ilves—Social Democratic Party (2006)

Lithuania

Population (million):	3.4
Area in Square Miles:	25,174
Population Density per Square Mile:	136
GDP (in billion dollars, 2005):	$49.1
GDP per capita (PPP, 2005):	$14,405
Joined EC/EU	May 1, 2004

Performance of Key Political Parties in Parliamentary Elections of October 2004

Farmers' Party—New Democratic Party (LVP-NDP)	6.6%
Homeland Union (TS)	14.7%
Liberal and Centre Union (LCS)	9.2%
Lithuanian Poles' Electoral Action (LLRA)	3.8%
Order and Justice (UTT)	11.4%
Labour Party (DP)	28.4%
Working for Lithuania (UDL Uz)	20.6%

Main Office Holders: President: Valdas Adamkus (2004); Prime Minister: Gediminas Kirkilas—Social Democrats (2006)

Latvia

Population (million):	2.3
Area in Square Miles:	24,942
Population Density per Square Mile:	92
GDP (in billion dollars, 2005):	$30.0
GDP per capita (PPP, 2005):	$13,054
Joined EC/EU	May 1, 2004

Performance of Key Political Parties in Parliamentary Elections of October 7, 2006

Fatherland and Freedom (TB-LNNK)	6.9%
For Civil Rights (PCTVL)	6%
Harmony Centre (SC)	14.4%
Latvia First—Latvia's Way (LPP-LC)	8.6%
New Era (JL)	16.4%
People's Party (TP)	19.6%
Social Democrats (LSSP)	3.5%
Union of Greens and Farmers (ZZS)	16.7%

Main Office Holders: President: Vaira Vike-Freiberga (1999); Prime Minister: Aigars Kalvitis—People's Party (2004)

Romania

Population (million):	21.6
Area in Square Miles:	92,042
Population Density per Square Mile:	235
GDP (in billion dollars, 2005):	$207.6
GDP per capita (PPP, 2005):	$9,566
Joined EC/EU	January 1, 2007

Performance of Key Political Parties in Parliamentary Elections of November 2004

Hungarian Democratic Alliance of Romania (UDMR)	6.2%
Justice and Truth Alliance (PNL-PD)	31.5%
National Union (PSD-PUR)	36.8%
Party of Great Romania (PRM)	13.0%

Main office holders: President: Traian Basescu (2004); Prime Minister: Calin Popescu-Tariceanu—PNL (2004)

Bulgaria

Population (million):	7.7
Area in Square Miles:	42,822
Population Density per Square Mile:	181
GDP (in billion dollars, 2005):	$68.7
GDP per capita (PPP, 2005):	$8,877
Joined EC/EU	January 1, 2007

Performance of Key Political Parties in Parliamentary Elections of June 25, 2005

Bulgarian People's Union (BNS)	5.2%
Coalition for Bulgaria (KzB)	31.0%
Democrats for Strong Bulgaria (DSB)	6.5%
Movement for Rights and Freedoms (DPS)	12.8%
National Movement for Simeon II (NDSV)	19.9%
National Union "Attack" (NOA)	8.1%
Union of Democratic Forces (ODS)	7.7%

Main office holders: Prime Minister: Sergey Stanishev—Socialist Party (2005); President: Georgi Parvanov—Socialist Party (2002)

CHAPTER 12

Beyond European Security: Europe, the United States, and NATO

Jeffrey Simon and Sean Kay

The Twenty-First Century Challenge

Contemporary European politics have witnessed extraordinary transformation over the last two decades. Beginning in 1986, a new Soviet leader emerged, Mikhail Gorbachev, who brought an end to forty years of Cold War between the U.S.-led North Atlantic Treaty Organization (NATO) and the Soviet Union and its Warsaw Pact allies in Eastern Europe. Dramatic events followed with the withdrawal of Soviet troops from Eastern Europe, the fall of the Berlin Wall, the unification of Germany, and movement by the European Union toward political, economic, and foreign policy integration. By 1992, the Soviet Union was gone and NATO evolved into a new role facilitating the geographic integration of a Europe "whole and free" as the new continental geopolitics were often called. Yet, at the same time, the collapse of Yugoslavia placed tremendous pressures on NATO and the European Union, at times straining the credibility of their claims of a new relevance based on shared values. Meanwhile, a range of new security challenges developed, including terrorism, technology and weapons proliferation, immigration, the environment, and major wars in Afghanistan and Iraq. Could the transatlantic relationship withstand these pressures?

NATO at the Crossroads

At the core of the transatlantic relationship lies the North Atlantic Treaty Organization. NATO is a political-military institution that serves to facilitate the common security interests of its twenty-six members from North America and Europe.[1] Traditionally, NATO was a collective defense alliance, which means that an attack against one of the members would be considered an attack on all the members. This underlying purpose is bolstered by multilateral political consultation, military planning, and exercises. NATO's headquarters is in Brussels, Belgium, and its military command center is nearby in Mons, while both are connected to an array of command centers based around Europe. NATO operates on a rule of consensus, meaning that for it to act, all its members must be in agreement. During the Cold War, the threat from Soviet forces to the east made this consensus relatively easy to achieve. Since the end of the Cold War, NATO has reflected a general agreement on core Euro-Atlantic values, though its members have not always agreed on the means through which to advance them and whether this implied a commitment to a more global alliance.

The U.S. and European negotiators who forged the alliance after World War II faced four basic challenges. First, it was necessary to meet the growing Soviet threat. Though the Soviet Union is gone, NATO now faces the new challenge of simultaneously hedging against any future Russian challenge while promoting stability in NATO's eastern periphery and creating incentives for a peaceful and democratic Russia to engage with the West. Second, NATO served to achieve this goal by keeping the United States engaged in European security on a permanent basis. Since the presidency of George Washington, the United States had avoided entangling alliances with Europe. But after World War I and World War II, a means was clearly needed to facilitate a more permanent stabilizing role for the United States in European security. Third, NATO served to reassure its European neighbors that, after the defeat of the Nazi leadership, Germany would be integrated into a peaceful, democratic West. This internal function was also important after the end of the Cold War as Germany was unified within the context of NATO. Fourth, NATO has made a sustained effort to rebalance the transatlantic relationship by fostering European integration in a way that complements the shared interests of the transatlantic security relationship.

The emerging challenges of the twenty-first-century security environment have required that NATO depart from its traditional mission of conventional territorial defense of the member states. Drawing on the consultative functions inherent in the organization, and decades of multinational military planning, NATO's members set out during the 1990s to incorporate a range of new political and military missions as directed by its member states. While basic theory of international relations would predict that, as an alliance, NATO would disappear in the absence of a threat, the shared democratic values of its members and institutional mechanisms have sustained the organization.[2] New missions have included major peace support operations in the Balkans and Afghanistan, and incorporating counterterrorism as part of its defense mandate. Meanwhile, NATO continues to reach out to the east to promote stability in key regions such as the Black Sea.

NATO persists mainly because its member states continue to see a shared interest in both sustaining and adapting its institutional functions. Institutions must adapt to new conditions if the international situation requires it. In fact, as the British minister of defense, John Reid, warned in early 2006 at a speech in Munich, institutions should not survive for their own sake. NATO would have to have relevance to new security challenges if its survival was to matter.[3] The dilemma for NATO is that the central strategic functions are the easiest to perform. In fact, NATO's strategic functions remain important, but largely as a reserve asset. Meanwhile, NATO has become more of a tactical tool on which to draw—and this requires making painstaking efforts to forge agreement when interests among members diverge.[4] Critics of this architecture increasingly suggest that the European Union should take primary responsibility for security in and around Europe while the United States tends to its more "global" responsibilities.[5]

The transformation to NATO's new missions culminated in the 1999 war against Yugoslavia over Kosovo. In this case, NATO went to war not to defend territory but rather to secure human rights. NATO emerged victorious in the conflict. However, fighting the war through NATO's rules and procedures left a major impact on some of its leading members, particularly the United States, which tended to see NATO as inhibiting their preferred way of waging war. In some quarters, the Kosovo war was seen as having drawn the United States into a war to save NATO, not to advance a cause that was vital to its own more immediate national interests.[6] Nevertheless, the transatlantic community is more than NATO, and if the values inherent in the idea of a better, more peaceful Euro-Atlantic space were to have any meaning, Europe and the United States could not stand by while ethnic cleansing was carried on in the Balkans. The impact of the war, however, appeared to be the harbinger of a divide in strategic culture, with the United States capable of and willing to project power, and the Europeans largely unable or unwilling to do so. Meanwhile, the United States might want its NATO allies engaged after a war for peace operations and nation building, but it did not want to experience a condition where allies without troops at risk were deciding how the United States wages war. Thus, when the United States invaded Afghanistan in the fall of 2001 after the September 11 attacks, NATO member offers of assistance were effectively met with a "thanks, but no thanks." Suddenly the primary institutional reflection of the transatlantic security relationship had gone from winning the Cold War to claiming as its main activity offering some Airborne Warning and Control System planes to protect U.S. airspace, providing some hurricane and earthquake relief, and protecting the 2004 Olympic games. These were useful missions, though there was nothing inherent in them that they had to be carried out by NATO per se. Most significantly, the strategic divide both over Iraq and also how to fight a war against terrorism, would lead to a significant transatlantic breakdown. Nonetheless, NATO had performed two very significant acts during the 1990s—NATO enlargement and intervention in the Balkans.

NATO ENLARGEMENT

Since the fall of the Berlin Wall and the expansion of democratic revolutions throughout Central and Eastern Europe, NATO has sought to extend a "hand of friendship" to former adversaries and thus to facilitate their integration into modern Europe. Achieving this outcome was a major initiative for NATO, and it took considerable time and effort to forge a working consensus to implement the policy. After the Cold War ended, the unification of Germany was a major new question mark on the international scene. How could Germany continue to be locked into the West, maintain its historical peaceful reconciliation with its neighbors, and extend that process to the East? Indeed, how would the West manage the simultaneous rise of Germany and decline of Russia? The answer was first posited by the Germans themselves—to begin a transparent and gradual process of enlarging NATO to include new members.[7]

For the countries of Eastern Europe, emerging from the shadow of communism and returning to Europe, both in terms of their political identity and security commitments, became a dominant factor of international relations in the 1990s. Countries ranging from the Baltic to the Black Sea began pressuring NATO to establish direct relationships with them, to eventually include membership. The administration of U.S. president Bill Clinton saw significant gains from an enlarged NATO, but sought to promote a gradual process that would lead to a strengthened alliance while at the same time not alienating Russia—which strongly opposed NATO's growth. Moreover, NATO collectively recognized that by setting clear criteria for new membership, the organization could serve as a means to promote reform to the East. To begin the process, states that were interested in joining NATO were asked to participate in a "Partnership for Peace," which allowed for affiliation with NATO and a gradual enhancement of political reform and military capabilities that would strengthen NATO as it eventually enlarged.

NATO enlargement was an important and logical extension of the adaptation that NATO undertook with the end of the Cold War. While some countries' membership made more strategic sense than others, once having proceeded to enlarge, it was difficult to say to other like-minded countries that they were not welcome. In retrospect, NATO's first historic success was overseeing and guaranteeing the reconciliation between Europe's two former great adversaries, Germany and France. By providing a secure environment for these long-standing rivals, NATO helped build the confidence necessary for the growth of European political and economic integration. NATO's institutionalization of transparent defense budgeting and force planning, common defense resources management, and communications, command, and interoperability standards, also has contributed to building confidence and security among European allies.

NATO had already enlarged a number of times. The core states that first began negotiating the alliance in 1948–1949 began with just three countries—the

United States, Canada, and Great Britain. This quickly expanded to include France, Belgium, Luxembourg, and the Netherlands. This group then added Italy, Portugal, Denmark, Norway, and Iceland as founding members. Following the treaty signing in 1949, NATO enlarged three more times during the Cold War, adding Greece and Turkey (1952), West Germany (1954), and Spain (1982). Generally, Cold War enlargement was based on pragmatic strategic criteria more relevant to collective defense than to Euro-Atlantic values. For example, strategically located Portugal, despite being under Salazar's authoritarian rule, was an original member in 1949. Spain, however, ruled by another dictator, Franco, was left out because of European objections, but it still benefited from a unilateral U.S. security commitment. Greece underwent a coup in the 1960s, which NATO did nothing to prevent or end, and Turkey has experienced extraconstitutional changes of government and suppression of minority populations. Yet, at the same time, it can be argued that NATO played an important role in facilitating both Spain's transition to democracy after Franco's death in the 1970s, and also more peaceful relations between long-standing adversaries Greece and Turkey.

The enlargement of NATO that commenced in the 1990s reflected an extension of this process—though with more extensive requirements for membership so as to consolidate reforms among candidate countries. To be invited to negotiate membership, candidates were expected to emphasize five key principles first articulated by U.S. secretary of defense William Perry including: conforming to basic political principles of democracy and the rule of law; economic liberty and free markets; accepting international norms concerning treatment of ethnic minorities and social justice; resolution of territorial disputes on the basis of good neighbor relations; and democratic, civilian control of the military.[8] Candidates were also expected to show that they would be "contributors to, and not consumers of" security from NATO. It was very important to consolidate these criteria before admission into NATO because, once a country has become a member, the organization has no mechanism to punish, or even expel, a violator of such general principles. Thus NATO would enshrine these principles in a formal enlargement study published in 1995.[9]

By 1997, Poland, Hungary, and the Czech Republic were identified as acceptable candidates for membership and they formally entered NATO in 1999, just ahead of NATO's fiftieth anniversary. The decision to limit the first round of NATO membership enlargement to these three most democratic and prosperous countries to the east was not without controversy. A majority of European states had lobbied hard for Romania and Slovenia to be invited as well. Interestingly, of these five countries, Poland and Romania had the most to offer geostrategically in terms of location, size, and military capabilities. However, Romania still had significant political and economic progress to make, while the others offered important contributions to the political goal of consolidating the values inherent in the transatlantic relationship. NATO thus developed a package to keep open the prospect for membership for those who were not joining in 1999. While continuing to allow suitors to develop their relationship with NATO via the Partnership for Peace, NATO also developed a more targeted "Membership Action Plan" for the remaining candidates. While the early track record on military reform in the initial three invitees was not promising, NATO continued with the enlargement process, culminating in the 2002 Prague Summit invitations for seven more members to join—Estonia, Latvia, Lithuania, Slovakia, Slovenia, Romania, and Bulgaria. By 2006, NATO still had key candidates remaining, including Ukraine and Georgia. Meanwhile, the Partnership for Peace would continue to play an important role by facilitating relationships between NATO and neutral countries in Europe such as Austria, Ireland, Finland, and Sweden so as to facilitate contributions to NATO-led peacekeeping missions. NATO would also expand on a "Euro-Atlantic Partnership Council" to broaden its relationship with nonmember countries in Central Asia, and a range of dialogue programs and other initiatives to reach out to countries from North Africa and the Middle East.[10]

A central challenge for NATO enlargement was to ensure that the process would proceed in a way that would not undermine reform efforts in Russia. Under President Boris Yeltsin, Russia had sent formal and informal messages indicating strong opposition to NATO enlargement—even warning of a new Cold War. In the end, there was nothing that Russia could have done to stop enlargement, and arguably the stabilization of the region between Russia and Germany was as much in Moscow's interest as in that of its new friends in the West. Nonetheless, a major basis for opposition to NATO enlargement, even in NATO countries, was that the policy could have a negative impact on relations with Russia. NATO thus proceeded to assuage Russian opposition by building a special NATO-Russia relationship. Also, NATO promised Russia that it would not deploy new troops or nuclear weapons infrastructure on the territory of the new NATO members. This was a problem for the new members as it signaled they were mainly joining NATO politically and not gaining significant security guarantees. However, this concession was important not only to satisfy Russia, but also the U.S. Congress and European parliaments who worried about potential costs associated with extending these new security commitments into Europe's east. Russia was effective in securing even more commitments from NATO of a deepening partnership during the 2002 round of enlargement. Nevertheless, Russia largely failed to take advantage of these opportunities to build a working relationship with NATO. Moscow feared simultaneously losing influence within NATO if it did not participate, but also that too much participation would legitimate the NATO process.

Ultimately, the most difficult problem in the unique strategic relationship with Russia remains to be dealt with, i.e., future Ukrainian membership in NATO, which Russia would view with serious concern. While former Soviet countries such as the Baltics had uneventful entry into NATO, Ukraine would be a serious red line for Russia, which continues to see it as a vital part of its geostrategic priorities. In theory, Russia too could become a candidate for NATO membership. However, its size, human rights record, border conflicts, and declining commitment to democracy, make it an unlikely candidate for serious consideration. Eventually, Russia acceded to NATO enlargement—and probably made gains in the process. Indeed, if the end result of its enlargement was to turn NATO primarily into a political talking shop, then this outcome was consistent with Russian hopes to dilute the military and strategic effectiveness of NATO. Nevertheless, NATO was successful in persuading Russia that it was purely a defensive alliance. This reassurance was something Russia appeared comfortable with, that is until NATO launched an offensive military campaign to advance human rights in Kosovo in 1999.

THE BALKANS

While NATO had undergone a dramatic institutional adaptation to post–Cold War realities, its greatest challenge would arise in the Balkans. In 1992, NATO began recognizing the risk that major instability on its periphery could spread, drawing its members into conflict, or leading to large refugee movements within Europe. Initially, the collapse of Yugoslavia was left to the nascent European Union to manage, but it quickly became too much for the EU, and later the United Nations. In 1992, NATO began a process of developing peacekeeping capabilities and rapid reaction forces while signaling threats toward warring parties in the region. In practice, there was no consensus on how and when to use military power. For several years, NATO's involvement in the Balkans was mainly one of containment. Approximately 250,000 people would be killed or missing in the region during this time of genocide. Still, NATO refused to intervene and this would seriously undermine the credibility of its commitment to secure Western values across the new Europe. There was even a danger that a lack of credibility relative to the extension of NATO values into the Balkans could erode the strategic foundations on which the transatlantic relationship stood. NATO's survival was no longer in doubt, but its relevance was severely challenged by crises in the Balkans.

North America and Europe were well-intentioned in various efforts to end spreading conflict in the Balkans—highlighted by a major intervention in Bosnia-Herzegovina in 1995 and Kosovo in 1999. However, the trends in the Balkans also exposed a major challenge for NATO. The inability of the member states to agree on a common approach to the Balkans showed the limits of what NATO could do to be a provider of security. Often international organizations—including NATO—became obstacles to ending the Balkan war. For example, the United Nations imposed an arms embargo on all parties in the former Yugoslavia in 1991. The embargo exacerbated an imbalance of power favoring aggressive Serb forces (which had inherited most of the military apparatus of the Yugoslav National Army), allowing them to make territorial gains against Muslims and Croats and carry out a policy of "ethnic cleansing"—or more accurately, genocide. In the United States, there was significant support for lifting the embargo, even unilaterally if necessary. However, lifting the arms embargo became politically impossible once the UN had deployed peacekeepers on the ground in 1992. Contributing states, particularly NATO members Britain and France, worried that their troops would get caught up in increased fighting if more weapons flowed into the region. Because they had a veto in the institutions that were attempting to manage the crisis, the result was institutional paralysis and inaction. Ironically, one of NATO's missions by 1994 was to work under a UN mandate to protect safe havens for civilians in Bosnia-Herzegovina. Yet these so-called safe havens actually served to attract more people into concentrated areas for Serbs to attack.

By 1995, its members began to escalate NATO's operational role in the Balkans. NATO authorized more robust engagement through air attacks on Serb positions when they violated ceasefires. Meanwhile, a Croat-Muslim alliance made major gains on the ground in Bosnia-Herzegovina. When Serb forces shelled civilians in August, NATO had reached the limits of its members' patience and authorized the launching of Operation Deliberate Force. This operation was a limited air campaign that served to tip the balance, when combined with the Croat-Muslim ground offensive, and push Bosnian Serbs toward a negotiated settlement; the settlement was formalized later that fall at the Dayton peace conference sponsored by a five-power contact group (the United States, Great Britain, France, Germany, and Russia).[11]

The preconditions for peace in Bosnia-Herzegovina went deeper than NATO's engagement. There had been dramatic shifts in the balance of power on the ground, and the Yugoslav patrons of the Bosnian Serbs in Belgrade needed to gain favor with the West to end devastating UN economic sanctions. The Dayton Accords, which created an integrated federal state of Bosnia-Herzegovina, depended on NATO's earlier institutional planning to provide for a climate of peace. Without strong and credible peacekeeping forces ready to deploy, the peace accord might have unraveled. Rapid deployment was necessary to reassure the Muslims and Croats, who feared that the Bosnian Serbs might negotiate a cease-fire only to regroup in the hope that the Serb-led Yugoslavia would intervene and annex eastern Bosnia in the name of "Greater Serbia." Such Serb actions might have prompted Croatia to annex Western Bosnia.

The peace in Bosnia-Herzegovina was less than perfect, and NATO members were especially reluctant to take risks in hunting down indicted war criminals—a necessary precondition for a lasting peace. By 2006, NATO had moved to a support role in Bosnia-Herzegovina, and the European Union had taken lead responsibility, thus suggesting that while the risk of a return to war is greatly reduced, it is still a function of an international presence to facilitate peace. Nonetheless, NATO's intervention through the Bosnia Peace Implementation Force and the subsequent follow-on force showed that the alliance had become more flexible, could field new and creative command structures, and could use force to back up diplomacy. NATO's role also validated the outreach to its new friends in the East. Eager to show their willingness to contribute to a NATO operation, thirteen Partnership for Peace countries and sixteen non-NATO states joined the effort. Even Russia would send troops serving alongside North American forces in some of the most dangerous areas of operation.[12]

The NATO intervention in Bosnia-Herzegovina continues to be considered a model for stability operations, particularly in light of the less than ideal long-term international engagements in Afghanistan in 2001 and Iraq in 2003. First, the NATO intervention in Bosnia came only after a peace settlement had been reached and after it had been granted legitimacy by the United Nations. There were no major local actors who sought to overturn the new status quo NATO was intervening to enforce. Second, even if there were resistance fighters or insurgents, NATO deployed a very sizeable force of 60,000 well-trained troops with a clear mandate to enforce the peace agreement. Third, NATO's military missions under the Dayton Accords were achieved relatively quickly. NATO thereby contributed to infrastructure rebuilding but, more importantly, provided a stable environment in which other institutions—including the United Nations, World Bank, Organization for Security and Cooperation in Europe, and the European Union—could participate in long-term nation building. While it is not necessarily the case that this model can apply in other regions of the world, it does depart significantly from both the efforts in Afghanistan and Iraq, which resulted in the growth of revisionist insurgency movements that severely challenged the United States and its coalition partners. NATO also could not escape the fact that its intervention in Bosnia, while successful, arrived about three years too late for the 250,000 people killed or missing there in the absence of international intervention.

One major gap in the Dayton accords was that, while it successfully focused on the conditions in Bosnia-Herzegovina, other sources of conflict in the Balkans were not fully addressed. This unfinished nature of the Balkan peace became painfully apparent with a growing crisis within Yugoslavia in 1998–1999 in Kosovo. Kosovo is a provincial area within Serbia which, along with Montenegro, had by 1998 come to represent what was left of the country of Yugoslavia. Kosovo was an area with about 2 million people, comprising a population that was about 90 percent ethnic Albanian Muslim and about 9 percent Serb. Kosovo is a place where Serbs have deeply emotional historical ties; it is often referred to as the cradle of Serb civilization, and it motivates nationalist Serb sentiments dating back to the fourteenth century. Nationalist Serb leaders—in particular Slobodan Milosevic—used Serb feelings toward Kosovo as a rallying point to gain political support during the 1980s. During the 1990s, Milosevic gradually stripped the Albanian majority in Kosovo of the political, cultural, and ethnic autonomy that had sustained its ongoing quest for independence. More radical elements involved in that quest became the Kosovo Liberation Army, which began an extended insurgency campaign—including terrorist attacks—against Serbs in Kosovo. Refusing to concede Kosovo, Milosevic responded with a brutal oppression of ethnic Albanians there. By late summer 1998, several hundred thousand ethnic Albanians had been internally displaced or forced out of the country into neighboring Albania and Macedonia.

By spring 1998, NATO saw Kosovo as a growing threat to stability in the Balkans, and possibly even beyond. The risk was geostrategic in that a heavy influx of ethnic Albanian refugees into Albania and Macedonia could lead to severe economic destabilization in these very unstable Balkan countries. Such an outcome could prompt intervention by the Albanians or Macedonians and eventually draw in larger neighboring countries, including Greece and Turkey. Equally important, NATO leaders also felt a historic sense of guilt for not having intervened early in the Bosnia-Herzegovina conflict. Nevertheless, in its eagerness to redress mistakes of the past, NATO pushed forward with a war that created an entirely new set of dilemmas for the organization and raised new questions about its long-term relevance.

Through March 1999, its members used NATO as a tool to combine a threat of force with aggressive diplomacy to compel Milosevic into a political settlement that would provide for a high degree of autonomy for Kosovo but still retain the overall territorial integrity of Serbia. In the end, neither the Kosovar Albanians nor Serbs were satisfied with this approach and diplomacy failed. In late March 1999, NATO agreed to launch its first war. Rather than acting as a defensive alliance, NATO was on the offensive—and it was fighting not for territory but to enforce the credibility of its commitment to secure Western values in the European area. Yet, in waging a war for values, NATO would soon be exposed to a variety of internal contradictions regarding the relationship between its strategic objectives and its willingness to employ sufficient military force to attain them with the lowest degree of cost. NATO would go to war, and would eventually win. Milosevic's ethnic cleansing of Kosovo was halted and, until his death in 2006, Milosevic was on trial in the Hague for war crimes. However, NATO's first war could have been its last because of a variety of political and operational challenges within the organization. Once the war started, Milosevic began a massive ethnic cleansing campaign, and 800,000 ethnic Albanians were forcibly expelled into nearby Albania and Macedonia, putting enormous strain on these fragile neighbors. Meanwhile, what was meant to be a three-day air campaign intended to coerce a return to diplomacy turned into a three-month war that raised doubts about NATO's new purpose.

A major concern for some NATO members was the absence of an international legal mandate to begin the war. The United Nations did not authorize NATO to use military force, though one could easily conclude it was the UN that in fact was not living up to its commitment to protect human rights. This action was technically problematic for NATO's own founding treaty, which states in Article One that the members must "refrain from the use of force in any manner inconsistent with the purposes of the United Nations." Article Seven of the NATO treaty requires its members to respect "the primary responsibility of the Security Council for the maintenance of international peace and security." Concerns about the legal mandate for the operation combined with alliance-wide political constraints to impact the operational concepts that NATO would deploy in war. When NATO bombed, it did so only above 15,000 feet to protect allied pilots and aircraft. NATO members seemed to signal that the lives of hundreds of thousands of ethnic Albanians were not worth risking the lives of Western pilots or even their airplanes. Indeed, scores of innocent civilians—including a large convoy of misidentified Albanian refugees—were accidentally killed by NATO bombs because of poor target identification. NATO's bombing strategy eventually led it to target and bomb civilian infrastructure, particularly electric power grids, damaging civilian drinking water facilities and hospitals. Attacking civilian targets was necessary to pressure Milosevic and his political allies in Belgrade. However, critics asserted that this strategy was a violation of humanitarian laws of war, ironically principles of international law that NATO had gone to war to uphold in the first place. NATO thus found itself in an institutional conundrum in that it went to war to protect human rights, but its own political constraints prevented it from waging war in a way that would allow the military objectives to be accomplished effectively.

NATO leaders had failed to learn the full military lessons of the 1995 success that compelled a peace in Bosnia-Herzegovina. Some allied decision makers believed that it was the limited NATO bombing that had forced the Serbs to negotiate, neglecting to account for the Croat-Muslim ground offensive. Thus it was assumed that the same would occur in any engagement with Yugoslavia over Kosovo—that a limited use of air power would result in a quick negotiated settlement. Yet sound military doctrine would have also taken into account at least the threat of a ground invasion to make the coercive application of air power successful. NATO's political leaders denied their military this essential tool of a ground threat while initially authorizing only three days' worth of air strikes. One of NATO's key institutional functions is to facilitate effective information exchange so that multinational military operations can be developed. However, in the case of Kosovo, members used NATO's rules and procedures to affect the consensus process, thereby limiting NATO's military effectiveness. Once war over Kosovo began, allied leaders had to spend as much time trying to keep NATO together as a political coalition as developing effective military tactics. Of the NATO allies, only Britain was enthusiastic about a ground campaign to liberate Kosovo. Several NATO members told U.S. president Bill Clinton that their governments might fall if a ground war option were even discussed. In Greece, over 90 percent of the public opposed the war. It was also unclear if U.S. congressional and public support could be sustained if a ground invasion turned into a protracted engagement with Serb formal and paramilitary insurgent forces embedded in the mountains and valleys of

Yugoslavia. NATO's rules and decisionmaking procedures seriously hindered the military's ability to effectively execute the mission they had been given.

Maintaining political cohesion in NATO ultimately became more important than selecting a military strategy to win the war. NATO practice was widely criticized as a "war by committee," and resonated especially poorly with U.S. military planners. This was especially true because, while the war had shown that European countries could have an equal say over political objectives, there was a major divergence in actual capabilities that they could bring to fighting a war. The United States dropped 90 percent of the war's high-tech precision weapons, dropped 90 percent of its Cruise missiles, and supplied 90 percent of all its electronic warfare and intelligence/reconnaissance capabilities. The United States did not need the Europeans to fight this war, and many U.S. military planners concluded that NATO created major costs in terms of strategy and operational efficiency. Conversely, the Europeans were increasingly frustrated with the notion that, in terms of boots on the ground, it was their forces that were already providing about 80 percent of all peacekeeping and peace-support operations in the Balkans. Politically and operationally, a major divide was growing across the Atlantic.

After three months of war, NATO eventually agreed to a far more aggressive use of air power. However, the key to victory probably had more to do with the likelihood that individual NATO allies—especially the United States and Britain—would eventually undertake a land invasion of Yugoslavia. Growing signs that a land invasion was inevitable appeared to combine with Russian diplomatic pressure on the Serbs to force them to negotiate a settlement favorable to NATO's objectives. NATO's objective of spreading Western values was, in the end, validated. Moreover, by 2004 the European Union was prepared to take over the stabilization operations in Bosnia-Herzegovina. Today Yugoslavia is making gradual strides toward political reform and integration with Europe, though serious challenges remain. Most importantly, people are no longer dying in Balkan wars. However, the war took a major toll on NATO. Leading NATO member states concluded that the primary lesson of the Kosovo war was not to do this again.[13]

The impact of the Kosovo war on the transatlantic security relationship was important for several reasons. First, the objectives of the war represented an extreme of what NATO was willing to do to carry out its new mission of extending principles and norms of "Euro-Atlantic values." If NATO was conflicted about how to implement such a mission in its immediate vicinity, it would raise questions about NATO playing any serious role in a global security environment. Second, the Kosovo conflict was signposted for about ten years—NATO had considerable time to anticipate and plan for the conflict, and yet at the moment of crisis, it was seriously unprepared for a range of contingencies. Third, it was NATO itself, with its rules and procedures requiring unanimity and consensus for decision-making, that was the primary cause of major military inefficiencies in warfare. Fourth, since the Kosovo war, NATO's key member, the United States, has moved away from NATO—skirting its institutional rules and procedures during the key high combat periods in Afghanistan and Iraq, and then entering Afghanistan belatedly and with insufficient forces. Finally, the Kosovo war sparked a new debate over the role and efficacy of international institutions, a debate which would culminate in transatlantic disagreements over the Iraq war in 2003. The Kosovo war contributed much to U.S. opinion that it is better to avoid binding multilateral institutions for the conduct of war. Meanwhile, the Europeans began more persistent efforts to invest in the foreign and defense aspects of the European Union.

In spring 2006, the Serb leader Slobodan Milosevic died while awaiting the end of his trial in The Hague for war crimes. Nonetheless, major challenges continued to confront the future of the Balkans. The future of Bosnia-Herzegovina still contained constitutional uncertainties as did the capacity of the European Union to fully manage its responsibility for military operations that it had inherited from NATO. Moreover, in spring 2006, the people of Montenegro decided in a referendum to endorse independence, raising broad questions as to what this move would mean for governance in Belgrade and for stability in the broader region. Perhaps most significantly, the final status of Kosovo had still not been resolved after the 1999 NATO war with Yugoslavia. Meanwhile, on the positive side of the equation, over the previous ten years NATO and the European Union had significantly grown their ranks of members and partners from the Balkans, and this would create considerable new opportunities for creative cooperative security building projects in the region. In particular, the entry of Hungary, Slovenia, Bulgaria, and Romania into NATO has formed a stable security boundary around the five states presently comprising the Western Balkans. Meanwhile, NATO's membership action program keeps Albania, Macedonia, and Croatia constructively focused and engaged in cooperative security activities consistent with NATO principles. The incentive of joining NATO's Partnership for Peace program has helped to keep the remaining Serbia, Montenegro, and Bosnia-Herzegovina focused on reforms that they need to undertake as an initial pathway to Euro-Atlantic structures and legitimacy. This institutional network is particularly key for facilitating NATO's ongoing coordination with the European Union in Bosnia-Herzegovina, for ongoing peace support operations in Kosovo, and for helping resolve constitutional status questions between Serbia and Montenegro and over Kosovo.

The European Union has also played an increasingly critical role in efforts to stabilize the Balkans. Along with the support of EU members Greece, Hungary, and Slovenia (and Romania and Bulgaria after 2007), the EU's Stabilization and Association Agreements with the Western Balkans contain provisions for future membership. Nevertheless, internal questions about the EU's own constitutional future have also placed its ability to move forward in its Balkans engagement into a more distant context. The Western Balkan countries themselves have made some, albeit halting, progress with the EU. Across the region, key problems include corruption and its impact on the rule of law—particularly in Albania and in Bosnia-Herzegovina which has outstanding issues of police reforms. The Serbs had made some initial progress in this direction, but this was suspended when they failed to deliver former General Ratko Mladic to the Hague Tribunal for trial on war crimes during the Bosnian war.

The Western Balkans provides a unique opportunity for the EU and NATO to work together. When the wars started in 1991, no international organization responded. Ever since, NATO and the EU have engaged in stabilization, cooperation, and integration activities in the region. One example of successful cooperation involved the Ohrid Agreement to prevent war in Macedonia. In February 2001, when war looked likely in Macedonia, NATO and the EU coordinated negotiations that led to the Ohrid peace agreement that August. In Bosnia-Herzegovina, the European Union has assumed responsibility for 6,000 troops that are shifting from stabilization to integration operations—while coordinating closely with NATO in supporting the police and providing basic military deterrence for the country. What makes the European Union mission unique is that it has assumed many of the previous NATO responsibilities, but also fights organized crime and is directly connected with police around the country.

Despite this successful institutional cooperation, even relatively stable Bosnia-Herzegovina faces major questions about the future of the country's constitution, thus making the question of the end date for European Union operations there ambiguous. Ultimately, the mission will only be accomplished when functional state-level institutions are created and working reliably. Meanwhile, around the Balkans, there has been an explosion of organized crime involving human, drug, and arms trafficking. As a result, NATO and the EU have found it necessary to coordinate their programs and activities to combat organized crime and counter terrorism. In sum, the Balkans continue to challenge NATO and the European Union to develop an effective common strategy for the region and to move beyond "stabilization" missions to improve "cooperation and integration" activities on the ground. This has had to be done in an environment in which there are increasing pressures to move the security perimeter of North America and Europe onto an even more global basis, to a range of new issue areas and regions far beyond the scope of even the Balkans.

This ongoing Balkan commitment is a challenge for the European Union, which has staked much of its defense and security credibility on having assumed responsibility for the Bosnia mission. It is an even greater challenge for NATO, which has tied its credibility to the future of Kosovo. NATO's commitment to Kosovo in 2006 (roughly 16,000 troops) was larger than its commitment to Afghanistan (15,000 troops). Interestingly, Kosovo is a tiny region in southeastern Europe while Afghanistan is the size of France. There might be increased pressure to redeploy troops out of Kosovo to new NATO missions. Yet there has been ongoing violence in Kosovo, including major uprisings in 2004 that surprised everyone involved and nearly proved disastrous for NATO. At the time, NATO had no crowd control capacity but it has since learned from the operation and is now increasingly prepared to engage in riot control.

Nonetheless, a general lack of progress on Kosovo's final status has raised larger strategic questions about the future of the region, which the Serbs continue to insist must remain a part of their sovereign territory. Meanwhile, Kosovo's ability to stand on its own remains limited without international agreement on its status and with economic conditions that are very poor. Kosovo has about 50 percent unemployment, inadequate infrastructure to sustain economic development, and a significant lack of foreign direct investment. Of approximately 200,000 Serbs who left Kosovo since 1999, only 14,300 returned, as most Serbs feared poor economic conditions as well as for their own safety. Experts close to the situation in Kosovo have asserted that the international community was "sugar coating" and was not paying adequate attention to "standards" in ongoing status negotiations. There is little convergence of interest in the region on the future status of Kosovo. For example, while Albania wants Kosovo independence, Macedonia will support any agreement as long as existing borders are recognized. Slovakia and Romania have concerns about Kosovo becoming a model for secession within their own territory and thus they prefer "autonomy" for Kosovo. Ukraine and Georgia see potential for spillover into Abkhazia and South Ossetia, but Poland views the situation differently in that Kosovo is not a part of Russia. Bulgarians perceive disintegrative pressures in Macedonia, while Hungarians express concerns about the status of the ethnic Hungarian Serbian province of Vojvodina. Hence, if Kosovo achieves independence through a "forced" decision, there will likely be significant regional disagreement over the outcome.

While it has slipped to a large degree off of the daily television screens, the Balkans continues to be a significant security challenge for NATO and the European Union. Together, these two key institutions can provide sufficient ballast to weather the storm, though to do this they will have to enhance integration prospects in the region, coordinate their security sector reforms to tackle the new security threats, and link their efforts to regional organizations to facilitate cooperation. If integration prospects were to lose credibility, security in the Balkans could be severely undermined because some nations might be tempted to move in unhelpful directions. Thus NATO and the European Union will need functional ways, even if not implemented for the immediate future, to keep their mutual "open doors" for these aspiring members and partners. A NATO-EU Balkans strategy would provide the necessary conditions for nurturing military cooperation and coordination with border troops, police, and intelligence agencies to enhance Balkan security and stability. Examples of such activity could include facilitating cooperation among defense ministries, and interior ministers' participation in regional emergency planning, while also broadening NATO engagement with partners to include police activities to combat organized crime. The end result could be to facilitate cross-border interagency coordination and cooperation both within and among Balkan states, thus building confidence across the region.

Emerging Threats—Diverging Strategic Culture?

The United States, Canada, their European allies in NATO, and their partners in the European Union have been working to refocus these institutions to reflect the new reality that most threats increasingly come from outside the European area. Nonetheless, aligning ambition and resources has proven to be a significant challenge. Moreover, most challenges, including immigration and the environment, require civilian responses, where a military alliance like NATO has decreasing value. NATO, in particular, faces problems coming to consensus on threats and preventing divergent risk assessments from developing among allies, providing the requisite capabilities, determining when and for how long to participate in coalition operations, and agreeing on what conditions are necessary for further engagement of NATO in meeting emerging threats. Meanwhile the European Union has an emerging capability, particularly in the areas of diplomacy, economics, and nascent military and multinational police functions. Nevertheless, the European Union has also struggled to find consensus on precisely what its role is—either to balance and influence the power of the United States, or to work together to complement a reinvigorated transatlantic relationship.

Since 1994, the NATO allies have focused attention on efforts to halt the proliferation of weapons of mass destruction and their means of delivery. In 1999, NATO's new strategic concepts referred to terrorism as a threat requiring coordination among NATO allies. Nevertheless, these issues remained in the background until September 12, 2001 when NATO declared the terrorist attacks on the United States to be an attack on all NATO members. For the United States, perceived degree of risk had changed dramatically—and was made evident in a rapid increase of $48 billion in defense spending. The European reaction, on the other hand, was to provide some resources, but generally to perceive terrorism as something that must be lived with, and managed mainly through civilian-police functions, not large-scale military actions. President George W. Bush illustrated this divergence in June 2006 when he stated, after a meeting with European Union leadership, that for the United States September 11 was a "change in thinking," while for Europe it was a "moment."[14]

The United States perceives itself to be in a war with terrorism, while Europe does not—or at least not to the same degree. Even in the face of major terrorist attacks in Madrid in 2004 and London in 2005, this European perception has not changed dramatically. In fact, this gap widened dramatically as European public opinion indicated a serious turn against the United States by spring 2006. According to the PEW Global Attitudes survey published in June 2006, favorable opinion toward the United States had dropped since 2000 by 27 percent from 83 to 56 percent, in France by 23 percent from 62 to 39 percent, and in Germany by 41 percent from 78 to 37 percent. Even for leaders that might want to invest in their relationship with the United States, it is a difficult proposition in a democracy to turn so hard against widespread public opposition to U.S. global policies. Reflecting the depth of these attitudes, only 7 percent of people in Spain had confidence in U.S. president George Bush to make wise decisions on international issues. In Britain, a majority of public opinion (41 to 34 percent) saw the United States presence in Iraq as a greater danger to world peace than Iran.[15] These countries are remarkable in that they are vital to long-term U.S. national interests, particularly in terms of combating international terrorism. Of course, nearly 100 Europeans were killed on September 11, making it more than simply a "moment" for Europe. Moreover, between fall 2001 and summer 2006, the total number of Europeans killed on their soil from terrorist attacks was 248 (in Madrid and London) and the total number of Americans killed in the United States was zero. Europe too has spilled blood in attacks by terrorists and, by this measure alone, they would certainly have the right to generate their own conclusions as to how best to combat terrorism—something that they had already actually been grappling with for decades. Ultimately, the gap was not over the nature of the threat, but the means with which to meet it.

The difficulty in bridging this growing gap lies at the heart of the challenge that terrorism poses as a threat. In a total reversal from the Cold War, when the United States and its allies knew their opponent's capabilities but not its intent, in the war on terrorism they know the intent of the opponent, but not his capabilities. Thus the various possible means of response are open to interpretation. This is a unique challenge for NATO because it is by definition a "defensive" alliance, intended to respond to an adversary's attack. However, the United States has interpreted terrorism as requiring "offensive" operations, including "preemptive" war often far beyond the territories of NATO members. This mentality shift strains the transatlantic relationship, particularly for those European allies (such as France and Germany) who had come to see NATO's main role as providing reassurance and stability rather than defending Europe. Meanwhile, the U.S. propensity to act unilaterally if necessary, and let the "mission shape the coalition" rather than via multilateral efforts, would further exacerbate this growing divergence in strategic culture between North America and Europe. The costs for both sides have been high, as Europe lost influence over many key decisions with the operations in Iraq in 2003. Yet the United States found itself providing 90 percent of the troops, paying 90 percent of the costs, and suffering 90 percent of coalition casualties.

This divergence between North America and Europe is particularly pronounced in the area of capabilities that the various countries in the transatlantic community are prepared to invest in. The transatlantic defense spending gap had already by 2001 become significant, with the United States spending an average 3.5 percent of its GDP on defense, while many European nations spent less than 2 percent.[16] The United States spent more than all the other NATO members combined. Europe spent collectively about two-thirds of what the United States spent, but got only about one-third the capability because they spent so much on salaries for a conscript-based military. In 1999, NATO had launched a Defense Capabilities Initiative. However, by 2006 the gap was as large as before, if not larger. While the U.S. substantially increased defense expenditures after 2001, most NATO allies' budgets remained unchanged. The gap also increased after the accession of NATO's seven new allies in 2004. In recognition that the gap cannot be closed, but rather "filled," the Prague Summit of 2002 saw NATO launching a new NATO Response Force and yet another "Capabilities Commitment" effort, while in 2004 at Istanbul, NATO narrowed its focus toward getting sufficient member states to commit enough resources to meet the mission requirements for reconstruction in Afghanistan.

The NATO Response Force was a particularly important initiative for NATO. On paper, and by 2006 in practice, it consisted of an integrated capability including technologically advanced, deployable, interoperable, and sustainable forces that included land, sea, and air elements ready to move quickly to wherever they might be needed.[17] The basic architecture was to be operational by fall 2006 and was seen as an important catalyst for a major reinvestment in military capabilities among the NATO allies. Conceptually, this would mean that NATO would, through its defense planning cycle, identify the requirements for organizing a force of about 25,000 troops and associated logistics, transportation, command and control, and intelligence needs, etc. Then NATO would survey its member states and see what they might contribute in targeted areas of specialization.

By streamlining contributions into a multinational spearhead force, the NATO allies would not need to individually boost their defense spending. Instead, they would have to commit to rationalizing their military investment in terms of what they could contribute to such missions. Nonetheless, even once prepared in command architectures and exercised in the field, there remained significant limitations on the NATO Response Force. If, for example, new NATO members are primarily concerned about territorial defense rather than exporting stability to other parts of the world, then they are not likely to invest significant resources in these missions. Ironically, NATO members could conceivably argue that they are meeting their commitments to NATO by creating small, high-end niche forces for the NATO Response Force, but meanwhile avoid undergoing significant national military modernization programs that would be far more important for larger-end security contributions in and around Europe. The focus on niche capabilities also risks ignoring two fundamental lessons from the 1990s. First, NATO has never been a "spearhead" force as envisaged in this new operational design. Most of the national militaries in Europe have remained land-based and primarily defensive in posture. Second, the NATO Response Force, even if well constructed, still requires NATO consensus to approve its use. A veto by any of the twenty-six NATO countries can prevent its deployment in a crisis. And if deployment is authorized, but some members choose not to contribute militarily, then the resultant absence of key troops or equipment could undermine the entire operation. Additionally, the deployment size of 25,000 troops is probably too small given the scope of crisis around the world. A force of 25,000 that is sustainable for only thirty days raises the question of what comes after the thirty days. Realistically, even for one mission, a force that is deployed also requires resting and exercising periods, thus meaning that for a single operation, a force closer to 60,000 troops is necessary. Even worse, however, would be a situation in which two or three crises happen simultaneously, requiring multiple rapid NATO force deployments. To illustrate the range of problems in actually using NATO for such missions, when Israel suggested in July 2006 that it would accept a NATO force to stabilize the southern areas of Lebanon to its north, NATO was unable to respond. Key members were not interested, and as a spokesman suggested: "The possibility, the shape, the structure of any international force—none of them has been seriously addressed."[18]

Also at the 2002 Prague Summit, NATO members endorsed a new military concept for contributing to counterterrorism efforts to include: first, antiterrorism—essentially defense measures to reduce vulnerabilities to attack; second, consequence management, which is dealing with and reducing the effects of an attack after it has occurred; third, counterterrorism, which involves offensive military action to reduce terrorist capabilities where NATO plays a lead or supporting role; and fourth, military cooperation, which involves efforts to coordinate with military and civil authorities, such as police, customs and immigration, ministries of finance and interior, and intelligence and security services, to maximize effectiveness against terrorism. Additionally, NATO would improve intelligence sharing and crisis response arrangements, including implementation of a civil emergency action plan against potential attacks by chemical, biological, or radiological agents. Similar efforts at achieving an integrated approach to counterterrorism included reaching out via the Euro-Atlantic Partnership Council, which called on NATO's partner countries to: intensify political consultations and information sharing on armaments and civil emergency planning; enhance preparedness for traffic management, and armaments and logistic cooperation; impede support for terrorist groups by enhancing exchange of banking information; improve border controls of arms ranging from weapons of mass destruction to small arms and light weapons; and also to facilitate civil emergency planning.[19]

While NATO has proved to be a good military instrument to deal with European security challenges during and after the Cold War, counterterrorism efforts require the application of wider sets of tools than traditional military actions, many of which are already available in the European Union. In other words, while NATO is a good "hammer," not all modern security problems are "nails." In addition, some Europeans feel that NATO's invoking of collective defense in September 2001 was a mistake in that, like Pandora's box, once opened, it generated further and more difficult problems. In sum, the wider regional and functional security requirements after September 11 oblige NATO to coordinate capabilities with the European Union. Regrettably, NATO as an institution has not grappled with the basic question of what constitutes common risks and obligations under its new mandate to respond to international terrorism. Postponing this transatlantic discussion because it is either too difficult or might demonstrate the weakness of common values in the face of increasingly divergent national interests, demonstrates the present state of NATO's declining role in global security. Beyond NATO, however, there has been some key convergence on issues of major importance to both Europe and North America. All countries in the transatlantic relationship agree as to the danger of Iran with nuclear weapons. Indeed, the United States and Europe have pursued a common multilateral strategy offering incentives and threats to bring pressure to bear on Iran to uphold its international commitments. Even on Iraq, all countries agree that an unstable Iraq is a threat to stability for the United States and Europe—though by 2006, Europe still had not offered up major commitments to Iraq, and the general trend was toward countries disengaging from, not entering, Iraq.

Stepping Out: The Black Sea, Afghanistan, and Africa

In areas where there has been convergence between North American and European interests, NATO has helped coordinate common policy objectives. Though a far cry from the strategic emphasis historically placed on it, NATO's primary activity has been to play a role in building cooperative security engagement in some pivotal crossroads of global security. Notably, the NATO members have been very reluctant to see the organization used as a lead force as it was in the Kosovo campaign, and to deploy ground forces on the same scale as in Bosnia-Herzegovina. NATO members have been particularly keen to avoid situations where combat is likely, thus illustrating that the divide between the United States and its allies remains.

THE BLACK SEA: REGIONAL COOPERATION

Though not often high on the radar screen of global politics, the Black Sea is increasingly understood to be a region with high potential to import instability into Europe. These instabilities come in various forms such as organized crime, and trafficking in humans, drugs, and weapons. The region is particularly important as an East-West energy supply bridge. For example, in 2004, 60 percent of Turkey's natural gas came from Russia, which had also become Turkey's second main trading partner. Correspondingly, Russia depends upon Turkey for free access through the Bosporus and Dardanelles for export of its energy supplies. It is also a region that has experienced, and continues to face, many consequence-management challenges ranging from the Chernobyl nuclear disaster in Ukraine, to earthquakes from Turkey to Georgia, and perennial flooding of Romania's and Ukraine's Danube delta region. If successfully stabilized, this region would also serve as a cooperative model for the remainder of Central Asia to its East. Since NATO deploys naval patrols in the Mediterranean (Operation Active Endeavor), engages in Afghanistan, and provides some limited support in Iraq, Black Sea bases provide NATO not only with a bridge, but also, in theory, with a buffer zone to close this trafficking road into Europe. While the NATO Istanbul Summit in 2004 produced a communiqué acknowledging the Black Sea's importance, this initiative was met with French reluctance—with Paris not wanting to cede too much responsibility in new security initiatives to NATO.

With Romania and Bulgaria now members of NATO, and with Ukraine and Georgia expressing interest in membership, the Black Sea is being gradually transformed geopolitically from a former Soviet area to a NATO "lake." Though the Istanbul agreements also acknowledged this new reality by putting a special emphasis on Partnership for Peace participants in the Caucasus and Central Asia, whether the Black Sea actually becomes a bridge or buffer will largely depend on Russia. Specifically, it remains to be seen whether Russia will support or work to prevent Ukraine's and Georgia's outreach to NATO. Optimists note that Russia's firm opposition to Baltic accession to NATO in 1996 turned into tacit acceptance by November 2002. Pessimists argue that most Russians still see the world as a zero-sum game, particularly in this region where several so-called "frozen conflicts" remain: in Moldova's Transdniestria, in Georgia's South Ossetia and Abkhazia, and Nagorno-Karabakh in Armenia-Azerbaijan. It is also difficult to get Black Sea NATO allies (Turkey, Bulgaria, and Romania) and partners along the littoral (Ukraine, Russia, and Georgia) and in the "wider" region (Moldova, Armenia, and Azerbaijan) to focus beyond their narrow national interests. Regional cooperation in the Black Sea remains elusive.

NATO and the European Union thus have limited engagement in the Black Sea area. However, it is possible that each could facilitate a "bottom-up" and "locally generated" approach to regional security by building on maritime cooperation, airspace reconnaissance, border controls and coastal security, and civil-military emergency planning. Two central questions pertaining to the Black Sea are those of Turkey and Ukraine. Turkey, already a NATO member, seeks an accelerated path toward membership in the European Union. Long a frontline state during the Cold War, Turkey now serves as a strategic bridge into Central Asia and the Middle East. Yet Turkish membership in the European Union remains a distant prospect because of economic issues. Keeping Turkey satisfied as a major strategic actor for Europe, even if its economic aspirations are not achieved in the near term, will be a significant challenge for the transatlantic relationship.

In late 2004, Ukraine underwent a dramatic "Orange Revolution" in which reformists successfully rejected irregular elections and external Russian influence. Long a keystone state between East and West, Ukraine itself is divided internally along these lines. It has announced aspirations to join NATO but it confronts significant challenges. First, Ukraine's defense establishment, which has been replete with incompetence, corruption, and operational disasters, appears to have stabilized, though it faces serious continuing challenges to reform the defense ministry, to transform and modernize the military, to rebalance the armed forces to be more interoperable, and to provide stability for its new leadership. Second, Ukraine's implementation of foreign, security, and defense policy has failed due to internal problems with policy coordination. Third, public support in Ukraine for membership in NATO has actually fallen since the Orange Revolution, making it harder for its leaders to bolster their arguments for seeking NATO membership. Ukraine has sought to complement Western activity by sending troops to Iraq. However, this proved costly in terms of resources and lives, with eighteen soldiers killed. In December 2005, Ukraine withdrew from Iraq.

AFGHANISTAN AND IRAQ: WAGING WAR, NATION BUILDING, OR COUNTERINSURGENCY?

Afghanistan has been identified by NATO officials as a key test for the future relevance of the organization. NATO was circumvented by the United States in the initial invasion, and also in the first years of postinvasion rebuilding and counterinsurgency fighting. NATO had contributed indirectly through the years of outreach into Central Asia via the Partnership for Peace and the Euro-Atlantic Partnership Council, which facilitated overflight rights and basing agreements that helped ease the initial deployments into Afghanistan. By 2003, NATO had agreed to undertake responsibility for stabilization operations in Afghanistan, commanding the International Security Assistance Force (ISAF). This was NATO's first major security mandate outside of the European area as classically understood. The ISAF mandate also included responsibility for supporting Provincial Reconstruction Teams. By 2004, there were roughly 6,500 NATO troops deployed in Afghanistan.

For much of the time, stabilization operations were limited to the capital, Kabul, leaving large parts of Afghanistan outside the control of international or Afghan forces. This allowed the defeated Taliban and Al-Qaeda time to regroup for future fighting. Not only was the force very small for rebuilding a country the size of California, it was also restricted in its mandate and capabilities. NATO's mission has been conceived by key European allies, including the United Kingdom, Germany, and France, as mainly a peacekeeping and reconstruction mission—not a combat operation. Meanwhile, the United States, which had a sizeable presence of about 18,000 troops in Afghanistan by 2006, has preferred to keep its troops outside the NATO command structure, operating in counterinsurgency engagement in Operation Enduring Freedom. This coalition-of-the-willing has included British, Dutch, and Canadian, as well as Afghan forces, operating alongside those of the United States. In 2005, NATO agreed to eventually take over all operations in Afghanistan, and to significantly increase its deployment there, perhaps allowing the United States to reduce its operations. However, just as this transition began, insurgent attacks and suicide bombings accelerated in an attempt to complicate the NATO turnover. These events called into question whether NATO was adequately prepared for taking on this strategic mission, particularly if it was uninterested in counterinsurgency combat operations. The NATO mission was even further complicated by a lack of airlift for mobility, and national caveats limiting what exactly troops could do while in ISAF.

NATO's newest members have made concerted, though limited, efforts to contribute to ongoing missions in Afghanistan. The Czech Republic sent its Sixth Field Hospital (thirty medical doctors and 120 troops) to Bagram to provide medical support to ISAF, though to pay for this it was necessary to float government bonds. Hungary sought to contribute within its means by increasing its presence in the Balkans to replace forces that were transferred from there into Afghanistan. Bulgaria provided a nuclear, biological, and chemical decontamination unit to ISAF. Romania was one of the initial participants in ISAF, sending a twenty-five troop military police platoon and one C-130 aircraft with staff officers and fourteen crew members. It also deployed a 405-troop infantry battalion to Operation Enduring Freedom. Slovakia sent a 40-troop engineering platoon to Operation Enduring Freedom to help restore the Bagram airfield, and also sent 17 engineering troops in 2004. The Baltic states sent small, but symbolically welcome, troops as well. Thus Afghanistan operations were based upon a sense of shared risk across the NATO alliance. Both its traditional and new members as well as additional partners shared an incentive to show that NATO still had relevance. However, it is also the case that some allies volunteered troops to Afghanistan to avoid pressure from the United States on providing troops to the U.S.-led coalition efforts in Iraq.

At the nexus between NATO's role in Afghanistan and Iraq is a basic question of whether NATO has the capacity to engage in counterinsurgency operations. A common form of combating more powerful conventional forces, insurgency using terrorist tactics to alienate a population away from a government is a unique form of warfare to which great powers have yet to establish an effective response. This is a tactic in warfare often employed by weak actors against large conventional powers, and it is most apt to succeed against democracies that emphasize humanitarian rules of war and act with self-imposed restrictions in warfare. More pointedly, it has been especially utilized against democracies, which might question a mission and recoil at suffering casualties and the loss of treasure. It is hard enough for national militaries to win the necessary "hearts and minds" that fuel insurgency movements—it is even more difficult to envisage doing so with a twenty-six-member military organization where the consensus process gives all countries a veto.

NATO faces severe limitations as a tool for counterinsurgency warfare. First, its consensus process makes NATO highly vulnerable to asymmetrical attacks intended to produce political and diplomatic gridlock in the decision-making process—which can in turn seriously hamper collective military action. NATO provides insurgents with more political targets to hit with terrorist attacks, and thus raises the question of the extent to which NATO members are willing to go to bear costs in engaging in counterinsurgency. Even a NATO member that is not contributing forces to a mission can find itself a target for insurgent-driven terrorist attacks. Second, while some NATO members such as Britain and Spain have a range of experience with counterinsurgency, the European members of NATO generally see this as a political and civilian police, rather than military, operation. Also, many Europeans view insurgency through the prism of their colonial experience and generally conclude that the best way to treat insurgency is to avoid it in the first place. Moreover, two NATO members, Turkey and the United States, have responded to insurgency with some tactics that their other European allies view as outside the norms and traditions of international human rights law. Thus, to the extent that NATO has engaged in counterinsurgency, it has been more as a tactical support operation than as a strategic tool for winning a war.

The war in Iraq significantly illustrated the limits of the transatlantic relationship in out-of-area security operations. Unable to agree on how to manage the threat posed by Saddam Hussein, the United States proceeded over the strong opposition of key allies such as Germany and France to invade and occupy Iraq in 2003. The United States would subsequently find itself entrenched in a slow and often devastating insurgency-driven war of attrition. The United States hoped to defeat terrorists and empower an elected Iraqi government to assume responsibility for the country's future, but it did so with only Britain among its NATO allies offering sizeable military assistance. In many respects, the tactical divergences over how to deal with Saddam Hussein obscured the more fundamental shared interests that the United States and its European allies had in Iraq. Whatever the debates about the merits of an invasion, all the parties shared interests in the building of a stable, democratic, and peaceful Iraq. Ironically, however, so long as the United States was taking major responsibility for Iraq, the European allies were able to disengage knowing that the United States would remain. Likewise, the U.S. presence would also increase Iraqi dependence on the United States for stability in the country. With over 2,500 Americans killed and a complex insurgency operating around the country, the United States certainly needed all the friends it could get in Iraq by 2006. Yet by then the number of allies offering troops was in decline.

Since Saddam Hussein's attack on Kuwait in 1990, the United States had preferred his removal from power. During the Clinton administration, the Iraq Liberation Act of October 31, 1998, endorsed the policy of regime change. The Bush administration emphasized regime change after the 9/11 attacks, but President Bush downplayed such efforts in his September 12, 2002, speech before the UN General Assembly, stressing the need to enforce UN resolutions requiring Iraqi disarmament. When Iraq failed to comply with Resolution 1441, the Security Council failed to reach consensus on what consequences to impose. Russia, China, and NATO allies France and Germany felt inspections should be given more time, whereas the United States, United Kingdom, Spain, and Bulgaria disagreed. NATO's small countries and new allies were caught in a dilemma of having to choose one or the other side—often bucking public opinion, which across Europe was generally opposed to a military intervention in Iraq.

In contrast to the Balkans and ISAF in Afghanistan, the absence of a shared threat perception among some NATO allies contributed to a lack of political will to directly confront Saddam Hussein, or later to provide substantial peace support forces. Thus, when the United States went to war on March 19, 2003, it did so with a coalition-of-the-willing that comprised 255,000 U.S., 45,000 British, 2,000 Australian, and 200 Polish troops. Illustrating the serious challenge to NATO, in advance of the war the alliance struggled to come to consensus on whether, as a result of a war in Iraq, NATO would give collective defense guarantees to Turkey—Iraq's northern neighbor and well within missile range. To some European members of NATO, the best way to prevent having to defend Turkey was not to start a war in the first place, and they worried that preparing for that defense might make that war more likely. Conversely, key U.S. diplomats felt that the best way to avoid a war was to speak with one voice across the Atlantic to pressure Saddam Hussein to leave power. NATO had engaged in the Middle East both with a Mediterranean Dialogue modeled in part on the Partnership for Peace, and also in a regional security initiative announced at its 2004 Istanbul Summit. Nonetheless, on the major issue of Iraq NATO was unable to agree on a role to play.

NATO did eventually play an important support role in Iraqi stabilization efforts. New NATO member Poland served as a major part of the United States' postinvasion stability operations in Iraq by taking command of a multinational division. Poland faced a range of operational challenges in assuming this command, but also gained vital experience for future military force projection. Challenges included: limits on the rules of engagement for each nation under its command; problems with compatibility of equipment and diverse languages making interoperability difficult to achieve; platoon level leadership and professionalism in civil affairs functions new to military-operational concepts in the field; and Poland's being primarily prepared for crisis response and not for war (and thus highly vulnerable once the insurgency in Iraq grew). Poland thus turned to NATO for assistance in its Iraq mission. NATO agreed in June 2003 to provide support to Poland's command in the form of intelligence, logistics expertise, movement coordination, force generation, and secure communications support. Poland, though, would also undergo serious internal debates about the usefulness of its engagement in Iraq, with public debates suggesting a desire to withdraw. However, in 2006 Poland had continued to resist these trends and remained engaged in Iraq.

AFRICA: PROMOTING VALUES AND INTERESTS

While North America and Europe were intervening in the Balkans in the 1990s, and in Afghanistan and Iraq later, one of the major conceptual challenges was the question of why its members would intervene in these places while largely ignoring genocide in Africa. The failure of the international community to prevent and then halt the killing of 800,000 people in Rwanda in the early 1990s has remained a stain on the record of NATO countries, which place human rights at the center of their Euro-Atlantic values. Even worse, it seemed that just ten years later, genocide was again occurring in Africa, this time in the crisis in Darfur, Sudan. After many years of pronouncements appealing for an end to conflict there, NATO's members agreed in June 2006 to respond affirmatively to a request by the African Union to provide support for its plans to expand its peacekeeping mission in Darfur. NATO's role would be limited mainly to providing air transport for peacekeepers from African countries contributing troops. NATO would also engage in training African Union troops in strategic-level planning and operational procedures, and also provide support for mapping exercises to facilitate effective planning for troop deployments. NATO's work in Darfur is done mainly out of Europe; thus NATO is not directly employed in the region and its overall engagement is minimal. Nonetheless, it does represent an additional step for NATO in expanding its support role in global security challenges in the twenty-first century. This direction could prove essential beyond the compelling moral challenge of crises like Sudan. It is countries like Somalia, for example, where transnational terrorist movements are gaining a new foothold, and it is instability in North Africa that is growing the immigrant population in European countries.

SMALL STEPS—TOWARD A MORE RELEVANT NATO?

NATO's engagement in new missions represents important supporting roles, though they fall far short of expectations many of its supporters had in the 1990s for a major reshaping of the transatlantic relationship based on common values and shared threat perception. Even in these limited areas, NATO has experienced significant deficiencies. NATO needs to provide specific advice for specialized force planning, more capacity for international training support, agreement on a new system for financing international military operations, improved methods for public information both locally in its operations and strategically in building domestic support for sustainable operations—and North America and Europe need to engage in a transatlantic dialogue that addresses the limitations of collective defense and out-of-area operations in a global security environment. If NATO is to remain relevant as an alliance, it must be aligned to the major threats its members confront. In an emerging environment where many threats will include not only terrorism and insurgency, but also those stemming from the environment and natural disasters, transnational disease, immigration, access to energy, and other new challenges, North America and Europe will have to develop essential complementary assets so that those countries that still share core values can operate together most effectively to advance their common security interests. In this regard, the development of the European Union as a security actor might prove to be the most significant strategic opportunity, or challenge, depending on how it evolves. In effect, while there is increasing demand for NATO, it comes at a time when its capacity is increasingly diminished. NATO has more to do, and fewer resources to do it with. It is possible, therefore, that an effective development of the European Union is essential to NATO's future, or it could serve to undermine NATO if the European Union emerges as a competitor.

What Role for the European Union?

Increasingly, the United States and Canada assess their transatlantic agenda in a new context of their individual bilateral relationship with the European Union. This is already the case in economic and other nonsecurity-related issues. While there is not a particular enthusiasm in Europe for investing resources to complement NATO, there does remain enthusiasm for developing the capabilities of the European Union. The key question is whether the European Union will consolidate around diverging strategic cultures between the United States and Europe, or in a way that identifies complementary assets allowing North America and Europe to work together to meet global challenges. On many issues, there is considerable convergence of interests including in Iran, the Middle East peace process, and over North Korea. Additionally, in some key areas, particularly Bosnia-Herzegovina, the European Union is taking primary responsibility for security operations. The European Union is also developing a rapid-deployment capacity and multinational police function. In a global security environment where diplomacy, economic investment, multinational police functions, and infrastructure development are critical tools of security management, the

European Union has a major role to play. Generally the world benefits from a united Europe that is peacefully integrated, whole, and free, and the European Union is the central mechanism to achieve this. All too often, "red lines" are put up to protect existing bureaucratic pipelines between NATO and the European Union. In a world where interior ministries, finance ministries, and police can be as vital to security as defense ministries, the development of the European Union in these areas can complement the transatlantic relationship in ways that significantly enhance the common interests of North America and Europe.[20]

Despite a convergence of diplomatic interests, there remain significant questions about the capacity of the European Union to emerge as a serious actor in global security. The major European countries—Britain, Germany, and France—are individually no longer the world powers that they once were. While Europe is internally at peace, the threats to it stem from its periphery and on a more global basis. While Europe does exert significant collective economic power, it does not have commensurate military capabilities with which to complement its diplomatic functions. Meanwhile, its global responsibilities are increasingly moving the United States out of Europe. Typically seeing NATO more as a mechanism from which to pick coalitions-of-the-willing, the United States has not prioritized its relationship with a Europe that it often sees as creating diplomatic obstacles to the projection of U.S. power, but not offering substantial military capabilities when the United States needs its help.

Individually, Europe's countries are not significant military actors. Only Britain and France have high-end military capabilities that allow them to project significant power at far ranges. Most European armies are large conscript forces that were well suited to the Cold War but lack the professionalism, efficiency, and deployment capabilities necessary for modern power projection.[21] The history of the European Union includes on-and-off efforts to build a European defense capability. Indeed, the creation of a Europe strong enough to handle its own security responsibilities was one of the early missions for NATO. Ironically, however, as the structure of the Cold War was embedded, Europe became mainly dependent on the United States for military protection, and failed to invest in force projection capabilities for managing crises outside Europe. Since 1992, the European Union countries have committed to a Common Foreign and Security Policy and to build an independent military capability complementary to NATO's.

The incentives for the European countries to pool military resources are strong. A common EU defense capability can provide these states with a measure of influence in global security that, alone, none would have. The European Union includes twenty-five countries, which combined spend over $150 billion a year on defense. The EU membership includes two nuclear powers and over 2 million troops among the member states. If it could coalesce, the European Union is well positioned to become a major global actor. In December 1999, the European Union agreed on an ambitious plan to create its own rapid-deployment force of 50,000 to 60,000 troops for use in humanitarian and rescue tasks, peacekeeping, and crisis management.

Nevertheless, the European Union faces significant constraints on its potential for military development commensurate with its strategic interests. Europe lacks a unified military industrial capability and faces dramatic short-comings in capabilities relative to the United States. Meanwhile, European forces are not integrated and exercised in the European Union, leading many observers to argue that the European Union should not duplicate that which already exists in NATO. Yet independent capabilities are also seen as essential to full development of the European Union, particularly as the United States stresses its commitments that are more global than those it has historically had to Europe. The European Union has agreed to establish a modest military planning center that will coordinate national contributions to a future European military force. The objective is to harmonize contributions through an eighty-person planning operation to be coordinated by the EU high representative for foreign and security policy. The European Union will have a political and security committee, and a military committee including military staff.

While formally intended to be a complement, not a competitor, to NATO, the European Union would nevertheless be able to plan for, and control, military operations not involving NATO.[22] Since attaining general agreement in fall 2003, the European Union has moved forward with three principal activities: first, deploying a small group of operational planners to NATO headquarters in Mons, Belgium; second, those states most ambitious about European defense cooperation would, if they chose, work to accelerate cooperation on military capabilities; and third, the European Union has agreed to a renewed collective defense commitment while reaffirming that NATO is the primary tool for collective defense in Europe.[23] Meanwhile, Europe has agreed to a "headline goal" of capability commitments to be achieved by 2010, undertaken small but important missions in Macedonia, and assumed control of all forces in Bosnia-Herzegovina. Most significantly, the European Union is developing vital complementary capabilities that do not currently exist in NATO and that the United States seriously lacks—multinational, trained and exercised, deployable civilian-police forces. In many respects, this is an ideal mission for the European Union to undertake in that the emphasis on multinational police cooperation is consistent with the priority Europeans place on civilian solutions to security challenges while giving Europe influence with the United States, which needs help in this area. The general need for well-trained multinational police forces that can deploy to regional crisis locations, provide immediate public security, and train local personnel for long-term security missions, is especially urgent. In 2004, the European Union announced plans to create a 3,000-person gendarmerie force for global deployment, including police from France, Italy, Spain, Portugal, and the Netherlands. The plan is to have a core of 800 to 900 members available for rapid deployment within thirty days and a reserve of 2,300 reinforcements on call.

Squaring the Circle in Transatlantic Security

The transatlantic relationship between North America and Europe is one of history's truly unique success stories. It is, indeed, so successful that it risks being taken for granted by a new generation on both sides of the Atlantic who do not remember the fall of the Berlin Wall, let alone the Cold War, the Marshall Plan, and World War II. In the search for new missions, it is worth recalling that having paved the way to European integration is a good definition of "mission accomplished"—though still more needs to be done to achieve a Europe that is truly whole and free. Moreover, the threats to North America and Europe today come from outside the relationship. Agreeing on how to square the circle in securing common values and interests in the twenty-first century is one of the most crucial challenges confronting a new generation of transatlantic leadership. In particular, it is essential to develop a balance between the need for broad political support for military operations, efficiency in waging war, and responsible burden sharing in postwar stability operations, so as to include both nation building and counterinsurgency. Some broader historical perspective on the importance of the relationship between North America and Europe is also important. In the momentary passion of anti-Americanism that grew out of the differences over Iraq, it was easy to forget that modern Europe exists in peace and prosperity because of the opportunities for freedom that were brought to it by the United States. Meanwhile, the United States is often quick to dismiss the wisdom of experience from countries with centuries more engagement in world affairs. Regardless of who is in political office, there is far more to unite North America and Europe than divide them. Working together, North America and Europe can serve as a center of gravity for the world, illustrating how the benefits of cooperation far outweigh the costs of conflict and isolation.

Notes

1. For official background on the North Atlantic Treaty Organization visit www.nato.int for detail on its historical development, organizational structure, member states, and key personnel.

2. For analysis of why NATO persisted after the Cold War, see Charles Glaser, "Why NATO Is Still Best: Future Security Arrangements for Europe," *International Security*, 18(1), summer 1993, 5–50; Robert McCalla, "NATO's Persistence After the Cold War," *International Organization*, 50(3), summer 1996, 445–475; and Celeste Wallander, "Institutional Assets and Adaptability: NATO After the Cold War," *International Organization*, 54(4), autumn 2000, 705–735.

3. See http://www.securityconference.de/index.php?menu_2006=&menu_konferenzen=&sprache=en&.

4. Joseph Lepgold, "NATO's Collective Action Problem," *International Security*, 13(1), summer 1998, 78–106.

5. For example, see Sean Kay, "What Went Wrong with NATO?" *Cambridge Review of International Affairs*, 18(1), April 2006, 69–83.

6. This concern is explored in detail in Sean Kay, "NATO, the Kosovo War, and Neoliberal Theory," *Contemporary Security Policy*, 25(2), August 2004, 252–279.

7. For detailed analysis of the decisionmaking behind NATO enlargement, see James Goldgeier, *Not Whether, But When: The U.S. Decision to Enlarge NATO*, Washington, DC: Brookings Institution, 1999; and Ronald Asmus, *Opening NATO's Door: How the Alliance Remade Itself for a New Era*, New York: Columbia University Press, 2002.

8. Jeffrey Simon, "Romania and NATO: Membership Reassessment at the July 1997 Summit," *Strategic Forum*, 101, February 1997.

9. See http://www.nato.int/issues/enlargement/index.html for official documentation of the NATO enlargement process.

10. For further analysis, see Jeffrey Simon, "Partnership for Peace: Charting a Course for a New Era," *Strategic Forum*, 206, March 2004.

11. For detailed analysis, see Sean Kay, *NATO and the Future of European Security*, Lanham, MD: Rowman & Littlefield, 1998, especially chapter 4; and Ivo Daalder, *Getting to Dayton: The Making of America's Bosnia Policy*, Washington, DC: Brookings Institution, 2000.

12. Jeffrey Simon, "The IFOR/SFOR Experience: Lessons Learned by PFP Partners," *Strategic Forum*, 120, July 1997.

13. For detailed assessments of NATO's engagement in Kosovo, see Ivo Daalder and Michael O'Hanlon, *Winning Ugly: NATO's War to Save Kosovo*, Washington, DC: Brookings Institution, 2000; Benjamin S. Lambeth, *NATO's Air War for Kosovo: A Strategic and Operational Assessment*, Santa Monica, CA: Rand Corporation, 2001; and Wesley K. Clark, *Waging Modern War: Bosnia, Kosovo, and the Future of Combat*, New York: Public Affairs, 2001.

14. See http://www.whitehouse.gov/news/releases/2006/06/20060621–6.html for full text of President Bush's remarks while visiting Austria.

15. See http://pewglobal.org/reports/display.php?ReportID=252 for the entire PEW survey.

16. For detail on transatlantic defense spending, see the International Institute for Strategic Studies, *Military Balance 2006*, London: International Institute for Strategic Studies, 2006.

17. See http://www.nato.int/issues/nrf/index.html for official background on the NATO Response Force.

18. Elaine Sciolino and Steven Erlanger, "Turmoil in the Mideast: International Force; U.S. and NATO Balk over Lebanon," *New York Times*, July 25, 2006, p. A1.

19. See http://www.nato.int/issues/terrorism/index.html for official NATO summaries of its engagement in the international effort to combat transnational terrorism.

20. See Stephen Flanagan, "Sustaining U.S.-European Global Security Cooperation," *Strategic Forum*, 217, September 2005.

21. See Sean Kay, *Global Security in the Twenty-First Century: The Quest for Power and the Search for Peace*, Lanham, MD: Rowman & Littlefield, 2006, pp. 112–117.

22. "European Defense 'Deal' Reached," *BBC News*, November 28, 2003.

23. Charles Grant, "Big Three Join Forces on Defense," Center for European Reform, March 2004.

Suggested Readings

Asmus, Ronald, *Opening NATO's Door: How the Alliance Remade Itself for a New Era*, New York: Columbia University Press, 2002.

Daalder, Ivo H., and Michael E. O'Hanlon, *Winning Ugly: NATO's War to Save Kosovo*, Washington, DC: Brookings Institution, 2000.

Drew, S. Nelson, *From Berlin to Bosnia*, Washington, DC: National Defense University Press, 1995.

Goldgeier, James, *Not Whether, But When: The U.S. Decision to Enlarge NATO*, Washington, DC: Brookings Institution, 1999.

Hendrickson, Ryan C., *Diplomacy and War at NATO: The Secretary General and Military Action After the Cold War*, Columbia, MO: University of Missouri Press, 2006.

Kaplan, Lawrence S., *NATO Divided, NATO United: The Evolution of an Alliance*, New York: Praeger, 2004.

Kay, Sean, *NATO and the Future of European Security*, Lanham, MD: Rowman & Littlefield, 1998.

Kugler, Richard, *Commitment to Purpose: How Alliance Partnership Won the Cold War*, Santa Monica, CA: RAND Corporation, 1993.

Lambeth, Benjamin S., *NATO's Air War for Kosovo: A Strategic and Operational Assessment*, Santa Monica, CA: RAND Corporation, 2001.

Michta, Andrew (ed.), *America's New Allies: Poland, Hungary, and the Czech Republic in NATO*, Seattle: University of Washington Press, 2000.

Serfaty, Simon (ed.), *Visions of the Atlantic Alliance: The United States, the European Union, and NATO*, Washington, DC: Center for Strategic and International Studies, 2005.

Simon, Jeffrey, *Hungary and NATO: Problems in Civil-Military Relations*, Lanham, MD: Rowman & Littlefield, 2003.

Simon, Jeffrey, *NATO and the Czech and Slovak Republics: A Comparative Study in Civil-Military Relations*, Lanham, MD: Rowman & Littlefield, 2004.

Simon, Jeffrey, *Poland and NATO: A Study in Civil-Military Relations*, Lanham, MD: Rowman & Littlefield, 2004.

Simon, Jeffrey (ed.), *NATO Enlargement: Opinions and Options*, Washington, DC: National Defense University Press, 1996.

Sloan, Stanley R., *NATO, the European Union and the Atlantic Community*, 2nd edition, Lanham, MD: Rowman & Littlefield, 2005.

Sperling, James, Sean Kay, and S. Victor Papacosma (eds.), *Limiting Institutions: The Challenge of Eurasian Security Governance*, Manchester, UK: Manchester University Press, 2003.

Yost, David, *NATO Transformed: The Alliance's New Roles in International Security*, Washington, DC: United States Institute of Peace, 1999.

CHAPTER 13

European and U.S. Approaches to Counterterrorism: Two Contrasting Cultures?

Wyn Rees and Richard J. Aldrich

There have been a series of terrorist attacks around the world since 9/11, including in countries such as Indonesia, Turkey, Kenya, and Jordan. Yet it was the two attacks in Spain in 2004 and the United Kingdom in 2005 that have excited particular attention because they have led analysts to draw out the contrasting responses to international terrorism between the United States and Western Europe. The attacks have served to underline the differing circumstances and strategies of the transatlantic allies. This chapter draws out these differences and seeks to place them within the broader context of historically determined strategic cultures.

The context in which the attacks occurred was very different in the cases of the UK and Spain compared to that of the 9/11 attacks in the United States. The two European countries have long experience of fighting a serious domestic terrorist menace: Spain has suffered with Basque terrorism, while the UK faced the Provisional Irish Republican Army until the Good Friday Agreement in 1998. The United States has been fortunate not to have experienced any large-scale domestic terrorist challenge. The presence of sizeable Muslim populations at home was a factor in the European attacks in contrast to the United States. Prior to 2003, most European countries were seen as indifferent supporters of U.S. policy in the Middle East and were not identified by Islamicists as a main source of aggression against Muslims around the world.

A remarkable gulf in strategic culture between the two sides of the Atlantic was visible. The U.S. declared a "global war on terrorism" and directed the full resources of a "national security" approach towards the threat posed by a "new terrorism." Overseas policy has been shaped by the identification of a nexus between international terrorism, weapons of mass destruction, and "states of concern." The United States conducted a military campaign that unseated the

Taliban in Afghanistan and then used force against Iraq to topple the regime of Saddam Hussein. At home the United States has undertaken major changes to its governmental structure, tightened the points of entry into the country, granted greater powers to its law enforcement officers and courts, and over-hauled its intelligence and security agencies.

In contrast, Europe has conceived of the problem differently. It has concep-tualized radical Islam in less absolute terms, and accordingly its approach to counterterrorism has emphasized "regional multilateralism" rather than "global unilateralism." Its military forces have participated in peacekeeping, reconstruc-tion, and security-sector reform as well as in grueling counterinsurgencies. Their foreign policies have continued to emphasize the containment of risk, consensus building, and balance of power. Domestically, European govern-ments have emphasized the countering of terrorism by law enforcement and judicial means. Their legal changes relating to surveillance and civil rights have been less sweeping than those of the United States, while the enhancements to internal security architecture have been more modest. Underpinning this differ-ent approach have been two key objectives: first, a desire to draw on some of the lessons derived from decades of fighting national terrorist movements; and sec-ond, a conviction that the "newness" of the threat posed by Al-Qaeda has been exaggerated. The implications of these divergent cultures are enormous for the future of the relationship between Europe and the United States. In the face of a security challenge that Washington has regarded as dominant, the transatlantic allies risk pulling in opposite directions.

From the spring of 2005 there was evidence that the United States was mov-ing closer to the European position by adopting a new strategy of counterter-rorism and seeking greater multilateral engagement. In March 2005, the U.S. National Security Council began a review of U.S. national policy designed to address a more "diffuse" terrorism, and, over the next twelve months, a new National Security Presidential Directive on counterterrorism gradually emerged. The entire framework of the U.S. National Security Strategy was revisited.[1] Meanwhile the Pentagon adopted a new strategic plan that empha-sized nonmilitary instruments and more cooperation with allies.[2] In bureau-cratic terms the appointment of Condoleezza Rice as secretary of state in the Bush administration's second term also accelerated this change. To what extent did this presage a more convergent transatlantic approach to international ter-rorism that was more sympathetic to European thinking? This chapter argues that while strategic doctrines may change, recent evidence suggests that the more immutable nature of strategic culture is making convergence difficult. Moreover, while some officials have begun to identify the shape of current problems more accurately, the slippery nature of those problems means that nei-ther Europe nor the United States yet has convincing answers.

European and U.S. Strategic Cultures

The concept of strategic culture remains ill-defined and underutilized. Its employment must be accompanied by an acknowledgment of its limitations, accepting that even amongst political sociologists, ideas such as "culture" remain contested.[3] Discussions on the nature of strategic culture have focused on the extent to which it can be employed to understand or explain national strategy. Some of the initial adherents of strategic culture have preferred to see it as "context" and therefore, to a large extent, inseparable from other factors, including the policy itself. More recent investigators have preferred to isolate strategic culture and to seek to employ it as a variable that one might hope to measure, despite the obvious methodological challenges. This chapter tends towards the former approach, viewing strategic culture as an emotional and attitudinal environment within which national security policy is made. [4]

Strategic culture is based on the understanding that states are predisposed by their historical experiences, political system, and culture to deal with security issues in a particular way. Other factors may influence a state's strategic choices, such as its level of technological development, but its preferences will be shaped most strongly by its past. These institutional memories will help to determine how threats are perceived, as well as condition the likely responses.[5] Officials quickly absorb a strategic culture's unspoken norms, which may be as important in ruling out policy options that are "inappropriate" as they are in determining the precise nature of paths taken.[6]

Notions of a strategic culture or strategic personality have been most closely connected with defense issues and above all war-fighting problems.[7] Caroline Ziemke, one of the first to make use of this approach, has suggested that it is about a state's self-conception, mediated through the historical experience of its past conflicts. Historical experience and strategic culture are often connected through a process of reasoning by analogy. Decisionmakers tend to focus strongly on the commanding heights of their past strategic experience, navigating in terms of major episodes that are regarded as successes or failures.[8] These seminal experiences have burned themselves deeply into the national psyche and have significant unconscious meaning.[9] Munich and Suez, more recently Vietnam and Somalia—perhaps soon Afghanistan and Iraq—are all examples of what Dan Reiter has called the "weight of the shadow of the past."[10]

Applying the concept of strategic culture to the phenomenon of international terrorism presents difficulties because the latter crosses a number of established boundaries. First, international terrorism blurs the boundaries between external security and internal security—the perpetrators may originate from abroad but commit acts of violence against citizens in the homelands of their targets. Second, state responses are likely to be mixed, ranging from the use of force against the sources of terrorism to increasing internal security measures such as law enforcement and judicial action.[11]

Nevertheless, the classical literature on counterterrorism identifies, at least in outline, typologies of state response to terrorism that can be grouped into three broad categories: first, military-led approaches focused on a mixture of preemption, deterrence or retribution; second, regulatory or legal-judicial responses that seek to enhance the criminal penalties for terrorist activities and improve civil/police cooperation; and third, appeasement options ranging from accommodation to concession.[12]

The United States has evolved a sharply defined strategic culture. Its approach has been shaped by a belief in U.S. exceptionalism: that its democratic system, capitalist economy, and moral values are superior to those of the rest of the world and justify its position of leadership. This has given it a sense of mission in the world and a confidence that its actions are in the broadest interests of humanity.[13] This self-belief has been allied to strategies that seek ways to leverage its vast material and technological power. It has predisposed U.S. policymakers toward a national security culture that favors a military response. As a superpower, the United States sees the use of force as an important signal of resolve within the international community. Its military gives the United States a global reach and ensures that no targets are beyond its ability to strike. Since 9/11, increased U.S. spending on defense, on defense research and especially on Special Forces relative to other major powers, has accentuated this phenomenon.

It was only after the Iran hostage crisis of 1979 that counterterrorism featured regularly on the presidential agenda. The United States has consistently displayed an underdeveloped and somewhat two-dimensional counterterrorism culture. In part this is because counterterrorism has been seen as an unattractive political issue. In the White House there was a fear of encouraging public expectations that could not be fulfilled and a tendency towards blame-avoidance. Meanwhile the US intelligence community was narrowly focused on the Cold War, playing to its strengths in technical collection, and relying on allied expertise for coverage of less important subjects. Terrorism was frequently perceived as something sponsored by the Soviet bloc and was regarded as a minor subset of the "real problem."[14]

A diet-and-binge approach to covert action and aggressive human intelligence collection has also dogged U.S. counterterrorist operations. After its generous support during the first three decades of the Cold War, covert action became mired in the foreign policy struggles between the Congress and the White House during the 1970s. Special activities were shackled under President Carter and covert action appeared to be a dying art form. The Reagan era heralded the "unleashing of the CIA" only for it to become bogged down once again in the Iran-Contra fiasco of 1986.[15] During the late 1980s covert action was rehabilitated, partially by success in Afghanistan against the Soviets, only to meet a renewed downturn after the end of the Cold War. A risk-averse culture in the CIA was reinforced by a decision in the mid-1990s to drop agents that were either "unsavory" or politically risky.[16] Inevitably, 9/11 signaled a further swing of the pendulum toward a more ambitious use of intelligence to counter a threat that was perceived to have grown urgent in nature.[17]

Terrorism was principally an overseas phenomenon for the United States, whether in terms of attacks upon its armed forces, citizens or interests. In 1983, the United States suffered the devastating loss of 241 of its Marines serving in the peacekeeping force in Beirut. Just a few years later, U.S. citizens were murdered in the bombing of Pan Am flight 103 over the Scottish town of Lockerbie, and in 1998 two of the U.S. embassies in Africa were the targets of terrorist outrages. Yet it was not until the attack on the World Trade Center in 1993 and the federal building in Oklahoma City in 1995, that the United States experienced significant acts of terrorism on its own shores—the former perpetrated by foreigners but the latter the work of homegrown extremists.

This absence of a major domestic terrorist threat resulted in a false sense of invulnerability becoming prevalent in the United States. This misperception was cruelly exposed by the attacks of 9/11. The enormous loss of life suffered on that occasion—2,783 dead—had two galvanizing effects upon the U.S. government. First, it gave the Bush administration the political will to use force more readily on the international stage. Second, it led the United States to pour efforts into protecting its own territory and to create a dedicated Department of Homeland Security. The defense of its own shores has become a major preoccupation in the U.S. war on terror. Although the United States has long been perceived as "trigger happy," in reality, prior to 9/11, all presidents—even Ronald Reagan—have agonized before taking action in the realm of counterterrorism.[18] After 2001 the constraints that hitherto made the United States a "reluctant sheriff" were stripped away and a new predisposition toward preemptive action was inaugurated.[19]

U.S. strategic culture has also led to international terrorism being linked to a nexus of other threats. The United States' sense of its global responsibilities has meant that it has long been concerned with the proliferation of weapons of mass destruction (WMD) and states that reject the prevailing order. Even prior to 9/11, the Clinton administration was warning of the potential linkages between international terrorist groups and "states of concern."[20] It was clear that the interaction between these issues was regarded as the foremost threat to U.S. security. Once again, military power was perceived to be the principal instrument to address these challenges.

In contrast, a European strategic culture is more elusive. The most obvious reason for this is that Europe comprises a mix of nations, each with its own particular histories. Until the latter part of the twentieth century there was intense politico-military competition between major European states that precluded the development of a common strategic culture. In the Cold War period, the overarching nature of U.S. power within Western Europe ensured that the strategic values of Washington held sway, and the emergence of a specifically European strategic culture was further constrained.

European countries now share important attributes, namely liberal-democratic governments, market economies, and adherence to the rule of law. Yet, in relation to terrorism, their experiences have often been divergent. Some countries have experienced protracted difficulties: West Germany struggled with the Baader Meinhof movement, and Italy with the Red Brigades, while French support for the Algerian government led to acts of terrorism by the Armed Islamic Group. Other European countries, such as the Netherlands and Belgium, experienced little in the way of terrorist attacks. This resulted in European countries being exposed to terrorist groups that were national in their focus, and militated against the emergence of common European threat perceptions and counterterrorism cooperation across state boundaries.

European states tended to disagree over terrorism issues, leaving a legacy that has needed to be overcome in the context of the contemporary terrorism challenge. In the past, European states were unable to agree on a common definition of terrorism. National courts frequently refused to extradite individuals charged with terrorism to other countries because they were willing to accept the defense plea that these were "political" crimes. There was an absence of structures to facilitate counterterrorism cooperation between states and so states were reliant on ad hoc forms of collaboration.

Another factor that has influenced the development of a European strategic culture in the fight against terrorism has been the emergence of the political will to forge closer European integration. In the Treaty on European Union, which was ratified in November 1993, the member states agreed to build closer cooperation in a number of policy areas. One of these was in the field of internal security or "Justice and Home Affairs." For the first time the European Union (EU) has been capable of cooperating over matters relating to terrorism as well as engaging in the construction of common institutions that can harness the counterterrorist activities of the member states. The shock waves caused by the 9/11 attacks in the United States speeded up the efforts of EU countries to build structures and design policies to combat terrorism.

Notwithstanding these complications, elements of a European strategic culture in relation to counterterrorism have developed. It has focused upon a law enforcement and judicial response, seeking to deny terrorists a sense of political legitimacy, and to prosecute them as criminals. This was a hallmark of French responses to Islamicist extremism during the 1980s and 1990s. It was increasingly evident in the UK campaign against the Provisional IRA, in which the role of the military became to support the civil police, and the emphasis was placed upon catching terrorists and prosecuting them before the courts. These same priorities can be found in speeches by Gijs de Vries, the EU's counterterrorism coordinator. He stresses that the EU's police agency (Europol) and its judicial

Box 13.1   Gijs de Vries outlines five key aspects of the European Union's approach to counterterrorism after 9/11 in a speech in Washington

Already a few days after 9/11, the European Council adopted an ambitious action plan. . . . Allow me to just give you five examples.

—First, we created the European Arrest Warrant. When Swedish prosecutors now issue an arrest warrant, for instance, the police of any other EU country has to arrest the criminal and extradite him or her. No country can refuse to surrender nationals. What used to be politics is now just judicial. Governments are not involved anymore. This makes things much faster. It is much harder now for criminals to escape arrest and to find a safe haven in another EU member state.

—Second, we started joint investigation teams. This means that law enforcement authorities of two or more member states can set up teams for criminal investigation. Hence, German and Danish police and prosecutors could work together with their Portuguese colleagues in Lisbon.

—Third, we created Eurojust, our nascent law enforcement agency. Its job is to improve the coordination of member states' law enforcement activities to help with assistance and extradition requests, and to support investigations.

—Fourth, we adopted legislation on terrorist financing. In line with UNSCR 1373, we establish lists of persons, groups and other entities involved in terrorist activities and freeze their assets. The EU has also beefed up its laws against money laundering.

—Fifth, our police agency, Europol, was given a new role in the fight against terrorism. It is collecting, sharing and analysing information about international terrorism and can participate in the joint investigative teams. It also assesses EU member states' performance in fighting terrorism and other forms of serious international crime.

(*Source: http://ue.eu.int/uedocs/cmsUpload/CSIS_Washington.13_May_2004.pdf*)

cooperation forum (Eurojust) must have a leading role in the counterterrorist efforts of the member states.[21]

The preference for civilian agencies rather than the military accords with the particular circumstances in which Europe finds itself with regard to its Muslim communities. Concentrations of Muslim populations in Western Europe far exceed those of the United States: for example, the Netherlands is home to 1 million Muslims, the UK 1.5 million, Germany just over 4 million, and France some 6 million.[22] While the vast majority of those citizens are law abiding, the July 2005 bombings in London demonstrated that small pockets of second-generation resident Muslims can be won over to the cause of violent jihad. By focusing upon a law enforcement and judicial approach, European countries are seeking to minimize the frictions within their own domestic populations and limit the radicalizing effects that can result from more aggressive policies.

Debating the "New Terrorism"

Strategic cultures, and indeed cultures of counterterrorism, are shaped by history and represent significant elements of continuity in a realm of change. Few things underline this better than the different ways in which the United States and Europe have conceived of the "new terrorism." One of the historic traits associated with U.S. strategic culture has been a tendency to assert the importance of new developments that break with the past. In the 1990s this was most clearly illustrated by the Revolution in Military Affairs debate. After 9/11 the assertions of a "strategic revolution" were quickly transferred to the field of terrorism. Al-Qaeda was deemed to be an example of "new terrorism"—perhaps even a "catastrophic terrorism"—that confounded the old lessons about this seemingly well-understood phenomenon. Indeed, more recently, commentators in both the United States and Europe have begun to speak of a "new Al-Qaeda" that is different yet again from the "new terrorism" of 9/11.[23]

The most plausible assertions about the emergence of "new terrorism" were made in the mid-1990s by Bruce Hoffman, a senior analyst with RAND. Hoffman argued that terrorism was changing, with "new adversaries, new motivations, and new methods," which challenged many of our most fundamental assumptions about terrorists and how they operate. Hoffman noted that while instances of attacks were going down, casualties were going up. He explained this in terms of a new religious terrorism that defied the old dictum that terrorists wanted only a few people dead, but many people watching. Now, it appeared, killing was no longer an ugly form of political communication, or a form of bargaining with violence—instead it was becoming a religious duty. In other words, the new terror was more apolitical and casualties were themselves the objective. This conjured up an alarming world without restraint in which the realist world of bargains, deterrence, and rational behavior evaporated, offering the prospect of terrorists who might seek to use weapons of mass destruction if they could obtain access. It also implied that militant Islam might attack the developed states of the West, not because of what they were doing in the Middle East, but simply because of what they were. The catastrophic events of 9/11 seemed to herald such an era and offered an obvious rationale for a hard-nosed military response.[24]

There is now some disagreement about the novelty of the "new terrorism," and four years after 9/11 the picture stands in need of reassessment. On the one hand, the rise of religious terrorism generally since the early 1990s, and of terrorism by Islamicist groups in particular, is undeniable. The exit of a quarter of a million trained and radicalized Mujahadeen from South Asia at the end of the war against the Soviets in Afghanistan has fuelled this development. They headed for their home countries, from the Mahgreb to Indonesia, or for new conflicts in Chechnya or Bosnia. Their organization is more fissiparous than the old terrorism, an ideological community rather than a fixed hierarchy. Al-Qaeda has tended to invest sporadic training and expertise in particular groups, rather than directing them. For many radical Islamicist groups, Osama bin Laden is now an icon rather than leader.[25]

Nevertheless, important elements of the old terrorism remain. Since 9/11, many terrorist attacks have been modest in scale and have targeted members of the coalitions fighting in Afghanistan and Iraq. Indeed, the overwhelming balance of effort by radicalized groups since 2003 has been to provide volunteer foreign fighters for the conflict in Iraq. The much vaunted use of WMD by terrorists has not materialized. Increasingly it appears that Al-Qaeda and its affiliates see themselves less as terrorists and more as a global insurgency with certain objectives. They may lack an explicit list of political desiderata, but they are waging an effective war of political communication, most obviously via the Internet.[26]

Europe has been more skeptical of the idea of "new terrorism," instead suggesting that the rise of Islamicist terrorism remains rooted in some old political and economic problems. It has suited European attitudes to interpret this phenomenon more in terms of a reaction to specific policies and military deployments, rather than to a general anathematizing of the West. Gijs de Vries has pointed specifically to lack of progress on the Middle East peace process and in Iraq as key factors in terrorist recruitment.[27] Others have been inclined to talk about a situation in which there is not so much a new terrorism as a new and more globalized environment that presents the perpetrators of violence with enhanced opportunities. There is a globalized world in relation to communications, ideologies, and capacity for violence. Newness may be more about context, specifically the ability of social and religious movements to exploit opportunities provided by globalization. In other words, developed states have encouraged a porous world in which networks move elegantly, but states move clumsily. The Internet as the "network of the networks" is a good example of this.[28]

In retrospect, the "new terrorism" of 2001 does not look quite so innovative. There are likely to be few further 9/11s, but sadly more attacks similar to Bali, Madrid, and London. Politicians on both sides of the Atlantic were quick to seize on the rhetoric of "new terrorism" because it mobilized elected assemblies, delivering enhanced budgets and robust packages of security legislation. However, it has also provided a convenient excuse to forget awkward lessons expensively learned in past decades. Europeans have argued that in the rush to address the "new terrorism," the United States in particular has neglected some of the basic conventions governing the related fields of counterterrorism and counterinsurgency. These concern the primacy of political warfare, the use of minimum force, the need for good human intelligence, and maximum efforts to ensure the legitimacy of one's actions. History, in almost any decade, underlines that few low intensity conflicts have been successfully resolved by a predominantly military approach, and never by applying large-scale formal military power.

Together with doubts about the nature of "new terrorism," there has also been a growing tendency in Europe to ponder the issues of relative risk. While proponents of the strong connection between new terrorism and WMD have emphasized the possibility of major catastrophe, others have emphasized the extreme difficulty of creating a device that would result in more casualties than conventional explosives. As the EU high representative Javier Solana has remarked, the last documented terrorist use of WMD was in 1995 when the Aum cult killed only twelve people in Japan. Two years earlier they had tried to spray anthrax spores on a Tokyo street but killed only birds and animals.[29] Subsequent real WMD events have proved to be scarce. On June 7, 2006, the UK security agencies conducted a large-scale raid on a house in London in a search for an alleged chemical device. They shot one resident but found nothing. Contemporaneously, Canadian success against a large-scale Islamist conspiracy in the summer of 2006 revealed plans that focused on conventional explosives.

More broadly, European policymakers have tended to observe that interstate war, civil war, organized crime, and even traffic accidents are all killing more people than terrorism. Meanwhile the cost of the war against terror has run into many billions. Europeans still regard counterterrorism as a high priority but question whether it should be quite so preeminent as a foreign policy objective. The matter is one of nuance. Although President Bush's speeches have been less triumphalist during 2005 and 2006, they still hold fast to the absolutist objective of eradicating terrorism, expressed in phrases such as "the final outcome of this struggle" and "the defeat of terrorism threats."[30] Europeans have wondered whether this warfare analogy—with its prospect of final victory—is realistic. Europeans have tended to look to their own historical experience and have drawn the gloomy lesson that terrorism in some form will always be with us. Some would even go so far as to see terrorism as a regrettable characteristic of all open societies that has to be addressed vigorously but that also has to be endured.

European and U.S. Counterterrorism Cultures Post-9/11

The different strategic cultures of the United States and Europe have resulted in contending approaches to combating terrorism. In the realm of external security, the most striking difference has been in their preparedness to use force. As part of its integrated plan for countering terrorism, founded on the National Strategy for Combating Terrorism, the United States has accorded priority to its military and intelligence assets. The experience of 9/11 galvanized the United States into a willingness to use its military power against a range of threats. This has extended to using military power preemptively, before the United States is attacked. The administration has argued that such actions are legitimate because the United States is a democratic nation with vital interests to secure.

The Pentagon has been in the driving seat of policy execution. Special Forces have increasingly been deployed in a military role and are now more the preserve of the Pentagon than the CIA. They have assisted in the retraining of local security forces in dozens of countries, with large contingents in Djibouti and the former Soviet republic of Georgia. A vast military deployment in Colombia is also increasingly justified on the grounds of counterterrorism rather than counternarcotics. Training operations are under way in dozens of other countries. Most recently in North Africa, a stream of newly arrived advisers is seeking to upgrade the capabilities of local forces. Underpinning all this is a substantial development of overseas bases to allow the greater projection of force.

Another reason why the United States has been predisposed toward the threat and use of force is the threat it has identified between state sponsors, terrorist groups, and weapons of mass destruction. In his speech to Congress in 2002, President Bush argued that states hostile to the United States and its allies could furnish terrorist groups with the capacity to inflict enormous destruction. He alleged that states such as Iran, Iraq, and North Korea constituted an "axis of evil"—by seeking weapons of mass destruction, these regimes could provide these arms to terrorists, thereby constituting a threat to the United States of a qualitatively different magnitude. The state sponsorship of Al-Qaeda provided the grounds for the U.S. military attack on Afghanistan at the end of 2001, the removal of the Taliban, and the rise to power of the pro-Western Karzai government. The fear of the linkage between Iraq, WMD, and terrorism provided the pretext for the subsequent U.S. military assault and victory over the government of Saddam Hussein in 2003.

In contrast, the view of European governments has tended to be that military force is a blunt instrument, particularly against the elusive targets presented by transnational terrorism. Europe has been more circumspect than the United States in identifying a nexus between states of concern, WMD, and international terrorism. This was the core of the difference between the Bush administration and France and Germany over the war in Iraq. While countries such as the UK, Italy, and Spain were prepared to support the hard-line U.S. stance, France and Germany were of the opinion that the International Atomic Energy Agency inspectors who were investigating Iraq's alleged nuclear weapons program should be granted a longer period to do their work. They were justifiably suspicious that U.S. pressure for military action against Iraq was motivated by its desire to remove a regime that Washington had long regarded as destabilizing in the region. The cost, however, was an iciness in transatlantic relations that has not been easy to overcome. As the U.S. position in Iraq has deteriorated,

France and Germany have barely contained their *schadenfreude* over the deepening quagmire.

The U.S. response to Europe's reluctance to use force has been to argue that this is because of the structural disparity in power between the transatlantic allies. Elite opinion in Washington has alleged that the European attitude was consistent with its past predilection to rely on the United States to take care of global threats, such as nuclear proliferation. Neoconservative critics in Washington have argued that the Europeans choose to ignore threats because of their relative military weakness. They point out that European countries have reduced their defense spending and thus lack the military capability to enforce their will within the international community. In the words of Robert Kagan, "the incapacity to respond to threats leads not only to tolerance. It can also lead to denial."[31]

The significance accorded to multilateralism is the second major transatlantic difference. Europe's experience of overcoming its own internal rivalries after World War II has led it to pursue policies based upon building consensus and adhering to the rule of law. The creation of the European Union exemplifies this approach and results in European states working for the broadest degree of international support. It was the perception of European opponents of the war that the United States had abandoned these principles when it attacked Iraq. That is not to say that Europe has always opposed the use of force. If an action has appeared to be proportionate to the aggression, and if it is in accordance with Article 51 of the UN Charter on self-defense, then Europe has been willing to support the use of coercive means. For example, there was widespread support in Europe for the actions the United States took against the Taliban government in Afghanistan in 2001. The only European criticism was that the United States did not draw on the military forces Europe had offered for the operation and thereby limited the breadth of the coalition that toppled the regime.

In contrast, U.S. military might has left it fearful of being constrained by the veto power of allies. In the post-9/11 environment, the United States was reluctant to wait for the support of its allies before undertaking those tasks it believed to be in its vital interests. This has reflected a wider sense of unease within the U.S. government since the end of the Cold War. U.S. officials have come to question the relevance of organizations such as NATO in the face of radically new threats such as international terrorism. The Bush administration has expressed its preference for the informality of "willing coalitions" to tackle crises rather than reliance on structured alliances. The administration has been selective about its international partners and openly critical about waiting for the United Nations to sanction international action.

A third difference between the transatlantic allies has been over European advocacy of long-term strategies aimed at conflict prevention. European countries have identified issues such as enhanced overseas aid as instruments capable of mitigating some of the underlying causes of terrorism. Such funding can help to alleviate some of the factors that lead to the radicalization of politics and the sense of despair. This resonates with the EU's own sense of strength: after all, it disburses approximately 55 percent of the world's official development assistance.[32] The United States has been willing to increase its foreign assistance but has targeted its resources more narrowly towards those countries, such as Egypt, Pakistan, and Indonesia, that it considers to be in the vanguard of the war against terror.

The Europeans have been willing to carry through this commitment to long-term structural projects by providing troops and resources for postconflict peace-building projects. In the case of Afghanistan, for example, the United States rapidly drew down its military presence in the country after 2001, maintaining only enough troops to carry out "search and destroy" missions against Al-Qaeda and the Taliban. This was consistent with the United States' traditional skepticism about the value of "foreign policy as social work"[33] and the Pentagon's reluctance to tie down large numbers of troops in peacekeeping situations. In contrast, the Europeans have taken the lead in establishing the International Security Assistance Force (ISAF) in Afghanistan, and have provided the lion's share of resources to rebuild its society. NATO's decision to take over running the ISAF has meant that the militaries of several European countries are now responsible for spreading government control from the region around Kabul to the south and west of the country.

Consistent with their reluctance to threaten the use of force, Europe has preferred to offer positive incentives to states accused of supporting terrorism to reform their behavior. Trade, diplomacy, and cultural contacts have been viewed as more likely instruments to modify the errant behavior of governments such as Libya, Iran, and Syria during the 1990s, rather than the threat of the use of force. Individual European states, as well as the European Union, pursued regular interaction in the name of a "critical dialogue." Critics in the United States accused European states of self-interested action that was more concerned with improving their economies than addressing security concerns. The European response was that although their policies might take longer to bear fruit, they offered the possibility of changing the minds and long-term behavior of the countries in question.

Europe could point to real achievements in their dealings with President Ghaddafi of Libya.[34] In 2004, the Libyan government announced that it was suspending its attempts to acquire WMD and was establishing a compensation fund for the families of the Lockerbie victims, in return for the suspension of economic sanctions. It was evident that several factors had influenced Libya's change of policy. The effect of the U.S. assault upon Iraq the previous year had been salutary, demonstrating that the Bush administration was prepared to use force to alter the actions of states of concern. Yet alterations in Libya's approach had been apparent for some time, motivated by the economic isolation in which the government had found itself. European governments deserve much of the credit for encouraging the regime to alter course and providing it with a face-saving formula for the reversal of its position.

Iran has been more problematic. Three European countries—the UK, France, and Germany (E3)—have been the principal interlocutors with the government in Tehran. They have sought to discourage Iran from supporting terrorism and to convince it to desist from developing a nuclear weapons program. In return for such policy changes the E3 have offered trade benefits and possible admission to the World Trade Organization. Yet Iran spurned the opportunities presented to it by the E3, resulting in the case being referred to the UN Security Council. The White House has been persistent in its public saber rattling toward Tehran,[35] warning that unless European efforts made progress the United States would have to step in and pursue a harder line. In June 2006 the United States announced it was willing to undertake face-to-face negotiations with Iran if the country agreed to halt its uranium enrichment program.

Internal security has also revealed some remarkable contrasts between Europe and the United States. Both sides of the Atlantic believe in the importance of combating terrorism through law enforcement, and judicial and intelligence cooperation. The Europeans place more emphasis on these instruments because they do not accord the military instrument the prominence it is given by the United States. The Europeans are also predisposed toward weighing the balance that is struck between more stringent security measures against terrorism and the penalties that are incurred in terms of human rights. They are more wary about investing law enforcement personnel with powers that could damage the core values of their society.[36]

However, the effort of the U.S. in homeland security since 9/11 should not be underestimated.[37] The National Strategy for Homeland Security has sought to construct a defense system based upon overlapping circles. In the first circle, focused overseas, the United States has relied upon its FBI legal attachés working in embassies, and customs officials deployed in European ports to monitor cargoes destined for the United States. The next security circle concerns entry into U.S. territory by foreigners, and here the United States has enhanced the security of airlines, introduced biometric identifiers into travel documents, reappraised its visa waiver programs, and tightened its borders. Since November 2002, the various agencies responsible for U.S. domestic security have been amalgamated into the Department of Homeland Security, the largest reorganization of the federal government since 1947. The United States' last line of defense has focused on promoting cooperation between its plethora of police and intelligence agencies emergency responders, and the enhancement of security for critical infrastructure such as power plants and refineries.

Since 2001, Europe has taken steps to close some of its vulnerabilities to terrorist activity. Several EU member states have drafted new legislation to prosecute terrorist activities and have afforded greater operational powers to their police forces—information has been circulated more freely among intelligence services, new policies to target fund raising have been implemented, and there has been a tightening of border controls. A common definition of terrorism, which had hitherto eluded agreement, was reached in draft form in December 2001 and entered into force in June 2002. As well as defining the types of crimes that comprise terrorism, it also determined stiff penalties to be imposed for terrorist offences.[38] Furthermore, efforts to speed up the process of continent-wide extradition were achieved with the signing of a European Arrest Warrant. This designated thirty-two offenses, including terrorism, punishable by imprisonment of at least three years' duration.

Problems persist in Europe's internal security in spite of greater resources and attention over the last four years. First, the priority attached to counterterrorism varies amongst EU states. While countries such as Spain, the UK, France, and Germany have made strenuous efforts, such as drafting new laws, to address the new challenges, other countries have languished because they do not perceive an imminent threat to themselves. Several countries have been reluctant to increase resources for security and unwilling to transfer additional competences to the EU level because they have sought to preserve their sovereign powers. Second, some states have proved unwilling to implement agreements that have been made at the EU level. While all states have ratification processes that have to be respected, some have made little effort to draft domestic legislation to bring EU-wide conventions into effect. For example, in the case of a Framework Decision on the freezing of terrorist assets, the measure was agreed in March 2002, but as late as mid-2004 there were still states that had not enacted its provisions. Third, the European Commission still struggles to coordinate counterterrorism measures between the member states and the level of the Union. The EU has no internal security structure with the equivalent remit of the U.S. Department of Homeland Security, and its counterterrorism coordinator, Gijs de Vries, has no special budgetary authority.

The Future of Transatlantic Counterterrorism

What are the prospects for transatlantic convergence on counterterrorism? The practical business of everyday internal security cooperation and joint intelligence operations has continued in spite of transatlantic political storms.[39] Moreover, there has been no simple split comprising the United States versus Europe—the UK, Italy, Spain, and the Netherlands all deployed troops to Iraq. Yet longer-term tensions across the Atlantic have remained undiminished. The failure to find WMD in Iraq confirmed suspicions that U.S. explanations of the war were a smoke screen, and the exposure of prisoner treatment at Guantanamo Bay and Abu Ghraib prisons appeared to confirm the worst fears about its actions. At the same time, tensions over Iran have every prospect of escalating as Tehran seeks to play off European and U.S. positions.

Contrasting cultures have also thrown up persistent difficulties in both the internal and external security domains. First, the United States and Europe differ over such issues as electronic surveillance. The recent decision by the U.S. government to end the separation between information obtained by the law enforcement and intelligence communities could prove to be a major obstacle to cooperation as it could risk undermining a prosecution in a European court if it could be shown that the information on which it was based was inadmissible. Second, the United States has expressed exasperation with the length of time it takes to obtain judicial cooperation with European countries. Third, there has been tension over sharing intelligence. The Europeans have been alarmed by what they perceive to be inadequate U.S. attention to issues of data protection. This has resulted in lengthy negotiations between the United States and Europol before personal data could be transferred. Again, the media have been a factor since European security agencies fear leaks of operationally sensitive information to the U.S. press.

The media spotlight has focused on heightened European anxieties about the troublesome issue of "extraordinary rendition." This focuses on the shadowy issue of the U.S. treatment of detainees who have been moved to prisons in third countries, including Syria, Jordan, and Egypt. Human rights groups have asserted, with considerable evidence, that "extraordinary rendition," initially developed in the 1980s to bring foreign terrorists to trial in the United States for crimes overseas, now represents a system for outsourcing torture. It is clear that this is a substantial program. In 2002, the director of Central Intelligence, George Tenet, told Congress that even prior to 9/11, some 70 people had undergone rendition. Congressman Edward J. Markey has suggested that since 9/11 the number is approximately 150. Confirmation of this has come from unexpected sources. On May 16, 2005, Egyptian prime minister Ahmed Nazif told a press conference that more than 60 suspects had been rendered to his country since September 2001.[40] Cases such as that of Benyam Mohammed, a former London schoolboy accused of being a dedicated Al-Qaeda terrorist, illustrate the problem. For two years U.S. authorities moved him between Pakistan, Morocco, and Afghanistan, before he was sent to Guantanamo Bay in September of 2005.[41]

Secret warfare remains at the forefront of transatlantic discussions, with ambiguous results. In the summer of 2006 the Council of Europe completed an enquiry into what many have referred to as "CIA Secret Prisons in Europe." There can be no doubt that a shift from the intelligence doctrine of "watch and wait" to the more preemptive "seize and strike" has increased the numbers of detainees and captives in circulation around the world. On June 6, 2006, Dick Marty, a Swiss senator and chairman of the Committee on Legal Affairs and Human Rights, produced a report on the transshipment of suspects through Europe that reflected the Council's historic focus on human rights. The movements were well documented but the location of alleged "secret prisons" remained elusive. European responses to the enquiry were by no means uniform. Most Western European governments said little while those in Eastern Europe vigorously contested the Council's findings.[42] Nevertheless, the European Parliament endorsed the report and voted to continue the enquiry for another six months. Rather than reinforcing the transatlantic divide, this report has revealed the fissiparousness of European thinking. Some governments were clearly unaware of activities by the CIA or their own secret services, while others were supportive. Some governments have cooperated with the enquiry, while others have not. Perhaps the efforts of the Council of Europe underline a different lesson of rather a depressing sort—in both Europe and the United States national mechanisms of intelligence accountability have weakened, while no one seems to have proper oversight of growing activity by special forces.

These issues alarm European intelligence and security officials because secret warfare runs contrary to their own culture. Since the end of the Cold War, European clandestine agencies have undergone a quiet revolution. Legality and regulation have been at the center of this, with services being placed on the statute books and the elements of the European Convention on Human Rights being written into their regulations.[43] European services have embraced the new approach, which has increased their transparency and legitimacy and allowed them to develop a wider customer base and conduct more operations. It is not only that the utility of these U.S. renditions is unclear, it is also that the European culture of public expectations is very different.[44] As recently as July 2005, intelligence officials in Washington expressed dismay that their British counterparts blocked their efforts to have a suspect, Harron Rashid Aswat, seized in South Africa and moved to one of the undisclosed detention centers run by allied states, possibly Egypt. Aswat is a British citizen of Indian descent, and London hesitated at the idea of an extraordinary rendition of someone with a UK passport.[45]

Notwithstanding these public indicators of continued trouble, privately there have been sustained efforts at transatlantic convergence. At the center of this has been a substantial reshaping of both U.S. national security strategy and its more detailed counterterrorism strategy. Even in 2003, it was obvious that alongside the dominant military culture of U.S. counterterrorism was an alternative view. This alternative view was propounded largely by officials in the CIA and the State Department who emphasized political warfare, economic instruments, patient diplomacy, and counterproliferation as an alternative to coercive interventions. There was a growing recognition that while the core terrorist groups may be impervious to political engagement, they draw support from a wider environment of anti-Westernism throughout the Middle East, and indeed Muslim communities throughout the world. Specific policies in the Middle East were thought to be a substantial part of the problem. There was perceived to be too much emphasis on Osama bin Laden and not enough on the wider hostility that was developing in the Muslim world toward the United States. By 2004 this alternative view had been given a higher profile by a number of vocal figures who were concerned about the lack of progress in the global war on terror. This included an "anonymous" CIA officer, soon revealed as Michael Scheuer, who was formerly head of the CIA's unit specializing in

Al-Qaeda.[46] In February 2004 it was echoed by none other than George Tenet in a statement given to the Senate Committee on Intelligence urging less focus on Al-Qaeda and more attention to the general growth of extremism.[47]

In March 2005 there was evidence that this alternative view was receiving official attention. The National Security Council's Frances Fragos Townsend and her deputy, Juan Carlos Zarate, began a wide-ranging policy review. The arrival of Condoleezza Rice at the State Department was central to this shift. Shortly afterwards, Philip Zelikow, former 9/11 Commission staff director and now special adviser to Rice, was put in charge of a ten-member committee to reassess policy. The committee's meetings, which began in June 2006, have taken it to London and Paris with the support of the White House. Privately there have been admissions that this initiative owed much to European influence.[48] These moves have been complemented by the renewed emphasis on public diplomacy at the State Department, under the somewhat uncertain leadership of Karen Hughes.[49]

These developments reflect disillusionment with the war in Iraq and fears about Afghanistan. In Iraq, the Pentagon has accepted that the insurgency is growing more violent, resilient, and sophisticated. Economic reconstruction has been slowed, Arab diplomats have been targeted in Baghdad, and the prospect of an early drawdown of U.S. forces has been slipping away. The period July 2004–June 2005 saw approximately 500 suicide attacks.[50] Military leaders are also anxious about the war in Afghanistan. Although $11 billion per annum is spent on keeping 22,000 troops in the field, the shift of attention to Iraq allowed the insurgency in Afghanistan a crucial breathing space. Meanwhile the G8 five-pillar reconstruction program has stalled. More broadly, the State Department's most recent statistics paint a gloomy picture, showing that across the world there were three times as many terrorist attacks in 2004 as in 2003.[51]

The Pentagon overhauled its strategy during 2005 in response to the increasingly diffuse nature of Islamic terrorism. One example of this was a conference in June 2005 at the Special Operations Command headquarters in Tampa, Florida. Special Forces commanders and intelligence directors from the United States and many of its allies were gathered together to discuss the substance of the new counterterror strategy. The keynote address was given by General Bryan D. Brown, Head of U.S. Special Operations Command, who said that there had been an unambiguous change in U.S. thinking and a recognition that "we will not triumph solely or even primarily through military might."[52] Brown is an authoritative voice, given that the Pentagon has designated Special Operations Command as the global "synchronizer" for its new strategy.[53] Another example is that of General Richard B. Myers, chairman of the Joint Chiefs of Staff, who since July 2005 has expressed criticism of the idea that military instruments can offer the main solution to countering terrorism.[54] He instructed the Pentagon to join the State Department in emphasizing the "war of ideas." The Pentagon announced contracts amounting to $300 million awarded to companies to enhance its psychological operations.[55]

Some regard the expansion of Special Forces as the strongest evidence that the United States is attempting doctrinal change in the realm of counterterrorism. Special Forces are no longer viewed as a support element or a fringe activity but are increasingly viewed as a separate arm. Current proposals suggest that even regular forces will undertake some tasks currently undertaken by elite units, including training foreign security forces, thus liberating "real" Special Forces for more aggressive missions that involve growing fusion with intelligence, surveillance, and reconnaissance. Overall, U.S. spending on Special Operations Command capabilities has grown from $4.8 billion in FY 2003 to $8 billion in FY 2007. The Marine Corps is to establish its own Special Operations Command with 2,600 personnel.[56] However, this evidence is ambiguous. Some have argued that while this denotes a genuine shift to a more agile use of force, it also allows the Pentagon to advance a long-cherished desire to take paramilitary operations away from the CIA.[57]

Have there been corresponding changes in Europe? Restored confidence in transatlantic approaches will certainly require new attitudes on both sides. In December 2003, the European Council published a "European Security Strategy" (ESS) that attempted to bring together policy amongst the EU member states.[58] There was some evidence in the European Security Strategy that EU states have moved closer to U.S. thinking on security threats by acknowledging that terrorist acquisition of WMD was a priority consideration and that Europe would have to play a bigger part in addressing security challenges outside its region. In the earliest draft of the paper, reference was made to the possibility of military preemption, thereby narrowing the gap with U.S. thinking, but in the final draft this was diluted to talk of "preventive engagement." Furthermore, the ESS remained wedded to UN approval for military interventions, which remained at odds with the United States. In 2005, the United States showed a new willingness to consult with its European allies at an early stage of its policy process. The achievements made by the EU in internal security have made them a more important partner for the United States. In recognition of this, a new U.S.-EU forum entitled the "High Level Policy Dialogue on Borders and Transport Security" was created. This draws together the U.S. Departments of State, Justice, and Homeland Security with the EU Directorate General for Justice and Home Affairs, and the European Commission. It is a concerted attempt to build transatlantic cooperation from an early stage through the sharing of ideas.

The strongest signs of convergence are visible in the new U.S. National Security Strategy, unveiled in March 2006. Distinctive commitments to the active promotion of democracy and to preemptive action against proliferation remain. However, some of the strap lines of this high level document read almost as an atonement for past unilateralist indulgences. These included "Strengthening Alliances to Defeat Global Terrorism" and "Working with Others to Defuse Regional Conflicts," and indeed even "Developing Agendas for Cooperative Action with Other Main Centers of Global Power." Perhaps most

---

Box 13.2   The National Security Strategy
of the United States of America, March 16, 2006

. . . Like those who came before us, we must lay the foundations and build the institutions that our country needs to meet the challenges we face. The chapters that follow will focus on several essential tasks. The United States must:

- Champion aspirations for human dignity;
- Strengthen alliances to defeat global terrorism and work to prevent attacks against us and our friends;
- Work with others to defuse regional conflicts;
- Prevent our enemies from threatening us, our allies, and our friends with weapons of mass destruction (WMD);
- Ignite a new era of global economic growth through free markets and free trade;
- Expand the circle of development by opening societies and building the infrastructure of democracy;
- Develop agendas for cooperative action with other main centers of global power;
- Transform the United States' national security institutions to meet the challenges and opportunities of the 21st century; and
- Engage the opportunities and confront the challenges of globalization.

(*Source: http://www.whitehouse.gov/nsc/nss/2006/*)

---

notable was the overt commitment to avoid bilateralism in favor of genuine regionalism and a commitment to institutions both regional and global.[59]

Conclusion

Strategic culture remains the biggest challenge to transatlantic convergence on counterterrorism. Security doctrines are matters of fashion, but strategic culture is much more firmly embedded. During 2005 and 2006 there was clear evidence of new thinking in Washington. This was underlined by the strongly multilateral tone of the new National Security Strategy unveiled in March 2006. Yet skeptics doubt whether the new strategy being prepared by the White House will result in genuine convergence with Europe. Policy and implementation are two different things. Here again, history intertwines with strategic culture, and past experience points the way. As some of the most insightful U.S. commentators on counterinsurgency have remarked, one of the many ironies of the United States' long engagement with low intensity conflict in Vietnam was that the high-level strategy was exemplary. However, strategic concepts and workaday practice were worlds apart. The civilian agencies did not wish to touch the dirty business of counterinsurgency and, on the ground, mid-level military commanders determinedly ignored pious exhortations about the value of social engagement. At the operational level, the U.S. Army in Vietnam remained wedded to high technology and brute force.[60]

Accordingly, some Europeans remain skeptical about whether the United States is capable of implementing the new strategy because coercive policies have always tended to be the United States' instinctive first response. Officials in Europe also note that the sort of information operations that now seem to form the cutting edge of recent U.S. thinking have a nasty habit of backfiring if they are not done well. The available linguists and regional experts are already overstretched by the expanded intelligence effort, and it is hard to see where the personnel will come from for sophisticated political operations. In short, it is clear that the United States has changed its mind, but Europeans are unsure whether the United States is capable of, or indeed has the capacity for, a change of heart. There are also skeptics in Washington. Few believe that the White House can persuade the many agencies and departments to work more closely together. The new strategies have been long in the making for the very reason that Washington has been unable to resolve awkward debates over whether Iraq is making more terrorists and whether the United States needs to change its policy toward the Palestinian-Israeli dispute. Some observe that resolving to sell existing policies in the region better is an easier bureaucratic option than changing them.[61]

The remarkable slowness with which Washington has moved to redraw the gritty detail of its counterterrorism strategy—the process began in 2004—underlines just how difficult it is for the U.S. government machine to institute change. In part this is about ingrained culture, but it is also about bureaucratic infighting. Any serious reshaping of strategy results in winners and losers in Washington. All the signs are that defining the boundaries between an increased number of entities engaged in counterterrorism has been difficult. In turn, this loss of momentum favors those who want no change. Special Forces continue to expand, but the new doctrine hovers uncertainly between prioritizing information warfare or else emphasizing preemptive operations. Recent controversies have focused on the extent to which the Pentagon's secret soldiers based in embassies overseas—known as Military Liaison Elements—can take the war to the enemy even in neutral or friendly states. The Pentagon has pushed for a clear directive that allows these secret teams to accelerate their work. The CIA and the State Department have resisted, and the debate over exactly how beastly secret warfare should become seems unresolved. Meanwhile George Bush has conspicuously failed to eschew the rhetoric of "war fighting," partly because some of these activities are legal only within the realm of war.[62]

Looking to the future, the implementation of any new strategy will be especially hard because some of the problems are now so slippery that no one in the United States or Europe really knows what to do about them. Future problems may not be so much about a new global terrorism, but more about the nature of globalization itself. As early as February 2003, George Tenet warned the Senate Intelligence Committee that globalization, which had been the driving force behind the expansion of the world economy, had simultaneously become a serious threat to U.S. security.[63] The problem was not so much a new enemy as a new medium. A globalized world favors insurgent groups and puts developed states at a disadvantage. The uncomfortable truth is that while "globalization works," it works best for Al-Qaeda and its admirers.[64] The greatest challenge for both European and U.S. strategic thinking may be that a range of transnational threats is accelerated by globalization. Belatedly, this is now receiving more recognition with the latest U.S. National Security Strategy devoting a section to "the Challenges of Globalization." While this dawning realization is to be welcomed, neither Washington nor Brussels yet appears to have persuasive answers to these problems.[65]

Certainly, the EU and the United States must redouble their efforts to arrive at common perceptions of threats and responses in relation to countering international terrorism. They are two international actors that have a history of the closest cooperation, and only if they act together can this persistent and growing menace be addressed effectively. If they fail to work together, if their strategic cultures cause them to continue to diverge, then the prospects for the West's ability to address one of the most important issues on its security agenda are bleak.

Notes

1. Susan B. Glasser, "Review May Shift Terror Policies," *Washington Post*, May 29, 2005. The new document dealing with specifics of counterterrorism, NSPD-46/HSPD-15, was completed in early March 2006 and remains classified.

2. The Pentagon document finalized in March was entitled the "National Military Strategic Plan for the War on Terrorism"; see Linda Robinson, "Plan of Attack: The Pentagon Has a Secret New Strategy for Taking on Terrorists—and Taking Them Down," *US News and World Report*, August 1, 2005.

3. Lucian Pye, "Culture and Political Science: Problems in the Evaluation of the Concept of Political Culture," *Social Science Quarterly*, 53, 1972, 285–296.

4. Colin S. Gray, "Strategic Culture as Context: The First Generation of Theory Strikes Back," *Review of International Studies*, 25(1), January 1999, 49–71.

5. Alastair Johnston, "Thinking about Strategic Culture," *International Security*, 19(4), spring 1995, 32–64, and Jack Snyder, "The Soviet Strategic Culture: Implications for Nuclear Options," RAND, Santa Monica, 1977.

6. Errol Meidinger, "Regulatory Culture: A Theoretical Outline," *Law and Policy*, 9, 1987, 355–386.

7. Joanna Spear, "The Emergence of a European Strategic Personality and the Implications for the Transatlantic Relationship," *Arms Control Today*, 33(9), November 2003, 13–18.

8. Caroline F. Ziemke, "The National Myth and Strategic Personality of Iran: A Counterproliferation Perspective," in Victor A. Utgoff (ed.), *The Coming Crisis: Nuclear Proliferation, U.S. Interests, and World Order,* Cambridge, MA: MIT Press, 2000, pp. 88–89; Richard E. Neustadt and Ernest R. May, *Thinking in Time,* New York: Free Press, 1986.

9. On the unconscious life of administrative elements see Howell S. Baum, *The Invisible Bureaucracy: The Unconscious in Organisational Problem-Solving,* New York, NY: Oxford University Press, 1987.

10. Dan Reiter, "Learning, Realism, and Alliances," *World Politics,* 46(4), July 1994, 490–526; Dan Reiter, *Crucible of Beliefs: Learning, Alliances and World Wars,* Ithaca, NY: Cornell University Press, 1996.

11. An interesting use of the concept that crosses the international-domestic divide is that of intelligence culture. See Philip H. J. Davies, "Intelligence Culture and Intelligence Failure in Britain and the United States," *Cambridge Review of International Affairs,* 17(3), October 2004, 495–519.

12. Neil C. Livingstone, "Proactive Responses to Terrorism: Reprisals, Preemption and Retribution," in Charles W. Kegley (ed), *International Terrorism: Characteristics, Causes, Controls,* New York: St Martin's, 1990, pp. 219–227; Grant Wardlaw, *Political Terrorism: Theory, Tactics and Countermeasures,* New York: Cambridge University Press, 1982, pp. 121–127.

13. On the confluence of U.S. idealism and national interest see Christopher Thorne, "American Political Culture and the End of the Cold War," *Journal of American Studies,* 26(4), December 1992, 316–30. On recent lineages of exceptionalism see David Dunn, "Myths, Motivations and 'Misunderestimations': The Bush Administration and Iraq," *International Affairs,* 79(2), March 2003, 279–297.

14. The best summation of U.S. approaches in recent decades is Timothy Naftali, *Blind Spot: The Secret History of American Counterterrorism,* New York: Basic Books, 2005.

15. Rhodri Jeffreys-Jones, *The CIA and American Democracy,* 3rd edition, New Haven, CT: Yale University Press, 2003, p. 227.

16. Revelations about Central America had resulted in a "scrub order" that required high-level and somewhat laborious approval for the CIA recruitment of agents with an unsavory past, typically with strong terrorist connections or association with human rights violations. The rise of a "play it safe" culture during the 1990s is documented in Robert Baer, *See No Evil: The True Story of a Ground Soldier in the CIA's War on Terrorism,* New York: Crown Publishing Group, 2002.

17. Although Richard Clarke, U.S. counterterrorism coordinator in the 1990s, has contrasted the approaches of the Clinton and Bush administrations, there are also underlying continuities. See Richard A. Clarke, *Against All Enemies: Inside America's War on Terror,* New York: Free Press, 2004.

18. This somewhat counterintuitive observation is persuasively argued in Naftali, *Blind Spot,* pp. 117–165.

19. See in particular the 1990s critique of the United States' reluctance to intervene, by Richard Haas, *The Reluctant Sheriff,* Washington, DC: Brookings Institution, 1994. Haas, now president of the Council on Foreign Relations, has recently rethought his position in the light of Iraq and now advocates caution in *The Opportunity,* Washington, DC: Public Affairs Press, 2005.

20. President Bill Clinton, Speech to the United Nations General Assembly, New York, September 24, 1996.

21. In explaining the action taking by the EU, de Vries has chosen to emphasize criminal/judicial initiatives. Speech by Gijs de Vries, European coordinator for counter-terrorism, "European Strategy in the Fight Against Terrorism, and Cooperation with the United States," given at CSIS, Washington DC, May 13, 2004, http://ue.eu.int/uedocs/cmsUpload/CSIS_Washington.13_May_2004.pdf.

22. Oliver Roy, "EuroIslam: The Jihad Within," *The National Interest*, 71, spring 2003, 63–73.

23. The references to "newness" are innumerable. But see for example Bush's comments on "the new and changing threat" and the "new and very complex challenge" in his foreword to "National Strategy for Homeland Security," Office of Homeland Security, July 2002, http://www.whitehouse.gov/homeland/book/nat_strat_hls.pdf.

24. Bruce Hoffman, *Inside Terrorism*, New York: Columbia University Press, 1998. See also Ian O. Lesser, Bruce Hoffman, John Arquilla, David F. Ronfeldt, Michele Zanini, and Brian Michael Jenkins, *Countering the New Terrorism*, Washington, DC: RAND 1999.

25. Bruce Hoffman has used the persuasive analogy of a capital investment company. Others have talked of franchises. Bruce Hoffman, "The Leadership Secrets of Osama Bin Laden: The Terrorist as CEO," *Atlantic Monthly*, 291(3), April 2002, 26–27.

26. The first to engage with the "newness" problem was Thomas Copeland in his timely essay, "Is the 'New Terrorism' Really New? An Analysis of the New Paradigm for Terrorism," *Journal of Conflict Studies*, XI(2), fall 2001, 2–27. See also Alexander Spencer, "Questioning the Concept of the 'New Terrorism,'" *Peace, Conflict and Development*, 8, January 2006, 1–33, and Robert Jervis, "An Interim Assessment of September 11: What Has Changed and What Has Not?" *Political Science Quarterly*, 117(1), 2002, 37–54.

27. "Interview with Gijs de Vries on Terrorism, Islam and Democracy," September 6, 2005, Euroactiv.com http://www.euractiv.com/Article?tcmuri=tcm:29–136245-16&type=Interview.

28. This thesis is most clearly explored in Roger Scruton, *The West and the Rest: Globalization and the Terrorist Threat*, London: Continuum, 2002.

29. Javier Solana, "A Secure Europe in a Better World," European Council, Thessalonika, June 20, 2003, http://www.en-cps.org/documents/solana_draft.pdf.

30. President Bush, "Statement on the Death of Abu Musab al-Zarqawi," June 8, 2006, http://www.presidentialrhetoric.com/speeches/06.08.06.html.

31. Robert Kagan, *Paradise and Power: America and Europe in the New World Order*, London: Atlantic Books, 2003.

32. European Commission website, http://europa.eu.int/comm/echo/index-en.htm.

33. Michael Mandelbaum, "Foreign Policy as Social Work," *Foreign Affairs*, 75(1), January-February 1996, 16–32.

34. The initial dialogue with Libya over WMD was developed by the overseas intelligence services of the UK and Libya. See Julian Coman and Colin Brown, "Revealed: The Real Reason for Libya's WMD Surrender," *The Daily Telegraph*, December 21, 2003.

35. These were accompanied by private explorations of options. In 2002, Bush's deputy national security adviser had commissioned a paper that looked at options for regime change in Iran, citing the WMD issue as the driver.

36. On the issue of values see Alex Danchev, "How Strong Are Shared Values in the Transatlantic Relationship?" *British Journal of Politics and International Relations*, 7(3), August 2005, 429–436.

37. The DoD has absorbed about half of all emergency funding since 9/11. See "Security After 9/11: Strategy Choices and Budget Tradeoffs," Center for Defense Information, January 2003, 10–11. http://www.cdi.org/mrp/security-after-911.pdf.

38. Leading a terrorist group was punishable by a sentence of at least fifteen years, while financing its operations was punishable by a sentence of at least eight years. There are close parallels with the Italian "deep freeze" approach of long sentences for terrorism, adopted in the late 1970s.

39. See in particular the discussion of multinational "Alliance Base" activities run out of Paris, described in Dana Priest, "Help From France in Key Covert Operations," *Washington Post*, July 2005, 3.

40. George Tenet in 9/11 Commission Hearings, transcript for March 24, 2004; Edward J. Markey, *Boston Globe*, March 12, 2005; Shaun Waterman, "Egypt: U.S. Hands over Terror Suspects," *Washington Times*, May 17, 2005.

41. Stephen Grey and Ian Cobain, "Suspect's Tale of Travel and Torture: Alleged Bomb Plotter Claims Two and a Half Years of Interrogation Under U.S. and UK Supervision in 'Ghost Prisons' Abroad," *The Guardian*, August 2, 2005.

42. Craig Martin, "European Probe Finds Signs of CIA-Run Secret Prisons," *Washington Post*, June 2006, 7.

43. Jean-Paul Brodeur, Peter Gill, and Dennis Töllborg (eds.), *Democracy, Law, and Security: Internal Security Services in Contemporary Europe*, Aldershot: Ashgate, 2003. The process began as a Europe-wide response to the Leander case brought by the European Court initially against the Swedish Security Service.

44. The matter has been complicated by arguments over the relative advantages of long-term observation of suspects, versus capture and interrogation. See Jimmy Burns, Stephen Fidler, and Demetri Sevastopulo, "Different Approach to Tackling Terrorism Exposed," *Financial Times*, July 12, 2005.

45. Philip Sherwell and Sean Rayment, "Britain and America Clash over Tactics," *Daily Telegraph*, July 31, 2005.

46. Anonymous [Michael Scheuer], *Imperial Hubris: Why the West Is Losing the War on Terror*, New York: Brasseys, 2004.

47. George Tenet, "The Worldwide Threat 2004: Challenges in Changing Global Context," Statement to the Senate Committee on Intelligence, February 24, 2004, www.cia.com.

48. Guy Dinmore, "US Shifts Anti-Terror Policy," *Financial Times*, July 31, 2005. Rice and Zelikow have worked closely together over a long period and in 1997 co-authored a book on the final collapse of communism in Europe.

49. Susan B. Glasser, "Review May Shift Terror Policies," *Washington Post*, May 29, 2005.

50. Recently the Saudi government commissioned a study of Saudi foreign fighters making their way to Iraq. It found that it was the invasion of Iraq that was prompting jihadists to volunteer and most had not been in contact with radical organisations before 2003. Patrick Coburn, "Iraq: This Is Now an Unwinnable Conflict," *Independent on Sunday*, July 24, 2005.

51. Susan B. Glasser, "U.S. Figures Show Sharp Global Rise in Terrorism," *Washington Post*, April 27, 2005.

52. Interview with General Bryan D. Brown, *Special Operations Technology*, 3(4), June 7, 2005.

53. Robert Fox, "GWOT Is History: Now for SAVE," *New Statesman*, August 8, 2005.

54. Alec Russell, "Don't Mention War on Terror, Say Bush Aides," *Daily Telegraph*, July 27, 2005.

55. Renae Merle, "Pentagon Funds Diplomatic Effort: Contracts Aim to Improve Foreign Opinion of United States," *Washington Post*, June 11, 2005.

56. Testimony of the Honorable Thomas W. O'Connell, Assistant Secretary of Defense, Special Operations Low Intensity Conflict Before the U.S. House of Representatives Committee on the Armed Services Subcommittee on Terrorism, Unconventional Threats and Capabilities, Regarding the Special Operations Forces Command Budget for 2005, March 11, 2004.

57. Jennifer D. Kibbe, "The Rise of the Shadow Warriors," *Foreign Affairs*, 8(2), March-April 2004, 110–112.

58. Javier Solana, "A Secure Europe in a Better World," Office of the High Representative for CFSP, Brussels, www.ue.eu.int/ueDocs/cms/Data/docs/pressdata/en/reports/76225.pdf.

59. "The National Security Strategy of the United States of America," March 16, 2006, http://whitehouse.gov.nsc/nss/2006/.

60. Michael McClintock, *Instruments of Statecraft: U.S. Guerrilla Warfare, Counterinsurgency, and Counterterrorism, 1940–1990*, New York: Pantheon Books, 1992. See also Larry E. Cable, *Conflict of Myths: The Development of American Counterinsurgency Doctrine and the Vietnam War*, New York: New York University Press, 1986.

61. Some diplomats fear that the new strategy may remove the State Department's control over foreign security programs in favor of the Pentagon. Interviews, Washington, D.C., June 2005.

62. Jim Hoagland, "Terror Turf Wars: Bush's Secret Blueprint Stalled by Infighting," *Washington Post*, April 16, 2006.

63. Edward Alden, "Globalisation Cited as Threat to US Security," *Financial Times*, February 11, 2003.

64. Martin Wolf, *Why Globalization Works*, New Haven, CT: Yale University Press, 2004.

65. "The National Security Strategy of the United States of America," March 16, 2006, http://whitehouse.gov.nsc/nss/2006/.

Suggested Readings

Benjamin, D., and S. Simon, *The Age of Sacred Terror*, New York: Random House, 2002.

Boer, M. den, and J. Monar, "Keynote Article: 11 September and the Challenge of Global Terrorism to the EU as a Security Actor," *Journal of Common Market Studies Annual Review*, 40, 2002, 11–28.

Daalder, I., and J. Lindsay, *America Unbound: The Bush Revolution in Foreign Policy*, Washington, DC: Brookings Institution Press, 2003.

Dubois, D., "The Attacks of 11 September: EU-US Cooperation Against Terrorism in the Field of Justice and Home Affairs," *European Foreign Affairs Review*, 7(3), autumn 2002, 317–335.

Hoffman, B., "Is Europe Soft on Terrorism?" *Foreign Policy*, 115, summer 1999, 62–77.

Lansford, T., *All for One: Terrorism, NATO and the United States*, Aldershot: Ashgate, 2002.

Mahncke, D., W. Rees, and W. Thompson, *Redefining Transatlantic Security Relations: The Challenge of Change*, Manchester: Manchester University Press, 2004.

Stevenson, J., "How Europe and America Defend Themselves," *Foreign Affairs*, 8(22), March-April 2003, 75–90.

Glossary

acquis communautaire: A French term that cannot be precisely translated but that denotes the sum total of EU treaties, regulations, and laws developed since the 1950s; must be accepted by new member states as it exists at the time of accession.

Barcelona Process: Also known as the Euro-Mediterranean Partnership, it was negotiated in 1995 as a means of promoting more harmonious relations between the EU and the greater Middle East. Its key goals are to establish an area of peace and security in the Mediterranean, to implement a free-trade agreement by 2010, and to bolster institutional contacts between the EU and Middle Eastern countries. In 2007, the Barcelona Process is due to be absorbed into the European Neighborhood Policy (see below).

Bretton Woods system: The international monetary system created at the end of World War II in Bretton Woods, New Hampshire. It was designed to establish international management of the global economy and to provide for the cross-convertibility of national currencies through a fixed exchange rate with gold or with currencies backed by gold (such as the U.S. dollar). Its key foundations were the General Agreement on Tariffs and Trade, the International Monetary Fund, and the International Bank for Reconstruction and Development, which in 1956 was merged with other institutions to form the World Bank.

Common Agricultural Policy (CAP): A controversial, very expensive subsidy system established under the Treaty of Rome to increase agricultural productivity and sustain farm incomes in the European Community. It mainly benefits wealthy European farmers and damages developing countries' agricultural exports.

Common Assembly: The parliamentary arm of the European Coal and Steel Community (ECSC); precursor to the European Parliament.

Common Foreign and Security Policy (CFSP): The "second pillar" of the European Union, created under the Maastricht Treaty to replace European Political Cooperation. It establishes the broad foreign policy objectives of the EU and requires member states and the EU institutions to cooperate in promoting these objectives.

Conference on Security and Cooperation in Europe (CSCE): A process designed to promote European cooperation on trade and human rights. Its members include the United States, Canada, Russia, the former Soviet republics, and all of Europe. It was renamed the Organization for Security and Cooperation in Europe (OSCE) in 1994.

constitutional monarchies: The form of monarchy in which the monarch accepts the increasingly stringent limits on his or her power imposed by a constitution.

consumer price inflation: The rate of increase of the prices for goods and services weighted according to their share in a standard consumption bundle.

Copenhagen criteria: The Copenhagen criteria are the rules that define whether a nation is eligible to join the European Union. The criteria require that a state have the institutions to preserve democratic governance and human rights, a functioning market economy, and that the state accept the obligations and intent of the EU. These membership criteria were laid down at the June 1993 European Council in Copenhagen, Denmark, from which they take their name.

corporatism: Democratic corporatism provides for the representation of organized interest groups in the policymaking process. Most often such interests are economic, including business, labor, agriculture, etc. In practice such representation may be formal, such as on the EU Economic and Social Council and on national commissions (health, environmental protection, etc.), but most often it is informal through access to governmental policymakers and legislative committees.

Council of Europe: Organization established in 1949 to promote European integration after World War II. Has played an important role in promoting human rights and operates the European Court of Human Rights. Located in Strasbourg.

Council of Ministers: The decisionmaking institution of the EU comprising ministerial-level representatives from each of the member states. In cooperation with the European Parliament, it has the power to adopt or reject EU legislation. Subordinate to the European Council's overall authority.

Council for Mutual Economic Assistance (CMEA): Economic organization established by the Soviet Union in 1949 to coordinate trade among the communist countries of central and eastern Europe. Disbanded in 1991 after the fall of communism.

debt-to-GDP ratio: The ratio of gross public debt to gross domestic product across all levels of government.

euro: The single European currency.

EUROCORPS: A multinational military corps comprised of troops from France, Germany, Spain, Belgium, and Italy.

Eurogroup: The ECOFIN representatives of the euro-zone member states.

European Atomic Energy Agency (Euratom): One of the three European communities set up in the 1950s, established simultaneously with the European Economic Community (EEC) in 1958 to promote the peaceful use of atomic energy. Since 1967 has shared common institutions with the EEC and the ECSC.

European Bank for Reconstruction and Development: A London-based international development bank established in 1991 to promote economic development and political reform in central and eastern Europe. Main shareholders are the EU member states and EU institutions, along with the United States and Japan.

European Central Bank: The European Central Bank is located in Frankfurt, Germany, and is responsible for setting interstate policy for the whole of Europe's Economic and Monetary Union. Oversees the euro.

European Coal and Steel Community (ECSC): The first of the three European communities, created under the 1951 Treaty of Paris. Established a common pool for coal and steel products and strong institutions to regulate the coal and steel industries on a supranational basis.

European Commission: The executive body of the European Union. Initiates legislation, executes EU policies, negotiates on behalf of the EU in international trade forums, and monitors compliance with EU law and treaties by member states.

European Community (EC): Term used informally before 1993 for what the Maastricht Treaty named the European Union.

European Constitution: Also known as the Treaty Establishing a Constitution for Europe; was agreed by the European Council in October 2004. It was designed to provide a constitution for the EU that would allow the institution to function effectively with twenty-seven members following the enlargement of 2004. The treaty was in the process of ratification when it was rejected by the French and Dutch electorates in national referenda held May 29 and June 1, 2005. To date, Austria, Belgium, Cyprus, Estonia, Germany, Greece, Hungary, Italy, Latvia, Lithuania, Luxembourg, Malta, Slovakia, Slovenia, and Spain have ratified the constitutional treaty. The future of the Constitution is currently uncertain, though the German EU presidency (January–June 2007) intends to address the issue.

European Convention: Also known as the Convention on the Future of Europe, this was a body established by the European Council in December 2001 as a result of the Laeken Declaration. Its purpose was to produce a draft constitution for the European Union for the Council to finalize and adopt. The Convention finished its work in July 2003 with their draft treaty establishing a constitution for Europe, also known as the European Constitution.

European Council: The EU institution comprising the heads of state or government of the member states and the president of the European Commission. It meets at least twice each year and sets broad guidelines and directions for the development of the EU, as worked out in the Council of Ministers. (See above.)

European Court of Justice (ECJ): The judicial arm of the European Union, which may decide cases brought by EU member states, EU institutions, companies, and, in some cases, individuals. It ensures uniform interpretation of EU law by decisions that are binding upon the member states.

European Currency Unit (ECU): Artificial unit of account established to operate the exchange rate mechanism of the European Monetary System; consists of a basket of member-country currencies. Replaced by the euro on January 1, 1999.

European Economic Area: Members of the European Economic Area have full access to the European Union's single market in most areas of trade (agriculture and fisheries are exceptions) but do not have influence on the policy decisions of the European Union. The European Economic Area comprises the EU countries and Iceland, Norway, and Liechtenstein.

European Economic Community (EEC): The most important of the original European communities, set up under the 1957 Treaty of Rome to promote an "ever closer union" among the peoples of Europe through the development of a common market, common external tariff, and common policies in agriculture, transport, and other fields. Renamed the European Community in the Maastricht Treaty and made the major part of the first pillar of the European Union.

European Free Trade Association (EFTA): Organization formed in 1960 under British leadership to promote economic cooperation among European states not wishing to become members of the EC. Unlike the EC, did not have strong supranational institutions or a mandate to promote political union. Lost importance as most of its members decided to join the EC.

European Monetary System (EMS): Exchange rate regime, established in 1979, to limit currency fluctuations within the European Community. Operates an exchange rate mechanism (ERM) under which member states are required to maintain the value of their currencies relative to those of other member states. Laid the groundwork for monetary union and the single currency (euro), established in January 1999.

European Neighborhood Policy: The objective of the European Neighborhood Policy (ENP) is to share the benefits of the EU's 2004 enlargement with neighboring countries. It is also designed to prevent the emergence of new dividing lines between the enlarged EU and its neighbors. The vision is that of a ring of countries, drawn into further integration, but without necessarily becoming full members of the European Union. The policy was first outlined by the European Commission in March 2003. The countries covered include the Mediterranean coastal states of Africa and Asia, as well as the European members of the Commonwealth of Independent States (with the exception of Russia and Kazakhstan) in the Caucasus and Eastern Europe.

European Political Cooperation (EPC): Foreign policy cooperation among the member states of the EC, established in 1970, conducted on an intergovernmental basis by foreign ministries. Given treaty status in the Single European Act (1987) and replaced by the Common Foreign and Security Policy in the Maastricht Treaty.

European Rapid Reaction Force (ERRF): The European Union Rapid Reaction Force is a transnational military force managed by the European Union itself rather than any of its member states. Following the initial declaration in December 1999, the formal agreement founding the ERRF or EURRF was reached on November 22, 2004, and according to statements made by EU officials the first ERRF units would be deployable by 2005. The aim was to have 60,000 soldiers available, deployable for at least a year.

European Security and Defense Identity (ESDI): The ESDI was first established by the Western European Union as a means of creating a European pillar within NATO that could fulfill agreed "Petersberg Tasks": rescue and relief, peacekeeping, and peacemaking. Following the Anglo-French meeting at St. Malo in December 1998, responsibility for the ESDI was transferred to the EU. Currently, the ESDI is supported by a number of institutional bodies, including the Political and Security Committee (PSC) of the European Council, an EU Military Committee (EUMC), an EU Military Staff (EUMS), and a European Defence Agency (EDA).

European Security Strategy (ESS): Entitled "A Secure Europe in a Better World," the ESS was drafted in response to the controversial 2002 National Security Strategy of the United States. Approved by the European Council in December 2003, the ESS identifies a string of key threats Europe needs to deal with: terrorism, proliferation of weapons of mass destruction, regional conflict, failed states, and organized crime.

euro zone: The group of countries having adopted the euro; also known as the euro area.

exchange rate mechanism (ERM): A multilateral framework for the joint management of exchange-rate movements between participating countries to within set tolerance margins.

General Agreement on Tariffs and Trade (GATT): Multilateral trade treaty signed in 1947 establishing rules for international trade. Forum for eight rounds of tariff reductions culminating in the 1994 Uruguay Round agreements and the establishment of the World Trade Organization as successor to the GATT.

GDP (gross domestic product): Annual value of goods and services produced in a country.

High Authority: The executive body of the ECSC. Ceased to exist in July 1967 with the entering into effect of the merger treaty establishing a single commission for the ECSC, Euratom, and the EEC.

intergovernmentalism: Approach to integration in which national governments retain their sovereign powers and cooperate with each other by interstate bargaining and agreement. Opposed to federalism and supranationalism.

Lisbon Strategy: Also known as the Lisbon Agenda, this is an EU action and development plan adopted for a ten-year period in 2000 in Lisbon, Portugal, by the European Council. The Lisbon Strategy intends to deal with the low productivity and stagnation of economic growth in the EU, through the formulation of various policy initiatives to be taken by all EU member states. The long-term goal is to make the EU "the world's most dynamic and competitive knowledge-based economy" by 2010.

Maastricht Treaty: The Treaty on European Union (TEU), known as the Maastricht Treaty, was signed at Maastricht, the Netherlands, on February 7, 1992, the culmination of more than a year of negotiation and debate. By far the most sweeping revision of Community treaties ever attempted, the TEU amended the Treaty of Rome, which established the European Economic Community (EEC) in 1957. The TEU brought into being a new entity called the European Union (EU), a complicated structure of three pillars that has profoundly redefined European economic and political governance.

Marshall Plan: Officially known as the European Recovery Program, this plan was proposed in 1947 by U.S. Secretary of State George C. Marshall to foster postwar European economic revival through extensive U.S. aid.

nominal long-term interest rate: The rate of return on benchmark government bonds of a set maturity (usually equal to or greater than ten years).

North Atlantic Cooperation Council (NACC): Created by NATO at the Rome summit in November 1991. A U.S. initiative, the NACC was a new institutional relationship of consultation and cooperation on political and security issues open to all of the former, newly independent members of the Warsaw Pact. In July 1997, it was replaced by the Euro-Atlantic Partnership Council (EAPC).

North Atlantic Council: NATO's highest body; the decisionmaking arm of the organization.

North Atlantic Treaty Organization (NATO): A political-military institution founded in 1949 for the collective defense of its member states, which include the United States, Canada, and fourteen European countries.

Organization for Economic Cooperation and Development (OECD): An international organization established in 1961 comprising mainly industrialized market economy countries of North America, Western Europe, Japan, Australia, and New Zealand. Successor to the OEEC.

Organization for European Economic Cooperation (OEEC): Organization of European Marshall Plan aid recipients, created at the behest of the United States to administer the aid and serve as a forum to negotiate reductions in intra-European barriers to trade.

Organization for Security and Cooperation in Europe (OSCE): See Conference on Security and Cooperation in Europe.

parliamentary democracy: The form of democracy in which the composition of the executive branch is determined by the legislative majority, which may also dismiss the executive. The legislative branch of government is elected by the people.

Partnership for Peace (PFP): Framework agreements for non-NATO states to have a military relationship with the alliance.

PPP (purchasing power parity): Adjusts foreign currencies for dollar equivalents in purchasing power.

Schengen Agreement: The 1985 Schengen Agreement is an agreement among European states that allows for common policy on the temporary entry of persons and the harmonization of external border controls. A total of twenty-six countries—including all European Union states except the Republic of Ireland and the United Kingdom, but including non-EU members Iceland, Norway, and Switzerland—have signed the agreement and fifteen have implemented it so far. Border posts and checks have been removed between Schengen countries and a common "Schengen visa" allows tourist or visitor access to the area. The eight Central and Eastern European states that joined the EU in 2004 are expected to implement the agreement by 2008.

Single European Act (SEA): First major revision of the founding treaties of the European Community; went into effect in 1987. Increased the powers of the European Parliament, broadened the policy responsibilities of the EC, and, above all, scheduled the completion of a single economic market by December 31, 1992, as a member-state treaty commitment.

Stability and Growth Pact: Establishes several goals for fiscal policy beyond which EU member states are "admonished" or can even, in theory, be fined by the European Commission.

Stability Pact for South Eastern Europe: The Stability Pact was created by the EU on June 10, 1999, to provide a comprehensive, long-term conflict prevention and peace-building strategy for the Balkans. The Stability Pact is not an organization itself; rather it offers a political commitment and a framework agreement to develop a shared international approach to enhance stability and growth in the region.

supranationalism: Approach to integration in which participating states transfer sovereign powers and policymaking responsibilities to transnational institutions whose decisions are binding on those states. An important feature of the first pillar of the EU, and one that distinguishes the EU from international institutions such as NATO or the OECD.

Treaty of Nice: A treaty approved in December 2000 at the European Council that amended the Treaty on European Union to prepare the EU institutions for enlargement. The treaty established the number of seats in the European Parliament, weighted votes in the Council of Ministers, and determined the number of representatives on the Committee of the Regions and the Economic and Social Committee that the current and future members of the Union would receive. Nice was widely regarded as an awkward set of compromises, and dissatisfaction with the treaty led to the European Convention of 2002–2003.

The Treaty on European Union: See Maastricht Treaty.

unicameral parliament: A legislative body consisting of a single house.

unitary government: The form of government in which the national government is the only repository of sovereign power and in which the powers of subordinate levels of government are determined by the national government.

Warsaw Pact: A military alliance founded by the Soviet Union in 1955 in response to West Germany's entry into NATO. Its membership included the USSR and the countries of Eastern Europe.

Western European Union (WEU): An exclusively western European mutual defense organization established in 1954. Moribund through much of the Cold War, revived in 1984 as a vehicle to develop European defense cooperation, designated the defense arm of the EU in the Maastricht Treaty.

Index

Notes on Contributors

Richard J. Aldrich is Professor of Politics and Head of the School of Politics and International Relations at the University of Nottingham. He is the author of *The Hidden Hand: British and American Cold War Secret Intelligence* (2001).

Graham Bowley is a freelance journalist based in New York City. He writes for the *Financial Times, International Herald Tribune* and the *New York Times*.

Nicolas de Boisgrollier is Visiting Fellow at the Center on the United States and Europe at the Brookings Institution in Washington, DC.

Eric S. Einhorn is Professor of Political Science at the University of Massachusetts Amherst and is co-author, with John Logue, of *Modern Welfare States: Scandinavian Politics and Policy in the Global Age* (2003).

Mark Gilbert is associate Professor of Contemporary European History at the University of Trento. His work on Italy includes *The Italian Revolution: The End of Politics, Italian Style* (1995) and (with Anna Cento Bull) *The Lega Nord and the Northern Question in Italian Politics* (2001).

Jonathan Hopkin is Senior Lecturer in Comparative Politics at the London School of Economics. He is author of *Party Formation and Democratic Transition in Spain* (Macmillan 1999).

Erik Jones is Professor of European Studies at the SAIS Bologna Center of the Johns Hopkins University. He is author of *The Politics of Economic and Monetary Union* (2002).

Sean Kay is Professor of Politics and Government at Ohio Wesleyan University and Mershon Associate at the Mershon Center for International Security, Ohio State University. He is the author of *Global Security in the Twenty-first Century: The Quest for Power and the Search for Peace* (2006).

John Logue is Professor of Political Science at Kent State University where he also directs the Ohio Employee Ownership Center. He writes on Scandinavian politics and employee ownership.

Imelda Maher is Sutherland Professor of European Law at University College Dublin. She is author of *Competition Law: Alignment and Reform* (1999).

Bruce Parrott is Professor and Director of Russian and Eurasian Studies at the Johns Hopkins School of Advanced International Studies. He is editor and contributor to *The End of Empire? The Transformation of the USSR in Comparative Perspective* (1997).

Wyn Rees is Professor of International Security in the School of Politics and International Relations at the University of Nottingham. He is the author of *Transatlantic Counter-terrorism Cooperation: The New Imperative* (2006).

Jeffrey Simon is a Senior Fellow at the Institute for National Strategic Studies at the National Defense University. He is author of *Poland and NATO: A Study in Civil-Military Relations* (2004).

Ronald Tiersky is the Joseph B. Eastman '04 Professor of Politics Science at Amherst College and the general editor of the *Europe Today* series. He is the author of *Francois Mitterrand: A Very French President* (2004).

John Van Oudenaren directs the World Digital Library program at the Library of Congress. He is the author of *Uniting Europe: An Introduction to the European Union* (2005).

Helga A. Welsh is Associate Professor of Political Science at Wake Forest University. She is the author of numerous publications on German history and politics and one of the editors of *German History in Documents and Images* (published by the German Historical Institute, Washington, DC).